THE SPIRIT
OF
AMERICAN LAW

edited by

George S. Grossman

with a foreword by
Rennard Strickland

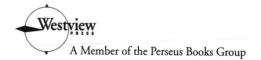

A Member of the Perseus Books Group

Copyright © 2000 by Westview Press, A Member of the Perseus Books Group

Published in 2000 in the United States of America by Westview Press, 5500 Central Avenue, Boulder, Colorado 80301-2877, and in the United Kingdom by Westview Press, 12 Hid's Copse Road, Cumnor Hill, Oxford OX2 9JJ

Visit us on the World Wide Web at www.westviewpress.com

Library of Congress Cataloging-in-Publication Data
The spirit of American law / edited by George S. Grossman.
    p.   cm.
  Includes bibliographical references and index.
  ISBN 0-8133-6782-4 (pbk.)
  1. Law—United States—History.   I. Grossman, George S.
KF351.S68   2000
349.73—dc21   99-048660
                                                                                 CIP

The paper used in this publication meets the requirements of the American National Standard for Permanence of Paper for Printed Library Materials Z39.48-1984.

10   9   8   7   6   5   4   3   2   1

In Memoriam
Ellen Rausen Jordan
1943–1996

CONTENTS

PART I THE ROOTS OF AMERICAN LAW

PART II   THE GROWTH OF AMERICAN LAW

PART III   AMERICAN LAW IN
THE TWENTY-FIRST CENTURY

ILLUSTRATIONS

FOREWORD

Stepping Through the Looking Glass: Reflections in the Magic Mirror of Law

The Law, wherein, as in a magic mirror, we see reflected, not only our own lives, but the lives of all men that have been! When I think on this majestic theme, my eyes dazzle.

—*Oliver Wendell Holmes, Jr.*
Speech to the Suffolk County Bar, 1913

Justice Holmes's oft-quoted metaphor of law as the magic mirror is at the same time strikingly accurate and surprisingly misleading. Rather than the hand-held mirror which Holmes is thought to have taken from Alfred Tennyson's *The Lady of Shallott*, the law's real mirror may be closer to the ones in carnival fun houses which shorten, lengthen, and distort images depending upon angle and light. I often think about Holmes's "Speech to the Suffolk County Bar" because he also analogizes the legal process to a princess "mightier than she who once wrought at Bayeux, eternally weaving into her web dim figures of the ever-lasting past." It seems to me that today Holmes's Princess and his mirror have become more like Lewis Carroll's Little Alice from Wonderland stepping through our contemporary carnival funhouse. Nonetheless, they still prove that Holmes was right when he observed that the law is, in the final analysis, a great anthropological document reflective of all who have been a part of its dazzling life and spirit.

George Grossman in *The Spirit of American Law* has collected thirty-three essays which, taken together, tell us much about the magic mirror of law and the women and men whose experiences are reflected therein. Each selection in this anthology was carefully chosen from literally thousands of works on law. Professor Grossman, a distinguished author, bibliographer, and librarian, demonstrates what prize-winning historian Barbara Tuchman meant when she said that great commentators search out hundreds of examples and then present their readers with the one which most perfectly tells their story. This anthology is composed of a series of almost-perfect examples that, taken together, help us see deeply into not only the spirit but the operation of law.

While Grossman notes in his preface that this anthology was originally compiled for potential law students, the work will prove to be invaluable to a much larger audience interested in knowing how the maze of law, the wonderland of regulation, and the hegemony of the legal profession came into being. Many law schools will make this recommended or required reading for students in the summer before their first year. *The Spirit of American Law* is a text ideally suited to prepare students for the study of law. Other citizens will discover and read it on their own as an insightful guide to the past, the present, and the future of American law.

The Spirit of American Law is much more than a collection of excellent essays. The brief introductory commentaries by Professor Grossman, read together, are a wonderful outline and summary of key ideas, movements, and individuals. I found them particularly insightful in preparing me to understand and appreciate the major selections. The author calls his book "an organized sampling," but, to me, *The Spirit of American Law* is much more than a loosely gathered anthology. It is a full and sustaining feast that, taken as a whole, provides a rich and rewarding reading experience not only for those to whom these selections are new, but also for those of us who are revisiting old friends.

I first met George Grossman over a quarter of a century ago. Since that time I have been impressed with the depth and diversity of his scholarly productivity. His work in legal history and Native American law, especially his pioneering bibliographic studies, has always inspired me. Only a mature and serious scholar, deeply read in the history and development of the legal system, could have assembled *The Spirit of American Law*.

As I read through the manuscript, I was reminded of the story of High Forehead, the Cheyenne informant. George's Minnesota colleague, the distinguished legal anthropologist E. Adamson Hoebel often told this tale. One summer, out on the great plains, Hoebel and High Forehead were sitting under a solitary tree talking about the Northern Cheyenne and their traditional law-ways. High Forehead, according to Hoebel, had resisted talking about difficult legal conflicts within the tribe. On that day, under the blazing sun, for the first time he began to tell the story of how the Cheyenne had used law before the blue coats came on the prairie and built guard houses for jails. High Forehead unfolded the who and the why and the how of Cheyenne law and order and of the people and their lives, their dreams, and their spirits. *The Spirit of American Law* has that same revelatory impact for American law and our legal system.

Rennard Strickland
Dean and Philip H. Knight Professor of Law
University of Oregon School of Law
and former President of the
Association of American Law Schools

PREFACE

*The special information that lawyers derive from their studies
ensures them a separate rank in society, and they constitute
a sort of privileged body in the scale of intellect.*

—*Alexis de Tocqueville, 1835*

At the end of the twentieth century, lawyers in the United States remain among the intellectual elite: Practicing lawyers are essential facilitators of commercial life and guardians of individual rights; the writings of legal scholars pour forth in over four hundred journals edited at law schools; and from city halls to the White House, from town councils to Congress, from traffic courts to the United States Supreme Court, lawyers predominate in government. From their privileged positions, lawyers must be ever aware of the social impact of what they do. Likewise, citizens at large must know at least the basics about law and the legal profession.

This anthology was initially compiled for law school applicants to read on their own during the summer between college and law school, but I hope it will be of interest to anyone curious about the culture of American law. I also hope it will prove useful in introductory courses in Legal Studies, Legal History, Constitutional History, and similar courses.

The readings have been selected largely from books with appeal to the general public; only in Part 3 are articles included from legal periodicals. The selections are not intended to help students get into law school or to provide advice on how to study law.[1] Nor is there self-help legal advice.[2] Rather, the

---

1. On studying law, Karl N. Llewellyn's classic, *The Bramble Bush* (1930), remains high on recommended reading lists, since legal education, especially the first year, has changed little since 1930. Some, however, prefer *An Introduction to Legal Reasoning* (1948) by Edward H. Levi. A more recent example of the genre is Sheldon Margulies's *Learning Law: The Mastery of Legal Logic* (1993). Other recent works written to allay the anxieties of law students include *Starting Off Right in Law School* (1997) by Carol J. Nygren, *Learning the Law: Success in Law School and Beyond* (rev. ed., 1997) by Steven J. Frank, *How to Study Law and Take Law Exams in a Nutshell* (1996) by Ann M. Burkhart and Robert A. Stein, and *Law School Without Fear: Strategies for Success* (1996) by Helene S. Shapo and Marshall Shapo. The Society of American Law

readings explore broader interests: the roots, development, and future of American law, including characteristics of the American legal profession, philosophical issues below the surface of legal problems, and the social consequences of legal solutions—all embraced in the term "spirit."

For those with such broad interests, there are two one-volume histories,[3] a somewhat dated coffee-table book,[4] a set of encyclopedias,[5] and thousands of books on specific legal topics. To help make choices among those thousands, two law librarians surveyed legal educators in the early 1980s and compiled a book-length, annotated bibliography of recommended readings.[6] But no one has yet prepared an anthology to provide an organized sampling of the available literature.[7]

This book is designed to fill that gap. The organization is largely chronological, with each selection preceded by an introduction. Footnotes are omitted from the selections and avoided in the introductions. Each introduction includes at least one quotation—often from a work I would have liked to include as a selection, but omitted for space considerations.

Part of the fun of preparing an anthology is the license to exercise a degree of arbitrariness. I selected readings for readability and entertainment value as well as content. I do not claim that the readings will lead to better grades in law school or greater success in law practice or will make the reader knowledgeable in any aspect of law. Rather, I hope the reader will find this book in-

---

Teachers commissioned a collection of essays edited by Stephen Gillers and published as *Looking at Law School* (4th ed., 1997). And there are two entertaining treatments of the first-year experience at Harvard Law School: Scott Turow's *One L* (1977) and John J. Osborn, Jr.'s novel *The Paper Chase* (1971) (the basis for the film and television series). For those interested in the history of legal education in greater detail, there is *Law School: Legal Education in America from the 1850s to the 1980s* (1983) by Robert Stevens.

2. See Jean Sinclair McKnight, *Law for the Layperson: An Annotated Bibliography of Self-Help Law Books* (2d ed., 1997).

3. Lawrence M. Friedman, *A History of American Law* (2d ed., 1985), and Kermit L. Hall, *The Magic Mirror: Law in American History* (1989). There are also a number of books for classroom use. Melvin I. Urofsky's *A March of Liberty: A Constitutional History of the United States* (1988) was especially useful in the preparation of this book.

4. Bernard Schwartz, *The American Heritage History of the Law in America* (1974).

5. *West's Encyclopedia of American Law* (1997–1998). Other useful reference sources are *The Oxford Companion to Law* (1980) and *The Oxford Dictionary of American Legal Quotations* (1993).

6. Julius J. Marke and Edward J. Bander, *Dean's List of Recommended Reading for Prelaw and Law Students Selected by the Deans and Faculties of American Law Schools* (2d ed., 1984).

7. One anthology with different aims was published for would-be law students in 1975: Thomas Ehrlich and Geoffrey C. Hazard, Jr., *Going to Law School? Readings on a Legal Career.* It is divided into four sections: (I) Some Profiles and Life Styles of Lawyers, (II) Law Schools, (III) The Job Market, (IV) The Profession and Its Ethics. Another anthology, John Honnold's *The Life of the Law* (1964), emphasizes the institutional sources of law, with sections on courts, legislatures, the administrative process, and the bar at the heart of the book.

teresting and enjoyable (although at times disturbing), and I hope these readings will contribute to the development of the sort of "practical wisdom" seen by the dean of Yale Law School as the core value in the life of a lawyer:

> [T]he outstanding lawyer—the one who serves as a model for the rest—is not simply an accomplished technician but a person of prudence or practical wisdom as well. It is of course rewarding to become technically proficient in the law. But earlier generations of American lawyers conceived their highest goal to be the attainment of wisdom that lies beyond technique—a wisdom about human beings and their tangled affairs that anyone who wishes to provide deliberative counsel must possess.[8]

The preparation of this anthology began at Northwestern University's Law Library, continued at the Law Library of the University of California at Davis, and concluded on a sabbatical leave at the University of California's Hastings School of Law's Library. I am grateful to the staffs of all three law libraries—especially to Chris Simoni, Marcia Gold Lehr, and Jessy Johnson at Northwestern; Judy Janes, Peg Durkin, Steve Langford, Jon Lin, Susan Llano, Erin Murphy, and Lisa Chance at Davis; and Jenny Parrish, Faye Jones, Linda Weir, and John Borden at Hastings. Thanks also to three other law librarians who have been my friends and mentors for over three decades—J. Myron Jacobstein, Morris L. Cohen, and Roy M. Mersky—and to my colleagues present and past, especially Richard Wydick, Bruce Wolk, and Rex Perschbacher.

George S. Grossman
Davis, California

---

8. Anthony T. Kronman, *The Lost Lawyer: Failing Ideals of the Legal Profession* (1993), p. 2.

PART I

The Roots of American Law

CHAPTER 1

The Origins of Law

Attempts to define the origins of law have drawn on the thoughts of philosophers, theologians, historians, and social scientists, as well as legal scholars. Such giants as Aristotle in Greece, Cicero in Rome, and Thomas Aquinas in the Middle Ages considered law to be a natural phenomenon subject to the same principles everywhere and for all time. Their theory of "Natural Law" was revived in the Renaissance and continues to influence modern legal thought and legal developments in such areas as international human rights.

In the late eighteenth century, in much of the western world, certainties began to unravel. The American colonies revolted; the French revolted; throughout Europe, established institutions and established ideas were challenged. Conceptions of law became unsettled as well. In Germany, philosophers Immanuel Kant and Georg Hegel came to view law as grounded not in immutable rules of nature, but in human free will: the legitimacy of legal rules lay in their "reason," their power to persuade. John Locke in England and the Baron la Montesquieu in France translated the ideas of the Age of Reason—or the Enlightenment—into principles of limited government based on "social contracts." Americans adopted many of these principles in the Constitution, the French in the codification of their laws, the Code Napoléon of 1803.

The codification of laws spread throughout continental Europe. But some resisted. In the early nineteenth century, the Historical School, led by Friedrich Karl von Savigny in Germany, rejected both nature and reason as the basis of law. Von Savigny saw law evolving organically from the spirit ("*Volksgeist*") of each nation and opposed codification as an interference with organic growth.

Codification was also resisted in England. But English Positivists, led by Jeremy Bentham and John Austin, campaigned for codification. Laws, they said, originate simply as commands of the sovereign and should be analyzed objectively through observation; speculative, subjective considerations of right and wrong should be left to moral philosophers.

Bentham, Austin, and their followers, however, did not shy away from moral philosophy. They called for the evaluation of laws on the basis of "utilitarian" values measured in terms of the "greatest happiness of the greatest number." Later in the nineteenth century, German jurist Rudolf von Jhering added that social, rather than individual, happiness should be paramount.

Many twentieth-century legal scholars took to the empiricism of the Positivists. In the United States, legal thinkers have been influenced by currents from Europe as well as by the work of native social scientists. Positivist, empirical research has been employed to investigate the social purposes and the social effects of law.

Among modern social scientists, some of the most fruitful work has been done by anthropologists who have studied societies in which laws were emerging in their rudimentary forms. In a seminal work, a leading legal scholar and a leading anthropologist joined forces to study a Native American tribe. The legal scholar, Karl N. Llewellyn, and the anthropologist, E. Adamson Hoebel, jointly published their study, *The Cheyenne Way*, in 1941. Llewellyn and Hoebel viewed law as "a batch of tools to get jobs done in a culture," as "processes of handling trouble and channeling behavior" (p. 42). The "jobs" for law include the establishment of "authority" among members of a group and the establishment of "norms and imperatives" for the conduct of war, the reaction to homicide and other hurtful conduct, the bonds of marriage and sexual relations, and the ownership and inheritance of property. The pioneering work of Llewellyn and Hoebel was followed by other anthropological studies of law, some based on historical sources.

Historical and anthropological sources have linked the origins of law to religious beliefs and practices. In a scholarly study of Cherokee law, *Fire and the Spirits* (1975), Rennard Strickland pointed out that, in the eighteenth century, "law was centered in the priestly complex of the native tribal religion" (p. 11). Offenses against the community were adjudicated by clan elders on the basis of oath taking:

Deviations from established norms which offended community expectations were tried in the courts of the villages. A Cherokee trial was essentially a matter of oath saying. . . . Violation of the oath would prevent the ghost from passing to the Nightland, and, therefore, the punishment for the offense with which the accused was charged would, in the view of the traditional Cherokee, be less grave than having one's ghost remain forever wandering as a result of violation of the oath. (p. 25)

Religious strictures also governed the avenging of homicides, the execution of witches, and the expiation of sins; and the Cherokee social order—its clans and classes, its governance in peace and war, its marriage relations—was considered to be "patterned after the system of the creating spirits" (p. 22). Another scholar of American Indian law, John Phillip Reid, viewed eighteenth-century Cherokee law in secular terms.

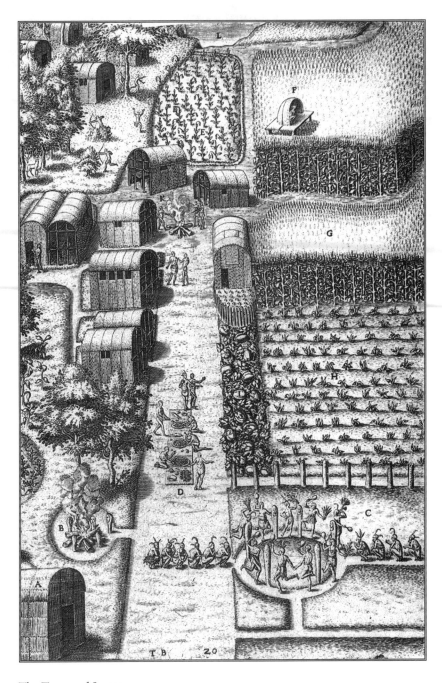

The Towne of Secota.

From Thomas Hariot, *A briefe and true report of the new found land of Virginia* ... (1590), based on a drawing by John White, 1587.

from John Phillip Reid, *A Better Kind of Hatchet: Law, Trade and Diplomacy in the Cherokee Nation During the Early Years of European Contact* (University Park: The Pennsylvania State University Press, 1976), pp. 1–12.

The Cherokee Way

The Cherokees were the mountaineers of aboriginal America, holding the lofty ridges and deep valleys of the southern Appalachian highlands, whence they could send predatory raiders swooping down on the less populous nations to the east, or they could retreat into a natural fortress that protected them from powerful enemies to the north and south. They were a people who both awed and puzzled the first Europeans who came into contact with them. . . .

[T]he Cherokees as a nation possessed several discernible characteristics that contributed to both their survival and their vulnerability. Their strength lay in their mountain homeland and in their numbers, for they were generally reckoned one of the largest, if not the largest, of the North American nations, with a population of up to 20,000 men, women, and children; at no time were there fewer than 10,000, and they usually were able to muster about 3,000 warriors when forced to make a stand. Their weakness lay in their divisions, for they were spread throughout 60 independent towns, connected by winding, narrow, difficult trails and partitioned by high mountain ridges. Their language was subdivided into at least three distinct dialects, and their nation was segregated into five regional groups, often competing against one another, and sometimes, when rival clusters of towns became antagonistic, even competing within themselves. [The five groups were known as the Lower Cherokees, the Valley Cherokees, the Middle Cherokees, the Out Cherokees, and the Overhills.]

. . .

. . . The governance of the Cherokees . . . was in the towns. There was no semblance of national government save in times of great emergencies when a single leader or the headmen of one town or region might assume the task of speaking for the nation. . . . For [the British] the concept of "national government" meant one thing; they could not understand that for the Cherokees it meant little except a response to individual crises which dealt with the problems at hand and functioned only until the immediate danger had passed away.

When utilizing their government of crisis, Cherokee headmen did not think in the manner of contemporaneous European leaders. They did not try to settle problems or resolve controversies, they tried to avoid them. In the legal, ethical, and governmental world of an eighteenth-century Cherokee the art of legislation was neither practiced nor understood. They had no need to enact laws, and what the Cherokees did not need, they did not pursue.

What the Cherokees did need was unity in their towns, and this they accomplished through town councils. The closest approach to a permanent government body, at any level of their society, the town council served the purpose of the Cherokees partly because the Cherokees did not require more. Again it was not a matter of legislation; it was a matter of consensus. Cherokee town government operated so closely to what we might describe as anarchy, that decisions called for unanimous consent, leaving the council without a need to restrain dissident minorities. Every Cherokee had a voice in the council, and every Cherokee had a right to be heard. The necessity to fit everyone into the town's council house was one reason why Cherokee villages were never large, usually dividing once the adult population reached 500 persons. Another was the terrain, for in the southern mountains it was rare to find a level tract along a stream sufficient to plant crops for a larger population. . . .

The town council may have divided the common fields and also may have settled the hours of sowing, tilling, and harvesting, for with Mohawks and Creeks lurking in the woods no worker was safe unless surrounded by a large band of well-guarded comrades. It is unlikely, however, that the town council performed other structured administrative functions, aside from designating the dates of festivals and ball plays. . . .

. . . One factor keeping government at a minimum was the high value placed on personal freedom. It is perhaps even wrong to think of Cherokee headmen as first among equals, for they were first only while supported by public opinion or public inertia. When they spoke for a town, or a region, or in rare cases for the nation, they did so in the hope, not the certainty, that their words would be listened to and their pledges honored.

Cherokee headmen did not exert authority, they exercised influence based on the intangible ingredients such as their personalities, the success of prior prophecies, tales told by conjurers, and the auguries of those whom they sought to sway. For headmen to employ coercion, even coercion applied through established legal institutions or social structures manipulated in predictable ways, would have been a violation of Cherokee constitutional premises. By way of contrast, the argument could be made that much of a headman's influence was derived from his native ability to invent *sui generis* solutions and to move around, not through, opposition. Political power came through personal credit, not government office. Headmen had no rank, no titles, no hereditary status. A contemporary European expressed the principle by saying that they could "only persuade." Somewhat later, a Cherokee informant put it another way. It was, he pointed out, by "native politeness alone . . . that the chiefs bind the hearts of their subjects." For Cherokee headmen government was more than the art of the possible or the art of compromise. It was the art of inducement coupled to the art of proselytism.

Government by the gentle hands of headmen who could not afford to antagonize may seem like no government at all. . . . It might even be wondered whether it is realistic to speak of Cherokee law: Could there have been uniformity in sixty mountain villages isolated into five regional clusters and divided by three dialects? What may have been custom among the Lower towns on the headwaters of the Savannah could have been outlandish among the Overhills on the upper reaches of the Little Tennessee. The answer is that the Cherokees did have a national law: a law derived from rules of conduct and attitudes of mind concerning their kinship system, with its seven matrilineal, exogamous clans.

The seven clans were what made the Cherokees a nation. A warrior from the Overhill town of Tennessee, going to hunt in the Middle settlements, knew that if he stopped in the town of Watuga, he would find fellow clan members to welcome him, men who called him "brother" and identified his interests with theirs. A woman who grew up in the Lower town of Estatoe and who, to escape the dangers of Creek raids, fled to the Out town of Tuckaseegee knew that she need not worry about leaving her family behind. In Tuckaseegee she would have an extended family, perhaps not the close-knit group of clan kin who formed the social family, but at least a legal group who would protect her rights and avenge wrongs done her.

The clans provided the framework through which the average Cherokee arranged society. Close to a Cherokee male were the members of his clan, closer still were his blood clan relatives—mother, siblings, mother's siblings, sister's children, and mother's sister's children. A second group was father's clan, for son and father did not belong to the same clan and had few legal ties, save one of much importance: he could not marry any woman who belonged to father's clan. He classified everyone in father's clan according to sex, not generation, calling all males "father" and all the females "father's sister" no matter their age. The members of father's father's clan and mother's father's clan formed a third group. He called the men "grandfather" and the women "grandmother," and could marry into both. In fact, because he had a kin term for them and could joke with them in a special way, the average Cherokee was more likely than not to marry a "grandmother." The final group into which he divided society was formed by the three remaining clans, with whom he had no ties of relationship or terminology and from whom he could select a spouse if he wished.

Anthropologists call it a "Crow" type system, and it was more than a method for classifying relatives or regulating incest. It was the adhesive of Cherokee life, giving form and substance to Cherokee society. As a body politic the Cherokees may not have yet been welded into a "state," but as a people they were a "nation": an ethnic group that possessed a fund of shared experience and had accumulated an identity of interest providing them with a distinctive character and a common culture.

Without the clans the Cherokees might have lacked the apparatus for expressing their nationhood. There were no national clan leaders, no national clan structure, thus the clans were instruments for unity, not division. In town councils the clans sat separately in seven sections, yet even here the Cherokee people were probably not divided by clan rivalry. Each clan section may have served as a caucus, helping to eliminate dissension and smoothing the way for the emergence of a consensus.

There are facets of clan membership that the passage of time hides forever from our view. For example, the termination of incestuous relationships, which surely was effected through the clan, must remain a mystery. Of what we do know, however, we may be certain as there are enough recorded cases to show us the way. From these we learn that in domestic law the chief activity of the Cherokee clan was to avenge or satisfy a homicide. If a member of the Wolf clan was killed by a Cherokee of another clan, the Wolfs were owed one life. If a Wolf killed a member of one of the other six clans, the Wolfs would have to pay.

. . .

. . . The Cherokees had an alternative for [intrafamily] situations, as well as for the difficult cases of accident or self-defense. They could accept compensation in place of the blood price. It may not have been the general rule, but its availability softened the strictures of absolute liability.

It is difficult to generalize about Cherokee homicides; so few are reported for the eighteenth century that generalities do not come easily. But one can be made without too much audacity: a large percentage of Cherokee homicides, perhaps we may safely assume most, were the result of accident. The Cherokee social system contained safeguards discouraging aggressive attitudes that might lead to acts of violence. One of the very basic safeguards was the doctrine of shared property, a difficult concept for us to recapture after two centuries of changing values. The Cherokees owned what they grew, hunted, captured, or manufactured; . . . they were not communists. They planted the open fields around their towns in individual strips, gathered their corn as personal property, and stored it in private magazines . . . behind each house. They did not, however, think of exclusiveness. They shared what they had. A hungry family could expect to find food, a traveler was welcomed for the night. Stealing may have occurred but there was little incentive for it. Men did not even covet horses, which had a marginal value in mountain warfare and, due to Cherokee inability to fence fields, were a detriment to their agricultural economy, and there is no indication that theft was a social problem. Permanent wealth accumulation was not a Cherokee characteristic, for the mores of their society despised the greedy man, and goods were never so plentiful that they were tempted to risk the sting of gossip.

A second reason why the Cherokees could avoid aggression among themselves was their war machine. They may not have been distinguished warriors, but they were always at war, and the aggressive Cherokee male had many outlets for his energy and frustrations. He did not have to quarrel with fellow Cherokees; he could quarrel with Creeks, Choctaws, Shawnees, and Catawbas. For him war was a personal affair, not a national duty or a clan obligation. Like the domestic blood feud, wars were often waged for retaliation, yet clans did not wage them. If any unit of society did, it would most likely be the town of the victim, with all seven clans participating. This rule, however, was not absolute, for war parties were generally private groups which gathered around a leader and followed him as long as he could maintain interest. The Cherokee warrior was an individualist, who fought when he pleased and seldom went to war except for pleasure. If the enemy pressed too hard and panic seized him, he would retreat into the woods to await a safer day. If he set off on a raid and became tired on the first night out, dreamed a bad dream, or decided that the trip was too much bother, he did not fret. He abandoned the expedition and went home. No one could keep him on the path against his free will, and public opinion praised caution without seeking explanations.

Unlike the domestic blood feud, retaliation between nations was not privileged, and a single killing could lead to an unending war. The most difficult challenge faced by eighteenth-century Cherokee law was the making and the keeping of peace. No Cherokee was empowered to speak for the nation, and every Cherokee had a right to dissent. A warrior who had recently lost a brother in a Creek raid might tell a Creek peace delegation that he would bury the bloody hatchet after he had taken one Creek scalp. If he succeeded, it would be for the brother of his Creek victim to decide if the war would continue. Peace negotiations therefore were largely promises to forgive and forget, to think good thoughts about one another, and to reject war talks from third parties. About the only means of enforcing peace was to exchange visitors. Creek headmen would come to Cherokee towns, and Cherokee headmen would go to Creek towns. It was not a foolproof procedure, but in the absence of coercive authority, it was the best method that the southern nations possessed. The presence of Creeks . . . not only was visible evidence to the Cherokees that their former enemy's heart was now pure and straight, but, more im-

portant, it meant that the Creeks were unlikely to attack them, for if they did the visitors would become hostages and their lives would be forfeited.
. . .

Without a law of coercion to restrain "bad thoughts," the Cherokee nation relied upon an ethical code which postulated as its ideal person the individual who deferred to the wishes of the majority, voiced demands in terms of respect, and never pushed fellow Cherokees beyond their voluntary inclinations. Circumspection was the social norm and the test of correct behavior. A Cherokee male who wished to sponsor a policy in the town council did so with caution, and if the emerging consensus was going against him, the ideal man did not argue—he avoided an open confrontation by withdrawing.

Corporal punishment not only had no place in the Cherokee legal system, it was abhorrence to the Cherokee legal mind. Without a state they had, of course, no state-imposed sanctions, yet they had sanctions, effective sanctions, imposed by clan members and neighbors. In situations of homicide, the certainty of vengeance was a sanction, while for other antisocial acts they employed ridicule, sarcasm, ostracism, withdrawal, and perhaps even gossip. To a Cherokee, these marks of ethical disapproval were at least as effective as was physical coercion in contemporary Europe. . . .

For some legal theorists, the test of law is the legitimate use of physical coercion applied in an adjudicatory proceeding, and by this definition the Cherokees would have to be classified as a people without law. It is a contention leading to a barren conclusion, as it would mean that many of the known societies in world history must be described as "lawless," apparently relegated to that state of anarchy which the human species has always found too intolerable for existence. To escape from this dilemma it is not enough to create new categories of law, to suggest, for example, that a system of feud, such as the Cherokee code of homicide, "is an absence of law, since blood revenge is more a sociological law than a legal one." The Cherokee blood feud was legal because society accepted it when executed according to a universally recognized formula of conduct. It was more than a vendetta—more than a vendetta sanctioned and controlled by law: it was a vendetta required by law, imposing a duty as well as a liability, and the Cherokee male who did not perform his duty was a Cherokee in disgrace.

The Cherokee who did perform his duty was acting within his rights, and "right" was defined by law. Today the emphasis might be upon the concept of rights. . . . The eighteenth-century Cherokee legal mind, however, probably did not think of "right"; it thought of "duty." The Cherokee's emphasis was on the brother's duty to support his sister and on the clan-brother's duty to avenge a homicide. That is, the legal emphasis was on the duty that custom dictated should be rendered, not on any right that could be enforced. Even the practice of standing passive while vengeance was being exacted was less a right possessed by the avenger of blood than a duty imposed upon the clan kin of the manslayer. The Cherokees had law because Cherokee men and Cherokee women performed their duty.

That some Cherokees escaped the consequences of acts for which other Cherokees suffered retaliation is immaterial. At most, such inequities meant that their system of "justice," in a narrow sense, was faulty or uneven. As far as "law" was concerned, the person who escaped "justice" did so by the same procedures that brought the less lucky to account. The regularity, the certainty, and the predictability of those procedures are what matter. If a woman escaped vengeance in kind it was because another was sacrificed in her place, or because her victim's kin were willing to accept other types of indemnification. The Cherokees had no difficulty with the doctrine that a man might be executed for the acts of his brother. Indeed, there may have been a right of substitution. An uncle who wished to shield his nephew from the consequences of some folly could ask to be killed in his place. From the Cherokees' point of view, the requirements of "law" had been fulfilled, and so intently did they concentrate upon law that there is every indication they did not consider questions of "justice" that readily occur to us. "Guilt" and "innocence" were not the operative elements in the Cherokee law of homicide. "Liability" was.

. . . A very few of the people with whom the Cherokees had contact possessed a more coercive law in the sense that their headmen or "kings" could maintain a folk peace by executing manslayers without fear of retaliation. These nations enjoyed a slight advantage over the Cherokees, for when they negotiated peace on the strength of promises that a wrongdoer would be punished, they might be making promises that could be kept. When it came to waging war, on the other hand, the difference was unimportant for none of the nations possessed the organizational skill that would have permitted them to employ the power of coercion to unite their people into an efficient disciplined group. Thus, the Cherokees' law was adequate while they lived in splendid isolation among their mountains and their valleys, in contact only with other aboriginal nations of the North American continent. With the arrival of Europeans, all would change.

CHAPTER 2

Ancient Law

The impact of geography on law would make an interesting thesis. While the mountains of North Carolina confined Cherokee communities, the mild climate and fertile river valleys of the Middle East produced growth and prosperity.

The distinct identity of law evolved with the growth of Middle Eastern civilizations. The turning point came with the development of writing. As English scholar Henry Sumner Maine expressed it in his classic study, *Ancient Law* (1861):

> When . . . law has once been embodied in a Code, there is an end to what may be called its spontaneous development. Henceforward the changes effected in it, if effected at all, are effected deliberately and from without. (p. 20)

Archaeologists began to dig in the Middle East in the eighteenth century. Their findings have thrown considerable light on the development of written law in ancient societies.

The earliest written codes of laws discovered, dating from more than 2,000 years before the Christian era, are from the Babylonian kingdom in Mesopotamia, an area that is now largely Iraq. Written codes are believed to have existed at about the same time in Egypt, and codes have been found from the Hittite civilization—now largely Turkey—dating a few hundred years later. Exciting as these discoveries have been, it may be an exaggeration to refer to the tablets as codes. They are merely disorganized statements of a variety of legal rules, not comprehensive restatements of the laws.

The most significant discovery has been the Babylonian Code of Hammurabi believed to be from the eighteenth century BC, the most systematic ancient code, though still a partial statement of the laws that must have existed at the time. The fragmentary nature of early codes indicates that written law continued to be supplemented by customary law. In most societies, law also continued to be commingled with religion and administered by priestly functionaries. One of the most notable features of the Code of Hammurabi is its establishment of a secular judiciary.

About 500 years after the Code of Hammurabi, in Palestine, Moses based law on divine revelation. Yet another six centuries elapsed before Draco produced Greece's first written code, the harshness of which has given rise to the word *draconian*. In the sixth century BC, Draco's code was mitigated by the milder laws of Solon, which, about 150 years later, influenced the Twelve Tables, the seminal code of Roman law.

Justinian and his ministers.
Mosaic in the Basilica of San Vitale at Ravenna, sixth century.

from J. M. Kelly, *A Short History of Western Legal Theory*
(Oxford, Eng.: Clarendon Press, 1992), pp. 1–29, 39–62, 79–82.
Copyright © 1992 by Delphine Kelly.
Reprinted by permission of Delphine Kelly and Oxford University Press.

The Greeks

Greece as a Starting-Point

The reason why Greece has a special place in the history of civilization is not merely that most departments of literature and the visual arts were there raised to levels which later ages agreed to regard as classical, that is, as permanent standards of excellence. It is also because the Greeks were the first people—at any rate, the first of whom Europe retains any consciousness—among whom reflective thought and argument became a habit of educated men; a training for some, and a profession or vocation for others, not confined to observation of the physical world and universe—in which the Egyptians and Babylonians had long preceded them—but extending to man himself, his nature, and his place in the order of things, the character of human society, and the best way of governing it.

Other ancient peoples had contained priests and prophets whose teaching or whose poetic insights included perceptions of human nature and moral precepts; a lot of the Old Testament of the Jews, for example, could be put into that category. Similarly, other ancient peoples, since they had laws, must have had some capacity to reason about the function of a law and how best to make it achieve a particular purpose; this can be presumed of the civilizations of Mesopotamia, from whose ruins the great code of the Babylonian King Hammurabi (about 1800 BC) and the laws of Eshnuna (about 200 years older still) have been excavated. This epoch antedates the high period of Greek civilization by roughly 1,500 years. Nevertheless it was among the Greeks that the objective discussion of man's relation to law and justice became an activity of the educated mind and was recorded in a literature which has been part, ever since, of a more or less continuous European tradition. It is therefore with the Greeks that the history of reflective jurisprudence in the West, or European legal theory, must begin.

. . .

The Political Structure of Ancient Greece

. . . In the seventh, sixth, fifth, and fourth centuries BC the people who spoke one or other dialect of the Greek language, and who recognized in their linguistic and cultural affinities a common Hellenic nationality, . . . lived in hundreds of "cities" (*poleis*), one of which—Athens—was of considerable size even by modern standards, but which varied greatly, down to something hardly bigger than a large village of the modern world together with a small immediate hinterland.

. . .

In any treatment of Greek civilization, including Greek law, there is a tendency for Athens to bulk very large, and often to seem synonymous with Greece itself. This is because, of the hundreds of Greek city-states, Athens was by far the greatest, in population, in power and influence, in wealth, in art and literature, until her defeat in the long Peloponnesian war with Sparta [in the fifth century BC] inaugurated a rapid decline. . . . It is, however, altogether wrong to assume that a constitutional or legal rule evidenced at Athens was mirrored in a similar rule everywhere else. Despite the features of broad family resemblance . . . , Greek cities differed as widely in their political systems—which ranged with numerous gradations from kingships through tyrannies . . . and oligarchies to democracies, in many places with frequent revolutions from one system to another—as they did in dialect; their legal systems, though we are very imperfectly informed about most of them, probably reflected this variety in regimes.

The Sources for Greek Law and Legal Theory

The materials for the history of Greek law are not to be found in Greek legal texts; the Greeks, so fertile in so many areas of the intellect, never produced a practical legal science; the Roman jurists were to be the first to give this to the world. Indeed such a thing as a Greek legal treatise does not exist, nor is there any hint that such a thing was ever written, even at Athens, or that any school of legal instruction ever operated there. What laws the people of Greece lived by must be gathered elsewhere; the best source is the physical remains of lawcodes or statutes engraved on stone or bronze, of which archaeology has uncovered a scattering all over the Greek world, most no more than problematical fragments. . . . Other evidence must be gathered wherever it can be found, chiefly in various departments of literature: a good deal, for example, is known of the law of Athens from the speeches of the fourth-century orators, while the works of historians, philosophers, and even dramatists also provide useful material. . . .

The position in regard to legal theory, as distinct from actual law, is similar. There was no such thing as a recognized and distinct branch of philosophy of specifically legal orientation; such questions as the origin and basis of the state, the source of obligation in law, or the relation of law to some higher or more fundamental standard, were not discussed in monographs on those themes alone, or by theorists specializing in them. Greek ideas on such matters are indeed recorded in great quantity, and are the first shoots of an intellectual growth which later ages cultivated in a more specific and organized way; but they must be gathered from a variety of literary sources, many of them quite unconscious contributions to the history of jurisprudence, a science for which the Greeks did not even have a name (just as there was no Greek word for "law" as an abstract concept). Thus not only philosophical works—although these are certainly the most important—but also the work of poets, dramatists, and historians must be drawn on to provide the first chapter in that history.

Archaic Greek Ideas on Law and Justice

The earliest coherent body of evidence we have about Greek life and thought is furnished by the Homeric epics, the *Iliad* (about the siege of Troy) and the *Odyssey* (about the wanderings of the Greek Odysseus trying to get home after the Trojan war); these poems seem to have been put into the form in which we know them about 800–700 BC, but this form represents the concretization of a long tradition of orally transmitted epic poetry, and it is agreed that the poems reflect a much earlier epoch of Greek society, very roughly 1300–1100 BC, the era to which the "siege of Troy" (which from the evidence of archaeology may have been a historical event) can be assigned.

This archaic society already rests on "cities," each with a political organization consisting of king, council of elders, and people. It is a society living according to an understood pattern, in which the supernatural plays an important part, and in which various moral virtues or faults are celebrated or deplored; but in which the idea of law, in a sense which the word conveys immediately to the modern mind—or conveyed to the Romans, or even to the Greeks of a later age—is fluid and elusive. We seem to be seeing, in Homer, the formative stage in the idea of law; indeed, if we appraise Homeric society from the standpoint of our own conception of law as something known, certain, and objective, we are seeing Europe in a pre-legal condition.

There is no "legislature." The king does not "make" laws, in the sense of rules which the people must obey. There is no apparent consciousness of custom as something normative. Instead, there is *themis*: a word whose force is difficult to grasp, but which is applied to an area at the centre of which is perhaps the idea of god-inspired decision or directive or finding. This finding is not arbitrary, but reflects a shared sense of what is proper. . . .

Side by side with *themis*, we find in the Homeric poems the notion of *dike*, a word which in the Homeric era had not acquired its later clear senses (abstract justice or a lawsuit or a judgment) but nevertheless had a somewhat sharper edge, a "severer countenance" than *themis*.

. . .

These hazy conceptual embryos, *themis* and *dike*, are the symbols of a world not yet conscious of law. . . . Of anything that can be called a theory of law, or reflection on the nature of society or the state or government, there is no trace in these epics, which otherwise transmit a very full idea of how Hellenic society lived and thought in the late second millennium BC.

In the age following Homer, in the eighth–sixth centuries BC, though the works of Hesiod and the lyric poets reflect a conception of justice—Hesiod (eighth century) complains of the evil of "crooked judgments"—there is still no sign that the concept of law has emerged. . . .

The Age of the Lawgivers

The earliest European appearance of something which obviously corresponds with our "law" in the positive, statutory sense is with the famous lawgivers Dracon (late seventh) and Solon (early sixth century BC). This is the era in which, all over the Hellenic world, and undoubtedly related to the recent development of the art of writing, the first efforts were made to inscribe in permanent and public form rules which formerly had the vaguer status of custom, the interpretation or even the statement of which was vulnerable to distortion through the self-interest of the aristocracies which ruled in most Greek cities and whose members were the repositories of whatever justice there was.

. . . The dramatist Euripides, writing in the late fifth century, presents the emergence of written laws as a progressive achievement, tending to equalize the ground of rich and poor; laws, once publicly written up on stone or bronze, were equally knowable and accessible to all, and so no longer subject to the arbitrary statement or interpretation of a closed and privileged caste.

Status (and Original Quasi-Sanctity) of Statute-Law

The earliest phase of Greek legislation was associated with individual lawgivers such as Dracon and Solon at Athens. . . . But the later legislative process, at any rate in cities which were democracies, rested on a majority vote of the people. . . . Once the wave of codes had passed over the Greek world, statute came to be thought of not just as a more effective vesture for law, but as its only source; there is no trace of custom being looked on as an independent or even complementary source of law. Indeed the prejudice in favour of statute reached the point that, where an ancient rule was actually practiced although not contained in a contemporaneously existing written law, it was attributed to a former lawgiver, even if he was a mythical one.

The Athenian democracy of the fifth century evidently saw in its *nomoi*, its laws, a characteristic feature which proudly distinguished them, as other Greeks were for the same reason distinguished, from their non-Greek ("barbarian") neighbours; the latter . . . were ruled by tyrants guided only by their own arbitrary discretion. . . .

This sense of a proud distinction in the possession of written laws may have something to do with the strong difference in attitude towards statute law between the Greeks and the medieval and modern (and to some extent even the Roman) world. Whereas no particular sanctity attaches, in the modern eye, to the original text of an enactment, in the sense that no inhibition is felt about amending it, perhaps frequently, in response to changed conditions, the Greeks were at first averse to altering their laws. A general predisposition in favour of the stability and permanence of a law once made is attested both by passages in literature . . . and by evidence about rules actually governing the process of proposing a new law (which necessarily must repeal or modify the old one). The most extreme example is reported by Demosthenes about the Locrians, a Dorian people living in the toe of Italy, who were reputed to have been the first of all the Greeks to adopt a written code; anyone who proposed an alteration in their laws had to make his proposal with a rope around his neck, which, if his proposal was rejected, was drawn tight. The Athenians . . . had no such spectacularly drastic law; but the process of legislation in Athens was hedged around with formidable barriers. . . .

In the following age this austerity was relaxed, at any rate in the era of Athens's incipient decline; new laws multiplied, the legislative process was degraded to an engine of political warfare, and even the recording of new laws became chaotic, so that it was often uncertain whether a supposed law existed or not, or whether a directly contradictory law might coexist with it. A further source of confusion was the unclear relationship of *psephismata* (resolutions, decrees) to *nomoi*, statutes more strictly so called; the most that can be said is that *nomoi* were envisaged as permanent general dispositions, while *psephismata* were *ad hoc* or supplementary or effectuating measures. . . . It is however clear from the expressions of the orators that this picture of uncertainty, and of the transfusion of the legislative process by political expediencies of the moment, was regarded as a shameful decline from the standards of an earlier age which had looked on the ancestral laws as immutable.

The Emergence of Legal Theory: Origin of the State and of Law

. . .

[T]he demoralized climate of Athens at the end of the Peloponnesian war, afflicted by disease and defeat, . . . contained a school or movement of minds called then and since by the name sophists. . . . A position maintained by the sophists . . . was that, since human customs are widely and visibly different from place to place, laws (even in the sense of deliberate statutory regulation of human behaviour) might perhaps be regarded as equally relative and contingent. . . . Why should disobedience to law be wicked, when no one could rationally stigmatize in this way the non-observance by one tribe of a custom recognized by another? Sophists tended to answer that all law is merely conventional, contingent, accidental, variable; this observation, evidently valid for mere custom, had however the effect of fixing law itself with the character of relativity and indifference, and thus of floating it off from the moral moorings which provide the sense of duty to obey it.

. . .

The first philosopher to challenge the sophistic position was Socrates (469–399 BC), who ended his life having been condemned to death for reasons which are still obscure—ostensibly for "corrupting the youth," but probably at least partly because of the spirit of critical detachment towards received ideas and ancestral beliefs which the whole tribe of philosophers—Socrates as well as the sophists—displayed. In prison under sentence, and waiting to be given the fatal draught of poison, Socrates could, apparently, have easily escaped; his friends were anxious to arrange this, and the authorities (it is suggested) might have been glad enough to turn a blind eye to the frustration of a sentence which some of them now regretted. Plato's dialogue *Crito* shows Socrates's friend of that name trying to persuade him to grasp the chance of life; Socrates firmly refuses, determined to remain obedient to the laws of his city, though he was himself the innocent victim of their unjust operation. He imagines the laws as personified, and as arguing with him the basis of his duty to obey them, a duty resting indeed on "convention," but in a far deeper and morally weightier sense than that intended by the sophists; convention in the sense, in fact, of implied but none the less binding contract. Socrates had had the benefit of those laws all his life; if he had not wished for their protection, he could have left Athens and gone to live elsewhere; and so by his conduct he has tacitly agreed to respect them. . . . [D]isobedience, if Socrates were to take the chance of escape, would amount (say the laws) to "doing what in you lies to destroy the laws and with it the whole state." This quixotic determination to uphold the laws even at the unjust sacrifice of his own life gives peculiar force to the element of agreement, of contract, as the rock on which state and laws are founded.

. . .

The Relation of Law to a Higher Standard

A central problem of jurisprudence is whether a law, in order to be recognized as such, need conform only to formal criteria, or whether its validity depends also on its not infringing some permanent, higher, "natural" standard. In other words, even assuming in general terms that the state and its laws are entitled to obedience, does this mean that any measure whatever, as long as it bears the formal marks of enactment, is entitled to this obedience, however repugnant it may be to the subject's moral values? Or is there a transcendent standard which is paramount?

This question, . . . which lies at the root of all modern discussion of "fundamental rights," was not posed by ancient Greek philosophy, but does appear in Greek literature. It is raised in mid-fifth century Athenian tragedy, in the *Antigone* of Sophocles, where it is presented in the form of a celebrated dilemma, handled by the poet so easily as to make us suspect that it was a commonplace even in his time. A civil war had divided two brothers, one of whom died in attacking Thebes, the other in its defence. The king forbids the burial of the former, wishing to leave his body to be devoured by beasts; but thus also, according to Greek religious ideas, preventing his soul from finding the repose which only burial—even a token interment under a handful of earth—can ensure. Antigone, the dead brothers' sister, is impelled by piety to disobey; she puts earth on the body lying exposed on the plain, and is arrested. The king asks her whether she knew of his order, and, if so, why she disobeyed it. She replies:

> . . . These laws were not ordained of Zeus,
> And she who sits enthroned with gods below,
> Justice, enacted not these human laws.
> Nor did I deem that thou, a mortal man,
> Couldst by a breath annul and override
> The immutable unwritten laws of heaven.
> They were not born today nor yesterday;
> They die not; and none knoweth whence they sprang.

Eternal laws of supernatural origin are mentioned by Sophocles also in another passage, though not in a context of similar dramatic confrontation. But otherwise the *Antigone* passage, although much cited in later classical literature, is isolated. . . .

Nevertheless the Greeks reveal, in two ways, a belief in the idea of something transcending positive laws, something which is "naturally" right and proper, something classifiable as "natural" law or justice. Firstly, Aristotle actually enunciated the theoretical distinction between that which is naturally just . . . and that which is just only in consequence of having been prescribed by positive law. . . .

Secondly, a series of Greek literary passages suggests that a certain range of relationships was felt to involve "natural" rights and duties. . . . The family relationship was seen as carrying with it the natural duty of children to give honourable burial to parents and to support them in old age, just as the parents had been under a natural duty to sustain their children in infancy. Again, . . . enslavement was regarded as the natural consequence of capture in war. The rights of intestate succession were attributed to the natural circumstances of blood relationship; the right of self-defense was equally located in nature, and . . . punishment for wrongdoing which exactly matched the mode of the offence (symmetrical retribution) was considered to be what nature suggested.

The Purpose and Scope of Law

. . . Plato . . . assigned to law not merely the regulation of conditions inherent or at least common in human society, [such as crime, property, inheritance, and contract,] but also the deliberate training (in the gardener's quite as much as in the teacher's sense) of that society towards an ideal state of perfection. Thus he visualized law in an extra dimension which, although various regimes have tried to make it a reality, the West has on the whole rejected.

The conception of a state in which law has this dimension was made articulate by Plato; but it existed in practice already in his time in the most individual of all Greek states, Sparta, and Sparta is thought to have been his inspiration. This city, a byword then as now for rigorous austerity, enforced its manners by education and training on the young, and maintained [its manners] among them as adults. These manners had no basis in what we might recognize as a religious morality, but were geared to the production and constant renewal of a militarist and irresistible state. Other Greeks, glimpsing, as they thought, something of the pristine simplicity and manliness of their race in a milieu which must have resembled that of a philistine boarding-school, felt a sneaking admiration for Sparta, expressed in Plato's case by proposing something like the Spartan model for his ideal polity and its rulers.

These rulers ("guardians") are central to the whole system. The first generation of rulers is to be selected by the legislator, who will also divide the remaining population into the second class (soldiers) and the third (common people); thereafter an official myth will be propagated, according to which these three categories correspond to a divinely preordained classification. The further breeding in the ruler class is to be governed by rigorous eugenic regulation, by which weaklings will be either avoided or eliminated. Between the rulers—who may, incidentally, be of either sex—a communism not only of property but of sexual partners and of children is to be observed. Anything like the nuclear family, the concept around which so much of Christian and even of non-Christian law and ethics revolves, will not be in the picture. The education of young people is to be subject to the most minute regulation, with certain modes of music excluded from the curriculum as tending to encourage softness or frivolity, the body is to be trained to endure hardship, the spirit to show courage; the formation of the intellect is to be aimed at producing rulers who will be philosophers (the "philosopher kings," in a phrase commonly used to sum up this idea of Plato's). The formidable austerity and the (to us, repellent) conformity which Plato sought for—and in some measure found in his Spartan model—was, however, not visualized as harnessed to the sort of imperialist or racialist ideology with which we might expect to find it associated in the twentieth century. It was simply a regime which he rather naively thought would produce a noble state in which justice could best be achieved. Thus it was a regime complying certainly at first sight with the doctrine that laws should be for the general benefit; but (at any rate, as we would think) conflicting with it at a deeper level because established at too great a cost in human freedom and dignity.

. . .

Aristotle's Analysis of Justice

The nearest thing to conscious legal theory in classical Greek literature is to be found in the fifth book of the *Nicomachean Ethics* of Aristotle, devoted to an analysis of justice and equity. . . . [J]ustice, he wrote in a classification which became celebrated, is of two kinds: "distributive" and "corrective." By distributive justice he meant "that which is exercised in the distribution of honour, wealth, and the other divisible assets of the community, which may be allotted among its members in equal or unequal shares." . . . [T]his definition corresponds evidently with "legislative justice," the kind we expect to see displayed in statutes or other governmental measures which distribute benefits or impose burdens in patterns and proportions which we can accept as fair or rational. . . . Aristotle's meaning emerges from some general propositions, for example, that equals are to be treated equally, unequals unequally, that justice is proportion, injustice is disproportion. . . . He does not, however, descend to discussing a hypothetical concrete situation to be regulated by law, which will of course not respond to measurement against an abstract formula, but only to a legislator's instinct of fairness.

"Corrective" justice, on the other hand, is not legislative justice, but rather what we might call judicial justice, the justice of the courts. Corrective justice is putting right something that has gone wrong, restoring an equilibrium where the just balance has been disturbed. . . . This corrective justice, moreover, comes in two forms: where it intervenes in situations which are "voluntary," and where it does so in situation which are "involuntary." . . . The distinction between "voluntary" and "involuntary" transactions corresponds superficially with the distinction which we would recognize between contract, on the one hand, and tortious or criminal wrongs, on the other. . . .

Law and Equity

In the fifth book of the *Ethics*, in which Aristotle discusses justice, he also deals with "equity" (*epieikeia*) as something distinct from it. The conception of equity . . . is a correction of legal justice, because a law speaks in general terms, and, because of the natural irregularity and variety of the material it tries to regulate, it cannot provide a perfectly just treatment for every possible case:

> When, therefore, the law lays down a general rule, and thereafter a case arises falling somewhat outside the general model, it is then right, where the lawgiver's words have turned out to be too simple to meet the case without doing wrong, to rectify the deficiency by deciding as the lawgiver would himself decide if he were present on the occasion, and would have enacted if he were aware of the case in question.

Effect is given to equity in this sense, he says, not by changing the general law but by a popular vote (*psephisma*) which bends, *ad hoc*, its application, also, apparently, by an arbitrator agreed on by the parties to a dispute, because in another work, the *Rhetoric*, he says that . . . people prefer an arbitrator, who looks to equity, rather than a judge who must stick to the strict law; indeed this is why (he says) such a thing as an arbitrator was invented.

. . .

Equality Before the Law

. . . Aristotle quotes verses of the venerated Solon . . . in which this archetypal Greek lawgiver disclaims all willingness to allow the base to have equal shares in the country with the noble; and in the celebrated funeral oration delivered by Pericles and reported by Thucydides the statesman mentions it as a proud feature of the Athenian system that personal merit will lead to honour and preferment. But in the same passage Pericles says that, despite a hierarchy of rank based on merit, "as regards the law, all men are on an equal footing so far as concerns their private disputes." . . .

The Romans

Rome and Italy

. . .

In the course of the fourth and third centuries [BC] the power of Rome grew from [a] modest beginning until it had become the dominant force in Italy. The pattern of this development was the gradual building of a network of relationships, mostly of alliance, with neighbouring peoples; the planting of colonies and settlements; and the progressive extension of Roman citizenship. This development was occasionally marked by wars, as this or that people revolted from an alliance which was in fact one of dependence, but on the whole the progress of Rome to supremacy in Italy was not a naked military conquest. A generous policy in regard to the grant of citizenship, and a prudent restriction of authority's exercise to what was necessary for military security—there was no attempt to impose a uniform system of local government, judicature, or religion—helped to produce a genuinely harmonious Italy, Roman in its standard language, sentiment, and allegiance.

. . .

The Greek Impact on Roman Law

. . .

[T]he Greek cities had laws, and traditions of lawgiving. But nowhere was there a legal science or any very sophisticated legal technique. A mid-fifth-century Greek law-code . . . might be as elaborate and as extensive in scale as the Twelve Tables enacted by the Roman legislative commission at about the same date; but the subsequent life of a Greek system was led without any jurists' profession to guide, organize, expound, and develop it. Moreover, . . . litigation was conducted less in the spirit of a contest about the objective applicability of a legal norm than as a rhetorical match in which no holds were barred. Even in Athens we do not know the name of a single person who worked as a legal adviser (rather than as a court orator), or who taught law to students, nor the name of a single book on a legal subject. . . .

In Rome, on the other hand, apparently already some time before the first encounter with the Greek mind . . . , there were the beginnings of a legal profession of a kind that never existed in Greece and remained, indeed, unique in the world until the rise of the common lawyers in the high Middle Ages. This profession, pursued in some measure through a sense of public duty and the responsibilities of their class by men of rank engaged in the running of public affairs, was entirely secular, even though its remoter origins may lie partly in the functions of the Roman priesthoods in an era when cult ritual, magic, and the activation of legal forms were different aspects of the same complex of ideas, namely, those connected in the involvement of the gods in bringing about results in human affairs. By the later republic all traces of this primitive association had disappeared. The lay jurists, who from about the mid-second-century BC became known to us individually by name, pursued the entirely secular and practical tasks of expounding rules of law, drawing up formulas for legal transactions, and advising magistrates, litigants, and judges. They also taught their science to the generation of students who would follow them, and they began to publish: commentaries, monographs, collections of their opinions, introductory textbooks for students. For a period of nearly 400 years, . . . until the turmoil of the third century AD, the science of these jurists represents—together with the Roman genius for imperial government—the most characteristic flower of Roman civilization, and the one least indebted to foreign models, evidently growing spontaneously from some part of the Roman national spirit without parallel elsewhere in the ancient world.

These jurists pursued a science which was the opposite of theoretical. The formulation of great first principles and grand generalities was quite foreign to them. They were strictly practical, concentrating on the concrete individual cases in regard to which they had been consulted as to the law (hence their name *iuris consulti*, "persons consulted about the law"), and giving their view tersely, without rhetorical or philosophical flourish, mostly also without any full statement of reasons (though often citing in support the congruent opinions of other or earlier jurists). Anyone seeking the underlying principles of their work in a particular area of law must do so by careful collation from the vast sediments of their case-material and commentaries. . . .

These jurists, then, practiced a science unknown to the Greeks. . . . And yet it would be wrong to say that the Greek intellect, as distinct from rules of Greek law, made no contribution to the Roman legal achievement; because the Roman jurists in fact owed extremely important elements of their *method* to the adoption of tools which they encountered in Greek philosophy and grammar, and perhaps to some extent also in Greek rhetoric.

The most important of these, one with which the study of Plato and Aristotle would have acquainted them, was the so-called dialectical method: this means the organization of material in an orderly system by a process of division and sub-division into genera and species, arrived at by establishing differences (*diairesis*) on the one hand, and analogies or affinities (*synagoge, synthesis*) on the other. . . .

In addition to the dialectic process, it may be that Roman ideas on the interpretation of statutes or other legal instruments and transactions were influenced by lessons and themes from Greek philosophy and rhetoric. . . . Roman jurists very often had recourse to the etymology, the real or supposed derivation of a word, in order to explain its legal force. . . .

Another interpretative rule . . . requires that words should be understood in the sense in which they are generally employed, and not in some sense which may have been special to the person using them in a particular case. This too may have a partly Greek origin. . . .

Greek Philosophy and Roman Equity

Roman equity . . . is meant here to convey . . . the impact on Roman theory and practice of Greek ideas about the superiority of the spirit to the letter, and the importance of the will or intention rather than mere words; and about . . . *aequitas*, meaning that which is fair or conscionable, and a value co-ordinate with *ius*, the strict law. . . .

The essence of equity, though not raised to the status of a legal doctrine, might be respected in a Roman court, in which the advocates would naturally deploy the weapons with which their education in Greek philosophy and rhetoric had furnished them. Thus Cicero . . . reports a case in which one party, who had resold to the person from whom he had originally bought it a piece of land which was subject to an easement, was being sued for failure to disclose the existence of this encumbrance. Strictly speaking, the law required such disclosure; but as it had existed at the time when it had been sold by the man who was now repurchasing it, who therefore knew about it perfectly well, was there not a case for treating the rule requiring declaration as inapplicable in these circumstances? . . .

. . . There was . . . a formal route by which what would today be called equitable values were . . . introduced into the law, namely, the jurisdiction of the praetor. . . . It was an absolutely central element in Roman administration of justice, the importance of which cannot be exaggerated. . . .

Without being himself a judge, the praetor was the gate of access to judicial hearing and decision; it was before him that the issues between the parties were clarified, whereupon he reduced them to a simple, one-sentence formula, expressed as a command to the judge. . . . [O]ut of his supervisory role in the administration of justice there grew what for all practical purposes was a legislative power. This happened in gradual stages by process of usurpation which was simply acquiesced in.

The key to this development lies in the fact that the praetor was the absolute, uncontrolled master of civil legal process. All actions were initiated before him, and the hearing of an issue by a judge was authorized by him; if he chose to deny a plaintiff the action he sought, there was no one to whom an appeal could be brought, and the plaintiff remained shut out from relief. Alternatively he might effectively guarantee the plaintiff's ultimate failure by letting him go ahead, but building into the written programme for the hearing (the conditional command to the judge, called the *formula*) a special defence, related to some plea which the defendant had raised, and directing the judge to dismiss the action if he found the facts did sustain that plea. From accumulated single instances, as may be imagined, firm practice emerged; thus by the last century of the republic a regular special defence, based on the plea that the plaintiff's behaviour had been or was now unconscionable, called the *exceptio doli*, had emerged, and sufficed to frustrate a plaintiff who might have the strict letter of the law on his side; a similar defence based on duress (*metus*) was established around the same time. Again, where someone who had purchased property and had actually got possession of it, but without the conveyancing formality requisite for property of that type, was sued for possession by someone claiming on the vendor's civil-law ownership (which still subsisted because of the ineffective conveyance), the praetor created, so to speak out of the air, a special defence . . . which cut the Gordian knot of civil law by simply directing the judge, if he found that the property had been subject of a contract of sale and had been physically handed over to the buyer, to dismiss the action founded on the seller's title notwithstanding that, at civil law, this title was perfect.

. . . Naturally the availability of these procedural devices to someone with a formally defective conveyance undermined the whole system of conveyancing formalities by making them irrelevant in practice; and so, in the result, the praetor effectively repealed the old law on the subject.

. . .

Roman Theory of Natural Law

. . .

It is in Cicero, writing in high-minded academic detachment, that we encounter a conception of natural law. . . . In his treatise *De legibus* ("On the Laws"), . . . he presents nature as the source of precepts to the human individual, a source accessible to every such individual through his or her reason; and this provision for human conduct has its origin in God. . . .

In the most celebrated of all such passages . . . he wrote:

> True law is right reason in agreement with nature, diffused among all men; constant and unchanging, it should call men to their duties by its precepts, and deter them from wrongdoing by its prohibitions; and it never commands or forbids upright men in vain, while its rules and restraints are lost upon the wicked. To curtail this law is unholy, to amend it illicit, to repeal it impossible; nor can we be dispensed from it by the order either of senate or of popular assembly; nor need we look for anyone to clarify or interpret it; nor will it be one law at Rome and a different one at Athens, nor otherwise tomorrow than it is today; but one and the same Law, eternal and unchangeable, will bind all peoples and all ages; and God, its designer, expounder and enacter, will be as it were the sole and universal ruler and governor of all things; and whoever disobeys it, because by this act he will have turned his back on himself and on man's very nature, will pay the heaviest penalty, even if he avoids the other punishments which are adjudged fit for his conduct.

. . .

On the positive side, Cicero presents several legally material principles as derived from the law of nature. . . . The right of self-defence is the most obvious instance; others are the prohibition against cheating or harming others, and the precept that one must positively defend others from harm.

. . .

[The] entirely practical, common-sense employment of the concept of nature by the jurists linked up in their minds with an element in the Roman legal system which arose in one important area of legal practice, namely commerce (in the broadest sense) with foreigners on Roman territory, or between such foreigners themselves. This element was called the *ius gentium*, "the law of (all) nations," as distinct from the *ius civile*, "the citizen-law," i.e. that pertaining only to Romans. . . . This . . . , taken in isolation, would suggest that the Romans had taken a scientific interest in the legal systems of other peoples, and by comparative study had established that certain rules were the same everywhere. In fact this is not the case. The Romans, like other ancient peoples, took very little interest in the institutions of their neighbours.

. . .

The Late Roman Empire and After

. . .

Three events of late Roman history—all three contained within the fourth and fifth centuries AD—may fairly be called of cardinal importance in the sense implied by the derivation of the word "cardinal" from the Latin word for a hinge: they were the hinges upon which a gigantic door of history turned, closing the era of the Graeco-Roman pagan world centered on the basin of the Mediterranean, opening that of the Western Christian world whose centre of gravity lay more and more to the north of the Alps. Those three events were, firstly, the formal division of the Roman empire into a western and an eastern half; secondly, the roughly contemporaneous adoption of Christianity as the official religion of the empire; and thirdly, the destruction and conquest of the western empire by the Germans [in 476].

. . .

[The] east-Roman, Byzantine empire survived the collapse of its western twin half by a thousand years, though in a condition of continual contraction and advancing debility, until the capture of Constantinople by the Turks in 1453, barely a generation before the discovery of America.

The culture of this Eastern Roman empire, though it has always appeared stifling and even sinister to the modern Western European mind, is of enormous importance for the history of European civilization (and of European jurisprudence). . . . The Eastern empire preserved in its Byzantine form the Greek language and with it the physical remains of classical Greek literature and science; in that era of fragile manuscript transmission, almost all knowledge of this vast culture had disappeared in the West when the Western empire lapsed into semi-barbarism with the German conquest; but at the epoch of the Renaissance it was chiefly from the libraries of the Byzantine empire that Greek learning, and scholars able to interpret it, once again reached the West. And, of central importance in the history of law, it was in the Eastern empire, under the emperor Justinian (527–65), that the mass of the inherited writings of the classical Roman jurists (which came to an end in the turbulence of the third century) was edited and compiled into the *Digest* which bears his name. This work . . . was apparently as good as unknown throughout the West during the Dark Ages, but it was rediscovered in the late eleventh century . . . and ultimately became the basis of the whole civil law of continental Europe and, later, of the many distant lands to which it was exported by colonialism or by cultural penetration.

CHAPTER 3

Medieval Europe

Following the sacking of Rome in 476, the Western Roman Empire disintegrated into a changing kaleidoscope of Germanic kingdoms. Ostrogoths, Visigoths, Franks, and others brought their customary laws to former Roman lands, but they were soon influenced by Roman law. Among Roman influences was the reduction of laws to writing. The Visigoths in France and the Salic Franks in the Lowlands produced written texts of customary laws before the end of the fifth century.

Conquered Romans were allowed to remain under Roman law, but with the deterioration of Roman culture, their texts were soon reduced to simplified abridgments. In contrast, in the unconquered Eastern Roman Empire, the Emperor Justinian summoned the best legal minds of the Empire and had them comb through the available sources of Roman law and distill them down to a *Code* of legislation, a *Digest* of juristic writings, and an *Institute* to provide an overview for the instruction of students. The whole, known as the *Corpus Juris Civilis*, was completed in 534. For a time thereafter, no other legal sources were allowed to be cited, and new law required the approval of the emperor.

By about 600, even the remote Anglo-Saxons of England had their written laws (the "dooms" of King Aethelberht). In their monumental 1895 study, *The History of English Law Before the Time of Edward I*, Frederick Pollock and Frederic William Maitland wrote of Aethelberht:

> Not improbably he had heard of Justinian's exploits; but the dooms . . . are barbarous enough. They are also, unless discoveries are yet to be made, the first Germanic laws that were written in a Germanic tongue. (p. 11)

In 643 the Lombards in Italy compiled the most influential Germanic laws. By then, Christianity had spread to the conquered Romans and to their conquerors alike. As the most organized and most universal institution in Europe, the Church developed its canon law not only to govern its clergy, but also to regulate aspects of secular life such as marriage and inheritance.

Other secular laws were localized for centuries under a feudal system which delegated legal jurisdiction as well as authority over land tenure and administration to local barons. Feudalism allowed for national unity under strong kings, such as Charlemagne, crowned Emperor of the Holy Roman Empire in 800, but weakness at the center and the fragmentation of authority were more prevalent.

Despite the shortcomings of feudalism, a cultural, commercial, and legal flowering occurred after the turn of the millennium. In the eleventh and twelfth centuries, law schools at Pavia and Bologna attracted students from all over Europe to study and edit both Germanic and Roman law. With Roman law as a model, canon law was systematized by Gratian's *Decretum* of 1141. Roman law was also "received" into secular legal systems throughout Europe—with the exception of England.

The Court of King's Bench, fifteenth century.
From Whaddon Folio, Inner Temple, London.

THE COMMON LAW OF ENGLAND

from R. C. Van Caenegem, *The Birth of the English Common Law,* 2d ed.
(Cambridge, Eng.: Cambridge University Press, 1988), pp. 85–110.
Copyright © 1973, 1988 by Cambridge University Press.
Reprinted by permission of Cambridge University Press.

English Law and the Continent

Let us start . . . with a paradox. . . . It is that English and continental law irrevocably took their different courses in the very century, the twelfth, when English civilization was closer to the Continent and less insular than at any other time. The Common Law and the "Romano-Germanic family," two of the systems of universal significance . . . are both of European origin, yet they differ greatly. To lawyers outside Anglo-Saxon lands the traditional Common Law is well nigh incomprehensible . . . because there are no codes that encompass it. . . . But Englishmen fully share this incomprehension mixed with aversion, as far as "the alien jungle of the *Code Civil*" is concerned. . . .

Why is the Common Law so different from the law of the European Continent? Why above all did this national law of England enter upon its different course precisely in the twelfth century?

. . .

The Common Law of England . . . —so different from the *jus commune* or common learned law of the European universities—is the oldest national law in Europe. It is the oldest body of law that was common to a whole kingdom and administered by a central court with a nation-wide competence in first instance. In the rest of Europe, the law was either European or local, not national. In consequence a number of countries paradoxically adopted the cosmopolitan *jus commune* to provide a national legal system which the divergent customs could not produce, because they were not sophisticated enough and regional pride resisted the imposition of the customs of one region on all others. . . .

For centuries, . . . this Common Law of England consisted of a system of actions or legal remedies, each commanding its own procedure, whereas continental law knew general procedural rules which governed all or large classes of causes. English law prefers precedent as a basis for judgments, and moves empirically from case to case, from one reality to another. Continental law tends to move more theoretically by deductive reasoning, basing judgments on abstract principles; it is more conceptual, more scholastic and works more with definitions and distinctions. In other words it was moulded by the Roman Law of the medieval universities. It was this professors' law, marked by exegesis and commentaries on learned books and glosses, which made continental law different from the Germanic and feudal customs and laws of England. . . . [I]n the Common Law, . . . the Year Books, with their reports of court cases, were typical. . . . In England lawyers received their training in the Inns of Court, technical colleges where they learnt their craft like every medieval craftsman, in contact with practising masters, not in universities at the feet of scholars who were apt to lose themselves in controversy. English law worked essentially within the existing feudal framework, whereas continental law incorporated a vast amount of extraneous elements, mainly of Roman origin. . . . A final difference is the absence of codification in England. The tradition of case law and empiricism makes very poor soil for codification . . . but with systematic theory and logical deduction from general premises, codes came naturally on the Continent.

. . .

The breach came with the momentous modernization of European society in general, and the law in particular, that took place in the twelfth and thirteenth centuries, a watershed of the greatest importance. In all Europe . . . a process began which led eventually to the sovereign national states of modern times, with their central bureaucracy, rational approach and modernized law. The towns in many lands broke with the old order, the universities rose and with them the study of Justinian's *Corpus Juris Civilis*. Monarchical government made great strides forward, the rulers of France undertook the unification of the kingdom and created in the Parliament of Paris a central high court, occupied by professional jurists educated in the universities. Politically speaking, feudalism had spent its force and vast new monetary resources allowed the state to employ non-feudal officials. . . .

. . . The breakthrough of a centralized and modernized legal system took place exceptionally early in England (and Normandy), before Roman law was in a position to exert any profound influence. . . . Nowhere in Europe is there a national legal system that had done away to all practical intents and purposes with the archaic modes of evidence [such as trial by ordeal] earlier than in England; nowhere do we find the practice of court enrollments as early as in England.

If the modernization of the law came exceptionally early in England, it was also remarkably systematic. The activity of the justices . . . and the various actions with which they dealt formed a coherent whole and were grasped and described as such. The new law and its judicial apparatus were national and royal. Not local magnates, but the king and his central justices were the bear-

ers of the whole system and its application was nation-wide. This was very unlike the Continent, where local and regional custom reigned supreme and even
the central courts judged according to local custom in appeal cases. This modernized law of England was essentially autochthonous, based on known rule
and familiar practice. It owed very little to Roman law. . . .

Not so on the Continent, where from the twelfth century onwards learned
commentaries on the *Corpus Juris Civilis* and Romano-canonical treatises on
procedure appear and, where, more important, we find from the thirteenth
century onwards a continuous stream of treatises on customary law and important royal legislation, which had absorbed Roman law to various degrees.
But by that time the Common Law and the Common Law courts were already
firmly and unshakably established. . . . This precocity, the premature character
of the rise of the Common Law is all-important. . . .

[W]hen at the turn of the twelfth century Romano-canonical learning began
to conquer the practice of Europe's ecclesiastical courts and, in the course of
the thirteenth century, to influence its lay courts and writers on customary law,
it was too late for the Common Law to be affected in any substantial way. . . .
The Common Law was set in its own techniques, practice, ideas and institutions, had created its own framework and had produced a technical terminology of considerable sophistication and precision that was to last for centuries
and constitute a barrier to civilian influence. . . .

Hardly have we, by drawing attention to the precocity of English modernization, answered one question, than another arises. Why this precocious development in England among European states? . . . No one will be simplistic
enough to explain this complex phenomenon by naming one single cause.
There must have been many, but some were more important than others and
one that we should certainly not overlook is the achievement of old-English
kingship in building a unified state. England had learned to live as one country, under one government with a national network of institutions, officials
and courts, during those very centuries when elsewhere the Frankish state and
its successors were falling apart and their administration disintegrating. The
old-English state, unified and consolidated in the tenth and eleventh centuries,
afforded the political basis on which later generations could build the Common Law. . . .

[Following the Norman Conquest of 1066,] the *Franci* and the *Anglici*
. . . were "two nations" in England, . . . separated by a wide gulf. The
"French" were of continental origin, ruled the country and its Church, controlled its wealth, were kept together by Anglo-Norman feudalism and held
land in Normandy and in England. They spoke French . . . were very close to
continental civilization and had a military, knightly way of life. They had
scant respect for the traditional values of the conquered English. . . . [T]he majority of the English were unfree *nativi*, so that the terms "naif," "rustic,"
"villein" and "Englishman" were interchangeable. This was the other nation,

the mainly unfree, English speaking, peasants, who were barred from high office and led a humble life in local agriculture, saving with difficulty such elements as they could of their own historical treasures, their kings, their saints
and their language.

. . . The Common Law was essentially feudal land law and feudalism came
from the Continent. . . . The royal officers and feudatories who shaped and defined the Common Law in its formative years were overwhelmingly members
of the "French" nation. . . . Also, . . . this Common Law was the "law of a
class" and not "of the whole kingdom and the men who dwell therein." The
Common Law took no interest in the unfree peasants who were harshly excluded. . . . The men who created it were members of a small dominant aristocracy and it was accessible to them and the free minority of the natives (an upper layer amongst the English), and they created it in order to preserve
harmony among the free, landowning top class. It is not surprising that the
technical language of this "English" Common Law was French and remained
so (though it became less and less understandable to French people) until the
seventeenth and eighteenth centuries. . . . It was in the thirteenth century that
the fusion of Norman and English into one nation took place and that Common Law, which bound together freemen of every descent became truly English, distinct from continental law and part of the country's identity. It was then
seen that the Common Law offered a way out of the difference between Englishman and Normans, held them together and solved existing contradictions.

. . . Thus in the thirteenth century the name of Englishman was something
to be proud of, whereas a century before it denoted servile status, and a system based on French feudal law, administered in French, became the pride of
the English nation. The Common Law helped to create a sense of nationhood
and greatness in late medieval England. It made people aware of their distinct-
ness, as compared with the other nations in the British Isles and on the Continent. . . .

[A]nother key element in the founding years of the Common Law [was] the
personality of Henry II [reigned 1154–1189], that "subtle inventor of new judicial forms," that man of genius—the word is not too strong—who was "by
instinct a lawyer." . . .

Under Henry II the Anglo-Norman complex reached its zenith. . . . In those
years the Common Law machinery was unshakably established and his personal drive was clearly of the highest importance. Modernization was on the
way in many countries, but it made all the difference whether the monarch
was a Henry II, full of initiative, or an indecisive and weak king like Louis VII,
his contemporary on the French throne. Many experiments had been going on
for some time in England and Normandy and no essential element of the
Common Law was invented in Henry's day, but he decided which elements
were finally to be selected and how they were to fit in with the others. He
made the whole work like a system.

We should also not forget that this king disposed of the necessary people and resources. England and Normandy were intellectually very alive and full of enterprising people who were in the forefront of European development. This is well known and applies to the legal field as well as to all others. . . . English libraries of the time contained a rich selection of books . . . and people made use of them. . . . General education, among laymen too, made great progress and it was possible to recruit for the royal bench a considerable number of justices of outstanding quality. Few had received a formal education in civil or canon law, but many must have had a passing acquaintance with it, since an elementary knowledge was widespread among clerics and ecclesiastical and lay litigation was often in the same hands. These justices, laymen and clerics, became real professionals and without them no Common Law could have developed.

. . .

Confidence in the customs of the realm and pride in the royal courts that administered them so efficiently were strong dams against the first civilian waves, whose strength at this early stage was not yet comparable to the maturity and prestige of later centuries. The smattering of Roman law found in the English judiciary probably exercised a liberating effect and gave people the intellectual stimulus to turn the pages of the past and to grasp and expound the judicial practice of the triumphant central courts in a systematic way. The Treatise called Glanvill, their greatest achievement, is typical: its substance is in no way Roman, but some Bolognese inspiration is unmistakable. It was not much, but probably just enough to inoculate the royal judiciary against . . . adopting Roman law wholesale.

If Henry II could call on good brains, he also had the wealth to employ them. Ever since Anglo-Saxon times England had been rich. . . . Henry II was possibly the wealthiest ruler in Europe, his financial administration was certainly the most efficient. . . . However, running the kingdom along more modern lines proved very costly. The judicial machinery he set up was on a scale that had never been seen before and those hundreds of royal justices and personnel, touring the country or sitting at Westminster, must have caused considerable expense. . . .

It is true that justice yielded profits. But it is easy to overstress this aspect. . . . It does not make sense to suggest that Henry's judicial initiatives were really so many devices to make money. . . .

Everybody in the twelfth century knew that you could not obtain justice for nothing, that it had to be paid for like anything else. . . . Even before the Normans came the wheels of justice had to be oiled by gifts to the king, without forgetting the queen who expected her percentage, and for many centuries afterwards the parties paid the men who had to judge them, like the students paid the professors who had to examine them and did so, we confidently hope, freely and objectively. . . .

It was in such circumstances that the new Anglo-Norman system of laws and procedure was born. . . . Thus, because the Common Law had become part and parcel of her political constitution, an element of her national conscience and the foundation of her social order, England became an island in the Romanist sea. Her semi-feudal, semi-modern Common Law, the most Germanic of Europe, was an anomaly, a freak in the history of western civilization, less modern because it was modernized earlier—a common phenomenon in the history of science and technology. The time factor was of crucial importance. In the rest of Europe legal modernization took place later, under the influence of Roman or Roman inspired doctrine, which had reached scientific maturity and was practised in the Church courts for everyone to see. Because there was a legal void to be filled the kings of England had accomplished a less radical modernization a few generations before Roman law and procedure were ready to offer a fully elaborated model for modernization and before the practical possibilities in terms of university trained personnel were available. Its product however was adequate for the needs of the time and the Common Law, this accident of chronology, continued on its own solitary course.

To a continental observer in the early sixteenth century the Common Law must have looked quaintly antiquated and hopelessly medieval, full of archaic elements, which elsewhere had been swept away like cobwebs by Romanist doctrines: a fossil from the days of western feudalism, of which the Anglo-Normans could hide the fact that it was rooted in antiquated and provincial French law . . . just as its technical language was outmoded provincial French. . . . [T]he first to modernize, was the last to remove certain procedural archaisms. Some of the Common Law's obvious imperfections were remedied from the late Middle Ages onwards by the Equity jurisdiction of the Court of Chancery, whose outlook was strongly Romano-canonical—a price paid for the precocious nature of the Common Law. . . . [B]ut the seventeenth century saw the triumph of the Common Law, which conserved its essential procedure until the great reforms of the nineteenth and much of its substantive law until our day.

. . .

The importance of timing can be seen all along in the historical difference between England and the Continent. . . . Not until after 1066 did feudalism reach [England's] shores. . . . In the twelfth century the English state was the most advanced model. . . . Feudalism in England has not been allowed to realize its disruptive potentiality and even strengthened royal power; but when . . . kingship began to overstep the boundaries, . . . and the personal rule of the monarchy undermined the rule of law, feudalism supplied the constitutional framework for resistance. The revolting barons took their stand on feudal law and followed its formalities. For, if the king was their divinely ordained ruler he was also their feudal lord and as such had obligations towards them; king and barons had entered into a contract and the contractual nature of medieval feudalism coloured the whole constitutional outlook of the period. Thus England ignored feudalism when it could have undermined the state, but had it ready at hand, when it served, without endangering the integrity of the state, to check royal power. This seems to be feudalism at its best and it is one of the paradoxes of history that kings and lords of French extraction built in England a better feudal system than at home: this feudal law, the stone which the continental builders disallowed, when they turned to Roman law, became the cornerstone of the Common Law. It played a great and rather unexpected role in the seventeenth century. When royal absolutism triumphed on the Continent, the English Parliament stood its ground and overcame the monarchy, the deplorable triumph—so it seemed to many—of a medieval relic over modern, progressive forms of government. The Common Law and the powerful lobby of the common lawyers in Parliament were instrumental in this victory, and we have here the amazing spectacle of a legal system inaugurated by French kings and a French feudal aristocracy in the twelfth century buttressing the English Parliament in the seventeenth. But what is backward and scorned in one century is modern and craved for in the next: the eighteenth and nineteenth centuries greatly admired England's institutions; her Gothic parliament, however medieval in origin and structure, became the dream of liberal revolutionaries and the keystone of modern civilized states on the Continent.

CHAPTER 4

The Rights of Englishmen

Following the Norman Conquest of England in 1066, William the Conqueror took stock of what he had conquered in the *Domesday Book*, a national inventory of land holdings, other wealth, and a variety of local customs and practices, intended largely to serve as the basis for assessing taxes. The *Domesday Book*, unique for its time, began the notion of an official "record" and evidenced the tight administrative control the Norman monarchy intended to maintain.

The powers of Norman monarchy, however, were not unlimited. Limits were recognized not only in the *de facto* interdependence of kings and barons, but also by express proclamations. By royal proclamation, William assured the conquered Anglo-Saxons of their right to preserve their ancient laws, and William's grandson, Henry I, proclaimed a Charter of Liberties to assure the barons of their rights and privileges. Henry I's Charter was confirmed and extended by the legal reforms of Henry II and by subsequent kings, but it was also at times disregarded. The reign of King John (1199–1215) was especially acrimonious, as he quarreled with the Church and united the barons against him. In 1215 the barons forced John to sign a Charter more sweeping than those of his predecessors. John's Great Charter, the *Magna Carta*, remains at the beginning of the statute books of England.

Late in the thirteenth century, in 1295, King Edward I called the three estates of the realm—the barons, the clergy, and the knights and burgesses (later called the commons)—to a Model Parliament and established the pattern which eventually evolved into the modern-day House of Lords and House of Commons. His success at consolidating and reforming English law through legislation earned Edward I the epithet of "the English Justinian."

Over the next five centuries, England developed its system of limited monarchy with power shifting from the Crown to Parliaments. At times, as in the weak reigns of the House of Lancaster (1399–1461), Parliaments gained significant powers, such as the power to impeach royal ministers; at other times, as in the era of the Tudors (1485–1603), strong monarchs reigned with compliant Parliaments.

The last Tudor, Queen Elizabeth, ruled over a golden age of culture, marred by religious strife resulting from the break of her father, Henry VIII, with the Roman church. When she died without heir, the throne fell to James I of the House of Stuart, whose claim to a "divine right of kings" threw into doubt any limits on royal power. James's son, Charles I, inherited a country made restless by James's absolutism. Unrest increased as Charles chose the autocratic Duke of Buckingham as his chief minister.

Resistance to James I and Charles I came not from underground rabble, but from highly respected men of the establishment. Preeminent among them was a lawyer, Sir Edward Coke, who not only distinguished himself in law practice and government service, but also as author of thirteen volumes of law reports and four volumes of the *Institutes of the Laws of England* (1628–1644) which continued to be cited as authorities until modern times. In a career of over fifty years, Coke served in all three branches of government: called to the bar at the age of twenty-six in 1578, he was made attorney general in 1594 and chief justice of the Court of Common Pleas in 1606 and of the King's Bench in 1613. He was dismissed as a judge in 1616 for resisting royal dictates. He then assumed a leading position in Parliament and continued to press for limits on royal authority. His views led to jail in the Tower of London for a time, but he was so well respected and so well connected that he was not easily repressed. Near the end of his career, in the Parliament of 1628, Coke faced one of his most significant battles and achieved one of his most significant victories—the Petition of Right, the most valuable document to limit royal power since the *Magna Carta*.

Charles I called the Parliament of 1628 to levy taxes the Parliament of 1626 had failed to levy. In the intervening two years, Charles I, embroiled in war and desperate for money, imposed a forced "loan," since the king had no authority to levy taxes without Parliament's consent. As legal historian J. H. Baker explained, in *An Introduction to English Legal History* (3d ed., 1990):

> Such powers would enable the Crown to raise money without the consent of parliament, and the forced loan was another sign of growing absolutism in Stuart government. (p. 539)

Charles encountered wide resistance. He had some resisters jailed, others banished from their home counties, and yet others pressed into military service. The Parliament of 1628 responded not only by challenging the forced loan, but by a more fundamental challenge to the powers of the Crown to impose punishment. Such powers had long been qualified by the right of Englishmen to *habeas corpus*—a writ commanding jailers to bring prisoners to court and establish the causes of detention. *Habeas corpus*, however, was ineffective in this instance.

Sir Edward Coke.

From the frontispiece of his *First Part of the Institutes of the Lawes of England* . . . (1629).

SIR EDWARD COKE

from Catherine Drinker Bowen, *The Lion and the Throne:*
The Life and Times of Sir Edward Coke
(New York: Little, Brown and Company, 1956), pp. 478–507.
Copyright © 1957 by Catherine Drinker Bowen. Copyright renewed.
Reprinted by permission of Harold Ober Associates, Incorporated.

[In 1627,] there came to King's Bench the celebrated suit known to history as the *Case of the Five Knights*. Formerly, the dozens of gentlemen who had been imprisoned as Refusers to the loan had sat in jail, writing letters to their wives and helplessly awaiting events. Five of them . . . now sued out their habeas corpus in the court of King's Bench. On November twenty-second they were brought to the bar and their case argued by four lawyers of great ability, among them [John] Selden and [William] Noye. The King had a right to imprison subjects on suspicion; counsel could not argue against it. But cause of committal must be expressed, said Selden, so that when the matter came to court, the judges could either bail or remand (return) the accused to prison. In support of this doctrine, Magna Carta and other ancient statutes were quoted. Attorney General [Sir Roger] Heath, for the Crown, argued *reason of state*: men, even though innocent, could be dangerous enough so that custody was indicated. In other cases, persons charged with serious crimes must be imprisoned while the facts were being ascertained. Witness the dangerous plotters of Elizabeth's time. Elizabeth's judges, said Heath, had declared the Crown need not show cause for sending a man to prison.

Chief Justice Sir Nicholas Hyde was in a quandary. Tudor sovereigns since Henry VIII had issued forced loans and flung Refusers into jail when they chose—yet never before on such a scale, with the whole country roused. The Crown now pleaded legal precedent and practice; Selden pleaded fundamental law and the ancient charters of the land. England, urged Selden, was not Spain; men could not be kept in durance indefinitely without showing cause. The Five Knights moreover were considerable landowners, gentlemen of probity, property and Protestantism, who paid their debts, fed the poor of their parishes and had the support not only of their counties but—as the trial made obvious—of most of London as well. "Gentlemen recusants of the loan," the prisoners were called. Westminster Hall was crowded. . . . Counsel for the prisoners, when their turn came, "pleaded with great applause," said a newswriter, "even of shouting and clapping of hands, which is unusual in that place."

Nevertheless, the Five Knights lost their case. . . . Hyde gave the deciding precedent which overrode all previous precedents of charter and ancient statute: In the 34th year of Elizabeth (1594) all twelve judges had declared that "a prisoner committed *per speciale mandatum* . . . at the King's command . . . was not bailable and cause for committal need not be shown." When a man is imprisoned by the King and cause given, he is bailable. But if the cause be not specified, the offense probably is too great for the general knowledge, dangerous for public discussion, perhaps not fit to be divulged for other reasons, or for the people to meddle with. "In brief," reported a newswriter, "the gentlemen are remanded to prison and there like to lie by it."

Nothing less than a Parliament could rescue the Five Knights; their lawyers needed the force of the realm behind them. Fortunately for the prisoners, the royal Treasury also needed a Parliament. . . . But with the jails full of Refusers, with principal gentry banished from their counties and popular feeling hot in their support, to call a Parliament would be awkward to say the least. In January, 1628, all prisoners for the loan were freed, including the Five Knights. Charles gave orders that writs be issued for a Parliament to assemble in March.

Elections went hard against the Crown. Every Refuser who ran was returned, including twenty-seven who had suffered imprisonment. . . . In London, excitement mounted. . . .

It was to be an extraordinary Parliament, one of the two most celebrated in English history. The roster of names is glorious. Selden and Noye were there, who had argued for the Five Knights. . . . On the right front benches were only three Privy Councilors [Councilors to the King]. No more had been returned; the King was poorly represented.

. . .

In the past two years, Englishmen had suffered extraordinary attacks upon their personal liberties. Nothing comparable could be remembered. . . . This Parliament might well be England's last, and the nation turn to arbitrary government, as every great nation on the Continent had turned. A plan of action was urgently necessary. Four days before the session opened, at a meeting in Sir Robert Cotton's house it was decided . . . [l]iberty of person . . . must be the theme of this Parliament: the right of subjects against imprisonment without cause expressed, their right against banishment, against foreign service without consent.

How these matters were to be accomplished, the men in Cotton's library did not know, or whether they could be accomplished. The Five Knights' Case had shown where the judges stood—Chief Justice Hyde, at any rate. To prove the King's power to imprison without cause, crown lawyers could marshal legal opinions and actual practice under the Tudors. Parliament must fall back upon the fundamental law, upon Magna Carta and the famous Chapter 39: "No freeman shall be taken or imprisoned or disseised of any free tenement or of his liberties or free customs, or outlawed or exiled, or in any other way destroyed, nor will we go upon him nor send upon him, except by the lawful judgment of his peers or by the law of the land. To no one will we sell, to no one will we refuse or delay, right or justice." Against the exaction of forced loans, other statutes existed. The fact that kings had subverted them did not annul these ancient agreements. . . . Parliament, in this emergency, must go above the statutes, appeal beyond the laws to The Law, to that universal right which Englishmen claimed as their inheritance. Scripture declared that it was against reason to send a man to prison without cause.

The practical problem was whether to proceed by bill, petition, resolution or remonstrance. Petitions to his Majesty's grace and clemency were, after all, no more than a confession of weakness. Coke and Wentworth were for attempting a bill—a law confirming the ancient rights of the subject. If the King showed himself against it—which meant eventual veto—then other means must be found. . . .

On Monday, March twenty-second, the Commons met for business. "This," Sir Benjamin Rudyerd told them, "is the crisis of Parliaments. We shall know by this if Parliaments live or die. . . . Men and brethren, what shall we do? Is there no balm in Gilead? If the King draw one way, the Parliament another, we must all sink." A magnificent orator, Rudyerd could portray gloom as only the silver-tongued can do. Coke rose next. At seventy-six, he stood up in his place with the sturdy confidence of an old man who has lived through trouble and danger and has seen bad days turn to better. . . .

None disputed the Englishman's right to his property, his goods, lands and inheritance. . . . Yet a man's person, it seemed, had become less secure than his goods. ". . . It is a maxim, *The common law hath admeasured the King's prerogative,* that in no case it can prejudice the inheritance of the subjects. It is against law that men should be committed and no cause shown. I would not speak this, but that I hope my gracious King will hear of it. Yet it is not I, Edward Coke, that speaks it but the records that speak it."

. . .

In the midst of debate on this vital subject, Coke, whose business was to cite precedents and explain them to the House, suffered a startling setback when the Solicitor General suddenly cited Sir Edward against himself. As Chief Justice, Coke had declared in a suit of 1616 (shortly before his dismissal) that the prisoners having been committed by order of Privy Council, the cause might be "*arcana regni,* or mystery of state, and need not be disclosed." Moreover, as Solicitor General in 1592, Coke had quoted the renowned Judge Stamford to the effect that "if Privy Council commit one, he is not bailable by any court of justice."

The Solicitor General, a lawyer of shrewd ability and energy, flourished the two statements triumphantly before the Commons. Taken aback, Coke floundered, blustering a little. Since the days of his Attorneyship under Elizabeth—since the time indeed of his Chief Justiceship—Sir Edward had changed his views more than he perhaps realized or had care to face. Attorney Generals do not think as Parliament men think, and a Privy Councilor may look east when a Commons man looks west. Coke believed that Stamford should be over-ruled. Two days after the Solicitor General's attack, Sir Edward rose in his place and without apology reversed himself, speaking with the rough simplicity of his years (at seventy-six, a man has no time left for flourishes): "I have not *veritatem ex cathedra*, or infallibility of spirit. I confess that when I read Stamford then [1616] and had it in my hands, I was of that opinion at the Council table. But when I perceived that some members of this House were taken away, even in the face of this House, and sent to prison, and when I was not far from that place myself, I went to my book and would not be quiet till I have satisfied myself. Stamford at the first was my guide, but my guide deceived me, therefore I swerved from it. I have now better guides. I have looked out precedents and Statutes of the Realm, whereby I am satisfied that such commitments are against the liberty of the subject. I desire to be free of the imputation that is cast upon me."

. . .

. . . Several days later, the Commons drew up four resolutions, strong, comprehensive, plain: no freeman to be imprisoned without cause shown, even at the King's command; habeas corpus not to be denied; a prisoner brought to court on habeas corpus must be either bailed or freed; no "tax, taillage, loan, benevolence" to be commanded or levied without consent by act of Parliament.

. . .

The Lords, however, were not quick to respond. "The greater part," reported a newswriter, "stand for the King's prerogative against the subjects' Liberties." Before the peers were ready to join in such resolutions they must hear more on the other side. Attorney General Heath was called in and . . . argued for the King. Between the two Houses, feeling grew warm. On Heath's suggesting that the liberties claimed by the Commons "might be moderated," Coke quoted from the scriptural story of the two harlots who came before Solomon: "The true mother would never consent to the dividing of her child." Buckingham chose to take offense. Did Sir Edward intimate that "the King his master, was a whore?" "Your Grace," Coke replied blandly, "misinterprets me."

. . .

By April twenty-fifth, the Lords were ready with their Propositions. There were five. . . . To the Commons the document must have come as a desperate disappointment. All of their hard work . . . resulted only in timorous paragraphs, each one opening with the phrase, "His Majesty would be graciously pleased to declare." The whole was sugared with assurance of "his Majesty's royal prerogative, intrinsical to this sovereignty, and entrusted him withal from God," and the Lords' conviction concerning the rightness of things done for reasons of state.

Coke attacked the Propositions with a kind of cold savagery. Was Magna Carta then to be accorded confirmation as a matter of grace? "When the King doth a thing 'of grace,' it implies that it is not our right. *Lex terrae* is the common law of the land." And what was this "intrinsical" prerogative? "It is a word we find not much in the law. Admit this intrinsic prerogative and all our laws are out." By the Lords' third proposal, his Majesty ratified to his subjects their "several just liberties, privileges and rights." What then were "just" liberties, and who might determine between liberties just and unjust? In the fourth proposal, the common law must yield to martial law. "The great question will be," said Coke, "When is time of peace and when of war?" A half-war was difficult to define. "It is certain that when the courts of justice are sitting, is time of peace." In the fifth proposition, if the King for "matter of state" commit a man, he will express the cause *at a convenient time*. "Who," demanded Coke, "shall judge of convenient time?" The Propositions had been written by a churchman, Bishop Harsnet of Norwich. "We see," finished Sir Edward, "what an advantage they have that are learned in the law, in penning articles, above them that are not, how wise soever. There was never yet any pillars or maxims of the common law shaken but infinite inconveniences have followed."

"I think," said Selden, "there is not one of the five [Propositions] fit to be desired and asked. Ours were resolutions of law. Their Lordships propound what they would have to be law."

In toto, the Commons rejected the Lords' proposals. "Reason of state," said Coke, "lames Magna Carta."

On the twenty-eighth of April, King Charles came to the House of Lords and calling for the Commons to stand at the bar, spoke through his Lord Keeper. The affairs of Christendom would wait no longer upon this Parliament. Delay, he had heard, was due to a debate "touching the liberty of the subject." To shorten the business he therefore declared his heart and intention: "He holdeth Magna Charta and the other . . . statutes insisted upon to be all in force. He will maintain all his subjects in the just freedom of their person and safety of their estates. You shall find as much security in his Majesty's royal word and promise as in the strength of any law ye can make. And therefore his Majesty desires that no doubt of distrust may possess any man, but that ye will all proceed unanimously to his business."

The Commons returned to their chamber, where the King's first Secretary of State pleaded with them to trust the royal word. Moderates of the House agreed. . . . Nevertheless the House stuck to its determination. A committee was appointed, a bill drawn up. Next morning, Coke presented it to the Commons: *An Act for the better securinge of every free man touching the proprietie of his goods and libertie of his person.* . . . "*Be it enacted,*" [italics in original] each brief section began, leaving no doubt as to the form of actual statute. There was provision against taxation without parliamentary consent, against imprisonment without cause given, . . . and a declaration that any freeman, "returned upon a *habeas corpus*, ought to be delivered or bailed."

Coke finished reading and debate broke out at once. The bill was not sufficient—a mere recital of old laws, with no penalties attached for infraction by the King's officers. To force the judges to give bail upon habeas corpus, something stronger was needed. For Coke an act of Parliament overrode judicial power. "What if the judges remand or remit a man?" he asked roughly. "What is that to acts of Parliament? I was committed to the Tower, and all my books and study searched, and thirty-seven manuscripts were taken away. Thirty-four were restored and I would give three hundred pounds for the other three. . . . After," continued Coke, "I was inquired what I had done. When a man is committed, it is easy to find causes against him. Cause found after commitment, this is fearful!"

A second royal message, brief and to the point, interrupted debate. His Majesty desired the House "clearly to let him know whether they would rest upon his royal word and promise, made at several times, and especially by my Lord Keeper's speech made in his own presence."

The House was struck dumb. "Upon this," says the reporter, "there was a silence for some time." The Secretary of State stepped forward with conciliatory words. They fell on deaf ears. . . . Painfully the House twisted and turned, seeking a way out. Impossible that they should trust the King; impossible also to pronounce the word of distrust. . . . Of course, Wentworth put in tactfully, the House trusted in the King's goodness. "But we are ambitious that his Majesty's goodness may remain to posterity. We are accountable to a public trust, and seeing there hath been a public violation of the laws by his ministers, nothing can satisfy them but a public amends . . . vindication of the subjects' rights by bill."

Next day—Friday, May second—a third message was delivered by the Speaker: his Majesty renewed his promises to maintain his subjects in liberty. But he would countenance no "encroachings upon that sovereignty or prerogative which God hath put into his hands for our good." Let the Commons contain themselves within the bounds and laws of their forefathers, "without straining or enlarging them by new explanations or additions in any sort." He could delay no longer. If the House were not done with their business by Tuesday week, then "it shall be their own faults."

The Commons returned answer next morning, begging that they might proceed by way of bill. They had no wish to "strain or enlarge the former laws in any sort" nor to encroach on the prerogative. They desired only to make "some necessary explanation" of the just sense and meaning of old laws, "with some moderate provision for execution and performance . . . as in times past, upon like occasion hath been used."

The King's reply came back in short order. He had expected "answer by action, not delay by discourse." Yet he would be content if Magna Carta be confirmed by bill, so long as the Commons did not add to it, paraphrase or "explain it." What need explanations, unless the Commons doubted their King's word? "It may well be said, What need a new law to confirm an old, if you repose confidence in the declaration made by his Majesty to both Houses?"

Blandly, King Charles ignored the Five Knights' Case, the Commons' assumption that committal without cause was against Magna Carta and a freeman's right to trial. Such matters were to be left to his Majesty's clemency and kingly justice. Should the Commons—the message ended—"seek to tie their King by new and indeed impossible bonds, they must be accountable to God and the Country for the ill success of this meeting."

. . .

. . . Coke referred to the royal promises. "Was it ever known," he asked, "that general words were a sufficient satisfaction to particular grievances? When grievances be, the Parliament is to redress them. Did ever Parliament rely on messages? The King's answer is very gracious; but what is the law of the realm, that is the question! I put no diffidence in his Majesty; but the King must speak by record and in particulars—not in general. Did you ever know the King's message come into a bill of subsidies? All succeeding Kings will say, 'Ye must trust me as well as ye did my predecessors, and trust my messages.' . . . But messages of love never came into a Parliament. Let us put up a Petition of Right! Not that I distrust the King; but that I cannot take his trust but in a Parliamentary way."

No one doubted Coke's meaning. Every member was familiar with petitions of right, which differed from petitions of grace as right differs from clemency and pardon. . . . [I]f a man had been wronged, if his fundamental rights had been subverted, he petitioned not for grace and pardon but for restitution or restatement of his rights—a very different matter. The thing that would set this petition apart was its public nature. It must be voted by both Houses as a bill is voted. And it must have the King's assent, given publicly before Lords and Commons assembled. In substance it would reiterate an Englishman's right to personal liberty, his security from arbitrary imprisonment without cause. . . . It would protest . . . the exaction of forced loans and taxes without consent by act of Parliament. In the end the petition would pray his Majesty to command his officers and ministers to serve him according to the laws and statutes of the realm as so laid down.

On Thursday, May eighth, the petition was ready. Coke had been chosen to present it to the Lords at a conference in the Painted Chamber. . . .

. . . After three days' hesitation, the Lords concurred, sending down the petition to the Lower House unchanged save for an added paragraph: "We humbly present this petition to your Majesty, not only with a care of preserving our own Liberties, but with due regard to leave entire that sovereign

Power, wherewith your Majesty is trusted, for the Protection, Safety, and Happiness of your People." This small alteration, the Lord Keeper assured the Lower House, was "no breach of the frame," but propounded only "that the Petition might have the easier passage with his Majesty."

As soon as the Commons were alone they broke into dismayed speech. *To leave entire that sovereign power*—The seemingly innocent, courteous little phrase could nullify their petition. . . .

"To speak plainly," Coke said, "this will overthrow all our Petition. It trenches to all parts of it; . . . This turns all about again. Look unto the petitions of former times! They never petitioned wherein there was a saving of the King's sovereignty. I know that prerogative is part of the law, but *sovereign power* is no Parliamentary word. Should we now add it, we shall weaken the foundation of law and then the building must needs fall. Take heed what we yield unto! Magna Charta is such a fellow that he will have no sovereign. I wonder this 'sovereign' was not in Magna Charta, or in the confirmation of it? If we grant this, by implication we give a sovereign power above all these laws. 'Power,' in law, is taken for a power with force: '*The Sheriff shall take the power of the country.*' What it means here, God only knows. It is repugnant to our Petition that is a *Petition of Right*, grounded on acts of Parliament. We must not admit of it, and to qualify it is impossible. Let us hold our privileges according to the law."

. . . The Lords, however, would not give in but persisted, clinging to their "saving words." Five days passed. The King sent two brief messages, urging haste. . . .

The Commons, meanwhile, used all art and persuasion to bring the Lords around. Concerning "sovereign power," Glanville and Sir Henry Martin suggested tactfully that the words were unnecessary. Did not members acknowledge the King's power when they took their oath at the Parliament door? "I . . . do utterly testify and declare in my conscience, that the King's Highness is the supreme Governor of this Realm in all causes, &c." To this skillful argument the Lords capitulated, but not until they had composed a declaration—separate from the petition—assuring his Majesty that the Lords did not intend "to lessen or impeach any thing, which by the Oath of Supremacy, we have sworn to assist and defend."

. . .

On the second of June, the King came down to Parliament and took his seat on the throne. "Gentlemen," he said, "I am come hither to perform my promise. I think no man can think it long, since I have not taken so many days in answering the Petition as ye have spent weeks in framing it. And I am come hither to show you that, as well in formal things as essential, I desire to give you as much content as in me lies."

The Petition of Right was now read aloud: "Humbly shew unto our Sovereign Lord the King, the Lords Spiritual and Temporal and Commons in Parliament assembled: That whereas it is declared and enacted by a statute made in the time of the reign of King Edward the First . . . that no tallage or aid shall be laid or levied by the King or his heirs in this realm, without the goodwill and assent of the Archbishops, Bishops, Earls, Barons, Knights, Burgesses and other the freemen of the commonalty of this realm. . . . Yet nevertheless, of late, your people . . . have been required to lend certain sums of money unto your Majesty, and many of them upon their refusal, have been imprisoned, confined and sundry other ways molested and disquieted. . . . And where also by the statute called 'The Great Charter of the Liberties of England,' it is declared and enacted, that no freeman may be taken or imprisoned or be disseised of his freeholds or liberties. . . . Nevertheless . . . divers of your subjects have of late been imprisoned without any cause shewed, and when for their deliverance they were brought before your justices by your Majesty's writs of *habeas corpus* . . . and their keepers commanded to certify the causes of their detainer; no cause was certified, but that they were detained by your Majesty's special command, signified by the Lords of your Privy Council, and yet were returned back to several prisons, without being charged with any thing to which they might make answer according to law. . . ."

On and on it went, the great roll and roster confirming the rights of Englishmen. Nothing was slurred over, nothing extenuated. About this petition was no fine language, no conscious "poetry" or philosophical argument concerning freedom and the soul of man. Penned by lawyers, it spoke the plain language of the common law: a practical instrument to keep innocent men out of prison, to relieve them if put there arbitrarily and to give each subject, whether innocent or guilty, his chance at trial. The petition could not be called a law; it did not include the law's penalty for infraction. (That would come later, in the year 1679.) Nevertheless it carried authority. The judges, Coke had said, must abide by it if the King gave consent in the traditional words: "*Soit droit fait comme il est desiré. . . .* Let right be done as is desired."

Charles sat on his throne and listened, until the voice ceased with the words "that your Majesty would be graciously pleased . . . to declare your royal will and pleasure, That in the things aforesaid, all your ministers shall serve you according to the laws and statutes of this realm, as they tender the honour of your Majesty, and the prosperity of this kingdom."

Lords and Commons waited for the King's reply. It came through the Lord Keeper: "The King willeth that right be done according to the laws and customs of the realm and that the statutes be put in due execution, that his subjects may have no cause to complain of any wrong or oppressions, contrary to their just right and liberties: to the preservation whereof, he holds himself in conscience as well obliged, as of his prerogative."

The Commons had failed. The traditional word had not been spoken, *Soit droit fait.* The King had not so much as mentioned the petition, let alone answered it. His words were soothing but meaningless, as to children who must be comforted. He had conceded nothing. . . .

Sitting in their ancient chapel of St. Stephen's, the Commons mourned as the exiled mourn, or those who have lost their country. . . .

. . . Pym rose, tried to speak and wept outright; Coke followed with a like dramatic result. "Overcome with passion, and seeing the desolation likely to ensue, Sir Edward Coke was forced to sit down when he began to speak, through the abundance of tears. Yea, the Speaker in his speech could not refrain from weeping and shedding of tears, besides a great many whose great griefs made them dumb and silent. Yet some bore up in that storm and encouraged others."

"That black and doleful Thursday," a newswriter called it. "Such a spectacle of passions, as the like had seldom been seen in such an assembly, some weeping, some expostulating, some prophecying the fatal ruin of our kingdom; some playing the divines in confessing their own and country's sins, which drew those judgments upon us; some finding, as it were, fault with those that wept. I have been told by a parliament man that there were above an hundred weeping eyes."

It was an extraordinary scene. These men who wept outright before their fellows were not the timid spirits of Parliament but members whose courage already had been tested, some of whom had suffered imprisonment for the cause. They wept from helplessness, frustration, a temporary loss of hope. . . . At last it was decided to go into Committee of the Whole and discuss freely some plan of action. The doors were locked, order given that no man go out "upon pain of going to the Tower." Only Speaker Finch, "with tears flowing in his eyes," asked permission to leave the House "for half an hour." It was granted, though the Commons knew he must go straight to the King, perhaps return with orders for a dissolution. But the fact of his departure—perhaps the very desperateness of their situation—seemed to renew the courage of the House. Coke rose, speaking this time with his accustomed resoluteness. "We have dealt," he said, "with that duty and moderation that never was the like, after such violation of the liberties of the subject. Let us take this to heart."

What Coke said now was to be his last recorded speech on the liberty of the subject. He told of precedents in history where men had spoken out. . . . "Now, when there is such a downfall of the state, shall we hold our tongues? How shall we answer our duties to God and men? Why may we not name those that are the cause of all our evils? In the fourth year of Henry III and the twenty-seventh of Edward III and in the thirteenth of Richard II, the Parliament moderated the King's prerogative. Nothing grows to abuse but this House hath power to treat of it. What shall we do? Let us palliate no longer! If we do, God will not prosper us. And therefore, not knowing if I shall ever speak in this House again, I shall now speak freely. I think the Duke of Buckingham is the cause of all our miseries. And till the King be informed thereof, we shall never go out with honour or sit with honour here. That man is the grievance of grievances! Let us set down the causes of all our disasters and they will all reflect on him. Our liberties are now impeached, we are deeply concerned. . . ."

At the word "Duke," Sir Edward was interrupted by cries from all quarters of the House. "The Duke! The Duke! 'Tis he! 'Tis he!" "As when one good hound" (wrote a country member) "recovers the scent, the rest come in with a full cry, so we pursued it, and every one came on home, and laid the blame where he thought the fault was." The great name had been spoken at last; the block that held them back was shattered. . . .

As the clock in the tower struck eleven, Speaker Finch hurried into the chamber. "Had he not returned at that very moment," wrote Mead, "I hear it from a Parliament knight they had voted the Duke a traitor and arch enemy to the king and kingdom, with a worse appendix thereto." His Majesty, said Finch, adjourned the House until tomorrow, "all committees to cease in the meantime." A like message went to the Lords. But the Peers, this time, stood out. After brief conference with the Commons they dispatched a joint deputation to ask his Majesty for "a clear and satisfactory answer," given in full Parliament, to their Petition of Right.

Long ago, Coke had told the Commons that no sovereign could resist a request if it came from both Houses. The prophecy was correct. King and Lords of Privy Council sat all afternoon "on the question whether the Parliament should be dissolved." Next morning, Speaker Finch brought word that his Majesty wished to meet again with Parliament, "that all Christendom might take notice of a sweet parting between him and his people." The words were winning and full of charm. The Commons however were not yet sure if they spelled dissolution or something better, nor had a time been set for the King's coming. Two days later, on Saturday at four in the afternoon, Black Rod knocked with his staff upon the Commons' door.

Members trooped upstairs, through the long corridors into the Lords' Chamber. When they were gathered behind the bar, as many as could find place, Lord Keeper Coventry addressed the sovereign in the Parliament's name. "Taking into considerations," he said, "that the good intelligence between your Majesty and your people doth much depend upon your Majesty's answer to their Petition of Right formerly presented; the Lords Spiritual and Temporal and the Commons in Parliament assembled, with unanimous consent do now become most humble suitors unto your Majesty, that you would be graciously pleased to give a clear and satisfactory answer thereunto."

He could not have imagined, Charles replied, but that his former answer should have given full satisfaction—it had been approved "by the judgments of so many wise men." But to show there was no doubleness in his meaning, he was willing to please "as well in words as in substance." Let the petition once more be read, and both Houses would have an answer that he was sure would satisfy.

Once more, the scroll appeared. Once more, the Commons heard their words as they had set them down, the confirmation of their ancient rights and liberties. Over and over, the ancient phrases repeated, after the legal fashion which leaves no loophole for misinterpretation. The Clerk's voice ceased and the Commons broke into applause, quickly subdued as the Clerk once more stepped forward, about to read aloud the royal answer.

"*Soit droit fait,*" he said, "*comme il est desiré.*"

As the words were pronounced, a great shout rang, and was repeated again and again. News spread to the street—"broke out," wrote a Privy Councilor, "into ringing of bells and bonfires miraculously." From steeple to steeple the joyous sound was echoed. . . .

The Commons had triumphed. For the moment, King and country were one. Above the City, night came down as bonfires flared, prophetic indeed of violence to come.

CHAPTER 5

The English Legal System

From 1628 to 1639, Charles I governed without parliaments. Financial necessity forced him to call a Parliament in 1640, but pent-up grievances so strained relations between Parliament and the royal court that civil war broke out in 1642.

The parliamentary party found a leader in Oliver Cromwell, a member of Parliament who proved to be an able general. Cromwell's forces prevailed. Unlike in previous depositions, England did not merely exchange one royal house for another, but put an end to the monarchical form of government—for the time being. Charles I was beheaded in 1649. For the next decade, England was governed by a "Protectorate" (some have called it a military dictatorship) headed by Cromwell until his death in 1658. When no suitable successor was found, England returned to being a monarchy with the "Restoration" of Charles I's son as Charles II in 1660.

Parliament again became restive under Charles II's successor, James II, in part due to James's Catholic religion. James was peacefully deposed in the "Glorious Revolution" of 1688 and replaced with his Protestant daughter, Mary, and her Dutch husband, William of Orange. William and Mary accepted a Bill of Rights drafted in Parliament with such stringent limitations on the Crown that English royalty eventually became mere figureheads.

One of the most frequent grievances raised in the Protectorate era, and under monarchy as well, was the uncertainty of English law. The English common law, having grown by the accumulation of cases since the twelfth century, was buried in hundreds of volumes of court reports. Abridgments of the reports provided some guidance, but both the reports and the abridgments were privately prepared and often unreliable. In addition, the legislative output of Parliaments was disorganized. No official organization—or even compilation—of statutes had ever been attempted (and was not to be attempted until the nineteenth century).

Early in the seventeenth century, Edward Coke's chief rival, Francis Bacon, proposed codification of the laws of England on the model of continental law. During the Protectorate, radical reformers proposed a simple, clear, brief statement of the laws which everyone could understand, eliminating the need for lawyers. In the eighteenth century, utilitarian philosopher Jeremy Bentham proposed less drastic, but no less comprehensive, codification.

No scheme of codification took hold in England, but much of the need was met by a treatise—Sir William Blackstone's *Commentaries on the Laws of England*, published between 1765 and 1769. Jeremy Bentham and others were critical of Blackstone for his uncritical acceptance of common law doctrines. Blackstone's conservatism also ran counter to the spirit of the time, which saw much legal innovation, especially in the Court of King's Bench where the innovative chief justice Lord Mansfield modified the leading principles of commercial law to fit the increasing commercial activities of the time. Nevertheless, Blackstone's *Commentaries* met with phenomenal success. In *The Mysterious Science of the Law* (1941), historian Daniel J. Boorstin has written:

> In the fourteen centuries since Justinian's *Institutes,* Blackstone's *Commentaries* are the most important attempt in western civilization to reduce to short and rational form the complex legal institutions of an entire society. (p. 3)

Sir William Blackstone.
Painting attributed to Sir Joshua Reynolds. National Portrait Gallery, London.

SIR WILLIAM BLACKSTONE

from Gareth Jones, *The Sovereignty of the Law:*
Selections from Blackstone's Commentaries on the Laws of England
(Toronto: University of Toronto Press, 1973), pp. ix–xiii.
Copyright © 1973 by Gareth Jones.
Reprinted by permission of Gareth Jones.

Sir William Blackstone

Blackstone was just eighteen when he graduated from Oxford and entered the Middle Temple. He seems to have worked as hard there as at Oxford. But after Oxford Temple life was profoundly depressing. His companions were "obscure and illiterate". His study was lonely and totally undirected. He gleaned his law from the solitary perusal of unreadable books, from the experience of "common attorneys" and from attending the Courts, a pedagogical experience which left an indelible and distasteful impression upon him.

Blackstone remained on and off in London from 1741 until 1753, practicing the law without great success. It is said that he had "no powerful friends to commend him". But there were more significant reasons for his initial failure at the Bar. He was a hesitant and diffident advocate, not being blessed with a "graceful delivery or a flow of elocution", and he must have spent little time in London and too much in Oxford and All Souls where he was elected a Fellow in 1743.

. . .

Blackstone was bitterly disappointed. . . . Oxford attracted him more and more and his practice at the Bar was meager. . . . Friends . . . urged him to retire to his Fellowship and "to read Law Lectures to such Law students as were disposed to attend him". He did so, and began "to execute [what] he had previously planned, . . . his Lectures on the Laws of England".

His lectures were an immediate success, despite the handicap of a delivery which [was] described as "formal, precise, and affected". The sudden injection of a competent and conscientious teacher of law into the moribund body of Oxford University must have been dramatic and would have ensured the presence of a captive audience. Besides his lectures were remarkable for their content and arrangement. They were comprehensive, uncomplicated, and above all literate, designed to appeal to a civilized listener. His exposition was clear and his explanation lucid. He set out to demonstrate that the study of law could be humane and need not be so "dry and disgusting" and so narrow or insular as to drive away gentlemen of ability from the Bar. Blackstone's exposure in the Temple to a non-existent course of study had led him to meditate "upon some Improvements in the Method of academical Education, by retaining the useful Parts of it stripped of monastic Pedantry; by supplying its Defects, and adapting it more peculiarly to Gentlemen of Rank and Fortune". It has been suggested that Blackstone's real concern for the future of legal education was snobbishly social, that he was worried about the reluctance of English gentlemen to practice at the Bar and was alarmed by the vulgarisation of the profession. It is true, as the *Commentaries* show, that he saw a real danger to the English Constitution if the law ceased to be "the prerogative of a privileged class"; but it would be unjust to him to deny his profound intellectual interest in "modernising the science of law".

Ironically the *Commentaries* had their greatest influence in the Old Colonies, where they served to educate in the law not only gentlemen but many of humbler birth. Nearly all the American states have accepted Blackstone's suggestion that law be studied at a University before practice, and the American Law School has convinced the practitioner of the value of the dialectic study of legal principles. In England Blackstone's suggestion that a University degree in law should be an essential preliminary to call to the Bar has only recently been given serious consideration. Blackstone would have been saddened that so little has been accomplished in the last two hundred years—even though he might be comforted by the fact that the Bar continues to attract gentlemen of birth and fortune!

Blackstone was not alone in his concern to foster the teaching of English Law at the universities. Charles Viner, who had made substantial sums of money through the sale of his *General Abridgement of Law and Equity*, expressed in his will made in 1752 (a year before Blackstone began lecturing) the wish to establish a professorship of the common law at the University of Oxford, "that young gentlemen who shall be students there, and shall intend to apply themselves to the study of the common laws of England, may be instructed and enabled to pursue their studies to the best advantage afterwards, when they shall attend the courts at Westminster, and not to trifle away their time there in hearing what they understood nothing of, and thereupon perhaps direct their thoughts from the law to their pleasures". His scheme to endow a professorship, fellowships, and scholarships for the study of English law was accepted, after some wrangling and dispute, by the University, and in 1758 Blackstone was elected the first Vinerian Professor.

Blackstone spent less and less time in Oxford after his election to the Vinerian Chair, and he was harried by political enemies for lecturing through a deputy and for allegedly committing other breaches of the Statute which had established his Chair. He was once more in London, having bought chambers there in 1759 with the object of resuming practice; for his lectures had established for him a reputation "which he justly thought might entitle him to some particular notice at the Bar." But he did not break completely with Oxford until 1766. . . . His practice had grown to such an extent by that time that he found "that he could not discharge the personal duties of the [Professorship], consistently with his professional attendance in London, or the delicacy of his feelings as an honest man". Academic and literary success had for him proved to be the touchstone of professional advancement.

Blackstone's increasing practice brought him the inevitable legal honours and material prosperity, although he still found advocacy and the bustle of Temple life somewhat distasteful. But his return was less lonely, for in 1761 he married the sister of his biographer, Sarah Clitherow, "with whom he passed near nineteen years, in the enjoyment of the purest domestic and conjugal felicity". She bore him nine children.

. . .

Blackstone was thirty when he first began to lecture on the laws of England. The lectures, burnished over fifteen years and scrutinised by the Bench, were to form the basis of his *Commentaries*, the four volumes of which were published between 1765 and 1769. In these volumes, in about two thousand pages, Blackstone sought to describe the structure of the English legal system and to formulate the main principles, both substantive and procedural, which were the basis of the contemporary common law. He was not writing for legal antiquarians and specialists but for "young gentlemen" who were "desirous of some general acquaintance with the constitution and legal policy of their native country". His were "mere elementary institutes", an "introductory discourse", which sought to avoid technicalities "which chiefly result from the special circumstances of the case". Legal minutiæ were passed over with notes of apology and regret. Blackstone's aim was "to examine the great outlines of English law, and [to trace] them up to their principles".

No critic of the *Commentaries* should dismiss as irrelevant these self-imposed limitations or ignore the rudimentary state of English jurisprudence before the appearance of the *Commentaries*. . . . The Inns of Court provided [students] with no formal instruction; and their books, generally written in law-french, were chaotically arranged, obscurely phrased and interminably long.

. . .

Blackstone's arrangement of his topics did not seriously confuse the ordinary reader. It was convenient, and the easy, if humourless, clarity of his prose made up for any structural shortcomings. Principles are neatly set out and aptly illustrated, with classical allusions; recapitulation is discreet and never laborious, and the order and balance of the exposition is sustained throughout the four volumes. Each chapter can be read isolated from the others and yet is seen to form an integral part of a whole. Above all, his analysis of common law principles is, by and large, scrupulously correct. Rarely does he sacrifice accuracy to generalization. In a text of two thousand pages it is remarkable that there are so few errors of law; and those that can be found are generally venial. It is this technical and mature ability to distill a principle from a mass of confusing authorities which makes lawyers admire the *Commentaries* so profoundly. . . .

[But some were] infuriated by Blackstone's complacency and satisfaction with the established order. . . . [Blackstone's leading critic, Jeremy Bentham,] condemned Blackstone for his servile apologia on behalf of a society which had dismally failed to fulfil its social responsibilities and for his readiness to use any intellectual weapon, including philosophical argument and historical analogy, to justify a *status quo* which indulgently rejoiced in the perfection of its legal constitution and the glory of its common law.

. . .

To assess the force of these criticisms, it is necessary to recall something of Blackstone's background and to probe more deeply into his views as they are expressed in the *Commentaries*. Born, on his mother's side, into the minor squirearchy of England, he spent his life among men who had been brought up to believe that "by studying the country's past, especially its law, they could unravel those mysteries of authority and obligation which so baffled them". He was a member of a University steeped in inert tradition, and like many of its members he was impatient of dissent and dissenters. . . .

He was a lawyer, a profession which does not intuitively welcome reform, and he represented the interests and ethos of a highly influential segment of English society which was prepared to venerate institutions it was "not able presently to comprehend". He and his peers revered the common law as the embodiment of right reason:

> And hence it is that our lawyers are with justice so copious in their encomiums on the reason of the common law; that they tell us, that the law is the perfection of reason, that it always intends to conform thereto, and that what is not reason is not law. Not that the particular reason of every rule in the law can at this distance of time be always precisely assigned; but it is sufficient that there be nothing in the rule flatly contradictory to reason, and then the law will presume it to be well founded.

The common law was incomparably more perfect than statute law. When the legislature attempted "to improve" the native law, its intervention was rarely helpful and frequently inept.

> For, to say the truth, almost all the perplexed questions, almost all the niceties, intricacies, and delays, (which have some times disgraced the English, as well as other courts of justice,) owe their original not to the common law itself, but to in-

novations that have been made in it by acts of parliament; "overladen (as Sir Edward Coke expresses it) with provisoes and additions, and many times on a sudden penned or corrected by men of none, or very little judgment in law". . . . And if this inconvenience was so heavily felt in the reign of Queen Elizabeth, you may judge how the evil is increased in later times, when the statute book is swelled to ten times a larger bulk: unless it should be found, that the penners of our modern statutes have proportionably better informed themselves in the knowledge of the common law.

The defects of the poor law could be traced to the poor law statutes which "remain very imperfect, and inadequate to the purposes they are designed for: a fate, that has generally attended most of our statute laws, where they have not the foundation of the common law to build on". The number of crimes which were punishable by death was difficult to justify because the death penalty was "inflicted (perhaps inattentively) by a multitude of successive independent statutes, upon crimes very different in their natures".

. . .

Roman law did not escape Blackstone's strictures. It was "partly of pagan origin", and as luxury, politeness, and dominion increased in their society, "it swelled to that amazing bulk which it now occupies". And it was the civil law "which established in the twelfth century a new Roman empire over most of the states of the continent; states that have lost, and perhaps upon that account, their political liberties; while the free constitution of England, perhaps upon the same account, has been rather improved than debased".

England was indeed fortunate to have such a perfect body of law. "Everything is now as it should be"; and little should be changed.

. . .

The ancient and excellent laws of England are the birthright, and the most ancient and best inheritance that the subjects of this realm have, for by them he enjoyeth not only his inheritance and goods in peace and quietness, but his life and his most dear country in safety.

These words are Coke's; but they could well have been written by Blackstone. . . . With Coke, Blackstone . . . equated the sacred and inviolable rights of Englishmen with the sacred and inviolable rights of his own propertied class.

. . .

It is rare that Blackstone ventured to criticize institution or principle. Admittedly it can be said that his self-appointed task was to write an elementary commentary on the laws of England, and that was difficult enough in two thousand pages without worrying about more sophisticated questions which could only be discussed when the literate student had a sound grasp of legal principle. Nevertheless, judged on the highest standard, it remains a serious criticism of even an elementary commentary that Blackstone does not give his reader a glimpse of the inadequacies of the English legal system.

. . .

[H]is paeons of praise to the common law would not have appeared unctuous to those nurtured on Coke's dictum, that "reason is the life of the law, naye the common law itself is nothing else but reason". For the great majority, the *Commentaries* were nothing more than what they purported and appeared to be, an excellent primer of English law.

Blackstone in America

Nowhere could this have been more true than in the New World where the *Commentaries* were an immediate success. The English editions which were exported just did not meet the demand, so that in the years 1771–1772 Robert Bell, the Philadelphia publisher, was able to sell an American edition of 1,400 copies at £3 a set, and then print a second edition barely a year later at a slightly increased price. The rumour that the *Commentaries* "have sold nearly as many . . . in America as in England" had a solid basis of fact.

Those who bought the *Commentaries* were not exclusively students of the law. It was in America that Blackstone's dream that the *Commentaries* should educate laymen in the law was realised. He would have been delighted that the gentlemen of Virginia and South Carolina should turn to his volumes to decide knotty boundary disputes and tiresome family feuds, but he might have been surprised that men of humbler origins in Philadelphia and Boston should find them equally instructive. As Burke remarked, in his speech on *Conciliation with the Colonies*, "in no country perhaps in the world [was] the law so general a study".

It was not until the middle of the eighteenth century that the common law began to take root in the colonies; and after the Revolution, in some states such as New York, its future was obviously not assured. Blackstone's *Commentaries* played a considerable part in establishing the common law before and after the Revolution. In the colonies trained lawyers were few and tended to practice in the larger towns. Law books were expensive so that even second-hand legal advice was hard to come by. The *Commentaries* filled these gaps and provided a rounded picture of the common law and its institutions. In its four volumes there was enough hard law to satisfy the appetite of the profession and enough elegant exposition to attract the literate. For the colonist the great merits of the *Commentaries* were their comprehensiveness and their lack of subtlety. The answer to most of his legal problems could be found there, and the relevant principles of law were stated in terms which left little doubt as to their scope and application.

. . .

It was inevitable that there would be in the post-revolutionary period a reaction against England and English institutions. Among lawyers this took the form of a deep suspicion of the common law. . . . Statutes which forbade the citation of English decisions were not uncommon. But some colonists . . . who had been markedly hostile to the law and all lawyers in the immediate post-revolutionary era, came to recognise that the traditional safeguards of the common law were infinitely preferable to "the vagaries of politicians".

Blackstone's *Commentaries* may have indirectly contributed to the survival of the common law. Their practical utility outweighed the contempt that might have been felt for their author's political views. . . .

. . . The *Commentaries* gave more than an impetus to self-directed reading. America needed lawyers and men of affairs. In the new American Law Schools of Harvard, Yale and Columbia, Blackstone's *Commentaries*, edited and annotated by a succession of editors, became the popular text book and served to educate generations of students in the principles of the common law, thereby fulfilling Blackstone's wish that law should be studied in the humane surroundings of a University. The *Commentaries* [according to Harvard professor James Bradley Thayer] "furnished the stimulus and exemplar for [American] attempts at systematic legal education" and came to exercise "an influence upon the jurisprudence of the new nation, which no other work has since enjoyed."

PART II

The Growth
of American Law

CHAPTER 6

From Thirteen Colonies to United States

As colonists from England settled in America in the seventeenth century, they brought with them not only English law, but also the dissenting political and religious ideas that led many of them to leave England. Although royal charters granting English colonies required adherence to English law, and royal governors and the Privy Council back in London had the power to veto colonial legislation, the colonists managed to go their own ways. According to the leading treatise on U.S. legal history—Lawrence M. Friedman's *A History of American Law* (2d ed., 1985):

> [E]ach colony had a legal system built up out of various and diverse materials. These were of three general types: First, there was what might be called remembered folk-law—those aspects of living English law which the settlers brought with them. Second, there were those norms and practices which developed indigenously, to cope with new, special problems of life in the settlements. England, for example, had no need to consider, in its law, the problem of hostile native tribes. Third, there were norms and practices that the colonists adopted because of who they were—the ideological element. Puritans in power made law which was certainly different from English law, and which was not dictated by climate, conditions, or crisis, but by their own tight set of beliefs. (p. 35)

However, in the eighteenth century, as Britain prevailed over France in their struggles to colonize North America, colonial administration was tightened and the flow of English-trained lawyers to the colonies increased. At the same time, little was done to record and preserve colonial law. The desire of colonists to develop their own laws contributed to the tensions leading to the Revolution.

In the wake of the American Revolution, as in revolutionary England over a century earlier, a simplified codification was urged by some as a way to liberate the people from dependence on the common law and on lawyers. The help of France during the Revolution also led some colonists to espouse the codified continental system over the common law. Adding fuel to the anti–common law sentiment was the fact that a large number of lawyers sided with England and took refuge in Canada after England recognized the independence of the United States in the Treaty of Paris in 1783. But codification did not succeed. Francophiles could not overcome the language barrier and the lack of French law books, while the common law received a boost from Blackstone's *Commentaries,* which became the standard text for law study and practice.

Although some states initially prohibited the citation of English authorities, eventually, most state legislatures enacted "reception" statutes accepting the common law of England except for "repugnant" provisions. Americans also continued to develop their own laws. The first American court reports were published in 1789; by the 1820s, lawyers were complaining of having too many reports. Legislation also increased at a rate leading to frequent compilations of statutes.

The newly independent states did not create a codified alternative to the common law, but they codified their form of government in instruments without precedent—written constitutions. Each state enacted a constitution enshrining a government limited by the separation of powers between the executive, legislative, and judicial branches, with a representative, elected legislature, and, in most states, with a popularly elected, but weak, governor. Some state constitutions included a bill of rights protecting individuals, but the right to vote and hold office was invariably limited to white males with property and, in some states, further limited by religious qualifications.

The need remained to define the government of the union. For over a decade after the outbreak of the Revolution, the union functioned with the Articles of Confederation, which was somewhere between an instrument for an alliance of sovereign states and a federation. The shortcomings of the Articles were dramatically highlighted by runaway inflation in Rhode Island, deliberately induced by the state's legislature to relieve debtor farmers, and by an uprising of debtor farmers in Massachusetts, known as Shays' Rebellion. Both crises were related to the inability of the Confederation Congress to adequately regulate the issuance of currency. In 1787 the states called for a Constitutional Convention to create a true union with a true government.

Back of the State House, Philadelphia.
From William Birch, *The City of Philadelphia* (1800).

THE UNITED STATES CONSTITUTION

from Richard B. Bernstein, *Are We to Be a Nation?*
(Cambridge, Mass.: Harvard University Press, 1987), pp. 149–81.
Copyright © 1987 by the President and Fellows of Harvard College:
Reprinted by permission of Harvard University Press.

An Assembly of Demigods?

On 25 May 1787, picking their way through a driving rain, thirty men representing seven states assembled in the Pennsylvania State House, now known as Independence Hall, and the Federal Convention began. . . . Eventually fifty-five men representing twelve states attended at least some sessions of the Convention. Writing from his post in Paris to John Adams, Thomas Jefferson described the delegates as "an assembly of demigods." Other observers, though less adulatory than Jefferson, were also impressed with the range of talent and experience assembled for the Convention. The gathering included states' governors, chief justices, attorneys general, and many delegates to the Confederation Congress, as well as several distinguished Americans who had agreed to come out of retirement to participate one last time in American affairs.

Two of the delegates were regarded by common consent as the greatest living Americans. George Washington had not had an easy time deciding whether to accept or decline his appointment to the Virginia delegation. For eight grueling, frustrating years he had served his country as commander-in-chief of the Continental Army. He had wrestled with the problems of an ill-trained, poorly equipped, and undisciplined army; a recalcitrant, faction-ridden, and impotent Congress; an erratic, touchy officer corps that had conspired once against his own leadership and another time against Congress itself; and even his elderly, querulous mother, who complained bitterly and unfairly to Congress and anyone else who would listen about her son's neglect of her. At the end of 1783, with American independence won, Washington retired to his estate at Mount Vernon; renouncing power and popularity, he was determined to settle back into the life of a vigorous, hard-riding planter and country squire. And yet he never abandoned his interest in American affairs. For one thing, he was a shrewd land speculator who kept a vigilant eye on all factors that might affect his investments. For another, his experiences during the Revolution had strengthened his belief that the United States needed a stronger, more vigorous government than that provided by the Confederation.

. . .

Washington's only possible rival in the estimation of the Western world was Benjamin Franklin. At eighty-one the oldest delegate to the Convention, Franklin could look back on an enormous range of careers and a dazzling constellation of talents and achievements. Printer, inventor, essayist, scientist, public servant, founder of learned societies, propagandist, politician, revolutionary, diplomat, peacemaker—by 1787 the self-educated Franklin was firmly enshrined in the role of sage. At this time, Franklin was visibly old and enfeebled. Almost certainly he realized that his part would be that of conciliator—to ease tensions, turn aside wrath with soft or amusing words, and help to frame compromises. A younger generation would take the lead in the theoretical work.

To forestall any possible contest between Washington and Franklin for preeminence, Franklin and his Pennsylvania colleagues decided to propose Washington for the presidency of the Convention. To Franklin's disappointment, bad weather on the first day prevented him from attending the session to nominate Washington himself; Robert Morris stood in for Franklin, and all who were present understood and welcomed the Pennsylvanians' graceful gesture.

Seated at a desk just in front of the president's chair at this first—and every later—session was the thirty-six-year-old James Madison of Virginia. Madison was perhaps the most learned and best prepared delegate; indeed, he had arrived two weeks before the scheduled opening date. Now, as the proceedings got under way, he carried out a resolution that he had made as a result of his careful study of the histories of ancient and modern confederacies. Using a self-taught system of shorthand, he began the single most detailed, authoritative, and reliable record of the Convention's labors. Each evening he copied out his shorthand notes, occasionally referring to the full texts of speeches lent him by other delegates. Several other delegates kept notes of the debates for their own reference, and the Convention had elected an official secretary, Major William Jackson of Georgia, but he turned out to be lazy and inefficient, and his *Journal*, published in 1819, is unreliable.

. . .

After the election of officers, the Convention appointed a committee . . . to draft rules of procedure. Most of these were based on the rules of the Confederation Congress and were designed to preserve civility during the debates and to ensure a spirit of harmony, cooperation, and mutual respect. Two, however, require extended discussion.

The rule of secrecy prohibited delegates from making copies of entries in the Convention's journal without leave of the full Convention. Further only delegates were permitted to examine this journal or to attend meetings of the Convention or of its committees. Finally, delegates were barred from revealing or discussing with outsiders any business of the Convention. This rule of secrecy was consistent with the general practice of legislatures on both sides of the Atlantic until the 1790s. The "public's right to know" did not have the same meaning in 1787 that we give it today. Although there was much good-natured curiosity and well-meant speculation about what was going on behind the closed doors of the Convention, no one inside or out made a serious effort to breach this rule while the Convention was in session. The city of Philadelphia did its part by posting armed sentries around the State House to discourage inquisitive passersby and ordering loose dirt to be spread in the streets to muffle the sounds of passing wagons and carriages.

The other important rule adopted by the delegates was what might be called the "rule of mutability." The delegates rejected a proposed rule entitling delegates to require that the yeas and nays be entered in the journal and accepted the proposal of Richard Dobbs Spaight of North Carolina that the Convention grant itself the ability to reconsider votes already taken by a majority. The delegates had reason to congratulate themselves on having adopted Spaight's suggestion, for the Convention retraced its steps many times in the course of the summer, backing off from false or hasty starts and reaping the benefit of sober second thoughts.

. . .

This manner of doing business created severe pressures on the delegates. Because of the rule of secrecy, they were unable to thrash out matters, complain to sympathetic friends, or simply release their pent-up emotions. As the Convention dragged on through the summer, delegates began to wilt under the unusually oppressive heat. . . .

Despite all the frustrations inherent in attending the Convention and the many temptations to leave Philadelphia for home, more than half the delegates (twenty-nine) attended every or nearly every session, with another ten missing only a few weeks. Forty-two delegates showed up on the last day, including three—Elbridge Gerry of Massachusetts and George Mason and Edmund Randolph of Virginia—who refused to sign the Constitution.

Why were so many so faithful to their duties? First, many delegates sincerely feared for the nation's future under the Articles of Confederation and believed that the Convention provided a last clear chance to restructure the government of the United States to preserve the American experiment. Second, the delegates were aware that the interests of their states and sections as well as those of the United States depended on what the Convention did. They were there as much to safeguard state and local interests under whatever new system was devised by the Convention as "to render the constitution of the federal government adequate to the exigencies of the Union." Third, especially for younger and more intellectual delegates such as James Madison, Alexander Hamilton, and Charles Pinckney, the challenge of framing a new government and participating in deliberations critical to the future of republican government was irresistible.

Fourth, and closely related to the third, participation in the Convention gratified many delegates' desire for fame. Considered the reward of virtuous conduct, fame was the goad to virtuous behavior in public and private life. And, as the delegates knew from their familiarity with Sir Francis Bacon's essay on the subject, the greatest fame and highest honor were reserved for "founders of states and commonwealths."

There was also the hope that distinguishing oneself at so important an assembly and among so remarkable a gathering of notables might well be a spur to one's later political career. Witness Charles Pinckney, whose desperate desire to shine led him to knock five years off his own age (he was twenty-nine) in order to lay claim to the distinction of being the Convention's youngest delegate—an honor properly belonging to twenty-six-year-old Jonathan Dayton of New Jersey. Even more questionable were Pinckney's later claims about his influence at the Convention.

Did the delegates write the Constitution in order to protect their economic interests? In 1913 Charles A. Beard, relying on his research into lists of holders of United States securities in the 1780s, maintained that the delegates to the Convention and the supporters of the Constitution in the state ratification controversy were bent on protecting their holdings in these securities. A strong constitution and powerful federal government, Beard asserted, would guarantee the rights of property against encroachments by radical state governments such as Rhode Island or by armies of desperate debtors such as the Massachusetts farmers led by Daniel Shays. Later research has shattered the foundation of Beard's claims and restored a measure of patriotism to the framers' motives. But the threats posed to the security of the rights of property by state governments and by the possibility of more debtors' rebellions like Shays's Rebellion galvanized politicians . . . who otherwise would not have pursued that object with energy or commitment.

. . .

On 29 May 1787, once the Convention had adopted its rules and elected its officers, Governor Edmund Randolph of Virginia opened the main business on behalf of his state's delegation. . . . Virginia had taken the leading part in campaigning for this gathering, and the delegates were probably not surprised to see Virginians at the head of this effort as well. Tall, handsome, a polished speaker, Randolph was one of the most popular figures in Virginia politics. In a long and eloquent speech, Randolph decried the unsettled state of the Union, pointed out the many defects of the Articles of Confederation, extolled the advantages of strengthening the general government, and concluded by presenting . . . fifteen resolutions drawn up by Madison and his colleagues. Later historians have dubbed these resolutions the Virginia Plan.

. . .

[The Convention] chose to scrap the Articles of Confederation and frame a completely new instrument of government for the United States, one having the authority to operate directly on the American people rather than having to rely on the cooperation of the state governments. . . . [The Virginia Plan] was the foundation of the Convention's effort to create a fully developed system of government. The drafters of the Articles of Confederation had made no effort to embody the principle of separation of powers in the document, because it was intended to be not an instrument of government but a covenant among sovereign states. . . . [The Virginia Plan] brought the cherished constitutional principle of separation of powers to the federal level, after more than a decade of fruitful experimentation in state constitution-making.

The Virginia Plan provided for a national legislature in two branches, each to be apportioned on the basis of population. The members of the first branch would be elected by the people; those of the second would be chosen by the first branch from a list of persons nominated by each state legislature. Members of the national legislature would be ineligible for other state or federal offices. They would receive liberal stipends to be paid by the United States, and thus would not be dependent on the whims of state governments, as were delegates to the Confederation Congress. The national legislature would have the legislative powers vested in Congress by the Articles, as well as the authority to legislate "in all cases to which the separate States are incompetent, or in which the harmony of the United States may be interrupted by the exercise of individual [states'] Legislation" and the power to veto state laws contrary to the new federal charter. The national legislature would also have the power to summon the armed forces of the United States against any state failing to fulfill its duties to the Union.

The Virginia Plan merely sketched the structure of the national executive, not even specifying how many persons would constitute it; but the plan did provide that the executive would be chosen by vote of the national legislature and would join with "a convenient number of the National Judiciary" to exercise a qualified veto power over the national legislature. The national judiciary would include one or more supreme tribunals and several lower courts; the judges of these courts would be named by vote of the national legislature. The national judicial power would extend to piracy, maritime cases, suits involving foreigners or citizens of other states, federal revenue cases, impeachments, "and questions which involve the national peace or harmony." The plan also included a proposal to devise a method to admit new states to the Union, a guarantee of a republican form of government for the states, an amendment procedure more flexible than that of the Articles, a requirement that state officeholders swear to support the new charter of government, and a ratification clause under which the new charter would be submitted to specially chosen assemblies in the states rather than to the state legislatures.

The first incarnation of the Constitution of the United States, the Virginia Plan contained the seeds of most of the issues that agitated the delegates, and some of its omissions proved just as controversial as its terms. For the rest of the Convention, using the Virginia Plan as a basis, the delegates struggled to frame a national charter sufficiently powerful, flexible, and well checked and balanced to hold the nation together without injuring the legitimate rights of the states.

The Dilemma of Representation

The dispute that posed the greatest threat to the unity and harmony of the Federal Convention focused on the system of representation governing the structure of the national legislature. Ever since the first Continental Congress of 1774, every assembly convened to discuss American affairs or to deal with American problems had adhered to the rule that each colony—or, later, state—had one vote, regardless of population or the number of delegates its government appointed. The large states, such as Virginia, Pennsylvania, Massachusetts, and New York, often chafed at this system of representation, which in their view gave an unfair advantage to small states such as Delaware, Rhode Island, and Georgia.

Even before the Convention began, the rule of equal representation posed problems. In the preliminary caucus of Virginia and Pennsylvania delegates, the Virginians had managed to scotch the Pennsylvanians' suggestion that the Convention itself do away with the rule of equal representation. . . . On the other hand, the Virginia Plan startled and disturbed the delegations from the smaller states by apportioning *both* houses of the national legislature on the basis of population.

From the vantage point of two centuries' experience, the solution seems obvious. Nonetheless, it took ten weeks of heated debate, false starts, and even threats of disunion and disruption of the Convention before the delegates finally arrived at a compromise.

For the first few weeks the supporters of the Virginia Plan enjoyed an almost unbroken string of successes, as provision after provision and clause after clause fell into place. . . . On 13 June 1787 the committee reported its revisions of the Virginia Plan to the full Convention. The report made several important changes in Randolph's original resolutions. First, the members of the second branch of the national legislature would be elected by the individual legislatures of the several states rather than by the cumbersome multilevel system proposed by the Virginians. Second, the powers of the national legislature were expanded by the addition of a clause permitting it to veto state laws that contravened treaties entered into by the United States—a clear threat to state laws punishing Loyalists and confiscating their land, which were invalid under the Treaty of Paris of 1783. Third, the report included the first suggestion that slaves be counted in some fashion in determining representation in the national legislature; this provision was familiar from earlier practice, and the northern delegates knew from the outset that some such concession was necessary to satisfy the southern delegates. Fourth, the report did away with the shared veto power given to the national executive and a "council of revision," instead vesting a qualified veto power solely in the national executive. . . . Fifth, the national executive would consist of a single person.

. . .

. . . In the succeeding weeks some large-state delegates, including Madison, James Wilson of Pennsylvania, and Rufus King of Massachusetts, could not resist making sarcastic comments about what they saw as the pretensions of the small states and the desirability of dismantling them. In response, on 1 July, Gunning Bedford, Jr., of Delaware exploded. . . . Later Bedford apologized for the warmth of his remarks, asking that "some allowance . . . be made for the habits of his profession"—he was a lawyer and attorney general of Delaware—"in which warmth was natural & sometimes necessary." Bedford also reminded the tactless large-state delegates that they had offered more than ample provocation.

Not until 16 July did the delegates finally arrive at a solution, or, more accurately, a compromise of competing state claims. . . . Under the resolutions adopted that day, each state would receive an equal vote in the second branch of the legislature of the United States; seats in the first branch would be apportioned on the basis of the number of free inhabitants in each state plus three-fifths of the number of "other persons" (that is slaves); a census every ten years would allow for adjustment of representation in the lower house according to population growth; the lower house would have the power to originate revenue bills, with the upper house having no power to change them.

. . .

Creating a National Government

From the first days of the Convention, the delegates abandoned the idea of merely framing amendments to the Articles of Confederation. Both in the original Virginia Plan of 29 May and in the . . . report of 13 June, the delegates agreed that they were working to create a *national* government. On 20 June, however, Oliver Ellsworth moved that the Convention replace the word "national" with the phrase "of the United States" wherever appropriate. Randolph agreed to the motion, and the delegates dutifully marked up their copies of the 13 June report to reflect this change.

Despite this rewording the delegates continued to assemble a government that was in fact more "national" than "federal"—a distinction disregarded today but considered significant in the eighteenth century. In the 1780s a federal government was a confederation or league of separate and otherwise independent governments; the federal government would act on the individual governments under it rather than directly on the people of each political unit. By contrast, a national government acted directly on the people and not on intervening governments. Were the United States a completely national government, the states would have the same relation to the national government as counties have to a state: they would function as mere administrative units, with no share in *sovereignty*, or ultimate political rule. It was an axiom of classical political theory that sovereignty could not be divided between two governments or two levels of government claiming authority over the same people and territory.

The Constitution created a completely new kind of government, however— one that . . . was neither completely national nor completely federal but a mixture of both. In some areas, the central government would have final power or sovereignty; in others, the state governments would be supreme; in still others, the federal and state governments would have overlapping, or concurrent, power. This intricate solution to the problem of strengthening the government of the United States while paying due respect to the authority of the state governments evolved more by accident than by design. The consequences of this new form of federal government are shown in one key debate from which emerged the linchpin of the supremacy of the government of the United States in federal-state relations.

One of the principal features of the Virginia Plan was the national legislature's power to veto state laws violating the "articles of Union," a device proposed by James Madison. This assault on state sovereignty alarmed delegates such as Hugh Williamson of North Carolina, John Lansing, Jr., of New York, and Luther Martin of Maryland. In Williamson's words, this provision "might restrain the States from regulating the internal police"—that is, the states would be discouraged from making laws necessary to protect the safety, health, morals, and welfare of their citizens. Lansing and Martin predicted that such a veto power over state laws would provoke resistance by the states, particularly the smaller states, to the entire plan. The proposal also contained disquieting echoes of the old power of the king in council to disapprove laws passed by colonial assemblies, a procedure that had been attacked in the Declaration of Independence.

The delegates substituted for Madison's veto power over state laws . . . [a] provision . . . making the laws of the United States the supreme law of the land despite the states' laws or constitutions. Originally drafted by Luther Martin as a tactic to head off Madison's proposed negative on state laws, this provision was recast to become what is now the Supremacy Clause of the Constitution (Art. VI, Sec. 1). The Supremacy Clause makes the Constitution, federal laws, and treaties the supreme law of the land, elevating them above state constitutions and laws. The clause thus confers on the federal courts the power to enforce the Constitution against the states, giving implicit sanction to the federal courts' power to declare state laws unconstitutional. Neither Madison nor Martin expected the Supremacy Clause to assume this importance. Madison was the last delegate to give up the fight for a national legislative power to disapprove state laws, and he saw the Supremacy Clause as an inadequate substitute. . . .

Creating a National Executive

After the issue of representation, the most difficult task the Convention faced was the creation of a national executive. At the outset, the Committee of the Whole took a long, hard look at James Wilson's proposal that "a National Executive to consist of a single person be instituted." Madison recorded that the delegates greeted Wilson's motion with "a considerable pause." Finally Benjamin Franklin broke the silence, urging his colleagues to deliver their opinions on the proposal. George Mason and Edmund Randolph argued that a single executive would be the "foetus of monarchy," and Roger Sherman claimed that, because the executive was simply an institution to carry out the will of the legislature, the legislature should have the power to choose the executive *and* to fix its numbers. Ultimately, on 4 June, by a vote of seven states to three, the Committee of the Whole adopted Wilson's motion. . . .

The next major stumbling block was the means of choosing the national executive, an issue closely linked to the duration of his term and his eligibility for reelection. The delegates could not make up their minds, adopting and then dropping several competing proposals. The main choices before them were election by the national legislature as opposed to election by either the state legislatures or some body of "electors" chosen by the states in some way. When the delegates favored electing the executive by the national legislature, they also chose to give the executive a single, relatively long term; seven years was the term most frequently mentioned, though some delegates suggested a term as long as twenty years and Alexander Hamilton favored lifetime tenure "during good behavior." When the delegates supported assigning the choice of the national executive to the states, they also favored a relatively short term— three or four years—with no limit on eligibility for reelection.

Eventually the Convention referred the whole matter to its Committee on Postponed Matters. . . . On 24 August this committee recommended that the president be elected by electors selected by the states—by whatever means they chose—to a four-year term without restrictions on reelection. Each state was assigned electoral votes equal to its combined representation in both houses of Congress. The idea of this "electoral college" had surfaced repeatedly in the Convention's deliberations, but each time the delegates had rejected it. They accepted the committee's recommendation now because they recognized that their ingenuity had reached its limits and that the electoral college was the least objectionable method before them.

Only a handful of delegates favored James Wilson's proposal that the president be chosen by popular vote. Wilson was perhaps the most consistent advocate at the Convention of a strong central government founded directly on the American people. He favored popular election not only of the president but also of both houses of the national legislature, as well as proportional representation in both houses.

A former scholarship student at St. Andrews University, Wilson emigrated from Scotland to Pennsylvania in 1765. He was trained as a lawyer . . . and became perhaps the foremost legal theorist in America in the 1770s and 1780s. Wilson published notable pamphlets refuting British assertion of authority over the colonies in the years leading up to the Declaration of Independence but was reluctant to take the final step of revolution, though he did sign the Declaration. His . . . generally conservative stands in Pennsylvania state politics earned him the dislike of many of his fellow citizens, some of whom once organized a mob to lay siege to his Philadelphia home, thereafter nicknamed "Fort Wilson." In many respects Wilson fits the pattern of most other self-made Americans of this period. Yet in the Federal Convention he outstripped every other delegate in his commitment to the cause of democratic nationalism. Robert G. McCloskey, the most astute interpreter of Wilson's life and thought, maintains that of all the delegates Wilson had the clearest and most accurate vision of America's eventual constitutional development, and most historians of the Convention rank him as second only to Madison in his contributions to the making of the Constitution.

Wilson may have lost the fight for a popularly elected president, but he was generally successful in working to create a strong and independent presidency. He and his fellow delegates were strongly influenced by the New York and Massachusetts constitutions, which created independent, popularly elected governors, rejecting the principle of legislative supremacy enshrined in the constitutions of Virginia and Pennsylvania. They saw the need to create an executive capable of maintaining the balance of powers in a government of three coequal branches. Finally, they took courage and inspiration from the silent presence of George Washington. Believing that Washington would be asked to serve as the nation's first chief executive under the Constitution, the delegates were willing to entrust greater powers to the presidency in the expectation that Washington would exercise them responsibly and set unassailable precedents for his successors. Thus, the delegates gave the president the power to appoint judges and other government officials and to negotiate treaties with the advice and consent of the Senate—a survival of the old conception of the upper house of the legislature as a council to advise and act with the executive. They also gave the president the sole power to veto legislation, despite Madison's proposal to league him with a Council of Revision drawn from the national judiciary for that purpose. This veto power was qualified, however; a two-thirds vote by both houses of the national legislature could override a presidential veto. The Constitution thus created a presidency that would be what the holder of the office wanted to make of it.

The Judiciary

Beyond agreeing that there should be a judicial branch of government and one supreme court, the framers gave relatively short shrift to the national judiciary. Some delegates . . . maintained that there should be no lower federal courts at all, on the ground that the state courts would be bound by oath to enforce the Constitution and thus could be relied upon to handle cases involving the United States or its Constitution or laws. Most delegates agreed on the need for a system of lower federal courts but ultimately decided to leave this matter to be worked out by the national legislature.

Much ink has been spilled over whether the delegates to the Federal Convention intended to grant the federal courts the power to declare federal or state laws unconstitutional—what we now call the doctrine of judicial review. Nowhere does the Constitution explicitly confer the power to pass on the constitutionality of federal laws or actions, but references by several delegates to state courts' exercises of the power to review state laws in the 1770s and 1780s suggest that they would not have been surprised by federal courts' assertions of this power in the 1790s and early 1800s. As for the federal courts' power to review the constitutionality of state laws and actions, a stronger case can be made that the delegates expected the federal courts to have and exercise this power under the Constitution. The Supremacy Clause is the locus of this power, clothing the Constitution with supralegal status and commanding its enforcement against contrary state laws or constitutional provisions. In addition, by bringing the Constitution into the sphere of judicially enforceable law, the Supremacy Clause ensures that controversies over the meaning of the Constitution will resolve themselves, sooner or later, into judicial questions coming before the federal judiciary and eventually the Supreme Court.

The Constitution leaves the structure of the federal court system, the number of members of the Supreme Court, and the jurisdiction of all federal courts to the discretion of the national legislature. Article III merely sets forth the maximum grant of jurisdiction beyond which Congress may not go, but it seems to permit Congress to give the courts less than the full measure of constitutionally authorized jurisdiction. One of the most important acts of the first Congress meeting under the Constitution was the adoption of the Judiciary Act of 1789, which completed the work deliberately left unfinished by the delegates to the Federal Convention.

Sectionalism and Slavery

Although the initial division in the Federal Convention was that between the large and small states, the split that occurred most often and ominously was that between northern and southern states. Two issues became the focal points for these divisions—the apportionment of the lower house of the national legislature (linked with the apportionment of direct taxes) and the regulation of trade.

Some historians have claimed that the South Carolina and Connecticut delegates forged a "deal" early on in the Convention to link these two issues and pursued this strategy throughout the drafting of the Constitution; through this arrangement they created a consensus on which delegates from both sections could agree. Although such a "deal" would explain neatly the evolution of the compromise between proslavery and antislavery interests, it seems more likely that the delegates worked and argued and dealt their way into the eventual compromise, step by step, without a clear vision of the final result.

The original Virginia Plan contemplated a proportional representation based on the number of free inhabitants of the several states. The 13 June report . . . modified this ratio to include three-fifths of "other persons," a euphemism for slaves. . . . In late August the problem reached a crisis as the delegates from the deep South pressed for limits on the power of the general government to regulate trade, specifically the slave trade. Delegates from northern states . . . and Virginian delegates . . . resisted these efforts, fearing that they would interfere with the natural erosion of slavery as a workable institution.

To resolve this controversy, the Convention appointed yet another committee, which reported a compromise designed to please no one but to propitiate everyone. The United States could not interfere with the slave trade before 1800—a date later extended by eight years—but could within limits tax the importation of slaves. Further, only a simple majority in both houses of the national legislature would be needed to pass navigation acts—that is, tariffs, quotas, embargoes, and discriminations in favor of local products. This clause was a concession by the South Carolinians, who had previously demanded a two-thirds vote in both houses for the enactment of such laws. . . . In this atmosphere of tense and punctilious conciliation, the Federal Convention sidestepped the explosive issue of slavery, wrapping up its work on the issue by adopting a fugitive-slave clause. . . .

Many later historians and politicians have denounced what they see as the Convention's failure of nerve, moral courage, and ingenuity in dealing with the problem of slavery. Indeed, in the 1830s and 1840s abolitionists . . . staged public burnings of the Constitution, denouncing it as "a covenant with death" for its compromise with the slaveholding states. But the delegates to the Convention were fully aware of the southern states' commitment to their "peculiar institution" and believed . . . [the] threat that South Carolina and the other deep southern states would leave the Union unless the Constitution contained some protection for slavery. In a choice between striking a blow against slavery and holding the Union together, the delegates decided to preserve the Union. They showed equal sensitivity to the growing antislavery sentiment in the northern states by taking care to avoid mentioning slavery or slaves by name anywhere in the document. . . .

. . .

The other element of this sectional compromise was the southern delegates' willingness to abandon the requirement of a two-thirds vote by both houses of the national legislature to pass laws regulating foreign trade. This was the South's concession to the New England delegates, whose states conducted most of the United States' "carrying trade" and manufacturing. The southerners would have preferred to make it more difficult for the United States to regulate trade, as this power would increase the price of imported goods on which the South relied.

Virginia, alone of the southern states, stood to gain from the restriction on the slave trade. Although its delegates, such as Madison and Mason, opposed on principle restrictions on the power of the United States to ban or restrict this trade, Virginia enjoyed large profits from the sale of native-born slaves across state lines. Prohibiting or restricting the overseas slave trade would thus benefit Virginians active in the domestic slave trade, for they could be assured of a market in those slaveholding states, such as South Carolina, that otherwise would buy slaves more cheaply from overseas. In this as in other instances, principle was mixed with baser motives for political decision-making in the Convention.

Omission of a Bill of Rights

None of the plans for a new form of government or for amendments to the Articles of Confederation nor any of the drafts produced by the Convention's several committees contained a declaration of rights. Of course, neither did the Articles of Confederation. Although only a few delegates felt that a bill of rights should be incorporated in the Constitution, the Convention's omission of one proved to be the single greatest obstacle to the ratification of the Constitution.

Throughout the late spring and summer of 1787, the delegates focused on devising and adjusting the machinery of government under the Constitution. Few if any—not even such staunch libertarians as James Madison—bothered to think in terms of that government's potential effect on the rights of individual Americans. Some isolated procedural safeguards did find their way into the Constitution, such as the ban on suspending the writ of habeas corpus (a writ commanding an official detaining or incarcerating a person under color of law to bring that person before a judge to explain the legal authority under which the person is being held); the strict definition of a treasonable offense and the standard of evidence needed to support a conviction for treason (the only crime so treated in the Constitution); the guarantee of trial by jury; the bans on bills of attainder (legislative acts imposing punishments on named persons) and *ex post facto* laws (laws making acts criminal though committed before enactment of the law); the omission of property qualifications for holding federal office; and the prohibition on religious test oaths for voting or holding office. Hamilton cited all of these . . . to support his argument that the Constitution itself was a bill of rights.

A few delegates were not convinced, however. George Mason and Elbridge Gerry unsuccessfully raised the issue on 12 September, a few days before the end of the Convention. Their failure to persuade their colleagues to act to recognize individual rights prompted their refusal to sign the Constitution and their later opposition to it in the campaign for ratification.

One of the grand figures of Virginia politics, Mason was born in 1725, the fifth of a long line of rich, powerful planters. Only rarely could Mason be tempted to take part in public life; he preferred to remain at Gunston Hall, his opulent plantation in Tidewater, Virginia. His most important contribution to his state and nation was his participation in the convention that drafted the Virginia constitution of 1776; Mason was the principal draftsman of the Virginia Declaration of Rights, a model for all later bills of rights. . . . To everyone's astonishment, however, he agreed to serve as a senior delegate from Virginia to the Federal Convention. This trip to Philadelphia was the farthest he had ever traveled from Gunston Hall. As a delegate, Mason followed an independent line, voting to strengthen the government of the United States yet opposing efforts to create a single, independent executive. Weeks before the climactic exchange of 12 September, Mason had begun hinting that he might not be able to support the emerging Constitution.

Elbridge Gerry, nicknamed the "Grumbletonian" for his supposed refusal to support any measure he did not himself propose, had also moved away from his early belief in the need for a stronger general government. A . . . signer of both the Declaration of Independence and the Articles of Confederation, in 1785 Gerry had opposed his state legislature's proposal that amendments to the Articles were necessary. Shays's Rebellion had changed Gerry's mind, and he accepted appointment as a Massachusetts delegate to the Federal Convention. Gerry distrusted many of the tendencies he saw in the Constitution, however, and it became clear that he too would not automatically go along with his fellow delegates.

On 12 September Mason urged the Convention to add a bill of rights to the Constitution. He pointed out that, by reference to the state bills of rights (including his own), "a bill might be prepared in a few hours." Gerry backed Mason's proposal and made a formal motion in its support, which Mason seconded. Despite Mason's hopeful prediction that a bill of rights prefixed to the Constitution "would give great quiet to the people," Roger Sherman argued that such a measure was not needed: he "was for securing the rights of the people where requisite. The state declarations of rights are not repealed by this Constitution; and being in force are sufficient." No one else spoke to Mason's and Gerry's motion, or to Mason's reply to Sherman that "the laws of the United States are to be paramount to state bills of rights." When the motion was put to a vote, every state present on the floor rejected it, and the move to add a bill of rights to the Constitution perished.

Despite Mason's estimate of how quick and simple it would be to draft a satisfactory bill of rights, his fellow delegates realized that his proposal, if adopted, could add days or even weeks to the life of the Convention. Having spent more than four months in Philadelphia away from their families, business affairs, and political and other commitments, they were eager to finish their work and depart. Having weathered one crisis (over representation) that nearly wrecked the Convention, and another (over slavery and the regulation of trade) that carried with it ominous signs of future sectional divisions, and having exhausted their ingenuity and patience, the delegates were not willing to tackle yet another difficult assignment. Further, the delegates had never included the task of writing a federal bill of rights as part of their mandate, and they did not believe that the Constitution might pose a threat to individual rights. Had they been less exhausted, they might have realized that the creation of a government having the power to operate directly on the people of the United States carried with it at least a potential threat to individual rights. As it was, though they brushed aside the Mason-Gerry proposal, the delegates would have to come to terms with it in the public arena for months thereafter.

CHAPTER 7

Federalists versus Republicans

The Constitution drafted in Philadelphia required ratification by elected conventions in nine states. The campaign for ratification led to the formation of the Federalist party and gave rise to an enduring classic, *The Federalist*, a collection of eighty-five newspaper columns by Alexander Hamilton, James Madison, and John Jay, explaining the Constitution and urging its ratification.

Following ratification, Congress moved quickly to correct the Constitution's lack of a declaration of individual rights. Ten amendments to the Constitution were passed by Congress as the Bill of Rights in 1789 and ratified by the states in 1791. The all-important First Amendment protects freedom of religion, speech, the press, and assembly from congressional abridgment; other amendments provide protections against unreasonable searches and seizures, excessive bail or excessive fines, double jeopardy, self-incrimination, and cruel and unusual punishments; yet other amendments protect the right to keep and bear arms, the right to a trial by jury, and the right to "due process of law"; the Sixth Amendment, dealing with criminal trials, provides the right to a speedy and public trial, the right to be informed of accusations, to confront adverse witnesses, to summon favorable witnesses, and to have the assistance of counsel.

Opposition to the Constitution, however, was not entirely mollified. Abuses by a strong colonial authority gave rise to the Revolution, and some feared that a new central government—with constitutional powers to control currency, tax, regulate interstate commerce, control foreign policy, raise an army, and enact legislation "necessary and proper" to carry out its enumerated powers—might become equally oppressive. The proponents of a strong federal government were seen as favoring commercial, industrial interests concentrated largely in the northern states; they rallied around the Federalist party led by John Adams and Alexander Hamilton. Their opponents advocated agrarian, small-scale communities and strong state governments; in 1791 they formed the Republican party (no relation to today's G.O.P.) with Virginians Thomas Jefferson and James Madison as its leaders.

The administration of George Washington managed to remain above party politics and sectionalism. Both Hamilton and Jefferson served in Washington's cabinet. But strife continued to threaten the stability of the government. In 1794 an agrarian antitax insurrection in Pennsylvania, the "Whiskey Rebellion," led to the dispatch of 15,000 federal troops. In the same period, the threat of war with England was ever present (it became a reality in the War of 1812) and a new foreign threat emerged: Although the French Revolution of 1789 was initially kindred to the American Revolution, the revolutionary government of France harassed U.S. shipping, refusing to honor U.S. neutrality in hostilities between England and France.

Perhaps most threatening to the fabric of U.S. government was the federal government's repressive reaction to the French threat—the Alien and Sedition Acts of 1798, which made it a crime to "write, print, utter, or publish . . . false, scandalous, and malicious, writing or writings, against the government of the United States, or either house of the congress of the United States, or the president of the United States." John Adams had succeeded Washington as president in 1797 and Republicans, not without cause, saw the Alien and Sedition Acts as attempts to suppress criticism of Federalist policies. The Acts were also denounced on the basis of states' rights in the Virginia and Kentucky Resolutions drafted by Jefferson and Madison. After a number of prosecutions, the Acts were repealed or allowed to expire.

Several defendants charged under the Alien and Sedition Acts pleaded that the acts were unconstitutional under the First Amendment's guarantee of freedom of speech and of the press. But the Supreme Court avoided the issue. It was not clear whether the Court had the authority to refuse to enforce an act of Congress on constitutional grounds. The Constitution was silent on the issue, and many believed that each branch of government had the final word on the constitutionality of its own actions. As Alexander Bickel points out in *The Least Dangerous Branch* (2d ed., 1986):

> Congress was created very nearly full blown by the Constitution itself. The vast possibilities of the presidency were relatively easy to perceive and soon, inevitably, materialized. But the institution of the judiciary needed to be summoned up out of the constitutional vapors. (p. 1)

In its early years, the Supreme Court was rather inactive. The first chief justice, John Jay, resigned largely out of lack of interest; two chief justices followed with brief tenures. As John Adams lost the election of 1800 to Thomas Jefferson, one of his last acts as president was to appoint John Marshall as the fourth chief justice. John Marshall remained chief justice for the next thirty-four years.

Portrait by St. Memin.   Copyright, 1901, by Thomas Marshall Smith.

John Marshall.

From John F. Dillon, *John Marshall: Life, Character and Judicial Services* (1903), based on a painting by Charles Saint-Memin, 1801.

from Kent R. Newmyer, *The Supreme Court Under Marshall and Taney*
(New York: Thomas Y. Crowell, 1968), pp. 18–38.
Copyright © 1968 by Thomas Y. Crowell Company.
Reprinted by permission of Harlan Davidson, Inc.

John Marshall and the Consolidation of National Power

From Independence to the Treaty of Ghent in 1815*, the overriding question in American history was whether the nation—besieged without by hostile governments and within by provincialism and factionalism—had sufficient power to survive. . . . Though the Supreme Court under John Marshall (1801–1835) was as much concerned with this crucial issue as Congress and the executive, it did not seem likely in 1801 that it could profoundly affect the outcome. Little had happened during the Court's first twelve years to contradict Hamilton's observation of 1788 "that the judiciary is beyond comparison the weakest of the three departments of power" or to dispose of Chief Justice Jay's fear that the Court's weakness was permanent. President Adams' appointment of John Marshall—supported unenthusiastically even by the Federalists—did not particularly brighten the outlook.

Yet . . . , within ten years the Court consolidated far-reaching judicial power and in fifteen more put the authority of Congress on a broad and permanent constitutional footing. Not only did the Court legitimize national power but also influenced . . . the manner in which power was used to achieve policy goals.

The gulf between promise and accomplishment presents the first interpretive problem about the Marshall Court. . . . The Jeffersonians were certain of two things: that the Constitution was a limiting document and that John Marshall was a malignant force. They charged the Chief Justice with usurping power not in the Constitution and with converting his weak-willed colleagues to his plans for aggrandizement. The Federalists, on the other hand, expected

---

*The Treaty of Ghent ended the War of 1812 between the United States and Great Britain, ceding the Oregon Territory to the United States and submitting the United States–Canadian boundary to an arbitration commission.

the Court to consolidate national power and contain the emerging forces of democracy. And the more the Jeffersonians inveighed against Marshall, the more heroic he became to the party of conservative nationalism. The result— and it has been incorporated into historiography—was that the Chief Justice appeared to be the whole Court and to make history single-handedly.

It must be conceded that John Marshall was a natural for the heroic role. Few Americans, with the possible exception of Washington, were so appealing. He was an aristocrat by birth and political philosophy (in an age when gentlemen still ruled) but a democrat in manner (when democracy was the coming thing). Whether outracing his comrades in rare moments of leisure at Valley Forge, playing quoits with Richmond cronies, tempting Justice Joseph Story away from his Puritan habits with a bit of Madeira, or guiding the Court in conference, his democratic demeanor, openness, humor, and natural grace won the affection of many men. His writing was lucid and sometimes eloquent, informed by a mind that was superbly logical and incisive. And, again as the age demanded, Marshall tempered reason with experience. He had long been involved in the business of law, as well as in service to state and nation—as an officer in the Revolution, as a member of the Virginia House of Burgesses and delegate to the state ratifying convention, as special ambassador to France in 1797, as a Congressman, and, briefly, as Secretary of State under John Adams. His devotion to the Republic was beyond question. As the *North American Review* (January, 1836) aptly put it, "one could hardly help thinking that the office was made for the man, or the man for the office."

. . .

Revisionist historiography, for the most part, has not gainsaid the genius of the Chief Justice or the lasting achievements of his Court. However, it has been more concerned with Marshall as a man among men, a judge among judges, than with his heroism. Also, recent scholarship has been dissatisfied with the formal approach to law which removed the Court and justices from the political process, which denied judicial discretion and obscured genuine historical alternatives. Quite simply, the burden assumed by modern students is that of putting the Marshall Court back into history, of measuring its accomplishments in light of its institutional limitations and against the potential of the historical moment. Such was the implication of Oliver Wendell Holmes' heretical pronouncement that Marshall presented "a strategic point in the campaign of history, and part of his greatness consists in his being *there*."

. . .

The "campaign of history," to follow Holmes' interpretive lead, in which Marshall and his colleagues were engaged concerned the issue of national union—and they found abundant opportunity for creative action. It is clear in retrospect that ingredients for success were not lacking. National statesmen could count on the deep patriotism of one generation of Americans who had waged a successful national revolution and of a second whose zeal was replenished by another war with the same enemy. Moreover, the nationalist impulse had been institutionalized by the Federal Constitution: rooted in practical wisdom, buttressed with untapped national power, and equipped with a method of change, the Constitution was an immeasurable boon to national survival. Constitutional government was also bolstered by an inherited tradition of popular respect for legal order which had survived the upheaval of revolution. Both the moral authority of Washington and a dozen successful years of nationhood gave momentum to the young republic. And the security provided by three thousand miles of ocean plus the prospect of prosperity rooted in an enterprising people and a rich continent were additional advantages that few emerging nations had.

Yet national union was as much potential as it was fact. Each advantage had a less auspicious side. If the Revolution was, as some historians insist, constructively conservative, it also set in motion social and political forces that could undercut the very foundations of the Constitution. Provincialism—and with it an indifference to national welfare and suspicion of national power—continued to embarrass effective central government. Given the diverse natures of the sections, the individual pursuit of economic happiness could easily divide the nation. And continental expansion could diffuse as well as enhance national unity.

In these ambivalent circumstances, it was far from certain whether the nation could last. Conceivably it might do so on terms other than those laid down by the Philadelphia Convention. More likely though, if national union was not attained with the Constitution of 1787, it would not be attained at all. The future of the republic, then, rested on the capability of that document to contain and accommodate the forces of political, economic, and intellectual change and harness them to the national purpose. A crucial question, therefore—and a great unknown in 1801—was how and by whom the Constitution would be interpreted.

When he assumed the duties of Chief Justice in March, 1801, two things were clear to John Marshall: first, that his Court must reinforce the movement toward a stronger national government; second, that it would have to establish its position as an authoritative interpreter of the Constitution in order to do so. It was the latter contingency that was problematical.

The institutional future of the Marshall Court was not entirely without promise. The constitutional grant of power, however ambiguous, was still considerable, and the pre-Marshall Court had begun to build on it. The jurisdictional and organizational gaps had been filled in with the passage of the Judiciary Act of 1789. The Court had established internal rules and procedures and set up working relationships with Congress and the executive, with the lower federal courts and the state judiciaries. The judiciary also began to consolidate its position as a separate and independent branch of the government.

. . .

Yet in 1801, the Court had not established itself as *the* authoritative interpreter of the Constitution. The Republicans supported the right of the states to interpret the constitutional powers of the federal government in the Virginia and Kentucky Resolutions of 1798 and 1799. And the Republican view was supported by the electoral victory of 1800. Presidents, senators and representatives, as well as justices, took an oath to uphold the Constitution, and they all insisted on their right to interpret the document. The claim of Congress was especially strong. The tradition of legislative dominance, dating from the revolutionary and confederation period, was still vital in the 1790s. . . . With the Republicans in control of Congress after 1801 and the Federalists barricaded in the judicial branch, congressional claims were certain to be pressed with new vigor.

Not only had the Court failed to capture the high ground, but the power it did hold was in jeopardy. . . . Want of litigation was one reason: the Court had been open for business for a year and a half before deciding a case. By 1801 it had decided only sixty-three cases, averaging less than one of real significance each year. As the rapid turnover in membership and the difficulty in finding talented replacements indicated, aspiring statesmen were not interested in positions on the Court. . . .

On top of its other woes, the Court was deeply involved in the bitter political battles of the day—and on the losing side. The Republicans, who had gained the Presidency and both houses of Congress in the election of 1800, were in a position to humble the Court. By their own lights they had ample justification for doing so. . . . The enthusiasm with which Federalist judges enforced the Sedition Act of 1798 against Republican critics aroused bitter resentment, and their refusal to consider the Act's constitutionality further inflamed sentiment against the Court. The anti-Jeffersonian political harangues which Justice Chase delivered from the bench brought these feelings to a boil. Finally, the Judiciary Act of 1801—which created sixteen new judgeships for Federalists and reduced the Court from six to five so that President Jefferson would not be able to appoint a Republican justice—made it inevitable that the Court would be attacked by both the President and Congress.

Here then was the unpromising historical material from which judicial power had to be molded. What could be done? Immediate action was imperative lest judicial weakness become an institutional habit. But the Court had few offensive weapons in its arsenal. Its vulnerability to the aroused Republican forces, moreover, made dramatic action inadvisable. Marshall escaped this dilemma by undertaking, as the first order of business, to unify the Court and order its internal affairs. He thus turned the weakness of his colleagues to advantage and precluded reprisal from the Republicans. Relying on the unifying effect of Republican threats, the Federalist sympathies of the other justices, and on his own charisma, Marshall persuaded his associates to abandon seriatim opinions for a single majority opinion. And, to make the most of this new procedure, Marshall was to write the final opinion of the Court himself. From 1801 to 1805, he wrote twenty-four of the Court's twenty-six opinions; the other two were cases on which he did not sit. . . . During this period there were no dissents and only one separate opinion. Up to 1810, Marshall had written 147 of 171 opinions, including all the important ones. The appointment of stronger minds to the Court was soon to reduce Marshall's dominance. But for the time it was an expedient and successful means of regaining lost ground against heavy odds.

But unity alone was not enough. What the Court needed was a victory—and this did not seem likely. During Marshall's first two years, the Court had decided only seven cases and there had not been a significant one since 1798. Moreover, the Republican juggernaut had begun to roll. In 1802, in the midst of ominous anti-Court rhetoric, the Judiciary Act of 1801 was repealed, returning the judiciary to the system of 1789. On the heels of the repeal came another bill establishing new terms for the Court—in effect adjourning it for fourteen months (from December, 1801, to February, 1803). During this time, the Republicans sharpened their impeachment weapons and talked of wholesale slaughter.

There was the possibility, of course, that the Court might take the offensive itself and invalidate the Judicial Repeal Act of 1802. Ultra-Federalists imprudently urged it to do so. But, fortunately for the Court, John Marshall was more intrigued with the unemployment problem of one William Marbury. Back in February, 1801, the Federalists had passed a bill authorizing the President to create as many justices of the peace for the District of Columbia as he thought expedient. Forty-two offices were created and, at the last minute, filled with trustworthy Federalists. When Secretary of State Madison assumed his new duties on March 5, he found the commissions duly signed, sealed, and ready for delivery. None were delivered. Jefferson later commissioned thirty justices of the peace, including twenty-three of those nominated by Adams. During the December, 1801 term, Marbury and three other dispossessed officials requested a writ of mandamus from the Court ordering Madison to show cause why he should not be compelled to deliver their commissions.

Marbury v. *Madison* (1803) clearly was not one of those cases that was ready made for greatness. If it promised anything, it was disaster, for the facts seemed to be leading the Court to a fateful confrontation with Republican power. Should the Court issue the writ and the President ignore it, judicial power would be humbled. If the Court refused to issue the writ, the Republicans—and the executive department, for it was also a struggle between departments—would win by default.

Marshall's opinion in behalf of the unanimous Court was austere in its simplicity. The key questions and the Court's answers amounted to one paragraph: Had Marbury a right to his commission? If so, did the law afford him a remedy? If it did, was the remedy a mandamus issued by the Court? Affirmative replies to the first two questions led the Court to a direct confrontation with Republican power. A negative reply to the third, justified by Marshall's unique reasoning, allowed it to escape and turned retreat into victory. The Court cannot issue a writ of mandamus, declared the Chief Justice, because the power to do so (granted in Section 13 of the Judiciary Act of 1789) was not specified in Article III of the Constitution as being within the original jurisdiction of the Court. Though Congress might control the appellate jurisdiction of the Supreme Court by Article III, it had no authority to regulate the Court's original jurisdiction. There was no choice, therefore, but to hold that Section 13 was an unconstitutional exercise of congressional power. William Marbury had lost his job, and the Supreme Court had made good its claims to review acts of Congress.

Behind the facade of simplicity . . . were some crafty legal tactics. . . . Marshall's first coup was to reverse the regular order of questions (he warned counsel that there would be "some departure in form" from the points stated in argument). He could have disposed of the case straight off . . . by holding that Marbury could not bring a case on original jurisdiction before the Court. . . . Instead, Marshall asked questions one and two, which gave him an opportunity to expound the doctrine of vested rights and to remind the President of the United States that he was not above the laws of the country (a lecture he would surely not have dared give to Washington or Adams).

More daring yet was his declaration that Section 13 was unconstitutional. For this large proposition, Marshall did not offer a single precedent; nor did he reason from the wording or intention of the act itself. He merely asserted. In doing so, he ignored previous circuit and Supreme Court rulings upholding Section 13, as well as the axiom of constitutional interpretation expounded by the Framers and repeated by state judges and Supreme Court justices, that no act ought to be voided if a plausible argument for its constitutionality could be made. A less ingenious mind than Marshall's could have supplied an argument for issuing a writ of mandamus in Section 13 by viewing it as a power incident to the original jurisdiction granted by Article III rather than as an addition to it—a position which, in fact, he later acknowledged.

After disposing summarily with Section 13, Marshall expanded in Olympian fashion on the general theory of judicial review. The substance of his argument came, without acknowledgment, from Hamilton's *Federalist* No. 78. The principles he deduced were simple and "long and well established": The "original and supreme will" of the sovereign people created the written Constitution, which is the supreme and paramount law of the land. That Constitution imposed on the Court the burden of explaining what that law was. All else followed. (Jefferson once cautioned against granting Marshall the toehold of a premise.) If the legislature passed an act in conflict with the supreme law of the Constitution, the Court, in explicating the law, had no choice but to uphold the Constitution and void the act of Congress. The duty was simple and straightforward; not to perform it would be "immoral." In the midst of such simple truths, the central question of whether Section 13 was in conflict with the Constitution was forgotten.

Despite its boldness, Marshall's opinion left the Court well protected from Republican reprisal. It avoided the inevitable insult that would have come with an issuance of the writ and, in the process, salvaged the principles of judicial review. Marshall made this powerful blow for judicial power seem almost innocuous. Section 13 was of small overall importance and concerned the Court's own business; voiding it appeared to be an act of judicial self-denial—especially when six days later *Stuart* v. *Laird* sustained the constitutionality of the Republican Repeal Act of 1802. Marshall's emphasis on the doctrine of limited government, moreover, reminded the Jeffersonian opposition that judicial review was congenial with their own philosophy of government. In fact, the brunt of the Republican attack was not against the principle of judicial review but against Marshall's brusque censure of the President.

Because the mandamus decision has been the focal point of debate over the Court's rise to power, historical evaluations of it have varied sharply. The present tendency is to abandon the hero-villain approach for a less dramatic and more sophisticated assessment. Few scholars now blame Marshall for radical usurpation or credit him with the single-handed creation of judicial power. The Constitution, after all, paved the way for judicial review, while Hamilton's *Federalist* No. 78, judicial precedents, and the debates over the Repeal Act of 1802 all supported Marshall in his decision. Moreover, it is clear now that the decision was neither comprehensive—since it dealt only with an act concerning the judiciary, which even Jefferson agreed was within the Court's purview—nor conclusive—since no precedent can underwrite a power persistently abused. Nor was the precedent of immediate use. Not until *Dred Scott* v. *Sanford* fifty-four years later did the Court void another congressional statute. And not until the . . . late nineteenth century was the full power of judicial review realized. Finally, as Justice Holmes reminds us, the foundation of constitutional nationalism was the Court's power to review *state*, not national, legislation. By 1803, that power had been solidly established by the Supreme Court. . . .

Marshall's mandamus decision may not have changed the course of constitutional history, as the romantics insisted, but it was a constructive "coup" . . . that determined which direction the historical current would run. For the first time, the Supreme Court claimed the power to review acts of Congress and, because of Marshall's strategy, made good its claims. Though not immediately of value, the prescriptive authority of this decision, adorned as it was with Marshall's eloquence, was ready ammunition for the Court in its constant struggle to justify its use of power. Saying "no" to Congress in 1803, moreover, gave authority to the Court when it said "yes." . . . Certainly, the successful assertion of judicial prerogative in 1803 was just what the Court needed to boost its sagging spirits and prestige until better days.

To talk of consequences, however, is to run ahead of events. Because of the impending impeachment campaign, it was uncertain in 1803, and for two years thereafter, whether the mandamus opinion was a victory or a swan song. Republicans had threatened removals since the late 1790s, and now they meant to act. Federal District Judge John Pickering, who unwisely mixed alcohol with his Federalism, was the first to go. In 1805, Justice Samuel Chase was charged with misconduct . . . for his political harangues. . . . A conviction would seriously jeopardize judicial separateness and equality, for, as John Quincy Adams noted, the whole Court, "from the first establishment of the national Judiciary," was on trial. Chase's acquittal (helped by a brilliant defense and inept Republican management) rested finally on the recognition that he was guilty not of "treason, bribery, or other high crimes and misdemeanors," which were the constitutional grounds for removal, but of political intemperance. The Senate's decision was scarcely less significant than the Court's mandamus opinion, since it virtually eliminated impeachment ("a mere scarecrow of a thing," concluded Jefferson in disgust) as a means of controlling the Court. The judicial claim to power—suggested by Hamilton, aspired to by the early Court, and asserted by Marshall in *Marbury* v. *Madison*—was validated. The Republicans, it should be added, salvaged a small victory by teaching the judges to subdue their political passions and improve their judicial manners.

However, Chase's good luck did not entirely lift the Republican siege. Two years later, in the treason trial of Aaron Burr, the Jeffersonians and the judiciary (or rather President Jefferson and Chief Justice Marshall) were again in battle.

. . .

The clash between the President and the Chief Justice could not obscure the fact that the Court and the Republicans had come to share enough ground for a rapprochement. There had, in fact, always been a theoretical affinity between judicial power and the Republican policy of limited government. And the Republicans' acceptance of judicial review in 1803 suggests they recognized this. . . . In 1809, with three Republicans on the bench . . . and Jefferson in retirement, the stage was set for a new period of harmony.

United States v. *Peters* (1809) signaled the change. Since 1779, the state of Pennsylvania had resisted a decree of the Committee on Appeals of the Continental Congress reversing a prize decision of the state admiralty court. When in 1803 Federal District Judge Richard Peters affirmed the Committee's decision, the state legislature ignored the decision and reasserted Pennsylvania's rights threateningly. By 1808, when the Supreme Court was asked for a writ of mandamus compelling Peters to execute his decision, the cause had assumed ominous implications for the nation. . . .

Marshall quashed . . . [Pennsylvania's claim] in a powerful opinion upholding the power of the nation to enforce its laws by the "instrumentality of its own tribunals." When the Pennsylvania legislature petitioned President Madison for redress, he firmly refused; when Governor Snyder threatened to call out the militia, Madison made it clear that such a move would be met by national authority. The victory, based on the harmony of the Court and the executive, signified the successful consolidation of judicial power.

United States v. *Peters*, in 1809, marked the start of a new age for the Court. But it was not until *Martin* v. *Hunter's Lessee* seven years later that the Court formally completed the circle of judicial power. The *Martin* case . . . originated during the American Revolution when Virginia passed an act confiscating Tory lands within the state and subsequently sold those lands to private citizens. Other citizens claimed the same lands by titles that ran back to the original Tory owners and for thirty-odd years they contested the validity of the state confiscation act. The Supreme Court voided the act in *Fairfax's Devisee* v. *Hunter's Lessee* (1813), on the ground that it conflicted with the Treaty of 1794 with England. After consulting with Jefferson and Monroe, the Virginia Court of Appeals not only refused to obey the Court's decision, but also denied the constitutionality of Section 25 of the Judiciary Act under which the case had been heard. It was this refusal and denial which came, on another writ of error, before the Supreme Court in the *Martin* case.

In a unanimous opinion, Republican appointee Joseph Story chastised the Republican state of Virginia for following the states' rights course. . . . Fusing together law, logic, and policy, he made a case for appellate jurisdiction that was "unanswerable and conclusive," as Chancellor James Kent later put it. Because some constitutional questions (which came under the Supreme Court's jurisdiction by Article III) could be heard in state courts, Story argued, it was imperative that those state court decisions be reviewable by the Supreme Court. Section 25 provided for this essential process of review; to deny that section would curtail the powers granted to the Court by the Constitution. It is a "doubtful course," Story continued, to argue that the Supreme Court should not have the final power of review because that power might be abused. "From the very nature of things, the absolute right of decision, in the last resort, must rest somewhere." Before and after this powerful assertion, Story delivered obiter dicta which carried judicial nationalism even further. Operating on the now familiar premise that it was not the states but the whole people who created the Constitution, Story . . . set a new precedent for judicial aggressiveness by informing Congress that it was constitutionally obliged to maintain the final review power of the Court. . . . Ten years earlier the *Martin* ruling would have run headlong into the unyielding resistance of the executive, Congress, and the states. But, instead, in the euphoric climate of nationalism after the war of 1812, it became . . . the "keystone of the whole arch of Federal judicial power."

John Jay, who was still alive, must have gladly retracted his gloomy pronouncement of 1801, that the Court lacked and would never acquire "energy, weight, and dignity." For in these formative years it was the Court—and not

Congress or the President or the states—that presented itself as the most authoritative interpreter of the Constitution. The record was impressive. Over bitter opposition, the Court had confirmed its power to review state acts and to pass final judgment on federal questions coming from state courts. It had turned the implications in the Constitution concerning judicial review of congressional acts into solid precedent. And in the process of acquiring power, the Court developed techniques for using it: the united bench delivering a single opinion, the convenient device of obiter dicta, the leeway afforded by constitutional and statutory interpretation, and the educative possibilities of judicial opinion were all explored. Finally, the Court had begun to justify itself to American democracy. The Court insisted that when it spoke, it did so in the people's name and from an allegedly certain Constitution that left no room for judicial partiality.

. . .

Neither the states, nor the President, nor the Congress surrendered its right to interpret the Constitution and all continued to influence constitutional law. But it was the Supreme Court that emerged from the struggles of the early nineteenth century as best qualified to speak fully and authoritatively on the Constitution. Authority—and this is where John Marshall made his mark—followed demonstrated ability.

CHAPTER 8

The Golden Age

During the long tenure of Chief Justice John Marshall, the Supreme Court continued to enhance the power of the national government. In *Dartmouth College* v. *Woodward* (1819), corporate charters granted by states were protected from state alterations under the "contract clause" of the Constitution prohibiting state laws from "impairing the Obligation of Contracts." In *McCulloch* v. *Maryland* (1819), the Supreme Court breathed life into the clause of the Constitution giving the national government unspecified powers "necessary and proper" to carry out its specified powers. The case upheld the "implied" power of the national government to charter a national bank and prohibited the state of Maryland from taxing such a bank. In *Gibbons* v. *Ogden* (1824), a navigation license granted by the national government was held to take precedence over a state license in interstate waters, providing a precedent for the broad interpretation of the Constitution's "commerce clause" empowering Congress "To regulate Commerce with foreign Nations, and among the several States, and with the Indian Tribes."

Federal power was enhanced not only by judges, but also by legal scholars. As a native legal literature replaced law books imported from England, the most successful authors embraced Federalist ideas. Most widely read was James Kent's *Commentaries on American Law* (1826–1830), often called the "American Blackstone," written after Kent's retirement as Chancellor (chief judge) of New York. Another retired lawyer, Nathan Dane, published *A General Abridgment and Digest of American Law* (1829), giving the United States its first national legal research compendium. The success of Dane's work enabled him to endow the Dane Chair at Harvard Law School.

The first holder of the Dane Chair was Associate Justice Joseph Story of the United States Supreme Court. (It was accepted practice then for justices to teach on the side.) Appointed to the Supreme Court in 1811 at the age of 32, the youngest justice ever, Story became phenomenally productive both on the Court and as a teacher and scholar. Although nominally a Republican, Story embraced much of Marshall's Federalism and bolstered it with impressive scholarship. Outside the Court, Story did even more to solidify the emerging national jurisprudence by writing a series of treatises, or *Commentaries*, in the 1830s and 1840s, among them *Commentaries on the Constitution* (1832), which he dedicated to John Marshall. Most of Story's other *Commentaries* were devoted to private law, largely commercial law, which was then undergoing changes, not only to "Americanize" the common law inherited from England, but also to adjust to new realities in the economic environment.

Among the many economic changes accompanying the growing industrialization and urbanization of the era, the early nineteenth century witnessed the introduction of railroads, the invention of the steamboat, and massive public works—foremost among them the Erie Canal. The legal community responded through courts, legislatures, and newly formed regulatory bodies.

The early nineteenth century has been labeled the "Golden Age" of American law—an age of "instrumentalism" when law was used creatively to accommodate to social conditions. Creativity flourished not only in the constitutional decisions of the Marshall Court, but perhaps even more in the case-by-case adjustment of the common law in the decisions of state courts.

The Golden Age, however, is not without its critics. The most widely cited critique of the era is Morton J. Horwitz's book, *The Transformation of American Law, 1780–1860* (1977):

> During the eighty years after the American Revolution, a major transformation of the legal system took place, which reflected a variety of aspects of social struggle. That the conflict was turned into legal channels (and thus rendered somewhat mysterious) should not obscure the fact that it took place and that it enabled emergent entrepreneurial and commercial groups to win a disproportionate share of wealth and power in American society. (p. xvi)

The "social struggle" underlying the evolving legal system can be seen most clearly in the law of torts. For example, as industrialization and the spread of railroads led to more and more accidents, employers were not required to compensate employees for injuries sustained on the job unless the injured employees could prove that the injuries were caused by the negligence of the employers themselves. Employers could escape liability if the injuries were caused by "fellow servants," if the injured employees could be said to have "assumed the risk" of injury (as in occupations known to be dangerous), or if the injured employees could be found guilty of "contributory negligence."

The pathbreaking doctrines on industrial accidents were penned by Chief Justice Lemuel Shaw of the Massachusetts Supreme Judicial Court, widely regarded as the most influential judge of the Golden Age. However, he sided with workers when he refused to follow the established rule treating labor unions as "criminal conspiracies."

The struggle between labor and capital was one of the most visible sources of legal tensions in the first half of the nineteenth century. But some have seen other reasons behind the legal innovations of the Golden Age—as exemplified in the criminal law, the law of property, corporation law, and the law of contracts.

The blessings of the American way of life.

Lithographic print by Nathaniel Currier, 1855. Library of Congress Prints and Photographs Division.

from William E. Nelson, *Americanization of the Common Law:*
The Impact of Legal Change on Massachusetts Society, 1760–1830, 2d ed.
(Athens: University of Georgia Press, 1994), pp. 117–44.
Copyright © 1975, 1994 by William E. Nelson.
Reprinted by permission of William E. Nelson.

Liberty and the Breakdown of Stability

The gradual breakdown of ethical unity in Massachusetts over a thirty-year period beginning in the 1780s did not mean that all the rules of law inherited from the prerevolutionary period were reversed. Some rules, notably the rules of property, which had protected the economic and social stability of colonial communities, were enforced with increasing rigor after independence was achieved. But, as we shall see, the social effects of enforcing those rules were quite different from what they had been before.

[Criminal Law]

One area where concern for property continued to appear was in the criminal law. Indeed, concern for the protection of private property began to dominate the criminal law after the Revolution, and, as it did, it superseded the ethical concerns that had underlaid that body of law during the colonial period.
. . .

Despite these new concerns, however, the old conception of the purpose of criminal law still prevailed at the outset of the Revolution. Thus in 1776 the General Court urged the people to "lead sober Religious and peaceable Lives, avoiding all Blasphemies, contempt of the holy Scriptures, and of the Lord's day and all other Crimes and Misdemeanors, all Debauchery, Prophaneness, Corruption, Venality, all riotous and tumultuous Proceedings, and all Immoralities whatsoever." In this statement, though, one can also see the beginning of a new apprehension of political and economic disorder. Although this anxiety was at first peripheral, by the early 1780s it was becoming a central one, as men came to view criminal law as having a dual function "to discourage [both] vice . . . and disorders in society."

Although quite real, the new anxiety had little support in the events of the time. During the 1760s and early 1770s Massachusetts experienced relatively few violent attacks on property or serious breaches of ethical unity. The same was true during the Revolution itself. In the 1780s, however, fears previously unfounded became real, as a number of attacks on authority and property occurred. Between 1780 and 1785 there were in Middlesex County alone four prosecutions for rioting and five for assaults on tax collectors, in one of which eighteen codefendants had participated. Conditions were even worse in the western counties. Between 1782 and 1785 there were two attempts in Berkshire to prevent the courts from sitting and transacting business and numerous attempts in several counties, successful and unsuccessful, to rescue prisoners. On one occasion in 1782 authorities in Northampton had to release three hostages taken from insurgents, since they lacked the military power to resist an insurgent force camped in the nearby hills. The culmination was reached in Shays's Rebellion in 1786, when for several months Massachusetts was engaged in a civil war in which rebel forces controlled most of Hampshire and Berkshire counties as well as parts of Worcester and Middlesex.

Ending as they did in open rebellion, these seven years of violence undoubtedly heightened the fear of social breakdown and disorder. The simultaneous increase in the incidence of theft appears to have contributed to both a strengthening and a modification of the fear. . . . Governor Hancock perhaps best summed up this new view when in an address to the legislature in 1793 he suggested that the primary function of criminal law was to insure "the good order of Government . . . [and] the security of the people."

Hancock's address, which said nothing about the preservation of religion and morality, is another indication that the ancient reasons for protecting property rights and preserving social stability were being forgotten. The protection of order and property was becoming an end in itself rather than merely a means to the pursuit of community morality—an end to which men with differing ethical ideals could adhere. . . .

[Property Law]

Prerevolutionary rules regulating competition among resource users—a key element in the preservation of stability in the colonial era—were reaffirmed in the half century after the Revolution. Indeed, the rules were often extended in the postrevolutionary period to apply to new forms of wealth generated by changes in the economy. The law continued, for example, to confer on a man who had customarily exploited a particular economic resource an absolute and "despotic dominion" over it, "in total exclusion of the right of any other individual in the universe"—a policy that . . . promoted the economic security of the individual. In suits between neighboring landowners that arose because one owner sought to use his land in a manner harmful to the other, this policy, as before the Revolution, meant that the older claimant's usage would be elevated to the level of a property right and that a more recent claimant would have to use his land so as not to interfere with the older right. A postrevolutionary plaintiff could thus recover damages for a nuisance if a defendant built a stable, a blacksmith's shop, or a factory that emitted noxious smells next to an existing dwelling house or tavern; if he polluted water on or adjacent to the plaintiff's existing estate, causing the water to emit noxious smells, pollute the plaintiff's well, or to be otherwise unfit for continued use; if by constructing a drain or a necessary house, by failing to make due repair to his property, or by placing gravel on his land he caused noxious water to flow onto the plaintiff's land; if he obstructed the plaintiff's ancient drain, as a result of which water flowed back onto the plaintiff's land; or if he drained a nearby pond, causing the plaintiff's immemorial well to dry up. If, however, the defendant had an ancient prescriptive right older than the plaintiff's right, he would not be liable in damages. That is, the courts would enforce whatever land use was older.

. . .

Courts also continued to protect existing patterns of resource use in water rights and flooding cases. Thus a landowner who constructed a dam across a stream running through his land acquired a property right in the stream's water and could bring suit for damages if an upstream owner diverted water needed to run the plaintiff's mill or if a downstream owner built a dam and so raised the level of the stream that the plaintiff's mill wheels could not function properly. The owner of a subsequently constructed dam was entitled to use only such water as would not interfere with the first owner's use. Similarly, the owner of land along a stream could sue an upstream owner whose dam deprived him of water used for agriculture or a downstream owner whose dam caused his land to be flooded. In all these cases, however, a plaintiff could not recover if a defendant had an ancient prescriptive right older than the plaintiff's right or if the plaintiff had suffered no damage, as would occur if he had never improved the land for whose loss he was bringing suit. In short, the law would confer a property right only on the prior user of an economic resource that others subsequently sought to use.

Postrevolutionary property law did not, however, limit itself to protecting rights that had been protected in the colonial period; it also began to accord protection in cases where protection had not previously been given. For example, . . . [t]he Supreme Judicial Court . . . held that the soil beneath tidal waterways on which wharves were built was owned not by the public but by the owner of the adjoining land—which, as the court expressly recognized, was contrary to the English common law rule. An owner of land along a nonnavigable stream was even held to have property rights in the entire bed to the point of midstream.

. . .

The courts also extended the legal protection accorded to holders of various sorts of licenses. After the Revolution a person could not become a ferryman, innkeeper, retailer of spirituous liquors, auctioneer, or harbor pilot without first obtaining a license from state-created authorities. In addition, many towns prohibited people from entering occupations such as butchering, chimney sweeping, acting as an intelligence officer, selling tea or sugar or running a confectionary, acting as a measurer or weigher of grain, or producing plays without first obtaining a license from town selectmen. Licenses, of course, remained a sort of property right that sometimes conferred upon their holders monopolistic privileges that could be transmitted to others. As before the Revolution, ferry and liquor licenses could be conveyed as property and would descend, upon their owners' deaths, to their heirs or successors. Owners of land at which ferries had customarily docked induced courts to rule in several cases that the right to a ferry license was appurtenant to their land, while owners of buildings that had customarily been licensed as inns obtained rulings that they had a legal right to have their licenses renewed even when town selectmen opposed renewal. Holders of licenses could be deprived of their property right only if they failed to fulfill the various obligations to the public imposed on them by law—the obligation, for example, of charging a reasonable fee for their service. As in the prerevolutionary period, the holder of a liquor license had no legal right to prevent competitors from entering into business if they could procure licenses, but the holder of a ferry license did. . . .

The important development in the postrevolutionary period was that the rules in the ferry cases were extended to cover analogous problems. Thus the owner of a turnpike was permitted to sue someone who built a road around his tollgate, thereby depriving him of his tolls. Similarly, the owner of a fishing boat possessed a cause of action against the owner of another boat who intentionally operated it in a noisy and disorderly manner for the purpose of driving fish away from the plaintiff's vessel. In fact, the courts appeared to be moving in the direction of developing a generic cause of action permitting an established businessman to recover damages against a new competitor who, as a result of his competition, had deprived the plaintiff of his business. Although the Supreme Judicial Court refused in 1783 to decide whether a millowner could maintain an action against a new competitor solely for "loss of custom," it did hold that such a claim could be joined to a claim for diversion of water. Similarly, a businessman could recover for "loss of custom" resulting from a breach of contract; an employer, for example, could recover damages from an employee who, in leaving his employ, enticed his customers to leave him or otherwise caused him to lose business, while an innkeeper could recover for "loss of custom" resulting from a supplier's fraudulent sale of noxious lemon juice.

. . .

A similar trend can be seen in the rules of law regulating laborers. Although slaves in Massachusetts had been freed after the Revolution, the law continued to recognize the right of the head of a household to the labor and the wages of his "servants," his wife, and his children. It also continued to recognize the right of a master to the labor and wages of his apprentice and, in the event of a default by the apprentice, not only would permit the master to sue the person from whom he had acquired the apprentice or the person who had induced the apprentice to default, but would even permit the master to invoke the criminal process to secure obedience from the apprentice. Of course, a master also had authority to inflict corporal discipline on an apprentice without invoking the judicial process.

In the nineteenth century the courts began to expand these rules to cover industrial laborers, whose economic position was quite different from that of children, apprentices, and traditional sorts of servants. Thus in one case a plaintiff recovered damages against a defendant who had induced minors employed at his factory to resign. . . . [A]lthough the employer could bring suit against one who interfered with his right to an employee, the employee possessed no action against a third party who sought to induce his employer to discharge him. The analogy was . . . to ancient concepts of property in children, apprentices, and servants; the courts slowly were coming to place factory workers under the same legal rubric as the older categories of servants, although in the 1820s they were not as yet prepared in Massachusetts to permit the invocation of the criminal process to insure that workers remained on the job.

The reasons for the expansive application of property concepts in the postrevolutionary period are unclear. Part of the explanation might be that the courts were merely following traditions and applying rules inherited from the prerevolutionary period. This explanation is not, however, entirely satisfactory by itself, given the undeniable extension of prerevolutionary property doctrine by the courts.

Perhaps the extension of property doctrine may best be explained by a tendency of the postrevolutionary generation to equate the protection of property with the preservation of liberty. That generation often associated the "rights" of "life, liberty, and property" with each other, arguing that "property must be secured, or liberty . . . [could] not exist." The association of property and liberty was so close that men classified property among their other fundamental "unalienable rights" and viewed "the freedom of property from the indefinite despotism of sovereignty . . . [as] the best security to be found against those laws by which social liberty . . . [was] so often injured." As a result, challenges to property rights were labeled by litigants as "arbitrary and unprecedented . . . in this free Country where property is held secure by the laws and constitution," and the courts, when confronted with an argument that to deny a claimed property right would undermine liberty, almost invariably granted the property right for which a claim was made.

But while the concepts of private property and liberty may have been closely allied, the postrevolutionary rules allocating property did not result in increased individual liberty; they merely identified the individuals who would enjoy it. For every person who gained liberty by obtaining protection of a property right, some other person usually lost at least an equivalent amount of liberty. When one miller, for example, gained a property right to use water in a stream, another lost the right to use the same water. Likewise, when an employer obtained a right to prevent his employee from working for another, the employee effectively lost the liberty to improve his wages or working conditions by threatening to leave his master's employ. The effect of the postrevolutionary rules of property law considered above was simply to insure that the individuals who had possessed property and hence liberty in the past would continue to possess it in the future.

There is evidence that some members of the postrevolutionary generation consciously sought legal protection of property as a means of insuring economic and social stability. John Adams, for example, believed that it was essential to social order and stability that the property rights of the poor as well as the rich be protected. Fisher Ames likewise thought that "the rights of property and the tranquillity of society" were related and that the duty of government was to secure both. The very idea of property, in sum, may have become a code word for a broad constellation of genuine conservative values, including the preservation of upper-class wealth, community stability, and, perhaps, even ethical unity.

. . .

The direction in which the law of property was being pushed by a majoritarian democracy can be seen most clearly in the 1823 case of *Callender* v. *Marsh*. The plaintiff, the owner of a house located on a hill in Boston, had brought suit against a surveyor of the highways who, without compensation to the plaintiff, had lowered the grade of a highway in front of the plaintiff's house, thereby weakening the foundation of the house and making access to the house more difficult. The plaintiff claimed that his property had been taken from him without compensation, in violation of the Massachusetts constitution, but the court ruled that no taking had occurred. The case, argued the court, was analogous to "the location of schoolhouses upon public land," which, although it might "materially diminish the value of an adjoining or opposite dwellinghouse, on account of the crowd and noise which they usually occasion," would not require "the public . . . to consult the convenience of the individual so far as to abstain from erecting the schoolhouse, or to pay the owner of the dwellinghouse for its diminished value." The constitution required the public to pay for land physically taken from its owner but did not require compensation for a diminution in the value of the land resulting from a public improvement made without any actual taking.

What is most important about *Callender* v. *Marsh* is the court's analysis of the contending policy interests. On the one hand, as in the colonial period, there was the owner of private property. But since the colonial period the interest on the other side had changed. A selfish, rapacious, and authoritarian crown, which threatened the liberty and stability of Massachusetts communities had been replaced by the majoritarian and egalitarian democracy of the Age of Jackson. The interests of community and of selfish individualism had changed sides. Absolute and total protection of the owner in his enjoyment of property no longer seemed necessary to the interests of community; instead, the individual now appeared as an obstruction to continued social progress, liberty, and equality. . . .

[Corporations]

The corporation was another institution transformed in the early nineteenth century from a device furthering community values into one furthering the self-interest of individuals. Before and even immediately after the Revolution, the corporate form had been used largely by institutions like religious parishes and owners of common fields as a means of pooling the energies and resources of individuals in the pursuit of common ends. By 1830, on the other hand, the typical corporation was the business corporation, in which individuals sought personal economic aggrandizement, often at the expense of others in the community.

The key question in corporation law, the resolution of which resulted in the transformation of the corporation, was "whether the *private* property of any proprietors . . . [could be] held liable to satisfy the debts of the propriety, or the property of the Corporation only." Men began to argue that to hold shareholders liable for a corporation's debts would be to take "a citizen's property . . . from under his own controul," contrary to the "the best provisions of the constitution"; they also argued, rather emotionally, that "the great increase of corporations for almost every purpose . . . [was] seriously alarming" and threatened "the independence and integrity of every branch of . . . government."

But at the turn of the century it was not yet clear whether such arguments would be accepted by the courts. For in the colonial and immediate postrevolutionary years, municipal and similar corporations had had unquestioned authority to levy taxes or assessments on their members in order to raise funds to discharge debts or for other authorized purposes. The 1800 case of *Thompson* v. *Russell* upheld the existence of a similar power on the part of private business corporations. The *Thompson* case was a suit in which the president of the Haymarket Theater Corporation recovered upon an assessment voted by the members of the corporation which the defendant had refused to pay. No agreement to pay the assessment was pleaded, and ... the obligation to pay it arose not as the result of an agreement but as a matter of law from the defendant's membership in the corporation. The *Thompson* case, in short, rejected the doctrine of limited liability for shareholders of business corporations.

In the first decade of the nineteenth century, however, that doctrine triumphed. Its victory was assured by the 1807 decision of *Ellis* v. *Marshall*, which tested the validity of a claim by a street improvement corporation in Boston that a resident of the street whom the legislature had made a member of the corporation could not decline that membership. The corporation's argument, in substance, was that its members had a status analogous to that of residents of a municipal corporation, who could not decline the obligations imposed on them by the municipality. The court, however, thought the two types of corporation different, since municipal corporations were created by "public acts, promotive of general convenience," while the street improvement corporation had been created by "a private act, obtained at the solicitation of individuals, for their emolument or advantage." It therefore held that the private business corporation, unlike the municipal corporation, could not "press into service" unwilling individuals or their wealth.

Two years later, in *Andover and Medford Turnpike Corporation* v. *Gould*, the court took another step in holding that even a person who had voluntarily become a member of a business corporation could not be sued for unpaid corporate assessments unless he had expressly promised to pay them; the corporation's only remedy against a delinquent member was to sell his shares for whatever price they would bring on the market. In reaching this decision, the court sought not only to protect private property but also to encourage investors to join corporations. It recognized that investors, who could no longer be forced to join, would be more willing to do so if they knew that when "assessments bec[a]me grievous, they [might] abandon the enterprise." The central significance of the *Gould* case, however, lies in the transformation that it wrought in the underlying concept of shareholder liability. The *Thompson* case, it will be recalled, held that a shareholder was liable to pay assessments simply because he was a member of the corporation. That is, liability was imposed in *Thompson*, as it had been imposed pursuant to the colonial law of obligations, on account of a relationship rather than an agreement. *Gould*, however, put the emphasis on agreement; after *Gould*, not only the existence but even the scope of a shareholder's liability to pay assessments above and beyond the purchase price of his shares was determined by looking to the contract with the corporation by which he had purchased the shares.

Having held that a corporation could not levy assessments on its members without their consent, the courts in 1808 found it easy to take the next step, which was to rule that "the bodies or private property of the individual members cannot be taken in execution to satisfy a judgment against the corporation." This rule of limited liability to creditors followed from the rule of limited liability to the corporation. As Chief Justice Parsons explained, creditors of towns could seize property of individual inhabitants upon execution of a judgment obtained against the town, since the town itself had power to tax the inhabitants in order to pay the judgment. But a business "corporation ha[d] not this remedy." . . . Parsons, analyzing the problem of liability through the shareholder's eyes, viewed a creditor as a mere subrogee of the corporation; of course, a shareholder could have no greater duty to the corporation's subrogee than to the corporation itself.

Thus, within a span of two years, the common law rules of shareholder liability had been rejected as inapplicable to the new species of corporation—the business corporation. . . .

In the 1820s the legislature, in response to fears that the perpetuation of shareholder liability might drive business and capital to other states, began to move in the same direction as the courts. New charters ceased to impose shareholder liability. . . . By 1830, in short, the modern rule of limited liability was fully established in the law of business corporations.

The statutory application of the rule of limited liability to manufacturing corporations marked the end in Massachusetts of the notion that coercive nongovernmental corporations could exist for the purpose of pooling individual resources for the common good. Thereafter people were free to join nongovernmental organizations only if they wished and to contribute to them only whatever resources they wished. And, as the subsequent history of the corporation in the nineteenth century shows, individuals would join largely to further their own economic well-being.

[Contracts]

In contract as well as property and corporation law it became a postrevolutionary maxim that "a man ha[d] a right to use his property as he please[d], provided by doing so he . . . [did] not injure another's." Two complementary principles followed. One was that a man ought to be permitted to enter into whatever contracts he wished and that the law ought to enforce all contracts he entered into. The other was that a man ought not to be compelled to enter into contracts when he did not wish to and that the law ought not to enforce liabilities to which parties had never given their consent. Over the course of several decades these two principles undermined the traditional customary and ethical basis of contract law and led to a new understanding of the essential nature of contract.

The former principle soon provided a basis for challenging the usury laws and the ethical concepts underlying them. As early as 1789 it was asked "with some degree of plausibility, why a man . . . [should] not set a price on his own money, as well as on his own goods." . . .

The corollary principle that men ought not to be compelled to enter into contracts to which they did not consent received similar articulation. Courts thought it only "conformable to the principles of justice, and to the essential nature of contracts . . . [that] an obligation . . . [could] not be converted into a different engagement" from that which the parties had made. That is, a party could not be subjected "to perils not undertaken by his contract." . . .

To hold explicitly that individuals should themselves determine whether to undertake contractual liability did not, however, effect any fundamental change in existing law, for even in the colonial period persons other than slaves, children, and servants were rarely held to liability without their consent. The postrevolutionary changes in contract law were more marginal, being concerned chiefly with questions about the scope and the terms rather than the existence of contractual liability. In the colonial period, . . . the terms of contracts were usually determined by reference to customary usage, but after the Revolution the intentions of the parties at the time of their entry into a contract became key. The new approach was an inevitable consequence of the new underpinnings of contract law. As one judge explained, the rule that a contract could "not be carried *beyond* the intent of the parties *at the time of entering into it* . . . [was] clear from the nature of its constitution; one essential ingredient being, that it is entered into freely, of the parties' own accord." The essential point, of course, is that the terms of contractual liability are as important as its existence; a requirement that a contract conform to certain customary terms and that it contain no others can effectively impose liabilities on individuals to which they have never given their consent and can effectively bar them from making contracts that they seek to make.

Such a requirement can be especially burdensome in periods of rapid change, when custom makes no provision for new kinds of commercial relationships and for new and unanticipated business needs. In early nineteenth-century Massachusetts, the breakdown of traditional ethical standards combined with rapid economic development was having precisely this effect, and the courts as a result found themselves confronted by many issues that were "not determined by uniform usage and practice" on the part of the commercial community or by past judicial decisions. In one case involving the "duty of an agent of a hat manufacturing company," for example, the court observed that the duty could "not be well ascertained by usage, because probably this was the first company of the kind ever established in this commonwealth"; thus it was necessary to decide the case by inquiring into "the essential nature of contracts." Or, as the court said in another case in which there were "no authorities directly in point . . . [,] the action must then be determined by the meaning" of the contract made by the parties. Indeed, there was little else besides the meaning of the parties to which the courts could look. To have attempted to search for custom that in fact did not exist would only have given juries free reign to impose liabilities incapable of prior anticipation. This, in turn, would have made economic planning impossible and would, in the minds of contemporaries, have rendered property insecure. Hence it became settled that "in every contract, the first and most important consideration . . . [was] to discover the intention of the parties" and "to effectuate . . . [that] intention" "if consistent with the rules of law."

Courts determined the parties' intentions not only by reference to their express declarations, however, but also by inferences drawn from their course of conduct and from the facts and circumstances surrounding their relationship. Evidence of a usage or custom of trade was thus admissible to aid in construction of the parties' contract, provided that the usage or custom was known to the parties or was "of so general a nature as to furnish a presumption of knowledge." Evidence of usage and custom was admitted not because, as in the colonial period, usage and custom constituted rules of law for the decision of a case, but because usage and custom were "useful, in many cases, to explain the intent of the parties." Contracting parties were therefore free to reject customary usage as the basis of their contract, and, when they had in fact rejected a usage, they would not be bound by it.

. . .

Kettell v. *Wiggin*, a marine insurance case, marked . . . [an] occasion on which the courts gave effect to the apparent intentions of the parties, even though their decision contributed to the disruption of economic patterns that had prevailed since the colonial era. Colonial mercantile ventures rarely had followed carefully planned or otherwise preordained trade routes: colonial sea captains did not leave Boston with a cargo of rum knowing that they would sell the rum in Africa for slaves, that they would then sell the slaves in Jamaica for molasses, and that they would finally return to Boston and sell the molasses to a distiller of rum. Commerce was much more haphazard and flexible. A sea captain might leave Boston with a cargo of rum that he planned to sell in Jamaica, but if on his arrival in the Caribbean he learned that the market was unfavorable in Jamaica or that some other market was more favorable, he would go to that other market. In fact a vessel might stop at several ports other than that originally planned before unloading its cargo and might pick up a return cargo at one or several of these ports or even at different ports. The vessel in *Kettell* v. *Wiggin* was engaging in precisely this kind of trade. Its insurance provided that the vessel should proceed first to Gibraltar, where the outward cargo would be sold; then to one of the Cape Verde Islands for a cargo of salt; and finally back to Boston. The vessel did in fact sail to Gibraltar and then to the Cape Verde Islands, but upon its arrival at one of the islands the captain learned that seventeen vessels were waiting in port for salt and that he would not be able to obtain a cargo for approximately five weeks. Being short on provisions, the captain concluded that he could not wait. The island's governor, however, offered to expedite the loading of a cargo of salt if the captain would first take the vessel to a neighboring island on a mission for the governor, and the captain agreed. As a result, he was able to load his vessel considerably sooner, but his early departure from the Cape Verde Islands for Boston led to the vessel's being captured by pirates on the return voyage. When the owners sought to recover their loss from their insurers, the insurers contended that the mission on behalf of the governor amounted to a deviation from the voyage, which invalidated the insurance, and the court agreed, holding that the voyage on which the vessel had sailed was not the same as the voyage that the defendants had insured and hence "was not within the terms of the policy," even though the voyage had, according to the jury, been in accordance with the customary usage of merchants trading in the Cape Verde Islands. Thus the colonial doctrine that "a Voyage performed in the usual manner doth not affect ye Insurance" was overruled; usage had simply come to be of less weight in the scales of justice than the right of a promissor to enforce the explicit terms of his promise and not to be held liable to contractual provisions to which he had not freely consented.

In upholding the principle in *Kettell* that a party could not be held to contractual liability beyond the terms of his express promise, the court actually did far more than merely adhere to the intentions of the parties. It had, in fact, made a significant policy judgment about who should bear the burden of loss in a case where the parties had had no intentions. The parties in *Kettell* had not and, indeed, could not have anticipated the need for the deviation that the captain later made; the real question in the case was whether liability would be imposed when the parties had made no provision either for or against it. The plaintiff's position, in effect, was that liability flowed from the fact that the vessel's deviation was sanctioned by customary usage not inconsistent with the express contract of the parties. The court, however, held that usage that had not been incorporated into an express contract could not be the basis of legal obligation in a case where parties had entered into such an agreement. By making an express contract the parties "suspended" rights . . . that might otherwise have existed on the basis of customary usage.

. . .

The new rules of law permitting parties to ignore custom and usage . . . undermined but did not totally destroy prerevolutionary ethical standards. Indeed, a few of those standards persisted throughout the postrevolutionary period. In *Boynton* v. *Hubbard*, for instance, the Supreme Judicial Court vigorously reaffirmed ancient moral standards in holding that an individual could not make a contract for the sale of an inheritance that he expected to receive in the future from an ancestor who was living at the time the contract was made. It reasoned that if such contracts were upheld,

> Heirs, who ought to be under the reasonable advice and direction of their ancestor, who has no other influence over them than what arises from a fear of his displeasure, from which fear the heirs may be induced to live industriously, virtuously, and prudently, are, with the aid of money speculators, let loose from this salutary control, and may indulge in prodigality, idleness, and vice; and taking care, by hypocritically preserving appearances, not to alarm their ancestor, may go on trafficking with his expected bounty, making it a fund to supply the wastes of dissipation and extravagance. Certainly the policy of the law will not sanction a transaction of this kind, from a regard to the moral habits of the citizens.

Likewise the legislature throughout the period had rejected pleas that the usury laws violated the right of individuals freely to make and enforce contracts; "the experience of mankind," as one commentator noted, demonstrated the necessity of preventing "the horrid oppression of usury," for usury would "ripen . . . into a disease that . . . [would] gangrene . . . the whole course of money transactions." Similarly, the courts continued to hold wagering contracts void and unenforceable, despite arguments that "men . . . [were] masters of their own property" and that the law ought "not enquire minutely into the value of the consideration, which may induce them to part with it." The contrary argument—that "every man of experience, and [with] a knowledge of the human character" knew "that it would be hostile to the welfare of society, that . . . such contracts, should be protected by judicial authority"— carried much greater weight, since many men still believed that "'the practice of gaming . . . pervert[ed] the activity of the mind, taint[ed] the heart, and deprave[d] the affections.'"

The important effect of the postrevolutionary changes in contract law was the undermining not of the ethical standards but of economic and social stability. The new rules of contract undermined stability primarily by giving individuals freedom to make economic bargains purely in their own interest. Postrevolutionary bargainers no longer needed to assume that they should receive only a fair equivalent in return for their goods or services; they no longer needed to assume that hard work resulting in the production of goods or services was the only legitimate means of accumulating wealth. Instead, the new law of contract permitted men to accumulate wealth by turning a sharp bargain or by anticipating the fluctuations of the market. Whereas prerevolutionary contract law had rested on an assumption that economic values and economic relationships were fixed and unchanging and had impeded efforts by individuals to alter their inherited place in the economy, postrevolutionary law assumed that a fluctuating market-place was the central institution in the economy and left individuals free to manipulate its workings so that they rather than their neighbors would most benefit from it.

The shift in the philosophy of contract was merely one part, however, of a broader shift in men's understanding of the role of law in the economy. In the prerevolutionary period the function of law had been to render the distribution of wealth stable by granting individuals property rights in that wealth and by making it difficult for them to lose it in exchange transactions. After the Revolution property ceased to be viewed as a man's stable portion of the community's resources. Instead, his property became his starting stake in a rapidly changing economy—which he could use as he wished, by combining with other entrepreneurs or by making sharp bargains so as to promote his own aggrandizement. Massachusetts, in short, had been transformed from a society where men with stable places in the economy concentrated on pursuing ethical ends to a society where economic place was uncertain and many men used their wealth chiefly for the purpose of acquiring even greater wealth. The prerevolutionary legal system, in which community was the primary social value, had largely been destroyed. A new system emphasizing rugged individualism as its fundamental value had begun to take its place.

A new legal system did not emerge fully developed merely by virtue of the destruction of the old system, however. Although the destruction of the colonial system finally settled the question whether the state could impose ethical values on individuals who did not freely accept them, it did not settle the question of how resources would be distributed among individuals possessing different values; that is, it did not settle whether some values would be favored over others in a distributional scheme. The decline of the colonial legal system and the establishment of a system permitting individuals to select their own values did not produce the classical nineteenth-century laissez-faire state with its emphasis on competition and material well-being. Competition and materialism came to be favored not only because old traditions and old patterns of stability broke down but also because Massachusetts law after the Revolution developed a concern for economic development.

CHAPTER 9

The Jacksonian Era

Among the most active—and most successful—reformers of the Golden Age were those advocating prison reform. Starting in New York and Pennsylvania, prison systems were established with the assumption that criminals could be rehabilitated by isolation from each other during imprisonment. Reformers disagreed on the degree of isolation necessary for rehabilitation, and faith in the efficacy of the reforms faded by mid-century, but there was enough coherence to the reforms in their early stages to draw international attention.

Among the Europeans who came to study America's new prisons was a French aristocrat, Alexis de Tocqueville. During his visit, in the 1830s, his interests expanded to other aspects of American society. He took a special interest in the legal profession. In his classic *Democracy in America,* he observed that lawyers in the United States "form the highest political class and the most cultivated portion of society."

By 1830, however, public disaffection with the legal profession was rife. Andrew Jackson had been elected president in 1828 on a Populist platform containing a good deal of lawyer bashing, and legal reform became a hot topic of popular debate.

As in the immediate post-Revolutionary period, a wave of codification proposals swept the nation. Some proposals were influenced by the English philosopher Jeremy Bentham, who advocated a utilitarian, detailed, all-encompassing code to replace the common law. Others were influenced by the polemic of a colorful Irish revolutionary, William Sampson, an immigrant to New York after years of exile in France, who had in mind a more general, more flexible code modeled on the Code Napoleon of 1803. Justice Story participated in a codification effort in his native Massachusetts. In New York, in addition to Sampson, a respected lawyer, David Dudley Field, devoted much of his career to codification. The Massachusetts effort failed, but in New York, Sampson and Field had partial success. As historian Maxwell Bloomfield relates in *American Lawyers in a Changing Society, 1776–1876* (1976):

> As a direct result of his [Sampson's] labors, the New York legislature passed a statute in 1828 that revolutionized the real-property law of the state, forming in effect a partial code. Other states in turn began to explore the possibilities of systematizing certain branches of their law by taking into account not only prior statutes but related judicial decisions as well. The new trend assumed major proportions after 1848, when New York abolished the intricate common law rules of pleading and practice in a Code of Civil Procedure that was soon adopted by twenty-three other states and territories.
>
> . . . Partial codification thus emerged as the answer of the professional bar to the mounting clamor for changes in the law after 1828. (pp. 86–87)

New York's Code of Civil Procedure of 1848 was largely the work of David Dudley Field, who continued to champion codification proposals, with partial success, into the 1880s. His opposition came largely from the professional bar and was spearheaded by a leading New York lawyer, James C. Carter. Carter and other opponents of codification feared a shift in power from courts to legislatures. They were convinced that popularly elected legislators were less trustworthy, more subject to factional, sectional, and special-interest influences than judges.

Public opinion on codification was divided. Simplification of the law was desired, but some feared a code drafted by lawyers and enacted by legislators. More popular were Jacksonian reforms to open the legal profession to popular control. Measures were adopted for reducing the standards for entry into the legal profession, for the popular election of judges, for limited judicial terms, and for giving juries greater powers vis-à-vis judges. Accompanied by other "democratizing" measures—such as the elimination of the property qualification for voting and the elimination of required qualifications for many government posts (opening the way for the so-called "spoils system")—these measures have generally been seen as the causes of fundamental change in the character of the bar.

A Vermont lawyer.
Painting by Horace Bundy, 1841. National Gallery, Washington, D.C.

Decline of the Legal Profession

from Robert A. Ferguson, *Law and Letters in American Culture*
(Cambridge, Mass.: Harvard University Press, 1984), pp. 11–29, 199–205, 273–85.
Copyright © 1984 by the President and Fellows of Harvard College.
Reprinted by permission of Harvard University Press.

In America the Law Is King

. . .

The centrality of law in the birth of the republic is a matter of national lore. "In America the law is king," Thomas Paine the prophet of revolution proclaimed in 1776, and so it has remained ever since in the political rhetoric and governmental councils of the nation. Revolutionary orators and pamphleteers . . . were members of the profession. Their writings were heavily scored with the citations and doctrines of legal study and contributed decisively to what historians have called the conceptualization of American life. Twenty-five of the fifty-six signers of the Declaration of Independence, thirty-one of the fifty-five members of the Constitutional Convention, and thirteen of the first sixteen presidents were lawyers. All of our formative documents—the Declaration of Independence, the Constitution, the Federalist papers, and the seminal decisions of the Supreme Court under John Marshall—were drafted by attorneys steeped in Sir William Blackstone's *Commentaries on the Laws of England* (1765–1769). So much was this the case that the *Commentaries* rank second only to the Bible as a literary and intellectual influence on the history of American institutions.

. . .

Ascendancy came in a rush with the Revolutionary lawyer's reach for cultural legitimacy. John Adams' first inclination had been to preach. That was the conventional ambition of colonial intellectuals, and Adams had to struggle to establish vocational self-respect for a second choice in law. . . . Subsequent generations would have no need for qualms. By 1787, in his last year at Harvard College, John Quincy Adams debated a loftier proposition: "the profession of law against physic and divinity as being most beneficial to man." . . . Thirty years before Alexis de Tocqueville's famous equation of the legal profession to an intellectual aristocracy, American lawyers already arrogated that status to themselves.

Law attracted men of talent because the profession was lucrative and secure, but the intellectual ascendancy of the lawyer—his virtual monopoly as republican spokesman—came from ideological factors. It was an immense advantage that the rhetoric of revolution had been so patently legalistic. The inalienable rights of rebellion could be and were derived from right reason and natural law, but American vehemence depended on the particular expression of these rights in the common law of England, the statutory enactments of Parliament, and the various royal charters pertaining to colonial government. Participation in the central Revolutionary debates over parliamentary jurisdiction in the colonies required a detailed knowledge of the same historical, legal sources.

. . .

The English legal tradition enabled Anglo-American intellectuals to *assume* a visible link between the observance of natural law and the attainment of civic happiness. Since providence had provided Americans with a continent unspoiled by human history, they could confidently order their new country through a correct, theoretical application of man-made or positive law in harmony with the natural order around them. . . .

The assumption of a connection between nature, order, and positive law in Revolutionary America appears most dramatically in that embodiment of popular wisdom, the rabble-rousing Tom Paine. For while *Common Sense* is an electrifying call to arms, it is also a demand for a country defined entirely through law. Paine was no attorney, but in *Common Sense* what he fears most is the "truly alarming" absence of a legal plan. "We may be as effectually enslaved by the want of laws in America," he warns, "as by submitting to laws made for us in England." . . . In this situation "the law is king" because it remains the only principle of order once the constitutional bonds with England have been sundered. . . .

While Tom Paine's use of law was superficial, his easy reliance on it and the phenomenal popularity of *Common Sense*—half a million copies were published in 1776 alone—confirm a basic familiarity with and acceptance of legalistic conception in the language of Revolutionary culture. The American lawyer's achievement was to use this familiarity and acceptance to gain control over general discourse in the public domain. With remarkable skill, he converted his own conceptual needs into weapons against his intellectual rivals, seizing upon his advantages as Revolutionary spokesman to drive the American clergy and military away from civic podiums and the positions of communal control.

. . .

The rise of the doctrine of judicial review early in the nineteenth century made the lawyer's hegemony as republican spokesman official and reveals a great deal about the profession's centrality within American culture. Long before the doctrine became national policy in *Marbury v. Madison* (1803), lawyers were assuming its general validity in America. . . . In a sense, the lawyer's background *made* him call for a new kind of interpretation and confirmation of fundamental law.

. . .

. . . James Madison believed that . . . [t]he most the drafters at the Constitutional Convention had been able to do was "to avoid the errors suggested by the past . . . and to provide a convenient mode of rectifying their own errors as future experience may unfold them." . . . In a statement central to English legal thought . . . , he added: "All new laws, though penned with the greatest technical skill, and passed on the fullest and most mature deliberation, are considered as more or less obscure and equivocal, until their meaning be liquidated and ascertained by a series of particular discussions and adjudications." Only the ongoing legal process could define the republic.

. . .

Judicial review would become the cultural paradigm for the lawyer's scrutiny. . . . [J]udicial review was designed primarily to catch the dangerous mistakes that every lawyer feared and assumed within the accelerated lawmaking of the new republic.

. . .

The power of determining the constitutionality of law also gave both sides of the bench the confidence and latitude to argue vital policy instead of dead-letter law. In a developing nation obsessed with its own future glory, no audience could be held by the traditional forms and rhetoric of the past. Before everything else the American lawyer wanted to be heard; the strongest sense of legal propriety would bend before that primal need. Even the conservative Hamilton sounded more like Tom Paine than like learned counsel when he announced that "the rules of legal interpretation are rules of *common-sense,* adopted by the courts in the construction of the laws."

John Marshall was the perfect model and logical extension of the need to speak a contemporary language that all Americans could understand and heed. The architect of judicial review in the federal courts, Marshall was also dismissive of case law in general. In fact, his five greatest constitutional opinions as chief justice of the Supreme Court failed to cite a single previous court decision as authority. Each argument was grounded instead upon appeals to the *principia* of American civilization. . . . Obviously, recourse to judicial review as such was infrequent, but the implications of possible use were sufficient to frame every discussion of constitutional principle. Marshall made the most of this situation, and his methods helped to turn important cases into high ceremonial occasions within republican culture. Already the final arbiter of the law in 1803, the Supreme Court was the great oracle of Americanism by the time of Marshall's retirement in 1835.

In republican society generally, the courtroom speech of both attorney and judge quickly became one of ... "the active centers of social order"—a point within a culture where leading ideas come together with leading institutions and where a governing elite uses the set of symbolic forms involved to express the fact that it is in truth governing. With members of the bar already in control of the legislative and executive processes of government, judicial review meant that lawyers alone would create and evaluate practical policy. The courtroom represented a final and exclusive podium for analyzing and testing formulations within the American experiment. Others might comment, but the business of defining the republic remained the particular prerogative of those who joined the legal profession.

. . .

The frailty of new institutions turned the lawyer's business of definitions into a mission for every American to ponder. Most eighteenth-century observers feared that a national government based on republican principles would prove impossible when stretched to the unheard-of scale of the American continent. "You might as well attempt to rule Hell by Prayer," wrote a typical anti-federalist in 1787. . . .

These anxieties were based upon hard realities and a negative course in events that later Americans have ignored in their eagerness to trace the developing nation. Between 1790 and 1860 virtually every state, major faction, and interest group tried, at least once, to weaken the federal government or break up the union. Political unrest, war, rebellion, economic depression, and uncertain geographic identity were the common lot of the former colonies as they struggled to establish themselves in a union never far from collapse. . . .

Amidst pervasive uncertainty, lawyers assigned themselves to what they conceived to be the crucial problems. They became, in Chancellor James Kent's terms, "*ex officio* natural guardians of the laws" and "sentinels over the constitutions and liberties of the country." Since many construed the emergence of the United States as the first important step in a new age of human progress, the role of guardian easily assumed cosmic overtones. "Of the learned professions, nay of all the sciences," remarked the *American Quarterly Review* in a typical encomium for the period, "it [the law] may well put in a claim for even the highest rank. What, indeed, can be more noble than the aim of that science which is to direct the actions of mankind, and whose foundations rest upon the will of the great ruler of the universe."

. . .

Supporting the lawyer's assertiveness as ideological guardian was a peculiar and overwhelming self-confidence. His comprehensive sense of relevance and purpose encouraged him to dominate republican culture. . . . When the Supreme Court justice Joseph Story came to bolster the faculty of the Harvard Law School in 1829, his inaugural lecture urged every student to "addict himself to the study of philosophy, of rhetoric, of history, and of human nature."

. . .

Although the lawyer's emphasis upon general literature represented what many would call a pre-professional stage of American law, . . . it was an emphasis reinforced by the same men who were creating the complex legal system to follow. Their influence within the profession meant that the movement toward more technical definitions of expertise came slowly. . . . [T]he impact of this narrower focus came in the decades after the Civil War. Until then, the assumed role of republican guardian and westward expansion preserved the conditions that caused the lawyer to rely on general literature. It is no coincidence that the final dominating exponent of the generalist tradition came out of the West. Abraham Lincoln's oratory combined equal portions of Blackstone, Shakespeare, and the Bible. In the first half of the nineteenth century the bond between knowledge, general literature, and law remained paramount.

. . .

James Kent gave the configuration of law and letters its most accurate early expression while lecturing at Columbia College in 1794. He urged every American lawyer to master the Greek and Latin classics as well as moral philosophy, history, logic, and mathematics, and his emphasis was on the ability that flowed from general knowledge. Only an attorney "well read in the whole circle of the arts and sciences" could form "an accurate acquaintance with the general principles of Universal Law." . . . Every aspect of what Kent called "the attractive chain of classical studies" was relevant to an infinitely expanding sphere of legal control: "The science of law . . . reaches to every tie which is endearing to the affections, and has a concern on every action which takes place in the extensive circles of public and private life."

Thomas Jefferson's more famous lists of readings for law students were a practical demonstration of the science of law reaching toward every tie. Jefferson . . . also found "history, politics, ethics, physics, oratory, poetry, criticism, etc. as necessary as law to form an accomplished lawyer." Jefferson's plans of study were virtual bibliographies of the Enlightenment, requiring fourteen hours of reading a day across a five-year period. His students read physical science, ethics, religion, and natural law before eight each morning; law (in at least three languages) from eight to twelve; politics and history in the afternoon; and poetry, criticism, rhetoric, and oratory "from Dark to Bed-time."

The law student's assigned task was nothing less than a practical omniscience in human knowledge. David Hoffman's *Course of Legal Study; Respectfully Addressed to the Students of Law in the United States* (1817) was the standard manual of its kind well into the 1830s; it covered six years of study and opened with the Bible, Cicero's *De Officis*, Seneca's *Morals*, Xenophon's *Memorabilia*, Aristotle's *Ethics*, and a long list of other readings in general literature and political philosophy. Hoffman expected his law student to seek "that comprehension of expression peculiar to the poet," and he insisted on the usual litany that "every species of knowledge may prove necessary." . . .

To be sure, few possessed the intellectual dedication that . . . Hoffman's guide required. For every Jefferson devoting five full years to legal training, scores of "Blackstone lawyers" entered the profession after a few months of study, self proclaimed masters of one text. . . . The supposed "golden age of American law" in the first half of the nineteenth century was really a period of very weak collective standards, and many of its greatest leaders from beginning to end . . . joined the bar after minimal preparation.

. . .

Breakdown and Resolution

. . .

Still central to republican experience in 1825, the configuration of law and letters disappeared with the Civil War. . . . One by one the conditions supporting the configuration became less relevant in republican life. . . .

The priorities that held the early American lawyer to literature were brittle, and this was a period of extraordinary social, economic, and intellectual flux. Serious erosion began in the second decade of the century. Between 1789 and 1815 American law developed through basic constitutional issues and through a delineation of general problems in property, contracts, debt, and ejectment. "I saw where justice lay," wrote Chancellor Kent, "and the moral sense decided the court half the time. . . . I might once in a while be embarrassed by a technical rule, but I most always found principles suited to my views of the case." The War of 1812 undermined this broad philosophical approach by creating many of the more complex branches of modern law. The British blockade disrupted coastal shipping, ruined intercontinental trade, and forced new efforts in domestic manufacturing, internal transportation, and mechanical invention. Overnight the law required experts in admiralty and insurance law to handle the tangled aftermath of confiscations and losses. Similar needs quickly developed in corporation and patent law.

Technical competence triumphed over general learning and philosophical discourse as case law accumulated. Where only three appeals in corporation law came before the Supreme Court prior to 1815, the case load in this new area required a textbook by 1832. In fact, there were suddenly too many textbooks on American law rather than too few. "The multiplication of books is becoming, or rather has become, an evil that is intolerable," wrote Kent in 1830, referring to the growing mass of case reports and legal digests. . . .

Philosophically, the shift from general principles to textbook law created a very different sense of subject. It dictated a relative stress on positive or manmade law over natural law. The early lawyer searched for a declaration derived from common usage and consistent with nature. His successor, the reader of case reports, thought in terms of the specific commands that society had placed upon itself. Each had a particular approach to the printed page. The first looked for connections and resemblance; the second, for distinction and precision. The first, for eloquence and ethical foundation; the second, for material support. Their respective needs made general literature useful to the former and increasingly irrelevant to the latter. And the second kind of lawyer inevitably swallowed the first.

. . .

The lawyer's more frequent choice of technical expertise over general learning was also a reaction to Jacksonian influences. While anti-lawyer sentiment stretched back as far as the Revolution, the egalitarian tendencies of the 1830s exacerbated hostility by segregating a professional elite. Jacksonian democrats spoke of subjecting the bar to popular controls. To protect themselves, lawyers moved toward a narrower, but safer, basis of identification. Abdicating the sweeping assertiveness of their predecessors, the new practitioners of the 1840s claimed legitimacy through specific utilitarian skills that lawyers alone could perform. Political service, literary enterprise, and public speaking belonged in a different (and increasingly suspect) category. By 1850 the expansive post-Revolutionary lawyer, the courtroom orator who relied on general jurisprudence, belles-lettres, and the classics, was an anachronism. . . .

The law itself began to serve radically different national needs. In the decades following the Revolution, Americans depended on formally structured legal institutions because they lacked functional equivalents for ordering their society. The law supplied a vital image of cohesion, a useful paradigm for order in the world. It expressed corporate harmony, a crucial ingredient of every republican's moral sense of self. Fixed standards, firm precedents, and immutable law were part and parcel of an ideology of union, an aesthetics of cohesion. But by 1830 the same premises were blocking a radically different sense of national development. Precedent and fixed law were clumsy tools for coping with a burgeoning economy of land speculators, textile mills, turnpike companies, and railroad corporations. Moreover, Americans no longer needed expressions of communal solidarity in quite the same way. Jacksonian individualism accepted national identity as a given, stressing instead personal freedom from artificial social institutions and arguing for unrestrained self-interest as the surest guarantee of communal growth and virtue.

Always a function of communal expression, the law adjusted to Jacksonian impulses. By 1850, "law, once conceived of as protective, regulative, paternalistic and, above all, a paramount expression of the moral sense of the community, had come to be thought of as facilitative of individual desires and as simply reflective of the existing organization of economic and political power." This shift transformed the lawyer's role in American society. As long as law reflected the order and virtue of the republic, lawyers could speak for the entire community. But once law became a deliberate instrument of social policy for particular kinds of individuals, the attorney who operated in this process became a narrower agent of competing concerns. As the increasingly technical representative of vested interests, he found less and less reason to function as the ideological guardian of his culture.

Significantly, the role of ideological guardian was a growing problem even for the established generation of lawyer-orators. In the decades before the Civil War, republican principle began to founder on a basic incompatibility in the American experiment. Sectional strife over slavery in a free republic made national identity a dangerous subject. Leaders . . . spoke less of principle and more of compromise between conflicting ideals. . . .

The lawyer's centrality to compromise glorified his position as the American peacemaker. . . . However, the price of the peacemaker's inflated role was bankruptcy in the face of war. Because the failure of compromise was peculiarly the lawyer's own, it paved the way for a broader rejection of his influence.

. . .

As Jefferson exemplifies the original form and direction of the legal mind in America, so Daniel Webster illustrates the changing nature of that mind in the first half of the nineteenth century. . . . In the 1820s Webster was his country's foremost courtroom advocate, over-shadowing others in his mastery of constitutional law and in the importance of cases argued. But the rapidly growing complexity of the law soon robbed him of the ability to hold his own in many cases and led to an embarrassing dependency on friends for knowledge of the law. In the 1830s and 1840s colleagues . . . , fresh out of Harvard Law School, were catching the great orator in simple ignorance of the law during courtroom disputes.

. . .

End of the Configuration

. . .

Virtually every lawyer-writer in America viewed the changing nature of his country with alarm. Most feared and rejected the democratic impulses that recast republican culture between the Revolution and the Civil War. A minority from Thomas Jefferson through Andrew Jackson and beyond welcomed democratization but condemned other trends like the growth of commercialism, the consolidation of political power, the emergence of special interests, and the rise of corporations. Both groups assumed for themselves the role of ideological guardian; both saw symptoms of corruption and decline; both gave way to anger and despair in the face of change. Among the conservatives, every transition provoked an expression of loss. . . . For the democrats, the same transitions were marred by an overwhelming sense of danger. . . .

At its worst the lawyer-writer's pessimism stifled insight and effort. . . . One after another the wise men, patriots, and heroes of the early American bar lamented their unavoidable decline. . . . No major event of the period passed without some leading lawyer predicting imminent and utter ruin.

. . .

Such gloom came out of a sharp debate over the meaning of American civilization. At issue was the role of law in government, and at stake was the nature of the republic itself. John Adams, John Marshall, Joseph Story, James Kent, Daniel Webster, and other conservative members of the early American bar all believed in what they called "an empire of laws, not of men." Their republic enshrined the law of nature, a rule of right and reason, within organs of government that protected the rights of men against the encroachment of minorities *and* majorities. Accordingly, they emphasized the form of government created by a constitution, and they looked for a finely articulated arrangement of institutions to distribute and to check power. In essence their rule of law was a "method of counterpoise" that skillfully mixed and balanced refractory and antagonistic parts. Self-regulating, that rule nonetheless required highly educated managers to maintain and explain its balanced intricacies. This was the ground on which the conservative bar established its own importance. Because each intricacy derived from a general notion of right and reason, a theorist could also hope for its universal expression and enforcement. . . .

From the beginning, however, another theory of republicanism influenced post-Revolutionary politics. This second theory looked to the inalienable power of the people as the source of all government and emphasized the right of those outside government to reach and restrict those within. The two theories—what can be termed the institutional view and the participatory view—were implicitly antithetical, but it was the democratic continuum in American politics that turned abstract alternatives into clashing orthodoxies. The move toward universal manhood suffrage, the direct election of government officials, the shift from political caucuses to public nominating conventions, and the growth of the party spoils system forced a constant reiteration of differences between 1800 and 1850. Each change, depending upon the observer's orientation, signaled either a terrible loss of institutional integrity or a vital gain in the people's access to government. The shrill tone of antebellum politics—its hysteria, its paranoia, its plain nastiness—owed much to a deliberate spirit of contradiction as the second view slowly displaced the first in the American mind.

Although most conservative intellectuals found themselves on the losing side of this acrimonious debate, the lawyer-writer expressed the deepest sense of defeat. In his case democratization threatened identity itself because he alone had included political expertise in his definition of professionalism or claim to special knowledge. He *professed* to know more about republicanism than others—precisely the claim that a participatory theory of republicanism could not allow. No, the people alone knew their best interest. Moreover, if true wisdom resided in the people, then the special knowledge of an elite was a dubious contribution to republican virtue. By the 1830s an expert's knowledge was a dangerous thing, and all of the professions were under attack as strongholds of aristocratic privilege. The Jacksonian's faith in spontaneous action and self regulation made the rule of law a contradiction in terms.

. . .

Two exceptions prove the rule of the lawyer's pessimism: Charles Grandison Finney (1792–1875) and David Dudley Field (1805–1894). Finney, practicing in upstate New York, saw the face of Jesus across his darkened law office one evening in 1821 and immediately abandoned one profession for another. Soon he was the leading revivalist in America. . . . Field, for his part, developed into the most powerful corporate lawyer of the age. . . . More memorable than any courtroom triumph, however, was Field's lifelong attempt to reform the American legal system. He became famous as the heart and soul of the codification movement in nineteenth-century legal thought. Joining the very different careers of Finney and Field was an essential optimism—an optimism that embraced the early lawyer's belief in comprehensiveness. Significantly, both men fought hardest against the narrow professionalism of immediate colleagues. Mere evil and lawlessness stood in their way less than "false instruction given to the people" and "the theories and prejudices of the profession, hardened by the incrustation of centuries." Charles Grandison Finney and David Dudley Field were embattled generalists in an increasingly specialized age.

. . .

. . . Finney's new evangelism plunged him directly into the major democratic movements of the period. . . . It opened the way for a communal spokesman to regain the popular audiences that the conservative legal profession had been losing. Conversely, the one time lawyer remained to help control those audiences. Finney curbed the excess emotionalism of his listeners when he could, and his background in the law supplied much of his skill in crowd manipulation. Old training and new fervor combined in the preacher's sense of mastery. . . .

David Dudley Field brought the same untiring zeal to a different idea of reaching the people. As he put the central concern of his life, "It is the first duty of a government to bring the laws to the knowledge of the people." Codification, reducing the chaotic mass of nineteenth-century law to order, was the great means to this end. It involved neither more nor less than "writing [the law] in a book of such dimensions and in such language that all can read and comprehend it." The people, of course, could never write such a book; that was the task of "the true lawyer" who understood what was needed and knew best how to supply it. In fact, Field went much further. "A code is or should be an homogeneous work," he wrote. "It should have the impress of one mind, or at most of a few minds." Here was a sense of mission at least as exalted as Finney's. Field, with perhaps a few others, wanted "to look at the law of the land as a whole, to lop off its excrescences, reconcile its contradictions, and make it uniform and harmonious." As a first step he meant to transform the hundreds of volumes of New York case law, the entire common law tradition, and all relevant statutes, commentaries, and court procedures into "four or five pocket-volumes" that every American could understand. . . . Field hoped for the highest of stations. He would be the lawgiver of millions for all time to come.

Defeats—and there were many—never punctured the codifier's assurance or resolve. Field began his drive for legal reform in 1839, and within ten years New York had a preliminary Code of Civil Procedure. Largely the work of Field, this preliminary code became law in nine other states before the Civil War. But . . . the Code of 1848 was only the first step in a master plan that failed. Four other codes . . . never gained acceptance in New York. Even the preliminary enactment lost its integrity; relentless modification soon tore it apart, leaving a jumbled mass, seven times the size of the original pocket-volume. Beyond New York just five states out of forty-two embraced the full intent of codification. Field did not hide his exasperation. "Are we to go on forever in a hopeless search for something certain and something stable?" he chided the legal profession in 1884. The question, asked in Field's eightieth year, carried a direct challenge. "Order can be brought out of this confusion," he insisted. "It is only our own profession that has hitherto prevented it." . . .

His self-confidence came from the methodological certainties and ideological hopes of the early bar. Field dismissed "the mere practicing lawyer" of his own day. The ideal man of the law was a scholar: "He must have comprehended the greatness of the whole, the harmony of its parts, and the infinite diversity of its particulars." . . . Against these aspirations, opposition could sound like ignorance. But what if such a code—"as simple as so vast a work can be made"—proved too simple? Field's detractors included most of his colleagues, and they denied his first premise. The legal profession had lost its faith in the power of abstraction. Generalization no longer explained experience.

CHAPTER 10

Slavery

The Golden Age of American law was tarnished by an air of tension. Underlying Federalist-Republican disagreements was a sectional division that threatened to turn—and eventually did turn—into national catastrophe.

The division surfaced in a number of contexts. The industrial-urban economy of the North contrasted with the agricultural-rural economy of the South and led to divergent interests. President Andrew Jackson's opposition to a national bank was resented by the North and applauded by the South. Tariffs on the importation of industrial goods were favored by the North to protect its infant industries, but resented by the South. Most divisive of all was the South's reliance on the labor of enslaved blacks.

In ancient times, slavery was often imposed on war captives regardless of race. In the New World, the practice of race-based slavery was started by Spanish colonists who impressed native Americans into an *"encomienda"* system, which, though technically distinguishable, amounted to slave labor in practice. (The enslavement of native Americans was never widely practiced in the English colonies.) As the Spanish colonists decimated native populations, they turned to importing slaves from Africa. Trade in African slaves became a mainstay not only for Spanish, but for English and colonial ships as well, by the mid-1700s.

England briefly flirted with slavery, accepting the status of slaves brought into England in a 1677 case, but the case was overruled thirty years later, and in 1772 Lord Mansfield could write: "By the common law, no man can have a property in another." English shipping, however, continued to prosper in the slave trade until prohibited by statute in 1807, and England continued to tolerate slavery in its colonies until 1833.

The first shipment of slaves to the English colonies arrived in 1619 in Virginia. The legal backing for slavery, however, developed slowly. As recounted in Kenneth M. Stampp's *The Peculiar Institution: Slavery in the Ante-Bellum South* (1956):

> Not until the 1660's did Maryland and Virginia make the first important legal distinctions between white and Negro servants. During this decade various statutes provided that Negroes were to be slaves for life, that the child was to inherit the condition of the mother, and that Christian baptism did not change the slave's status. Even then it took many more years and many additional statutes to define clearly the nature of slaves as property, to confer upon the masters their required disciplinary power, to enact the codes by which slaves' movements were subjected to public control, and to give them a peculiar position in courts of law. (pp. 22–23)

By its very nature, slavery tended to eliminate law as a factor in the relationship between master and slave. As Judge A. Leon Higginbotham, Jr., wrote in his book, *In the Matter of Color: The Colonial Period* (1978):

> While never reluctant to protect and maximize their property rights in the slaves, many judges and legislators were reluctant to recognize that slaves had, in their own right, any basic human rights. Many feared that any judicial protection of the slave would trigger further challenges to the legitimacy of the dehumanized status of blacks and slaves. (p. 8)

In the colonial era, slavery was practiced in both northern and southern colonies, although it never became as significant an economic factor in the North as it was in the tobacco and cotton plantations of the South. (Judge Higginbotham's book deals with the legal treatment of slavery in six colonies—three in the South and three in the North.) Following the Revolution, northern states abolished slavery. New York and New Jersey were last in 1804.

About two decades later, influenced by a religious revival movement labeled "The Great Awakening," reformers in the North, most notably Frederick Douglass and William Lloyd Garrison, campaigned to abolish slavery in the South as well. They received popular support, but they also encountered opposition from moderates hoping for accommodation with the South.

In the Constitution, slavery was left up to individual states. Without much discussion at the Constitutional Convention, a clause was inserted into the Constitution requiring the return of slaves fleeing slave states. In 1793 Congress enacted a Fugitive Slave Law to enforce the constitutional clause. As the abolitionist cause gained momentum, a number of northern states enacted "personal liberty laws," withdrawing state cooperation in the enforcement of the 1793 federal law.

The North succeeded in limiting slavery in a number of respects. With the acquiescence of the South, the slave trade was prohibited by federal statute in 1808. Northern law also freed slaves taken into free states by their masters. Extralegally, abolitionists organized "underground railroads" to help fugitive slaves escape to Canada, which did not force their extradition. The question of fugitive slaves in northern states, however, remained one of the most divisive issues and a moral and legal quandary for northern courts.

The quandary is exemplified by the rulings of Chief Justice Lemuel Shaw of the Massachusetts Supreme Judicial Court. Opposed to slavery on moral grounds, Shaw was torn between his sympathy for abolition and the countervailing considerations of upholding the Constitution and, above all, preserving peace. Shaw was the father-in-law of novelist Herman Melville, whose well-known short story, "Lord Jim," is said to have been based on Shaw's dilemma.

Broadside of Boston's Vigilance Committee, 1851.
Library of Congress, Rare Book and Special Collections Division.

THE FUGITIVE SLAVE LAW

from Leonard W. Levy, *The Law of the Commonwealth and Chief Justice Shaw*
(Cambridge, Mass.: Harvard University Press, 1957), pp. 72–108.
Copyright © 1957 by Harvard University Press. Copyright renewed by Leonard W. Levy.
Reprinted by permission of Leonard W. Levy.

The Fugitive Slave Law

Remanding Runaways

I. The fugitive-slavery issue was freighted with perils to the nation. Shaw's thought on the subject was filled with apprehension for the security and harmony of the Union. He was earnestly a man of peace who would not consciously aggravate a situation offering the menace of a "great national calamity." To persons of like sensibilities, the histrionics of extremists, who rasped unceasingly on the sinful nature of slavery, were exasperating. In October 1835, two months after conservatives in a mass meeting at Faneuil Hall had apologized to the South for the abolitionism in Boston, a mob of several thousands . . . stormed a meeting of the Boston Female Anti-Slavery Society, cowed the defenseless praying women, and nearly lynched William Lloyd Garrison. A quietus on agitation was devoutly wished by persons of standing. Frenzied provocateurs, vowing obedience not to law and order and the Constitution, but to an unwritten "higher law" of conscience, endangered the political stability. . . . Article IV, section 2, of the United States Constitution had provided for the return of fugitive slaves, and Congress had passed the Act of 1793 to that end. As a judge, Shaw felt duty-bound to enforce the Constitution as law regardless of whatever moral twinges he may have experienced. When the abolitionists hurled their barbs at him, they aimed at a man who reluctantly regarded the return of runaways as a legal necessity.

II. It was not until 1842 that the first bona fide case of a fugitive slave came before Shaw; but in 1836 there occurred a case that clearly indicated his desire to avoid giving effect to the Fugitive Slave Act unless the facts at issue presented no other recourse. . . .

[In August 1836] the brig *Chickasaw,* Henry Eldridge, Captain, had sailed into Boston harbor carrying two Negro passengers, Eliza Small and Polly Ann Bates. . . . While the *Chickasaw* lay in the stream, she was boarded by one Matthew Turner who represented himself to the captain as the agent of John B. Morris, a wealthy slave-holder of Baltimore. The women were asserted by Turner to be fugitives from Morris' service. . . . [F]rom the evidence, it is not clear whether the women were fugitives or whether they were the victims of a mean plot by their former master to repossess them.

In any case, Captain Eldridge detained his passengers on the brig at the request of Turner until the latter obtained a warrant for their arrest as escaped slaves. News of the events on the *Chickasaw* quickly circulated. A large and excited group of Negroes collected on the wharf. During Turner's absence, a Negro citizen appeared before Chief Justice Shaw and secured a writ of habeas corpus directed against Eldridge, forcing him to release the unfortunate women pending a hearing on the question of his authority to hold them in restraint. Deputy Sheriff Huggerford, who served the writ, found the women in a state of agitation, locked in their cabin. One of them, a mulatto of about thirty, upon learning that friendly proceedings had been instituted, burst into tears, crying that "She knew God would not forsake her and send her back to the South."

. . . As the Court opened that August first, the Chief Justice took the bench, sitting alone. Spectators, mostly Negroes, packed the room. The few whites present were, in the main, abolitionists concerned with the freedom of two of God's children. If there were any in the audience friendly to the cause of Eldridge or the slaveowner's agent, they were lost in a sea of sympathizers for the alleged slaves.

The Chief Justice, rising to give his opinion, stated the issue simply: "Has the captain of the brig *Chickasaw* a right to convert his vessel into a prison?" He decided that the defendant had not the least right to hold the women. They had been detained in his custody in a most unlawful manner, since he in no way brought himself within the provisions of the federal statute of 1793. Shaw concluded his opinion by saying "the prisoners must therefore be discharged from all further detention."

Turner, the agent, then arose and implied that he would make a fresh arrest under the provisions of the Fugitive Slave Law, and he inquired of the Court whether a warrant would be necessary for that purpose. At the same moment a constable was sent to lock the door leading downstairs. These actions created a wave of excitement among the spectators. The general impression was that the slave-hunter was about to make a fresh seizure right on the spot, even though the prisoners appeared to have been discharged by the Chief Justice.

Tension charged the air for a moment. Before Shaw could answer Turner, word was passed to the women informing them that they were discharged and advising that they clear out before the agent got them again. . . . Someone called to the people in the room, "Take them." A chant of "Go—go!" rang out. Instantly, the tumult broke: the spectators, both white and colored, turned into a disorderly mob, rushed over the benches, and stormed down the aisle toward Eliza and Polly Ann. Shaw protested, "Stop, stop," but the mob tore on, yelling "Don't stop." Shaw climbed down out of his bench and endeavored vainly to hold the door against them. Huggerford, the only officer in the room, was grabbed, throttled, and "maltreated to the peril of his life." The crowd, bearing away the prisoners, disappeared through the private passageway of the judiciary and dashed down the stairs of the Court House. In Court Square, the fugitives were shoved into a carriage and driven out of the city, followed for a short distance by the screaming mob. Huggerford and a posse took up the pursuit. The carriage crossed over Mill Dam—where toll money was thrown out while the horses were driven at a gallop—and was gone.

The story of the shocking rescue was a sensation in Boston's newspapers. The *Columbian Centinel* excoriated the seditious "Abolition Riot," and estimated that ninety percent of the public shared its views. "A Friend of the Union," in a letter to the editor, wrote heatedly that if a few fanatics and Negroes were suffered to browbeat and put down the highest tribunals of the nation, "then adieu to its peace and union." Only exemplary punishment of the leaders and abettors of the mob, stated the writer, would "satisfy our Southern brethren, and convince them that their *rights* and *property* will be protected, at least here in New England. . . ." But the fugitives were never recaptured; nor were their rescuers ever brought to trial, because, most curiously, no one came forward to identify any of them.

. . .

Shaw, it should be noted, had not only refused, under the facts of the case, to allow the alleged fugitives to be held at the agent's pleasure; he had not granted a postponement of the hearing as requested, so that evidence could be brought from Baltimore to prove that they were the property of Morris. Obviously Shaw was disinclined to enforce the Fugitive Slave Law except in a case of unavoidable necessity. . . .

There was a shocking postscript to this first "rescue" of alleged fugitive slaves in Boston. Four weeks later, a United States naval officer from Baltimore entered Samuel Eliot Sewall's office [Sewall had been volunteer attorney for Small and Bates] and after announcing that he was a relative of Morris the slaveowner, proceeded to insult the abolitionist lawyer "with opprobrious epithets," and then struck him "a number of blows with the butt end of a horsewhip." The assailant, who immediately thereafter left town, had informed his victim that he had no right to interfere with Southern property rights.

III. Six years later the famous Latimer case occurred. On October 19, 1842, a Constable Stratton, furnished with a warrant issued by the Boston Police

Court, arrested George Latimer, "a fine looking colored man." A complaint of theft in Virginia had been brought against him by James B. Gray, a Norfolk slavemaster, who simultaneously claimed the fugitive from justice as his slave. Soon a crowd of "nearly three-hundred, mostly male blacks," assembled before the Court House where the prisoner was held. To defeat a rescue, he was slipped out by the back door and locked up in the Leverett Street jail. . . . Fearing that Gray and his men might smuggle Latimer out of the city late at night, parties interested in freedom's cause successfully petitioned Chief Justice Shaw for a writ of habeas corpus.

The following evening, Stratton, in compliance with the writ, produced Latimer before Shaw in the Supreme Court room. The Court was not officially in session, but since the judges were present for other purposes, they also heard this case. At the time, "immense crowds" were milling about the Court House "in a very feverish state of anxiety." . . .

After consultation with the other judges, Shaw discharged the writ and ordered Latimer returned to the custody of his captors. . . . He ruled that Gray and Stratton showed sufficient authority to detain the prisoner under the Act of 1793, which the United States Supreme Court had recently upheld. . . . State courts could not interfere with the operation of a constitutional statute under whose terms Gray as claimant was entitled to arrest Latimer wherever he fled, prove his ownership before a federal court, and obtain therefrom a certificate to carry his slave away with him. . . . When Stratton and his assistants escorted the slave back to jail, they were riotously attacked by the mob outside the Court House. The rescue attempt failed, but one officer was given "a touch of the nose bleed" and another was "struck by a brickbat, and severely hurt. . . ." Eight of the mob were arrested, all of them Negroes.

. . .

On October 24, a final legal effort was made by Latimer's friends to free him. They sued out a writ of personal replevin, under a state personal liberty law of 1837, passed to guarantee trial by jury "on questions of personal freedom." This law did not exclude fugitive slaves from its protection. . . .

. . . In the account of Shaw's opinion as reported by Garrison, . . . an important paragraph reveals much of Shaw's thought on the fugitive-slavery question. He said, "in substance," reported *The Liberator* (November 4), that

> he probably felt as much sympathy for the person in custody as others; but this was a case in which an appeal to natural rights and the paramount law of liberty was not pertinent! It was decided by the Constitution of the United States, and by the law of Congress, under that instrument, relating to fugitive slaves. These were to be obeyed, however disagreeable to our own natural sympathies and views of duty! . . . By the Constitution, the duty of returning runaway slaves was made imperative on the free states, and the act of Congress . . . was in accordance with the spirit of that instrument. He repeatedly said, that on no other terms could a union have been formed between the North and the South.

...

As to Latimer's rights under the Massachusetts Personal Liberty Law of 1837, they were non-existent, ruled Shaw. That law had been passed by state officers sworn to support the Constitution and laws of the nation; they could not pass any law in conflict with these superior obligations. Therefore, the statute relied upon by the prisoner could not be construed to embrace runaways. Such persons must be regarded as exceptions to its provisions. The statute, Shaw concluded, . . . was unconstitutional and void insofar as it concerned fugitive slaves. Accordingly, the writ of personal replevin was inapplicable in Latimer's case. Shaw then ordered that the slave once more be remanded to the custody of the agents of Gray, whose claim was properly pending before a federal court.

The abolitionists countered this opinion with abuse most galling. At their Faneuil Hall meeting on October 30, Sewall imputed to Shaw the "basest motives of personal feeling." Wendell Phillips pronounced his famous curse upon the Constitution, and Francis Jackson, Frederick Douglass, and Edmund Quincy did their best to incite a crowd to rescue. The intemperate Garrison wrote that Shaw's opinion proved his readiness to aid "in kidnapping a guiltless and defenseless human, and to act the part of Pilate in the Crucifixion of the Son of God. . . ." Where, asked Garrison, did Shaw's guilt differ "from that of the slave pirate on the African coast . . . ?" When "A Subscriber" protested that it was "unchristian" to classify with slavers "one of the best men in the community," Garrison replied that Chief Justice Shaw had betrayed the honor of Massachusetts "when Liberty lay bleeding." . . .

Chandler [editor of the conservative *Law Reporter*] undertook "to deal a blow" against the "false morality, born from the sophistry of fanaticism" which sought to undermine public confidence in the judiciary and the laws of the nation. He referred indignantly to critics who insisted that Shaw should have freed Latimer in accordance with the "law" of conscience, in spite of the Constitution and Congress. Did not the abolitionist know, asked Chandler,

> that a judge has nothing to do with the moral character of the laws which society chooses to make, and which, when made, it places him upon the bench to apply the facts before him? Does he not know that the judiciary is the mere organ of society, to declare what the law is, and having ascertained, to pronounce what the law requires?

. . . The zealots who made civil disobedience sound doctrine, however, had their own image of the ideal judge. He was a Judge Harrington of Vermont who, rejecting documentary proof that a Negro claimed was in fact a fugitive slave, had allegedly remarked: "If the master could show a bill of sale, or grant, from the Almighty, then his title to him would be complete: otherwise it would not."

With such a judge in mind, Garrisonians were not given to pause in a scrupulous regard for fact or moderation when discussing Lemuel Shaw. They meant to whip public opinion into a froth of hysteria, and fortune favored them. Justice Story was too ill to hear the case [in federal court] as scheduled on the fifth of November, and the date when Gray might apply before a federal court for a certificate was advanced to the twenty-first. The abolitionists made the most of the opportunity which time gave to them. They bellowed animadversions at mass meetings up and down the state. A propaganda sheet, the *Latimer Journal and North Star,* rife with a sense of bitter injustice, was published tri-weekly, beginning with November 11. The editors, Dr. Henry I. Bowditch and William F. Channing, sons of famous fathers, circulated twenty thousand copies of each issue. "The slave shall never leave Boston even if to gain that end our streets pour with blood," they wrote. The judiciary was their special target. "The whole of the Latimer Journal," stated the *Law Reporter,* "was largely devoted to the most positive assertions, that the chief justice's decision upon the *habeas corpus* was grossly illegal, and he and Mr. Justice Story are accused of using their offices to oppress their fellow men."

Bowditch, Channing, Charles Sumner, and others of similar persuasion got up a petition threatening the Sheriff [Eveleth] of Suffolk County with removal from office if he did not order his subordinate, jailor Coolidge, to release Latimer. . . . Spurred by the threat of removal and by public demonstrations against the use of the jail by Gray and his agents for their personal advantage, Eveleth ordered Latimer's release by noon of the eighteenth. This new development, just a few days before the slaveowner could get a certificate, put Gray in a quandary. He still had legal custody of Latimer, but if he held him privately, his slave would be rescued from him. As his counsel, Austin, explained in his letter "To the Public," "to attempt to keep Latimer in any other place than the jail, was to raise at once a signal for a riot, if not bloodshed." Consequently Gray consented to sell his claim for $400. Immediately after the sale, Latimer was set free.

The Fugitive Slave Law was yet to be enforced in Massachusetts. Whittier stated its defiance in "Massachusetts to Virginia": "No fetters in the Bay State,—no slave upon our land!" An immense petition for repeal of the law, bearing 51,862 Massachusetts signatures, rolled up into the size of a barrel, was presented in Congress by "Old Man Eloquent," John Quincy Adams. Under "gag law," the petition was not received. The state legislature, however, favorably responded to anti-slavery protests. Outraged citizens had held meetings in every county and in almost every town "to demand that their ancient Commonwealth should never again be insulted by the conversion of her jails into barracoons, and her sworn servants and judicial officers into the minions of the slave catcher." On February 17, 1843, following a great demonstration in Faneuil Hall, a petition with 65,000 names, borne on the shoulders of six men, was delivered to the State House where it was presented by Charles

Francis Adams. The "Latimer Law," an act "further to protect Personal Liberty," was passed. It prohibited state judges from recognizing the Act of 1793 . . . ; it prohibited officers of the Commonwealth from assisting in the arrest of alleged fugitive slaves; and it prohibited the use of state jails for the confinement of fugitives. . . . Other northern states also passed personal liberty laws, converting the Act of 1793 into a nullity by the withdrawal of state aid in its enforcement.

IV. Southern anxiety for the loss of runaways was allayed by a new Fugitive Slave Law passed by Congress, with Webster's endorsement, as part of the Compromise of 1850. The peculiar ingenuity of the new legislation was that it brought the law of bondage home to a free state. It was a law of flint, providing federal officials for its effective enforcement. When hateful scenes of slavery were transferred from the South and enacted in the streets of Boston, the old city was confronted with a choice among cherished alternatives: liberty or union? freedom or property? The new law produced a curious moral spectacle, for the question which distracted the minds of free men was whether to catch slaves or not to catch slaves.

To the anti-slavery hotspurs, fanatically devoted to a "higher law" than the Constitution, the measure was diabolical; it violated the purest promptings of conscience and Christianity. Wendell Phillips resolved for "the Abolitionists of Massachusetts" that "CONSTITUTION OR NO CONSTITUTION, LAW OR NO LAW" they would fight the sins which Black Daniel symbolized. Those who praised Webster's patriotism and defended the Act of 1850 denied that the . . . [abolitionists] had a monopoly on moral justification. If the conservatives like the Chief Justice had retreated from the cause of individual freedom, it was in an anxious regard for even greater moral values: peace and Union. Or so they reasoned.

Charles Francis Adams wrote that while a shallow veneer of anti-slavery sentiment had been fashionable among them, it was "mere sentiment," without roots either in conviction or in material interests. "On the contrary," contended Adams, "so far as material interests were concerned, a great change had recently taken place. The manufacturing development of Massachusetts had been rapid, and a close affiliation had sprung up between the cotton spinners of the North and the cotton producers of the South,—or as Charles Sumner put it, between 'the lords of the loom and the lords of the lash.'"

By mid-century a great majority of Boston's "best people" no longer concealed their warmness toward Southern interests. Their eagerness to keep on the best of terms with the South was later recalled by Edward L. Pierce, a student at Harvard Law School (1850–52). "A southern slave holder, or his son at Harvard," he wrote, "was more welcome in society than any guest except a foreigner. . . . The deference to rich southern planters was marked." Almost all the wealth of the city was controlled by the "Cotton Whigs," and as social and business Boston gradually became "almost avowedly a pro-slavery community," its self-justification of loyalty to the Constitution and to national security approached hysteria. When the news came from Washington that the Fugitive Slave Act had been safely passed, one hundred guns roared a joyous salute across the Common.

A few weeks later, opponents of the law swelled Faneuil Hall to fire their invective against its supporters, to pledge their aid to Negro fellow-citizens, and to demand "INSTANT REPEAL." A group of fifty—it soon grew to two hundred and ten—was appointed to act as a Committee of Vigilance and Safety which determined to render the abominable act a nullity. Then in the same hall, in November, defenders of the law swore their allegiance to it at a "Constitutional Meeting."

V. In the furious climate of irreconcilable loyalties and thunderous rallies engendered by the Act of 1850, men waited apprehensively.... A month after the law was passed, slave-hunters arrived in Boston searching for William and Ellen Craft, fugitives from a Georgia planter. Here was the first test—and the vigilance committee ... tracked down the slave-hunters and chased them out of town. Then on February 15, 1851, the Shadrach affair began.

From Norfolk there came to Boston a "hired kidnapper," with documents prepared in Virginia, claiming a waiter at Taft's Cornhill Coffee House as a slave. George Ticknor Curtis, "Cotton Whig" and Commissioner of the United States Circuit Court, issued a warrant for the arrest of the alleged runaway, one Frederick Wilkins, alias Shadrach. Seized as he unsuspectingly served breakfast to United States Deputy Marshal Patrick Riley, Shadrach was hustled through a back street to the Court House.... In the meantime, word had spread that the marshal had captured a fugitive slave. Vigilance men Samuel Eliot Sewall, Charles Davis, Ellis Gray Loring, Charles List, Robert Morris, and Richard Henry Dana—he who had sailed before the mast—all volunteered for the defendant.

As a turbulent crowd, increasing by the moment, assembled in Court Square, Dana prepared a petition for habeas corpus addressed to Chief Justice Shaw.... With this petition Dana sought out Shaw, whom he found in the lobby of the Supreme Judicial Court Room with Associate Justice Metcalf, and explained that with the writ he hoped to bring a test case on the constitutional power of a commissioner to issue a warrant under the Act of 1850. Shaw flatly refused to grant habeas corpus in Shadrach's behalf, revealing a positive disapproval of the anti-slavery efforts. In his diary, under the entry for that Saturday, February 15, the ardently partisan Dana recorded in detail his conversation with the Chief Justice. In what Dana considered "a most ungracious manner," Shaw had replied after reading the petition, "This won't do. I can't do anything on this." And laying it on a table, he turned away to busy himself with something else; but he was not rid of Dana so easily. To an inquiry into the defects of the petition, Shaw gave the impression of trying to "bluff" off his questioner. Finally he yielded to Dana's persistence with the objection that Shadrach had not signed the petition. The lawyer then reminded the judge that state law permitted the petition to be made on behalf of the petitioner. Dana thought to himself that the Chief Justice certainly knew that in extreme cases, when the writ was most needed to protect personal liberty, circumstances might make it impossible for the prisoner to sign personally. Shaw was obstinate:

"There is no evidence that it is in his behalf. There is no evidence of his authority."

"Do you require proof of his authority? What proof do you require, sir?"

"It is enough for me to say that the petition is not sufficient. The petition shows on its face that the writ cannot issue. It shows that the man is in legal custody of a United States marshal."

Again the lawyer instructed the judge: the fact of legal custody must appear on Riley's return to the writ *after* it was granted. Shaw tried another tack, this time complaining that Shadrach could not properly swear ignorance of the charge against him. Dana called attention to the fact that the petition stated fully the pretence of arrest. Finding this to be true, Shaw fell back on his original objection that there was want of evidence from the prisoner. He then added his final objection—"and not made," wrote Dana, "until after he had positively refused to issue the writ"—that the petition required an appended copy of the warrant of arrest or a statement that a copy had been applied for and could not be obtained. Yet the petition clearly stated that Shadrach did not know whether his imprisonment was under a warrant or not. Moreover, the Act of 1850 permitted arrests without a warrant. Dana was disconsolate: "I felt that all these objections were frivolous and invalid, but seeing the temper the Chief Justice was in, and his evident determination to get rid of the petition, I left him for the purpose of either procuring the evidence he required or of going before another judge."

Dana returned to the United States Court Room. Extending from its door into the street was a crowd of about two hundred Negroes. Inside the court room, Shadrach's counsel requested time to consult with him and to prepare the defense. Commissioner Curtis held the proceedings over until the following Tuesday. Officiously, Riley ordered the room cleared of spectators, reporters, and attorneys so that Shadrach might be left alone with his guards. . . .

As the door was opened a yell went up from the Negroes milling in the passageways. Instantly a tug of war began over the door, the officers inside straining to keep it shut, the crowd pressing to force it open. Shadrach headed for the unguarded opposite exit, and as about fifteen men streamed into the room, jamming Riley into a corner behind the door, the marshal screamed from his place of safety, "Shoot him! Shoot him!" But the rescuers had already escorted Shadrach out of the room, down the stairs, and into the streets. . . .

The amazing rescue threatened the success of "peace measures," and the nation protested. The Washington correspondent of the New York *Journal of Commerce* telegraphed from the capital: "Some sensation was produced here by the intelligence of the negro insurrection in Boston." Secretary of State Webster thought the rescue was "a case of treason." On February 17, President Fillmore called a special cabinet meeting to discuss measures to be taken, and on the next day, issued a proclamation commanding all civil and military officers to assist in recapturing Shadrach and to prosecute all persons who took part in the "scandalous outrage" committed against the laws of the United States. On the Senate floor, Henry Clay demanded to know whether a "government of white men was to be yielded to a government by blacks." Boston's reputation had been "badly damaged," especially in the South. The *Savannah Republican* scourged the city as a "black speck on the map—disgraced by the lowest, the meanest, the BLACKEST kind of NULLIFICATION."

In Boston, the press fulminated against the "mischief which mad Abolitionism will wantonly perpetrate." On February 18, the Board of Mayor and Aldermen expressed regret that the Commonwealth's dignity had been criminally insulted, and ordered the City Marshal to make "the whole police force" available to quell a similar breech of law should one be anticipated. Two days later, the Common Council approved unanimously the Board's action and "cordially" endorsed the President's proclamation.

The abolitionists, in their turn, ridiculed the furor which the rescue had occasioned. "Warrington" attacked as Tories the leading citizens who pretended outrage: "State-street brokers and Milk-street jobbers who . . . hold mortgages on slave property . . . dared not to disturb the good understanding between the planters and the manufacturers. . . ." And was not the rescue for the greater glory of God and His children? Dr. Bowditch marked down the day in his calendar as "a holy day," and [Theodore] Parker thought the rescue was "the noblest deed done in Boston since the destruction of the tea in 1773." Impishly, vigilance men recalled that Mrs. Glasse, the celebrated cook, had prudently premised in her recipe for cooking a hare, "First, *catch* your hare!"

Richard Henry Dana shared the rejoicing of his fellows, but in the aftermath of the rescue, he set down in his diary the one event that marred the day and disturbed not only him, but Judge Metcalf too. "The conduct of the Chief Justice, his evident disinclination to act, the frivolous nature of his objections, and his insulting manner to me, have troubled me . . ." wrote Dana. Shaw's conduct, he concluded perspicaciously, "shows how deeply seated, so as to affect, unconsciously I doubt not, good men like him, is this selfish hunkerism of the property interest on the slave question."

. . .

VI.   It was notorious that no fugitive slave had ever been returned from Boston. Webster Whigs were dismayed that the whole state of Massachusetts was known as the cradle of "mad Abolitionism." It had become a matter of pride, not alone in the South, that a fugitive should be seized in Boston and taken back to slavery. Then, on Thursday evening, April 3, 1851—before the excitement of the Shadrach case had subsided—the city government of Boston was presented with an opportunity to make good on its promises of loyally enforcing the Fugitive Slave Act: Thomas Sims was taken into custody as a fugitive slave belonging to Mr. James Potter, a rice planter of Chatham County, Georgia.

Sims spent that night, and the rest of his nights in Boston, confined to the jury room of the Court House which was reserved for use in federal cases. He was thus technically imprisoned in a federal jail. This expedient was resorted to, as in Shadrach's case, because there was no United States prison in Massachusetts, and because the 1843 "Latimer Law" of the state prohibited the use of its prisons for detaining any person accused of being a fugitive slave. In the court-room prison, Sims was kept under close guard by the men of Charles Devens, the United States Marshal.

On the next morning, Boston awoke to witness one of the most extraordinary spectacles in its existence. During the night, the Court House had been barricaded. Under the direction of City Marshal Francis Tukey, iron chains had been girded entirely around the building. Its approaches were cleared by a belt of ropes and chains along the sidewalks, and heavy links stretched across its doorways. The Court House was in fetters, "bound . . . to the Georgia cotton presses." Here was a visible answer, thought Bronson Alcott, to the question, "What has the North to do with slavery?" Tukey had concentrated his men on the scene. The entire regular police force, reinforced by great numbers of special police, patrolled the area and were stationed around and within the building. Wendell Phillips estimated the total number of police at no less than five hundred! Only authorized persons could get within ten feet of the Court House and pass the armed cordon. In effect, this meant that the city government of Boston had temporarily suspended the right of an ordinary citizen in a free Commonwealth to attend public sessions of its courts.

News of the arrest and of the exceptional scenes at the Court House hurried about the city. Several hundred people, infected with curiosity, clogged Court Square from early morning till ten at night. There was no organized attempt at disturbance, although the police were jeered at and scolded by women; on the other hand, repeated cheers were given for the Union. Not till midnight was the square emptied of the crowds for that day. Word of the whole affair reached Longfellow, who recorded in his journal: "April 4, 1851. There is much excitement in Boston about the capture of an alleged fugitive slave. O city without soul! When and where will this end? Shame that the great Republic, the 'refuge of the oppressed,' should stoop so low as to become the Hunter of Slaves."

Low indeed was the stooping, for the chains across the door of the temple of justice were neither low enough to step over nor high enough to walk under. Those who entered the Court House on special business, lawyers, city officers, members of the press (who could enter if their views on the slavery question were safe enough), commissioners, and judges—even the judges—all had to bow their backs and creep beneath the chains. Tukey, the satrap in charge, had ordered it so. Chief Justice Lemuel Shaw of the Supreme Judicial Court, the great Shaw, venerated for his wisdom and for his advanced age, was among the first that morning to stoop beneath the chains. Decades before, Shaw himself had commented that one of the many evils in legally sanctioning slavery was that it degraded ministers of the law and profaned the sanctuary of justice. . . .

At nine that same Friday morning, Commissioner Curtis opened his court to hear the case of young Thomas Sims. The scene was the United States Court Room, up two high and narrow flights of stairs. Six guards were at the door. The prisoner sat with two policemen on each side of him and five more directly behind. Only his counsel could approach him from the front. His counsel were men of first eminence—the vigilance committee had wasted no time in sounding out legal aid. Robert Rantoul was there, a volunteer in Sims' defense who was a United States Senator, and Webster's successor at that. In little more than a year Rantoul would be dead, and Whittier would write in "Rantoul": "We saw him take the weaker side, And right the wronged, and free the thrall." Charles G. Loring, a leader of the Boston bar, also appeared for the prisoner. Seth Thomas was present for the Southern claimants, such "despicable wretches" Dana had never beheld—"cruel, low-bred, dissolute, degraded beings!"

Thomas produced documents to prove that Sims belonged not to himself, but to James Potter of Georgia. Bacon, the agent, whom he had brought from Savannah as witness, took the stand to identify Sims as Potter's slave. There was no testimony on behalf of the defendant. It would have taken weeks before witnesses might be found in Georgia and brought to Boston to speak in court for him. But the law of 1850 envisioned no such delays, only an informal hearing in which the fate of the alleged fugitive was to be decided in a "summary manner," as the law said. The claim of the slave-catcher, made by affidavit or testimony, was in effect sufficient proof to identify the prisoner as the person in fact owing service.

Sims' attorneys moved to introduce as evidence for their client his sworn statement that he was born in Florida; that he had been free as long as he could remember; that his free papers were probably with Mr. Morris Potter of Savannah; and that he never knew nor heard of James Potter, the man who claimed him, until after his arrest. Curtis, however, rejected this affidavit by refusing to entertain the motion on ground that the law of 1850 stated: "In no trial or hearing under this Act shall the testimony of such alleged Fugitive be admitted as evidence." Curtis then held the case over till the next day, Saturday.

On the same Friday morning, when the hearing before Curtis had just begun, Samuel E. Sewall appeared before the Supreme Judicial Court and appealed to Chief Justice Shaw for a writ of habeas corpus to bring Sims before the Court on ground of illegal detention. After consulting with his associates a few moments, Shaw announced his decision to refuse the petition. He stated that if the writ were issued and the prisoner should be brought before the Court, its duty would be to remand him to the custody from which he was taken, by reason of no jurisdiction to decide whether he was or was not a fugitive. Sewall then requested permission to argue on the unconstitutionality of the law of 1850. Again Shaw refused, informing him, somewhat crustily, that the Court had already passed its judgment. "When a Court of Justice sits in fetters . . . the ancient and prescriptive safeguards of personal liberty must of course give way," recorded the abolitionist society.

Discouraged but resourceful, Sims' friends shifted to the familiar technique of agitation. Perhaps public opinion might pressure the courts to a more friendly view of the matter, or a crowd might even be incited to a rescue. The vigilance committee decided to hold a public meeting. The anti-slavery forces convened on the Common, and in the evening, reassembled in Tremont Temple, one thousand strong. Samuel Gridley Howe presided. Speeches of "the most extravagant character" were delivered. Wendell Phillips, the principal speaker was "treasonably violent"; he "maligned Chief Justice Shaw in terms that a gentleman would hardly apply to a pickpocket" for Shaw's refusal to grant the writ. Phillips advised resistance to the Fugitive Slave Act and declared that before a slave should be carried out of Massachusetts, its railroads and steamboats should be destroyed. He also counseled the Negro men of the city to arm and defend themselves.

The law-and-order element of the city was badly frightened. The *Daily Evening Transcript* (April 5) stigmatized the abolitionists as an "imbecile faction" and promised that the overwhelming majority of citizens were resolved at all hazards "to uphold the laws, the Constitution, and the Union." Because of the inflammatory appeals of the agitators, Mayor Bigelow and Marshal Tukey feared a repetition of the Shadrach affair. They doubtless considered the city police incompetent to deal with the poets, preachers, lawyers, and physicians who composed the vigilance committee. While the Tremont Temple meeting was in progress, three companies of the military were ordered out by the mayor: the City Guards, the New England Guards, and the Boston Light Guards. In addition, two hundred and fifty United States troops, with two pieces of ordnance, were kept on the alert at the Charlestown Navy Yard. All that Friday night, members of the vigilance committee, including the gentle Bronson Alcott, "beat the streets," in a gesture of supreme defiance, to protect other fugitives from being arrested.

On Saturday, April fifth, the Sims affair provoked sharp action in the state Senate. Sims requested by petition that the legislature intervene in his favor by passing a special law requiring a writ of habeas corpus to be issued to him. His petition stated that the writ had been refused by the Supreme Judicial Court, that he was a citizen of Massachusetts, and that he ought not to be "surrendered, exiled, or delivered to bondage, until proved to be a slave by a 'due process of law.'" Senator Keyes spoke at length in Sims' favor, declaring that as a result of Shaw's decision, the noble writ of habeas corpus lay a dead letter at the feet of the Fugitive Slave Act. Senator Robinson echoed these sentiments and claimed that the judiciary should be made responsible by popular election. He even hinted at Shaw's impeachment. However, the Chief Justice and his associates had many supporters who believed them to be "the purest and most incorruptible judiciary in the world." In the end, Sims' petition was laid on the table.

In Court Square, the events of Saturday—and of the following week—resembled those of the preceding day. Again there appeared the crowds, the armed cordon, and the judges passing under the chains. In the United States Court Room, Curtis listened to additional evidence that Sims was Potter's slave. That night, readers of the *Commercial Gazette* in New York learned that "The whole Union will probably know in a few days whether a fugitive slave can be arrested in the capital of Massachusetts, and in case the claim is made out, be delivered safely to his master in another State." And a sensitive poet added another entry in his journals: "April 5. Troops under arms in Boston; the court house guarded; the Chief Justice of the Supreme Court forced to stoop under chains to enter the temple of Justice! This is the last point of degradation. Alas for the people who cannot feel an insult!"

Over the weekend, a number of gentlemen of high standing, including Charles Loring, spoke privately to Shaw and his associates, persuading them to reconsider their refusal to hear an argument. Monday morning, Richard Henry Dana appeared with Rantoul before the Supreme Judicial Court.

. . .

The unanimous judgment of the Court, given at three o'clock the same Monday, was a denial of the writ. Shaw's opinion was the first full-dress sustention of the constitutionality of the Fugitive Slave Act of 1850 by any court. A decade later, Hurd, the historian of the law of bondage, wrote that the opinion was thereafter regarded as "the highest authority—to the degree that in opinions of judges in later cases who have maintained the action of commissioners in like circumstances, it has been taken to preclude all further juristical discussion."

That the Chief Justice had reasoned through his stand on the controversial law before that Monday may be surmised from the length and maturity of an opinion written in only a few hours. As early as . . . 1836, he had indicated his intention of giving effect to Congressional enactment should the duty of remanding a fugitive slave arise. In the 1842 Latimer case, he had voided a state personal liberty law in so far as it applied to fugitives, and had remanded Latimer to his master's custody. Shaw's conduct in the Shadrach case was also revealing. It would have been contrary to the man had his opinion in the Sims case taken any other turn than it did.

. . .

Many of the city's first merchants were present in the court room to hear Shaw's opinion—only a favored audience was permitted entry. George Bancroft, the historian, testified before a committee of the state Senate that while a plain citizen of Massachusetts could not obtain admittance within her halls of justice, he could do so by saying to the officers at the door, "I am a gentleman from the South!" When the opinion was read, the merchants in attendance, "who had swallowed their dinner in a hurry to get this as the dessert," muttered, "Good, good." The anti-slavery men grieved over the decision; "most painful," reported Elizur Wright's paper, the *Commonwealth*. "What a moment was lost when Judge Shaw declined to affirm the unconstitutionality of the Fugitive Slave Law!" exclaimed Emerson: "This filthy enactment was made in the nineteenth century by people who could read and write. I will not obey it, by God." Theodore Parker wrote to Charles Sumner that he never had had any confidence in the Supreme Judicial Court anyway, adding with spiteful glee: "But think of old stiff-necked Lemuel visibly going under the chains! That was a spectacle!"

For public consumption, however, the abolitionists trumpeted the theme of the ermine having been dragged in the dust, and they libeled Shaw for having "spit in the face of Massachusetts. . . ." Benjamin Thomas, later Shaw's associate on the high bench, was much closer to the truth in his estimate. He wrote that although there were "portions of that opinion which did not command our assent . . . it is not difficult to understand or to respect the position of the Chief Justice on the subject." Thomas added that Shaw "was so simple, honest, upright, and straightforward, it never occurred to him there was any way around, over, under, or through the barrier of the Constitution,—that is the only apology that can be made for him." But no apology need be made for him if one accepts his debatable premise that the decisions of the United States Supreme Court sustaining the Act of 1793 must be taken as controlling precedents for the Act of 1850.

After Shaw's decision, the abolitionists frantically redoubled their activity. From pulpit, press, and platform, they thundered condemnation. The ultras among them conspired to rescue Sims by lawless means. Fantastic schemes were plotted; all but one were abandoned as impractical. The one was to have Sims jump from the window of his Court House prison to a waiting carriage. But almost at the last minute the rescue was blocked: new iron bars were fitted in the window.

All week, while rescue plans were being discussed and public opinion agitated, Sims' lawyers tried to save him by due process. The proceedings before Curtis continued, and a bewildering number of new actions were instituted, before Judge Peleg Sprague of the United States District Court and Justice Levi Woodbury of the United States Supreme Court, on circuit. Every writ and petition was defeated. Then, on Friday, April 11, Commissioner Curtis delivered his opinion, remanding Sims to the custody of the agent who claimed him. So ended the legal proceedings against Thomas Sims. During the black hours of Saturday morning, a guard of three hundred armed men led the slave through the streets of the sleeping city. At Long Wharf the brig *Acorn*, armed with cannon, received him. Before dawn, he was on the way back to his master.

In Boston, most of the respectable citizenry were relieved to be done with a disagreeable but necessary job. To the benefit of peace and profits, the majesty of the law had prevailed. *The Commonwealth* of April 14 accurately summed up the city's press: "'Boston is redeemed!' shouts all hunkerdom, 'the Fugitive Slave Law has been enforced!'" The *Boston Herald* (April 14) was proud that the city had verified its mettle: "Our city has been redeemed from the opprobrious epithets which have been denounced against her, for her supposed inability and disinclination to yield to the laws of the Union, and the South will please accord us all the credit which is due therefore." As if in reply, Sims' "home town" paper, the *Savannah Republican*, acknowledged its "pleasant duty to accord to the authorities and people of Boston great credit for the firm and energetic manner in which they have demeaned themselves." The paper was particularly pleased with Chief Justice Shaw's decision. Another Savannah journal, however, was most crabbed about the manner in which Sims was returned. "If our people," it declared, "are obliged to *steal their property out of Boston in the night*, it would be more profitable to adopt a regular kidnapping system at once, without regard to law." The nearby *Augusta Republic* responded in much the same way, adding that the slave could never have been returned had it not been for "the countenance and support of a numerous, wealthy, and powerful body of citizens. It was in evidence that fifteen hundred of the most wealthy and respectable citizens—merchants, bankers and others—volunteered their services to aid the Marshal."

. . .

VII.   Not until the spring of 1854 was Boston again—and for the last time—convulsed by the fate of an escaped slave captured in its streets. Lemuel Shaw was not a participant in the Anthony Burns case, which was the most tragic and thrilling of its kind, but his Court did not wholly escape involvement. After Transcendentalist poets and preachers attacked the Court House in a vain effort to rescue Burns, the building was converted into an armored slave-pen, guarded by a detachment of United States marines, two companies of artillery with cannon, rifles, and fixed bayonets, and the United States Marshal's guard, "a gang of about one-hundred and twenty men, the lowest villains in the community, keepers of brothels, bullies, blacklegs, convicts. . . ." No one was permitted into the Court House, neither judges, jurors, witnesses, nor litigants, without first passing a cordon five men deep, and proving a right to be there. During this siege, the state courts were scheduled to be in session but adjourned in most cases, while United States Commissioner Edward G. Loring, in a mockery of the canons of judicial neutrality, consigned Burns to slavery. Burns' counsel, Dana, lamented in his diary:

> Thus the judiciary of Massachusetts has been a second time put under the feet of the lowest tribunal of the federal judiciary in a proceeding under the Fugitive Slave Law. Judge Shaw, who held the Supreme Judicial Court, is a man of no courage or pride, and Judge Bishop, who held the court of Common Pleas is a mere party tool, and a bag of wind at that. It was the clear duty of the court to summon before it the United States marshal to show cause why he should not be committed for contempt, and to commit him, if it required all the bayonets in Massachusetts to do it, unless he allowed free passage to all persons who desired to come into either of the courts of the State.

Dana was overwrought when he made his remark about Shaw. But the Chief Justice was entitled to no credit for his tacit submission to the bayonets which closed his court. By his inaction he permitted what was in effect the rule of martial law for the sake of "Union-saving" measures. In the critical years before the Civil War, few men who labored constructively under public responsibility escaped unblemished from a compromise with slavery.

Less than two weeks after President Pierce signed the Kansas-Nebraska Act, destroyer of sectional peace, Anthony Burns' freedom was sacrificed to the Fugitive Slave Law. A military escort of two thousand men marched the lone slave out of black-draped Boston, its flags at half-mast, while the people of the city watched in shame. Just as the rendition of Sims had helped elect Sumner to the Senate, so the rendition of Burns, together with the despised Kansas-Nebraska Act, led to a new and drastic Massachusetts Personal Liberty Law.

This statute, which Shaw opposed, obligated the justices of the Supreme Judicial Court to take fugitive slaves from the custody of the federal marshal, by habeas corpus, and to have the slaveowner's claim tried by a jury in a state court. The governor, upon advisement by the Supreme Judicial Court, returned this bill unsigned, quoting the Court's opinion that state authorities could not interfere with a person in the custody of federal officers under United States law. The measure, adopted without the governor's signature, provided in addition that a federal commissioner empowered to issue certificates of rendition could hold no state judicial office; nor could any lawyer who acted as a counsel to a slaveowner in a fugitive slave case practice thereafter in the courts of the state. In these provisions, the personal liberty law was probably an unconstitutional bill of attainder, but neither in whole nor in part was it ever tested before the Court. The statute was partly directed against Commissioner Loring for his rendition of Burns, and under its terms he was removed from office as Judge of Probate. Popular resentment against him was so feverish that he was also dismissed from his post on the Harvard Law School faculty, despite a recommendation in his favor by Lemuel Shaw, Fellow of the Harvard Corporation.

VIII. On August 21, 1860, Shaw resigned from the bench. He was free at last to express himself on public matters as a private citizen. . . .

[I]n his final public act, Shaw headed a group of prominent conciliationists who hoped to appease the South by recommending unconditional repeal of Massachusetts' Personal Liberty Laws. In an "Address" published on December 18, the signatories, "impelled by no motive save the love of our country," warned:

> The foundations of our government are shaken, and unless the work of destruction shall be stayed, we may soon see that great union . . . broken into weak, discordant, and shattered fragments; and that people, who have dwelt under its protection in unexampled peace and prosperity, shedding fraternal blood in civil war.

Urging their fellow citizens first to examine their own conduct for "causes which threaten a great people with ruin," before demanding loyalty to the Constitution from the South, the signers documented their conviction that Massachusetts itself "has violated our great national compact" by its personal liberty laws. Such laws, commanding interference by the state with the laws of the national government, were "laws commanding civil war." There followed a fervent plea for sanity in the conduct of state affairs. Were Massachusetts "honestly and generously" to discharge its obligations under the Fugitive Slave Act and to repeal the provoking statutes, then secession might be given pause and the Union preserved. Five days later, South Carolina seceded.

CHAPTER 11

The Civil War

The cooperation of northern states in the enforcement of the Fugitive Slave Law was an emotionally charged issue, but it involved relatively few slaves and a relatively minor threat to slavery in the South. Far more consequential was the issue of slavery in the territories.

The territorial issue surfaced as early as 1787 when the Northwest Ordinance prohibited slavery in the Northwest Territories. No such provision was made at the time of the Louisiana Purchase in 1803, and the issue surfaced again in 1820 when Missouri petitioned to be admitted as the first state carved out of the Louisiana Territory. A compromise was reached by the admission of Missouri as a slave state and the simultaneous admission of Maine as a free state. To keep the lid on the issue for the future, Congress also agreed to draw a line across the western territories designating south of the line as slave, north of the line as free.

The Missouri Compromise held for over two decades, but both the South and the North became dissatisfied with it in the 1840s. As Texas split off from Mexico and the United States won the 1846–1847 Mexican War, huge new lands were added south of the Missouri Compromise line. Northern congressmen attempted to keep slavery out of the new southwestern territories by the so-called Wilmot Proviso, a bill which lost in a closely divided Congress. Another compromise—the Compromise of 1850—admitted Texas as a slave state and California as a free state, but the issue continued to fester as southerners agitated for slavery in Kansas Territory north of the Missouri Compromise line. Their effort led to another divisive session in which Congress passed the Kansas-Nebraska Act in 1854 giving settlers "popular sovereignty," allowing them to choose whether to become free or slave states. Popular sovereignty, in turn, led to armed violence between the settlers, foreshadowing the Civil War.

Two political parties dominated the political scene at mid-century: the Democrats represented populist, Jacksonian tendencies; the Whigs, formed in the 1830s, opposed such tendencies and favored manufacturing and commercial interests. In the 1850s, the Whigs self-destructed largely over sectional divisions. At the same time, the Democrats became largely sectional, adopting a pro-South, proslavery position. In response, a sectional party, the Republicans, organized in the North.

The Republicans took an uncompromising position against further extension of slavery in the territories, but they were not abolitionists. They were willing to reassure existing slave states of their right to retain slavery—even proposing a constitutional amendment to that effect. Southern states did not consider that protection enough.

Although the South feared becoming a minority in Congress, there was a southern, proslavery majority on the Supreme Court. The majority's opportunity to support the southern cause came in 1857 as a slave, Dred Scott, taken by his master to the free Wisconsin Territory, sued for his freedom. The Supreme Court ruled against Dred Scott 7 to 2 , with an opinion written by Chief Justice Roger B. Taney and supported by six separately written concurrences.

Chief Justice Taney pronounced that Dred Scott, even if freed, was not a "citizen" and, therefore, had no standing to bring a suit. Although this was sufficient to dispose of the case, Taney's decision went on to a more sweeping dictum. According to Don E. Fehrenbacher's *Slavery, Law, and Politics: The Dred Scott Case in Historical Perspective* (1981):

> Rightly or not, permanently or not, the Supreme Court had written two new rules into the fundamental law of the nation: first that no Negro could be a United States citizen or even a state citizen "within the meaning of the Constitution"; and second, that Congress had no power to prohibit slavery in the territories, and that accordingly all legislation embodying such prohibition, including the Missouri Compromise, was unconstitutional. (p. 4)

As the North elected a Republican president in 1860—the relatively inexperienced Illinois lawyer, Abraham Lincoln—some still hoped to preserve the union. Lincoln gave voice to such hope on several occasions. But soon after Lincoln's inauguration, South Carolina declared its secession, followed rapidly by six other slaveholding states, and on April 12, 1861, South Carolina troops fired on Fort Sumter to wrest it from federal control. War was never officially declared, but exactly one week after the Fort Sumter attack, the North responded with an equally unambiguous act of war—the blockade of southern ports ordered by presidential proclamation.

Congress was in recess and the new president had to take charge. Resources, industries, transportation had to be harnessed to the war effort. Enlistment of volunteers was called for (later, military conscription would cause riots in the North) and internal security had to be assured.

The issue of internal security was far more challenging than it would have been in a war with foreign enemies. In a civil war—pitting "brother against brother"—it was extremely difficult to sort out citizens according to their loyalties, especially in the border states.

An immediate problem was the location of the capital. The slave state of Maryland lay between Washington and the free states. Maryland was not among the early secession states, but after Fort Sumter, many in Maryland agitated for secession, and some formed groups to prevent the passage of northern troops to the defense of Washington. President Lincoln gave the federal military extraordinary authority to secure the transport routes through Maryland by martial law, including the power to suspend habeas corpus. As the war progressed, the military's authority was extended to other areas of military operations, to territories wrested from the South, and eventually to citizens anywhere who expressed "sympathies for those in arms against the Government of the United States," or declared "disloyal sentiments and opinions, with the object and purpose of weakening the . . . Government in its effort to suppress the unlawful rebellion," or gave "aid and comfort to Rebels against the authority of the United States." Many thousands were thus interned summarily by military tribunals. Some accused Lincoln of using the suspension of habeas corpus to suppress the Democratic party. But court challenges were ineffective, and in 1863, Congress acted to validate the suspensions by statute.

Dred Scott.
Painting by Louis Schultze, 1881. Missouri Historical Society, St. Louis.

PRESIDENT ABRAHAM LINCOLN

from Mark E. Neely, Jr., *The Fate of Liberty:*
Abraham Lincoln and Civil Liberties
(New York: Oxford University Press, 1991), pp. 210–22.
Copyright © 1991 by Mark E. Neely, Jr.
Reprinted by permission of Oxford University Press, Inc.

Lincoln and the Constitution

Whig Heritage

Lincoln had been a Whig for most of the life of that political party—twice as long as he was a Republican. And the Whigs generally took a broad view of what the Constitution allowed the federal government to do (create a national bank and fund the building of canals, roads, and railroads, for example). As a victim of rural isolation and lack of economic opportunity in his youth, Abraham Lincoln proved eager as a politician to provide the country with those things that seemed wanting in his hardscrabble past. His desire to get on with economic development made him impatient with Democratic arguments that internal improvements funded by the federal government were unconstitutional.

After years of political struggle to implement improvement schemes, Lincoln, as a congressman in the late 1840s, saw "the question of improvements ... verging to a final crisis." The Democratic national platform in 1848 declared that "the constitution does not confer upon the general government the power to commence, and carry on a general system of internal improvements." Speaking on the subject in the House of Representatives, the 39-year-old Lincoln expressed plainly his mature judgment that "no man, who is clear on the questions of expediency, needs feel his conscience much pricked upon this."

Emphasis on the practical was characteristic of Lincoln, but his confidence in this instance stemmed in part from a belief that the constitutional arguments were also on his side. In the Civil War, Lincoln would again suggest practical reasons for action and then add assurances and proofs that the Constitution permitted it anyhow.

In his 1848 speech on the internal improvements crisis, Lincoln laid unusual emphasis on constitutional subject matter. Despite his assertion that practical demands for internal improvements should weigh heavily against constitutional doubt or controversy, Lincoln seemed preoccupied with constitutional questions in the speech, devoting eight of twenty-six paragraphs, almost a third of his time, to that issue. He began these arguments with a modest disclaimer:

> Mr. Chairman, on the . . . constitutional question, I have not much to say. Being the man I am, and speaking when I do, I feel, that in any attempt at an original constitutional argument, I should not be, and ought not to be, listened to patiently. The ablest, and the best of men, have gone over the whole ground long ago.

Lincoln followed this by quoting and summarizing at some length arguments from Kent's *Commentaries*.

The Democratic president, James K. Polk, had suggested that it would require a constitutional amendment to make such internal improvements possible. Lincoln did not much like this idea, in part no doubt because of its impracticability and time-consuming nature, but in the speech, he attacked it in the language of sweeping constitutional conservatism.

> I have already said that no one, who is satisfied of the expediency of making improvements, needs be much uneasy in his conscience about its constitutionality. I wish now to submit a few remarks on the general proposition of amending the constitution. As a general rule, I think, we would [do] much better [to] let it alone. No slight occasion should tempt us to touch it. Better not take the first step, which may lead to a habit of altering it. Better, rather, habituate ourselves to think of it, as unalterable. It can scarcely be made better than it is. New provisions, would introduce new difficulties, and thus create, and increase appetite for still further change. No sir, let it stand as it is. New hands have never touched it. The men who made it, have done their work, and have passed away. Who shall improve, on what *they* did?

Often quoted in later years, this passage had rather a different meaning in context from what constitutional conservatives since his day have imagined. What Congressman Lincoln was really saying was that no amendment was needed if a reasonably broad interpretation of the existing document were accepted.

. . .

Slavery and the Constitution

At the very time that Abraham Lincoln's awareness of constitutional questions was on the rise, the issue of slavery in the territories was injected into American politics. The Wilmot Proviso, which would have forbidden slavery in any territory acquired as a result of the Mexican War, came up several times while Lincoln was in Congress, and he consistently voted for it. But the slavery controversy did not make a constitutional thinker of Lincoln, any more than the old economic issues of the 1830s and 1840s had.

This sets Lincoln apart from his era. A leading historian . . . has criticized its era for a tendency to make every political question into a constitutional question: "The tendency to debate the constitutionality of issues rather than their expediency did little to temper the discussion; if anything, it exacerbated differences." This volatile constitutionalism became even more a factor in the era that followed. The 1850s . . . witnessed the increasing "fashion of constitutionalizing debate on slavery." When pressed, Lincoln voiced an antislavery interpretation of the Constitution, but he was not one to constitutionalize the debate over slavery or anything else.

Lincoln did think more about the Constitution after 1848 than in previous decades, but his ideas were quite unoriginal. He viewed the document as most antislavery moderates did, shunning the anti-Constitution "covenant-with-death" views of the abolitionists and their unconstitutional political positions as well. He embraced the interpretation of the Constitution as a reluctant guarantor of the slave interest existing at the time of the country's founding. The Constitution betrayed the basically antislavery sentiments of its authors by hiding slavery "away, . . . just as an afflicted man hides away a wen or a cancer, which he dares not cut out at once, lest he bleed to death; with the promise, nevertheless, that the cutting may begin at the end of a given time." Like many of his fellow Republicans, Lincoln attributed great importance to the absence of any explicit mention of slavery or the Negro race in the document. It seemed a sure sign that the founders looked forward to the day when, with slavery eradicated by time, there would be "nothing in the constitution to remind them of it."

Lincoln was a lawyer, but antislavery sentiment and Whig tradition go farther than professional outlook to explain Lincoln's views of the Constitution. The influence of Lincoln's profession on his political ideas has been exaggerated in recent years: "the last Blackstone Lawyer to lead the nation," one writer calls him. Such views have been expressed especially by biographers and historians interested in what is widely regarded as "Lincoln's first speech of distinction," his address to the Young Men's Lyceum of Springfield, delivered January 27, 1838. This speech contained not so much constitutional views as cheerleading for the laws of the land and was widely quoted in later years:

> Let reverence for the laws, be breathed by every American mother, to the lisping babe, that prattles on her lap—let it be taught in schools, in seminaries, and in colleges;—let it be written in Primmers, spelling books and in Almanacs;—let it be

preached from the pulpit, proclaimed in legislative halls, and enforced in courts of justice. And, in short, let it become the *political religion* of the nation; and let the old and the young, the rich and the poor, the grave and the gay, of all sexes and tongues, and colors and conditions, sacrifice unceasingly upon its altars.

Lincoln mentioned the Constitution itself at the end of the speech, when he invoked "Reason, cold calculating, unimpassioned reason" to "furnish all the materials for our future support and defense. Let those [materials] be moulded into *general intelligence*, [sound] *morality* and, in particular, *a reverence for the constitution and laws.*"

Thus, Lincoln gave "eloquent expression to the developing ideology of his profession," according to historian George M. Fredrickson, who sees "Lincoln's early speeches as an aspiring young lawyer and Whig politician" as part of a "'conservative' response to the unruly and aggressive democracy spawned by the age of Jackson." Indeed Fredrickson finds this conservative law-and-order strain in Lincoln's political thought substantially unshaken until the *Dred Scott* decision of 1857 undermined "Lincoln's faith in the bench and bar as the ultimate arbiters of constitutional issues." The problem with such an interpretation stems mainly from its approach, that of "intellectual history," for Abraham Lincoln was neither an intellectual nor a systematic political thinker. He was a politician, and historians ignore the instrumental side of his political thought only at great peril. He rarely thought abstractly about the Constitution and the laws. He usually thought about them when a particularly pressing political problem arose. At the time of the Lyceum speech in 1838, Lincoln's recent admission to the Illinois bar was surely a less important circumstance than the political situation. The purpose of the speech was to urge the protection of unpopular minorities. Lincoln mentioned recent headlines describing mob violence and vigilante justice that victimized Mississippi gamblers and unfortunate black people. Most other interpreters of Lincoln's speech in modern times have assumed that the real shadow hanging over it was that of the martyred Elijah Lovejoy, killed just prior to the address by an anti-abolition mob in Alton, Illinois. To say that Lincoln here was at odds with democracy in the age of Jackson is either unfair to Lincoln or paints a dark caricature of Jacksonian democracy.

Lincoln was not searching so much for order and community as for usable arguments and instruments. That is not to say that his constitutional thinking was nakedly opportunistic or embarrassingly shallow, but only that he changed his mind from time to time and that he did not characteristically reach first for a copy of the U.S. Constitution when confronted with a political or social problem. Even to survey Lincoln's ideas on the Constitution is to run the risk of overemphasizing his constitutional concerns, because thinking in constitutional ways did not come naturally to him. It was more often forced on him. . . .

Whatever the Lyceum address may seem to mean, it is, in fact, difficult to find any threads of legalistic, procedural, or constitutional conservatism woven into Lincoln's political thought of the 1850s, even before the *Dred Scott* decision. Lincoln quickly embraced a moralistic antislavery ideology that pointed to the Declaration of Independence and the political libertarianism of Thomas Jefferson as its fundamental source while relegating the Constitution and the laws to a rather pale secondary role. Shortly after the passage of the Kansas-Nebraska Act in 1854, Lincoln told an audience in Springfield on October 4 that the "theory of our government is Universal Freedom. 'All men are created free and equal,' says the Declaration of Independence. The word 'Slavery' is not found in the Constitution." His political message varied little from this until 1861.

Jefferson and the Declaration of Independence assumed a conspicuous place in Lincoln's political imagery in this period. Nevertheless, careful readers of the previous paragraph will have noted, perhaps a little impatiently, that the Declaration did *not* say that all men were created "free" and equal. Lincoln did not take his political ideas straight and by rote from any single printed source, but of their many sources, the slogans of Thomas Jefferson proved to be of greater importance than the words of the Constitution and of increasing importance to Lincoln after 1854. On October 16, 1854, he spoke of "Mr. Jefferson, the author of the Declaration of Independence," as "the most distinguished politician of our history." He justified his anti-Nebraska stand by saying that "the policy of prohibiting slavery in new territory originated" with Jefferson and the Northwest Ordinance. The policy began "away back of the constitution, in the pure fresh, free breath of the revolution." . . .

[A]ntislavery Republicans like Lincoln embraced an antislavery interpretation of (or created an antislavery myth about) the Constitution. "This same generation of men," he said, "mostly the same individuals . . . who declared this principle [of self-government]—who declared independence—who fought the war of the revolution through—who afterwards made the constitution under which we still live—these same men passed the ordinance of '87, declaring that slavery should never go to the north-west territory." With such language as this, Lincoln made of the founders a single cohort of heroes who drafted the Declaration of Independence, won the Revolution, and wrote the Constitution.

In truth, the Constitution stood as an embarrassment to the antislavery cause. It protected slavery in the states as surely as it did anything, and all politicians, Republican and Democrat alike, knew it. The best the antislavery politicians could do was to find antislavery tendencies in the document. In building a mythical past for his political platform, Lincoln preferred to state the antislavery interpretation of the Constitution and get on quickly past that document to the Declaration of Independence. In a speech in Chicago on July 10, 1858, for example, he said, "We had slavery among us, we could not get our constitution unless we permitted them to remain in slavery, we could not secure the good we did secure if we grasped for more, and having by necessity submitted to that much, it does not destroy the principle that is the charter of our liberties. Let that charter stand as our standard." The spirit of the Constitution, properly and carefully looked at, was antagonistic to the Kansas-Nebraska bill, Lincoln could say after elaborate argument, but it was easier to say that the "spirit of seventy-six" and "the spirit of Nebraska" were "utter antagonisms."

After the *Dred Scott* decision, Lincoln's constitutional views changed little, and his overall political thought, less. The Taney court's decision may have accelerated his rush to the Declaration of Independence. In a Springfield speech after the decision, Lincoln asked: "I should like to know if taking this old Declaration of Independence, which declares that all men are equal upon principle and making exceptions to it where will it stop. . . . If that declaration is not the truth, let us get the Statute book, in which we find it and tear it out!" Of course, the Declaration of Independence was not law, as the Constitution was, and could not properly be located in a "statute book." Lincoln knew this and, when not on the stump, could write about it in more lawyerly fashion. In an 1858 letter to an Illinois politician named James N. Brown, Lincoln said more soberly: "I believe the declara[tion] that 'all men are created equal' is the great fundamental principle upon which our free institutions rest; that negro slavery is violative of the principle; but that, by our frame of government, that principle has not been made one of legal obligation." The *Dred Scott* decision merely forced Lincoln to articulate his view of what makes a lasting Supreme Court decision, which he did with characteristic avoidance of Latinate distinctions. Speaking rhetorically to the Southern people early in 1860, Lincoln pointed out what he thought were good reasons for doubting the force of this Supreme Court decision:

> Perhaps you will say the Supreme Court has decided the disputed Constitutional question in your favor. Not quite so. But waiving the lawyer's distinction between dictum and decision, the Court have decided the question for you in a sort of way. The Court have substantially said, it is your Constitutional right to take slaves into the federal territories, and to hold them there as property. When I say the decision was made in a sort of way, I mean it was made in a divided Court, by a bare majority of the Judges, and they not quite agreeing with one another in the reasons for making it; that it is so made as that its avowed supporters disagree with one another about its meaning, and that it was mainly based upon a mistaken statement of fact—the statement in the opinion that "the right of property in a slave is distinctly and expressly affirmed in the Constitution."

Here, in challenging Taney's careless opinion, the Republicans' emphasis on the absence of the words "slave," "slavery," or "property" in connection with the idea of slavery, was all the constitutional doctrine Lincoln needed.

War and the Constitution

Once Lincoln became president and faced civil war, his clear record on the Constitution became paradoxical and unclear. To be sure, his constitutional outlook all along had left room for the argument of "Necessity." Lincoln demonstrated this years before the Civil War, and not only in recognition of the founders' necessary protection of slavery in the U.S. Constitution. In 1854, while reviewing the history of the slavery-expansion controversy in a speech in Bloomington, Illinois, Lincoln stated matter-of-factly: "Jefferson saw the necessity of our government possessing the whole valley of the Mississippi; and though he acknowledged that our Constitution made no provision for the purchasing of territory, yet he thought the exigency of the case would justify the measure, and the purchase was made." As a Whig and a critic of the Mexican War, Lincoln's record was not as pro-expansion as that of most western politicians, but he admired Jefferson and agreed that the Louisiana Purchase was too good an opportunity to miss, no matter what the Constitution said. The prompt development of an attitude of indifference to the niceties of constitutional interpretation involved in suspending the writ of habeas corpus might have been predicted from the unpricked constitutional conscience of Lincoln's pre-presidential career. He naturally responded vigorously to the exigency of civil war. But on the question of emancipation, Lincoln appeared to some antislavery advocates at the time and to many historians since to have been strangely stricken with a paralyzing constitutional scrupulousness. When it came to putting the spirit of seventy-six into action, Lincoln as president grew suspiciously reluctant.

The most telling event was his revocation of Fremont's emancipation proclamation in Missouri in 1861. In a moment of pique . . . President Lincoln now lectured fellow Republican Orville Hickman Browning on the constitutional issues involved. . . . Lincoln had not bothered to mention the Constitution or to dwell on law in first reprimanding Fremont, but once Browning brought it up, the president waded in:

> Genl. Fremont's proclamation, as to confiscation of property, and the liberation of slaves, is *purely political,* and not within the range of *military* law, or necessity. If a commanding General finds a necessity to seize the farm of a private owner, for a pasture, an encampment, or a fortification, he has the right to do so, and to so hold it, as long as the necessity lasts; and this is within military law, because within military necessity. But to say the farm shall no longer belong to the owner, or his heirs forever; and this as well when the farm is not needed for military purposes as when it is, is purely political, without the savor of military law about it. And the same is true of slaves. If the General needs them, he can seize them, and use them; but when the need is past, it is not for him to fix their permanent future condition. That must be settled according to laws made by law-makers, and not by military proclamations. The proclamation in the point in question, is simply

"dictatorship." It assumes that the general may do *anything* he pleases—confiscate the lands and free the slaves of *loyal* people, as well as of disloyal ones. I cannot assume this reckless position; nor allow others to assume it on my responsibility. You speak of it as being the only means of *saving* the government. On the contrary it is itself the surrender of the government. Can it be pretended that it is any longer the government of the U.S.—any government of Constitution and laws,—wherein a General, or a President, may make permanent rules of property by proclamation?

I do not say Congress might not with propriety pass a law, on the point, just such as General Fremont proclaimed. I do not say I might not, as a member of Congress, vote for it. What I object to, is, that I as President, shall expressly or impliedly seize and exercise the permanent legislative functions of the government.

When he finished that part of the letter, Lincoln wrote, "So much for principle. Now as to policy." And then he proceeded to talk about Kentucky. It seems striking that when delaying freedom for the slave, Lincoln thought first of constitutional principle, then of policy. But policy considerations came first with him in dealing with the crisis following the firing on Fort Sumter. Was he willing to go farther to save the Union than to free the slaves? Did he value the Union more than liberty after all?

To answer those questions will require a quick review of American thinking on the subject of emancipation and war before Abraham Lincoln faced both as live subjects rather than abstract possibilities. The review can be brief because there had been little thought on the subject and because what little thought there was had been clearly and succinctly put by an intelligent politician, John Quincy Adams. After his return to Washington as a member of the House of Representatives, "Old Man Eloquent" attempted to avenge his loss of reelection to the presidency in 1828 by attacking Southerners and the "Slave Power." In a debate in Congress as early as 1836, Adams expressed the belief that from "the instant that our slaveholding states become the theater of war, civil, servile or foreign . . . the war powers of Congress extend to interference with the institution of slavery in every way by which it can be interfered with." During the early rounds of the Texas controversy in 1842, when war was much spoken of, Adams again warned Southerners that Congress would have "full and plenary power" over slavery in a state at war. . . .

Lincoln's constitutional journey was similar to Adams's. When President Lincoln revoked the Missouri proclamation in September 1861, he had already abandoned any belief that slavery, because of the Constitution, could not be touched in the states where it then existed. Generals could not fix the "permanent future condition" of the slaves in Missouri but the slaves' status could "be settled according to laws made by law-makers." Such an idea, daring though it was, did not fully anticipate the constitutional grounds of Lincoln's actions a year later when he announced his own Emancipation Proclamation, because Lincoln was no "law-maker." He was head of the executive branch; Congress made the laws. . . .

What has never been noticed in the furor over the Fremont proclamation is how far Lincoln already had traveled down John Quincy Adams's constitutional road in 1861. Although Lincoln would never reach the point where he believed a general could proclaim emancipation, within less than a year of the Fremont episode, he had reached Adams's view that the president could do so. What Lincoln learned, between September 1861 and the drafting of the Emancipation Proclamation in July 1862, was not Adams's view that war threatened slavery; Lincoln knew that already. He learned, perhaps from William Whiting's *War Powers of the President,* published in 1862, that war gave the president and not law-makers only the power to abolish slavery in enemy territory.

Lincoln moved faster in adjusting his prewar ideas about the Constitution and slavery than most historians have previously believed. What he said to Browning, admittedly, was said in private. In public, Lincoln's utterances sounded more skeptical, but his constitutional doubts had clearly been dispersed well before the public announcement of the Emancipation Proclamation on September 22, 1862, and he wanted the public to know it. His famous letter of August 22, 1862, to Horace Greeley, counseling patience on the slavery question, said nothing of constitutional obstacles to action and expressed a willingness to free slaves, if such action would save the Union. On September 13, he explicitly told a delegation of Chicago Christians urging emancipation: "I raise no objections against it on legal or constitutional grounds; for, as commander-in-chief of the army and navy, in time of war, I suppose I have a right to take any measure which may best subdue the enemy." Emancipation was for him "a practical war measure" and as soon as military circumstances at the front seemed to require it and political circumstances in the border states seemed to permit it, Lincoln acted to end slavery in the Confederacy.

Lincoln did worry more about the consequences of emancipation than the consequences of suspending the writ of habeas corpus—and for good reason. Lincoln regarded the suspension of the writ as an exception for a temporary emergency, and he felt sure that the American people would never want to continue the condition when the emergency was over. He put it more vividly, of course, comparing such an unimaginable course to that of a man fed emetics in illness and then insisting on "feeding upon them the remainder of his healthful life." . . .

Emancipation was different. Though it might be adopted as a practical measure to end the war, it could not be reversed when the crisis was over. As Lincoln put it in his letter to Browning about the slaves in Missouri, "If the General needs them, he can seize them, and use them; but when the need is past, it is not for him to fix their permanent future condition. That must be settled according to laws." Emancipation, though perhaps a matter of situational ethics in the midst of war, would necessarily affect American society for all time to come. Lincoln was a practical man, all right, but he did occasionally think about the country's "permanent future condition." He saw no danger in the temporary suspension of habeas corpus during rebellion or invasion, but the case of black people was clearly different. Only rigid safeguards would protect freedmen from popular race prejudice and possible reenslavement. Black freedom might prove as temporary and situational as the whites' brief loss of customary liberties during the Civil War. So Lincoln's thoughts necessarily turned to a constitutional amendment to end slavery in the United States.

This was a major change in his constitutional thinking. The Constitution was last amended five years before Abraham Lincoln was born. He was on record in a speech in Congress recommending that the document be left alone and that the American people not get into the habit of changing it. In the desperate throes of the secession crisis, he did agree to a proposed amendment that would have explicitly guaranteed slavery where it already existed. But this was redundant in Lincoln's view, merely reassuring the South of what it already had. In 1864, he wanted an amendment to guarantee that there would be nothing temporary about emancipation.

This ability to balance short-term practicality and long-term ideals is perhaps the essence of statesmanship. In Lincoln's case, the one helped preserve the Constitution as the law of the land, and the other brought such changes as made it worth preserving "throughout the indefinite peaceful future."

CHAPTER 12

Reconstruction and Formalism

Amendments to the Constitution following the Civil War promised an era of racial justice. The Thirteenth Amendment abolished slavery; the Fourteenth prohibited abridgment of the "privileges and immunities of citizens" or deprivation of "life, liberty, or property, without due process of law" and provided for "equal protection of the laws;" the Fifteenth protected voting rights. But the promise was betrayed soon after the war as the assassination of Abraham Lincoln brought the nation an administration more interested in conciliation with the southern states than with justice for the freed slaves. An effort to impeach Lincoln's successor, Andrew Johnson, was defeated by one vote and the promise of the Reconstruction era was abandoned for an era of "Jim Crow" laws that placed freed slaves in a disenfranchised, segregated, and disadvantaged status. The courts abetted the process. In the *Civil Rights* cases (1883) the Supreme Court limited civil-rights protections to "state action," and in *Plessy* v. *Ferguson* (1896) even state-imposed segregation was upheld.

The main interests of the country in the following decades turned from issues of racial justice and federal-state relations to issues of economics. Rapid industrialization created huge concentrations of wealth as well as a huge urbanized working class increased by a swelling tide of immigration. Unruly financial practices brought on an economic depression in the 1870s. But attempts to regulate business were thwarted by the courts. In the "Golden Age" of the early part of the century, statutes and judicial opinions in such fields as contracts, torts, corporations, and labor relations largely favored business interests. In the postwar era, the judiciary resorted to a "formalism" in interpretation, limiting legislative attempts to swing the pendulum back.

The judges were not alone. Their formalist tendencies received support from legal scholars and the bar. Under the sway of the then-fashionable ideas of three Englishmen—the eighteenth-century economist Adam Smith, prophet of *laissez faire*; the nineteenth-century philosopher Herbert Spencer, who applied the concept to society at large; and his contemporary, the naturalist Charles Darwin, whose theory of evolution extended the concept to the whole animal kingdom—scholars, lawyers, and judges alike interpreted law formalistically to shield business from government regulation.

Thomas M. Cooley, a judge as well as a law professor, wrote the most influential American law book of the late nineteenth century: *A Treatise on the Constitutional Limitations Which Rest upon the Legislative Power of the States of the American Union* (1868, with seven subsequent editions). The title reveals the prevalent distrust of legislatures. Cooley considered both legislative favoritism toward business and legislative attempts to regulate business as beyond the powers of legislatures, except in circumstances within the "police powers" of government. Cooley was willing to grant considerable scope to "police powers," but most courts interpreted Cooley's treatise to limit legislatures. Cooley's follower, Christopher G. Tiedeman, in his book *A Treatise on the Limitations of Police Power in the United States* (1889), went even further than the most formalist judges, questioning the constitutionality of legislation regulating usury, gambling, and drugs—as well as wages, hours, and tariffs.

Some have attributed the formalism of the era to the class biases of the judiciary and the bar. But, as in evaluating the early part of the century, some have seen a variety of motivations. One of the most respected legal historians, James Willard Hurst, in his *Law and the Conditions of Freedom in Nineteenth-Century United States* (1956), has written:

> It has been common to label nineteenth-century legal policy as simple laissez faire, and political debate of the last sixty years has propagated a myth of a Golden Age in which our ancestors—sturdier than we—got along well enough if the legislature provided schools, the sheriff ran down horse thieves, the court tried farmers' title disputes, and otherwise the law left men to take care of themselves.
>
> The record is different. Not the jealous limitation of the power of the state, but the release of individual creative energy was the dominant value. Where legal regulation or compulsion might promote the greater release of individual or group energies, we had no hesitancy in making affirmative use of law. (p. 7)

State courts took the lead in limiting the powers of legislatures to regulate the economy. The U.S. Supreme Court held back, reluctant to overturn legislation, although some of the justices had the opportunity to act on their own since, in that era, Supreme Court justices also sat as Circuit Court judges. In 1873, in the *Slaughter-House* cases, the Supreme Court upheld a Louisiana statute granting a monopoly of the animal slaughtering business to one company. Two years later, in *Munn* v. *Illinois*, the court refused to strike down an Illinois statute regulating the rates of grain elevators. The majority of the Court reasoned that state police powers extended to the regulation of private property "affected with the public interest."

In both the *Slaughter-House* cases and in *Munn* v. *Illinois*, dissents were filed by Justice Stephen J. Field, one of the most colorful justices ever to serve on the Supreme Court. Though a Californian, Stephen J. Field was the brother of New York's David Dudley Field. The two brothers not only lived on opposite coasts, they also had opposing views of legislatures. While David Dudley Field led the forces favoring codification, Stephen Field felt that legislatures were not to be trusted. According to Stephen Field, the judiciary had to be ever-vigilant to protect private property from the populist pressures of legislators. Stephen Field was appointed to the Supreme Court by President Lincoln in 1863, and he served long enough to see his dissenting views prevail.

Justice Stephen J. Field.
Photo from California Historical Society.

JUSTICE STEPHEN J. FIELD

from G. Edward White, *The American Judicial Tradition,* exp. ed.
(New York: Oxford University Press, 1988), pp. 92–108.
Copyright © 1988 by Oxford University Press, Inc.
Used by permission of Oxford University Press, Inc.

I. . . .

Business, of course, was an honorable word in the later nineteenth century, and . . . Stephen Field was . . . first a representative of and later an apologist for the swashbuckling entrepreneurs who emerged with expanding private enterprise. The son of a New England Congregationalist minister, Field shared the inclination of his brothers, Cyrus, an inventor, and David Dudley, a New York City law practitioner, to seek their fortunes outside the church. A graduate of Williams College, a member of the New York bar, and a sixth-year apprentice in his lawyer brother's office, Field set out for California in pursuit of gold at age thirty-three. He settled in Marysville, northeast of San Francisco, where he became a land speculator, a magistrate with expansive powers, and something of a lawyer. Here he made the first of his numerous enemies, William Turner, later a state judge, who once said in a letter to the Marysville newspaper that Field's life, "if analyzed," would be "found to be a series of little-minded. . . meanlinesses, of braggadocio, pusillanimity, and contemptible vanity." Field later settled his score with Turner by securing election to the California State Legislature and drafting a bill rearranging the state's judicial districts so that Turner's district was relocated in a remote area in northwestern California.

Field's actions in the Turner affair were characteristic: he hated fiercely and long, and was tireless in his efforts to avenge himself on those who had crossed him. When Grover Cleveland, the first Democratic President after the Civil War, was elected in 1884, Field, who had himself been prominent in Democratic circles, asked Cleveland not to appoint certain California enemies of Field to federal offices. When Cleveland subsequently did appoint some of those men, Field vowed never to enter the White House while Cleveland was President. Cleveland returned the compliment by pointedly overlooking Field's candidacy for Chief Justice when Morrison Waite died in 1888.

Field's capacity for controversy and his immersion in the roughest sort of human affairs were encapsulated in the Terry affair, perhaps the most sensational piece of drama in which a Justice of the Supreme Court has ever participated. David Terry, who had served with Field in the California Supreme Court in the 1850s, married one Sarah Hill. When a law suit involving a contested former marriage of Mrs. Terry came before Field, sitting on the Ninth Circuit, he delivered an opinion finding against Mrs. Terry, in the course of which he gave a detailed history of her less than solid past. Upon hearing this, Mrs. Terry jumped up from her seat in the courtroom and protested that Field had been paid to rule against her. Field ruled her out of order and asked that she be removed from the room. Terry responded by knocking down a marshal and brandishing a knife. He and Mrs. Terry were subsequently sentenced to jail for contempt of court. Both made threats against Field's life.

In the summer of 1889, just when the Terrys were due to be released from prison, Field was returning to California to sit on the Ninth Circuit. He was advised not to make the trip and could have avoided it, since circuit visits could be made at two-year intervals. He resolved to go, however, with the comment, "I should be ashamed to look any man in the face if I allowed a ruffian, by threats against my person, to keep me from holding the regular courts in my circuit." Protection was arranged for Field in the person of a bodyguard, David Neagle. In August, Field was returning by train from Los Angeles, where he had held court, to San Francisco, with Neagle accompanying him. The Terry couple happened to board the same train. While taking breakfast in the dining car, Field and Neagle encountered them.

Field had seated himself at a table between the Terrys and the door. Mrs. Terry, on seeing him, rapidly left the dining car. Slightly later, Terry rose and headed toward the door, but as he reached Field's table he suddenly struck Field twice on the side the face. Neagle leaped from his seat and cried "Stop, stop!" Believing that Terry was drawing a knife, he shot him twice, killing him. Mrs. Terry then returned, carrying a satchel with a gun to find her husband dead. Neagle was taken into custody and removed from the train at Stockton.

Mrs. Terry filed a complaint charging Neagle and Field with murder of her husband, and Field was actually arrested; but when the U.S. Attorney General's office put pressure on the local authorities, he was released. Neagle was subsequently exonerated, but not before his case had reached the Supreme Court on a question about the issuance of a federal writ of habeas corpus. The Court, with Field not sitting but rooting in the wings, held that the issuance of the writ in Neagle's behalf was proper. Field never buried the incident, and when, a year later, a California journalist who had written a moderately approving account of Terry's life was nominated by President Harrison to the position of Register of the U.S. Land Office in San Francisco, Field used his influence to force withdrawal of the nomination. "When Field hates," a contemporary observed, "he hates for keeps."

The Terry affair revealed much about Field: his stubbornness, self-righteousness, his vindictiveness, his penchant for arousing hostility in others. These qualities combined with a creative and innovative mind to make Field a formidable and controversial judge. Even Terry had called Field "an intellectual phenomenon," who could "give the most plausible reasons for a wrong decision"; Field's opinions had the self-assurance and righteous fervor of an Old Testament prophet, which numerous contemporaries thought him to resemble. It has been suggested that the increasingly strident and self-righteous tone of Field's opinions in his later years masked deep anxieties. He allegedly came to see dark threats to the private enterprise system in the radical philosophies, such as Communism and Socialism, that were emerging in late-nineteenth-century Europe.

Whatever the reasons, the balance of values Field weighed in his decision-making shifted decisively after 1870 to the side of private property rights. In his earlier opinions, especially those on the California Supreme Court, he had shown an inclination to tolerate legislative interference with private property in order to protect the public health or welfare; later he was to regard such activity as subversive and to generate a theory of judicial review that allowed the judiciary to function as a guardian of established economic interests. Although Field thought of himself as a conservative, . . . his theory of judging was in some respects a radical departure from the views that had come to prevail in the Taney Court. Field's success in securing acceptance for his view of judging—the view that dominated the Supreme Court by the time of his resignation in 1897—was a tribute to his creativity, his arrogance, and the energy and zeal of his attempts to dispel his anxieties.

II. After 1870 new factors were clearly affecting interpretations of the Constitution. . . . For one thing, . . . the Southern states, at least technically, were under military rule; moreover, three amendments directly affecting the rights of American citizens as against state governments had been added to the Constitution; finally, private enterprise had evolved from its original dependence upon the states for economic support to a position in which it could survive without state subsidization. Circumstances suggested the possibility of a more expansive reading of the two principal clauses of the Constitution limiting state regulation of private enterprise—the contracts clause and the commerce clause. In addition, language in the Reconstruction Amendments, particularly in the Fourteenth, was itself sufficiently broad to suggest a potential set of new constitutional limitations. Attention turned, in legal treatises, to the role of constitutions, federal and state, as negative checks on state activity. These developments, together with the increasing incidence of literature expressing confidence in private enterprise and propounding a theory of minimal governmental participation in economic affairs, foreshadowed a new chapter in American constitutional history and a new stance for the appellate judiciary. Changes, however, were to come slowly and seemingly without pattern or design. Antebellum theories of government persisted well after the Civil War, and few judges saw themselves as agents of change.

By the time of the Civil War, the contracts clause had diminished in importance. . . . The clause was construed more and more infrequently during the late nineteenth century, and by 1900 had ceased to be a factor in constitutional litigation.

The second potential constitutional protection for private enterprise against state regulation was the commerce clause. . . . Two kinds of questions arose in the commerce clause cases of the late nineteenth century, one set involving the proper subject matter of state regulation, and the other the appropriate scope of state taxation of goods in interstate commerce.

. . .

Field's opinions on the commerce clause illustrate the markedly ideological character of his judicial stance. He tended to see legal problems as symbolic of ideological conflicts and to analyze them primarily on that level. This tendency was illustrated by his slavish support of the fiction that a state could impose [otherwise] unconstitutional conditions on its grants of corporate charters, since it had the power to grant the charters in the first place. . . . Consequently, in this limited area Field tolerated a measure of state regulation of private enterprise, but for reasons that underscored his commitment to the autonomous exercise of private rights.

In the broader area of state regulatory powers Field . . . succeeded in shifting the area of focus, in cases involving state regulation of private enterprise, from the commerce clause to the due process clause of the Fourteenth Amendment. His approach had the virtue of clarity and ideological consistency in an area where confusion and temporizing appeared to reign.

III. Increasingly, the Fourteenth Amendment came to be the focus of judicial activity and controversy on the Court in the late nineteenth century. This amendment had been enacted in a period when race relations and civil rights were social issues of first priority in America, but by the 1890s those issues had been displaced in importance by issues involving economic theory. The flurry of Congressional activity in the years immediately following the Civil War testified to the dominant role of the legislative branch of government at that time; the Court, in contrast, had been disgraced by the *Dred Scott* decision and . . . partisanship. . . . By the end of the century Congress was virtually inactive, no further constitutional amendment was to occur for another twenty years, and the Court was at one of its highest points of prominence. There were distinct winners and losers in this saga: corporations and advocates of limited government generally profited, and blacks and other minorities generally suffered from the Court's approach to the Fourteenth Amendment. When Field, having established what was then a longevity record, finally left the Court in 1897, he could look with pride at having been on the side of the winners most of the time, and also at having played a major part in developing a new conception of the function of the appellate judiciary in America. . . .

The Fourteenth Amendment raised a spate of potentially troublesome questions. One set involved its assertion of natural rights against the federal government and the states: thus, was it merely declaratory of existing individual rights, or did it create new ones, and if so, for whom? Another set involved the allocation of governmental power it envisaged. Concededly, one of its purposes was to enhance the authority of the national government as against the states, but how far did that authority extend? Of particular interest here was the amendment's declaration that persons born or naturalized in America were both citizens of the United States and citizens of their respective states, and that state governments could not abridge the privileges and immunities of citizens of the United States. Finally, the amendment raised a set of questions about its enforcement. Was it self-executing, or did its implementation require additional legislation? Did its coverage extend to the infringement by private citizens of the rights of other citizens? And who was the ultimate judge of its reach—Congress and state legislatures, through enforcement statutes, or the judiciary, through scrutiny of allegedly discriminatory legislative action?

The framers of the Reconstruction Amendments apparently intended, among other things, to secure full citizenship rights for freed blacks, thereby ensuring that attempts on the part of Southern states to deprive blacks of citizenship rights would be constitutionally prohibited. Nonetheless, through the ingenious stratagems of counsel, the first case asking the Court to determine the scope of the Fourteenth Amendment's protection involved not the civil rights of blacks but the economic rights of butchers in Louisiana.

The *Slaughter-House* cases . . . tested the right of Louisiana to establish a twenty-five-year monopoly on the abattoir business. Louisiana's action was in the established tradition of state-created economic monopolies. The question, as raised by former Justice Campbell in behalf of competing butchers, was whether that practice was now impermissible under the Fourteenth Amendment. [Justice] Bradley [in circuit court] held that it was. . . . Among the privileges and immunities of national citizenship, he maintained, was the right "to adopt and follow [a] lawful industrial pursuit . . . without unreasonable regulation or molestation and without being restricted by . . . unjust, oppressive and odious monopolies." This "sacred right of labor" was "one of the fundamental privileges of an American citizen."

Bradley's decision (which was appealed to the Supreme Court) raised a delicate problem in political statesmanship. A measure of state regulation of private rights seemed essential. . . . Yet the Fourteenth Amendment was clearly designed to underscore the inalienable rights of American citizens—or so its privileges and immunities, equal protection, and due process clauses suggested. The choice, then, was between construing those clauses narrowly or establishing the federal judiciary as an omnipresent check on state regulation. [Justice] Miller, for a majority of the Court, chose the former option. The "one pervading purpose" of the Reconstruction Amendments, he argued, was protecting black freedmen; although others could share in this protection, Miller "doubt[ed] very much whether any action of a State not directed by way of discrimination against the [N]egroes as a class, or on account of their race [would] ever be held to come within the purview" of the equal protection clause. As for the privileges and immunities clause, that pertained only to privileges and immunities *peculiar* to national citizenship, such as the right to travel to the seat of government, the right to move freely from one state to another, and the right to claim diplomatic protection when out of the country. The Fourteenth Amendment, in Miller's view, did not change the relation between the national government and the states, it merely codified an existing relation. The privileges and immunities clause underscored the special rights attendant on national citizenship, rights that had been in evidence before Reconstruction; the equal protection clause was hypothesized as being exclusively designed to raise blacks to an equal footing with other citizens; the due process clause . . . pertained only to matters of procedure. "[W]e do not see in [the] amendments," Miller maintained, "any purpose to destroy the main features of the general [federalist] system."

. . . Field dissented from this reading. . . . Field saw the Fourteenth as giving "practical effect" to "the sacred and inalienable rights of man," and repeated Bradley's argument on circuit that the privileges and immunities clause conferred on private citizens the right to pursue a lawful calling unrestrained by monopolies.

The *Slaughter-House* cases represented a turning point in the history of judicial construction of the Fourteenth Amendment. From that point the privileges and immunities clause ceased to be an object of judicial interest and the due process clause became the focus of controversy. Through continued glosses on that clause the scope of the amendment's protection was widened to include economic rights as well as civil rights. And in counterpoint the rights of blacks under the Reconstruction Amendments were narrowed, as though racial inequality was to be made the price of expanded protection for free enterprise. . . .

Having rejected a substantive reading of the due process clause in the *Slaughter-House* cases, Miller then entertained such a reading in *Bartemeyer v. Iowa*, decided a year later. *Bartemeyer* raised the question whether an Iowa prohibition law deprived a liquor dealer of his property without due process of law. Miller avoided facing the due process argument squarely, but indicated that it should be taken seriously. Field . . . gave substantive meaning to the Fourteenth Amendment from that point on. . . .

Field's most important contributions to the development of the Fourteenth Amendment came, however, in his circuit opinions in California. Abandoning his early practice of deferring to legislative supremacy even against due process challenges, Field set out to make his Ninth Circuit the protector of private rights against state interference. From 1874 to 1882, in a series of cases involving California statutes discriminating against Chinese immigrants, Field extended the amendment's equal protection clause to cover aliens, implicitly announcing a very broad judicial power under the amendment to scrutinize the reasonableness of state legislation. At the same time he gave tacit support to attempts to secure for corporations the protection of the due process and equal protection clauses on the ground that they were "persons."

That question had received contradictory answers in the lower courts after Reconstruction. . . . If corporations were not persons within the meaning of the amendment, Field maintained, corporate property could be arbitrarily infringed by legislatures. "It would be a most singular result," he argued, "if a constitutional provision intended for the protection of every person . . . should cease to exert such protection the moment the person becomes a member of a corporation." Four years later a unanimous Supreme Court, aided by disingenuous testimony by advocate Roscoe Conkling as to the original purposes of the framers of the Fourteenth Amendment, summarily upheld Field's position, and the due process clause of the amendment became a vehicle for the judicial assertion of economic theories.

As the economic content of the Fourteenth expanded, the original purpose of the Reconstruction Amendments became increasingly neglected. . . . Congressional statutes penalizing persons who deprived blacks of their constitutional rights were struck down or circumscribed in opinions by Bradley; in his most celebrated opinion, the Civil Rights cases, he held that the Fourteenth Amendment prohibited only discriminatory acts by states, not private persons, and that the Civil Rights Act of 1875, which had attempted to outlaw racial segregation in inns, was unconstitutional. The combination of this decision and the Slaughter-House cases meant that blacks could not expect the federal government to protect them from discriminatory acts by private individuals. What citizenship rights they had were rights primarily against official state action. Such decisions set the stage for the plethora of discriminatory legislation that emerged in the South after 1880.

. . . Field was least sympathetic toward the rights of blacks. He supported . . . a construction of the Force Bill (1870), prescribing criminal penalties for conspiring to deny United States citizens their constitutional rights—a construction that exempted from its coverage the murder of a group of blacks participating in a political rally in Louisiana. He dissented from a case whose object was to insure black voters federal protection against those attempting to prevent them from exercising their rights, and maintained, in dissent, that states could constitutionally exclude blacks from jury service. The occasional sympathy he felt for the plight of racial minorities, as evidenced by some of his decisions in cases involving Chinese aliens, did not extend to blacks.

IV. By 1890, . . . the Court had prepared itself, through its interpretations of the Fourteenth Amendment, to re-emerge as a major political force in American life. Its preparation had been seemingly without design, for in its Fourteenth Amendment cases, as in its contracts and commerce clause decisions, it had shown neither uniformity of approach nor marked ideological trends. Tentative steps had been made in one direction and then another ... alternately tolerant, then suspicious of attempts to regulate private property; at once champions of an expansive jurisdiction for the federal courts and of extensive delegations to the states of control over civil rights issues.

Despite these ambivalences, tendencies were evident. By the 1890s the Court had claimed the power to scrutinize the reasonableness of legislative activity to insure that property had not been seized in violation of due process. It had also transformed what Miller had declared to be the original meaning of the Fourteenth Amendment to a meaning more harmonious with the temper of the late nineteenth century, in which the concerns of private enterprise were taken far more seriously, by most Americans, than the concerns of blacks. It had apparently abandoned its efforts to secure some compromise between antebellum theories of economic regulation and the post–Civil War spirit of laissez faire; a majority of its Justices in the 1890s viewed as presumptively suspect legislative attempts to regulate industrial enterprise.

The Court was ripe for the acceptance of Field's theory of the judicial function, a theory that combined a hostile attitude toward governmental infringements of broadly conceived economic rights, with a conception of the appellate judiciary as an active check on legislative excesses. Judicial power, as Field observed on his retirement from the Court in 1897, was a "negative power, the power of resistance." ...

In his conceptualization of the judicial function, Field referred to the power of the judiciary as power to declare the law. That phrase hearkened back to the oracular theory of judicial decision-making, in which judges merely interpreted the commands of legislatures, the sole "lawmakers." Although that theory had never been repudiated in the course of the nineteenth century, it had been de-emphasized in the works of creative antebellum judges ... who had tacitly made the judiciary a repository of wisdom on matters of social policy. With Field and those who shared his perspectives, however, came an apparent de-emphasis on policy considerations and a professed return to immutable guiding axioms of the law, axioms that the judge applied merely to the facts before him to reach a sound result. This emphasis underscored the apparently limited nature of judicial decision-making, while de-emphasizing the fact that the governing axioms judges faithfully applied were often synonymous with congenial economic and social theories. Field, of course, did not believe that the right to use one's property free from governmental interference was merely a "theory"; he viewed it as a self-evident truth about mankind. Neither did he suspect that in determining the content of the Reconstruction Amendments the federal judiciary was "making law" in the boldest sense, substituting their views as to the proper beneficiaries of those amendments for the admittedly vague views of the framers.

Or if he did, he kept silent about it. For the theory of judicial performance articulated by Field for the Court in 1897 was a declaration of judicial power of a radical kind. It allowed an institution of government that was largely unaccountable to immediate popular criticism to decide for itself what was the proper relation of government to free enterprise in late-nineteenth-century America, and whether or not the citizenship guaranties conferred on blacks by the Reconstruction Amendments were to be enforced. . . . In order to uphold substantively conservative philosophical positions, then, Field was advocating a radical augmentation of judicial power.

The judiciary in America, however, becomes a hostile object of public attention when its power has been perceived as being overly concentrated or aggrandized. One of the elements of the American judicial tradition has been a dialectic of power between the judiciary and its constituencies. The judicial branch has used its apparently limited power to enhance its stature, and yet has been reminded of the fact that it is ultimately responsible for the political effects of its decisions, so that the more it ventures into the realm of political statesmanship, the more it risks having its goals frustrated. A combination of favorable social circumstances, incompetence in other branches of government, and the presence of able, strong-willed men on the Court enabled it to become by the 1890s the chief overseer of American economic development and to maintain that position for another twenty years. But its boldness was eventually to be the source of limits on its supremacy. In 1905 one of its own members announced that a Constitution was not made to embody any particular economic theory, whether paternalism or laissez faire, and that judges should not use their office to read their own social or economic prejudices into the law.

CHAPTER 13

The Life of the Law

The decade of the 1870s was pivotal for the legal profession. It was the decade in which the American Bar Association was founded, signaling a rise in the standards and prestige of the profession; it was the decade in which West Publishing Company began the National Reporter System, bringing about a unified system for the publication of judicial opinions; and it was the decade in which Harvard Law School began teaching by the "case method," bringing greater respectability to the academic study of law. All three developments were indicative of a new philosophy of law as defined by Harvard's dean, Christopher Columbus Langdell, originator of the case method.

Dean Langdell first employed the case method in Harvard's class on contracts. Previously, most lawyers did not study law in law schools but gained admission to the bar through apprenticeships. For those who did attend law schools, legal instruction consisted largely of readings in treatises supplemented by professors' lectures. The case method replaced rote learning with a challenging, probing approach, using original appellate opinions to get at underlying rules of law through "Socratic" discussion. Eventually, the case method spread to law schools throughout the nation, and law schools became the gateways to the legal profession. As conceived by Dean Langdell, however, the case method largely ignored legislation and administrative regulation, and it was based on a questionable philosophical assumption. As an irreverent legal scholar, Grant Gilmore, has put it in *The Ages of American Law* (1977):

> Langdell seems to have been an essentially stupid man who, early in his life, hit on one great idea to which, thereafter, he clung with all the tenacity of genius. . . . However absurd, however mischievous, however deeply rooted in error it may have been, Langdell's idea shaped our legal thinking for fifty years.
>
> Langdell's idea was that law is a science. (p. 42)

The law-is-a-science approach had consequences not only for legal education, but also for judicial interpretation. It lent credence to the formalism of late nineteenth century judicial decisions and led to judicial resistance to legal change whether through legislation or through judicial interpretation.

The resistance came to a head in 1905 with the Supreme Court case of *Lochner* v. *New York* in which a state law regulating working conditions was struck down, in a 5-to-4 decision, on the ground that it interfered with employers' and workers' "liberty of contract." The majority opinion treated "liberty of contract" as an abstract, scientific principle and considered employers and workers to be in an equal bargaining position. In the same era, however, courts were using syndicalism laws, conspiracy laws, and labor injunctions to prevent the organization of effective labor unions that might have helped equalize the relationship.

The *Lochner* decision was true to the principles of Justice Stephen Field, who had dissented in the *Slaughter-House* cases in 1873 and had lived to see the majority of the court adopt his view; in turn, the *Lochner* case drew a dissent from Justice Oliver Wendell Holmes, Jr., who also served one of the longest tenures on the Court and lived to see his position replace that of Field.

Oliver Wendell Holmes, Jr., in 1872.
Photo from Harvard Law School Art Collection.

Justice Oliver Wendell Holmes, Jr.

from Bernard Schwartz, *Main Currents in American Legal Thought*
(Durham, N.C.: Carolina Academic Press, 1993), pp. 376–92.
Copyright © 1993 by Bernard Schwartz.
Reprinted by permission of Carolina Academic Press.

Oliver Wendell Holmes: Law as Experience

. . . Holmes, more than any other legal thinker, . . . set the agenda for modern American jurisprudence. In doing so, he became as much a part of American legend as law: the Yankee from Olympus—the patrician from Boston who made his mark on his own age and on ages still unborn as few men have done. To summarize Holmes's work is to trace the development from nineteenth-century law to that of the present day.

Oliver Wendell Holmes was the son of the famous American of the same name, whom Sir William Osler called "the most successful combination the world has ever seen, of physician and man of letters." The younger Holmes came from what his father termed "the Brahmin caste of New England"—the "untitled aristocracy" of early America. The great formative influence during the first part of Holmes's life was, however, not so much his family or his formal education; it was his military service during the Civil War. Immediately after graduation from Harvard College in 1861, he enlisted in the Union Army. The war for Holmes was anything but an academic exercise. He fought in major battles and was seriously wounded three times.

. . .

The literary critic, Edmund Wilson, once wrote an essay on Holmes in which he asserted that Holmes's war service was "to affect in fundamental ways the whole of his subsequent thinking." The war experience "cured him for life, of . . . social illusions." "Having lost in the war the high hopes of the Northern crusade and fallen back on a Calvinist position which will not admit the realization of the Kingdom of God on earth—[he] must simply, as a jurist . . . , submit to the dominant will of the society he has sworn to serve." This led directly to the doctrine of judicial restraint, which was to form the principal element in the Holmes judicial canon. "If the business men made the laws,

186

he would have to accept their authority; if the people should decide to vote for socialism, he would have to accept that, too."

When he left the army, Holmes decided to study law. He told his father that he was going to Harvard Law School, and Dr. Holmes is said to have asked, "What is the use of that? A lawyer can't be a great man." Holmes himself showed how mistaken his father was. Holmes's career illustrated the truth of his own declaration "that a man may live greatly in the law as well as elsewhere; that there as well as elsewhere his thought may find its unity in an infinite perspective; that there as well as elsewhere he may wreak himself upon life, may drink the bitter cup of heroism, may wear his heart out after the unattainable." ...

After his graduation from law school, Holmes was admitted to the Bar, joined a law firm, and became a part-time lecturer at Harvard. He wrote articles for legal periodicals and edited the twelfth edition of Kent's *Commentaries*. Then, in 1880, came the invitation to deliver a series of lectures. He chose as his topic *The Common Law* and the lectures were published in a book of that name in 1881. This was the book that was to change both Holmes's life and the course of American law.

The Common Law

Holmes was a historian of the law before he was a judge. His *Common Law* was the first American work to "have examined legal institutions and conceptions exclusively with a view to their historical development." ... For the first time, an American jurist viewed the law as anthropologists might view it—as an organic part of the culture within which it grew up.

But *The Common Law* was anything but a dry antiquarian account of the historical minutiae. ... As a state judge tells us, "The book propounds an idea audacious and even revolutionary for the time." The Holmes theme has become so settled in our thinking that we forget how radical it was when it was announced. ... The very words used must have appeared strange to the contemporary reader: "experience," "expediency," "necessity," "life." Law books at the time used far different words: "rule," "precedent," "logic," "syllogism." As Holmes's biographer tells us, "The time-honored way was to deduce the *corpus* from *a priori* postulates, fit part to part in beautiful, neat logical cohesion." Holmes rejected "the notion that a given [legal] system, ours, for instance, can be worked out like mathematics." Instead, he declared, "The law embodies the story of a nation's development through many centuries, and it cannot be dealt with as if it contained the axioms and corollaries of a book of mathematics."

But the great Holmes theme was stated at the very outset of *The Common Law*: "The life of the law has not been logic: it has been experience. The felt necessities of the time, the prevalent moral and political theories, intuitions of public policy, avowed or unconscious, even the prejudices which judges share with their fellow-men, have had a good deal more to do than the syllogism in determining the rules by which men should be governed."

When Holmes wrote these words, he was pointing the way to a new era of jurisprudence that would ... "break down the walls of formalism and empty traditionalism which had grown up around the inner life of the law in America." The courts, Holmes urged, should recognize that they must perform a legislative function, in its deeper sense. The secret root from which the law draws its life is consideration of "what is expedient for the community." ... The formalistic jurisprudence that the judges professed to be applying was actually the result of their view of public policy, perhaps "the unconscious result of instinctive preferences and inarticulate convictions, but none the less traceable to views of public policy in the last analysis."

In a lecture delivered in 1897, Holmes asserted "that the judges themselves have failed adequately to recognize their duty of weighing considerations of social advantage." The judges of the day looked at the law as anything but the instrument of transforming innovation it has since become. In law, as in nature, progress was then considered an evolutionary process, which could only be impeded by outside intervention. As it was put by James C. Carter, then considered the outstanding legal thinker, "The popular estimate of the possibilities for good which may be realised through the enactment of law is, in my opinion, greatly exaggerated." In law, as in the economics of the day, hands-off was the rule.

A noted Holmes statement has it that "a general proposition is simply a string for the facts." American law today differs sharply from that of a century ago, not only in general doctrines, but even more so in its approach to the facts. In determining legal issues, not too long ago, the blackletter approach was the only one permitted. . . .

The American judges at the turn of the century reached their restrictive conclusions deductively from preconceived notions and precedents. To them, the legal system was a perfect, but closed, sphere; the least dent was an invalid subtraction from its essence. During this century, the judicial method has become inductive, reasoning more and more from the changing facts of a relativist world. . . . The system has become fluid and inconstant, dependent upon the particular circumstances of time and place. As Holmes predicted in his 1897 lecture, the blackletter judge has been replaced by the man of statistics and the master of economics and other disciplines.

. . .

Judicial Restraint

The success of *The Common Law* led to a professorship in 1882 at the Harvard Law School. But Holmes taught there only a term, for he was appointed in December 1882 to the Supreme Judicial Court of Massachusetts. He served on that tribunal for twenty years (from 1899 as Chief Justice), when he was elevated to the United States Supreme Court. Though he was already sixty-one when he took his seat on that Court, he still had his greatest judicial years to serve. He did not leave the Supreme Court until his retirement in January 1932. During the thirty years he spent in Washington, he made the greatest contribution since Marshall to the American conception of law.

The jurisprudential foundation for much of twentieth-century American public law has been the doctrine of judicial restraint. The rule of restraint was primarily the Holmes handiwork. He was led to it by his innate skepticism, which made him dubious of dogma and decisions based upon dogmatic clichés. To his famous English correspondent, Sir Frederick Pollock, Holmes declared, "no general proposition is worth a damn." Delusive exactness he saw as a source of fallacy, particularly in the application of the purposed vagueness of constitutional provisions.

"Lincoln for government and Holmes for law," Justice Frankfurter once wrote, "have taught me that the absolutists are the enemies of reason—that . . . the dogmatists in law, however sincere, are the mischief-makers." For Holmes, the only absolute was that there were no absolutes in law. His philosopher's stone was "the conviction that our . . . system rests upon tolerance and that its greatest enemy is the Absolute." It was not at all the judicial function to strike down laws with which the judge disagreed. "There is nothing I more deprecate than the use of the Fourteenth Amendment . . . to prevent the making of social experiments that an important part of the community desires . . . even though the experiments may seem futile or even noxious to me." Not the judge but the legislator was to have the primary say on the policy considerations behind a regulatory measure. The judge's business was to enforce even "laws that I believe to embody economic mistakes."

Holmes articulated the rule of restraint even before his elevation to the highest Court. His tolerance toward legislative power was first expressed while he was still a state judge. In dissenting from an 1891 decision of the Massachusetts court, Holmes referred to the argument "that the power to make reasonable laws impliedly prohibits the making of unreasonable ones, and that this law is unreasonable." But, he went on, "If I assume that this construction of the constitution is correct, and that, speaking as a political economist, I should agree in condemning the law, still I should not be willing or think myself authorized to overturn legislation on that ground, unless I thought that an honest difference of opinion was impossible, or pretty nearly so."

The same theme was to be repeated many times by Holmes on the United States Supreme Court. It was sounded by him in the very first opinion which he wrote on that tribunal. In upholding a state regulatory law, Holmes, speaking for the Court, denied "that every law is void which may seem to the judges who pass upon it excessive, unsuited to its ostensible end, or based upon conceptions of morality with which they disagree. Considerable latitude must be allowed for differences of view, as well as for possible peculiar conditions which this court can know but imperfectly, if at all. Otherwise a constitution, instead of embodying only relatively fundamental rules of right, as generally understood by all English-speaking communities, would become the partisan of a particular set of ethical or economical opinions, which by no means are held *semper ubique et ab omnibus.*"

This was an early version of the view Holmes was to express in the 1905 case of *Lochner v. New York,* where he delivered perhaps his most famous opinion. In its *Lochner* opinion, the majority of the Court indicated that the reasonableness of a challenged statute, under the Constitution, must be determined as an objective fact by the judge upon his own independent judgment. In *Lochner* the state statute prescribed maximum hours for bakers. In holding the law invalid, the majority substituted its judgment for that of the legislature and decided for itself that the statute was not reasonably related to any of the social ends for which governmental power might validly be exercised. "This case," asserted Holmes in dissent, "is decided upon an economic theory which a large part of the country does not entertain." . . .

Holmes consistently rejected such an approach. "A constitution," he urged, "is not intended to embody a particular economic theory, whether of paternalism . . . or of *laissez faire.*" Holmes continually reiterated that, as a judge, he was not concerned with the wisdom of the social policy involved in a challenged legislative act. The responsibility for determining what measures were necessary to deal with economic and other problems lay with the people and their elected representatives, not the judges. The Constitution, Holmes declared, was not "intended to give us *carte blanche* to embody our economic or moral beliefs in its prohibitions." The Constitution was never intended to embody absolutes. Instead, "Some play must be allowed for the joints of the machine, and it must be remembered that legislatures are ultimate guardians of the liberties and welfare of the people in quite as great a degree as the courts."

Holmes recognized, with the majority in cases such as *Lochner v. New York,* that the question at issue was whether the challenged law was a *reasonable* exercise of the police power of the state. But, if Holmes, too, started with the test of reasonableness, he applied it in a manner very different from the *Lochner* majority. The Holmes approach was based upon the conviction that it was an awesome thing to strike down an act of the elected representatives of the people, and that the power to do so should not be exercised save where the occasion was clear beyond fair debate.

In the Holmes view, the test to be applied was whether a reasonable legislator . . . could have adopted a law like that at issue. Was the statute as applied so clearly arbitrary that legislators acting reasonably could not have believed it necessary or appropriate for public health, safety, morals, or welfare?

In the individual case, to be sure, the legislative judgment might well be debatable. But that was the whole point about the Holmes approach. Under it, the opposed views of public policy, as respects business, economic, and social affairs, were considerations for the legislative choice, to which the courts must defer unless it was demonstrably arbitrary or irrational. "In short, the judiciary may not sit as a super-legislature to judge the wisdom or desirability of legislative policy determinations. . . . [I]n the local economic sphere, it is only the . . . wholly arbitrary act which cannot stand."

Free Trade in Ideas

. . . It may now be fairly said that both the economic and the legal theories upon which *Lochner* rested have been repudiated. While the Supreme Court at the beginning of this century was increasingly equating the law with laissez faire, men turned to Holmes's dissents as the precursors of a new era. The at-first-lonely voice soon became that of a new dispensation which wrote itself into American public law.

Yet, if Holmes furnished the principal jurisprudential foundation for present-day public law, he did not necessarily concur in the assumptions upon which it was based. Holmes's attitude toward both law and life was grounded on an innate skepticism which made him doubt the economic nostrums that were acquiring increased currency as the century progressed. His personal views often ran counter to regulatory legislation based upon the new theories. To Sir Frederick Pollock, Holmes admitted that he shared to a great extent a "contempt for government interference with rates etc.," as well as a belief that the Sherman Anti-Trust Act was a "humbug based on economic ignorance and incompetence" and a "disbelief that the Interstate Commerce Commission is a fit body to be entrusted with ratemaking." As Justice Frankfurter once wrote, Holmes "privately distrusted attempts at improving society by what he deemed futile if not mischievous economic tinkering."

Edmund Wilson sums up the Holmes posture in this respect by noting, "Holmes . . . , in his economic views, . . . was . . . contemptuous of what he called 'the upward and onward.' . . . " Wilson then asks, "How, then in view of this philosophy, was it possible for Oliver Wendell Holmes to become . . . a great hero of the American 'liberals,' who were intent upon social reforms and who leaned sometimes pretty far to the Left?"

The answer is twofold. In the first place, the doctrine of judicial restraint was the necessary legal foundation for the soon-to-emerge Welfare State. The Holmes approach meant that the courts would uphold laws that coincided with liberal views on the proper scope of governmental regulation. American liberals applauded when Holmes rejected legal shibboleths that equated "the constitutional conception of 'liberty' . . . with theories of *laissez faire*." They recognized that the rule of restraint was essential if the law was to mirror the society in the transition from laissez faire to the Welfare State.

Even more important was the fact that, to liberals, Holmes appeared to be on the side of the angels in his opinions on freedom of speech. The theme of judicial restraint was overridden by another Holmes theme in cases involving the freedom of expression guaranteed by the First Amendment. In a characteristic letter Holmes wrote, "at times I have thought that the bills of rights in Constitutions were overworked—but . . . they embody principles that men have died for, and that it is well not to forget in our haste to secure our notion of general welfare."

Justice Frankfurter has shown that there was no real inconsistency in Holmes's abandonment of his basic rule of restraint in First Amendment cases. Restraint was the proper posture in cases like *Lochner v. New York,* where economic regulation was at issue. "The Justice deferred so abundantly to legislative judgment on economic policy because he was profoundly aware of the extent to which social arrangements are conditioned by time and circumstances, and of how fragile, in scientific proof, is the ultimate validity of a particular economic adjustment. He knew that there was no authoritative fund of social wisdom to be drawn upon for answers to the perplexities which vast new material resources had brought. And so he was hesitant to oppose his own opinion to the economic views of the legislature."

A different situation was presented in First Amendment cases. Here, says Frankfurter, history had taught Holmes that "the free play of the human mind was an indispensable prerequisite" of social development. "Since the history of civilization is in considerable measure the displacement of error which once held sway as official truth by beliefs which in turn have yielded to other truths, the liberty of man to search for truth was of a different order than some economic dogma defined as a sacred right because the temporal nature of its origin had been forgotten. And without freedom of expression, liberty of thought is a mockery."

The Bill of Rights itself, Holmes recognized, specifically enshrines freedom of speech as its core principle. "If there is any principle of the Constitution that more imperatively calls for attachment than any other it is the principle of free thought," he asserted in a 1928 dissent. "Naturally, therefore, Mr. Justice Holmes attributed very different legal significance to those liberties of the individual which history has attested as the indispensable conditions of a free society from that which he attached to liberties which derived merely from shifting economic arrangements." Because freedom of speech was basic to any notion of liberty, "Mr. Justice Holmes was far more ready to find legislative invasion in this field than in the area of debatable economic reform."

The Holmes concept of freedom of speech. . . . found its fullest expression in the Justice's dissent in the 1919 case of *Abrams v. United States,* which has been termed "the greatest utterance on intellectual freedom by an American." . . . The *Abrams* dissent sets forth the foundation of the First Amendment as "free trade in ideas," which through competition for their acceptance by the people would provide the best test of truth. Or as Holmes put it in a letter, "I am for aeration of all effervescing convictions—there is no way so quick for letting them get flat."

. . . Holmes stressed the ability of truth to win out in the intellectual market-place. For this to happen, the indispensable sine qua non was the free interchange of ideas. As the crucial passage of the *Abrams* dissent puts it, "when men have realized that time has upset many fighting faiths, they may come to believe even more than they believe the very foundations of their own conduct that the ultimate good desired is better reached by free trade in ideas—that the best test of truth is the power of the thought to get itself accepted in the competition of the market, and that truth is the only ground upon which their wishes safely can be carried out."

. . .

Clear and Present Danger: Law as Degree

. . .

The Holmes conception did not, however, mean that the Justice was an adherent of an absolutist interpretation of the First Amendment. Despite Holmes's deep faith in the free interchange of ideas, Justice Frankfurter tells us, "he did not erect even freedom of speech into a dogma of absolute validity nor enforce it to doctrinaire limits."

The Supreme Court, too, has rejected the absolutist view of freedom of expression. . . . It has been settled from the beginning that the Constitution does not provide for unfettered right of expression. Holmes's famous example of the man falsely shouting "fire!" in a theater is simply the most obvious example of speech that can be controlled.

But the fire-in-a-theater example was a far cry from the facts presented in the *Abrams** case. There, the Holmes dissent argued that the "silly" leaflets thrown by obscure individuals . . . from a loft window presented no danger of resistance to the American war effort. Not enough, he said, "can be squeezed from these poor and puny anonymities to turn the color of legal litmus paper."

---

*In *Abrams,* the majority of the Court upheld the conviction of six Russian-immigrant factory workers under the Espionage Act of 1917 for printing and distributing leaflets urging a general strike to protest U.S. intervention in Russia following the Russian Revolution.

According to Holmes, "Only the emergency that makes it immediately dangerous to leave the correction of evil counsels to time warrants making any exception to the sweeping command, 'Congress shall make no law . . . abridging the freedom of speech.'" But when does such an "emergency" arise? Holmes himself had provided the answer a few months earlier in another case: When "the words used are used in such circumstances and are of such a nature as to create a clear and present danger that they will bring about the substantive evils that Congress has a right to prevent."

. . . In the *Abrams* case, the legislature had the right to pass a law to prevent curtailment of war production; but, said Holmes, there was no danger, clear and present, or even remote, that the leaflets would have had any effect on production.

The Clear and Present Danger Test, as stated by Holmes, "served to indicate the importance of freedom of speech to a free society but also to emphasize that its exercise must be compatible with the preservation of other freedoms essential to a democracy and guaranteed by our Constitution. When those other attributes of a democracy are threatened by speech, the Constitution does not deny power to the [government] to curb it." As characterized by Justice Brandeis in a later case, the Holmes test "is a rule of reason. Correctly applied, it will preserve the right of free speech both from suppression by tyrannous, well-meaning majorities and from abuse by irresponsible, fanatical minorities."

Although even the Clear and Present Danger Test has been criticized by some as too restrictive, it represents a real step forward in favor of free speech. The Holmes test is above all a test of degree. "Clear and present" danger is a standard, not a mathematical absolute. "It is a question of proximity and degree," said Holmes. . . . As such, its application will vary from case to case and will depend upon the particular circumstances presented.

. . .

Holmes's Jurisprudence

The best statement that Holmes ever wrote on the nature of law is contained in his 1897 lecture, *The Path of the Law.* In this lecture, Holmes enunciated a new way of looking at the law. He said that if one wanted to know the law and nothing else, he must look at it as a bad man, who cared only for the material consequences which such knowledge enabled him to predict. Jurists of the time urged that the law was "a deduction from principles of ethics or admitted axioms or what not, which may or may not coincide with the decisions. But if we take the view of our friend the bad man we shall find that he does not care two straws for the axioms or deductions, but that he does want to know what the Massachusetts or English courts are likely to do in fact. I am much of his mind. The prophecies of what the courts will do in fact, and nothing more pretentious, are what I mean by the law."

Hence, to Holmes, "The only question for the lawyer is, how will the judges act? Any motive for their action, be it constitution, statute, custom, or precedent, which can be relied upon as likely in the generality of cases to prevail, is worthy of consideration as one of the sources of law." The object of jurisprudence, in the Holmes conception, "is prediction, the prediction of the incidence of the public force through the instrumentality of the courts." Hence, he once wrote, "I don't care a damn if twenty professors tell me that a decision is not law if I know that the courts will enforce it."

The Holmes concept of law is essentially positivist. Of course, Holmes recognized the importance of history in legal study. "The rational study of law is still to a large extent the study of history. History must be a part of the study, because without it we cannot know the precise scope of rules which it is our business to know." In fact, some of Holmes's best passages were devoted to the law's historical foundation. "When I think thus of the law," he once stated, "I see a princess mightier than she who once wrought at Bayeux, eternally weaving into her web dim figures of the ever-lengthening past."

The law which concerned Holmes, however, was not the passive product of the then-prevailing historical school. It was not enough that a legal doctrine was a product of the society's development over the centuries. Historical confirmation alone could not give validity to a legal precept. "It is revolting to have no better reason for a rule of law than that so it was laid down in the time of Henry IV. It is still more revolting if the grounds upon which it was laid down have vanished long since, and the rule simply persists from blind imitation of the past."

Holmes also made a sharp differentiation between law and morals. To be sure, "The law is the witness and external deposit of our moral life. Its history is the history of the moral development of the race." But, for a "right study and mastery of the law," the distinction between law and morals "is of the first importance." Nothing but confusion of thought can result from assuming that rights in a moral sense are equally rights in the sense of the law. Positive law must be given effect even if it conflicts with the limits "prescribed by conscience, or by our ideal, however reached." Indeed, "it is certain that many laws have been enforced in the past, and it is likely that some are enforced now, which are condemned by the most enlightened opinion of the time, or which at all events pass the limit of interference as many consciences would draw it."

To Holmes, the law was the positive law as seen by his bad man—the decisions which the courts would make to deal with conduct on his part. Indeed, Holmes once remarked, "I have regarded those who doubted that judges made law . . . as simply incompetent."

. . .

In a deeper sense, Holmes declared, the work of the courts is legislative: "It is legislative in its grounds. The very considerations which judges most rarely mention, and always with an apology, are the secret root from which the law draws all the juices of life. I mean, of course, considerations of what is expedient for the community concerned. Every important [legal] principle . . . is in fact and at bottom the result of more or less definitely understood views of public policy." Hence, "every rule [that a body of law] contains is referred articulately and definitely to an end which it subserves."

Holmes not only showed that the law was made in accordance with policy considerations; he also believed that it should consciously be so made. Instead of a system based upon logical deduction from a priori principles, the Holmes concept was one of law fashioned to meet the needs of the community. Law was once again to be a utilitarian instrument for the satisfaction of social needs.

CHAPTER 14

The Progressive Movement

As the formalistic, "scientific" decisions of courts came down in favor of business interests, farmers and industrial workers responded by organizing at the grass roots. Farmers organized the Grange movement of the 1870s and the Populist movement of the 1880s, gaining power in a number of state legislatures. In the 1890s and 1900s the main advocates for workers' interests came to be labeled "Progressives." Others embraced more radical ideas imported from Europe. The Socialist Party, under its charismatic leader, Eugene V. Debs, captured a number of seats in state legislatures. Communists and anarchists agitated at the fringes of the labor movement and in the burgeoning immigrant community.

Organized labor gained momentum with the formation of the Industrial Workers of the World (IWW) in 1905, bringing together previously disparate groups. Public sympathy for labor grew as the callousness of management was dramatically publicized by such events as the violent suppression of the Homestead strike of 1892 and the death of 146 workers in the Triangle Shirtwaist Company fire of 1911. Some of the sympathy, however, was dissipated when violence was blamed on the labor side. Prevailing public opinion put the blame on labor for a bomb explosion at a labor gathering in Chicago's Haymarket Square in 1886. The bomb killed seven policemen. Four anarchists were convicted in the subsequent trial and hanged (although they were never linked to the bombing itself). A strike against the Pullman Palace Train Company in 1894 led to violence and the jailing of Eugene Debs, then head of the American Railway Union. As labor-management strife continued, the IWW came to be widely condemned as a radical organization.

Much of the labor unrest was due to long-existing management practices—long hours, low wages, hazardous working conditions, lack of job security, payment in scrip redeemable only at company stores or for company housing at premium prices, "yellow-dog" contracts prohibiting unions, and other union-busting activities. Other causes can be found in new practices introduced in the 1890s and 1900s. Financial depression in the 1890s led a number of companies to arbitrarily reduce wages—a factor in both the Homestead and Pullman strikes—and mass-production, assembly-line manufacturing techniques—pioneered by the Ford Motor Company in the early 1900s and perpetuated by a new breed of "efficiency experts"—put workers under increasing strain.

Against this backdrop, the Progressive movement made political headway in both the Republican and the Democratic parties. Progressives won several elections, including victories by Governors Robert M. La Follette in Wisconsin, John P. Altgeld in Illinois, and Woodrow Wilson in New Jersey. Republican Progressives took over the White House when the assassination of President William McKinley in 1901 by a young anarchist brought the leader of the party's Progressive wing, Vice President Theodore Roosevelt, to the presidency. In one of a series of books commissioned by the American Bar Association, *Ordered Liberty: Legal Reform in the Twentieth Century* (1983), Gerald L. Fetner has written:

> It is hard to generalize about the Progressive movement, since it was geographically and institutionally heterogeneous. Yet if there was one theme that characterized Progressivism, it was the search for and imposition of new standards of ethical behavior for business, government, and the professions. The Progressives sought to bridle the excessive waste, inefficiency, corruption, and human suffering associated with American industrialization. Many Progressive-era spokesmen sounded this theme, none perhaps as forcefully as Theodore Roosevelt. (p. 8)

The young (he was forty-two in 1901) and dynamic new president captured the public's imagination by acting forcefully. He applied presidential pressure to get a mediated settlement in a dangerous coal strike; he had the Justice Department sue to break up trusts in a number of industries—including railroads, tobacco, and oil; and he was an early advocate of environmentalism, then called "conservation."

Theodore Roosevelt easily won the election of 1904. But in 1908 he declined to run again and turned the Republican nomination over to his hand-picked successor, William Howard Taft. Taft, too, won easily, but he went on to disappoint Roosevelt. In 1912 Roosevelt decided to make a comeback, but he was not able to recapture the Republican nomination from the incumbent Taft. Roosevelt then organized the Progressive party, later called the Bull Moose party, and ran against Taft, dividing the Republican vote and handing the election to the Democratic candidate, Woodrow Wilson, who won with a 42-percent plurality. (Nearly a half-million votes were drawn off by the Socialist Party's Eugene Debs.) As Roosevelt was embroiled in these struggles, he sought the advice of many fellow Progressives, including a young federal District Court judge from New York named Learned Hand.

Theodore Roosevelt, 1912.
Photo from Brown Brothers, Sterling, Pa.

JUDGE LEARNED HAND AND
PRESIDENT THEODORE ROOSEVELT

from Gerald Gunther, *Learned Hand: The Man and the Judge*
(New York: Alfred A. Knopf, 1994), pp. 118–23, 210–21.
Copyright © 1994 by Usingen Corporation.
Reprinted by permission of Alfred A. Knopf.

Learned Hand's most significant work during his early New York City years was the writing of a fifteen-page essay entitled "Due Process of Law and the Eight-Hour Day." Published in the May 1908 issue of the *Harvard Law Review*, the article was a response to a landmark decision by the Supreme Court in 1905, *Lochner v. New York*, a ruling that initiated three decades during which the Court intensively scrutinized and frequently struck down state and federal economic legislation. The name of the case still provides the colloquial label for those decades: the power wielded by the justices during "the *Lochner* era," when the Court engaged in "Lochnerizing" and frequently invalidated popularly supported laws, ultimately provoked public wrath. Hand's strong criticism of the ruling and the kind of judicial behavior it represented was one of the first published attacks on the decision, and one of the most trenchant. His analysis devastated the economic and jurisprudential underpinnings of the ruling and the reign of judicial supremacy—in his view, the abuse of judicial power—that *Lochner* initiated.

Hand's attack on *Lochner*, published in the nation's most widely read professional journal not long after his first, unsuccessful try for a judgeship, made him more visible, in New York and beyond. But ambition was not his prime motive. Rather, he was eager to elaborate a position on the proper role of the Supreme Court that he had first absorbed in James Bradley Thayer's classes at Harvard Law School, one that he believed in very deeply for the rest of his life. Hand's essay was not only a cutting critique of the legal justifications for the Court's behavior but also a sharp economic and political commentary, unusually blunt for the stately pages of the *Harvard Law Review*.

. . . The fate of the New York law struck down in *Lochner* was far less important than the approach that the Court's ruling signified: *Lochner* indicated that the justices would review very carefully, and would not hesitate to invalidate, many economic regulations, including the new worker-protective provisions that legislatures were beginning to adopt (decades after they had become commonplace in Europe). Hand's attack on *Lochner* presciently identified the harms that would flow from this judicial attitude, both in the obstruction of the popular will and in the abuse of judicial power.

. . .

When Hand was a law student in the mid-1890s, the Court had not yet struck down a single law on such "substantive due-process" grounds. But Professor Thayer spent much of Hand's constitutional-law course warning about the threatening cloud on the horizon—the risk that the justices would abuse their power and read their political and economic biases into the Constitution.

. . .

By 1908, when Hand wrote his article, the Court had reinforced its *Lochner* ruling with two similar decisions whose implications he also condemned. He emphatically agreed with Holmes's contention that the majority had "perverted" due process in *Lochner* and its progeny; indeed, he went beyond Holmes in narrowing the function of courts in cases claiming due-process violations. . . .

Hand's clear implication that the justices in the *Lochner* majority were reading their economic biases into the Constitution went further than most commentators were willing to go. But Hand had the youthful courage to speak out. A fervent plea for judicial restraint, a strong endorsement of legislative power to engage in experimentation, a sharp attack on exercises of judicial authority in the *Lochner* mode—these were Hand's central themes.

Hand set forth his supporting arguments succinctly and lucidly. In a passage revealing his deep convictions about the dangers of permitting judges to consider the wisdom or expediency of challenged laws, he stated:

> Whether it be wise or not that there should be a third camera with a final veto upon legislation with whose economic or political expediency it totally disagrees, is a political question of the highest importance. In particular it is questionable whether such a power can endure in a democratic state, while the court retains the irresponsibility of a life tenure, and while its decisions can be reversed only by the cumbersome process of a change of the federal Constitution. . . . [I]f the court is to retain the absolute right to pass . . . on the expediency of statutes passed by the legislature, the difficulty is inherent and in the end it may demand some change, either in the court or in the Constitution.

The risk, in short, was that the *Lochner* philosophy allowed unelected, politically unaccountable judges to decide whether a particular legislative purpose was or was not legitimate. Courts, Hand argued, were not super-legislatures: they exceeded their legitimate powers unless they deferred to elected legislatures on debatable issues.

Hand's second line of attack drew on his readings in economic theory. He argued that it was justifiable to restrict hours of labor, for this promoted the economic welfare of workers. Could it really be claimed that the protective laws made no contribution to that welfare, either under classic free-market theories or under more modern, paternalistic ones? In this part of his essay, Hand invoked recent "trades-unionist theory" and cited a book he had recently read, *Industrial Democracy,* by the British Fabian socialists Sidney and Beatrice Webb. So long as the economic arguments for a law existed, he insisted, that was "as far as the court can inquire." Nor were restraints on contract merely a fiction of socialist theory. Following Holmes, Hand cited the unquestioned validity of usury laws and argued further: "For the state to intervene to make more just and equal the relative strategic advantages of the two parties to the contract, of whom one is under the pressure of absolute want, while the other is not, is as proper a legislative function as that it should neutralize the relative advantages arising from fraudulent cunning or from superior physical force." . . .

Hand's essay elicited considerable attention and helped to make him attractive to those eager to place more articulate and independent individuals on the bench. A few years later, C. C. Burlingham would put it well in writing to President William Howard Taft's attorney general, George W. Wickersham, on behalf of another promising young New York intellectual, Van Vechten Veeder. C.C.B. told Wickersham that Veeder, although not well known at the bar, had a reputation as a fine writer: "I admit that in a way creates a prejudice against him because ordinary New York lawyers, worshipping at the shrine of Efficiency and Dispatch, are rather shy of learning." But, he insisted, an eloquent writing style, combined with a good mind, should be considered an attractive trait in a judicial nominee. A man who could write well *and* think well, turn out the work, and had a modicum of good sense to boot— such phrases described Hand even better than they did Veeder. And when C.C.B. made a similar appeal to Wickersham in Hand's case, it succeeded equally well, in part because of the trenchancy and eloquence Hand had demonstrated in criticizing the *Lochner* approach. [Hand was appointed United States district judge for the Southern District of New York in 1909.]
. . .

[In May 1911 Hand] sent [Theodore] Roosevelt his *Harvard Law Review* article on *Lochner.* . . . And in his cover letter Hand proceeded to summarize his views on judicial power—the first of many such letters to Roosevelt in the next two years.

. . . In a unanimous, highly publicized and much criticized decision handed down on March 24, 1911, . . . [New York's highest Court, the Court of Appeals] held, in a case called *Ives v. South Buffalo Ry. Co.,* that New York's recently enacted workmen's compensation law was unconstitutional. Judge William E. Werner's long opinion embodied the *Lochner* philosophy; indeed, the ruling was a blow to progressives such as TR and Hand not just because it struck down an important piece of pro-worker reform legislation, but because it illustrated with a vengeance the evils of Lochnerism.

The 1910 New York law had counterparts in many other industrialized nations, although few in the United States. The prevailing American rule governing compensation for work-related injuries was notoriously unsatisfactory: the injured employee could recover only if he showed the employer to have been at fault ("negligent"). And even if the employer had been negligent, the employee would recover nothing if he had been guilty of any "contributory negligence," or if any of the other rules favorable to employers came into play (such as the notion that an employee "assumed the risk" of being hurt by "voluntarily" going to work in a dangerous business). In practice, injured employees could rarely clear these hurdles.

The New York statute had been drafted by the Wainwright Commission, which the legislature had established to study the problem of industrial accidents. The commission prepared what even the New York judges called an "excellent," "comprehensive" report, the premise of which was that injuries to workers in especially dangerous occupations were a "necessary, substantially unavoidable" part of doing business. However, the report said, the common-law system of compensating employees was "economically unwise and unfair" and imposed the financial burdens of unavoidable industrial accidents on the group least able to bear them. In the view of the study commission and the legislature, imposing liability on employers made sense because they could spread the costs of accidents by passing them along to their consumers. Yet this reasoning did not persuade the court: the judges insisted that they "must regard all economic, philosophical, and moral theories, attractive and desirable though they may be, as subordinate to" the constitutional barriers; the very purpose of a constitution was to protect the people "against the frequent and violent fluctuations of ... 'public opinion.'" In short, the protections of property and liberty in the due-process clauses could not yield simply because the majority and good sense supported the legislation.

For Hand, the *Ives* decision dampened hopes that a line of recent Supreme Court decisions had kindled. Two months earlier, the unanimous Supreme Court, in the so-called Oklahoma Bank case, *Noble State Bank v. Haskell*, had taken a very broad view of the state's police power and a narrow view of due-process restraints. The opinion, by Justice Holmes ..., warned against "pressing the broad words of the Fourteenth Amendment to a drily logical extreme" and stated that "the police power extends to all the great public needs." Holmes added that this power may be used "in aid of what is sanctioned by usage, or held by the prevailing morality or strong and preponderant opinion to be greatly and immediately necessary to the public welfare." This approach was precisely what Hand had advocated in his *Harvard Law Review* article three years earlier. ... In the context of this cheery omen from Washington, the New York *Ives* decision seemed all the more a rude awakening. What Hand "especially deplore[d]" was the "kind of interpretation of such vague clauses as 'due process of law' [that] takes away from the legislature the power to do those things which are recognized as within the legislative power in every civilized country of the world." The idea that due process "embalms individualistic doctrines of a hundred years ago I believe myself to be heretical historically and very serious practically." Moreover, however permanent the Supreme Court's apparent change of course, Hand realized, the *Ives* case showed that state courts could block state legislative reform on their own: the obstructionist New York court in *Ives* was not even subject to review by the Supreme Court, since it had rested its decision not only on the federal Constitution, but also on the counterpart due-process clause in the New York Constitution.

. . . Unless the courts adopted a more receptive attitude toward legislation, Hand argued, "I am quite certain that . . . either the courts must give up their constitutional prerogative, a by no means unthinkable alternative," or most reform laws would have to be validated through constitutional amendments, with the result that constitutions would look like codes of legislation—surely, "a cumbersome form of making law."

Hand later regretted that his early advice to Roosevelt did not differentiate more clearly between the responses to judicial obstructionism that he approved of and those that troubled him. Hand was delighted to see TR advance arguments that would help persuade judges to adopt the Holmes-Hand due-process position, but he had serious reservations about TR's advocacy of direct popular restraints on judges. Roosevelt, whose capacity for sustained rational thought Hand . . . repeatedly had reason to doubt, either did not understand this distinction or was not persuaded by it. Roosevelt . . . insisted that "the people" must have the ultimate power:

> I wish to see the judge given all power and treated with all respect; but I also wish to see him held accountable by the people. [T]hey must have the power to act. And not only should they exercise this power in the case of any judge who shows moral delinquency on the bench, but they should also exercise it whenever they have been forced to come to the conclusion that any judge, no matter how upright and well-intentioned, is fundamentally out of sympathy with the righteous popular movement, so that his presence on the bench has become a bar to orderly progress for the right.

This idea of popular restraints on individual judges was a measure that a few western progressive states had already adopted, and it soon divided progressive and conservative Republicans when, a few weeks later, the proposed constitution for the new state of Arizona was drafted to allow the electorate to recall state judges. President Taft lambasted the scheme as one that would convert justice into "legalized terrorism," asserting that "the people at the polls no more than kings upon the throne are fit to pass upon questions involving the judicial interpretation of the law." By contrast, Roosevelt suggested that judicial recall was necessary, that it was in fact only a moderate reform, and that decisions such as *Ives* "would, in the end, render it absolutely necessary for the American people, at whatever cost, to insist upon having a more direct control over the courts."

Until early 1911, Roosevelt had resisted endorsing measures like judicial recall, so his attack on *Ives* was the first sign that he might flirt with western populist notions of direct democracy. These notions only alarmed eastern progressives like Hand . . . , for whom true progressivism required national policy-making based on expertise.

Two major causes account for Roosevelt's change in attitude. The first was his outrage at the *Ives* case itself. But as he moved ever closer to candidacy in late 1911, he also found the pressures from western progressives difficult to resist. And when he became a public candidate for the Republican nomination early in 1912, the furor over these direct-democracy proposals diverted attention from his New Nationalist platform and doomed his campaign. Roosevelt then abandoned his flirtation with the idea of recall of judges, but he did not retreat all the way to Hand's position. Instead, beginning in the fall of 1911, TR began to advocate the recall of judicial *decisions*. Rather than endorsing the removal of individual judges by popular vote, he now urged that the people be given the power to overturn state court decisions that interpreted due-process clauses in state constitutions as prohibiting state reform laws—a proposal that would meet the *Ives* decision itself but not the underlying problem of restrictive interpretations of due process generally, of Lochnerism.

. . .

Roosevelt announced his revised plan to curb the judiciary in a New York City speech to an overflow crowd at Carnegie Hall on Friday evening, October 20, 1911. Roosevelt's address was quaintly entitled "The Conservation of Womanhood and Childhood," and much of the speech was indeed devoted to a plea for laws to prohibit child labor and limit working hours of women as well as men. But these proposals went virtually unnoticed in the next morning's newspapers. What was new in Roosevelt's speech was his call for popular power over the decisions of the courts. He criticized judges "who have proved their devotion, not to the Constitution, as they thought, but to a system of social and economic philosophy which in my judgment is not only outworn, but to the last degree mischievous." Abuses of the courts' power to adjudicate constitutionality had to be curbed, and his preferred method of controlling the courts, he insisted, was not radical but the only alternative to radicalism: "The people should be enabled with reasonable speed and in effective fashion themselves to determine by popular vote whether or not they will permit the judges' interpretation of the Constitution to stand."

Despite Roosevelt's protests that his plan was moderate, his proposal, reiterated and elaborated for months to come, proved to be an egregious political mistake. . . . Astonishingly, Teddy Roosevelt took this important political step without consulting anyone. Apparently it was not until TR read the attacks on his Carnegie Hall speech, and realized that his general proposal raised knotty problems of detail as well as principle, that it occurred to him to seek advice. Some of his supporters pressed him to seek legal counsel. Brooks Adams, the pessimistic historian of the Adams clan, observed mordantly that it was highly desirable that "some thoroughly competent constitutional and economic lawyer—if you know such a one—advise you always before you speak." To consult someone before every speech was clearly not in Roosevelt's character, but he did know of a "thoroughly competent" lawyer, and he did seek his advice. The person he turned to was Judge Learned Hand.

Roosevelt sent Hand proofs of the "Conservation of Womanhood and Childhood," asking for comments. On November 20, 1911, Hand replied. Thinking that the speech was to be published within a week, Hand had little hope of changing the nature of the text, but he expected that this would not be the last word from TR on the issue, and he hoped to influence Roosevelt's future course. With respect to TR's general attack on abuses of judicial power, Hand made it clear, "I have said very often almost the same thing and there is really none of it that I can disagree with." But agreement as to the evil did not mean agreement with TR's remedies: "[T]o Appeal to the people not to endorse such opinions as [*Ives*] is to ask a remedy which is either impracticable, or, as I think, very dangerous." The danger was that recall of decisions threatened judicial independence, and indeed the very office of a judge:

> [I] cannot quite swallow the necessity of having public pressure put on a judge for any purpose, for it so utterly perverts the assumption which is fundamental in his function. He should properly have no duty, but to interpret words which have been used by the sovereign itself, and in doing that I think it is fatal in the end to his integrity to try to find the sovereign's meaning except in its formal declarations.

In short, so long as judges possessed the power of judicial review, a conscientious judge must try to interpret the words of the Constitution and not bow to the most recent referendum on the popular will. The problem, of course, was that general clauses such as "due process" were difficult to interpret in particular cases. But if it came to a choice between judicial independence and the general clauses, Hand made clear that he would opt for the former, not the latter:

> Really, we [judges] have got ourselves into the mess we are now in here in America, by failing to remember how strictly our duties should be interpretive. . . . In construing the vague clauses of the Bill of Rights we have done the most damage, and something must be done to change it, but I really think that I had rather take them out of the constitutions altogether than make the judges respond to any popular pressure.

Assuming, however, that the "vague clauses" were retained, judges had to make sure that they interpreted the text faithfully and did not merely give voice to personal or even popular opinion:

> The popular will, when clearly ascertained, cannot wisely be withstood in a democracy, but there are a good many occasions when before it has been authoritatively expressed [in the text of a constitution or statute], a judge is tempted to interpret what he finds about him in popular form. Except in so far as that helps him to an honest interpretation of what has reached authoritative expression, I have not the least doubt that he should, and indeed he must, wholly disregard them. If he does not, he is just as much a usurper of authority if they be popular . . . as though he followed his personal, but unpopular, predilections.

. . .

[W]hen Hand saw [another] article that TR had been writing, his hopes were once more dashed. The January 6, 1912, issue of *The Outlook* featured "Judges and Progress," Roosevelt's longest and most careful statement yet on the issue of judicial power. The conclusion was as provocative as ever: Roosevelt still advocated recall of judicial decisions. By now, Roosevelt had all but announced as a presidential candidate; the article was probably his misguided effort to attract support from the broadest possible coalition. Yet he was persisting in a stand that alienated many potential supporters. TR had reason to worry that westerners would prefer the more populist progressive, La Follette. Yet by continuing to advocate recall of decisions (though not recall of judges), and indeed making this position clearer than ever, he quickly lost the support of conservative Republicans, and moderate progressives such as Hand would view Roosevelt with mounting distrust.

. . .

On February 21, 1912, three days before Roosevelt announced, "I will accept a nomination for President if it is tendered to me," he delivered a major speech before the Ohio Constitutional Convention at Columbus in which he once again urged recall of judicial decisions and asserted he would support even the recall of judges as a remedy of last resort. This speech alienated many of Roosevelt's supporters and gave Taft and his cohorts their chief weapon for attacking TR in the ensuing primary campaign. Many of Roosevelt's allies abandoned him. . . . Hand, too, was distressed; he did not yet give up all hope of persuading Roosevelt to change his tune. Instead, for most of the spring, he sought to encourage TR to adopt still another moderate remedy, one that his longtime . . . acquaintance George Rublee had suggested. Hand had recently introduced Rublee to Roosevelt (and Rublee would soon join the inner circle of TR advisers). . . .

Rublee's idea, Hand wrote to TR, seemed to go "to the very heart of the difficulty" in a "more thorough-going fashion" than anything he had earlier suggested. The restrictive reading of due process that *Lochner* and *Ives* exemplified could be overcome, Rublee and Hand thought, by a constitutional amendment that would define "due process of law.". . .

Throughout March, Learned Hand and his closest friends bombarded Roosevelt with pleas that he embrace the Rublee-Hand constitutional amendment route. Rublee . . . joined this campaign, as did a new, soon to be intimate, friend of Hand.

This new face in the progressive movement was an effervescent, engaging young intellectual, Felix Frankfurter. Frankfurter was ten years younger than Hand, much younger than the other reformist lawyers in his circle, but this difference in age was no obstacle to a fast-developing friendship that deepened for the rest of Hand's life.

CHAPTER 15

Federal Regulation

Felix Frankfurter, a Jewish immigrant from Vienna, was the star student in Harvard Law School's class of 1905. After graduation, he spent an unhappy few months with a Wall Street law firm but then took a cut in pay and went to work in government jobs. In 1914 he returned to Harvard Law School as a professor and remained on the faculty until appointed to the U.S. Supreme Court in 1939. He retired from the Court in 1962.

Frankfurter never became wealthy. Instead of amassing wealth, he amassed influence. From his position at Harvard Law School, he remained active in public service, serving in the War Department during the First World War, mediating labor disputes, representing Progressive causes in litigation, advising the powerful, and publishing his ideas in popular as well as scholarly journals. He passed on his zeal for public service to his students, filling Washington agencies with Harvard alumni.

Foremost among Frankfurter's friends and mentors was another Jewish graduate of Harvard Law School, Louis D. Brandeis, who had been star of the class of 1878. In a dual biography of the two men, *Brandeis and Frankfurter* (1984), Leonard Baker has written:

> The association between Brandeis and Frankfurter . . . developed into a unique relationship. Their lives encompassed one-half the history of the United States; one remembered the Civil War, the other joined in the declaration that racial segregation in public schools was unconstitutional a century later. From the early 1900s to the early 1960s, the two of them, either singly or together, were involved in virtually every domestic struggle in the United States: civil liberties, civil rights, and criminal law, as well as economic rights. As lawyers they demanded courts acknowledge and deal with the grievances of the poor as well as the rich. They lobbied in the backrooms of the political houses for laws bene-

fiting the immigrant and the worker. They spoke to the rich and powerful on behalf of those not previously heard. (p. 45)

Both men also became active in the cause of Zionism. The relationship of Brandeis and Frankfurter became so close that Brandeis—who had stuck with private practice long enough to become rich—even helped Frankfurter financially to work for Progressive causes after Brandeis was appointed to the Supreme Court (where he served from 1916 to 1939), an arrangement that led to charges of impropriety when it was revealed many years after both men died.

Frankfurter graduated from law school in the year in which the Progressive agenda received a jolt from the Supreme Court's *Lochner* decision. Litigation on behalf of Progressive causes seemed almost hopeless. Brandeis demonstrated three years later that some Progressive cases could still be won, but for major policy changes, it seemed more promising to turn to Congress and to Theodore Roosevelt's White House.

A number of Progressive legislative victories had been scored in the late nineteenth century. Most notable was the establishment of the Interstate Commerce Commission (ICC) in 1887. Although the Supreme Court had upheld the regulation of railroads by states in *Munn v. Illinois* in 1877, it ruled nine years later, in *Wabash, St. Louis & Pacific Railway Co. v. Illinois*, that state regulations interfered unconstitutionally with interstate commerce. Congress responded by creating the ICC, the first independent federal administrative agency.

Many found the concept of an independent administrative agency difficult to accept. The Constitution defined the three branches of government, and some accused Congress of having created a fourth branch with powers of the other three branches—the power to legislate by issuing regulations, to adjudicate by holding hearings, and to execute by issuing and enforcing orders. On the other hand, Congress could not be expected to deal with the details of railroad regulation, and business interests as well as Progressives preferred regulation by a commission with expertise to the uncertainties of unregulated competition and case-by-case litigation. Nevertheless, a number of Supreme Court decisions over the next decade deprived the ICC of its most important power—the power to set rates—leaving the agency little more than a "sunshine" commission with power to investigate and throw light on the industry.

Another Progressive legislative victory was the Sherman Act of 1890 outlawing every "contract, combination . . . or conspiracy . . . in restraint of trade or commerce." The vagueness of the Act's terms left much of the specifics up to the courts. The Supreme Court responded by evolving a "rule of reason" by which the act was applied to some restraints of trade or commerce, but not others. The resulting uncertainty pleased neither Progressives nor the business world.

New legislation in 1906 restored the rate-making authority of the ICC. In that same year, the Pure Food and Drug Act and the Meat Inspection Act gave additional regulatory powers to the federal government after shocking exposés by "muckracker" journalists of unsanitary and dangerous conditions in the pharmaceutical and meat-packing industries.

In 1906 the Progressive cause also received a boost from an unlikely source: a speech by a young Nebraska law professor named Roscoe Pound to the annual convention of the American Bar Association on "The Causes of Popular Dissatisfaction with the Administration of Justice." Pound criticized the courts for their obstruction of legal reform, their archaic procedures, and other failings. Convention speeches are usually forgotten, but this one—and the bar's generally hostile and defensive reaction—caused quite a stir. It also helped propel Pound from Nebraska to Harvard Law School, where he eventually became dean and the leading American academic theorist of "sociological jurisprudence" emphasizing the social functions of legal rules rather than their forms or contents.

In 1907, in *Illinois Central Railroad Co. v. ICC*, the Supreme Court approved the restored rate-making authority of the ICC. There remained, however, the uncertainties of the Sherman Act, and some were calling for an entirely new approach to combat anticompetitive business practices.

Louis D. Brandeis, 1890s.
Photo from University of Louisville Law School.

JUSTICE LOUIS D. BRANDEIS

from Thomas K. McCraw, *Prophets of Regulation*
(Cambridge, Mass.: Harvard University Press, 1984), pp. 80–142.
Copyright © 1984 by the President and Fellows of Harvard College.
Reprinted by permission of Harvard University Press.

Brandeis and the Origins of the FTC

The formal regulation of business combinations in America dates from the passage of the Sherman Antitrust Act of 1890. The Sherman law in practice proved an unclear guide: its broad language raised problems of interpretation and left both business managers and government officials uncertain as to which commercial practices were being prohibited. During the first decade of the twentieth century, proposals to revise the Sherman Act appeared from every quarter. Neopopulists wanted a tough law to break up existing trusts and prevent additional ones from forming. Executives of center* firms sought greater reassurance about the legality of their operations. Managers of peripheral† firms wanted guarantees of immunity from prosecution for their own cartel-like activities. Although these groups disagreed about the specific provisions desirable in new legislation, there developed a consensus that a special federal regulatory commission might be helpful in interpreting and administering antitrust policy.

Theodore Roosevelt admired the commission form of government, and as president he encouraged the formation in 1903 of the United States Bureau of Corporations. The bureau's elite staff of economists and lawyers soon began to produce extremely useful studies of such center firms as Standard Oil, American Tobacco, and International Harvester. . . . Many of the bureau's admirers became convinced that its scope should be broadened. An "interstate trade commission," they believed, might combine the bureau's investigative activities with powerful new regulatory functions based on the model of the Interstate Commerce Commission. As the ICC oversaw railroads, the new

---

*The author defines "center" firms as "giant companies . . . requiring very large outlays of investment . . . technologically advanced . . . enjoy[ing] some significant scale economy." (p. 72)

†"Peripheral" firms are defined as "small, labor-intensive, managerially thin, and bereft of scale economies." (pp. 72–73)

trade commission would supervise manufacturing, wholesaling, and retailing. When Roosevelt once more ran for the presidency in 1912, his Progressive Party platform called for just such an agency.

Some Democrats also favored an interstate trade commission. The influential Senator Francis Newlands of Nevada, for example, introduced a commission bill in 1911 and worked diligently but unsuccessfully for its passage. Other Democrats, suspicious of bureaucratic government and fearful that a commission might indirectly accord legitimacy to big business, looked askance at Newlands' idea. One of these doubting Democrats was Governor Woodrow Wilson of New Jersey.

In the presidential election of 1912, Wilson defeated Progressive Theodore Roosevelt and Republican incumbent William Howard Taft, who took a pro-commission position less enthusiastic than that of Roosevelt. During the election campaign, Wilson departed from his anti-commission stance and supported the creation of a sunshine agency, to be coupled with tough and explicit new antitrust laws. But once in office, Wilson found it hard to decide on the shape of his antitrust program. Not until 1914 did he launch a two-part legislative package: one part would clarify the ambiguities of the Sherman Act through a specific enumeration of forbidden practices; the other would create a new regulatory agency. Finally, late in 1914, the Federal Trade Commission emerged, as a hybrid of proposals from Roosevelt, Newlands, and certain of Wilson's own advisers.

No individual person played the role of "father" of the Federal Trade Commission. . . . In truth, the FTC had many parents, but it captured the special attention of none. Troubled in infancy, awkward in adolescence, clumsy in adulthood, the agency never found a coherent mission for itself. . . . By common agreement of modern scholars, the FTC has been a singularly unsuccessful agency during most of the seventy-odd years since its creation. The primary reason behind this dolorous history has been identified as the persistent confusion and ambiguity of American public policy toward competition—the very problem that the FTC Act was intended to solve.

Insofar as the career of a single person illustrates both the problems that led to the FTC's creation and the reasons for its subsequent failure, that person is Louis D. Brandeis. The most influential critic of trusts during his generation, Brandeis served from 1912 until 1916 as Woodrow Wilson's chief economic adviser and was regarded as one of the architects of the FTC. Above all else, Brandeis exemplified the anti-bigness ethic without which there would have been no Sherman Act, no antitrust movement, and no Federal Trade Commission.

The Man and the Legend

As the "people's lawyer" of the Progressive Era, Brandeis embodied the popular revolt against the sudden domination of the nation's economic life by big business. His career as a practicing lawyer, which began in 1878 and ended with his appointment to the Supreme Court in 1916, coincided almost precisely with the principal phase of the rise of center firms. . . . Brandeis watched the business revolution as it developed, tried his best to understand it, and found it, on the whole, hostile to his own values of autonomous individualism. For that reason he fought it, and in his crusades against what he called the "curse of bigness" he was a formidable champion.

Several different forces in his background shaped Brandeis' individualistic values. Eight years before his birth in 1856, his Bohemian Jewish parents had fled Europe during the suppression of the democratic movements of 1848. Settling in Louisville, Kentucky, the family prospered in the grain-merchandising business but suffered setbacks during the depression of the 1870s. Louis Brandeis, an intellectually gifted child, was educated at the German and English Academy in Louisville and, later, when the depression in America drove the family temporarily back to Europe, at the Annen-Realschule in Dresden. He entered Harvard Law School in 1875, at the age of eighteen, and made a phenomenal record. Because he finished the standard course of study at Harvard before he reached twenty-one, a special ruling was required to allow him to graduate. . . .

. . . Brandeis' personal papers [have been] made widely available to scholars. In 1971, thirty years after his death, the first two volumes of his collected letters appeared, and by 1978 the remaining three volumes. For a number of scholars, these papers were a treasure; their publication represented an event that would illuminate the history of American Zionism, American reform, and the character and career of Brandeis himself. It was thought that the collected letters might force open the last unknown chambers of his life.

What they in fact showed was that Brandeis had been much less a man of thought than of action. None of the letters conveyed the impression of a deep conceptual intelligence. In them there was little evidence of reflection, none of rumination. There was no . . . agonizing over one's proper role in life or relationship with God, no self-doubt on any score. Instead, the letters depicted a quick, confident, and often rigid mind preoccupied with some immediate practical task—a controlled, carefully managed life with no wasted motion, little humor, and no frivolity.

Brandeis held himself aloof from other men. He encouraged awe and veneration, and he seemed impossible to know well. . . . As the editors of his letters put it, Brandeis "understood how to behave like a symbol." Today we see something of what that symbol represented. For Brandeis almost perfectly embodies some of the best and the worst elements in the American regulatory tradition. On the one hand, he epitomized the dogged militancy which has given that tradition its distinctive sense of righteousness and moral passion. On the other, Brandeis offered regulatory solutions grounded on a set of economic assumptions that were fundamentally wrong.

After graduation from law school, Brandeis associated himself in practice with Samuel D. Warren, a classmate whose wealth and family connections provided a ready clientele as well as entry into Boston social circles. Brandeis himself, with all his brilliance and his new Harvard connections, was yet a young Jew from Louisville, and Boston was one of the most snobbish and ingrown of American cities. As a social outsider, he could afford no false steps. . . . The firm of Warren and Brandeis enjoyed immediate success, in part because its first client was the paper-manufacturing company owned by the Warren family.

Brandeis' continued prosperity, however, depended not on the Warren connection but on his own drive and ability. Both were of the highest order. At Harvard, where he compiled what is still the best record in the law school's history, he had written of his "desperate longing for more law" and of the "almost ridiculous pleasure which the discovery or invention of a legal theory gives me." He referred to the law as his "mistress," holding a grip on him that he could not break. This passionate attachment served him well. In his career as a litigator, Brandeis became one of the most effective advocates the United States has ever produced. He had all the requisite talents: the persistent inquisitiveness, the quick study, the drive to win, the skepticism, the sympathetic style, the love of combat. He had two even more useful qualities. The first was a remarkable ability to convey a sense of the rightness of his client's cause. As one of his partners put it, "The prime source of his power was his intense belief in the truth of what he was saying. It carried conviction."

The second quality was the very close attention he gave to the care of clients. "Cultivate the society of men—particularly men of affairs," Brandeis once advised a young associate in his firm. . . . Brandeis himself took great pains to know men. During his early years in Boston, he kept a small notebook in which he listed the names of everyone he met at social gatherings. Gradually he accumulated dozens of thick scrapbooks on all sorts of personal, legal, and political subjects. . . .

Brandeis' careful development of his lawyerly skills reflected a characteristically shrewd management of his own career. "Know thoroughly each fact," he remonstrated in a memorandum to himself on the practice of law. "Don't believe client witness. Examine documents. Reason; use imagination. Know bookkeeping—the universal language of business: know persons. Far more likely to impress clients by knowledge of facts than by knowledge of law. Know not only specific case, but whole subject. Can't otherwise know the facts. Know not only those facts which bear on direct controversy, but know all facts and law that surround." Brandeis' emphasis on facts became a minor legend in itself, an important part of the sociological jurisprudence he advocated later in his career. "It has been one of the rules of my life," he once told a newspaper reporter, "that no one shall ever trip me up on a question of fact." Brandeis advised the young associate in his firm that the person "who practices law—who aspires to the higher places of his profession—must keep his mind fresh. It must be alert and he must be capable of meeting emergencies—must be capable of the tour de force." No American lawyer has ever been more capable of the tour de force than was Brandeis himself.

. . . As a busy attorney, Brandeis went rapidly from case to case, on a schedule set not by his own choice but by the dockets of courts and commissions. He became, as trial lawyers must, a quick expert on many different subjects: now railroads, now trusts, now conservation, now banking, now labor, now retailing. Of necessity, the expertise so rapidly acquired seldom ran very deep. . . .

As an outsider and a Jew, Brandeis did not attract the largest clients available to Boston law firms. These were the major banks and insurance companies, the railroads headquartered in the city, and the new giant manufacturing firms arising from the reorganizations and mergers of the period. His typical clients were not center firms, but peripherals: small and medium-sized manufacturers of boots, shoes, and paper, along with prominent Jewish wholesalers and retailers such as the Hechts and the Filenes. Following his own advice, Brandeis came to know these clients intimately. He impressed them with his factual knowledge of their businesses, and they employed him as counselor and adviser on a wide range of legal and business problems. Ultimately, this work on their behalf made him a millionaire. In turn, Brandeis also became identified politically with their interests; and much in his later campaigns as the "people's lawyer"—particularly his approach to the antitrust question—can be traced back to the problems and interests of these clients.

The most striking thing about Brandeis' triumphs as the people's lawyer was his almost extrasensory instinct for the winning ground. Here, time after time, he showed himself capable of the tour de force. He won his cases repeatedly, often against heavy odds, and the reputation for winning in turn became an essential element of the emerging Brandeis mystique. This talent for finding the winning ground, present in many great lawyers, in Brandeis reached extremely pronounced form, as several of his best known cases show. Three of these were *Muller v. Oregon* (1908), the Ballinger-Pinchot controversy (1910), and the Advance Rate Case before the Interstate Commerce Commission (1910). Together, these three episodes made him a celebrated national figure. In each, he deftly shifted the terms of the dispute away from his clients' weak points and onto novel ground. In all three situations, he caught the opposition by surprise, and in each he won the case.

The Winning Ground

In *Muller v. Oregon,* Brandeis defended the power of the state to enact a law limiting women's hours of work. The case represented a clash of two constitutional principles: on the one hand, freedom of contract, under which a worker and an employer could agree on any schedule of work, without limit; on the other, the right of a state to enact regulatory legislation for which it had a reasonable and not arbitrary basis. Three years earlier, in *Lochner v. New York* (1905), the Supreme Court had enunciated an extreme form of freedom of contract by overturning a statute that limited the working hours of New York bakers to ten per day. The controlling precedent, therefore, seemed squarely against the state of Oregon.

In defense of the Oregon statute, Brandeis . . . took the radical step of arguing on the grounds of statistical, sociological, and medical information concerning the physical consequences of overwork. If he could persuade the Supreme Court to accept his novel forms of evidence, he might win. One part of his brief before the court (pages 1–24) explored the relevant legal precedents and argument. But a much larger part (pages 24–113, which became famous in legal circles as the "Brandeis brief") detailed the testimony of numerous experts on the effects of overwork. In all, Brandeis cited or quoted from over ninety reports from American and European factory inspectors, commissioners of hygiene, and other authorities. Some of Brandeis' evidence in the *Muller* case strikes modern ears as a bit odd: "Long hours of labor are dangerous for women primarily because of their special physical organization." But the evidence showed clearly that the state had reasonable grounds on which to legislate. And from the time of *Muller* down to the present day, Brandeis' "sociological jurisprudence" has exercised a profound influence on the development of American law.

In a second case, Brandeis found a different kind of winning ground: management of publicity to discredit a political leader. This was in the Ballinger-Pinchot affair, the most sensational controversy of the Progressive Era. The case kept Brandeis in the national spotlight for much of the year 1910, and it confirmed his growing reputation as a legal magician.

The Ballinger-Pinchot dispute grew out of a disagreement over natural resources policy among former lieutenants of Theodore Roosevelt after his departure from the White House in 1909. Eventually the controversy precipitated a split between Roosevelt and his chosen successor, William Howard Taft. . . .

The affair began when Louis Glavis, a young employee of the Department of the Interior, went to his supervisor, Secretary Richard A. Ballinger, with a report that certain mining claims involving the wealthy Guggenheim family might be illegal. Ballinger, who had once done some legal work for the Guggenheims, dismissed Glavis' charges as unfounded. Glavis then took his tale to Chief Forester Gifford Pinchot, a holdover from the previous Roosevelt Administration and a symbol of Roosevelt's widely admired conservation policies. Pinchot, never one to miss an opportunity to score against an opponent, now brought Glavis' charges to the attention of President Taft. This act moved the issue beyond the mining claims and toward the question of Secretary Ballinger's integrity.

Taft responded by asking Ballinger for an explanation. The secretary went to see Taft at the president's summer home, taking along numerous documents bearing on the mining claims. Taft accepted Ballinger's explanation and in a long letter authorized him to dismiss Glavis for insubordination. Next Glavis, stung by his firing and egged on by officials within Pinchot's Forest Service, took his story to *Collier's Weekly*, a popular magazine that specialized in muckraking stories. *Collier's* editor Norman Hapgood, a friend and political ally of Brandeis, printed Glavis' article. (The cover of this issue depicted Secretary Ballinger in the middle of a large question mark with the caption, "Are the Guggenheims in Charge of the Department of the Interior?") An ensuing barrage of articles in newspapers and other magazines attacked Ballinger and focused public attention on the upcoming conservation hearings in Congress. . . . Brandeis appeared before the congressional committee as Glavis' attorney. Meanwhile, Pinchot heaped more fuel on the fire by ostentatiously challenging Taft and forcing the president to fire him from the post of chief forester.

In his role as Glavis' lawyer, Brandeis in effect was opposing Secretary Ballinger, President Taft, and Attorney General George Wickersham, who had advised Taft on the firing of Glavis. Unfortunately for Brandeis, a close examination of the evidence and of Ballinger's record as secretary yielded little ammunition for the Glavis-Pinchot-*Collier's* forces. The secretary was a capable public servant who would not be easy to discredit. But Brandeis found Glavis to be an articulate, appealing underdog who might excel on the witness stand, if only some focus could be provided for the contention that Ballinger was dishonest.

The necessary focus materialized when Brandeis discovered that members of the opposition had made a colossal error. They had antedated an important document pertaining to Taft's investigation of Glavis' original charges and had concealed the existence of a second such document. Brandeis decided to play out this discovery in small increments and thereby maximize the suspense. By shrewd management, periodic leaks to the press, and relentless questioning of witnesses, he gradually shifted the focus of the hearings from conservation policy and the propriety of Ballinger's conduct of the mining investigation to the honesty and integrity not only of Ballinger but also of Attorney General Wickersham and even of President Taft. The revelations about the antedating, which had little to do with the original issues but were intensely embarrassing to the administration, now became a national scandal, reported and embellished day after day by delighted journalists. Brandeis' management of the case, coupled with Ballinger's clumsy efforts to defend the administration, ended in total vindication of Glavis and Pinchot.

. . .

The fairest verdict on the Ballinger-Pinchot controversy has been provided by the historian James Penick: "Ballinger had to be labeled a 'high-toned crook' or there would have been no contest. 'If they had brazenly admitted everything,' Brandeis said, 'and justified it on the ground that Ballinger was at least doing what he thought best, we should not have had a chance.' It was the lying that did it, he added." . . .

In a third celebrated episode, Brandeis surpassed even his Ballinger-Pinchot performance. This was in the so-called Advance Rate Case before the Interstate Commerce Commission. The case began in 1910, when American railroads petitioned the ICC for an across-the-board increase in freight rates. The railroads alleged that their costs had risen rapidly because of much higher labor costs and inflationary pressures. Shipping interests hired Brandeis to oppose the railroads' petition, and he embraced their cause with great vigor. He identified them with the entrepreneurial firms he had long represented in Boston, some of which were significant shippers chronically involved in New England rate controversies. Also, Brandeis' father, a Louisville merchant, had dealt regularly with railroads, and Brandeis' brother Alfred was one of that city's major shippers of grain.

The national railroads, on the other hand, were . . . widely regarded as unduly wealthy and powerful. If there were a "curse of bigness," American railroads were among the most cursed institutions in the world. Their request in 1910 for the rate increase was neither well timed nor well managed. Indeed, the very idea of a jointly requested across-the-board increase for all railroad corporations (the profitable along with the unprofitable) and for all items of cargo (money makers and money losers) seemed to reflect a political arrogance that had characterized the industry since the 1850s. Yet in retrospect it is clear that the railroads did need a rate increase. Their costs were rising because of inflation and spiraling wages, and their roadbeds were deteriorating under pressures of extremely heavy traffic. The railroads' attorneys and financial officers presented a strong case before the ICC for a rate increase, buttressing their argument with page after page of persuasive statistical analysis.

Brandeis' response, breathtaking in its boldness, took opposition lawyers completely by surprise. He readily conceded that the railroad companies needed much more money. But he insisted that the proper source was not higher rates for shippers, but lower internal operating costs for the companies themselves. In his brief before the ICC, Brandeis stated: "As an alternative to the railroads' practice of combining to increase rates we offer cooperation to reduce costs. Instead of a dangerous makeshift, we offer constructive policy—scientific management, under which as costs fall wages rise."

As his most telling point, Brandeis impressed on the commissioners the "fact" that the railroads were operating inefficiently. The companies, he said, were ignoring "scientific management," a series of new techniques associated with . . . "efficiency experts" [who] enjoyed huge popularity during the Progressive Era. Their methods had already brought productivity gains to a number of manufacturing firms. When Brandeis called several of the experts to the witness stand, they made the most of this free publicity as an unpaid advertisement for their consulting services. And with their help Brandeis spun out, day by day, a tale of miracles, of almost certain efficiencies that would accrue from the railroads' conversion to the new system:

> Scientific Management [said Brandeis] differs from that now generally practiced by the railroads, much as production by machinery differs from production by hand. . . . Under scientific management nothing is left to chance. All is carefully prepared in advance. Every operation is to be performed according to a predetermined schedule under definite instructions, and the execution under this plan is inspected and supervised at every point. Errors are prevented instead of being corrected. The terrible waste of delays and accidents is avoided. Calculation is substituted for guess; demonstration for opinion. The high efficiency of the limited passenger trains is sought to be obtained in the ordinary operations of the business. The same preparedness is invoked for industry which secured to Prussia her victory over France and to Japan her victory over Russia.

As if all these remarkable results were not enough in themselves, Brandeis promised one final miracle. With his uncanny sense for the winning ground and ear for the catchy idiom, Brandeis elicited from expert witness Harrington Emerson the opinion that, under scientific management, the nation's railroads could save "at least $1,000,000 a day." This million-dollars-a-day slogan was taken up and broadcast throughout the country by newspapers. Cited again and again during the rate hearings, it took on a life of its own. Ultimately it seemed to be made true by virtue of endless repetition. Once more, Brandeis won his case. The ICC refused to give the railroads an additional penny.

. . .

Later on, railroad men and some disinterested analysts as well complained that Brandeis had simply dazzled the ICC and the public with promises of miraculous savings. Subsequent events in the railroad industry all but proved that scientific management had much less relevance for transportation and other service industries than it did for manufacturing. . . . And by the time of the war emergency of 1917–18, the railroads had fallen into such desperate financial straits that the federal government temporarily took over the entire industry. After a brief study, the government instituted by fiat very large across-the-board rate hikes of about the size of the combined increases the railroads themselves had requested in the years between 1910 and 1918. . . .

The rabbit-from-hat character of all three of Brandeis' celebrated victories foreshadowed the kinds of arguments he would make later against big business. There too he often substituted slogans for careful analysis. In his rhetoric against the trusts he appealed, as always, to the best moral instincts of his various audiences. But at the same time he misled them, perhaps unintentionally, about the practicability of his remedies.

. . .

Price Fixing, the Consumer, and the Petite Bourgeoisie

One of Brandeis' most characteristic campaigns was his energetic work on be-half of resale price maintenance (that is, price fixing or, in the euphemism of its proponents, "fair trade"). This controversy began in 1911, when the Supreme Court, in the patent-medicine case of *Dr. Miles Medical Co. v. John D. Park & Sons Co.*, ruled that price fixing was illegal, under both the com-mon law and the Sherman Act. The Miles company was a manufacturer of a popular elixir which it distributed through a network of 400 wholesalers and 25,000 retailers. The company's contracts with each of these dealers required that its elixir not be sold for less than a price specified by the company. If a wholesaler or retailer would not sign such a contract, the Miles company de-clined to do business with it.

John D. Park & Sons, a wholesale drug firm, refused to sign. Instead, Park procured the elixir from another wholesaler . . . for the purpose of reselling it to consumers at a price below the figure desired by the manufacturer. Dr. Miles thereupon sued Park. In deciding the case in favor of Park, the Supreme Court unshackled competition and opened a new era of price war-fare among retailers. In the process of doing so, the court provoked, in op-position to its ruling, one of the longest, most relentless, and best organized business lobbying efforts in American history. Brandeis spearheaded this lobbying. He lent his name to the crusade to overturn the court's decision, wrote articles and delivered speeches attacking the new doctrine, and drafted a bill to exempt small wholesalers and retailers from the Sherman Act so that they could resume their practice of fixing retail prices at uniform levels nationwide.

. . .

For Brandeis and his allies, to be simultaneously against bigness and for consumers was extremely difficult. From our perspective three generations af-ter this price-fixing controversy, it is clear that a substantial part of the battle represented an attempt by Brandeis to use governmental power as a means of reinforcing the strength of small shopkeepers in their war against large, price cutting retailers. To the extent that consumers voted with their pocketbooks for department stores and mail-order houses, the fight against these large re-tailers became a fight against consumers as well. In Brandeis' personal case, the justification for making such a fight lay in a powerful ideological aversion to bigness. For the small shopkeepers themselves, however, the issue involved stark self-interest. . . .

Brandeis' lament about the decline of autonomous individualism aptly il-lustrated one of the poignant themes of modern culture in an age of big business. This theme was the conflict between the small producer's values, which had characterized nineteenth-century American culture, and the emerging consumerist values of a twentieth-century mass society. Brandeis' hostility to the new consumerism found vivid expression in his own behavior. Though himself a millionaire, he disliked most other wealthy persons, being profoundly disturbed by their ostentatious consumption. He was incredulous, for example, when he read newspaper reports in 1911 that Elbert H. Gary of U.S. Steel had presented his wife with a pearl necklace valued at $500,000: "Is it not just the same sort of thing which brought on the French Revolution?" Brandeis also loathed such modern devices as automobiles and telephones. He practically never went shopping, even for his own clothes; he simply reordered suits and other items that had served him well in the past.

. . .

Politics, Economics, and Bigness

Early in his career, Brandeis decided that big business could become big only through illegitimate means. By his frequent references to the "curse of bigness," he meant that bigness itself was the mark of Cain, a sign of prior sinning. . . . He simply denied the possibility that size brought efficiency in any industry. . . .

This was fundamentally an *economic* argument. But in the absence of an adequate framework of economic theory, Brandeis, like many later reformers, had only his personal and political sensibilities to guide him.

. . .

The general problems Brandeis grappled with in trying to cope with the trust movement typified the larger dilemmas of national regulatory policy. How, in an age of big business, could the government preserve American democratic values? What steps should it take to balance the rights of producers against the new imperatives of consumers? How could government control bigness without interfering with personal liberty, let alone with economic efficiency? These questions dominated national political discourse during the twenty years surrounding the turn of the century, until they came to a head during the Wilson-Roosevelt Taft-Debs presidential campaign of 1912. The formal response in public policy culminated with passage of the Clayton Act and the Federal Trade Commission Act of 1914, after a classic legislative drama in which Louis D. Brandeis played a very curious part.

The Candidates and the Trust Issues, 1912

Brandeis took no serious role in presidential politics before 1910, when he squared off against the Taft Administration during the Ballinger-Pinchot controversy. . . . In the election of 1912, Brandeis' original choice for the presidency was his good friend Robert M. La Follette, but the candidacy of "Fighting Bob" collapsed, leaving Brandeis temporarily without a candidate.

The decision of the Democratic national convention in the summer of 1912 revived his spirits. "I have never met or even seen Wilson," Brandeis wrote, "but all that I have heard of him and particularly his discussion of economic problems makes me believe that he possesses certain qualities indispensable to the solution of our problems." Brandeis sent the new candidate a congratulatory note, and Wilson responded by inviting him to a private meeting at Sea Girt, New Jersey, Wilson's summer home. At this fateful meeting, the two men—both fifty-six years old, both transplanted southerners, both infused with a moralistic approach to politics—found an immediate rapport. In a three-hour discussion they discovered strikingly similar views on economic issues.

After the Sea Girt conference, which occurred just three months before Wilson's election as president, the informal position of influence that Brandeis had attained as the people's lawyer became institutionalized. . . . Even before he met Wilson, he had developed a program he called "the regulation of competition," in opposition to the platform of Theodore Roosevelt's Progressive Party, which Brandeis characterized as "regulated monopoly." . . . Brandeis' slogan about "the regulation of competition" had an appealing sound, and later in the campaign it seemed to help Wilson's cause significantly.

Wilson himself, however, never seemed certain about exactly what it meant. As the campaign progressed and his debate with Roosevelt intensified, Wilson telegraphed an urgent request to Brandeis to "set forth as explicitly as possible the actual measures by which competition can be effectively regulated." Brandeis replied with a detailed outline. . . . His suggestions took the form of an open letter that would appear over Wilson's signature. . . . In the open letter, Brandeis . . . propose[d] a series of measures designed to implement a Wilsonian antitrust program. First he advocated a strengthening of the Sherman Act by prohibition "of the specific methods or means by which the great trusts, utilizing their huge resources or particularly favored positions commonly crush rivals." Then he suggested an invigoration of the judicial process, so as to ensure that antitrust convictions were followed by reparations to the victims and also by genuine dissolutions. Indeed, the most significant difference between the programs of Roosevelt and Brandeis-Wilson lay in the latter's insistence that the government forcibly break apart the center firms formed over the last thirty years, whatever the resulting disruption to the national economy. Finally, Brandeis endorsed the creation of "a board or commission to aid in administering the Sherman law."

This new commission would investigate big business in much the same manner as the existing Bureau of Corporations had been doing; but unlike the bureau, it would have a close relationship with the Department of Justice. It would advise Justice on antitrust proceedings and help to enforce compliance with the law.

. . .

The Movement Toward the FTC, 1914

. . .

The roots of the support for a federal trade commission may be found in the history of antitrust prosecution under the Sherman Act. This legislation went on the books in 1890, but for a time indifferent enforcement made it almost a dead letter. From 1890 to 1905, the Department of Justice brought only 24 suits, or an average of only 1.5 per year. But the number leaped to an average of 18 per year over the next decade—a period of conspicuous trust busting by Presidents Roosevelt, Taft, and Wilson. This twelve-fold increase in the rate of prosecution meant that the targets of antitrust law now stood at much greater hazard than before. The surprising identity of these targets epitomized the dilemma Brandeis and his allies faced in attempting to strengthen the Sherman Act, for loose combinations of peripheral firms comprised by far the largest category of defendants. . . .

Thus, as unlikely as it seems, government antitrust action usually opposed not huge integrated firms, but loose associations of small companies—the very groups on whose behalf Brandeis spoke. The Department of Justice singled out these small companies not because of economic theory (which, incidentally, would have suggested these very targets), but because of the mechanics of prosecution. The department quite naturally gravitated toward cases it could win. The rudimentary methods of horizontal control employed by associations of small companies—local price fixing, market division, boycotting, and the like—were easy to detect and prosecute. Business managers in peripheral firms, therefore, had good cause for concern about antitrust enforcement.

Still their counterparts in center firms also remained apprehensive. These companies represented enormous investments that might at any time be endangered by antitrust prosecution. In the *American Tobacco* and *Standard Oil* decisions of 1911, the Supreme Court had shifted the already ambiguous terms of the Sherman Act toward even greater uncertainty. In the *Standard Oil* case, the court in effect determined that only "unreasonable" restraints of trade were illegal under the Sherman Act, not all such restraints. This "rule of reason," as it came to be called, satisfied none of the parties most directly concerned in the antitrust debate. For Brandeis and his allies, already dismayed at the focus of prosecution on small firms and associations, the court's new rule of reason appeared to weaken the potential for future prosecution of giant trusts. For business managers, on the other hand, the enunciation of the rule of reason implied a slight retreat by the court, but also a new unpredictability as to which business practices were permissible and which not.

More than anything else, executives of both peripheral and center firms wanted certainty: a bright line between legality and illegality. Many of them began to think that continuous administration of economic policy by a regulatory commission was preferable to what they saw as the spasmodic whims of individual judges. Detailed opinion surveys taken by the National Civic Federation and the United States Chamber of Commerce in 1911 and 1914 showed overwhelming support among all businessmen for a new regulatory commission. This enthusiasm derived not from a desire for more regulation, but rather from a sense that expert *administrative* regulation would be more stable and predictable than hit-or-miss antitrust litigation.

. . .

[B]y the time of Wilson's election in 1912, a national consensus had developed in favor of a commission; but Wilson . . . did not begin his legislative effort on the issue until 1914. The historical evidence suggests that this delay derived from the need of Wilson's advisers for more time to think through the administration's policy. A second reason was that Wilson himself, a close student of congressional government, carefully paced and sequenced his overall legislative program so as not to dissipate his supporting coalition on Capitol Hill.

. . .

During the year's delay in dealing with antitrust, the economic and political situation changed. By 1914 the country was facing a serious economic recession, and Wilson had used up some of the good will new presidents enjoy during their early months in office. By the time antitrust reached the top of his agenda, he had fewer bargaining chips. Furthermore, the autumn of 1914 would bring off-year congressional elections. The Democrats, the country's minority party, would have to be careful or their supremacy in the House and Senate might quickly disappear. . . . Yet if Wilson did nothing about antitrust, he would surely alienate his reformist supporters. This situation was hazardous for a president elected with only 42 percent of the popular vote.

. . .

Working on the assumption that some sort of commission must be formed, Brandeis strongly endorsed the creation of a type of sunshine agency. As its function, however, he had in mind not merely the accumulation of neutral facts but the tendentious use of selected facts to help peripheral firms, especially in their associational activities. "We should differentiate clearly," he wrote a member of Wilson's cabinet in 1913, "capitalistic industrial monopolies from those relations between competitors in industry which are really a regulation of competition." If this were not done, antitrust legislation would continue to hit the wrong targets. "Capitalistic monopolies have been fully investigated and we know how to deal with them. But we have no comprehensive detailed information concerning the character and effect of these trade agreements between competitors; and in the absence of such data we cannot deal with them intelligently. To obtain such information an investigation should be undertaken, and meanwhile those who supply the necessary data should be protected against criminal prosecution."

Wilson, after assessing the state of the economy, the mood of the country, and the divergent advice he was receiving, decided to go forward with his antitrust program. . . .

Writing the Legislation

A number of antitrust bills had been introduced since the *Standard Oil* and *American Tobacco* decisions of 1911. In addition, Congress had considered several interstate trade commission bills, including one submitted as early as 1908. . . . The administration pushed an antitrust bill sponsored by Representative Henry D. Clayton (Democrat of Alabama), chairman of the judiciary committee, and a trade commission bill offered by Representative James J. Covington (Democrat of Maryland), of the commerce committee. The curious progress of these two bills through the 1914 session of Congress—their repeated emendation, their intermittent support by Wilson—aptly illustrates the difficulty of balancing unclear economic policy with very clear political necessity.

As originally written, the Clayton antitrust bill took exceptionally stringent form. It enumerated a long list of prohibited practices. . . . The harshest aspect of the original Clayton bill lay in the criminal sanctions it imposed. Section 11, for example, provided:

> That whenever a corporation shall be guilty of the violation of any of the provisions of the antitrust laws, the offense shall be deemed to be also that of the individual directors, officers, and agents of such corporation authorizing, ordering, or doing any of such prohibited acts, and upon conviction thereof they shall be deemed guilty of a misdemeanor, and punished by a fine not exceeding $5,000, or imprisonment not exceeding one year, or by both said punishments in the discretion of the court.

If the bill passed in this form, and if the Department of Justice enforced it vigorously, tens of thousands of American businessmen might go to jail.

In contrast to the severe criminal sanctions of the Clayton bill, the Covington trade commission bill contemplated not an enforcement agency but a sunshine commission. . . . The commission would secure and publish information, conduct investigations as directed by Congress, and suggest methods of improving business practice and antitrust enforcement.

. . .

At first it appeared that all would go smoothly. Both the Clayton and the Covington bills passed the House of Representatives by large majorities in early June 1914. . . . Meanwhile, though, the president began to have second thoughts about the inconsistent approaches represented by the two pieces of the package: a strong antitrust bill and a weak commission bill. . . .

Business managers themselves were becoming disturbed—some almost panicky—at the criminal provisions of the Clayton bill. Many businessmen from peripheral firms objected vehemently because they engaged in the very practices enumerated in the bill. Like Brandeis and other administration spokesmen, they were running up against the central irony of antitrust enforcement. As the secretary of commerce put the issue in a letter to the White House, "Instead of striking at the things we mean to hit, it [the bill] does, as a matter of fact, seriously injure the small businessmen whom we are aiming to help." And as one small businessman from Mississippi expressed it,

> I respectfully submit that while Big Business is the alleged aim of these drastic laws, they hurt small business far more than they do the larger and stronger concerns for they can bear burdens that we can not. They can exist on a margin of profits fatal to us. . . . We may not combine to save costs, may not agree to desist from trying to take away markets from each other, may not agree to hold our goods for prices fairly remunerative. . . . Really we are being governed to our undoing.

The Clayton bill represented a very serious political hazard for the Wilson Administration.

The trade commission bill, on the other hand, had gained great popularity. Much milder in tone, it was also sufficiently general to be all things to all men. . . .

Brandeis' Abdication

Congress' consideration of the Clayton and Covington bills, during the spring and summer of 1914, was the climactic moment in the entire antitrust campaign. For Brandeis, it would seem to have been a unique opportunity to write into law and thereby institutionalize everything he had been fighting for. Nobody had more influence with President Wilson than did Brandeis, and this meant having direct access to the most capable manager of legislation to occupy the White House in many years. In these circumstances, one would expect to find the Boston lawyer working night and day with the congressional committees, shuttling back and forth between the White House and Capitol Hill, taking a major part in drafting and redrafting the bills until they were in exactly the right form. Surely Wilson himself would very much have liked to see Brandeis fill this role. But during these pivotal months, he instead continued to do lawyer's work, concentrating on an immediate task, which now happened to be an ICC rate case. What might have been Brandeis' greatest role in the making of national economic policy, then, was to be played by a stand-in.

That stand-in turned out to be George Rublee, a wealthy lawyer and former member of the Progressive Party. . . . The first graduate of the Groton School (in a class of one), Rublee was something of a dilettante and self-styled aristocrat. He had spent several years abroad, during which he occupied himself in such pursuits as playing tennis with the king of Sweden. Rublee practiced law intermittently with a Wall Street firm, but he always seemed to be available for special assignments. Thus he responded enthusiastically when, in 1914, Brandeis asked him to come to Washington and help with antitrust legislation.

A Roosevelt supporter in 1912, Rublee subscribed to the Progressive Party plank that called for a very strong interstate trade commission, quite unlike the sunshine agency favored by Wilson and Brandeis and contemplated by the provisions of the Covington bill. Accordingly, in his lobbying on behalf of Brandeis, Rublee tried somehow to work around the Covington bill. Initially he got nowhere. But when the negative national reaction to the harsh Clayton bill began to raise political problems for Wilson, Rublee saw his chance. Accurately sensing that the Clayton bill would be amended beyond recognition, Rublee conceived a strategy of accepting a milder Clayton bill but at the same time substituting a much stronger trade commission bill in place of the Covington measure. Rublee worked out his plan in cooperation with Representative Ray Stevens of New Hampshire, another ally of Brandeis. . . . Rublee's new bill, introduced by Stevens, provided for a commission very similar to the one advocated during the campaign of 1912 by Theodore Roosevelt and the Progressive Party. In 1914, however, the Democratically controlled House committee that was considering commission legislation still preferred the existing Covington bill and quickly voted down the new Stevens-Rublee draft. Next Rublee sought support from members of Wilson's cabinet, but to no avail. At this point in the fight, as he later recalled, he would have given up had his wife not kept urging him on:

> What we then decided was to go to the President and see if we could do anything with him. . . . Stevens made an appointment with the President to see us. Just before that, although I didn't know what Brandeis would think about it, I went to him and told him that we were going to do this. I knew this wasn't his approach to the problem and I hadn't thought of him as going along with our plan—I was afraid he wouldn't go or would oppose it. . . . I don't believe we should have succeeded if he hadn't gone along.
>
> It was such a beautiful summer day that the meeting was outdoors in the garden on the south side of the White House. I remember that the President was beautifully dressed—white linen—and looked very well. After Stevens' introductory statement I made the main statement. . . . I saw that it was making an impression on the President as I spoke and he listened very attentively and asked some questions. When I finished speaking, to my great surprise, Brandeis entered the fray with enthusiasm and backed me up strongly.

As Rublee implies, Brandeis' support of the Stevens bill represented a dramatic turnabout from his longtime stance on the nature of a new trade commission. Wilson, . . . hearing Brandeis' endorsement, decided to shift his own position as well and to go along with Rublee. Moving quickly now, the president asked the House committee to substitute the Stevens measure for the Covington sunshine bill, which the entire House had passed just five days previously. After several weeks of intense debate, resolved ultimately by Wilson's direct intervention, both the House and Senate passed the Stevens bill.

The outcome was the Federal Trade Commission Act of 1914, which provided for a board of five members, no more than three of whom could come from the same political party. The commissioners were to be paid salaries of $10,000 each, a high figure for 1914, intended to give prestige to the new agency. The core of the FTC's authority lay in three fundamental provisions Rublee had inserted into the bill: that "unfair methods of competition in commerce are hereby declared unlawful"; that the commission in effect had the power to determine which methods were unfair; and that it could order offenders "to cease and desist" from using such unfair methods. Altogether, the act envisioned a far more powerful and active agency than anything Brandeis had proposed.

According to his own recollection, draftsman Rublee developed the ideas behind these key provisions after studying a number of existing judicial decisions and after poring over the texts of other proposed legislation. "There were a number of other bills besides the Clayton Bill in which monopolistic practices were defined," Rublee said afterward. "I had noticed that in most of these bills at the end of the list of forbidden practices there was a general clause prohibiting all other forms of unfair competition. The same general clause appeared at the end of lists of specific practices enjoined in various decrees of Federal Courts in cases arising under the Sherman Law. . . . It therefore appeared that the phrase 'unfair competition' had a recognized meaning in the terminology of anti-trust law." Thus Rublee shaped his new bill in accordance with his own interpretation of these existing cases and legislative drafts. He intended that much of the new FTC's power would emanate from the "unfair methods" clause that he had gleaned from his study.

As it turned out, Rublee had been woefully naive in thinking that the phrase "unfair methods of competition in commerce" meant something clear and coherent. He had little experience in drafting this kind of law, and the ambiguity of his key phrase became an Achilles heel, raising insuperable problems during the very first months of the commission's operation. Rublee may have carried the day in 1914, but in so doing he had set off a time bomb that would soon explode. In the first full-scale judicial review of the FTC's authority, which came in 1920, the Supreme Court held that "The words 'unfair methods of competition' are not defined by the statute and their exact meaning is in dispute. It is for the courts, not the Commission, ultimately to determine as matter of law, what they include." And until the court softened its ruling a bit, some fourteen years later, the commission was unable to exercise many important powers.

Partly as a result of its ambiguous statute, the FTC got off to a rocky start. In no one's eyes did it represent a distinguished regulatory body. President Wilson tried to conduct a careful search for good appointees, but with the national economic outlook so uncertain, he worried about alienating business.

When Wilson asked Brandeis to serve as a member, the Boston lawyer declined, perhaps sensing that the tasks before the commission were impossible. The president did appoint George Rublee, but the Senate, bowing to the opposition of a senator from Rublee's home state, refused to confirm him.

Of the original five appointees, two were businessmen, one a career politician, one a lawyer-politician, and one (Rublee) a practicing lawyer [proposed by the president]. None had administrative talents of the first rank. By 1918, only three years after the commission's first meeting, not a single one of these first five members remained in office. The FTC itself, lacking strong leadership, drifted aimlessly from this task to that, making little impact. And on those few occasions when the commission did try to do something important, Congress or the Supreme Court intervened. Almost nobody connected with the FTC could take much pride in its early accomplishments. Looking back several years later, Brandeis himself provided a harsh verdict on the performance of the first FTC commissioners. "It was," he said, "a stupid administration."

The Confusion over the FTC's Functions

Besides weak appointments, many other reasons lay behind the commission's early failures. For one thing, the severe recession of 1914 placed Wilson and other Democrats in a difficult position. As leaders of the party committed to reform of the tariff, currency, and trusts, they now bore the stigma of having regulated prosperity out of the economy. . . .

Then too, the Great War in Europe erupted in August 1914, only a month before the passage of the Federal Trade Commission Act. The commission's first meeting, in 1915, came just a few weeks before the sinking of the *Lusitania,* an event that brought the first wave of war fever to the United States. Of course the war itself ultimately crowded trusts off the front pages; it ended for a time the national preoccupation with the dark side of big business. When the United States joined the conflict in 1917, the FTC was called upon to help in setting prices for essential commodities. By 1918, new and stronger appointees had begun to give more spirit to the commission's efforts. Yet, in a setting of war emergency, the FTC's investigations of business practices struck some critics as bureaucratic busywork—idle snooping that did nothing to facilitate economic mobilization.

In the longer run, the FTC's erratic career derived from its faulty enabling legislation and from a related absence of any coherent organizational strategy. "Unfair methods of competition" had no self-evident meaning. "Cease and desist," despite its acerbic ring, turned out to be just another formula for procedural delay. In the last analysis, Rublee's solution of 1914, so eagerly grasped by both Brandeis and Wilson as a means of resolving the dilemma raised by the Clayton bill, had been hollow at the core.

. . .

Advance Advice

Business groups in particular—both center and peripheral—were acutely disappointed when the commission failed to provide greater certainty in drawing the line between legal and illegal practices. As is abundantly evident from the congressional hearings, large numbers of businessmen supported the idea of a new commission because they anticipated receiving what they called "advance advice." That is, they expected to be able to go to the agency routinely with inquiries about the permissibility of contemplated business moves such as pricing decisions, mergers, and certain types of contracts. The commission could then declare that, if the transaction were carried out exactly as proposed, the commission itself would not enjoin it or prosecute the company for unfair trade practices. On the other hand, if the commission advised that it would oppose the contemplated move as a violation of the antitrust laws, then the transaction could be revised or abandoned, without placing the inquiring businessmen in jeopardy of prosecution.

Although advance advice could not confer total immunity from future prosecution, it could provide administrative guidelines tailored much more precisely than any of those available in statutory and case law. For many business managers, this was the great virtue of administrative regulation. Where litigation was formal and governed by elaborate rules of procedure, advance advice would be less formal and relatively unburdened by red tape. Where litigation looked to past acts and toward punitive resolutions, advance advice looked to the future and sought to be preventive. Where litigation occurred spasmodically, advance advice went on continuously. . . .

Later on, in the twentieth century, agency after agency developed different forms of advance advice. The Internal Revenue Service came to issue innumerable "private letter rulings" in response to questions posed by taxpayers. The Securities and Exchange Commission sent out hundreds of "no-action letters" regarding a wide range of securities transactions contemplated by corporations. Ultimately the Federal Trade Commission itself developed a set of trade practice conferences and merger guidelines for the use of corporate executives. Over the years, these forms of advance advice evolved into a type of administrative art characteristic of mature and intelligent regulatory procedure. It may be no exaggeration to say that the idea of regulation itself has hinged on the workability of one or another form of advance advice. . . .

Even so, advance advice flew in the face of some central tenets of Anglo-American jurisprudence. Because it avoided adversarial procedure, it offended the judicial principle that decisions be based not on conjecture but on the formal record of evidence developed by the parties at issue in some definite case or controversy. (When courts themselves have received requests for advance advice in the form of "declaratory judgments," they have refused the requests in the absence of prior statutory authorization.) Then too, because advance advice was negotiational—that is, discussed between a government agency on the one hand and a citizen or corporation on the other—it ran counter to the prevailing model of adversarial advocacy. Under the adversarial system, truth was assumed to be reached best through a contest between citizen and government (or citizen and citizen), played out under elaborate rules of advocacy before a judge who stood above the fray. With advance advice, both the judge and the contest disappeared. Finally, unlike court decisions, advance advice had no precedential value. Advisory opinions by agencies were directed only to the inquiring party and did not constitute authoritative statements of law on which others could rely directly. In practice, however, the knowledge of criteria consistently applied by an agency in its advance advice on a given subject created guidelines on which large numbers of business executives could rely informally in making decisions in the future.

For all of these reasons, advance advice initially encountered only lukewarm endorsement from the legal profession as a whole. . . . And because of the requirement that administrative rulings be subject to review by the courts, advance advice was certain to be circumscribed.

As soon as the Federal Trade Commission was organized in 1915, businessmen deluged it with requests for advance advice. Because the five commissioners themselves disagreed on what to do about these requests, they called on several outside consultants. One of these, as might have been expected, was Brandeis. On the afternoon of April 30, 1915, he spent several hours talking with the commissioners, and the unpublished stenographic transcript of this discussion shows in vivid detail the collision between adversarial and negotiational approaches to regulation and between legal and administrative mind sets. In this conversation Brandeis may be seen as expressing not just his own views but some of the core principles of the Anglo-American legal tradition.

The commissioners' first question was whether they should entertain applications for advance advice. Brandeis responded with an emphatic no. Determinations of legality, he declared, must come from courts and courts alone. If the commission gave advance advice, "the public would be tricked," and the commission itself "hoodwinked." Since determinations of legality had to be made on the basis of facts that "do not exist yet," the commissioners would have to regulate in the dark. On any controversial matter, said Brandeis, both sides of an issue had to be represented, but this would not be likely to occur under advance advice. Such advice was unnecessary anyway, he added—when businessmen were acting morally. Executives' consciences should be the best guide. As Brandeis told the commissioners (in what could not have been a very helpful comment, considering the problems they now faced), "Your conscience, if you are honest with yourself, would tell you, nineteen times out of twenty, whether you intend to restrain trade; and if you could say to yourself clearly, and honestly, that you did not intend a restraint of trade, you would not need to go to a lawyer at all." . . .

But if the commissioners were not to give advance advice or to have the power to determine the meaning of "unfair methods of competition," then why had Brandeis supported Rublee's draft of the FTC Act? . . . Whatever the reasons for Brandeis' inconsistency, the FTC in fact came into existence with a broad mandate to define "unfair methods of competition" but without power sufficiently explicit to survive judicial review. In its early regulatory activities, the FTC attempted halfheartedly to define unfair methods, but it also declined to give advance advice freely. This sort of timidity and tentativeness burdened the agency with the worst of both worlds.

. . .

Brandeis and Regulation

In January 1916 President Wilson nominated Brandeis to a seat on the United States Supreme Court. That nomination, which came as a complete surprise to nearly everyone concerned, touched off a national furor. There had never been a Jewish member of the court, and Wilson's action occasioned both open and covert expressions of antisemitism. Additional opposition came from the Boston establishment, which had turned against Brandeis. . . . The most serious chorus of objection, however, came from legal organizations. Seven former presidents of the American Bar Association sent a joint protest to the Senate, urging that the appointment not be confirmed: "The undersigned feel under the painful duty to say to you that in their opinion, taking into view the reputation, character, and professional career of Mr. Louis D. Brandeis, he is not a fit person to be a member of the Supreme Court of the United States." The confirmation fight, which went on for five months, became one of the year's most newsworthy events. In the end the defense, bolstered by Wilson's ringing affirmation of Brandeis' merits, carried the day. The nomination clinched Wilson's own claim to progressive credentials, and the event itself became a cause celebre in the history of American liberalism.

Once on the bench, Brandeis surprised his critics with his impartiality, wisdom, and judicial depth. His tenure on the court lasted for twenty-three years, until he retired in 1939 at the age of eighty-two, and he made a truly great judge. It was almost as if, having spent his entire previous career hurrying from one case to another and spreading himself too thin, he now at last could take the time for the kind of reflection essential in thinking through his positions. This is not to say that those positions changed in any important ways. The central themes of his court career accorded well with the chief interests of his earlier life: a preoccupation with actual social conditions, an insistence on individual rights and autonomy, and—most important for his decisions on economic issues—a powerful commitment to judicial restraint. Because of this emphasis on judicial restraint, it is difficult to separate law from economics in his judicial opinions. What is clear, though, is that he always retained a passionate feeling against the curse of bigness. And, despite his impartiality in most other matters, he also exercised a powerful preference for the interests of small producers, wholesalers, and retailers over those of consumers.

...

... Louis D. Brandeis endures as an American hero. In the minds of his countrymen he remains a properly revered symbol of individualism, integrity, self-reliance, and willingness to fight hard for cherished values. As we have seen, he also symbolizes one of the characteristic shortcomings of the American regulatory tradition: a disinclination to persist in hard economic analysis that may lead away from strong political preference. This shortcoming appears vividly in the subsequent tangles of twentieth-century antitrust policy, in the continuing institutional schizophrenia of the Federal Trade Commission, and in the frequent unwillingness of legislators to act on the unpopular principle that protection is usually anticompetitive and anticonsumerist, even when it is small business that is being protected.

CHAPTER 16

War and Civil Liberties

President Woodrow Wilson's main interest was in domestic reforms, but he had to devote much of his presidency to foreign affairs. Elected in 1912, he had only two years of peace before the Central Powers of Europe (Germany, Austria-Hungary, and Turkey) started the First World War. He was re-elected in 1916 in large part on the strength of the slogan "He kept us out of war."

In 1916 neutrality was patriotic. But neutrality was difficult to sustain as German U-boats sank American ships, and the Allied Powers (Britain, France, Italy, and Russia) seemed less and less able to hold their own.

As the United States entered the war in 1917, the demands of patriotism were reversed. Those who opposed the war were vilified by public officials and public opinion. A wave of intolerance toward German-Americans swept the nation and spilled over to immigrants in general as possibly infected by pacifist, communist, anarchist, and other imported radical ideas. The war also provided an opportunity to lash out against dissident citizens such as labor leaders and left-leaning politicians. Eugene Debs, head of the Socialist party, spent much of the war years in jail. He was still in jail in 1920 when he received nearly a million votes in the presidential election.

Federal legislation legalized much of the wartime repression: A Selective Service Act made it a crime to advocate resistance to the draft; an Espionage Act punished "false reports or false statements" with intent to harm the war effort; a Sedition Act prohibited "uttering, printing, writing, or publishing any disloyal, profane, scurrilous, or abusive language"; an Alien Act allowed the deportation of immigrants for their ideas. States enacted similar laws, including bans on red flags. The Supreme Court generally upheld convictions under the wartime statutes, as in the case of *Abrams v. United States* (1919), in which Justice Oliver Wendell Holmes's dissent formulated his "clear and present danger" test.

The war ended in 1919 with an armistice, without an occupation of Germany. Curiously, repression in the United States did not end but seemed to intensify. Upset by the denial of civil liberties, a Harvard law professor, Zechariah Chafee, Jr., was moved to publish a treatise, *Free Speech in the United States,* in 1920 (he updated it during World War II, and it is still considered a classic). He summed up the situation:

> Never in the history of our country, since the Alien and Sedition Laws of 1798, has the meaning of free speech been the subject of such sharp controversy as during the years since 1917. Over nineteen hundred prosecutions and other judicial proceedings during the war, involving speeches, newspaper articles, pamphlets, and books, were followed after the armistice by a widespread legislative consideration of bills punishing the advocacy of extreme radicalism.
>
> . . .
>
> So long as Congress refused to follow the disastrous precedent of 1798 and enact a peace-time Sedition Law, the federal government could not do much to suppress "evil-thinking" on the part of citizens. However, it could curb radical foreigners in our midst by seizing upon a new Alien Law and using it with relentless vigor. The hostility to immigrant workers, which had long been smoldering in this country, was now suddenly combined with hostility to heterodox thinkers and burst into a conflagration of hysterical hatred. (1941 ed., pp. 3, 196)

The explanation for the postwar continuation of repression may lie in Russia. The United States accepted the Menshevik revolution of 1917, which overthrew the autocratic tsarist regime, but Americans were alarmed when the Bolsheviks in turn overthrew the Mensheviks and made a separate peace with the Central Powers—so alarmed that the United States joined an unsuccessful Allied invasion of Russia to try to restore a pro-Allied government. The Bolsheviks became even more alarming as they formed a "Communist International" to spread revolution to other nations, and communists seized power briefly in Hungary and Bavaria.

In the United States, a postwar economic recession left many returning veterans unemployed and fueled a crime wave. Employers cut wages; workers went on strikes—including a police strike in Boston, the first by a police force. (The Boston police strike was broken by the Republican governor of Massachusetts, Calvin Coolidge, propelling him to the vice presidency in 1920.) Labor unrest was accompanied by racial unrest, manifest in several race riots and hundreds of lynchings. The Ku Klux Klan grew and became assertive. The Communist party organized in 1920. Also in 1920, the Eighteenth (or Prohibition) Amendment went into effect, turning the transportation and sale of alcoholic beverages into a criminal growth industry until the repeal of the amendment thirteen years later.

The attention of President Wilson, however, was focused on Europe. He personally attended the Versailles Peace Conference and hoped to inject his idealistic vision into the peace settlement. Central to that vision was a League of Nations. He succeeded in having the League organized, but he failed to get the U.S. Senate to ratify the Treaty of Versailles and join the League. He took his cause to the people in a national tour, during which he suffered a stroke. He spent the last seven months of his presidency incapacitated, and the United States never joined the League.

During President Wilson's incapacitation, his Attorney General, A. Mitchell Palmer, hoped to capture the Democratic nomination for president. With the aid of his young assistant, J. Edgar Hoover, Palmer initiated a "Red Scare" with a series of raids and over four thousand arrests, mostly of immigrants. The climactic event of the era, however, came not from Palmer's raids, but from the 1921 arrest of two obscure Italian anarchists by a small-town police force in Massachusetts.

The Passion of Sacco and Vanzetti.

THE CASE OF NICOLA SACCO AND BARTOLOMEO VANZETTI

from Osmond K. Fraenkel, *The Sacco-Vanzetti Case*
(New York: Alfred A. Knopf, 1931), pp. 3–25.
Copyright © 1931 by Alfred A. Knopf, Inc., 1959 by Osmond K. Fraenkel.
Reprinted with the permission of Nancy W. Wechsler.

Interest in the guilt or innocence of an accused person or in the adequacy of the legal machinery employed in determining a problem of this nature reaches at times the intensity of a social question. The conscience of a community, sometimes that of the whole civilized world, may feel itself under such circumstances involved in the fate of a person otherwise obscure; and partisanship may run so high that in the locality whose courts are under scrutiny the case at issue can hardly be discussed with reason.

Not since the time of the Dreyfus affair* has international feeling risen to so high a peak as it did in the case of Sacco and Vanzetti. Throughout Europe and America radical and conservative opinion locked horns over this conviction and the proceedings which followed it. . . .

The crime for which the two radicals went after seven years to the chair was the seizure in the streets of South Braintree, Massachusetts, on April 15th, 1920, of a pay roll amounting to $15,776.51 and the brutal murder of the men who had had it in charge. After fruitless attempts made in the courts of Massachusetts to save the accused men an appeal for clemency was submitted to Governor Fuller. The suspense pending his deliberations and those of the Advisory Committee he had appointed reached its apex with the announcement that a decision would be rendered on August 3rd, 1927. Upon its publication letters and petitions poured into Boston and Washington. In various cities of Europe the United States legations had to be put under guard. In others police reserves were called out to watch for violence at mass meetings held in condemnation of the decision. Everywhere parades and protests sprang up. Bombs, which the press laid at the door of sympathizers with the defendants,

---

*Captain Alfred Dreyfus, a Jewish officer of the French army, was convicted of treason in 1894. His court-martial received international attention due to charges of antisemitism and due to the flimsiness of the evidence, which, in the end, pointed to another officer. Dreyfus was cleared and reinstated in 1906.

were thrown in the New York subway and at the house of one of the jurors in the case. In Uruguay, Paraguay and Argentina the labor elements called general strikes. Newspapers in London and Paris deplored the outcome of the affair and in Germany twelve prominent lawyers prepared and signed a statement which decried a death sentence imposed after a judicial delay of seven years. In Morocco, Panama and Geneva popular demonstrations took place, and violence, both attempted and accomplished, was reported from Sydney, Montevideo, Bucharest, Stockholm, Berlin, Prague, Amsterdam, Athens and Copenhagen.

Indicative that not only the working men but also the middle and upper classes concerned themselves with the case, Secretary [of State] Kellogg received cables of protest from such prominent people as President Mazaryk of Czecho-Slovakia, Madame Curie, Professor Albert Einstein, the Marquis de la Steyre, a grandson of Lafayette, Fridtjof Nansen, Alfred Dreyfus, Louis Loucheur, Joseph Caillaux, and many others. A part, even, of that large body of opinion in the United States which maintained that justice had been done in the matter and the forces of anarchy put to rout, insisted that the dilatoriness of Massachusetts courts remained a disgrace to the country and agreed with the statement of the *London Morning Post* that Massachusetts had turned the law into an instrument of torture.

. . .

For days long lines of liberals marched before the State House of Boston. The arrival of Vanzetti's sister from Italy intensified the feeling of thousands of people. Many not radical in their beliefs expressed the hope that the efforts of the prisoners' counsel to induce the Supreme Court of the United States to interfere and stay execution might be successful.

Excitement grew as the date for execution neared. The paraders before the State House became more numerous and many of them were arrested. The police of Boston took precautions as though against a riot or a siege. Nevertheless, and to the surprise of many people, the streets of the city remained undisturbed by violence as Sacco and Vanzetti went to the chair.

Although it is not definitely known when Sacco and Vanzetti first met, the time must have antedated the war, for, in 1917, it was together they fled the draft. Both men belonged at the time to the Galleani group of philosophical anarchists, and both had been suspected by the United States Department of Justice of violation of the Selective Service Act and of holding views which made them liable to deportation. . . .

. . . During Wilson's administration one of those waves of hysteria to which most nations have at some period of their development been subject was breaking over the country. The government, under the leadership of Attorney General A. Mitchell Palmer and using as its weapon the newly passed so-called Espionage Act, had been instigating criminal proceedings against thousands of suspected radicals in all parts of the country. Lurid statements were being given out frequently to the press, and headlines such as these from the *Boston Herald* had become common occurrences, "Bolshevik Plan for Conquest of America"; "Reds Pervade Empire State"; "Bride Thinks Reds Kidnapped Missing Groom"; "Boston Armed at all Points Against Reds." . . .

During January Attorney General Palmer was quoted as stating about the extent of the Bolshevist infection in the United States: "The Red Movement is not a righteous or honest protest against alleged defects in our present political and economic organization of society. . . . It is a distinctly criminal and dishonest movement in the desire to obtain possession of other people's property by violence and robbery. . . . All their new words, 'Bolshevism,' 'Syndicalism,' 'Sabotage,' etc. are only new names for old theories of vice and criminality. . . . Each and every adherent of this movement is a potential murderer or a potential thief, and deserves no consideration."

. . .

In the New York Assembly the current emotion took astounding form. On the opening of the session of 1920 the Speaker of the House initiated the unseating of five members. Because they belonged to the Socialist party Orr, Claessens, De Witt, Solomon and Waldman, all duly elected members of the Assembly, were arraigned by Speaker Sweet, who accused them of "seeking seats in the Assembly after having been elected on a platform that is absolutely inimical to the best interests of the State of New York and the United States." It is amusing to recall that at this juncture George Bernard Shaw said: "It is high time for the Mayflower to fit out for sea again."

About fifteen hundred publications in thirty-three foreign languages and with a circulation of approximately eight million existed in this country at the time. Senator King proposed a bill to exclude these from second class mailing privileges, whereupon the Foreign Language Service of the government . . . sent out the following statement:

> We deplore the grave injustice which is being done to foreign-born peoples as a whole these days, by inaccurate and sensational newspaper stories; and the unfair and unfriendly treatment accorded them by Americans who are ignorant or misinformed concerning them and their press. Our eighteen months of intimate relations and work with the foreign language press have brought us indispensable proof that the large majority of these papers and peoples are American in the truest sense.

When Louis F. Post, Assistant Secretary of Labor, was criticized in the press and in Congress for too great indulgence towards radicals . . . he had said: "It is pitiful to consider the hardships to which they and their families (meaning the foreign-born) have been subjected by arbitrary arrest, long detention in default of bail beyond the means of hard-working wage-earners to give, for

nothing more dangerous than affiliating with friends of their own race, country and language, and without the slightest indication of sinister motive or any
unlawful act within their knowledge or intention."

In January, 1920, wholesale raids against alleged reds took place, accompanied in general by unlawful searches and seizures and other strong-arm methods on the part of government officers. Numerous arrests made under such
circumstances in New England resulted in habeas corpus proceedings on behalf of the accused persons which, in the spring of the year, came on to be
heard before Judge Anderson of the United States District Court in Boston.
During the course of his investigation the Judge denounced repeatedly both
the methods the officials used in their attempts to secure evidence and the
manner in which they carried out the actual arrests. . . .

Lawyers of distinction showed dissatisfaction with the official lawlessness
of these raids and some of them expressed their disapproval. Mr. Moorfield
Storey, in his introduction to Mr. Post's book, "The Deportations Delirium of
Nineteen-Twenty," said:

> When, therefore, the Department of Justice alleged that there was a very large
> body of 'Reds' in the country, aliens with the principles of Russian Bolsheviks,
> who were organizing here to overthrow the government of the United States by
> force, and followed the statement up by raids all over the country in which men
> and women, aliens and citizens, were seized and imprisoned, we did not disturb
> ourselves about questions of constitutional law. The men responsible for these ar-
> rests, the detectives and those who employed them, filled the newspapers with
> lurid accounts of what the 'Reds' had done and were planning and produced on a
> small scale a 'reign of terror' in which some thousands of innocent people were
> very cruelly treated and exposed to much suffering and loss. The statements in the
> newspapers were false and misleading. There was no conspiracy to overthrow this
> government and no evidence was ever produced which excused the action of the
> government. The safeguards of the Constitution were ignored, and any true
> American must blush at what was done and at the indifference with which he and
> all but a handful of his countrymen tolerated it.

Charles Evans Hughes, later Secretary of State, member of the World Court,
and now Chief Justice of the United States Supreme Court, wrote at the time:

> We cannot afford to ignore the indications that, perhaps to an extent unparalleled
> in our history, the essentials of liberty are being disregarded. Very recently infor-
> mation has been laid by responsible citizens at the bar of public opinion of viola-
> tions of personal rights which savour of the worst practices of tyranny.

Professor Zechariah Chafee, Jr., of the Harvard Law School, in his book,
"Freedom of Speech" . . . , dealt at length with numerous aspects of the arrests
and deportations and the hysteria of that period.

During the latter part of 1919 and in 1920 a countrywide "crime wave"
was being reported in the press of many of the large cities. Hold-ups, at-

tempts to blow up churches, safe-crackings, thefts by motor bandits and loot-ings of suburban homes were noted with increasing frequency. Editorials sug-gested a variety of causes for the condition, among them these: that drug ad-dicts were becoming more numerous, that organized seditious propaganda was being spread to inflame the radical minded, that the coal shortage had darkened the streets of the larger cities and so laid them open for miscreants, that prohibition had led to the use of a kind of liquor devastating in its ef-fects, and, of course, that the aftermath of all wars includes an increase in crime. In February, 1921, when time to analyze this crime wave had elapsed, George W. Kirchwey, for ten years Dean of the Law School of Columbia Uni-versity and at one time Warden of Sing Sing Prison, insisted that throughout the period the increase in the volume of crime had in actuality been slight. He described the nature of the crimes prevalent at the time as of the dare-devil, front-page sort, committed often by ex-soldiers who were both unemployed and accustomed to violence, and said he believed it was the nature of the crimes rather than any actual increase in their number which had gotten pub-lic opinion into a state of hysteria. While it continued the public sharply fo-cused its attention on the police and on the administration of the criminal law. Leniency against offenders was decried in the press; vigilance on the part of the police, frequently commended. As the most visible and vulnerable arm of the government, the latter stood most of the brunt of popular blame for the reported continuation of the deplored conditions. New England, with its shoe towns and their mixed populations, proved no exception to the current experience. Daring hold-ups, accompanied sometimes by violence and mur-der, took place there. And the brutal and apparently needless murders at South Braintree, Massachusetts, committed in broad daylight and in full view of many persons, called forth to the utmost the energies of police authorities in the State.

. . .

From Boston to the Cape the countryside revolted at this, the newest daring murder and hold-up in the current wave of crime. The police garnered de-scriptions of the murderers from eyewitnesses. Reported clues and promises of early arrest filled the front pages of the newspapers. According to the *Boston Herald* the rumored physical characteristics of the bandits tallied with those of several men concerned in an earlier unsuccessful hold-up in Bridgewater.

The crime attempted in Bridgewater early on the morning of December 24th, 1919, was held generally to be the work of a number of Italians or other foreigners operating in a touring car. This automobile had . . . blocked the passage of a truck containing a pay roll of the White Shoe Company. Two men in the street had tried to capture the truck. Their shots had been answered from the truck itself and they had fled back to their car and escaped. No one was hurt and nothing was stolen.

. . .

In actual fact the police remained for many days with no clues at all [for either the Bridgewater or the Braintree crime]. The work of investigation was conducted by Captain Proctor of the State Constabulary and Chief Stewart of Bridgewater. Braintree's Chief of Police, Gallivan . . . played only the slightest part in the ensuing events. The efforts of Proctor and Stewart were by now directed towards discovering a group of Italians with a machine.

. . .

During the spring of 1920 friends of Sacco and Vanzetti . . . were deported. In New York Elia and Salsedo had been taken into custody by agents of the Department of Justice and kept for weeks in one room of a building in Park Row. The group of Italian radicals to which Sacco and Vanzetti belonged was concerned about this confinement, contributed money to assist the two men and, late in April, 1920, sent Vanzetti to New York to find out what Salsedo's situation really was. Vanzetti made the trip and conferred with the prisoners' friends. He was told, among other things, that a new series of governmental raids should be expected around May 1st, and was advised to hide away all radical literature with the whereabouts of which he might be familiar.

On his return to Boston, therefore, he began arrangements to get the use of an automobile, intending by means of it to gather together all the radical literature he knew to be in the possession of his friends and acquaintances.

In New York, on the morning of May 3rd, Salsedo was found dead on the pavement outside the building in Park Row. Whether the man committed suicide or whether he was forced to his death has never since been established. . . . Sacco and Vanzetti, as they later claimed, were alarmed and disturbed upon learning of Salsedo's death. Just about the time it became known Sacco arranged definitely for the use of the automobile which belonged to Mike Boda. On the evening of May 5th Boda, Sacco, Vanzetti and a friend of all three, Orciani, started from Sacco's house for West Bridgewater to get the car [from Johnson's garage where it had been left for repairs]. Sacco and Vanzetti went by trolley, Orciani and Boda used the former's motor cycle. . . .

When Boda and Orciani reached the Johnson garage they found it closed and went to the owner's home near by. Sacco and Vanzetti followed them there and all four waited for Johnson. Mrs. Johnson answered the doorbell, found out what the men wanted, and then went over to a neighbor's house. Here, according to the arrangement made with the police to the effect that she notify them if Boda's car were called for, she telephoned the station. Boda was at the moment being advised by Johnson to leave his car where it was, because it had no license-plates for 1920. It seems the man accepted this advice because, while Mrs. Johnson was on her way back, he drove off on the motor cycle with Orciani.

Boda was never again seen in the United States.

Sacco and Vanzetti walked away from the garage and soon thereafter boarded a trolley car for Brockton. The police entered the car while it was passing through the Campello section of the town, arrested the two men and drove them in an automobile to the police station. Here Chief Stewart of Bridgewater at once examined them as to their political beliefs but asked them nothing which related in any way to the crime at Braintree or the earlier attempted hold-up at Bridgewater. On the following day District Attorney Katzmann questioned them. Like Chief Stewart he asked Vanzetti nothing which related to the Bridgewater crime or that at South Braintree, except that he wanted to know what Vanzetti had been doing on the Thursday before Patriots' Day, April 19th. He did ask Sacco whether he had read in the newspapers about the Braintree crime and what he had done on the day before he saw it reported in the press. Neither Sacco nor Vanzetti was at the time charged with participation in either hold-up. Both men were first held on charges, to which they pleaded guilty, of unlawfully carrying firearms. Sacco when arrested had a .32 Colt pistol and thirty-two cartridges of various makes; Vanzetti, a .38 Harrington & Richardson revolver with no extra cartridges, but he had a number of shotgun shells in his possession. At the time of the trial Vanzetti said he had purchased his gun a few months earlier as a protection against hold-ups. Sacco had owned his pistol for several years. His employer knew that he had one and had at one time suggested his getting a permit which, however, Sacco had failed to do. It was claimed by one of the officers that defendants made efforts to use their guns when arrested.

. . .

Immediately upon their apprehension pictures of Sacco and Vanzetti appeared in the press with a lengthy account of the circumstances of their arrest, a statement of their suspected connection with the Braintree crimes and further hints to the effect that the police believed them guilty of the Bridgewater hold-up as well, and of plans for a third crime and a subsequent escape to Italy. On May 8th the *Herald* announced that the police had clues to more of the bandit gang.

Orciani, taken into custody at the factory in which he worked, on the day following the arrest of the other two men, was dismissed because he proved at once that he had been working on April 15th.

Eyewitnesses of the Braintree murders were brought to look Sacco and Vanzetti over. Some could make no identification, some picked Sacco as one of the bandits who had done the shooting there, some identified him as having been near the spot before the crime and in the murderers' car after it. Originally no one claimed to have observed Vanzetti at the scene. Some time later he was identified as having been in the car after the shooting and was from then on accused of having had a hand in both crimes.

. . .

As soon as their friends discovered that the two men were charged with serious crimes they took steps on their behalf. Mr. John P. Vahey, of Plymouth, was retained to take charge of Vanzetti's interests. He cross-examined the witnesses who appeared on May 18th at the preliminary hearing of the Bridgewater case. At the conclusion of this hearing Vanzetti was held without bail for the Grand Jury on the statement of the Assistant District Attorney that he had witnesses identifying him in connection with the South Braintree affair.

On June 11th indictments were found against Vanzetti charging assault with intent to rob and with intent to kill, in connection with the Bridgewater hold-up. His trial on these indictments before Judge Webster Thayer and a jury took place at Plymouth, beginning on June 22nd and ending on July 1st. The defendant was not put on the stand in his own behalf. Found guilty and sentenced to a term of from twelve to fifteen years, he approached the murder charges with a conviction against him.

The District Attorney, Frederick Katzmann, has been criticized for trying Vanzetti on the lesser charge before trying him on the murder charges. Mr. Katzmann, it has been argued, should not have complicated the chances of two defendants in a capital case by seeking first to procure a conviction of one of them for attempted robbery. Later defendants' counsel went so far as to imply that Mr. Katzmann had deliberately arranged the order of the trials in the hope that a conviction for the Bridgewater hold-up would materially lessen Vanzetti's chances in the Braintree case, and would likewise injure Sacco's hope of acquittal on account of his association with a convicted criminal.

. . .

Friends of the prisoners had meanwhile been organizing a Defense Committee. . . . The Committee raised funds for the defense of both cases to the amount of more than fifty thousand dollars. And after the convictions it collected about two hundred and seventy-five thousand dollars more in the hope that new trials might be granted.

. . .

Just before the trial for the South Braintree murders took place articles appeared in the press commenting on the unusual interest aroused, especially in radical circles, by this case. . . . Some touched on the interest Sacco and Vanzetti had shown in the fate of Salsedo and one paper attributed the attention focused upon the affair to a claim that the defendants were being persecuted to cover the mistakes the United States Secret Service had made in the Salsedo matter. It was also remarked that the defendants had upon arrest been subjected to heavy grilling regarding their radical beliefs. There was no reference in any of these articles to Vanzetti's conviction for the Bridgewater crime; but on the day the trial opened many newspapers mentioned that Vanzetti had been brought to court from prison where he was serving time for another offense.

This thought, that the radical views of the defendants might enter prejudicially into the case, was expressed by the Italian Consul, the Marquis Ferrante, instructed by his government to attend the trial and express openly his hope that the defendants' views would not be allowed to affect proceedings.

The trial took place at Dedham, a residential suburb of Boston and continued from May 31st to July 14th [1921], during a spell of unusually hot weather. Judge Webster Thayer presided also at this trial. The leading news associations, as well as the Boston papers, had special reporters cover the case. The Greater Boston Federation of Churches sent a representative who later made an exhaustive report in which she expressed the opinion that the evidence at the trial had been insufficient to justify the convictions.

Such elaborate precautionary measures against danger were taken by the court authorities that on the opening day of the trial some one likened the progress of the defendants between the courthouse and the jail to a miniature police parade. In the second week of proceedings the practice was adopted of examining for concealed weapons all strangers who entered the court room; and whether or not the guards around and inside the courthouse were armed, became the subject of later discussion. There seems no doubt, however, that their numbers and their activity alike were unusual. The Judge himself took great pains on several occasions during the trial to make certain that even those firearms which were necessarily being handled as exhibits were not loaded.

When the verdict, guilty, was rendered the defendants seemed stunned at first. In the next moment Sacco, holding up two fingers, cried aloud. His cry came first in Italian: "siama innocente," then in English. Some of the jurors, according to the press, looked back as they were leaving the court room but no one stopped. Mrs. Sacco rushed to her husband and screamed: "Oh they kill my man, what am I going to do, my two children." Her cries grew more and more hysterical and she had to be taken away. Tears filled the eyes of some of the police officers who had had the defendants in charge during the trial.

Sacco and Vanzetti were led back to jail to await further legal proceedings, Sacco remaining in Dedham, Vanzetti being removed to Charlestown under his sentence for the Bridgewater hold-up. Since by Massachusetts law it is not customary to pronounce sentence in capital cases until all legal steps have been exhausted, sentence was not pronounced on the convicted men until April 9th, 1927.

After the trial supporters of the defense claimed that in a number of remarks Judge Thayer had fanned the patriotic prejudices of the wholly native jury and that he had permitted a cross-examination of Sacco which brought into unnecessarily devastating fullness the defendant's radical political views. On the other hand many people praised the fairness of the Judge's charge. These attributed the verdict of guilty to a combination of two factors: the positive evidence against the accused and the effect on the jury of the lies Sacco and Vanzetti told the police when first they were examined.

In the meantime propaganda against the verdicts spread through foreign radical and socialist groups. It was based in part on the mistaken suspicion

that in his charge Judge Thayer had discriminated against the defendants because they were Italians; but in the main the criticism of the verdicts rested on
the belief that it was the radical and pacifist views of the condemned men
which had been responsible for their conviction. Meetings of protest took
place during the month of October, 1921, in Milan, Brest, Rio de Janeiro,
Holland, Sweden and Switzerland. In Montevideo a strike was called. A bomb
thrown in Paris injured the valet of the American ambassador and troops were
called out in that city to prevent a demonstration. Italian newspapers demanded a revision of the trial. Anatole France, Romain Rolland and Henri
Barbusse joined in a cable to President Harding in which they asked his intervention.

As a result of all this agitation the Massachusetts police felt it necessary to
protect the home of Judge Thayer; and on the day set for hearing a motion for
a new trial based on the minutes of the case, they guarded the courthouse. Before that day came there had been bomb explosions in Havana and Lisbon
and protests in Lima and the Argentine Republic. After the argument, protests
continued to arrive from the Swiss Workmen's Union, from Mexican radicals,
from workers in New York. On December 24th, 1921, Judge Thayer handed
down his decision denying the motion.

. . .

The defense made great effort during the next few years to break down the
positive evidence against Sacco and Vanzetti. They filed a series of motions for
new trials, based either on alleged retractions by witnesses for the prosecution
or on new evidence relating to the guilt of the prisoners. All these motions
were, in accordance with regular practice, heard by Judge Thayer. He denied
them all at one time in a number of decisions, of which some drew down on
him further criticism for alleged intemperance in speech and errors of fact.

Several years had elapsed. Sacco, because he was not yet under sentence was
not allowed to take part in the regular activities of the prison. Early in 1923
he became despondent and attempted a hunger strike, with the result that he
was declared insane and was so considered for a time. Vanzetti, under sentence for the Bridgewater hold-up, had regular occupations to keep him active. He studied, besides, to improve his knowledge of English and kept up a
profuse correspondence with his friends and supporters. His letters, with
Sacco's, were published in 1928 by the Viking Press. Vanzetti took great interest in the progress of the case and kept in touch with developments. He too,
however, succumbed, early in 1925, to a deep depression and was removed for
a short period to the Hospital for the Insane. At this time he maintained that
the Fascisti were trying to get him out of the way and that some member of
that organization might be a prisoner and do him harm; wherefore he requested permission to carry a gun. He made disturbances in his room, abused
another prisoner for no apparent cause and reduced a chair to kindling wood.

State alienists reported to the Court their belief in his insanity and the view was confirmed by Dr. Abraham Myerson, an expert employed on his behalf. The prisoner himself invariably expressed the opinion that he was sane; and he insisted that he need not be removed from prison.

Much of the work for the defense in these later years was conducted by a prominent and conservative lawyer, William G. Thompson, member of the council of the Boston Bar Association. He argued some of the motions for a new trial and prepared the brief on the appeal from the judgment of conviction and from the denial of these motions. From the time he entered the case the prisoners and their supporters felt somewhat as though they had turned a corner and were looking on an altered and perhaps a fairer prospect.

A good deal was hoped for from the appeal which Mr. Thompson argued before the Supreme Judicial Court of Massachusetts in January, 1926. That court, however, decided that no errors had been committed by Judge Thayer at the trial or in his denial of the various subsequent motions.

All this time, although most witnesses of the murders at South Braintree had seen five men participate in the crime, the police had made no effort to find the other three bandits concerned. The charge against Orciani had been dismissed at the very beginning; Boda bore no physical resemblance to any of the men described; and . . . [a] trunk, suspected by some of containing the vanished loot, had been intercepted and found to hold nothing suspicious. Nor did the defense suggest any who might be guilty.

In November of 1925, however, while the appeal was pending undetermined, Sacco made the acquaintance in jail of a young Portuguese, Celestino Medeiros, there under sentence of death. Medeiros claimed he had been present at the Braintree shooting in the company of a gang of Italians he described but refused to identify. His statement entirely exculpated Sacco and Vanzetti; and from other sources the identity of the men he portrayed was established as that of the brothers Morelli and their associates, well-known criminals of Providence, R.I.

The supporters of Sacco and Vanzetti believed that evidence pointing to the Morellis as the murderers should constitute grounds for a new trial. But Judge Thayer took the stand that Medeiros, a criminal and unworthy of being taken seriously, was trying by the manufacture of this confession to prolong his own life. The defense called the Judge's opinion an irrational document, self-justificatory and evasive of the issues. At this juncture the *Boston Herald*, until now, like the rest of the press, hostile to the defendants, expressed grave doubt of their guilt and in an editorial later awarded the Pulitzer prize for the most outstanding piece of journalism during 1926, recommended an impartial review of the entire case. The *Springfield Republican* joined in this point of view and many men prominent in Massachusetts expressed the same opinion.

. . .

The feeling about the case was further complicated by the inclusion in the Medeiros motion of charges by the defendants' attorneys involving the United States Department of Justice.

Several people made affidavits, at the hearing to Judge Thayer, to the effect that an arrangement had existed between the District Attorney and the Boston office of the Department of Justice, whereby Mr. Katzmann was to have emphasized the anarchism of the defendants with a view to confirming them as material for deportation, and the Boston office was to have reciprocated by helping the District Attorney secure a conviction. Correspondence in proof of this cooperative arrangement was sworn to exist in the files of the Department of Justice in Boston. Mr. Katzmann never denied that there had been some cooperation.

When Mr. Thompson tried to get access to the files from United States Attorney General Sargent, in Washington, he was not permitted to do so. At the eleventh hour, just prior to execution, a last attempt was made by counsel to have the records opened. This time the Attorney General stated that he had had the files gone over and that no material bearing on the guilt of Sacco or Vanzetti was in them. He now expressed himself as ready to open these records upon order from the Governor. Governor Fuller gave no order. The files were never opened.

. . .

Public interest took on increased proportions during the interval between the argument of the appeal from Judge Thayer's denial of the Medeiros motion and the decision of that appeal by the Supreme Judicial Court. The United Mine Workers of America urged a new trial. In Paris posters demanding justice were placed all over by the Socialists and it was felt necessary to send guards to the United States Embassy. In the *Atlantic Monthly* for March, 1927, Professor Felix Frankfurter of the Harvard Law School wrote a review of the case in which he expressed the belief that defendants were entitled to a new trial. A book from his hand containing the same material in expanded form appeared shortly thereafter and a controversy developed about the case between Professor Frankfurter and Professor John Henry Wigmore, eminent authority on the law of Evidence and then Dean of the Law School of Northwestern University.

The appeal taken from the judge's decision in the Medeiros motion was unsuccessful. As no further legal steps remained to be taken sentence was now imposed. In addition to remarks made in Court by both prisoners, . . . Vanzetti made a public statement in which he said:

> If it had not been for these thing, I might have live out my life talking at street corners to scorning men. I might have die, unmarked, unknown, a failure. Now we are not a failure. This is our career and our triumph. Never in our full life could we hope to do such work for tolerance, for joostice, for man's understanding of man as now we do by accident. Our words—our lives—lives of a good shoemaker

and a poor fish-peddler—all! That last moment belongs to us—that agony is our triumph.

The defendants thereupon petitioned Governor Fuller for clemency, advancing as one of the grounds therefore the prejudice of Judge Thayer, which, they claimed, had been manifested partly in the legal proceedings and partly in various remarks made outside the court. Counsel announced that the Governor would be asked to appoint an impartial commission to review the cases.

At first Governor Fuller refused to appoint a commission; and he instituted instead a secret inquiry of his own. He denied the request of the defense that there be public hearings at this inquiry and also refused to permit counsel to be present during his interviews of witnesses. No record was kept of his proceedings nor were counsel ever informed as to what had been told him nor even as to whom he had seen, although they were permitted to suggest names of persons they desired him to interview and were also allowed to argue before him and his personal counsel, Mr. Joseph Wiggin.

In many quarters there now arose the insistent demand that the Governor submit this case for complete review to an impartial tribunal; at one time rumor had it that Mr. Charles Evans Hughes would be asked to preside over such a body. For a time, however, the Governor insisted that, as the responsibility for a decision rested with him, he could not divide it. Nevertheless, on June 1st, 1927, he announced the appointment of an advisory committee to report to him on the fairness of the trial and on the weight of evidence against the convicted men. Abbott Lawrence Lowell, President of Harvard University, a lawyer by education, but a teacher and administrator by experience, member of a distinguished Boston family, became its chairman. The other members were Samuel W. Stratton, President of Massachusetts Institute of Technology, a man without legal experience or training, and Robert Grant, a writer of fiction, formerly Judge of the Massachusetts Probate Court, that court which has to do with estates and guardianships. Counsel for the defense protested Judge Grant's appointment at once, on the ground that he had expressed views hostile to Sacco and Vanzetti. After interviewing Judge Grant the Governor refused to alter his choice.

The appointment of the Committee resulted in a general feeling that the case would now be lifted out of the atmosphere of propaganda into which the adherents of the defense had carried it. Some misgivings were expressed, however, when it came to be known that the Committee had refused the request of defendants' counsel for public hearings. The reason stated for this refusal was, that since the Committee could not compel the attendance of witnesses, the publicity might interfere with the ascertainment of the truth. Supporters of the defense asserted that this reason would not apply to any of their witnesses and also that people would be more likely to tell the truth if their statements were published.

While the Lowell Committee debated and Governor Fuller awaited their report he went on with his own inquiry. Suspense, acute while the hearings were in progress, reached a peak when the announcement came that a decision would be made public on August 3rd. Under the law the consent of the Governor's Council was necessary to a pardon or a commutation of sentence. When, therefore, a meeting of this council was called for August 3rd the announcement was interpreted by some people as a hopeful omen. On the other hand, reports from adherents of the defense who had been interviewed by the Governor seemed pessimistic. The defendants themselves, especially Sacco, had little hope. So well-informed a paper as the *New York Times,* however, carried on the morning of August 3rd a lengthy account of the steps it was expected the Governor would take to make possible a new trial. The article said he expected to call the Legislature in session to pass legislation to that end, and that it was a last minute interview with Judge Thayer which had apparently turned the tide. However, on the third it was announced that the meeting of the council had been adjourned for a day, which was interpreted by some of the afternoon papers as a sign of ill omen for the defendants.

In the meantime meetings of protest were taking place all over the world. The defendants, waiting together in Charlestown jail, had gone on a hunger strike in demonstration against the reported attitude of the Governor. On August 1st Vanzetti decided he would break his fast but Sacco, then already sixteen days without food, continued to abstain until August 15th when he succumbed to forcible feeding.

Late in the night of August 3rd Governor Fuller announced his own decision finding the trial fair and expressing his belief that the defendants were guilty. He stated that his Advisory Committee was unanimous in reaching the same conclusion. The execution of both defendants as well as that of Medeiros, whose life had been prolonged pending the investigation, was thereupon set for just after midnight in the night of August 10th to 11th.

Excitement over the decision spread rapidly. In the press and in messages sent to him directly Governor Fuller found himself praised for courage by some, sharply and bitterly criticized by others. Much dissatisfaction was expressed with regard to the tone of his report, particularly respecting its emphasis on the emotional aspects of the case and the brutality of the crime. A more reasoned explanation of the affair seemed to many people to be due the world. On Sunday, the 7th, the report of the Lowell Committee was released for publication. It seemed to be that reasoned consideration of all the issues for which the critics of the Governor had asked. Further study of it, however, led liberal journals such as the *New York World,* the *Baltimore Sun,* the *New Republic,* and the *Nation* to manifest their dissatisfaction. In Massachusetts the *Springfield Republican* alone voiced protest.

From all over Europe, however, and from the rest of the United States, came many statements of criticism to the effect that Sacco and Vanzetti had been persecuted partly for their convictions, and partly because they were foreigners in the United States during a period of anti-foreign hysteria. The *St. Louis Post-Dispatch* asserted that only a flimsy thread of evidence had been established between the prisoners and the crime "which they in all human probability did not commit." The *New York Evening World* was not satisfied that the bullet which killed Berardelli [the pay-roll guard] had been identified beyond reasonable doubt as having come from Sacco's pistol. It stressed Sacco's previous record and said that Vanzetti's also showed perhaps no association with a crime such as the one for which both men had been convicted. The *New York Telegram* said that a secret hearing such as had been had by the Lowell Committee, and a decision on evidence so heard, was far from constituting the new and open trial the public had demanded. This paper joined a number of others such as the *New York World,* the *Norfolk Virginian-Pilot* and the *Springfield Republican,* in expressing dissatisfaction with the Committee's treatment of the charge of prejudice against Judge Thayer; one of the newspapers wondered what the members of the Committee would consider prejudicial conduct on the part of a judge. The *World* devoted an entire editorial page to criticism of the reasoning and conclusions of the Committee's report. In a long letter to the *New York Times* Mr. Charles C. Burlingham, later President of the Association of the Bar of the City of New York, expressed similar views. Many of these papers insisted, as did also journals in other cities, that a civilized application of the principles of justice required commutation of the death sentence to life imprisonment.

A tremendous number of newspapers, on the other hand, took the view that all had been done that could be done and that the conclusions of the Committee and Governor Fuller would be acceptable to the conscience of America. "Human law can do no more," said the *New York Times.* "No men, convicted by due process of law, ever had greater consideration," the *Philadelphia Inquirer* stated. All over the country editors seemed to believe that the distinction and the accepted impartiality of the triumvirate who composed the Committee gave to the verdict a quality of dignified finality. And the belief that any decision other than the one arrived at would have been merely a cowardly weakening before anarchy and crime found thousands of advocates. "This case," said the *Boston Transcript,* "has been the vehicle of as vicious propaganda as ever deluged a community. Radicals the world over saw here an opportunity to further what they call their cause. And the strange circumstance is that many well-meaning citizens either thought these foreign agitators were in earnest or were afraid of what they might do. The advice that they then gave was, on the one hand, the counsel of misguided sympathy; on the other, the counsel of fear."

Mr. Thompson had retired from the case before the Committee's decision was made public, because he believed he had given all he could and new minds might better handle the steps still open to the defense. Mr. Arthur D.

Hill, former District Attorney of Suffolk County, in which Boston is situated, took over the further care of the interests of the condemned men. On August 6th, he made a motion for revocation of sentence and for a new trial on the ground of Judge Thayer's prejudice. Both motions were denied by Judge Thayer himself on the ground that the motions, being made after sentence, had come too late. On August 10th, just before the hour set for the execution, Governor Fuller granted a reprieve until the 22nd in order that there might be time for an appeal. On appeal to the highest court of the state Judge Thayer's decision was upheld.

While these proceedings were pending counsel for the defense made application to a number of Federal judges, including Justice Holmes of the Supreme Court, for a writ of habeas corpus.

Under the American Federal system the courts of the United States can review criminal convictions in state courts only where a question is raised under the United States Constitution, and then only when the point has been properly made in the state court. In this case no claim was made at the trial that any right of defendants under the Federal Constitution had been infringed. It was, however, argued by their attorneys, as the basis for the pending proceedings, that Judge Thayer's prejudice rendered the trial void and deprived the defendants of due process of law. The various applications for habeas corpus were denied on the ground that prejudice charged against the judge did not render the proceedings in the state court void. The United States Supreme Court has shown great reluctance in interfering with state courts where, as here, the question raised has been one of due process. . . .

On August 19th an attempt was made to appeal directly to the United States Supreme Court in an effort to have that body review the whole record. The execution was to take place, however, before this appeal could be heard. Counsel, therefore, requested a stay of execution from the three available Judges of the Supreme Court, Justices Holmes, Brandeis and Stone. Justice Brandeis refused to pass on the matter on the ground that his wife and daughter had been interested in the case. Justice Holmes and Justice Stone agreed that there was no prospect of the Supreme Court's being willing to take the matter up and that therefore they were not justified in granting a stay of execution.

At the last minute effort was made to obtain another respite from the Governor and to get the Department of Justice to open its files. As has already been said, the files were never opened.

On Sunday, the 21st, the day before that set for the execution, after large crowds had gathered and pickets had paraded, the Boston police put a stop to all meetings. Vanzetti's sister arrived from Europe and, with Mrs. Sacco, visited the condemned men in Charlestown jail. On the last day the Governor remained in his office all day receiving messages and visitors. Officials of the Federal Council of Churches wired that it "would shock the moral sense of the nation to allow their execution tonight"; President Green of the Federation of Labor made another effort to obtain commutation. The Governor is reported to have said to one group of visitors:

> I would be sorry to see any of you leave this room believing in the innocence of Sacco and Vanzetti. I can answer any question you may ask me about the case and convince you that they are guilty.

Around the prison elaborate preparations were made. A large section of the town was closed off and people living within this area were kept in their homes as though an air raid were in progress. The prison was barricaded, machine guns bristled, searchlights glared. Throughout the city the excitement grew more and more intense. Near the State House over one hundred and fifty persons were arrested for picketing, among them Edna St. Vincent Millay, Lola Ridge, John Dos Passos and the septuagenarian Professor Ellen Hayes of Wellesley. Outside the barred area around the prison great crowds gathered. Almost, Boston seemed besieged.

On the eve of the execution Mr. Thompson, Mrs. Sacco and Miss Vanzetti visited the prisoners. Medeiros had his sister with him. Mr. Thompson made a record of his conversation with Vanzetti which was published as an appendix to the book of letters written in prison by the defendants. This record shows Vanzetti to have been interested in the cause of anarchy to the end.

Medeiros was executed first of the three. According to the only reporter present at the execution, Mr. W. E. Playfair of the Associated Press, Sacco cried "Long live anarchy" in Italian, and then said in English: "Farewell my wife and child and all my friends. Farewell mother." Vanzetti was the last to die. Speaking calmly and slowly he said, first to the Warden, Hendry, and then to the others present:

> I want to thank you for everything you have done for me, Warden. I wish to tell you that I am innocent and that I have never committed any crime but sometimes some sin. I thank you for everything you have done for me. I am innocent of all crime, not only of this, but all. I am an innocent man. I wish to forgive some people for what they are now doing to me.

The warden was so much affected that he could hardly speak the words required by law to pronounce the death. Governor Fuller remained in his office to receive the report that the executions were accomplished.

CHAPTER 17

The 1920s and the New Deal

In 1925, while the convictions of Sacco and Vanzetti were being appealed, another trial captured the nation's attention. In Tennessee, a high school teacher named John T. Scopes was charged with violating a Tennessee statute prohibiting the teaching of Darwin's theory of evolution in public schools. The national visibility of the case was due not only to the nature of the charge, but also to the attorneys involved. Defending Scopes was the well-known Chicago lawyer, Clarence Darrow, who had made a career of defending labor organizers and high-profile criminal defendants. Assisting the state of Tennessee was William Jennings Bryan, three-time presidential candidate and a great orator. The clash between Darrow and Bryan has been immortalized in the play and film *Inherit the Wind*, and the case has come to symbolize the beginning of a new era.

With the new era came increasing respect for civil liberties. Palmer's raids, the Sacco-Vanzetti case, the Scopes trial, and other events had brought civil liberties issues to the forefront. The American Civil Liberties Union was formed in 1920. In that same year, the Nineteenth Amendment passed, giving women the right to vote. In 1925 a far-reaching decision of the Supreme Court, *Gitlow* v. *New York*, began to apply the most fundamental protections of the Bill of Rights to states (an unsettled issue until then, since the Bill of Rights refers only to "Congress").

In legal thought, too, it was a productive era. In 1923 the American Law Institute was organized to boil down the mass of judicial opinions, legislation, and other sources to clear, concise black-letter rules in a series of "Restatements of the Law." Staffed largely by Harvard law professors, the ALI project, which is still being maintained, seemed premised on Langdell's concept of the law as a science. At the same time, centered largely at Yale Law School, a very different approach to the law was being pursued by a group of professors loosely labeled "legal realists." With Professors Karl N. Llewellyn and Jerome N. Frank in the lead, and drawing on the insights of Holmes, Pound, and others, the realists stressed the indeterminacy of law, the influence of personal and class attitudes on judicial decisions, and the operation of law in society. They opened the law school curriculum to legislation and administrative regulation and made use of the social sciences, history, and psychology. In a history of this group, *Legal Realism at Yale, 1927–1960* (1986), Laura Kalman has written:

> For well over a hundred years, the structure and content of legal training have followed the strictures of Harvard and Langdell. During the 1920s and 1930s, however, a group of scholars known as legal realists developed a jurisprudence that challenged this education as having detrimental effects on unsuspecting students. Their attack grew out of their contempt for the conceptualistic legal theory upon which the Harvard training was based. The realists pointed to the role of human idiosyncrasy in legal decision making, stressed the uselessness of legal rules and concepts, and emphasized the importance of greater efficiency and certainty in law administration. (p. 3)

The decade of the 1920s also showed promise economically. Prosperity returned to the United States, and even war-torn Europe was recovering and entering an era of cultural creativity. The promise, however, was shattered at the end of the decade with the stock market crash of 1929. The resulting unemployment and economic misery tested the nation's institutions. Extraordinary measures seemed called for—but government was slow to respond.

After the Wilson presidency, three Republican presidents—Warren Harding (who died in office), Calvin Coolidge, and Herbert Hoover—followed a conservative, pro-business course. Harding called for "normalcy," and Coolidge declared: "The business of America is business." As the crash hit in the first year of Hoover's presidency, he took some corrective action, but his policies were too feeble to deal with the magnitude of the Depression. The Democratic party seemed to offer a real alternative—a "New Deal"—and, in 1932, not only was its presidential candidate, Franklin D. Roosevelt, overwhelmingly elected, but Democrats also gained overwhelming control of both houses of Congress.

The new administration mounted a two-pronged attack on the depression: public works (such as reforestation, public housing, even public arts projects) to create jobs, and new regulatory agencies (such as the Securities and Exchange Commission and the National Labor Relations Board) to police business practices. A "brain trust"—including an army of attorneys—gathered in Washington to draft the necessary legislation and staff the new agencies.

The first New Deal measures went too far in the direction of central economic planning even for some of the most ardent supporters of new approaches. The centerpiece of New Deal legislation was the National Industrial Recovery Act (NIRA), which gave the president authority to have codes of fair business practices drafted for individual industries. A number of codes, covering such issues as labor relations and fair competition, were drawn up with input from industry representatives. When the act was challenged in the Supreme Court case of *Schechter* v. *United States* (1935), a case involving a code drawn for the poultry industry, the court had a solid block of four justices who had opposed earlier Progressive measures and could be counted on to oppose the NIRA as well. But the Court also had three justices who were expected to be supporters: Justice Brandeis was still sitting; Justice Stone (soon to become chief justice) often voted to uphold Progressive economic measures; and a new justice, Benjamin N. Cardozo, had taken the seat of Justice Holmes, who had retired in 1932. Justice Cardozo had a reputation as an outstanding state judge (in New York), a superb writer, and a thoughtful Progressive.

Yet even the three justices most favorably disposed toward the New Deal joined in a unanimous decision holding the NIRA to be unconstitutional. The justices held that, in giving the president a blank check, without adequate standards and guidelines, Congress had simply delegated its legislative authority to the executive, violating the Constitution's separation of powers. As Justice Cardozo put it, the NIRA was "delegation running riot." The justices also insisted that federal legislation could regulate only interstate activity and could not extend to the intrastate sale of poultry.

The New Dealers went back to their drawing boards to correct some of the defects of their early legislative efforts, but the four conservative justices, usually joined by the swing voter, Justice Owen J. Roberts, continued to strike down New Deal statutes. Key attempts to stabilize agricultural and coal production were invalidated 5-to-4. Even more crucial tests loomed over the National Labor Relations Act (also known as the Wagner Act) and over the Social Security Act. The firm control of New Dealers in both elected branches of government seemed of little avail in face of the entrenched conservative justices.

The National Recovery Administration's "Blue Eagle" symbol.
Document from the New York Public Library.

THE CONSTITUTIONAL REVOLUTION
OF 1937

from William E. Leuchtenburg, "The Case of the Wenatchee Chambermaid,"
in John A. Garraty, ed., *Quarrels That Have Shaped the Constitution*, rev. ed.
(New York: Harper & Row, 1987), pp. 266–83.
Copyright © 1987 by William E. Leuchtenburg.
Reprinted by permission of William E. Leuchtenburg.

When on a spring day in 1935 Elsie Parrish walked into the office of an
obscure lawyer in Wenatchee, Washington, to ask him to sue the town's leading hotel for back pay, she little realized that . . . she was triggering a constitutional revolution that, even today, remains the most significant chapter in the
two centuries of existence of the United States Supreme Court. All Elsie knew
was that she had been bilked.

Late in the summer of 1933 Elsie Lee, a woman of about forty who would
soon be Elsie Parrish, had taken a job as a chambermaid at the Cascadian Hotel in Wenatchee, entrepot for a beautiful recreation area reaching from the
Columbia valley in Oregon to the Cascades and the country's foremost apple
market. . . . Here, in the land of Winesaps and Jonathans, where "in summer
and fall the spicy odor of apples is everywhere," Parrish worked irregularly
over the next year and a half, cleaning toilets and sweeping rugs for an hourly
wage of twenty-two cents, later raised to a quarter. When she was discharged
in May 1935, she asked for back pay of $216.19, the difference between what
she had received and what she would have gotten if she had been paid each
week the $14.30 minimum wage required for her occupation under state law.
The Cascadian, which was owned by the West Coast Hotel Company, offered
to settle for $17, but she would not hear of it. Instead, she and her husband,
Ernest, brought suit for what she insisted was due her.

The Parrishes rested their case on the provisions of a statute that had been
enacted by the state of Washington a quarter of a century before when, catching the contagion of reform from neighboring Oregon, it had taken steps to
wipe out sweatshops. The 1913 act declared it "unlawful to employ women
or minors . . . under conditions of labor detrimental to their health or morals;
and . . . to employ women workers in any industry . . . at wages which are not
adequate for their maintenance." To safeguard the welfare of female employees, the law established a commission that was authorized, after investigation,

to call together employers, employees, and representatives of the public to recommend a wage standard "not detrimental to health and morals, and which shall be sufficient for the decent maintenance of women." On receiving that recommendation, the commission was to issue an order stipulating the minimum wage that must be paid. Under provisions of the law, a commission had set a $14.30 weekly minimum for chambermaids. . . .

Alas, any law student in the land could have told [Elsie Parrish] that her case was hopeless, for twelve years before, the United States Supreme Court had ruled, in a widely reported decision in the case of *Adkins v. Children's Hospital,* that a minimum wage act for women was unconstitutional because it violated the liberty of contract that the Court claimed was guaranteed by the Constitution. Though the opinion by Justice Sutherland commanded only five votes and elicited vigorous dissents, it reconfirmed a notion incorporated in constitutional doctrine only a generation before: that a great corporation and its employee—even someone as powerless as a chambermaid—each had an equivalent right to bargain about wages, a fantasy that Justice Holmes dismissed as "dogma" and the renowned commentator Thomas Reed Powell of Harvard Law School called "indefensible." *Adkins,* said one commentator, "makes forever impossible all other legislation along similar lines involving the regulation of wages." The case involved an act of Congress rather than a state statute, but there was no difference in principle. . . . Though the Washington law remained on the statute books, it was presumed to be null and void. Hence, it startled no one when in November 1935, after hearing Elsie Parrish's case, the presiding judge of the superior court of Chelan County ruled against her, explaining that *Adkins* bound every court in the nation.

Surprisingly, the supreme court of the state of Washington took a different view. On April 2, 1936, it overturned the lower court's decision. To get around the huge obstacle of *Adkins,* the court pointed out that the U.S. Supreme Court had never struck down a *state* minimum wage law, which was true but irrelevant. The decision gave the Parrishes a moment of euphoria, but it hardly seemed likely that this opinion would survive a test in the Supreme Court, in the light of the *Adkins* ruling and given the manifest hostility of justices such as Sutherland to legislation of this nature.

Only eight weeks later, the Court settled any doubt on the matter by a decision on a case that, three thousand miles from Wenatchee, had begun to wend its way through the judicial system while Elsie Parrish was still making beds in the Cascadian Hotel. It arose out of the hope of social reformers in New York, especially women active in the Consumers' League, that the Court, despite *Adkins,* might look favorably on a minimum wage law for women and minors if it was drafted to relate wage setting not just to the needs of women but to the value of the services they rendered. To that end, Felix Frankfurter of Harvard Law School and Benjamin Cohen, a former Brandeis law clerk who was to be a prominent New Dealer, crafted a model law that New York State adopted in 1933, the fourth year of the Great Depression, which had reduced some young women, living on starvation wages, to sleeping on subways. Frankfurter warned that it was "foolish beyond words" to expect the Court to reverse itself, but he hoped that the justices might be willing to distinguish this statute, with its added feature of "value of services," from the one struck down in *Adkins*. "Every word" of the New York law, explained a prominent woman reformer, was "written with the Supreme Court of the United States in mind."

In accordance with the provisions of the model legislation, New York State obtained an indictment against Joseph Tipaldo, manager of the Spotlight Laundry in Brooklyn, who had been brutally exploiting his nine female employees, first by paying them far below the minimum wage and then by pretending to pay the minimum but forcing the sweatshop laundresses to kick back the difference between what he gave them and what the state required. When Joe Tipaldo went to jail to stand trial on charges of disobeying the mandatory wage order and of forgery, the hotel industry . . . rushed to his side with an offer to bankroll a test of the constitutionality of the New York law. Since hotels were working their employees twelve hours a day, seven days a week, they had a high stake in the case. In fact, the state had already begun minimum wage proceedings against them. Consequently, each hotel put money in a kitty to finance Tipaldo's petition for a writ of habeas corpus to compel Frederick L. Morehead, warden of Brooklyn's city prison, to release him from custody. While his case was being prepared, Tipaldo, utterly shameless, renamed his firm the Bright Light Laundry and made a big investment in expanding his business. He explained, "I expect to get it back eventually on what I save in wages."

On June 1, 1936, the United States Supreme Court appeared to justify his optimism when, in a 5–4 decision in *Morehead* v. *New York ex rel. Tipaldo,* it struck down New York's minimum wage law. In a sweeping opinion written by one of the most conservative justices, the Court declared that there was no meaningful difference between the New York statute and the District of Columbia act that had been invalidated in *Adkins:* both violated the liberty of contract that safeguarded equally the rights of employer and employee to bargain about wages. After quoting from *Adkins* with obvious approval, the Court declared, in language that shocked champions of social legislation, "The decision and the reasoning upon which it rests clearly show that the State is without power by any form of legislation to prohibit, change or nullify contracts between employers and adult women workers as to the amount of wages to be paid." Those words all but doomed Elsie Parrish's cause, and gave cocky Joe Tipaldo the victory of a lifetime.

That victory, however, turned out to carry a very high price. "After the court decision, business looked good for a while," Joe told a reporter three months later. "I was able to undercharge my competitors a little on what I saved in labor costs." But then business started to fall off, then fell some more. "I think this fight was the cause of my trouble," he said. "My customers wouldn't give my drivers their wash." Before the summer was over the Bright Light Laundry had folded, and Joe Tipaldo was one of the army of unemployed. "I'm broke now," he confessed. "I couldn't stand the gaff."

Elsie Parrish was made of sterner stuff. She was determined to carry on her struggle, though her prospects seemed bleak indeed. Given the precedent of *Adkins,* her case had never been promising. When the attorney for the West Coast Hotel Company asked the judge who had written the opinion of the supreme court of the state of Washington sustaining that state's minimum wage law in *Parrish* how he could possibly have done so in view of what the U.S. Supreme Court had said in *Adkins,* he replied, "Well, let's let the Supreme Court say it one more time." Now, in *Tipaldo,* the Court had "one more time" stated unequivocally that minimum wage laws for women were invalid. So gloomy was the outlook that, on the advice of Ben Cohen and Felix Frankfurter, the Consumers' League did not even file a brief in *Parrish.* "We are both rather pessimistic regarding its outcome," Cohen confided. Elsie Parrish had every reason to expect the worst.

The *Tipaldo* decision, though, engendered a powerful backlash, not least from some of the members of the Supreme Court. In a strongly worded dissent, Chief Justice Charles Evans Hughes upbraided the majority for failing to acknowledge either that the New York law could be distinguished from the act of Congress struck down in *Adkins* or that the state has "the power to protect women from being exploited by overreaching employers." Far more biting was the separate dissent filed by Justice Harlan Fiske Stone on behalf of himself and Justices Louis Brandeis and Benjamin Cardozo. In one of the most scathing criticisms ever uttered from the bench, Stone accused the majority of indulging its "own economic predilections." He found "grim irony in speaking of the freedom of contract of those who, because of their economic necessities, give their service for less than is needful to keep body and soul together." In an impassioned warning to his brethren to exercise more self-restraint, Stone wrote: "The Fourteenth Amendment has no more embedded in the Constitution our preference for some particular set of economic beliefs than it has adopted, in the name of liberty, the system of theology which we may happen to approve."

Much of the nation shared Stone's sense of indignation about *Tipaldo.* Secretary of the Interior Harold Ickes noted angrily in his diary: "The sacred right of liberty of contract again—the right of an immature child or a helpless woman to drive a bargain with a great corporation. If this decision does not outrage the moral sense of the country, then nothing will." People of the most diverse political views were appalled by the Court's ruling, for it seemed to deny government, state or federal, any kind of authority over working conditions. New Dealers were irate, and a Republican newspaper in upstate New

York declared, "The law that would jail any laundryman for having an under-fed horse should jail him for having an underfed girl employee." Even Herbert Hoover asked for a constitutional amendment to give back to the states "the power they thought they already had."

Only two groups applauded the decision. One was the press in a scatter-ing of cheap-labor towns undismayed by the fact that, following the ruling, the wages of laundresses—mostly impoverished blacks and Puerto Rican and Italian immigrants—were slashed in half. The other was a small faction of advanced feminists centered in Alice Paul's National Woman's Party. "It is hair-raising to consider how very close women in America came to being ruled inferior citizens," one of them wrote Justice Sutherland. Most women activists, though, were horrified by that view, which they believed reflected the dogmatism of upper-class ladies who had no familiarity with the suffer-ing of workers. They were as devoted as Alice Paul to equal rights, and they must have shuddered at the paternalism implicit in earlier opinions sustain-ing separate treatment for women on the grounds that they were wards of the state. But they were sure that female employees required protection, and they knew that insistence on the principle of equal rights meant no minimum wage law whatsoever, since the Court, as constituted during FDR's first term, would never sanction social legislation for men. "Thus," the historian Mary Beard wrote Justice Stone, Alice Paul "plays into the hands of the rawest capitalists."

. . .

Tipaldo, handed down on the final day of the term, climaxed an extraordi-nary thirteen months in which the Court struck down more important socio-economic legislation than at any time in history, before or since. During that brief period, it destroyed the two foundation stones of Roosevelt's recovery program, the National Industrial Recovery Act and the Agricultural Adjust-ment Act; turned thumbs down on a number of other New Deal laws and state reforms; and cavalierly rebuked the President and his appointees. The NIRA ruling had been unanimous, but almost all of the others had come in split decisions, most often with the "Four Horsemen," Pierce Butler, James McReynolds, George Sutherland, and Willis Van Devanter, a quartet of adamantly conservative judges whose ideas had been molded in the heyday of laissez-faire in the late nineteenth century, voting in the negative. They were often joined by the youngest member of the bench, Owen Roberts. At the end of the term, a nationally syndicated columnist wrote, "After slaughtering practically every New Deal measure that has been dragged before it, the Supreme Court now begins its summer breathing spell, ending a winter's per-formance which leaves the stage, as in the last act of a Shakespearean tragedy, strewn with the gory dead."

Despite the enormous setbacks the New Deal had sustained, Roosevelt gave every indication that he was accepting his losses virtually without complaint.

After being drubbed in the press for stating after the NIRA was struck down that the Court was returning the nation to a "horse-and-buggy" conception of interstate commerce, he had said nothing about the issue for the next year. *Tipaldo* moved him to break his silence to observe that the Court had created a "no-man's-land" where no government could function. But that was all he would say. While Elsie Parrish's feeble case was advancing toward its final reckoning in the United States Supreme Court, the President gave not the slightest indication that he had any plans whatsoever to make the justices any less refractory, for it seemed to him altogether inadvisable in the 1936 Presidential campaign to hand his opponents, who were hard put to find an issue, an opportunity to stand by the Constitution. As late as the end of January 1937, after Roosevelt had already delivered his State of the Union message and his inaugural address, the editor of *United States Law Week* wrote that "last week it was made plain that he does not at the present time have in mind any legislation directed at the Court."

But less than two weeks later, on February 5, 1937, the President stunned the country by sending a special message to Congress that constituted the boldest attempt a chief executive has ever initiated to remold the judiciary. He recommended that when a federal judge who had served at least ten years waited more than six months after his seventieth birthday to resign or retire, the President could add a new judge to the bench. Since this court was the most aged in history—its members were referred to as "the nine old men"—Roosevelt would be able to add as many as six new Supreme Court justices. He claimed he was presenting this proposal as a way of expediting litigation, but it was widely understood that what he really wanted was a more amenable tribunal. From the very first day, his program was saddled with a designation it could never shake off: "the Court-packing plan."

Though FDR's scheme provoked fierce protests, political analysts anticipated that it would be adopted. By winning in a landslide in 1936, Roosevelt had carried so many members of his party into Congress that the Republicans were left with only sixteen of the ninety-six seats in the Senate and fewer than one hundred of the more than four hundred seats in the House. So long as the Court continued to strike down New Deal reforms—and such vital legislation as the Social Security Act was still to be decided on—it was highly unlikely that enough Democrats would desert their immensely popular President to defeat the measure. The very first evidence of the attitude of the Court would come with its decision on Elsie Parrish's case, and there was every expectation that, acting not many months after *Tipaldo*, the Court would render an adverse ruling that would improve Roosevelt's already excellent chances of restructuring the Court. On the very day the *Parrish* decision was handed down, March 29, 1937, the president of the National Women's Republican Club declared, "I don't see how the President's bill can fail to get a majority."

March 29 came during the Easter holidays, always a gala season in Washington, D.C. On that bright Monday morning, a host of camera-toting tourists and children carrying Easter bunny baskets crowded the steps of the recently opened Supreme Court building and queued up in record numbers to enter the marble palace. . . . An hour before the session was scheduled to start at noon, four thousand visitors had already been admitted to the building. . . .

For some minutes it appeared that the spectators who had been fortunate enough to get into the courtroom were also to be frustrated, for the proceedings began with a recital of an opinion on another case by one of the Four Horsemen that left the audience nearly numb with boredom. But no sooner had he finished than the chief justice leaned forward in his chair, picked up some sheets of paper, and announced, "This case presents the question of the constitutional validity of the minimum wage law of the State of Washington." . . . [T]he spectators stirred in anticipation. Hughes, fully aware of the effect he was having and surely conscious of his magnificent appearance (with his patrician manner, sparkling eyes, and well-groomed beard, he was often likened to Jove), raised his voice to overcome the bustle, then paused and peered out over the crowded chamber for a moment before returning to his written opinion.

Anxious minutes passed as he labored through a reprise of the facts in the case. When he finally took up one of the arguments of Elsie Parrish's attorneys, he did so only to reject it disdainfully. It was "obviously futile," he said, for counsel to claim that the present case could be distinguished from *Adkins* on the ground that Mrs. Parrish had worked for a hotel and that the business of an innkeeper was affected with a public interest. As it happened, he noted, one of the cases *Adkins* had disposed of had dealt with a hotel employee. If the state of Washington law was to survive the day, it would need a better justification than this rickety effort. The Court was going to have to meet *Adkins* head on.

It took only a moment more for Hughes to reveal that the Court was prepared to do just that. In *Tipaldo*, the U.S. Supreme Court had felt bound by the ruling of the court of appeals of New York that the New York minimum wage act could not be distinguished from the statute in *Adkins* and hence was invalid; *Parrish*, the chief justice declared, presented a quite different situation. Here the highest tribunal of the state of Washington had refused to be guided by *Adkins* and had sanctioned the law in dispute. "We are of the opinion that this ruling of the state court demands on our part a reexamination of the Adkins Case," he continued. "The importance of the question, in which many States having similar laws are concerned, the close division by which the decision in the Adkins Case was reached, and the economic conditions which have supervened, and in the light of which the reasonableness of the exercise of the protective power of the State must be considered, make it not only appropriate, but we think imperative, that in deciding the present case the subject should receive fresh consideration." To do so properly, he observed, required careful examination of the doctrine of freedom of contract that had bulked so large in *Adkins*.

"What is this freedom?" Hughes inquired, his voice rising. "The Constitution does not speak of freedom of contract." Instead, the Constitution spoke of liberty and forbade denial of liberty without due process of law. The Constitution did not recognize absolute liberty, however. "The liberty safeguarded is liberty in a social organization," he declared. "Liberty under the Constitution is thus necessarily subject to the restraints of due process, and regulation which is reasonable in relation to its subject and is adopted in the interests of the community is due process." Hughes's delivery of the opinion in "a clear, resonant voice," noted one correspondent, "electrified and held spellbound the spectators who crowded every corner of the majestic Supreme Court chamber." As the chief justice spoke, members of the bar in the choice seats near the bench followed his every word as though transfixed.

The Court had long since established that the state had special authority to circumscribe the freedom of contract of women, the chief justice continued. In *Muller v. Oregon* (1908), he pointed out, the Court had fully elaborated the reasons for accepting a special sphere of state regulation of female labor. In that landmark case, the Court had emphasized, in the words of Justice Brewer, that because a woman performs "maternal functions" her health "becomes an object of public interest and care in order to preserve the strength and vigor of the race." Hence, Brewer had gone on, a woman was "properly placed in a class by herself, and legislation designed for her protection may be sustained even when like legislation is not necessary for men and could not be sustained." The state could restrict her freedom of contract, the Court had determined in *Muller*, not merely "for her benefit, but also largely for the benefit of all."

The precedents established by *Muller* and several later rulings had led the dissenters in *Adkins* to believe that the District of Columbia minimum wage law should have been sustained, and with good reason, Hughes asserted. The dissenting justices, he noted, had challenged the distinction the majority in *Adkins* had drawn between maximum hours legislation (valid) and minimum wage statutes (invalid), and that challenge remained "without any satisfactory answer." The state of Washington law was essentially the same as the Washington, D.C., act that had been struck down in *Adkins*, he acknowledged, "but we are unable to conclude that in its minimum wage requirement the State has passed beyond the boundary of its broad protective power." In that sentence, however convoluted, Hughes had in effect said what for some minutes it had been clear he was going to say: the Supreme Court was sustaining Washington's minimum wage law. Against all odds, Elsie Parrish had won.

Lest anyone miss the implication of the Court's reasoning, the chief justice spelled it out: "The *Adkins* case was a departure from the true application of the principles governing the regulation by the State of the employer and employed." In short, *Adkins,* written by Sutherland and carrying the votes of four of Hughes's other brethren, was being put to death in its fifteenth year. In truth, Hughes maintained, one could not possibly reconcile *Adkins* with "well-considered" rulings such as *Muller.* "What can be closer to the public interest than the health of women and their protection from unscrupulous and overreaching employers?" he asked. "And if the protection of women is a legitimate end of the exercise of state power, how can it be said that the requirement of the payment of a minimum wage fairly fixed in order to meet the very necessities of existence is not an admissible means to that end?"

With an eloquence, even passion, few thought him capable of, the chief justice added:

> The legislature of the State was clearly entitled to consider the situation of women in employment, the fact that they are in the class receiving the least pay, that their bargaining power is relatively weak, and that they are the ready victims of those who would take advantage of their necessitous circumstances. The legislature was entitled to adopt measures to reduce the evils of the "sweating system," the exploiting of workers at wages so low as to be insufficient to meet the bare cost of living, thus making their very helplessness the occasion of a most injurious competition.

Since many states had adopted laws of this nature to remedy the evil of sweatshop competition, the enactment of such legislation by the state of Washington could not be viewed as arbitrary or capricious, "and that is all we have to decide," Hughes said. "Even if the wisdom of the policy be regarded as debatable and its effects uncertain, still the legislature is entitled to its judgment." Delighted at what they were hearing, the New Deal lawyers in the chamber smiled broadly and nudged one another.

In his closing remarks, the chief justice advanced "an additional and compelling" reason for sustaining the statute. The exploitation of "relatively defenceless" employees not only injured those women, he asserted, but directly burdened the community, because "what these workers lose in wages, the taxpayers are called upon to pay." With respect to that reality, he said, the Court took judicial notice of the "unparalleled demands" the Great Depression had made upon localities. (That comment revealed how far he was reaching out, for the state of Washington had submitted no factual brief about any added responsibilities, and the statute in question had been enacted long before the Wall Street crash.) Hughes did not doubt that the state of Washington had undergone these tribulations, even if it had not troubled to say so. That deduction led him to state, again with unexpected acerbity: "The community is not bound to provide what is in effect a subsidy for unconscionable employers. The community may direct its law-making power to correct the abuse which springs from their selfish disregard of the public interest." Consequently, the chief justice concluded, "The case of *Adkins* v. *Children's Hospital* . . . should be, and it is, over-ruled," and the judgment of the Supreme Court of the state of Washington on behalf of Elsie Parrish "is affirmed." Some two years after she had changed sheets in the Cascadian Hotel for the last time, the Wenatchee chambermaid was to receive her $216.19 in back pay.

It would require some time for Court watchers to grasp the full implications of Hughes's opinion in *Parrish*—to write of "the Constitutional Revolution of 1937"—but George Sutherland's dissent revealed that the Four Horsemen understood at that very moment that their long reign, going all the way back to *Adkins* and even before, with only slight interruption, had abruptly ended. When he had spoken the final words, the chief justice nodded to Justice Sutherland seated to his left. Sutherland surveyed the chamber silently, almost diffidently, then picked up the sheaf of papers in front of him and began to read. Sensing his day had passed, Sutherland appeared barely able to bring himself to carry out his futile assignment. He started off speaking in a curiously toneless murmur, and even those near the dais had trouble at first catching his words. In the rear of the room, all was lost.

As a consequence, not a few missed altogether Sutherland's first sentence, and even those who did hear it needed a moment to take in its full import. "Mr. Justice Van Devanter, Mr. Justice McReynolds, Mr. Justice Butler and I think the judgment of the court below should be reversed," Sutherland began. A commonplace utterance. Yet that sentence signaled a historic shift in the disposition of the Supreme Court. Once again, the justices had divided 5–4, but this time, Owen Roberts had abandoned the Conservative Four to compose a new majority which on this day, and in the days and months and years to come, would legitimate the kind of social legislation that in FDR's first term had been declared beyond the bounds of governmental authority. The loss of Roberts did not go down easily. In the course of the afternoon, noted one captious commentary, "the Four Horsemen of Reaction whom he had deserted looked glum and sour."

After no more than a cursory paragraph saying that all the contentions that had just been advanced in *Parrish* had been adequately disposed of in *Adkins* and *Tipaldo,* Sutherland delivered a dissent that for quite some time constituted less a reply to Hughes and the majority in *Parrish* than to Justice Stone's 1936 calls for judicial restraint in cases such as *Tipaldo.* Undeniably, a justice was obliged to consider the contrary views of his associates, Sutherland acknowledged, "but in the end, the question which he must answer is not whether such views seem sound to those who entertain them, but whether they convince him that the statute is constitutional or engender in his mind a rational doubt upon that issue." . . .

Though Sutherland had been directing most of his barbs at Stone (Hughes's opinion had been all but forgotten), these last words may well have had a different target. His remarks, one writer conjectured, must have been intended as a rebuke to Roberts. Perhaps so, for the minority opinion did appear to be irritating Roberts, who, after looking toward Sutherland several times, raised a handkerchief to his mouth.

Sutherland, for his part, had hit full stride. After sipping some water he seemed to gain strength, and his voice resounded throughout the chamber. Indeed, the Washington *Post* characterized the reading by "the usually mild-mannered Sutherland" as nothing less than "impassioned." The elderly judge, described in another account as "pale, grim-lipped," even went so far as to rap his knuckle on the dais as he took issue with the President, though never by name; with Justice Roberts, no longer his ally; and even more vigorously, again without mentioning him directly, with Justice Stone. In rebuttal to the chief justice's assertion that the case before the Court required a fresh examination, in part because of "the economic conditions which have supervened," Sutherland stated bluntly "The meaning of the Constitution does not change with the ebb and flow of economic events."

When, having read nearly five pages of his opinion, Sutherland finally turned to the case before the Court, he said little more than that *West Coast Hotel* replicated the situation in *Adkins*. In every important regard, the two statutes involved had identical "vices," Sutherland maintained, "and if the *Adkins* case was properly decided, as we who join in this opinion think it was, it necessarily follows that the Washington statute is invalid." It was beyond dispute, he asserted, that the due process clause embraced freedom of contract, and Sutherland remained convinced, too, that women stood on an equal plane with men and that legislation denying them the right to contract for low-paying jobs was discriminatory. "Certainly a suggestion that the bargaining ability of the average woman is not equal to that of the average man would lack substance," he declared. "The ability to make a fair bargain, as everyone knows, does not depend upon sex."

If anyone thought that those last sentences had a hint of jocularity, they quite misperceived Sutherland's mood. The *Parrish* decision blew taps for the nineteenth-century world, and Sutherland, born in England in 1862 and reared on the Utah frontier, knew it. Having had his say, he understood that there was no point in going on any longer. Wearily, he concluded, "A more complete discussion may be found in the *Adkins* and *Tipaldo* cases cited *supra*." Then he carefully laid his opinion on the dais and, stern-visaged, settled back in his chair.

When news of the momentous decision, relayed swiftly to every part of the nation over press association wires, reached Sutherland's supporters, they shared his sense of dismay. Conservatives were outraged. If FDR wanted a political court, said a disgruntled senator, he had one now, for the decision was blatantly political, a transparent effort to kill the Court-packing bill by demonstrating that the judges would no longer misbehave. Ardent feminists were no less incensed. One of them wrote Sutherland: "May I say that the minority opinion handed down in the Washington minimum wage case is, to me, what the rainbow was to Mr. Wordsworth? . . . You did my sex the honor of regarding women as persons and citizens."

Most reformers, though, women as well as men, hailed the *Parrish* ruling as a triumph for social justice and a vindication for FDR, who had been accorded an altogether unexpected victory in the most improbable quarter. One outspoken Progressive, the columnist Heywood Broun, commented: "Mr. Roosevelt has been effective not only in forcing a major switch in judicial policy, but he has even imposed something of his style upon the majority voice of the court. There are whole sections in the document written and read by Chief Justice Hughes which sound as if they might have been snatched bodily from a fireside chat."

Partisans of the President jeered at the Court for its abrupt reversal of views on the validity of minimum wage legislation. Because of "the change of a judicial mind," observed Attorney General Homer Cummings sardonically, "the Constitution on Monday, March 29, 1937, does not mean the same thing that it meant on Monday, June 1, 1936." The head of one of the railway brotherhoods carried that thought a step further in noting, "On Easter Sunday, state minimum wage laws were unconstitutional, but about noon on Easter Monday, these laws were constitutional." That development perturbed some longtime critics of the Court—"What kind of respect do you think one can instill in law students for the process of the Court when things like this can happen?" Felix Frankfurter asked—but gave others no little satisfaction. A former United States senator from West Virginia wrote:

> Suppose you have noticed that the untouchables, the infallible, sacrosanct Supreme Court judges have been forced to put upon the record that they are just a bundle of flesh and blood, and must walk upon the ground like the rest of human beings. I got quite a "kick" out of reading that the Supreme Court said, right out loud in meeting, that it had been wrong. Like most of the wrongs done in life, there is no compensation for the great wrongs which that old court has been doing the country; but like all democrats, I am forgiving.

The performance of the Court proved especially embarrassing for the chief justice. Commentators, observing that Hughes had once said of a nineteenth-century decision that "the over-ruling in such a short time by one vote, of the previous decision, shook popular respect for the Court," pointed out that "Now, within a period of only ten months, the Supreme Court has reversed itself on minimum wages, again by one vote." . . . [Y]ears later Roberts claimed that he had voted with the Four Horsemen in *Tipaldo* only because New York had not presented the issue in the right manner. Furthermore, we now know that in *Parrish* Roberts was not responding to the Court-packing threat since he cast his vote before the plan was announced. Nonetheless, scholars, who have the advantage of information not generally known in 1937, find

Roberts's contention that he did not switch unpersuasive, and at the time, no one doubted that the Court, and more particularly Mr. Justice Roberts, had crossed over. "Isn't everything today exciting?" wrote one of the women who led the National Consumers' League. "Just to think that silly Roberts should have the power to play politics and decide the fate of Minimum Wage legislation. But, thank God he thought it was politically expedient to be with us." In a more whimsical vein, *The New Yorker* remarked: "We are told that the Supreme Court's about face was not due to outside clamor. It seems that the new building has a soundproof room, to which justices may retire to change their minds."

Yet despite all the ridicule directed at the Court, Hughes read the opinion in Elsie Parrish's case with an unmistakable note of exultation in his voice. For by being able to show that he had won Roberts to his side in *Parrish*, he had gone a long way toward defeating the Court-packing scheme. Once Roosevelt had a 5–4 majority for social legislation, there no longer appeared to be an urgent need for a drastic remedy. "Why," it was asked, "shoot the bridegroom after a shotgun wedding?" Not for nearly four months would FDR's proposal be finally rejected, and it would retain substantial backing almost to the very end, but never was it as formidable a proposition as it had been on the eve of Elsie Parrish's case. Within days after the decision was handed down, Washington insiders were regaling one another with a saucy sentence that encapsulated the new legislative situation: "A switch in time saved nine."

The Court's shift in *Parrish* proved to be the first of many. On the very day that *Parrish* was decided, . . . the Court also upheld a revised farm mortgage law (the original one had been struck down . . . in 1935) as well as other reform statutes. Two weeks later, once more by 5–4 with Roberts in the majority, it validated the Wagner Act (the National Labor Relations Act) and in the following month it turned aside challenges to the Social Security Act. Indeed, never again did the Supreme Court strike down a New Deal law, and from 1937 to the present, it has not overturned a single piece of national or state socioeconomic legislation. Many commentators even believe that the Court has forever abandoned its power of judicial review in this field. Little wonder then that analysts speak of "the Constitutional Revolution of 1937."

CHAPTER 18

War and Civil Liberties II

Like President Wilson two decades earlier, President Franklin Roosevelt in his second term was overwhelmed by foreign affairs. Adolph Hitler came to power in Germany in 1932—the same year Roosevelt was elected to the presidency—and by the middle of Roosevelt's second term, another European war seemed imminent. In the United States, isolationist sentiment was strong. In Congress, a Neutrality Act was enacted in 1935 and strengthened in 1937.

Following outbreak of war in 1939, despite the Neutrality Act, President Roosevelt took a number of actions favoring Germany's enemies. By executive agreements and executive orders, which do not require congressional approval, he traded fifty aging destroyers in 1940 for bases in British territories in the Caribbean and the Atlantic; in July 1941 he stationed troops in Iceland as a precaution; and in September 1941 he ordered naval ships to hunt down German submarines after a U-boat attack on an American ship. But the president's use of executive powers without congressional authorization was controversial.

The Japanese attack on Pearl Harbor in December 1941 ended the controversy. That attack also meant war with Germany and Italy due to a German-Italian-Japanese treaty of alliance. Thus, this time the United States faced war on two oceans, with its Pacific fleet severely damaged.

As in previous wars, the power of the executive was enhanced. Within two weeks of the attack on Pearl Harbor, Congress passed the War Powers Act, giving the president extraordinary authority to revamp federal agencies. Over two dozen new agencies followed to regulate war production, transportation, labor relations, prices, and other essential aspects of a war economy. Civil liberties, however, were not limited to the extent seen during and after the First World War. In 1940 Congress enacted an Espionage Act and an Alien Registration Act. In the same year, the Smith Act (passed over presidential veto) made it a crime to teach and advocate the forcible overthrow of the government or to belong to a group which does so. But the war-time attorney general, Francis Biddle, applied these statutes with moderation and asserted federal primacy in internal security matters to prevent repression at the state level. The Supreme Court also remained protective of civil liberties. As Paul L. Murphy has written in *The Constitution in Crisis Times: 1918–1969* (1972):

> Biddle . . . was on record as being intent upon avoiding the inexcusable excesses of World War I in the civil liberties area. Ten days following Pearl Harbor he informed United States Attorneys throughout the country that "prosecution of persons arrested for alleged seditious utterances must not be undertaken unless consent is first obtained from the Department of Justice."
>
> . . .
>
> As the war progressed, . . . pressure grew from many patriotic citizens and even from the President for the restriction of criticism of the war effort, particularly of right-wing pro-Nazi critics. Biddle was forced to walk a tightrope in his proceedings against such critics, notably against so stormy and controversial a figure as Father Charles Coughlin [a radio commentator], a number of ultra-right-wing, generally anti-Semitic self-proclaimed patriots, patently fascist in their views, and against the anti-administration Chicago *Tribune*, which had shockingly violated security matters by its sensational reporting. . . . [T]he Supreme Court offered wartime guidelines. In June, 1941, the Court considered an indictment . . . of an American citizen, charged through speaking and writing with willfully attempting to cause insubordination and disloyalty, and attempting to obstruct recruitment and enlistment in the armed forces. In a five-to-four ruling, [the Court] threw out the conviction. . . . The ruling, a literal application of Holmes's "clear and present danger" test, went a long way toward discouraging further prosecutions for unpopular oral or written expression during the war period. (pp. 225–27)

Given the prevailing respect for civil liberties, it is all the more perplexing why the era also saw what has been called "the greatest deprivation of civil liberties by government in this country since slavery"—the internment in "relocation camps" of over 120,000 West Coast Japanese Americans, about 80,000 of them born in the United States.

Discrimination was not new to Japanese Americans. Along with other Asians, their opportunities to immigrate to the United States were severely restricted by immigration laws; those who managed to immigrate were prevented from becoming citizens by naturalization laws—only their children born in the United States could attain U.S. citizenship; and the lives of both *Issei* (Japanese immigrants) and their U.S.-born descendants were limited by other racially discriminatory laws and practices of the time.

When the internment of Japanese Americans was first proposed, General John L. DeWitt, head of the West Defense Command, considered it "damned nonsense." But pressure from West Coast politicians and public opinion changed his mind. Once the idea was embraced by the military, most civilian authorities feared to challenge the military's prestige. Assistant Secretary of War John J. McCloy enthusiastically promoted internment and resorted to subterfuge to persuade Secretary of War Henry L. Stimson and Attorney General Biddle to drop their objections. The policy was then presented as a joint proposal of the War Department and the Department of Justice to President Roosevelt, who approved it in Executive Order 9066 in February 1942 without consulting Congress or even his cabinet. Advocates of internment then prevailed on Congress to pass Public Law 503 to endorse the president's order.

General DeWitt proceeded by imposing a curfew applicable to Japanese Americans and ordering Japanese Americans not to leave his area of command; he then ordered Japanese Americans to report to designated "Assembly Centers" from which they, with few exceptions, were transported to relocation camps in desolate, isolated areas, and kept there behind barbed wires under guard.

The first case challenging the general's orders to reach the Supreme Court became limited to the curfew order, since the defendant in the case, Gordon K. Hirabayashi, was given concurrent sentences for his curfew violation and his failure to report to an Assembly Center. The Court's decision, however, set the tone for later, more far-reaching challenges.

Posters, San Francisco, 1942
Photo by Dorothea Lange. Library of Congress, Prints and Photographs Division.

from Peter Irons, *Justice at War*
(New York: Oxford University Press, 1983), pp. 227–52.
Copyright © 1983 by Oxford University Press, Inc.
Used by permission of Oxford University Press.

[T]he nine members of the Supreme Court gathered for a closed-door conference on Monday morning, May 17, 1943 [to consider the case of *Hirabayashi
v. United States*]. . . . After the traditional exchange of handshakes that signified the bond of fraternity among men who would soon argue heatedly, Chief
Justice Stone—also by tradition—opened the conference.
. . .

When he opened the discussion, Stone looked down the long mahogany
table in the Court's conference room at a group dominated by the appointees
of Franklin D. Roosevelt. With the exceptions only of Stone and Owen
Roberts, the senior associate justice, every member of the Supreme Court in
1943 was a certified New Dealer. After the "Constitutional Revolution" of
1937 had broken the judicial logjam that had frustrated Roosevelt's efforts to
cope with the ravages of the Depression, the President had used his appointment power to reconstitute the Court. Stone's elevation to the post of Chief
Justice in 1941, after the retirement of Charles Evans Hughes, fit into Roosevelt's plan to project a "bipartisan" image during wartime. Although Stone
was a nominal Republican, he had generally voted in the 1930s to uphold
New Deal programs.

Roosevelt's expectation that his appointees would vote together as New
Dealers had quickly shattered on the shoals of dispute over First Amendment
issues. By the spring of 1943 . . . the justices had split into two factions whose
leaders were barely on speaking terms. Felix Frankfurter, whose charm and
wit in public masked an arrogant and abrasive manner in the conference
room, brought to the Court on his appointment in 1939 an undeserved reputation as a radical. His defense of real radicals against the paranoia of the
"Red Raids" that followed World War I, and his attack on the drive to execute Sacco and Vanzetti in 1927, had made Frankfurter an anathema to conservatives. In truth, however, he was an apostle of "judicial restraint" and
viewed his role on the Court as one of deference to legislative and executive

powers. Only in extreme cases, which rarely included challenges to restrictions on First Amendment rights, would Frankfurter step in as a judicial censor.

Justice Hugo Black, who sat at Frankfurter's left elbow on the bench, advocated a judicial role in First Amendment cases that was light-years away from that of his testy colleague. A constitutional literalist, Black sat in the conference room as a judicial policeman, ready to flag down errant officials. The command of the First Amendment that legislators pass "no law" that restricted the freedoms of religion, press, speech, and assembly was, in Black's mind, a constitutional stop sign. "No law means no law," he was fond of repeating. This brand of judicial activism made Black a special target for Frankfurter's scorn.

Although Chief Justice Stone generally remained aloof as Black and Frankfurter battled over First Amendment cases, his colleagues were loosely grouped under the contrasting doctrinal banners waved by the two justices. Three members of the Court often voted with Frankfurter in cases that raised issues of legislative and executive powers: Owen Roberts, a former corporate lawyer; Stanley Reed, a legal conservative who had loyally defended New Deal statutes before the Court as Solicitor General but who shared Frankfurter's views on judicial restraint; and Robert Jackson, a former Attorney General under Roosevelt. To Frankfurter's annoyance, the austerity of his judicial vision and the intervention of political factors produced occasional defections among this group, but these three members of the Court normally looked to him for leadership in the conference room.

Hugo Black headed a more cohesive bloc within the Court. William O. Douglas, who had zealously policed the financial community as head of the Securities and Exchange Commission, and Frank Murphy, who had served as governor of Michigan and as Attorney General under Roosevelt before his Court appointment, voted consistently with Black and shared his activist judicial philosophy. Frankfurter did not hide his contempt for this trio, whom he collectively derided as "the Axis." . . .

A quartet of cases on the Court's docket in 1943 illustrated the doctrinal chasm that separated the two factions. All four cases involved challenges by members of the Jehovah's Witnesses sect to state and local laws that restricted the First Amendment rights of this evangelical group. Over the dissents of Frankfurter and his three acolytes—Reed, Roberts, and Jackson—the Court struck down in the first three of these cases laws designed to erect barriers between the Witnesses and the subjects of their street-corner and door-to-door preachings.

The fourth case, in which Jackson deserted Frankfurter to write the Court's majority opinion, stung Frankfurter into a frenzy of denunciation. In striking down in the *Barnette* case a West Virginia law requiring schoolchildren, on pain of expulsion, to salute and pledge allegiance to the American flag, the Court abruptly overruled an opinion written three years earlier by Frankfurter in the *Gobitis* case, which involved a similar flag-salute challenge. The fact that the two laws were virtually identical rubbed in the affront. . . .

. . . Chief Justice Stone hoped on his part to heal the wounds opened by the Jehovah's Witnesses cases. Perhaps as his own contribution to the healing process, Black joined Frankfurter and Stone as an ally in the Hirabayashi case. One factor behind this unlikely alliance was Black's service in World War I as an Army artillery officer. Although all this service was stateside, Black was proud of his military record and became a lifelong member of the American Legion. Victor Brudney, who got to know Black well as law clerk to Justice Rutledge in 1943, later described him as a "jingo" who backed the war effort without question. In addition, Black had been a down-the-line New Dealer during his earlier Senate service and shared with Frankfurter a devotion to the President who had appointed both men to the Supreme Court. . . .

Black's statement at the outset of the May 17 conference forecast the outcome of the Hirabayashi case. "I want it done on narrowest possible points," he announced, according to sketchy conference notes made by Douglas. Along with Murphy's even briefer notes, these two sources constitute the only existing record of the closed-door conference. Douglas recorded Stone's quick agreement that the Court should confine its decision to the curfew violation alone. Stone offered two reasons for avoiding the evacuation issue. First, he stated, the concurrent sentences on the curfew and evacuation counts made a decision on the latter unnecessary. . . . Stone's second point was that Hirabayashi's "failure to report" for evacuation "did not necessarily mean he would be sent to camp." General DeWitt's exclusion orders provided "many exceptions" for those ordered to report, Stone told the conference.

The Chief Justice was in error on this question. Hirabayashi fit within none of the narrow exemptions to the exclusion order, a fact evident from the record before the Court. Had he reported for evacuation as ordered, Hirabayashi would inevitably have been shipped to the Puyallup Assembly Center to join his parents, brothers, and sister. None of his colleagues challenged Stone's erroneous assertion. The justices were obviously straining to evade the evacuation issue in the Hirabayashi case, and Stone's first reason for doing so satisfied them. Significantly, Stone's comments at the conference hinted at his doubts that evacuation could meet constitutional standards. According to Douglas, the Chief Justice admitted that there "may be difference between curfew of this kind and going to concentration camp." . . .

Douglas also recorded other doubts expressed by Stone in his conference comments. First noting a "grave question as to delegation," . . . Stone answered this question in the negative. In passing Public Law 503, he said, Congress had approved Roosevelt's decision to authorize the Army to exclude from the West Coast "any or all persons" designated by DeWitt, and had therefore "contemplated doing what was done." Stone finessed the after-the-fact implications of his statement with a rhetorical question: "does order have relation to espionage and sabotage—if it does problem of delegation drops out." The glaring absence of standards set out in Public Law 503 to confine DeWitt's orders within constitutional limits passed at the Supreme Court conference without any recorded comment.

The issue that most bothered the Chief Justice was the "discrimination" imposed on Japanese Americans by DeWitt's orders. "It is jarring to me that U.S. citizens were subjected to this treatment," Stone confessed at the conference. He had particular reason to be sensitive to the constitutional implications of racial and national discrimination in the Hirabayashi case. Five years earlier, . . . in the *Carolene Products* case, Stone had proclaimed that legislation directed at particular racial or national groups, and other "discrete and insular minorities" who had suffered histories of prejudice, should be subjected to "more exacting judicial scrutiny" than laws that affected the business community or other groups with unhindered access to the political process. In terms of judicial review, legislation in the latter category needed only a "reasonable" basis in fact, whereas laws that discriminated against minority groups placed on the government the burden of demonstrating a "compelling state interest" that justified the unequal treatment.

Despite his evident qualms about the discrimination against Japanese Americans, Stone told the conference (according to Douglas's abbreviated notes) that the constitutionality of DeWitt's orders "all depends . . . if there was reasonable basis as of time action was taken." Admitting that "no one doubts that many Japs are loyal," Stone found in the Pearl Harbor attack the "earmarks of treachery" that he attributed by implication to Japanese Americans. "In view of our whole history of relationship with them," Stone said of the group singled out for internment, there was "grave danger that these people would create damage." Justice Murphy's conference notes indicate that Stanley Reed and Owen Roberts both expressed doubts about the application of the curfew order to "a certain type of citizen" to the exclusion of others. Murphy's notes did not record a direct response by Stone to the question posed by Reed and Roberts. Douglas, however, reported that Stone told the conference that it was possible to "draw line between Japs and Italians."

Although Stone defended DeWitt's orders against the delegation and discrimination challenges, his arguments on these issues omitted an essential ingredient of constitutional analysis: that of locating in the Constitution itself the sources of legislative and executive authority for the challenged military orders and their statutory support. In his conference presentation, Stone raised the constitutional umbrella of the government's "war powers" for protection. These powers, he said, were "not limited to the conduct of hostilities" but included "all sorts of defensive activities" as well. The Chief Justice did not expand on the nature of the possible "defensive" measures covered by the war powers doctrine. Neither the Constitution nor Supreme Court precedent, in fact, put any flesh on this doctrinal skeleton. Stone himself had canvassed the potential sources of the government's wartime powers a year earlier, in a 1942 opinion [in the *Quirin* case] that upheld the convictions by military tribunal of eight German saboteurs who had landed by submarine on Long Island and the Florida coast. The saboteurs had been quickly captured and convicted; the military tribunal sentenced six of them to death and imposed life sentences on the other two. . . .

. . . The punishment of enemy saboteurs under existing provisions of federal law may well have fit under Stone's war powers umbrella. During the Hirabayashi conference, however, the Chief Justice could only point to an unspecified "grave damage" that Japanese American citizens, many of them concededly loyal, might inflict through espionage and sabotage, evidence of which was totally lacking in the record before the Court. He nonetheless concluded, in the conference remarks recorded by Douglas, that DeWitt's curfew orders were "not beyond war powers." . . .

Significantly, the conference produced none of the verbal fireworks that had exploded during recent sessions. Disarmed by Black's opening comment, Frankfurter apparently sat in silence through the meeting. By tradition, voting proceeded in reverse order of seniority, with the Chief Justice voting last. Stone looked first to Wiley Rutledge, and the junior justice voted to affirm Hirabayashi's convictions. One by one, his colleagues echoed Rutledge's vote. Frank Murphy, however, broke the string of votes to affirm and reserved his vote; he thus retained his right at a later time to cast a vote on either side. Unanimity in the Hirabayashi case thus hinged on Murphy's final vote.

Chief Justice Stone's final decision at the May 17 conference was to assign to himself the task of writing the Court's opinion in the Hirabayashi case. He recorded no reason for exercising this prerogative of his position; most likely, as in the *Quirin* case, Stone wished to place the imprimatur of his office on a case that raised basic constitutional issues during wartime, and hoped as well to head off potential conflicts that an assignment to a member of one of the Court's antagonistic factions might produce. Bennett Boskey, a 1940 Harvard Law School graduate who served as Stone's law clerk during this term, later confirmed this assessment. "Stone felt that certain types of cases of great national importance were cases that would be a good and proper thing for the Chief Justice to write the opinion," he said. Stone might also have felt, in view of Murphy's reservation of his vote, that his prestige as Chief Justice and skills as a mediator might succeed in forging the unanimity that he obviously desired.

With Boskey's help, Stone worked hard over the two weeks that followed the conference to draft an opinion that would satisfy his colleagues. He knew that members of the Court were entitled, up to the minute that an opinion was formally announced, to change their votes and to issue concurring or dissenting opinions. With this fact in mind, Stone and Boskey labored to produce a draft opinion that "put things on as narrow a ground as possible," as Boskey later said. The first draft, sent to the Court's basement print shop on May 30, ran to fifteen printed pages. The first seven recited in unexceptional manner the chronology of the Hirabayashi case and of Executive Order 9066, Public Law 503, and DeWitt's curfew and evacuation orders.

Stone's draft moved into uncharted constitutional waters on page 8, in its discussion of the ephemeral war powers of the government and the role of the courts in reviewing the exercise of these powers. Stone began with a phrase from a speech made by his predecessor, Charles Evans Hughes. "The war power of the national government is 'the power to wage war successfully,'" Stone wrote in quoting Hughes. The war power, Stone added in his own interpretation of this truism, "is not restricted to the winning of victories in the field and the repulse of enemy forces. It embraces every phase of the national defense, including the protection of war materials and the members of the armed forces from injury and from the evils which attend the rise and progress of war." With a citation to his own opinion in the *Quirin* case, Stone added that in reviewing "the choice of means" by which the legislative and executive branches of the government exercise the war powers granted to them by the Constitution, "it is not for any court to sit in review of the wisdom of their action or substitute its judgment for theirs."

Having thus limited the Court's reviewing role to that of deference to legislative and executive judgment, Stone adopted the test of "reasonableness" that he had seemingly rejected five years earlier in . . . the *Carolene Products* case. The only question that faced the Court, he wrote in addressing DeWitt's discrimination against Japanese American citizens, was "whether in light of all the facts and circumstances there was any substantial basis for the conclusion . . . that the curfew was a protective measure necessary to meet the threat of sabotage and espionage which would substantially affect the war effort." . . . Citing allegations that Japanese Americans posed a fifth-column danger, their concentration around West Coast defense facilities, their supposed adherence to Shintoism, the education of some 10,000 American-born Kibei* in Japan, and the system of dual citizenship maintained under Japanese law, Stone concluded that "the nature and extent of the racial attachments of our Japanese inhabitants to the Japanese enemy were consequently matters of grave concern" to General DeWitt.

Perhaps in light of the constitutional collision between the minimal standard of judicial review set out in his *Hirabayashi* draft and the "more exact-

---

*Children of Japanese immigrants (*Issei*) born and educated in the United States are referred to as *Nisei*; those born in the United States but educated in Japan are referred to as *Kibei*.

ing judicial scrutiny" he had promised in the *Carolene Products* case, Stone felt compelled to proclaim his devotion to the principles of racial equality. "Distinctions between citizens solely because of their ancestry," he wrote, "are by their very nature odious to a free people whose institutions are founded upon the doctrine of equality." Only those measures necessary "for the successful prosecution of the war," Stone explained, could displace this doctrine and justify military orders "which place citizens of one ancestry in a different category from others." In reaching this conclusion, Stone referred four times on one page to the "facts and circumstances" which, he claimed, "show that one racial group more than another" constituted "a greater source of danger" to the Army's wartime efforts.

Stone's draft opinion sparked flares of protest among four of his colleagues. The first was easily extinguished. Stone's careless discussion of the delegation question troubled Stanley Reed, the Court's most cautious member. Reed was particularly sensitive to delegation issues since as Solicitor General in the 1930s he had twice been burned by the Supreme Court in opinions that rejected crucial New Deal statutes on this ground. In his *Hirabayashi* draft, Stone had written that in passing Public Law 503, Congress had both reached back to ratify Executive Order 9066 and reached forward to authorize DeWitt's curfew orders. "The question then is not one of the congressional power to delegate," Stone asserted, "for Congress has itself approved the orders."

Reed objected to Stone's formulation. "It seems to me that the contrary is true;" he wrote the Chief Justice on May 29, "that the question is of the congressional power to delegate and that Congress has not approved the order under which this man was convicted." Reed suggested that the opinion merely state that Public Law 503 "is a sufficient delegation of the power to issue curfew" orders and that Stone avoid any implication that "Congress has approved the curfew orders." Stone willingly conceded on this technical but important point. The delegation question, he wrote in later drafts and in the final opinion, was that of "whether, acting together, Congress and the Executive could leave it to the designated military commander to appraise the relevant conditions" and to act accordingly. His sole objective met, Reed signed on with a letter of praise to Stone: "It seems to me that you have stated a very difficult situation in a way that will preserve rights in different cases and at the same time enable the military forces to function. It is a thankless job but you have done it well."

Justice Douglas raised more serious objections to Stone's first draft and proved more tenacious than Reed in pressing them. He sprinkled his copy of the draft with question marks in the margins and wrote to Stone on May 31 with "some suggestions on your first circulation. They are aimed at the most part to eliminate any suggestion of racial discrimination." The only member of the Court from the West Coast, Douglas had lived from the age of five in

Washington state and spent his summers at a remote cabin in Goose Prairie. Douglas was throughout his thirty-six-year career on the Court a consistent supporter of racial equality and sympathized during World War II with the Japanese Americans evacuated from his home state, some of whom he had grown up and gone to school with.

In his letter to Stone, Douglas objected particularly to a sentence in the draft opinion asserting that, because of prejudice against them, Japanese Americans "have maintained here a racial solidarity which has tended to prevent their assimilation as an integral part of the white population . . . and has encouraged their attachment to Japan and Japanese institutions. Douglas responded that "'racial solidarity' and lack of 'assimilation' do not show lack of loyalty as I see it. They may of course give rise to conditions which may breed disloyalty. But that is quite a different matter." Douglas also felt strongly that the opinion should put the government on notice that, in supporting the curfew orders as necessary but temporary measures, the Court questioned the necessity of evacuation and internment. "Is not the justification for dealing with Jap citizens as a group," he asked Stone, "the fact that the exigencies of war and the necessities of quick action in defending the nation against invasion do not necessarily permit enough time to sort out the sheep from the goats? Is it not necessary to provide an opportunity at some stage (although not necessarily in lieu of obedience to the military order) for an individual member of the group to show that he has been improperly classified?"

Stone apparently did not respond to this letter from Douglas, who promptly drafted a four-page concurring opinion which he circulated on June 3. Whether Douglas felt slighted by Stone's silence and wrote his opinion as a rebuke is unclear, but his move (in which Justice Rutledge initially joined) had a shock effect on his colleagues. It was an almost schizophrenic opinion, displaying simultaneously two sides of Douglas's complex personality. He began with a saber-rattling speech that matched the jingoism of the Hearst press: "We are engaged in a war for survival against enemies who have placed a premium on barbarity and ruthlessness. Self-preservation comes first. The United States wages war to win. And the war power in its command over the people and resources of the nation is ample for that purpose." Douglas then outdid Frankfurter in judicial deference to military judgment. "The decisions necessary for victory are largely military ones. . . . [C]ourts cannot sit in judgment on the military necessities which underlie those decisions." Douglas professed his belief that General DeWitt had acted in "good faith" in his conclusion that "among citizens of Japanese ancestry there were those who would give aid and comfort to the Japanese invader and act as a fifth column before and during an invasion."

The first protest against this abdication to military authority came, not from a member of the Court, but from Douglas's law clerk. Vern Countryman, a Montana native and a 1942 graduate of the University of Washington Law

School, had lived in Seattle during the evacuation. He had several Japanese American classmates in law school "and one day they weren't there anymore," he recalled. "I knew them very well and I thought the whole thing was ridiculous." Countryman later attributed Douglas's position to the influence of General DeWitt. "Douglas encountered DeWitt on the West Coast the previous summer and he filled him with horrible stories about Japanese submarines lurking off the coast. He really thought we had a hell of an emergency, and DeWitt sold him a bill of goods. I argued with him about paying so much attention to the military but I didn't get anywhere."

In the second half of his concurrence, Douglas displayed his contrasting passion for individual rights and procedural fairness. He expanded in this section on the points made in his letter to Chief Justice Stone. "I think it is important to emphasize that we are dealing here with a problem of loyalty not assimilation," Douglas wrote. "Loyalty is a matter of mind and heart not of race. That indeed is the history of America." Douglas then boldly raised the evacuation issue his colleagues had voted to duck and went even further in questioning the internment program. In noting that "guilt is personal under our constitutional system," Douglas held out the prospect that Japanese Americans could test the legality of DeWitt's exclusion orders and their subsequent detention. He pointed out that a conscientious objector to military service, after his induction, "may obtain through *habeas corpus* a hearing on the legality of his classification by the draft board." If a person detained solely "on account of ancestry" could adequately "demonstrate his loyalty to the United States," Douglas suggested, "the reason for the continued application of the order to him would cease." He concluded by urging that the Court "make certain that we leave no inference that American citizens could be denied for the duration of the war all opportunity to show that they were improperly classified as actual or potential fifth columnists and therefore were unlawfully detained."

There is no doubt that Douglas sincerely believed the views expressed in his draft concurrence, both the patriotism of the first section and the hostility to internment in the second. But the process by which the Court reaches agreement in contentious cases, between the initial conference vote and the announcement of opinions, often resembles a judicial poker game. Douglas may have intended his draft as a bargaining chip, intended to bluff Stone into making concessions in the Hirabayashi opinion. If so, he miscalculated the reactions of other players in this high-stakes game. Felix Frankfurter was outraged by the draft opinion and immediately launched a lobbying campaign designed to persuade Stone to call Douglas's bluff. Frankfurter had already indicated his down-the-line support for Stone's own first draft: "I go with you cheerfully all the way," he had written the Chief Justice.

Philip Elman, a recent Harvard Law School graduate who served as Frankfurter's law clerk in 1943, later explained a possible source of the justice's heated reaction to the implication made by Douglas that the War Department was unlawfully holding Japanese Americans in detention. "Frankfurter was not only very close and devoted to Roosevelt, but he was even more devoted to Henry Stimson. There was also Jack McCloy, a close friend who owed his job to Frankfurter. I don't think he regarded McCloy as a litigant" in the Japanese American cases, Elman said. Under his judicial robe, Frankfurter wore a symbolic uniform during the war. "He saw himself as a member of the President's war team," Elman added. "He went to war on December 8, 1941, literally." Within the week that preceded his outburst against Douglas, Frankfurter had met with both McCloy and Stimson to hash over War Department policies and problems; there is no evidence that the three friends discussed the Japanese American cases, but Frankfurter's intimate involvement in War Department business hardly made him a neutral in Douglas's attack on the Army's internment program.

As soon as Frankfurter read his copy of Douglas's draft opinion, he rushed to Black's chambers and enlisted the leader of "the Axis" in the crusade to stiffen Chief Justice Stone's spine. In a letter to Stone on June 4, the day after Douglas circulated his draft, Frankfurter reported the "two-hour talk I had with Brother Black who put my anxiety about this business vividly when he told me that he had been arguing against Douglas' invitation to bring 'a thousand *habeas corpus* suits in the district courts.'" According to Frankfurter, Black said that "so far as he was concerned, if he were the Commanding General he would not allow [the Japanese Americans] to go back even if the Court should establish their loyalty." Frankfurter added his own view that it would be "deplorable beyond words to hold out hopes . . . that there may be modes of relief for those now in the internment camps." He urged Stone to "overcome your natural hesitation and send for Brother Douglas and talk him out of his opinion by making him see the dangers that he is inviting."

. . .

. . . The pressure on Douglas increased at the Court's conference on June 5. At this meeting, Frankfurter wrote in his diary, Black repeated his statements that "he did not think that the courts could review anything that the military does," that "he would not allow a thousand habeas corpuses to be brought," and that "if he were the commanding General, he would not let the evacuated Japanese come back even if the Court directed that to be done." Justice Jackson then added his opinion that Douglas's draft "was a 'hoax' in that it promised something that could not be fulfilled." After these strong words, Chief Justice Stone moved to reduce the tension around the table by voicing "the eager hope that all who have ideas as far as expression or omission should let him know them and he would do his best to meet the variant suggestions."

Douglas reacted in two ways to this application of peer pressure. He first sent a note to Justice Rutledge, whose name was still on the draft of Douglas's concurrence, asking that Rutledge "turn over in your mind this week end the question whether I should stick with my concurring opinion in the Jap case if the C. J. takes out all the stuff in his opinion on assimilation and mistreatment." The following Monday, on June 7, Douglas made a final appeal to Stone on the "racial characteristics" issue, asking that the Chief Justice eliminate from his draft opinion four paragraphs that cast doubt on the loyalty of Japanese Americans. Douglas then matched this request with a veiled threat to change his concurrence to a dissent, should Stone fail to meet his demands on the internment issue: "The nub of the matter is that I could not go along in an affirmance of the judgment below except on the assumptions (a) that the group treatment was temporary; (b) that the individual must have an opportunity to be reclassified as a loyal citizen." In view of Stone's determination that the Hirabayashi case did not raise either the evacuation or internment issues, Douglas acknowledged the probable futility of his threat: "That may be too great a gap for us to bridge."

Conscious that both Frankfurter and Black were adamant on the issue, Stone stood pat and called Douglas's bluff. "I am anxious to go as far as I reasonably can to meet the views of my associates," he wrote to Douglas on June 9, "but it seems to me that if I accepted your suggestions very little of the structure of my opinion would be left, and that I should lose most of my adherents." Stone told Douglas that he intended "to stand by the substance of my opinion" and suggested that Douglas "express your views in your concurring opinion as you have already done." By the time Douglas received this letter, Rutledge had abandoned the joint concurrence and had decided to write his own, more moderate, concurring opinion. Forced to play his cards alone, Douglas tossed in his hand. Subsequent drafts of his concurrence softened the suggestion that habeas corpus offered an escape from internment and omitted entirely the hint that Douglas would vote to support such suits.

In the published version of his concurring opinion, Douglas stated his views in circumspect fashion. The remedy of habeas corpus as a challenge to internment "is one of the large and important issues reserved by the present decision," he wrote. . . . Douglas refused, however, to surrender unconditionally on the issue. If it "were plain that no machinery was available whereby the individual could demonstrate his loyalty as a citizen in order to be reclassified" and thus be released from internment, he wrote, "questions of a more serious character would be presented." This partial retreat satisfied Stone. . . .

Chief Justice Stone faced a more serious challenge to his campaign for unanimity in the Hirabayashi case from Justice Murphy, who had reserved his vote on the case at the Court's initial conference on May 17. According to Felix Frankfurter, admittedly a biased participant in the internal debate over the Japanese American cases, Murphy shared his scorn for the draft opinion that Douglas had initially circulated. "The most shocking thing that has ever been written by a member of this Court," Frankfurter recorded Murphy as telling him before the subsequent conference on June 5. Calling the Douglas draft "a regular soapbox speech," Murphy reported to Frankfurter that Douglas considered the section of Stone's opinion discussing the war powers issue "partly addressed to the American Legion." "Well, if the Chief's was addressed to the American Legion," Murphy said to Frankfurter, "Bill's was addressed to the mob."

If Frankfurter concluded from these comments that Murphy disagreed with the substance of Douglas's opinion, he quickly learned better. . . . Of all the Court's members, Murphy was perhaps the most sensitive to racial issues and the most likely to dissent in the Hirabayashi case. He had dealt sympathetically with racial and ethnic minorities during his career in politics and public service. As mayor of Detroit and governor of Michigan during the 1930s, he won the votes of blacks and Polish Catholics alike and welded these and other minorities into a potent New Deal coalition. During his short term as Attorney General, Murphy created the Civil Liberties Unit in the Department of Justice, and in a 1939 speech pledged that his office would "protect civil liberties for . . . the people of all racial extractions in our midst." He had also lived in Asia as Governor-General and Commissioner of the Philippines, and had brought back from that experience "a devotion to the Philippines as a new nation," according to John Pickering, his law clerk in the 1943 term.

Another factor that affected Murphy's attitude in the Hirabayashi case was his identification, as a member of the Irish and Catholic minorities, with the Japanese Americans as a group subject to prejudice and hostility. Murphy "had a terrible streak of religious fervor in him," Jo Pickering recalled, "and felt very strongly about religious freedom and race." . . . [O]n the same day as the *Hirabayashi* opinion, Murphy expressed some of these views in his majority opinion in the *Schneiderman* case. A longtime official of the Communist Party, Schneiderman was a naturalized American citizen who had been stripped of his citizenship for his political activities and beliefs. Murphy wrote for the Court in restoring Schneiderman's citizenship, over a dissent by Chief Justice Stone in which Frankfurter and Roberts joined. Murphy expressed his belief in America as a melting pot in writing that "we are a heterogeneous people. In some of our larger cities a majority of the schoolchildren are the offspring of parents only one generation, if that far, removed from the steerage of the immigrant ship. . . ."

Just as Douglas had done, Murphy marked his questions about Stone's draft opinion in the Hirabayashi case in the margins of his copy. Next to Stone's claim that the existence of Japanese-language schools gave evidence of "attachments to Japan" among the Japanese Americans, Murphy noted that this statement could apply with equal logic to "Catholic and other church schools." He voiced his concern with the racial issue at the Court's conference on June 5, which led Frankfurter to record in his diary that "we are all agreed" on the case "with the possible exception of Brother Murphy who still has his worries about drawing the line on the score of what he calls 'ancestry.'"

Frankfurter's own worry that Murphy might follow his doubts into dissent led to an exchange of hastily scribbled notes during the conference. At the time, Murphy was writing an opinion in a set of cases that upheld Indian tribal rights, and Frankfurter "good humoredly chided him" about the disparity between these and the Japanese American cases. "Are you writing Indian cases on the assumption that rights depend on ancestry?" Frankfurter asked in his first note. "If so—I cannot give my imprimatur to such racial discrimination!" Murphy let the sarcasm pass in his reply: "Felix, I would protect rights on the basis of ancestry—But I would never deny them." Later that day, after Murphy announced that he intended to dissent in the Hirabayashi case, Frankfurter switched from sarcasm to sermon in an appeal for unanimity: "Please, Frank—with your eagerness for the austere functions of the Court and your desire to do all that is humanly possible to maintain and enhance the *corporate* reputation of the Court, why don't you take the initiative with the Chief in getting him to take out everything that either offends you or that you would want to express more ironically." Murphy ignored this plea for judicial pacifism from the Court's war hawk and went ahead with the drafting of his dissent.

Three of his colleagues felt the lash of Murphy's displeasure in the first draft of his Hirabayashi dissent. Chief Justice Stone's assertion, based on the alleged "facts and circumstances" of the religious and cultural traits of the Japanese American population, that the Court could not "reject as unfounded the judgment of the military authorities . . . that there were disloyal members of that population" who "could not readily be isolated and separately dealt with, and constituted a menace to the national defense and safety," prompted a scathing rebuttal from Murphy: "If there were substantial evidence that citizens of Japanese ancestry were generally disloyal . . . the curfew order and other restrictions imposed on them might be defended. . . . But such evidence is lacking. On the other hand, there is good reason to believe that the action of the military authorities was based primarily if not solely on a widespread belief that persons of Japanese descent had not been and could not be assimilated and that by and large they gave primary allegiance [to] the Empire of Japan. It does not appear that any serious effort was made to segregate aliens, or isolate disloyal elements, or apprehend those who fomented and encouraged the spread of Japanese ideas and propaganda, such as members of the Society of the Black Dragon. Instead of this, by a gigantic round-up no less than 70,000 American citizens are placed under a special ban and deprived of their liberty because of a particular racial inheritance. . . . This is so utterly inconsistent with our ideals and traditions, and in my judgment so contrary to constitutional sanctions, that I cannot lend my assent."

Murphy next took a swipe at Douglas, whose draft concurrence he considered fainthearted and an invitation to military absolutism. In the "soap-box speech" Murphy had denounced to Frankfurter, Douglas had compared the military orders applied to the Japanese Americans with the military draft: "A nation which can require the individual to give up his freedom and lay down his life . . . certainly can demand these lesser sacrifices from its other citizens." Murphy denounced this language as simplistic. "We are told that the restrictions on personal liberty imposed by this statute," he answered Douglas, "are less severe than those established in pursuance of the draft law and previously upheld by this Court in Selective Draft Cases. . . . But the latter make no discrimination between citizens on the basis of ancestry, in contravention of due process and the fifth amendment." Murphy also criticized his colleague's flag-waving claim that a country that "wages war to win" cannot "sit in judgment" on the decisions of its generals. "Undoubtedly we must wage war to win, and do it with all our might," replied Murphy. "But the might of America lies in something else, something that is unique. It will avail us little to win the war on the battlefield and lose it at home. We do not win the war, on the contrary we lose it, if we destroy the Constitution and the best traditions of our country."

. . .

As the day for final decision approached, Murphy developed second thoughts about his isolated position as the only dissenter in the Hirabayashi case. Justice Stanley Reed applied the first gentle push. "Murphy had a considerable rapport with Justice Reed, their chambers were next to each other, and Reed had been making various suggestions about the Schneiderman case" on which Murphy was writing the Court's opinion, John Pickering recalled. The first draft of Murphy's dissent in Hirabayashi had conceded that if "substantial evidence" existed that Japanese Americans were "generally disloyal," or had "otherwise by their behavior furnished reasonable ground" for dealing with them as a group, the curfew order "might be defended and upheld against legal attack in the light of the conditions and the military situation which then prevailed." Reed found this argument "appealing" but not totally convincing. "If you admit this you give your case away," he wrote Murphy. "Military protection only needs reasonable grounds, which this record has. You cannot wait for an invasion to see if loyalty triumphs." Murphy bowed to this criticism. "Whether the record provides reasonable grounds, whether the evidence shows 'general disloyalty,' is a question of opinion," he informed Pickering on June 8. "I assumed it did not." Nonetheless, he instructed Pickering to strike the offending sentences from the draft.

The final push from Frankfurter was less gentle. "Of course I shan't try to dissuade you from filing a dissent," he wrote Murphy on June 10 in attempting just that task, "not because I do not think it highly unwise but because I think you are immovable." He asked Murphy, however, to consider whether "it is conducive to the things you care about, including the great reputation of this Court, to suggest that everybody is out of step except Johnny, and more particularly that the Chief Justice and seven other Justices of this Court are behaving like the enemy and thereby playing into the hands of the enemy? Compassion is, I believe, a virtue enjoined by Christ. Well, tolerance is a long, long way from compassion—and can't you write your views with such expressed tolerance that you won't make people think that when eight others disagree with you, you think their view means that they want to destroy the liberties of the United States and 'lose the war' at home?"

Reed's appeal to precedent more likely affected Murphy's decision to withdraw his dissent than Frankfurter's appeal to patriotism. In any event, Murphy took a pencil to the printed version of his dissent. He first changed "Mr. Justice Murphy, dissenting," to "concurring." Next to go was the language that had denied to the military "unlimited authority" over civilians "outside the actual theatre of military operations," and his conclusion that the curfew order "is discriminatory and therefore fails to comply with the requirement of due process of law contained in the Fifth Amendment." In its place, Murphy wrote that, in light of "the risk of sabotage and espionage, the military authorities should not be required to conform to standards of regulatory action appropriate to normal times." In response to Reed's criticism, Murphy conceded that "the military authorities could have reasonably concluded" that individual determinations of the loyalty of Japanese Americans "could not be made without delay that might have had tragic consequences." His final concession to unanimity was agreement that General DeWitt "made an allowable judgment at the time the curfew restriction was imposed."

Murphy made little attempt to hide his true feelings behind the cosmetic changes in his concurrence. Six of the eight paragraphs of the published version, in fact, read like the dissent they were intended to be. The result of the curfew, he wrote, "is the creation in this country of two classes of citizens for the purposes of a critical and perilous hour—to sanction discrimination between groups of United States citizens on the basis of ancestry. In my opinion this goes to the very brink of constitutional power." Finally allied with his colleagues, Murphy stepped back from the constitutional cliff over which his initial dissent had thrown DeWitt's orders.

For the sacrifice of his individual doubts to the Court's collective certitude, Murphy received a battlefield commendation from the Court's symbolic Provost Marshal General, Felix Frankfurter: "Frank—I congratulate you on the wisdom of having been able to reach a concurrence." John Pickering later said that Murphy "expressed to me unhappiness that he had not persisted in a dissent. If he'd gotten any adherents to that circulated dissent I don't think he would have changed." It seems clear that Justice Douglas, despite the implicit threat made to Chief Justice Stone that he might dissent, had no real intention of doing so. Justice Rutledge, however, came close to adding a second vote to Murphy's initial dissent.

After removing his name from Douglas's concurrence, Rutledge drafted one of his own. "I have strong sympathy with Mr. Justice Murphy's views," he wrote. "Judged by peacetime standards, the statute involves a delegation of concentrated, unconfined power over civilian citizens and the order a racial discrimination only war's highest emergency could sustain." He labeled De-Witt's curfew order "something which approaches the ultimate stain on democratic institutions constitutionally established." Seemingly on the brink of joining Murphy's dissent, Rutledge retreated and finally filed a more moderate one-paragraph concurrence. He took exception in his published concurrence to Stone's suggestion that "the courts have no power to review any action a military officer may 'in his discretion' find it necessary to take" in situations that required "some degree of military control short of suspending habeas corpus." Speaking of General DeWitt, Rutledge wrote that there may be "bounds beyond which he cannot go. . . . But in this case the question need not be faced and I merely add my reservation without indicating an opinion concerning it." Rutledge later admitted his doubts in a note to Stone: "I have had more anguish over this case than any I have decided, save possibly one death case in the Ct. of Appeals. I am now clear to go with you," he added, hinting that he had given serious thought to joining Murphy's dissent.

. . .

. . . The withdrawal of Justice Murphy's dissent cleared the last obstacle from this path, the *Milligan* case. Lawyers on both sides had devoted dozens of pages of their briefs and hours of argument before the Court of Appeals and the Supreme Court to this significant precedent, and Murphy had scribbled a note to himself during the Supreme Court argument: "Ex parte Milligan . . . governs this case." His draft dissent stressed its importance as a barrier to military control over civilians. "Having elected to proceed without resort to martial law, the government was necessarily subject to the Constitutional limitations which govern the exercise of the war power," Murphy had written, including in those limitations the due process protection against racial discrimination. Murphy's removal of this language from his published concurrence allowed Stone to dismiss he troubling precedent in a single sentence: "The exercise of [the war power] here involves no question of martial law or trial by military tribunal." Put in these narrow terms, Stone's conclusion was correct. But the holding implicit in *Milligan*, that military restrictions on the rights of citizens could be imposed only through martial law, escaped his analysis. The Chief Justice simply drove a constitutional bulldozer over this central issue.

During the month that began with the Court's conference on May 17, five members of the Court—Roberts, Reed, Douglas, Rutledge, and Murphy—had voiced serious doubts about the legality of DeWitt's orders and their constitutional basis. Compromise, cajolery, and their own concerns that the Court should maintain unity in wartime finally persuaded this potential majority for reversal to make Stone's opinion unanimous. The Chief Justice had labored through four printed drafts of his *Hirabayashi* opinion to meet the objections of the doubters and to blunt the sharp edges of the three concurring opinions.

With characteristic flattery, Frankfurter placed his benediction on Stone's final product: "You have labored with great forbearance and with concentration to produce something worthy of the Torah."

. . .

The Supreme Court's opinions came at a time of heated debate over the treatment of Japanese Americans in the internment camps and second thoughts about the necessity for their continued detention. Press reactions to the decisions reflected the geographical and political split over these issues. The Washington *Post* expressed liberal opinion on the East Coast in a June 25 editorial entitled "Stigma by Ancestry." Observing that "the Supreme Court has performed a duty for which it obviously had little relish," the *Post* cited the three concurring opinions in the *Hirabayashi* case as evidence that "some of the justices entertain grave misgivings" about the evacuation and detention issues the Court had avoided. The *Post* urged the Court not to evade its duty to "pass upon the constitutionality of our continuing discrimination against American citizens because of their racial heritage. The outright deprivation of civil right which we have visited upon these helpless, and, for the most part, no doubt, innocent, people may leave an ugly blot upon the pages of our history."

On the West Coast, in contrast, the Los Angeles *Times* hailed the *Hirabayashi* opinion as "heartening news for the Pacific Slope, where opinion has held with similar unanimity that the presence of any Japs here is dangerous in wartime." The *Times* welcomed the Court as an ally in the campaign for continued internment: "Agitation for the return of Japs to the Pacific Coast—which has gained recruits in high circles in Washington—gets its devastating answer from the clear analysis of the situation by Justice Stone and the unanimous opinion of the Supreme Court." Public officials on the West Coast voiced similar sentiments. Representative J. Leroy Johnson, a California Republican, promptly proposed to Congress the postwar deportation of all Japanese aliens and "disloyal" citizens. "This is a way to get rid of a group that may make future trouble," he explained. And California governor Earl Warren told the press that "nothing more destructive to our defense could happen than to release the potential fifth columnists." Warren predicted that the return of Japanese Americans to the West Coast would result in widespread sabotage and "a second Pearl Harbor in California."

. . . [I]t seemed certain that the Supreme Court would soon confront the issues of evacuation and detention. . . . [But] an entire term of the Supreme Court passed before its members confronted the challenge posed by the *Post* editorialist. In the meantime, the Japanese Americans . . . endured their second full year of internment.

CHAPTER 19

The Aftermath of War

The internment of Japanese Americans was directly challenged in the Supreme Court, in *Korematsu* v. *United States* (1943). Justice Black wrote the opinion of the Court upholding the criminal conviction of Hiroshi Korematsu, a United States citizen, for failing to report to an Assembly Center. But unanimity had broken down. Justices Murphy, Roberts, and Jackson filed dissents, Justice Murphy bluntly calling the majority opinion a "legalization of racism."

The Court again reached unanimity, however, in *Ex Parte Endo* (1944) in which the Court upheld the *habeas corpus* petition of an internee. The seeming paradox can be explained by the government's fatal admission that the challenger, Mitsuye Endo, was "loyal and not dangerous."

By the time of the *Endo* decision, the military had worked out procedures to establish the loyalty of individual internees and some had been released to areas away from the West Coast. The war in the Pacific was nearing the end, and the military was prepared to release a large number of internees to the West Coast as well. President Roosevelt, however, did not authorize release until after his election to a fourth term in November of 1944.

Forty-four years later, in 1988, another president, Ronald Reagan, signed a congressional enactment apologizing to the Japanese Americans interned during the war and providing compensation of $20,000 to each surviving internee. Previously, in 1984 and 1987, the convictions of both Gordon Hirabayashi and Hiroshi Korematsu were vacated by federal courts on findings that the government had misrepresented and concealed potentially decisive evidence related to the threat posed by Japanese Americans on the West Coast.

The approach of victory in both Asia and Europe also raised issues of international law. As President Wilson sought to establish the League of Nations in 1919, the World War II leaders of the Allies planned to establish a new framework for postwar international cooperation. The concept of a United Nations organization was first proposed at the Atlantic Conference of President Roosevelt and Prime Minister Winston Churchill in 1941. It was given final form in the United Nations Charter at a conference of fifty nations in San Francisco in 1945. This time, the participation of the United States was assured. The United States, along with Britain, France, China, and the Soviet Union, received the power to veto resolutions of the United Nations' key decisionmaking body, the Security Council.

In the decades following the establishment of the United Nations, several international crises—in the Middle East, the Congo, Cyprus, and elsewhere—were mitigated by United Nations actions. In Korea, a "police action" was fought from 1950 to 1953 under the United Nations flag to repel North Korea's attack on South Korea. The United Nations has also labored to develop a body of international law through its International Law Commission and through its International Court of Justice, located in The Hague. Nevertheless, the United Nations disappointed many who envisioned it as the foundation for an international legal order. As international law scholar, Quincy Wright, expressed in *International Law and the United Nations* (1960):

> It is not surprising . . . that the efforts of the United Nations to develop international law, and the judicial settlement of disputes has lagged. The International Law Commission has produced some draft codes, but its effort to define aggression and offences against peace and security have not produced practical results. . . .
>
> The International Court of Justice has been less frequently utilized than was its predecessor in the League of Nations period, the Permanent Court of International Justice. The organs of the United Nations have seldom asked for advisory opinions on matters affecting their own competence, and states seldom submit for decision disputes of political importance. . . .
>
> The apparent dominance of politics over law in contemporary international relations stems from the excessively disturbed condition of the world consequent upon the devastation of World War II, upon the unsettled political issues of that war, upon the major political differences between colonial and anti-colonial states, upon uncertainty arising from new weapons of destruction, and especially upon the vigorous ideological split between democratic and communist states. (pp. 16–17)

The Allies also faced the problem of how to deal with captured enemies accused of war crimes. History provided little guidance. The Spanish theologian Francisco de Vitoria in the sixteenth century, the Dutch jurist Hugo Grotius in the seventeenth century, and a host of other commentators set down principles for the conduct of war. From the mid-nineteenth century, a number of international agreements covered such topics as the treatment of the wounded, the rights of prisoners of war, and the use of chemical and bacteriological weapons. But neither the juristic writings nor the international agreements provided significant protections to civilian populations. It was also unclear how high up the chain of command responsibility should be traced, and there was no established mechanism to try and to punish war crimes.

International custom, as established by past practices, was even less satisfactory. Still fresh in the minds of World War II decisionmakers was the experience following the First World War. Although the Versailles treaty laid blame for the war and its atrocities squarely on the leaders of the German government—all the way up to the Kaiser—and called for the establishment of Allied military tribunals to try war criminals, in the end, the matter was left to the postwar German government. The Allies prepared a list of nine hundred alleged war criminals, and trials were duly held in Leipzig in 1922. Not surprisingly, the German judges acquitted or dismissed the cases against all but a handful of defendants. Those who were convicted at Leipzig received light sentences, and among the few who were incarcerated, some managed to escape with the suspected complicity of their jailers. But even if past experience had been more creditable, it would hardly have served as an adequate guide in light of the magnitude of the atrocities committed during World War II.

Nazi defendants on trial, Nuremberg, 1945.
Photo from Culver Pictures, Inc., New York.

WAR CRIMES

from Ann Tusa and John Tusa, *The Nuremberg Trial*
(London: Macmillan Publishers, 1983), pp. 20–31, 50–60.
Copyright © 1983 by Ann Tusa and John Tusa.
Reproduced by permission of the authors c/o Rogers,
Coleridge & White, Ltd., 20 Powis Mews, London W11 1JN.

[U]ndeterred by previous failure and the lack of existing machinery, every Allied nation between 1939 and 1945 demanded punishment for those who committed war crimes. . . . Yet, even more strongly than in the First World War, there was the conviction that the enemy's leaders constituted a criminal regime, that the incidents of atrocity were part of a deliberate policy of crime and that those who were most responsible and deserving of severest punishment were the Nazi leaders themselves. . . .

. . . No matter if the full horror of the concentration camps was only understood when they were liberated, there was always at the very least an awareness that such camps held people without charge, trial or right of appeal and treated them cruelly. No one might be able yet to calculate the figures for murders, enslavement and pillage by the Nazis but partizans and Resistance workers had given enough indication of the bestial nature of Nazi rule. The Nazis themselves had publicized such outrages as the destruction of the Czech village of Lidice, the murder of its menfolk and deportation to concentration camps of its women and children—all in reprisal for the assassination of Heydrich, the Protector of Bohemia. As a French government memorandum to the European Advisory Commission on War Crimes put it: crimes were taking place on such a scale "by an enemy who has sought to annihilate whole nations, who has elevated murder to a political system, that we no longer have the duty of punishing merely those who commit but also those who plan the crime."

As awareness of these crimes grew throughout the War and public disgust increased, the Allied governments issued threats of punishment, both to express the general sense of revulsion and in the hope of deterring Nazis from criminal acts in the future. For the first time, the punishment of war crimes became not just the automatic result of a war but a declared official policy in fighting it. Even so, the wording of that policy remained vague for several years. There was to be much procrastination, confused thinking, tortuous negotiation, and haphazard decision before it was clarified. It was a long road between the determination to punish and the establishment of an International Military Tribunal to decide who should be punished.

In October 1941, while the United States was still neutral, President Roosevelt drew attention to the wholesale execution by the Germans of hostages in France and he warned that "one day a frightful retribution" would be exacted.... Warnings of punishment were also issued in response to specific incidents. The British government, for example, threatened retribution for the killing after recapture of fifty British airmen who had escaped from the prisoner-of-war camp Stalag Luft III at Sagan. During the 1944 Rising in Warsaw, they also warned the Nazis that captured Polish soldiers must be treated as lawful combatants. . . .

But who was to exact justice? Under what conditions? Was it enough after this war to fall back once again on leaving each country to try its own criminals and as many of the enemies as could be caught? . . . In January 1942 the representatives of nine occupied countries in Europe held a conference at St James's in London to discuss such questions. They issued a declaration on 13 January that: "international solidarity is necessary to avoid the repression of these acts of violence simply by acts of vengeance on the part of the general public and in order to satisfy the sense of justice of the civilized world." The declaration announced that punishment for war crimes, whoever committed them, was now a principal war aim of the governments at the conference. It also made clear an additional intention: to bring to justice not only those who themselves perpetrated crimes, but—more ambitiously—those who ordered them. After this war at least it seemed that the leaders would not escape punishment. The St James's Declaration was approved by Britain, the United States and the USSR.

. . . The declaration, however, was expressed in general terms. It did not come down to the nuts and bolts—no names of alleged criminals were given, no machinery for trial was outlined. The St James's Conference was followed by only one practical step. The United Nations War Crimes Commission [UNWCC] was set up in London in 1943 to collect and collate information on war crimes and criminals. It was made up of representatives of seventeen nations—but had no Russian member. Stalin would only join if every Soviet Republic were given separate representation. This was refused.

It was a bad start to an experiment in international co-operation. From then on, things only got worse. A memorandum from Sir Cecil Hurst, the British Chairman of the Commission, sent to the Lord Chancellor's office in March 1944, said that the body was incapable of doing the job it was designed for—collecting evidence. They relied on the assistance of the governments represented and their help was not forthcoming. Hurst complained that after four months of work the Commission had only received seventy cases; half of them were so incomplete as to be useless and most were trivial.

The governments had made a lot of noise about war crimes but did not seem to be making a lot of effort to substantiate their allegations. Hurst was clearly irritated by what he regarded as laziness or incompetence. Perhaps he did not recognize the major problem of the governments he criticized: they were in exile, cut off from the scenes of the alleged crimes and without access to witnesses or documentary evidence. What worried him even more than the paucity and flimsiness of the cases presented to the Commission was the members' sense of frustration that the UNWCC was "limited by its present terms of reference." It was limited to investigating war crimes pure and simple. These, he said, were not the incidents which had most outraged public opinion and distressed the governments in exile. The biggest demand was for punishment of those who murdered and terrorized civilian populations (what the legal committee at Versailles had called crimes against humanity) and Hurst himself felt that it was a major priority to investigate charges of acts against Jews.

Many people too had come to believe that Nazi institutions as well as individuals were guilty of crimes. The organization most often accused of crimes against humanity was the Gestapo, and Hurst put forward a radical UNWCC proposal that not only should individuals be arrested and held for trial but that "all members of a body like the Gestapo should be responsible for the acts of the individual members" and interned until proceedings could be instituted.

. . .

The UNWCC continued to collect evidence and names of suspected criminals. It had never been asked to define crimes, consider whether distinction should be made between major and minor criminals, or to decide what form judicial proceedings against them should take.

A significant move to clarify some of these issues had been taken at the Moscow Conference of Foreign Ministers in November 1943. Here, Britain, the United States and the Soviet Union had issued a joint declaration condemning Nazi atrocities in occupied Europe. This stated that "at time of the granting of any armistice to any government which may be set up in Germany, those German officers and men and members of the Nazi Party who have been responsible for or who have taken part in the above atrocities, massacres and executions, will be sent back to the countries in which their abominable deeds were done in order that they may be judged and punished according to the laws of those liberated countries and of the Free Governments which will be erected therein."

The Moscow Declaration broke no new ground thus far; the return of criminals to the scenes of their crimes was a standard procedure. But the foreign ministers then tackled the harder questions raised at the St James's conference—how to deal with those Nazi leaders who had condoned or ordered crimes all over Europe and the need for international solidarity in seeking their punishment. In so doing they began to categorize the war criminals and create a class of criminal leader. They stated that "the above declaration is without prejudice to the case of major criminals whose offences have no particular geographical location and who will be punished by a joint declaration of the Governments of the Allies." So the foreign ministers had created two groups of war criminals and proposed two forms of treatment: national action for localized offences, and international action for those whose criminal orders had applied in several countries. But there was one important omission in the Moscow Declaration—there was no mention of trial before punishment for the major criminals. Indeed talk of punishment by "joint declaration" seems to preclude trial. Why was there no mention of judicial proceedings? Was it the memory of the practical difficulties and the final farce of the Versailles discussions and the Leipzig trials? Or was it that the foreign ministers reckoned that justice was too good for such men?

There is no record that Leipzig was mentioned at the Moscow Conference. There is however evidence that those present did not think the fate of leading Nazi criminals merited much time or trouble. At Moscow the US Secretary of State, Cordell Hull, actually said: "If I had my way I would take Hitler and Mussolini and Tojo and their accomplices and bring them before a drumhead court martial, and at sunrise the following morning there would occur an historic incident."

At the Tehran Conference at the end of 1943 Roosevelt's son, Elliott, gained the impression that Stalin was prepared to go even further. In the boozy atmosphere of a banquet the Russian leader gave to the other Allied statesmen, Stalin proposed a toast: "to the quickest possible justice for all German war criminals . . . I drink to the justice of the firing squad." He estimated that the firing squad should rid the world of about 50,000 leading Germans, mainly military. Churchill expressed shock. Roosevelt tried to cool the atmosphere with a jocular suggestion that perhaps the number could be cut to 49,000. Stalin and Molotov then claimed that the whole idea had only been a joke. Perhaps indeed it was. When discussing policy on official occasions Stalin always recommended that war criminals be given a judicial hearing before (inevitably) being shot. Churchill, on the other hand, can only have been shocked by Stalin's proposal because of the huge number of executions suggested, not the method. For a long time his government would argue against any form of trial and would favour some kind of dressed-up summary execution.

By the end of the war many people would have been content with summary execution, naked and unashamed. The public would have found it easy to draw up lists of ogres who had haunted the imagination in recent years; their deaths would have occasioned little soul-searching. The shock expressed when Mussolini and his mistress, Clara Petacci, were shot by Italian partisans in 1945 came less from the fact that they had been summarily executed than because their bodies [were] hung upside down from lamp-posts, then left to lie in the gutter. There are, it seems, a few decencies which ought to be observed even in a lynching. . . .

Cordell Hull's idea of a drumhead court martial only applied a little cosmetic to the procedure of shooting out of hand. This roughest form of justice would allow several minutes to be spent establishing that the prisoner really was *the* Adolf Hitler or whoever, and the charges to be read to him to explain why he was about to be shot; and would provide the court with the authority to give orders to a firing squad. When the British Foreign Office was considering this method with some enthusiasm in 1944, it reckoned that the whole process from the moment of arrest would be over and done within six hours.

Others considering what to do with major war criminals rejected the solution of short, sharp military action. . . . [They] saw the responsibility for dealing with top criminals as a political rather than a military or indeed legal matter. Those who shared his views argued that since the charge against Hitler and his colleagues was not based on a series of isolated incidents but on the totality of their acts, since the aim in punishing them was to give expression to international condemnation of their entire policy and to cleanse the moral atmosphere of their polluting presence, then what was involved was a political indictment and what was appropriate was political, executive action by the international community. Underlying this argument was the belief that no kind of hearing was required to establish guilt—as the Lord Chancellor put it: "Fancy 'trying' Hitler!" Many felt his guilt and that of his leading associates did not need proving. What was left to the international community was to settle punishment. In Lord Simon's view that was not a question to be left to "a posse of jurists"; it was a responsibility for world leaders, and they could look to history for an example of successful international action.

For there was a precedent for executive action by allies against a former enemy whose acts seemed abhorrent: that of Napoleon. His case offered interesting parallels with the problems faced after the Second World War and persuasive arguments for those who favoured joint political decision on the fate of major war criminals.

When Napoleon escaped from Elba, broke the terms of the 1814 Treaty of Fontainebleau, and marched again on Europe, he was declared "*hors la loi*" by the representatives of all the European states attending the peace negotiations at Vienna (significantly France herself was one). A unanimous condemnation having been passed, the states then had to decide what to do about the man they had outlawed. The Prussian military leader, Blucher, said he would shoot the Emperor if he fell into Prussian hands. . . . The Russians pressed for summary execution. . . . Finally, however, the Powers agreed to exile Napoleon permanently on St Helena. Here he would be out of harm's way and kept at British expense without incurring the embarrassment of executing a sovereign. (All European rulers had condemned the execution of Louis XVI and did not want their subjects to imagine that killing rulers was an acceptable way of expressing their opinion of them.) This was a decision reached by the entire European community (including France)—and it was a purely political decision. No one had seriously considered a trial for Napoleon; it was not deemed necessary since his crimes seemed self-evident, condemnation was universal, and the European statesmen had no qualms about punishing him for them.

However, the idea of a form of trial for major Nazi war criminals was attractive to many even though the form they favoured might seem repugnant to others. There were recognized advantages in more recent precedents than that of Napoleon—show trials. Stalin had punished his opponents and frightened others by the trials he had mounted in the 1930s; Hitler had made a public spectacle out of the trial of those who had plotted against his life in July 1944. Should the nations now decide on a show trial for Nazi war criminals, they could present massive evidence of their guilt to convince any wavering public opinion, to put on record their abhorrence of the crimes and to justify the inevitable punishment. In a show trial it is even possible to allow a little defence—just enough to demonstrate how feeble it is.

There was one final option open for those who were shocked by the roughness of military justice, convinced that executive action is no justice at all, and worried by the practical problems, political repercussions and moral implications of punishing war criminals. It was to do nothing at all. For those whose consciences were too tender to throw the first stone, it was appealing to tell the targets of international loathing to go away and sin no more. Doing nothing could become a high moral stance.

. . .

Torn between the conflicting alternatives for dealing with major war criminals, aware of the demand to find some way to meet public aspirations for some better way to run the world, the Allied leaders had made little progress by 1944 beyond the St James's and Moscow Declarations. . . . Despite occasional stabs of conscience and flashes of rhetoric, war crimes had a low priority; the politicians had an alliance to keep together, a war to win, all the complexity of the post-war settlement of Europe to consider.

. . .

America, thanks to geography, had been insulated against the horrors of the War. Only in December 1944 did the American public have its first direct experience of Nazi brutality. Seventy American prisoners-of-war were shot by the First SS Panzer Regiment at Malmedy in Belgium. . . . And as the Allied armies advanced through Europe and into Germany the concept of crimes against humanity took on meaning as well. Newsreels showed the squalor and degradation of the slave labour camps and the horror of the gas chambers; newspapers were filled with stories of the conditions suffered by prisoners-of-war, eyewitness accounts of extermination squads, the piles of corpses discovered by the liberating armies in the concentration camps. . . . The public put more pressure on the politicians after a visit to Buchenwald and Dachau concentration camps by sixteen newspaper editors and publishers in May and similar tours by Senators and Congressmen at the same time. . . . Those visitors had all reached the same conclusion—that the Nazis had had "a master plan . . . based on a policy of calculated and organized brutality." They all called for speedy action by the United Nations.

So too did the general public. The National Opinion Research Centre of the University of Denver had carried out a small poll at the end of 1944 and in January 1945 to discover how Americans viewed Germans. They found then that a large section of the population had friendly feelings towards them (though the more educated tended to be harsher); most people spoke of a need for "re-education," approved of sending relief to the Germans, objected to the country's dismemberment and hoped the Allies would help to rebuild German peacetime industry. But by the middle of the year many of those friendly feelings had evaporated. . . . They were thinking of punishment.

There had been clamour for a clearly defined policy from other quarters too. Once Europe was invaded by the Allies governments in exile feared, rightly, that Hitler would inflict a final programme of death and destruction in their countries as he was forced to withdraw his troops. They called for specific declarations by all the Powers on how such action would be punished. Jewish organizations hoped to save some of the Jews still in Nazi hands. They lobbied governments to issue threats of retribution for any future murders.

The governments of the major powers resisted public outcry and military requests for a long time. . . . Indeed, it could be seen as desirable to postpone a decision. They expected German maltreatment of Allied prisoners-of-war if they emphasized at this stage the intention of punishing Nazi war criminals. This was the reason for stopping the war crimes trials in Sicily in 1943 and the Anglo-American decision in 1944 not to segregate suspects in their prisoner-of-war camps.

However, as public opinion grew more bitter, and once the Allied armies crossed into Germany itself and top Nazis began to fall captive, the statesmen could delay no longer. They were faced with the realities of an occupation of Germany and the reconstruction of Europe. They must decide now, what to do with the high-ranking Nazis who had led their country into war, decimated and destroyed much of Europe, and who in consequence were thought of as criminal by most of the rest of the world.

. . .

The impetus to establish an international tribunal to try . . . major Nazi war criminals had come from America. It was accelerated by the outcry over the Malmedy massacre and direct experience of other atrocities once American forces invaded Europe, but it had begun and was sustained by the debate over the post-war settlement of Germany and Europe. Indeed it can almost be said that the Nuremberg Tribunal originated in an inter-departmental row in Washington over plans for the future of conquered Germany.

Tentative thinking about what should ultimately be done with Germany had started in March 1943 when the American President, Franklin Roosevelt, asked his Secretary for War, Henry Stimson, and his Secretary of State, Cordell Hull, to outline their views. Both men had agreed that the Allies should insist on Germany's unconditional surrender, full Allied military occupation, de-Nazification, disarmament, and the dismantling of war industries. Neither wished to destroy German industry as a whole—they saw a tolerable standard of living as an essential condition for a flourishing future German democracy—and the only slight difference between them was that Hull thought subsistence adequate whereas Stimson preferred to allow for something slightly more comfortable.

These suggestions were not taken up by the President. While Allied victory remained a distant prospect, he preferred to devote his time and energy to winning the War rather than considering the peace. Thereafter, once Europe was invaded, he became increasingly sensitive to the argument that this time Germany must be taught more thoroughly than in 1918 the lesson of what happened to those who started and lost wars; he also became alert to public demands for punitive action against war criminals.

In this mood Roosevelt rejected two occupation policy guides which had been drawn up by the War Department in the autumn of 1944 for the use of the military, on the grounds that they were too lenient towards the Germans. He was prepared to lend a ready ear to strongly contrasting proposals from another member of his government.

In the United States Treasury, the Secretary, Henry Morgenthau, conceived and nurtured from August 1944 a dreadful retribution to be visited on Germany. The country which had waged war on Europe, exploited its peoples and resources, committed atrocities and exterminated millions, was to be torn to shreds. Germany must suffer—and must never again be capable of causing suffering to others. Under Morgenthau's plan, Germany must be demilitarized. . . . The Nazi Party must be destroyed: Germany must be de-Nazified, its officials at all levels of government and administration must be removed from their posts and interned. In view of their treatment of others it seemed fitting that they should in their turn be exploited—let them now be directed to forced labour, repairing some of the damage they had caused in Europe. Above all, Morgenthau saw German industry as the source of that country's seeming capacity for evil. German industrialists had backed Hitler, enthusiastically joined the Nazi Party in its schemes and finally and fatally provided the materiel for a second war. So German industry must be destroyed. For ever. Germany must be pastoralized: the country stripped of its industrial plant and reduced to a nation of farmers. Within this ruthless and bleak conception, where Morgenthau saw an entire nation as criminal, dealing with war criminals became a simple matter. Minor offenders could be sent back to the countries where their crimes had been committed. The names of major criminals should be issued to the Allied Forces. As the men were captured, they would be identified and shot.

The Morgenthau plan was repulsive to Henry Stimson, the Secretary for War. Stimson too wanted to achieve a permanent peace, but he . . . saw lasting peace as the fruit of two strains: international co-operation and international legality. In principle, therefore, he could not accept a plan for the future of Europe which was based on Allied destruction of Germany—because Germany too must become a collaborator in the settlement. Neither could he accept a plan which countenanced Allied diktat and summary executions—from the beginning the new Europe must found its relations on legal processes and justice. . . . Furthermore, . . . Morgenthau's plan was both simplistic and self-defeating. As Stimson saw it, the destruction of German industry would seriously damage the economy of the whole of Europe. . . . In addition, by reducing Germany to starvation, the Allies would be creating all the conditions needed for dictatorship and war to breed again; the marginally more lenient treatment of the Versailles Settlement had provided ample scabs for the war-mongers to pick and infect, and Germans could not be secured as valuable contributors to the new European order if they were treated as criminals.

Stimson's criticisms of Morgenthau's plan for the Germans did not, however, involve any softness towards war criminals. He wanted to substitute more discriminating methods; to shift the approach from one based purely on punishment to one aimed at some degree of rehabilitation. He was unwilling to criminalize the entire German nation, but saw a therapeutic value in punishing internationally recognized war criminals: cleanse the German body politic to obtain a healthy partner for the future.

On 5 September 1944, Secretary Stimson sent a memorandum to the President and to Morgenthau: "It is primarily by the thorough apprehension, investigation and trial of all the Nazi leaders and instruments of the Nazi system of terrorism such as the Gestapo, with punishment delivered as promptly, swiftly and severely as possible, that we can demonstrate the abhorrence which the world has for such a system and bring home to the German people our determination to extirpate it and its fruits forever." Given Stimson's views on establishing international legality, there could only be one way in which this lesson could be delivered to the Germans and in which other nations could share in the educative process. Stimson wrote to Roosevelt on 9 September: ". . . the very punishment of these men in a dignified manner consistent with the advance of civilization will have the greater effect on posterity . . . I am disposed to believe that, at least as to the chief Nazi officials, we should participate in an international tribunal constituted to try them." In taking this stand, Stimson . . . added his voice to those who had called for international action in the St James's Declaration.

. . .

. . . Stimson might have opposed the Covenant of the League of Nations in 1919, but he had been influenced strongly by the views of Elihu Root, head of the law firm he had joined as a young man, and championed instead a World Court and the increased effectiveness of international law to control relations between states. For Stimson, the defeat of Germany in 1945 seemed to offer the chance of advancing this cause. Morgenthau, on the other hand, was more influenced by memories of the 1930s when he had been appalled by what he saw as the timorousness of American policy towards Japanese militarism and European fascism. He had urged a strong line then. . . . He felt the result, of ignoring his advice had been disastrous. Soft words and conciliatory action had not secured the peace in 1939; Morgenthau was certain they would not be adequate bases for lasting peace in 1945.

. . .

If Stimson wanted to dish the Treasury and see the triumph of his own principles over those of Morgenthau, he needed . . . an attractive solution to the niggling problem of what to do with the major war criminals. Quite obviously Morgenthau's plan to dispose of them by firing squad had the instant appeals of simplicity and cheapness. Stimson's proposal of an international tribunal would probably involve the President in lengthy and intricate diplomatic wrangling, then risk incurring public irritation at incomprehensible legal procedures and the time and trouble involved. Was it possible to package a scheme which at one and the same time would embody Stimson's demand for legality, yet seize the imagination of the President and public?

On 9 September, Stimson sent a memorandum to his Assistant Secretary, John McCloy, which condemned Morgenthau's plan for summary execution of Nazi leaders. He insisted that: "the method of dealing with these and other criminals requires careful thought and a well-defined procedure. Such procedure must embody, in my judgement, at least the rudimentary aspects of the Bill of Rights, namely notification to the accused of the charge, the right to be heard and, within reasonable limits, to call witnesses in his defence." Obviously then, Stimson . . . wished the Nazi leaders to be tried by an international tribunal which applied the rules and safeguards normally used in a court of law.

Having laid down the principles, Stimson left the details to be filled in by McCloy, and he speedily passed the buck down to . . . Colonel Murray C. Bernays, in civilian life a not very distinguished New York lawyer. . . .

By 15 September Bernays had produced a six-page scheme for a trial. . . . [H]e drew up a concise, logical plan by which not only all the individual defendants but also all the Nazi institutions whose policies had been denounced by the Allies could be tried at once. As if all this were not enough, in a plan covering a mere six pages Bernays stretched the concept of Nazi criminality to cover not just occupied Europe but Germany itself and extended it back in time to the very beginning of the Nazi regime.

In doing so, according to Bernays, the Nazi regime would implicitly be on trial. The defendants would be tried not just as individuals accused of specific crimes but as representatives of the organizations in the Nazi state to which they had belonged and which were allegedly criminal. As leaders and organizations were tried at the same time, evidence against an individual could be held against his organization and vice versa. Finally Bernays wove a net to hold them all and enmesh them with Nazi crimes at any period. All would be charged as criminal conspirators. The Nazi regime, its leaders and its institutions would be seen as plotting from the very beginning all the crimes of which they were now accused. They would be indicted for a series of acts which must all be seen as part of the same criminal intention—plotted for many years, begun at home and then gradually extended all over Europe to fulfill the intention to dominate, to establish Aryan supremacy, and to subject all human and physical resources to German needs.

At first glance a proposal which only covers six pages can seem simple. Indeed, the Bernays proposal had the supreme bureaucratic attraction of brevity. . . . Out of the jumble of abhorrent acts, evil men and the complexities of law incomprehensible to the layman, Bernays had composed a single theme to explain it all and capture the imagination—one huge, criminal plot carried out by a group of criminal conspirators. And more than this—after the trial was over, what a contribution the plan could make to the speedy de-Nazification of Germany; how quickly lesser officials and military men could be rounded up and tried. Thanks to the evidence against the Nazi organizations on which the Tribunal would be asked to make declarations of criminality, the subsequent proceedings would not get bogged down in defence claims that their defendants were innocent cogs in the State machine or patriots performing a duty to their country. Once these declarations were on record, later courts would know that the accused were members of criminal organizations. . . . The plan was gratifyingly coherent and seductively comprehensive. So much so that many of its elements were to shape the Nuremberg Tribunal—for good and bad.

Whatever its immediate attractions, however, Bernays' plan showed all the signs of having been written in a few weeks to a departmental brief, and by a not very distinguished lawyer. It hinged on the idea of conspiracy. Conspiracy is a fairly familiar charge in American and British law. It is a useful one to bring against a gang leader who does not himself blow the safe, kill the bank guard or drive the getaway car; who cannot therefore be charged with the actual crimes, but who has played the vital part in planning them and in hiring and directing those who committed them. The charge of conspiracy had been much used in the United States; it is a catch-all which was often the only effective way of dealing with large-scale, organized crime. Even so, conspiracy is always difficult to define and the charge can cause problems in court. . . . Implied in the conspiracy charge can be the idea that all members of a gang share guilt for all its acts. In Anglo-American law, defendants can be accused of conspiracy to commit all its acts whatever their length of stay in a gang and regardless of whether they even met most of its members. These are concepts found dangerous by many judges and ludicrous by many juries. If such a wide definition of the charge could be difficult to prove in cases involving relatively small numbers, how much more difficult it would be to pin it on an entire regime whose acts were allegedly criminal for twelve years. Bernays had recommended a wide definition of conspiracy when experience showed that many judges tended to narrow it: and to endeavour to impose limits of time during which they would accept that the conspiracy was active and to look for incontrovertible evidence to prove criminal purpose and criminal action on the part of individual defendants.

Worse still, the charge of conspiracy is viewed with even greater suspicion on the Continent, even though there it is not as widely defined as in Anglo-American law. Yet Bernays was suggesting that the charge be heard by an international tribunal, in which Continental judges would expect charges of criminal acts rather than of criminal intentions. Furthermore, he was recommending trying German defendants on a charge relatively unfamiliar in German law and unknown in international law. Even more disturbing, the potential defendants had received no prior warning that the charge would be brought against them. Most of the charges relating to war crimes were already well-established in international law (any German murdering a prisoner-of-war, for example, knew that he was committing a war crime). There had been plenty of warnings from the Allies that men committing these categories of crime would be punished. But there had been no specific warnings that men would be accused and punished for conspiring to commit them. All legal systems condemn the idea of *ex post facto* law—law which retrospectively makes criminal acts which were not illegal at the time they were committed. It is a fundamental principle of justice that a man can only be accused of committing a crime if he knew in advance, or should have known, that his acts would be crimes.

Bernays was on equally weak legal ground in extending the conspiracy charge to include the pre-war period in his anxiety to cover such policies as the persecution of German Jews, the Trades Unions, the Christian Churches, the establishment of concentration camps and the euthanasia programme. Before the War, most of these allegedly criminal acts had been committed by the sovereign German state against its own German nationals. International law recognized the right of a nation to try foreigners who committed crimes in war against its subjects; it accepted that once Germany had surrendered unconditionally, the occupying Powers were sovereign and could establish tribunals to try German nationals for war crimes against others. But there was no precedent in international law for other nations to try defendants on charges relating to domestic acts by a sovereign state. International law dealt only with the relations between nations and the acts committed by one nation against another.

Similarly without precedent not just in international but in every national legal system was Bernays' idea of trying organizations as well as individual defendants. It carried with it a dangerous possibility—that mere membership of a group might automatically make a man criminal; that there was no need to show the nature of his membership (whether it was voluntary, active, and based on full information about all the aims and activities of the group). Like conspiracy at its widest definition, the idea of asking a court to declare whole organizations criminal could be seen as creating a "catch-all" charge. This, unless severely limited by the most scrupulous safeguards, can easily become an instrument of injustice.

To be fair to Bernays, he had done his best to cobble together some working suggestions. It was now up to better lawyers to turn them into something more viable and in conformity with accepted legal principles and procedures.

Better lawyers abounded in the US War Department . . . , the State Department and in the Justice Department. From the second half of September they began to sink their teeth into Bernays' plan. Not surprisingly the Justice Department, though in favour of a trial in principle, was extremely critical of what was seen as Bernays' sloppy thinking. On 29 December, Assistant Attorney General Herbert Wechsler, in a memorandum to his superior Francis Biddle, urged dropping the charges concerned with pre-war acts and acts against German nationals on the grounds that they were *ex post facto*. He objected to the idea of trying organizations since it was without precedent and involved too great a risk of injustice. He considered the charge of conspiracy to be purely Anglo-American and therefore inapplicable in an international court, and against German defendants. Biddle was in full agreement. So were many others—not just in America, but even more so later when the trial was under discussion in Europe and the charge came under heavy criticism from Continental lawyers. Even so, though the Bernays plan drew heavy fire from all sides, though much of it was damaged and even wiped out, the essentials were to remain. Their seductions were irresistible.

. . .

. . . Stimson now threw into [the] discussions an idea totally unfamiliar which was viewed by many with deep distaste. During the War, several of the leaders of the smaller Allied states had revived the possibility . . . that launching aggressive war was in itself a crime. They suggested that one day Nazi leaders should be punished for it. Stimson had found this proposal most attractive at the time; it would now fit neatly into Bernays' wide concept of a trial. If this element were added, it could be argued that the war crimes and crimes against humanity with which the Nazi leaders were charged had inevitably and intentionally resulted from the aim and act of waging war to dominate Europe. To obtain that domination the conspirators had committed all their crimes—those against German nationals to strengthen their grip on Germany, the war crimes to ensure victory, the crimes against humanity to terrorize and enslave captured populations. The central crime, to and from which all the others flowed, was war.

The intellectual neatness of this idea and its acceptability to several nations might in themselves have been enough to win Stimson's support. But there was an even deeper appeal. As a constant and vocal proponent of the development of international law, Stimson had hailed as a crucial step the signing by sixty-three nations (including Germany) of the Pact of Paris (or the Kellogg-Briand Pact) in 1928. The signatories of that Pact had renounced war as an instrument of national policy for the solution of disputes. Some people regarded this as little more than yet another expression of pious hope. They pointed to the considerable number of similar agreements since the end of the First World War, to the constant vows not to resort to violence, then to the constant failure of the nations to make them binding. Stimson, and others, however, believed that the Pact was not mere aspiration but the expression of a legal commitment on the part of its signatories. Previous international agreements, starting with the Covenant of the League of Nations, had expressed the nations' belief that aggressive war should be seen as a crime; this Pact had made it so. Stimson had acted on his belief. Convinced that Germany was an aggressor, he justified escalating action against her while America remained neutral: economic pressure, embargo, naval threat. As he told a congressional hearing in 1941, he interpreted the Kellogg-Briand Pact as having changed international law so as to free nonbelligerents from any obligation to withhold aid when given against an aggressor.

But though Stimson and many others might think that war was now illegal, some did not. They argued that the Pact did not have the character or force of true law. It failed on two counts. Firstly, like innumerable scholars and politicians from Grotius to the drafters of the Covenant of the League of Nations, it had not succeeded in giving a clear, unambiguous definition of aggression. Next, critics of the Pact pointed out, it neither specified punishments for those who committed aggression nor proposed courts to try those accused of it. Real laws, they said, need sanctions and recognized institutions to apply them. Stimson was never impressed by any of these arguments. He believed that not only had the sixty-three nations made war illegal by their denunciation, they had also implied their preparedness to impose sanctions. They may not have done so this far but, as he put it in 1947, "a legal right is not lost because it is not used."

Morgenthau's plan for the treatment of Germany had stirred up one hornet's nest; Stimson's plan for a trial had stirred up another. . . . Many maintained that the international community must clarify its wishes in adequately drafted law before . . . a trial could take place. The reply of Stimson and his supporters was that the wishes of the nations and their condemnation of crimes had been adequately expressed in dozens of declarations and agreements in the inter-war years; in the Common Law tradition, at least, law develops through court decision, as well as by statute. The law was not being pushed into a dangerously extended leap as the opponents of this trial alleged; it was being encouraged to take a natural step along the line indicated by the international community.

Lawyers thrive on precedent. Critics of Stimson's proposals were not only hostile to the charges to be heard in the trial, they condemned the idea of trying a country's leaders as being without precedent. The Stimson camp could reply that there always has to be a first time; at some moment there had been the first trial for murders so why not now the first trial of criminal leaders of a state? Indeed, they would urge, this was the perfect time. Sufficient international agreement and law had been established; there was a strong demand for punishment of war criminals, a need to prevent blind vengeance, an intense desire to deter future criminals and aggressors and a cry for a just and permanent peace in Europe. What better justifications could there be for holding such a trial? What better moment for edging forward the rule of law than after a period of such lawlessness and resultant suffering? The detractors of the proposed trial would counter: are such responsibilities appropriate tasks for an *ad hoc* court, hearing disputed law in the atmosphere of hatred and recrimination following such a war?

Lawyers still wrangle over all these arguments. The proposal to set up an international tribunal to try Nazi war criminals had raised some of the most fundamental questions lawyers must ask about the law itself and the nature of judicial proceedings. . . . It was now up to the politicians to make that choice.

For a brief moment it looked as if Morgenthau's policies would prevail. Roosevelt went to a meeting with Churchill in Quebec from 11 to 19 September 1944. Roosevelt was concerned to assist British post-war recovery and Churchill had come to Quebec with the intention of asking for American financial assistance. It was logical, therefore, that Morgenthau, as Secretary of the Treasury, should be brought into the talks, and inevitable that he should take the opportunity of presenting his Plan for Germany. He found the British leader receptive. Whether or not Churchill suspected that support for the Plan was a *quid pro quo* for American financial aid, he was certainly in favour of one of its elements—summary execution for major Nazi war criminals. Before he and Roosevelt left Quebec they initialled the entire Plan. Morgenthau seemed to have scored a decisive victory.

He had not. His Plan had only been initialled, not signed. The two heads of government had kept their options open, and had decided to consult Stalin before reaching a decision even on the punishment of major war criminals. By sticking his head above the parapet at Quebec, Morgenthau had become an easy target. Details of his Plan were leaked to the Press, and all hell broke loose. The American public may have demanded punishment for war criminals, may have wanted all Germans taught a sharp lesson, but they had never envisaged anything as ruthless and vicious as this; Morgenthau's measures went far beyond anything they could find acceptable.

Public indignation was kept boiling by a Press campaign denouncing Morgenthau himself. Meanwhile he came under bureaucratic assault from the formidable alliance of the War, State and Justice Departments. These allies might still not agree over details, but their principles were the same, and they were united by a departmental ambition—to stop Morgenthau. It was a daunting combination for Roosevelt to face.... He was faced too with criticism of the Morgenthau proposals from a man for whom he felt as much trust and affection as he did for Morgenthau—Judge Sam Rosenman. Rosenman was Roosevelt's favourite speech writer and his special legal adviser. He was in favour of a trial. So too was one of the most respected figures in Washington, Justice Felix Frankfurter of the Supreme Court.

Roosevelt could not possibly withstand such a tide for long. A final wave hit him at the end of September. The Allied advance in Europe was stopped dead by German resistance. Once details of the Morgenthau Plan reached Goebbels, he had had a field day: "I myself am Number One on the list of war criminals," he boasted. The Nazi media cried for a fight to the last—why not, since the Allies demanded not only unconditional surrender but threatened to be merciless in victory? However unfairly, everyone in America blamed Morgenthau for the military setback; the Press campaign against him reached a new pitch of antagonism. With Roosevelt now a tired and sick man, there was no longer any possibility of standing up for Morgenthau.

So it was that Roosevelt was swept into the opposite camp. On 22 January 1945 he received a memorandum from Stimson, Hull and Biddle. In it they proposed setting up an Allied court to try Nazi leaders and organizations for "atrocious crimes" and for their part in a "broad criminal enterprise" to commit them. They recommended that the charges to be heard should include those concerned with acts committed before the outbreak of war against German citizens and suggested that a military tribunal was preferable to a civil body, since it would be "less likely to give undue weight to technical contentions and legalistic arguments." Having taken Morgenthau and his Plan to Quebec, Roosevelt took this altogether different memorandum to his meeting with Churchill and Stalin at Yalta in February 1945. Stimson, Hull and Biddle had decisively won the battle in Washington. They now had to see if Roosevelt would win a campaign with the European leaders.

Until now the odds had been heavily against winning British support for an international tribunal. In London, the views of politicians and officials had been perfectly clear at least since 1942. None of them wanted a trial of major war criminals.... [T]he Foreign Office ... had argued that no international court should be set up to try arch-criminals such as Himmler since "the guilt of such individuals is so black that they fall outside and go beyond the scope of any judicial process." Lord Simon, the Lord Chancellor, had felt his lawyer's conscience slightly bruised by this declaration. He commented that he did not think "that this programme will either satisfy public opinion or achieve a measure of substantial justice," and he drew attention to the wishes expressed in the St James's Declaration. Lord Simon's legal conscience was not so very tender, however. He expressed the hope that "the principal criminals will be disposed of by their fellow countrymen before peace comes"—presumably meaning that he hoped the Allies would be relieved of the problem by prior German resort to the lamp-post or firing squad rather than judicial process. If not then ... [h]e appears to have believed that "public opinion," the criteria of "substantial justice" and the aspirations of the St James's Declaration could be satisfied with rather quicker and rougher methods than those to be expected from an international tribunal.

. . .

Thereafter British official opinion simply hardened—a process assisted by finding plenty of justifications for sticking to their policy. Most of these were summarized in a brief prepared by Sir William Malkin of the Foreign Office for [Foreign Minister Anthony] Eden in February 1944. It was uncompromisingly entitled *Against the Establishment of an International Court.* In Malkin's opinion such a court would take too long to establish, it would look no more impartial than a national body, its proceedings would be intolerably slow thanks to language and procedural problems, it might very well not be recognized by those being tried and they would be given plausible grounds for contesting its legality. Send the minor criminals to be tried in whatever country seemed appropriate, said Malkin, and reserve the arch-criminals for the Four Powers. Lord Simon noted his approval of every word. He agreed too with a Cabinet paper from Eden in May which proposed drawing up a list of less than fifty top criminals "whose position or reputation is such public opinion will not object to their guilt being taken for granted without being established by any form of legal proceedings." Once the world was convinced that action against these men was "justified on the highest moral and political grounds" they could be punished by summary action.

Thus far, the British had always taken for granted American approval of their views. They had been somewhat startled back in November 1942 when the Soviet Foreign Minister, Maisky, had written to Eden suggesting setting up a tribunal for major criminals. . . . Whatever Stalin might say *sub rosa* at Tehran, his official line was constant. By late 1944 the Foreign Office had to admit with some bewilderment that Stalin wanted leading Nazis to be put to death—but only after a trial. . . .

So by the time the Big Three met at Yalta no one could be surprised when Stalin demanded that "the grand criminals should be tried before being shot" and there had been a complete reversal of the American position—Roosevelt had brought the Stimson-Hull-Biddle proposals and not the Morgenthau Plan.

The British were isolated. The question of war criminals was discussed only briefly, but in that short time a major step was taken. The Big Three reaffirmed the decision of the Moscow Conference to send minor criminals back to the scene of their crime, but they adjusted the Moscow intention to punish the major criminals by joint "declaration" into a specific commitment to a trial. The British had been routed.

They preferred to believe that they lived to fight another day. They issued an invitation in March for an American delegation to come to London to discuss the entire problem of how to deal with major war criminals. It was their undoubted intention to talk the Americans out of the idea of a trial. But when the delegation arrived in the first week in April, it was made up of three convinced proponents of the idea who had come to London with the aim of inspiring the British to buy the entire American package, give or take some minor adjustments to suit British taste. Judge Sam Rosenman was accompanied by Colonel Cutter (assistant executive officer to McCloy in the War Department) and Major General Weir (the Deputy Judge Advocate General).

. . .

The . . . British tried to douse American enthusiasm with some cold legal water. Rosenman, Cutter and Weir went to the Lord Chancellor's room in the House of Lords and were presented with a very full memorandum by Simon forcefully setting out British objections to holding any trial of major Nazi war criminals. In it he agreed that Hitler and others should suffer death for their actions, but he then argued that a trial would be "exceedingly long and elaborate" and would undoubtedly give rise to the comment that "the whole thing is a put-up job designed by the Allies to justify a punishment they have already resolved on." Besides, he said, such a trial would have to allow a proper hearing to the defence and full consideration of evidence and in so doing it would give the Nazi leaders a chance to turn the tables on the prosecution and score points. He hinted darkly that they might raise in their defence topics of Allied foreign policy and aggression which could prove "embarrassing" and he expressed the doubt that many unprovoked German attacks after the beginning of the War could "properly be described as crimes under international law." He was most scathing of the suggestion that Hitler himself might be tried, repeating the long-held British view that the totality of Hitler's acts made him "the scoundrel he is" but that they could never be adequately examined in a judicial proceeding however long and complex. The attempt to do so, said Simon, would be seen by the public as a farce; they would declare "the man should be shot out of hand."

. . . However, he then revealed a minute softening of the British hard line. He put forward the suggestion, as if it were a compromise, of dealing with the arch-criminals by means of an Instrument of Arraignment. Under its terms they would be charged as common criminals on counts which could include plotting to dominate Europe, breaches of the laws of war, and maltreatment of the

Jews. Those accused would be allowed to defend themselves before a tribunal (which need not be composed of lawyers) who would report their findings to the Allies. The Allies would then determine judgement and sentence.

"Instrument of Arraignment" is a most impressive title. Under it Lord Simon had put charges which the Americans wanted to pursue and included provision for a form of hearing. Even so . . . it was certainly not the kind of full judicial proceeding the Americans were calling for, not one where final decisions rested with judges rather than politicians. . . . Rosenman's instant response was that the idea was "novel, ingenious and sound in principle." Not that he was considering abandoning his plan in favour of Simon's. He was merely wondering if it was possible to arrange a marriage between them by offering acceptance of Arraignment as a dowry.

[T]he discussion for the remainder of the week only served to prove, how very different were British and American forms of hearing and charges and how impractical it was to try to join the Arraignment procedure with the plan for a fully-fledged trial. . . . Simon announced on 10 April that his Arraignment procedure would not actually allow for witnesses to be introduced for the prosecution or defence. That was not a trial in any normally accepted definition and the Americans inevitably retorted that they could not possibly countenance such a denial of an elementary right for the accused.

By the time Rosenman left London, the only concession he had wrung from the British was their agreement to sound out the feelings of the French and Russians. To make matters worse, Churchill had leapt at Simon's idea of Arraignment, passed it through his historian's mind and brought it forth transformed into a Bill of Attainder: get Parliament to pass one, he urged. He and his Cabinet colleagues were unanimous on 12 April: "for the principal Nazi leaders a full trial under judicial procedure was out of the question." By all means publish a formal statement of the case against them, but on no account give them much of a chance to answer it.

Whatever gloom the American delegates might have experienced at their failure to budge the British, it paled into insignificance on that very day when the news reached them that President Roosevelt had died. Their sadness was natural faced with the death of a great leader and a man who had been a close personal friend of Rosenman. To be callous, however, Roosevelt's death can be seen as a positive advantage. He had never been more than a reluctant supporter of the plan for a trial. . . . His successor, Harry S. Truman, on the other hand, was a wholehearted supporter. He had a profound belief in the beneficent power of law and the wisdom of judges, an abhorrence of summary execution, sensitive antennae to the balance of political forces in Washington and greater drive and disposition to make decisions than his ailing predecessor. Truman wanted a trial and he wanted agreement of its details quickly—preferably in time for the next great international meeting scheduled to take place in San Francisco from April.

John McCloy was also determined to get the trial plan implemented. He was in Europe when Roosevelt died. He asked De Gaulle for his views; the General favoured a trial. As at Yalta, so now, the British could be out-gunned. McCloy could use a combined American, French and Russian barrage. Thus equipped, and staunchly backed by Truman, McCloy arrived in London . . . in mid-April. He brought a new vigour and passion to the joint talks. While the British niggled about the "political and practical dangers" of a trial, McCloy issued a clarion call to take the chance history was offering to show that "Hitler and his gang had offended against the laws of humanity." The British might be beset with anxieties; McCloy was "prepared to take any risks or embarrassments which might theoretically ensue" if a trial were instituted. He dismissed the suggestion of summary execution with contempt; it was "contrary to the fundamental conception of justice." He swatted away the Napoleonic precedent; it was a "retrogressive step" when a "great opportunity now presents itself to move forward."

The British continued to worry about the administrative problems of mounting a trial; McCloy confronted them with a memorandum in which he accused them not of arguing against a trial as such but against "the ability of Allied brains to produce a fair, expeditious, reasonable procedure to meet the novel situation which is present." He swept aside the British plaint that it was impossible to deal with the totality of acts over twelve years of the Nazi regime: "the very breadth of the offence is not in itself an argument against judicial action." He scoffed at British fears that the Nazis would use the trial for propaganda and counter charges: "the advantages of the trial method over political action are so fundamental that we should not allow the bug-a-boo of possible embarrassment to hinder us from establishing the principle" of bringing international law into action against the whole "vicious broad Nazi enterprise."

Such certainty, such energy, so roundly expressed would have been hard to resist. The British were in no position to do so. McCloy had also brought to the talks the weight of Truman's commitment (emphasized by a telegram the President sent to the Cabinet on 24 April) and the support of the French and Russians for an international court and full legal hearing. The only wonder is that the British held out for so long. They struggled until 30 May. Then the Cabinet, sweetening capitulation with such humbug as "the United States has gone a long way to answer Cabinet objections," and calling the proposed procedure "carefully designed to prevent the accused from using the court as a platform" for propaganda, gave its approval to the draft American proposals.

It would hardly have mattered if they had not—though an international tribunal would have looked less international without them. Without waiting for their decision, Truman had gone ahead. At the end of April he had appointed a man to lead a prosecution team and prepare a case. His choice for the post was a decisive one with immense repercussions on the future trial. He appointed [Supreme Court Justice] Robert H. Jackson.

CHAPTER 20

The Cold War

On August 8, 1945, in London, representatives of the United States, Britain, the Soviet Union, and the provisional government of France signed an agreement to set up an International Military Tribunal to try the major Nazi leaders. The agreement specified three categories of war crimes: violations of the laws of war, crimes against peace, and crimes against humanity. The Tribunal was also empowered to criminalize membership in groups and organizations.

Adolf Hitler having committed suicide, twenty-four other Nazi leaders were placed on trial in Nuremberg, one in absentia. The defendants were given the opportunity to be represented by counsel, to introduce evidence, and to cross-examine witnesses. The trial lasted nearly a year. The Tribunal rejected the two main defense allegations: that guilt lay only with the state and not with individuals, and that the crimes charged were not considered crimes at the time they were committed. During the trial, one defendant committed suicide, and one was declared too ill to go on. Of the remaining twenty-two, twelve were sentenced to hang, seven received jail terms (three for life), and three were acquitted. Several Nazi organizations were declared criminal, but the Tribunal declined to criminalize the governing cabinet or the high command of the armed forces.

Lesser Nazis were tried by each of the four occupying powers in their respective zones of occupation or by German courts after the establishment of the West and East German governments. Trials were also held in other nations where prominent Nazis were caught. The most publicized trial—that of Adolf Eichmann—was held in Israel from 1960 to 1962, after Eichmann was abducted by Israeli agents from his hiding place in Argentina.

An international tribunal to try war crimes was also established in Japan by order of the Supreme Allied Commander, General Douglas MacArthur. Twenty-five defendants were tried; seven were executed; eighteen received prison sentences (sixteen for life). Two of the sentenced defendants appealed to the Supreme Court of the United States, which rejected their petitions.

The Nuremberg trial has been cited in national courts—including in the U.S. trial of its own soldiers following the massacre of civilians in the Vietnamese hamlet of My Lai in 1968—but no further international trials were held until the establishment of international tribunals for the former Yugoslavia and for Rwanda in 1996. In 1997 a United Nations commission recommended the establishment of a permanent International Criminal Court.

In postwar Germany, few war criminals sentenced to jail served out their full sentences. As relations between the Soviet Union and the West deteriorated into a cold war, the reconstruction of Western Europe became a cornerstone of Western policy. In support of that policy, German cooperation was courted by the early release of many convicted war criminals.

When the cold war turned hot on the Korean peninsula in 1950, it was accompanied by the familiar wartime domestic tensions regarding economic regulation and national security. In response to a national steel strike, President Truman attempted to seize the nation's steel mills. The seizure was ruled unconstitutional in *Youngstown Sheet & Tube Company* v. *Sawyer* (1952).

On the security front, the United States reacted to the cold war with a Loyalty and Security Program, begun in 1947, to screen federal employees. At about the same time, the attorney general began to compile a list of subversive organizations, and the Federal Bureau of Investigation began to maintain a Security Index of persons who should be rounded up in case of national emergency. Also in 1947, the House Committee on Un-American Activities (unaffectionately labeled HUAC) began hearings on the alleged penetration of the United States by the Communist party. Among the first hearings were those focused on the Hollywood film industry. In the course of the hearings, witnesses were pressured to inform on others, and the film industry was pressured to "blacklist" uncooperative witnesses. Victor S. Navasky, in *Naming Names* (1982), described the process:

The congressional hearing into Hollywood had begun in 1947, when ten objecting witnesses (who came to be called the Unfriendly Ten or the Hollywood Ten) had been cited for contempt of Congress when they refused to give a yes or no answer to the question that marked the era: Are you now or have you ever been a member of the Communist Party? The hearings [were] suspended until the convicted Ten had exhausted their appeals and were imprisoned for terms of up to a year.

. . .

From that day forward those called to testify were advised by their attorneys that they had three choices: to invoke the First Amendment, with its guarantee of free speech and association, and risk going to prison for contempt of Congress like the Hollywood Ten; to invoke the Fifth Amendment, with its privilege against self-incrimination, and lose their jobs . . . ; or to cooperate with the Committee and name names and hope to continue working. . . . The ground rules for the decade were set. (pp. viii–x)

In 1949 leaders of the American Communist Party were indicted under the Smith Act of 1940 for "teaching or advocating the forcible and violent overthrow of the United States government." In a trial before Federal District Court Judge Harold Medina, not only were the defendants convicted, but their attorneys were also jailed for contempt of court. The convictions of the defendants were upheld by the Supreme Court in *Dennis* v. *United States* (1951), and a series of Smith-Act trials of lower-ranking Communist party members followed.

In 1950 Alger Hiss, a high-ranking State Department official, was convicted of perjury after being accused of having been a Communist party member. In the following year Ethel and Julius Rosenberg were convicted of spying and sentenced to death (they were executed in 1953). The year 1951 also marks the rise to national notoriety of the member of Congress who gave his name to the era: Senator Joseph McCarthy of Wisconsin. Beginning that year, and until his censure by the Senate in 1954, McCarthy's Senate hearings eclipsed the House hearings.

The tensions of the era also had their impact on the legal profession. Although the increase in government legal jobs in the New Deal had created opportunities for upward mobility, the positions of power in the profession—including those in the American Bar Association—were still dominated by the old-line elite. In 1937 a group of lawyers organized the National Lawyers Guild as an alternative to the ABA. In the 1950s they became special targets.

Hearing of the House Un-American Activities Committee, 1947. Congressman Richard M. Nixon is second from right at podium.

Photo from United Press International.

Cold War Conformity

The Second World War, unlike the First, created minimal internal stress for
the legal profession. . . . With the Soviet Union a valued, if uneasy, ally there
was no significant protest from the left against the war effort and, therefore,
no hostility directed against political dissenters. Immigration restriction and
the absorption of second-generation Americans had reduced ethnic-group an-
imosity. The external foe was the only enemy; national unity bound lawyers
to the nation without exacting any sacrifice of their professional obligations.
. . .

. . . For the first time, minority-group lawyers in significant numbers gained
access to the professional elite in private practice. Ethnic and religious lines
still held fast in the older corporate firms. . . . But the expertise accumulated
by lawyers in New Deal Washington increased their market value in private
practice to newer corporations dependent upon the federal government for
contracts and profits. These lawyers, skilled navigators of the federal regulatory labyrinth which they had themselves designed, quickly became insiders
looking out as their days as professional pariahs receded. Professional mobility and elite circulation, set in motion during the 1930's, yielded their rewards
abundantly, if belatedly, to those who followed the traditional path to success
in corporate practice.

But for other lawyers the postwar era turned sour, then ominous, and finally
disastrous. The Cold War brought a menacing reminder of an earlier postwar
era: the Red Scare. . . . [L]iberal and radical lawyers identified their own obligations as attorneys with political reform, civil liberties, minority rights, and
the quest for social justice—especially in labor relations. Professionally, [the
legacy of the New Deal] signified an enlarged conception of the responsibility
of lawyers to provide service to clients regardless of their economic resources.
But the politics of the Cold War transformed these pursuits into subversive ac-

tivities. The professional elite, encouraged and abetted by two attorneys general, by the House Un-American Activities Committee, and by politicians eager to ride anti-Communism to political power, attempted to purge the profession of lawyers whose political and professional commitments deviated from Cold War orthodoxy. To bar leaders, convinced that they confronted "a campaign directed from Moscow, aimed especially at our capitalistic system," nothing less was tolerable.

Attorney General Tom Clark was the first to warn of impending danger and to propose palliatives. In a speech in 1946 to members of the Chicago Bar Association, reprinted in the American Bar Association *Journal,* Clark described a plot by Communists, "outside ideologists," and "small groups of radicals" to undermine the nation. He condemned the "revolutionary" who "uses every device in the legal category to further the interests of those who would destroy our government, by force if necessary." These lawyers, he suggested, should be taken by bar associations "to the, legal woodshed for a definite and well-deserved admonition." Clark's warning went unheeded for nearly two years. But as American relations with the Soviet Union deteriorated, the American Bar Association explored its woodshed for admonitory weapons.

At first there were only editorials, warning that "forces of disorder and disruption are gathering for strife that will come if and when the orders for it are issued from the faraway Kremlin." Occasionally an article criticized lawyers whose dogmatic adherence to constitutional rights impeded their response to the Communist threat. At its annual convention in 1948 the association adopted a resolution declaring that any lawyer who provided assistance or support to the "world communist movement" was "unworthy" of ABA membership. The Board of Governors resolved that no member of the National Lawyers Guild should be accepted in the association....

[The National Lawyers Guild]

The National Lawyers Guild was a primary target for the government and for the American Bar Association.... The Smith Act trial of Communist Party leaders, with the hysteria it both expressed and generated, was the turning point. Each of the defense attorneys cited for contempt by Judge [Harold] Medina was a guild member; three were officers. With guilt by association endemic in postwar public life, vilification of the guild inevitably followed. The House Un-American Activities Committee issued a report denouncing it as "the foremost legal bulwark of the Communist Party, its front organizations, and controlled unions." Guild lawyers, it declared, "substitute insult for argument" and "resort to intimidation of judges." The committee recommended that the guild be placed on the attorney general's list of subversive organizations. If intimidation of guild lawyers was not the intent, it certainly was the consequence. The guild quickly lost half its membership and was compelled to expend the major portion of its energies to save itself from annihilation.

The Un-American Activities Committee opened the government assault against the guild, but Herbert Brownell, President Eisenhower's attorney general, turned the campaign into a crusade with an address to the American Bar Association in 1953. Brownell conceded that in the past the guild had attracted "some very well-known and completely loyal American citizens." But professional groups, he noted, were not exempt from Communist infiltration. Indeed, "at least since 1946 the leadership of the National Lawyers Guild has been in the hands of card-carrying Communists and prominent fellow travelers. . . . It has become more and more the legal mouthpiece for the Communist Party. . . . The evidence shows that . . . [it] is at present a Communist-dominated and controlled organization." Therefore, he concluded, the guild must show cause why it should not be placed on the attorney general's list of subversive organizations. . . . For five years the guild was engaged in protracted litigation to avoid listing; finally, in 1958, after it filed for dismissal of the suit, a new attorney general withdrew the recommendation to designate it as a subversive group.

. . .

The political vulnerability of the guild during the Cold War was obvious. Less evident was the extent to which the anti-Communism of the bar camouflaged ABA efforts to undercut guild proposals for public funding of legal services for low-income groups. The broad dissemination of legal services had been a primary guild objective since its birth during the Depression. After World War II the guild, disappointed with the failure of charitable legal aid, advocated expanded government responsibility. Encouraged by the report of the Rushcliffe Committee in England, whose recommendations for government-subsidized legal aid were enacted in 1949, guild attorneys urged the appropriation of public funds for legal services for those who could not afford the fees charged by private attorneys. . . .

Leaders of the American Bar Association were appalled at the prospect of federally subsidized legal services. According to a member of the Board of Governors, federal legal services, like the "undermining influences of Communist infiltration" with which he equated them, would inevitably substitute state regimentation for professional independence. . . .

. . . The guild was triply vulnerable: for the politics of some of its members; for the willingness of its attorneys to defend clients and causes which other lawyers would not touch; and for its innovative recommendations for federally subsidized legal services. The socioethnic identity of its membership doubtlessly was an additional impediment, although one that is impossible to measure with precision. It is at least worth noting that the five guild lawyers sentenced for contempt after the Smith Act trial included three Jews, one black (who later became a Detroit judge), and one Irish Catholic—hardly representative of the most privileged professional groups. . . .

[Loyalty Oaths]

The Cold War objectives of the American Bar Association went far beyond the elimination of a professional rival and the defense of free-enterprise legal services. "We are faced with a constant attack from within upon our form of government and our American way of life by proponents of foreign ideologies," declared ABA president Cody Fowler in 1950. The association explored proscriptive and punitive measures of professional discipline, imploring other professional groups to follow its lead.

. . .

Among various proposals for professional orthodoxy none elicited more criticism than the resolution approved by the association without debate in 1950 demanding that all lawyers attest to their loyalty with an anti-Communist oath. Zechariah Chafee, Jr., of Harvard Law School, a patrician turned libertarian by World War I violations of the Bill of Rights, observed that the loyalty oath was adopted "with less discussion than would have been devoted to the menu at the next annual banquet." Chafee, author of the classic *Free Speech in the United States* and a charter member of the association's Bill of Rights Committee, decided that "if nobody else stood up on his hind legs and yelled, I was going to do so." Chafee, characteristically, yelled gently but effectively. He spoke and wrote vigorously against the proposal, which in his opinion violated the First and Fifth Amendments, portended "a purge of the American bar," and was, he concluded, "the worst thing the American Bar Association has ever done." Chafee directed his appeal to bar leaders within the association. Twenty-six prominent members . . . co-signed a petition in opposition to the oath which denounced it as "unfounded in its implication of widespread disloyalty."

. . .

Although the loyalty oath proposal expired at the state level, it was only part of a sustained, invidious, and more successful effort to intimidate lawyers for unpopular defendants and to discipline those whose beliefs or associations were adjudged subversive. . . . There was, one scholar concluded, "an open season on lawyers who defend hated men."

[The Smith Act Trial of 1949]

Overt repression began after the Smith Act trial in 1949. That trial was the key that unlocked Attorney General Clark's legal woodshed of discipline and harassment. It was long, frequently acrimonious, and laced with anti-Communist hysteria from the indictment stage through its "bizarre" culmination, when Medina found five defense attorneys guilty of criminal contempt and imposed prison sentences upon them without providing them with notice, a hearing, or the opportunity to defend themselves. After Medina pronounced sentence, defense attorney Abraham Isserman . . . accused the judge of "an effort to intimidate members of the bar. . . ." It may be difficult, as a special bar association committee on courtroom conduct recently concluded, "to decide whether the obstructive behavior at the trial arose out of the lawyers' individual, vigorous assertion of their clients' cause or was planned beforehand . . . , or whether their conduct was the result of a self-fulfilling prophecy, a consequence of Judge Medina's own behavior." But there is no question that Medina conducted the trial with an attentive eye to the press and to his approving audience in Washington government circles. He solicited information about newspaper coverage from a friend in a Washington law firm; he received letters of praise from the attorney general and from FBI director J. Edgar Hoover; and he sent a copy of his charge to the jury to Senator Joseph R. McCarthy.

. . . Medina, haunted by the memory of a tumultuous Smith Act trial five years earlier during which the judge had died of a heart attack, . . . observed that before the trial had progressed very far he "was reluctantly forced to conclude" that the lawyers' actions "were the result of an agreement . . . deliberately entered into in a cold and calculating manner" to provoke incidents that would cause confusion and delay and impair his own health. Medina indicated that he would have overlooked the conduct of the lawyers, or merely reprimanded them for it, had it come from the heat of controversy or from zealous defense. But the "agreement . . . deliberately entered into" made all the difference. . . .

The contempt citations triggered appeals, disciplinary proceedings, and collateral litigation which culminated in the first instances of disbarment for forensic misconduct. For the two lawyers most directly involved, Harry Sacher and Abraham Isserman, these proceedings, stretching over twelve years, can only be described as diabolic. They were veteran attorneys of acknowledged ability who had devoted substantial portions of their careers to civil liberties and labor defense efforts. During the Cold War they paid the price exacted by their profession for their commitments. . . .

On appeal the *Sacher* contempt case (involving all the defense lawyers) posed a dilemma for the Second Circuit. Medina's citation was challenged on the ground that summary punishment was proper only if it followed immediately upon commission of the contemptuous acts, not when it was administered weeks or months later, after the trial had ended. But reversal of Medina in the contempt case would substantiate the claim being pressed in the *Dennis* appeal (involving the Smith Act defendants) that the trial was unfair. This dilemma threatened to become an acute embarrassment to the government and to Medina when Judge Jerome Frank, "tentatively and most reluctantly" (he claimed), voted to reverse and remand for a hearing before another judge. Frank was convinced that the lawyers had acted contemptuously, but he also thought that the trial judge could not punish summarily after the trial. Since Judge Charles Clark had also concluded that the lawyers were entitled to a hearing and to an opportunity to defend themselves before a contempt citation was imposed, their votes were sufficient for reversal.

Judge Augustus Hand, the third member of the Second Circuit panel, believed that Medina had acted properly. He also was distressed by the implications of reversal. He apparently persuaded Frank to change his vote, thereby upholding the contempt citations. Hand, now joined by Frank, declared that the lawyers had committed "willful obstruction" which need not be punished immediately (thereby risking an interruption of the trial), but only as speedily as circumstances permitted. Yet the Hand-Frank majority, by resolving this problem, created new ones. . . . Frank, joining with Clark in voiding the "agreement" or conspiracy specification, joined with Hand in sustaining the other specifications—although Medina himself had conceded that but for the "plan" there would have been no contempt. This doubtlessly troubled Hand, who attempted to have his conspiracy cake yet not choke on it. Medina's statement about an agreement, Hand reasoned, meant nothing more than that the acts were "deliberate." It was, he concluded, quite unimportant whether Medina believed in a conspiracy. If the reasoning was tortured the result was clear: contempt citations, justified by the trial judge solely on the presumption that conspiracy existed, were upheld on appeal notwithstanding the finding that no conspiracy existed.

Frank, in his concurring opinion, dismissed fears expressed in *amicus* briefs that prospective lawyers for unpopular defendants would be intimidated by the contempt citations. "The fears are unfounded," he observed. But they were quite well-founded indeed. Reports of difficulty in obtaining counsel soon reached the Supreme Court, which earlier had denied a petition for review of *Sacher*. Justice Robert Jackson, who concurred in the denial, changed his mind when he realized that "the difficulties of obtaining counsel in these cases has increased since we denied review and . . . it threatens to become impossible." The Court heard the appeal and, by a 5–3 vote (with Jackson writing the majority opinion), upheld the power of a trial judge to defer summary contempt until the completion of the trial if he believed that the exigencies of the trial required it. Justices Black and Frankfurter issued stinging dissents and strong rebukes to Medina for his evident demonstrations of hostility toward the defense lawyers. Black, referring to the proceedings, declared: "I cannot reconcile this summary blasting of legal careers with a fair system of justice. Such a procedure constitutes an overhanging menace to the security of every courtroom advocate in America. The menace is most ominous for lawyers who are obscure, unpopular or defenders of unpopular persons or unorthodox causes." Frankfurter added that Medina had "failed to exercise the moral authority of a court possessed of a great tradition." It was, he concluded, "a disservice to the law to sanction the imposition of punishment by a judge personally involved and therefore not unreasonably to be deemed to be seeking retribution."

Sacher and Isserman went to jail (as did the other Smith Act trial defense attorneys), but their professional travail had barely begun. The Association of the Bar of the City of New York brought disbarment proceedings against Sacher, who already had been suspended for two years. The Second Circuit, again over Clark's dissent, upheld disbarment on appeal. Judge Augustus Hand, again for the majority, insisted that disbarment was necessary to protect the court and to increase respect for it by assuring that lawyers displayed "good professional character." Clark, however, observed that Sacher had a twenty-four-year record of "unblemished conduct" and that in appellate appearances on his own behalf, in trying circumstances, he had demonstrated "courteous and dignified" behavior and professional ability of "unusually high order." Clark expressed the hope that his disbarment would be rescinded when "the present atmosphere of hysteria has somewhat abated." His dissent concluded with the plaintive question: ". . . why must the most serious wounds to justice be self-inflicted?" By 1954, when the disbarment appeal reached the Supreme Court, the hysteria cited by Clark had begun to abate. In a *per curiam* opinion reversing the Court of Appeals, the Court declared that permanent disbarment was "unnecessarily severe."

Sacher's ordeal almost pales in comparison with Isserman's. Isserman, who had shared Sacher's two-year suspension in New York, was disbarred in New Jersey in 1952 for his "scandalous and inexcusable behavior." After his disbarment there the United States Supreme Court ordered him to show cause why he should not be disbarred from practice before it, since the high court ordinarily followed the findings of state courts in disbarment proceedings. With the Court evenly split, disbarment resulted (a third disbarment, in New York, followed). The four dissenting justices observed that disbarment for contempt was rare, if not unprecedented. Indeed, they noted, Elihu Root and David Dudley Field, two earlier titans of the bar, had been cited for contempt after the trial of Boss Tweed without additional penalty—in fact Field was subsequently elected president of the American Bar Association. In 1953 the Court denied a petition for certiorari appealing the New Jersey disbarment. But in 1954, the year that Sacher's disbarment was set aside, the tide turned. Isserman's Supreme Court disbarment was reversed under a new rule providing that no order of disbarment could be entered without the concurrence of a majority of the participating justices. Five years later Isserman's New York disbarment was set aside as "discriminatorily severe," with the Court of Appeals noting that Isserman had endured *de facto* suspension for nearly a decade. In 1961, twelve years after the first house of disciplinary cards was built upon its foundation of conspiratorial sand, Isserman's application for reinstatement to the New Jersey bar was granted. The state Supreme Court, writing the final page to a sordid chapter, concluded that a nine-year "stigma of disbarment . . . is more than enough."

. . .

[Professional Harassment]

Within months after the Smith Act trial concluded, its ripple effect was apparent. In California two defense lawyers for Harry Bridges, the left-wing union leader who was a venerable target of government prosecution, were summarily cited for contempt and served jail sentences for courtroom conduct which, in language strikingly reminiscent of the Medina contretemps, was described as "designed and calculated to contemptuously provoke the court." (One of the lawyers, Vincent Hallinan, became the vice-presidential nominee of the Progressive Party in 1952.) In Pennsylvania lawyer Hyman Schlesinger was defending a client in a trespass case when the trial judge interrupted the proceedings to inquire if he had ever belonged to the Communist Party or to its front organizations. Schlesinger, refusing to answer, was pronounced "morally unfit" and held in contempt. (The judge, who a year earlier had wrongfully dismissed a grand juror whom he had concluded was a Communist, was rebuked and reversed for conducting "arbitrary and unjudicial proceedings.") In separate proceedings Schlesinger was charged with "professional misconduct" by a bar disciplinary group. For a period of eight months he was unable to find defense counsel, "a lamentable commentary" according to the Pennsylvania Supreme Court which set aside his disbarment—a decade later.

In Florida a lawyer was disbarred for claiming his Fifth Amendment right against self-incrimination in declining to answer questions regarding his alleged membership in the Communist Party. The appellate court reversed, noting that, although a lawyer who was a party member forfeited his right to practice (because he was "guilty of a species of treason"), mere refusal to answer questions about party membership was insufficient for disbarment. In Maryland a lawyer convicted under the Smith Act of conspiring to advocate the forcible overthrow of the government was disbarred upon termination of his three-year jail sentence for a crime involving moral turpitude and for being "a subversive person." (Eighteen years later, when he sought reinstatement, a three-judge panel agreed that his conviction had been "largely political in nature.") In Hawaii a lawyer for Smith Act defendants addressed a public meeting while the trial was in progress at which she claimed that "shocking and horrible things" were occurring in court and that there could not be a fair trial in a Smith Act case. The trial judge invited the Hawaii Bar Association to scrutinize her professional conduct. A one-year suspension resulted which the Court of Appeals upheld on the ground that she had made "a willful oral attack" upon the administration of justice. In a 5–4 decision the Supreme Court reversed on the narrow ground that the evidence was insufficient to support the conclusion that her speech impugned the integrity of the judge. Only four justices could agree that lawyers "are free to criticize the state of the law."

. . . In Michigan two lawyers were called before a local ethics committee to account for their criticism of the Rosenberg trial. Lawyers appearing before legislative investigating committees and grand juries frequently were questioned about their political beliefs and associations and those of their clients. An American Bar Association committee concluded in 1953 that even lawyers who were conspicuously identified as anti-Communists were subject to "severe personal vilification and abuse" if they defended Communists or suspected Communists.... Lawyers who were spared disciplinary proceedings by their local bar association suffered economic reprisals and damaged reputations. It was, Justice Douglas concluded, "a dark tragedy."

Lawyers were not the only victims of professional reprisals. Defendants in political cases found it difficult in some instances, and virtually impossible in others, to obtain counsel. The deterrent effect of disciplinary harassment and economic risk was apparent when the government began its prosecution of second string Communist Party officials, who approached one hundred and fifty lawyers before they could obtain defense counsel.... Finally, a panel of willing lawyers was obtained through the combined efforts of the National Lawyers Guild and two bar associations. Steve Nelson, defendant in a Pennsylvania sedition trial, was compelled to represent himself after he unsuccessfully approached local bar associations, visited twenty-five lawyers in Pittsburgh, and wrote to fifty others in Philadelphia, New York, and Chicago—none of whom would defend him. Other Smith Act defendants, in Baltimore and St. Louis, encountered identical difficulties. For political nonconformists the right to counsel disappeared into constitutional limbo.

[Bar Admissions]

The pool of lawyers willing to defend unpopular defendants, reduced by expulsion and intimidation, was further depleted by the diligent efforts of bar associations to exclude prospective applicants who did not satisfy prevailing political tests. A reliable old weapon—good moral character—was refurbished for Cold War service. In Texas the Houston Bar Association issued an adverse recommendation against an applicant who had participated in activities on behalf of Julius and Ethel Rosenberg and had associated with a lawyer suspected to be a party member. The federal district court affirmed, suggesting that admission to the bar required that "private and personal character shall be unexceptional." The Supreme Court reversed. In New Mexico an applicant who belonged to the Communist Party between 1932 and 1940, used aliases to escape anti-Semitism in employment, and was arrested (but never tried or convicted) for organizing workers and recruiting volunteers for the Spanish Loyalist cause was prevented from taking the bar examination because he lacked the requisite moral character. The Supreme Court again reversed.... This disqualification, it suggested, had no rational connection to the applicant's fitness for practice. Neither unorthodox ideas, nor party membership, wrote Justice Black, demonstrated questionable moral character.

In a companion case the Supreme Court reversed a California decision which upheld the exclusion of an applicant [Raphael Konigsberg] who refused, on First Amendment grounds, to answer questions regarding his past or present political beliefs and associations. His examiners claimed that he had failed to demonstrate good moral character; the Supreme Court reversed on the ground that the record did not support reasonable doubt about his character. Without reaching the issue of whether the failure to answer was an independent ground for exclusion the Court, in another opinion by Black, declared that "good moral character" was "unusually ambiguous" and that any definition would reflect "the attitudes, experiences, and prejudices of the definer." It was, therefore, "a dangerous instrument for arbitrary and discriminatory denial of the right to practice law."

The New Mexico and California decisions, an attorney suggested in 1957, represented a "return to reason" by the judiciary. Disclosures of past party membership apparently were insufficient to sustain inferences of bad character. That interpretation gained credence when the Supreme Court also vacated an Oregon decision under which an expelled party member was excluded from the bar on the ground that his disclaimer of belief in the forcible overthrow of the government was a lie that demonstrated bad character. The Court asked Oregon to reconsider in the light of its recent rulings. Bar associations, rebuked by the Supreme Court in four consecutive cases that turned on definitions of good character, seemed to have exceeded their exclusionary limits.

But optimistic assessments were premature. Bar associations did not relent, and the Supreme Court ultimately acquiesced in their exclusionary efforts. First, the Oregon Supreme Court, again ruling that the expelled party member swore falsely when he declared his belief in the party's (and his own) nonviolent objectives, upheld his exclusion on character grounds. The Supreme Court denied certiorari. The Konigsberg case in California returned to the Supreme Court in 1961. Again the applicant had been asked about party membership; again he refused to answer; again the bar examiners refused to certify him on the ground that his silence obstructed a full inquiry into his qualifications. The first time around the Court had declined to reach the issue of whether refusal to answer was ground for exclusion; but this time, by a 5–4 vote, it affirmed, holding that a state could deny admission if an applicant refused to answer questions relevant to his qualifications.

The second *Konigsberg* opinion, written by Justice Harlan, was as tortured in its reasoning as the earlier *Sacker* opinion in the Court of Appeals had been. In *Sacher*, contempt charges resting necessarily upon a conspiracy were upheld even though the conspiracy claim was rejected. In the [second] *Konigsberg* case the Court . . . held that Konigsberg's refusal to answer left the record in sufficient doubt—even though his acknowledgment of party membership would *not* justify exclusion. . . . Konigsberg, wrote Black in dissent, was "but another victim of the prevailing fashion of destroying men for the views it is suspected they might entertain."

In another case decided the same day the Court upheld exclusionary proceedings in Illinois that made the California bar seem almost libertarian by comparison. Back in 1950 the Chicago bar committee on character and fitness, reviewing the application of George Anastaplo, discovered that the applicant had quoted from the Declaration of Independence about the right of the people to abolish their government if it was destructive of the ends for which it was established. The specter of Jefferson disturbed committee members, who questioned Anastaplo about membership in the Communist Party and about his belief in a Supreme Being. When he refused to answer on the ground that such questions constituted illegitimate inquiries into his political beliefs, the committee refused to certify him. The Illinois Supreme Court upheld the relevance of the inquiry for determination of Anastaplo's qualities of citizenship and affirmed. Anastaplo's appeal to the United States Supreme Court was dismissed.

In 1957, encouraged by the ray of hope cast by the first *Konigsberg* decision, Anastaplo sought a rehearing on his application. The character committee refused, but the state Supreme Court reversed and directed a rehearing. The committee again declined to certify, claiming that Anastaplo's refusal to answer was tantamount to a failure to demonstrate good character. Anastaplo argued his own case before the Illinois Supreme Court, which agreed with the bar committee that his "recalcitrance" prevented him from demonstrating good character, notwithstanding uncontroverted evidence of good character in numerous testimonials from lawyers and faculty members at the University of Chicago, where Anastaplo was teaching and studying for his doctorate. Anastaplo carried his case to the Supreme Court, again arguing his own appeal. By another 5–4 vote the Court affirmed his exclusion. Justice Harlan, relying upon [the second] *Konigsberg,* declared that the state's interest in learning about party membership out-weighed "any deterrent effect" upon the freedoms of speech and association.

To Justice Black, again in dissent, the case illustrated the consequences of permitting bar members to deny the protection of the First Amendment to applicants for admission. "To force the Bar to become a group of thoroughly orthodox, time-serving, government-fearing individuals is to humiliate and degrade it," Black wrote. "But that," he concluded, "is the present trend." Throughout the proceedings, ironically, Anastaplo had concealed his desire to retain his air force reserve commission so that he might fight against the Soviet Union if war came. Some years later Chicago law professor Malcolm Sharp would refer to Anastaplo as "the staunchest anti-Communist" he knew. After Anastaplo was expelled from the Soviet Union for taking too many photographs, Sharp observed: "The similarity between the Russian police and the

Character and Fitness Committee of the Chicago Bar must strike a detached observer."

. . . It may only be coincidental that an ethnic profile of the lawyer-defendants in admission and expulsion cases which were appealed to the Supreme Court reveals that, of a total of thirteen lawyers, there were eight Jews, two Irish Catholics, one Greek-American, and two probable Protestants—one of whom was female. Then again, it may not have been coincidental.

. . .

[Rhetoric and Reality]

There was no shortage of rhetorical obeisance to the lawyer's responsibility. . . . It was, of course, an article of professional faith that when constitutional freedoms were jeopardized established lawyers would rise to the responsibility of defending the unpopular and beleaguered.

. . .

. . . But the dismal record of the professional elite and the organized bar is beyond dispute. Grenville Clark, senior partner in the Root, Clark firm, with a long record of concern for the Bill of Rights, attributed the erosion of civil liberties to "the supineness of the organized Bar," which "appalled" him. The historian of the Association of the Bar of the City of New York . . . concluded that those lawyers "who had the courage [to defend freedom] had not the stature; and of the few who had the stature, apparently not one had the courage." A prominent Washington lawyer not only refused to take loyalty cases but declined to recommend lawyers who might do so. "I wouldn't be caught dead sending them on to another lawyer—for fear he would think I think he's a Communist, or something. I know that's bad, but most lawyers feel the same way." By the end of the Cold War decade elite irresponsibility had sifted down to law schools: among one group of law students who conceded overwhelmingly that a probable Communist was entitled to defense, only half said that they would take the case themselves. Eighty percent of those who said they would decline attributed their delinquency to the fear of unfavorable public opinion. The students had learned what their professional leaders taught.

. . . Lawyers who sought uneasily to balance their professional responsibility against their personal fear occasionally accompanied their appearance for an unpopular defendant with a statement of disaffiliation from their client's beliefs and associations in an attempt to shield themselves from the taint of their client's politics. A double standard of professional service plagued defense lawyers: they received unfavorable notoriety for efforts on behalf of political dissenters which no lawyer questioned when such efforts were made in defense of property and privilege. Elite lawyers, who split politics from professionalism whenever corporate practice was the issue, asserted the principle of guilt by association when political radicals were on trial.

[The Few Who Responded]

Evidence bearing on the motivation of lawyers who did defy professional complicity in Cold War repression is elusive and fragmentary, but it does suggest that, courage aside, professional and political marginality, reinforced by personal associations, were crucial determinants. The law firm most prominent for its defense work in loyalty cases was Arnold, Fortas & Porter, the new firm of New Deal lawyers. Its involvement may have been inadvertent; the victims of McCarthyism it represented were often Depression liberals who were referred to the firm by New Deal acquaintances of the partners. Yet there was empathy, generated by "the background and ideological identification of the members of the firm." As Fortas said: "We were 'liberals.' We were 'New Dealers.'" Renunciation of the New Deal was a primary component of Cold War politics; predictably, the most concerned law firm also was the most conspicuously New Deal firm.

But the most vigilant lawyers seldom came from prominent Washington or New York firms. They came disproportionately from among the children of politically radical parents and entered the legal profession during the Depression. They were drawn to labor law, practicing either for a CIO union or for the National Labor Relations Board. Their network of personal relationships provided contacts with labor radicals who, as targets of McCarthyism, turned to lawyer-friends for assistance. Responsive lawyers were quickly inundated; as one of them said, "if you take one or two of these cases you find you're not handling any others." These lawyers, receptive to the politics of the harassed radicals, were an alienated and disaffected professional group whose members shared similar career patterns, friendship bonds, political values, and Lawyers Guild membership. "They perceived their function in the [loyalty-security] litigation as defenders of the political left against government harassment." For some, the fusion of political commitment and professional activity offered personal fulfillment which they had never before experienced. As George Crockett told Judge Medina, in reference to his defense efforts, after his citation for contempt at the conclusion of the Smith Act trial: "For the first time in the 15 years that I have been practicing law I have had an opportunity to practice law as an American lawyer and not as a Negro lawyer. I have enjoyed that brief trip into the realm of freedom."

Occasionally a lawyer who did not fit into any of these categories emerged from obscurity to offer his services. Royal W. France had left a successful New York corporate practice in 1929 to teach economics in a Florida college. "I had become a servant, even if a highly paid one, of big business and I did not feel at home with myself." He taught for twenty years and became active in

Socialist Party politics. In 1951, nearing the age of seventy, he relinquished his second career to resume his first. Disturbed by the political climate, by the vulnerability of unpopular lawyers and defendants, and by the timidity of the bar, he returned to practice. He met with Harry Sacher and was drawn into the defense of second-string Communist Party leaders. He joined the Lawyers Guild and served on its executive board. A self-described "old fashioned type of liberal who believes that the First Amendment means what it says," he explained: "I could not be at peace with myself until I had genuinely and without reserve offered myself, at a crucial moment in history, to defend the principles which lay at the basis of my philosophy of life. To do so required defending Communists."

Measured by need there were too few New Deal firms, radical lawyers, mavericks like France, or vigilant defense organizations. The professional tone was set not by the few who responded but by the many who were silent. . . .

[Intellectual Gloss]

Even as the Cold War thawed, the political values of the professional elite remained frozen. Indeed, just as the Supreme Court showed signs of rousing itself from acquiescence in Cold War politics, influential voices on the bench and in the leading law schools articulated an ideology of professional craft and reason which added intellectual gloss to Cold War values. Their outcry was triggered by the hostile reaction to a series of decisions. . . . The first *Konigsberg* decision, in May, had marked the prelude; then in [other cases] the Court toppled important props supporting loyalty-security proceedings, sweeping forays by the House Un-American Activities Committee, and the prosecutorial zeal of the Department of Justice under the Smith Act. These decisions elicited stinging criticism from Congressional conservatives and some ABA leaders and vigorous efforts to restrict the appellate jurisdiction of the Supreme Court. . . .

A group of influential scholars . . . attempted to deflect the Supreme Court from its activist libertarian course. These spokesmen . . . remembered the attacks against the pre-New Deal Court for its conservative activism in defense of property and privilege; now they found it difficult to accept the proposition that the Court should defer to legislatures in matters of economic regulation, but aggressively protect fundamental constitutional freedoms from legislative abridgement. . . .

Learned Hand, deliver[ed] the prestigious Holmes lectures at Harvard Law School in 1958. . . . Asserting canons of judicial self-restraint which Thayer and Holmes had articulated at a much earlier time when the Court had persistently nullified social legislation, Hand was critical of broad judicial review and apprehensive about judicial choice. He advocated definitions of First Amendment freedoms and due process which did nothing more than reflect "an honest effort to embody that compromise or adjustment that will secure the widest acceptance and most avoid resentment. . . ." A judge should be "the mouthpiece of a public will, conceived as the resultant of many conflicting strains that have come, at least provisionally, to a consensus." . . .

Professor Herbert Wechsler of Columbia, who delivered the Holmes lecture the following year, shared Hand's yearning for "neutral principles" of adjudication. Wechsler wanted criteria "that can be framed and tested as an exercise of reason and not merely as an act of willfulness or will." Rejecting "*ad hoc* evaluation," which measured decisions against "the interests or the values" of personal choice, he insisted that courts must make principled decisions which rested upon "reasons that in their generality and their neutrality transcend any immediate result that is involved." Professor Henry M. Hart, Jr., of Harvard added his authoritative voice. Calling for judicial opinions "which are grounded in reason and not on mere fiat or precedent," for opinions which articulated "impersonal and durable principles," Hart, co-author of an influential text on the legal process, pleaded with the Supreme Court to be "a voice of reason." Reason, he insisted, was "the life of the law."

A school of jurisprudence had emerged that was perfectly attuned to the end-of-ideology politics of the Cold War. . . . At a deeper level it expressed what Thurman Arnold [Federal Court of Appeals judge and former Yale law professor], in a rebuttal to Hart, described as the new professional "theology." Hart had complained that a sharply divided Supreme Court, insufficiently committed to reasoned decisions, was "threatening to undermine the professional respect of first-rate lawyers." To Arnold this merely meant that corporate lawyers in the American Bar Association were critical of the Court's decisions protecting individual rights—as indeed they were—and that it was Hart's desire that the Court regain the admiration of the corporate bar. At this level, therefore, "Professor Hart's theology" not only represented an attack upon the competence of libertarian judges but an appeal to the politics of the professional elite as the valid standard of judicial decision making.

The political implications of the Hand-Wechsler-Hart doctrines, which Arnold and others spotted, were less significant than the camouflage of neutrality that disguised political preferences as reason and craft. Political disagreements were debatable. But . . . a debate over political values was transformed into a choice between politics and craft. . . .

The advocates of judicial self-restraint, neutral principles, and reasoned elaboration either did not comprehend, or could not acknowledge, that their jurisprudential preferences incorporated deeply conservative, even anti-libertarian, political values. This was not the first time in modern professional history that lawyers offered neutral principles to achieve particular results—and to preserve the powerful, magical image of their own professional skill as a mysterious science incomprehensible to unreasoning laymen.

CHAPTER 21

The Civil Rights Revolution

The Cold War was a world war in even broader terms than the two actual world wars. The end of World War II was also the beginning of the end for the empires of Britain, France, and other colonial powers. As each colony gained independence, it was pressured to join one of the Cold War camps. Some resisted alignment, proclaimed neutrality, and sought advantages from both East and West. The rivalry of the superpowers in the "Third World" largely took the form of economic and military aid, but it was also carried on by propaganda campaigns.

In the propaganda realm, the moral authority of the United States was greatly undermined by its laws and policies denying equal rights to African Americans. International pressure coincided with growing sentiment at home, as World War II caused widespread revulsion toward racism. International and domestic pressures combined to ready the nation for a revolution in civil rights.

The revolution was foreshadowed in the 1930s and 1940s. In 1935 the much publicized "Scottsboro" cases created public sympathy for nine black youths sentenced to death in Alabama after highly dubious evidence of having raped two white women. The youths' appeals to the Supreme Court brought rulings on the right to effective legal representation in capital cases and on the exclusion of blacks from juries. None of the nine defendants was executed, but some remained in prison as late as 1950. In June of 1941 President Franklin D. Roosevelt issued an executive order prohibiting discrimination in federal job-training programs and in industries working on defense contracts. President Harry Truman followed by desegregating the armed forces and establishing a blue-ribbon Committee on Civil Rights. The Committee's 1947 report, *To Secure These Rights*, was widely read. It called for equal opportunities in education, housing, and employment.

But Congress failed to translate growing public sentiment into legislation. Congressional delegations from southern states, though in the minority, had the power to block legislation through filibusters and through the control of congressional committee chairmanships based on seniority. A number of state legislatures passed antidiscrimination laws, but it was the U.S. Supreme Court that turned the creeping pace of reform into a revolution.

A carefully planned program of legal challenges by the National Association for the Advancement of Colored People (NAACP), spearheaded by future Supreme Court Justice Thurgood Marshall, began by winning modest victories. Whites-only primary elections in Texas were declared unconstitutional in *Smith v. Allwright* (1944); state laws requiring segregated seating on trains and buses were declared inapplicable to interstate carriers in *Morgan v. Virginia* (1946); and racially restrictive covenants in the sale of housing were rendered unenforceable in *Shelley v. Kraemer* (1948). The main target of the NAACP campaign, however, was segregation in education.

The segregation of education was endorsed by *dictum* in the Supreme Court's 1896 case of *Plessy v. Ferguson*. In that case, the Court accepted "separation of the races" as long as "equal" facilities were provided for blacks and whites.

The NAACP began its attack on *Plessy* at the graduate school level. The attack partially succeeded in *Sweatt v. Painter* (1950), in which the Court ordered the University of Texas Law School to admit a black applicant, Texas having failed to provide an equal law school facility for blacks. The opinion, written by Chief Justice Fred Vinson, went further in *dictum,* indicating that even if black and white law schools were provided equal physical facilities, the Court should also take into account such intangible factors as the reputations of the faculty and the influence of the alumni in determining whether the schools were truly equal.

The stage was set for an attack on the separate-but-equal doctrine itself on all levels. When the attack reached the Court in 1953, consideration was postponed for a year. During that year, Chief Justice Vinson died and was replaced by the governor of California, the Republican vice presidential candidate of 1948, Earl Warren. As his biographer, Ed Cray, describes in *Chief Justice: A Biography of Earl Warren* (1997):

The new chief justice knew where justice lay. He had come of age in a state with a long history of discrimination against Asians. In ignorance, in fear, in obedience to his perceived patriotic duty, he himself had urged the wartime confinement of those of Japanese descent. Since then, he had championed civil rights.

When the army decided to release the Japanese evacuees, Warren defended their right to live where they chose. When the National Guard's 40th Infantry Division returned to state control at war's end, he had desegregated the unit. (Proudly he claimed to be the first governor to desegregate the Guard.)

Not long after, Warren's Department of Justice chose not to appeal a federal court order that prohibited California school districts from maintaining segregated schools for "Indian children, or children of Chinese, Japanese or Mongolian parentage." (p. 278)

Remarkably, the newcomer to the Supreme Court—a court divided by serious differences in ideologies and personalities—managed to forge unanimity in overruling the separate-but-equal doctrine of *Plessy* in *Brown* v. *Board of Education of Topeka* issued on May 17, 1954. Relying heavily on social science research documenting the negative effects of segregation on black students, the Court's opinion, written by the new Chief Justice himself, forcefully declared: "Separate educational facilities are inherently unequal."

Unanimity, however, came at a cost. All justices could agree to strike down segregation in education but not on how such a decision must be implemented. The issue, therefore, was split into two and the second phase—the potentially divisive question of enforcement—was scheduled for reargument the following year.

Thurgood Marshall (standing), with attorney Charles H. Houston (right) and a client, 1935.

THE SECOND *BROWN* DECISION

from Richard Kluger, *Simple Justice: The History of Brown v.* Board of Education *and Black America's Struggle for Equality* (New York: Alfred A. Knopf, 1976), pp. 714–45. Copyright © 1975 by Richard Kluger. Reprinted by permission of Alfred A. Knopf, Inc.

One year and two weeks would pass between the Court's decision in *Brown* and its issuance of a decree explaining how it wished the process of desegregation to unfold. No one could claim the Justices were acting precipitously.

. . .

During the fifty-four-week cooling-off period between the Court's pronouncements on school segregation, rancor in the South was modulated, as the Justices had hoped, but apprehension grew rather than subsided during the long wait. The dimension of the issue at stake could not be mistaken.

. . .

[T]he school-segregation cases were not like most other cases that came to the Court. To start with, the Justices had reviewed earlier Court rulings on the question and pronounced them no longer applicable. Times and the nation had changed. The Court, then, had no ready example of its own devising to lean upon in determining how the mechanics of desegregation ought to be arranged. Beyond that was the realization that, however narrowly the Court tried to confine its implementation decree, the great social question at issue would pry it open and seek to apply it universally. . . .

Should the Court ignore, moreover, or did it really have to take cognizance of the prevailing racial attitudes in segregating communities as it handed down its orders? What judicial notice might it or should it take of the likely difference in parental responses in Topeka, where true integration would place 2 or 3 Negroes in every classroom with 22 or 23 white youngsters, and Summerton, South Carolina, where the process would place 2 or 3 white children in every classroom with 22 or 23 black youngsters? And if the Justices did recognize the difference, under what principle of law might the Court rule that the higher the ratio of black children in a school system, the longer a period of adjustment would be allowed to extend? How, indeed, could any period of delay be legally justified by the Court? Once having been told by the Court that their children had the right to attend unsegregated schools—and assume the full membership in American society emblemized by that right—most Negro families naturally wanted the process to begin as soon as possible. Every day a black youngster was denied admission to desegregated schools—and the educational advantages derived from them—was a fresh deprivation of his constitutional rights, and a day that child could not repurchase at any price.

The segregating South, for its part, wished to postpone the commanded commingling of schoolchildren as long as possible. . . . The South would yield, to be sure, but in its own sweet time. It was neither fair nor reasonable, the region indicated, to expect the South's prompt abandonment of its most strongly held customs and beliefs.

Between the newly proclaimed rights of the Negro and the freshly voided prerogatives of the South, the Supreme Court now had to negotiate without seeming to. It did not quite develop into a collision of unmovable object and irresistible force, largely because of moderating influences on both sides.

Among the more enlightened moderates on the Southern white side was Harry Ashmore, executive editor of the Arkansas *Gazette* in Little Rock, who was well regarded in the black community as a decent, liberal thinker. The day before the *Brown* decision came down from the Court, the University of North Carolina Press, probably the most broad-minded book-publishing enterprise in the South, brought out Ashmore's extremely timely book *The Negro and the Schools*. Though it carried his byline, the book was really a composite effort by forty scholars and commentators funded by the Ford Foundation. What the book had to say was immediately seized upon by both camps as the desegregation fight moved into its new phase of recommending to the Court how the process should unfold.

The depth of the American public's concern with education was what made the desegregation of schools an explosive issue, for, as Ashmore wrote, "Interest in the schools is universal, and it is an interest that directly involves not only the taxpayer but his family, and therefore his emotions. Those who are indifferent to all other community affairs tend to take a proprietary interest in the schools their children attend, or will attend, or have attended." Since that was so, said Ashmore, drawing his examples from the non-South, the most important factor in integrating the public schools was "community attitudes." He went on: "It is axiomatic that separate schools can be merged only with great difficulty, if at all, when a great majority of the citizens who support them are actively opposed to the move. No other public activity is so closely identified with local mores." The attorneys general of the South read those words, underlined them, and called them to the attention of the Supreme Court in the briefs submitted to it for the final round in *Brown*. Ashmore had based his findings on communities where segregation was not legally required but was extra-legally countenanced. How much more severe the problem of desegregation was likely to be in the South, where, without much question, "a great majority" of the citizenry actively opposed the step. The process must not be shoved down our throats, said Southern officials, invoking Ashmorean moderation.

But there was grist in Ashmore for the Negro side as well. "One thing that stands out in these case histories," he wrote, "is the frequency with which those who have had experience with integration—professional educators and laymen alike—have steeled themselves for a far more severe public reaction than they actually encountered." Not only that, but there was evidence to counter the proponents of gradualism who argued that it minimized public resistance to integration. Ashmore noted that "some school officials who have experienced it believe the reverse is true. A markedly gradual program, they contend, particularly one which involves the continued maintenance of some separate schools, invites opposition and allows time for it to be organized." Whatever the merits of the gradualist approach, it was clear that unsavory pressures mounted in the community whenever policies remained unsettled for a protracted period. It was important, furthermore, to understand that resistance to integration was not always specifically racist in origin:

> ... In many cases the basis of objection might be the demonstrable fact that the great majority of American Negroes are still slum-dwellers; many a parent who proudly considers himself wholly tolerant in racial matters will object to having his child associate with classmates of inferior economic and social background. . . .

Most of the findings in the Ashmore book were no surprise at Thurgood Marshall's NAACP Legal Defense Fund office. While Ashmore's task force of researchers was exploring the state of black education, Kenneth Clark [a psychologist who served as an expert witness in *Brown*] had undertaken a parallel effort on integration for the NAACP. . . .

Clark's most significant position, perhaps, was one that contrasted sharply with the Ashmore group's conclusions about the importance of favorable "community attitudes" as a prelude to the integration process. Where the South's lawyers latched on to this finding and cited deeply hostile community attitudes as a prime reason to delay desegregation, Clark in effect advised NAACP planners that that line of argument was so much baloney. He did not put it quite that way in his paper. What he said, in the classic jargon of his field, was: "The hypothesis that attitudinal and other subjective changes are necessary antecedents to behavioral changes is not supported by the empirical data examined in this survey. On the contrary, these data suggest that situationally determined behavioral changes generally precede any observable attitudinal changes." Translated from academese, that meant Clark found people who were faced with altered conditions were likely to change the way they acted before the way they thought. Practically speaking, that meant those opposing desegregation were likely to go along with its being imposed on them, even if they did not much like the idea, but if the process did not begin until those opposing the idea changed their minds about it, the wait might be a long one.

One of Clark's contributors, Gordon Allport of Harvard, whose major work, *The Nature of Prejudice,* had just appeared, argued that the Southern white masses knew deep down that segregation was un-American but were impaled by their own prejudices. "When we try to solve the conflict to accord with their consciences as Americans, we naturally arouse all the protests and threats and dying gasps of their prejudices," wrote Allport. "But let the backbone come from the Supreme Court, and it will strengthen the moral backbone of those who now live in conflict. . . . People do accept legislation that fortifies their inner conscience. . . . Protests are short-lived and readjustment rapidly sets in. Let the line of public morality be set by authoritative pronouncements, and all the latent good in individuals and communities will be strengthened. . . ."

. . .

Clark's findings stressed what Ashmore had far more gingerly suggested—that gradual integration could be a lot more painful than prompt and total integration. The longer the process was drawn out, the greater the likelihood that opposition would gather itself. Immediate desegregation of Catholic schools in St. Louis, for example, had been achieved more effectively than in Washington, D.C., where the process unfolded more gradually. The likelihood of violence developing, Clark added, had far less to do with the expressed racial virulence among whites prior to desegregation than with the disinclination of police to intervene effectively once the process was begun; slack law-enforcement encouraged violence. The size of an institution or jurisdiction undergoing desegregation, furthermore, had little to do with the ease or difficulty of the process. What evidence there was suggested, in fact, that the larger a community, the easier the process.

As the first Southern communities desegregated their schools voluntarily over the summer of 1954 following *Brown,* Clark monitored the process and remained in the midst of Thurgood Marshall's inner circle. First reports, mostly from the border states, were encouraging. Washington officials pushed hard to convert the capital's Jim Crow school system to an integrated one by the opening of the new term. Baltimore put its freedom-of-choice school-attendance policy on a non-racial basis, so that nearly 3,000 black students were going to previously all-white schools during the 1954–55 school year. Louisville swung over all its schools in a single semester, and St. Louis spread the process over two. Twenty-five counties in West Virginia, eleven junior colleges in Texas, and one small community in Arkansas desegregated. And in Delaware, Wilmington and other places where 28 percent of the state's Negro population lived began the process.

One of the more unlikely communities in Delaware to have started racially mixing its schoolchildren before it had to was the little agricultural town of

Milford in downstate, Southern-minded Sussex County. The Milford board of education opened up a white school to ten Negroes. In no time, a strong resistance movement developed. More than 1,500 whites attended a heated rally at the local American Legion Hall, picketing began, and violence threatened. Black leaders were asked to consider withdrawing the Negro youngsters voluntarily, but they declined, arguing that with desegregation about to begin in many places, it was essential for the first blacks who experienced the abuse of die-hards to stand fast and not be intimidated. The local school board, fearing the worst, closed the schools temporarily and appealed to state authorities to intervene. Milford looked like a test-tube example of the sort of resistance that might lie ahead in the surliest sectors of the Southland. The NAACP dispatched Kenneth Clark to investigate toward the end of September.

Aside from being trailed in a car soon after reaching the area, Clark suffered no firsthand brushes with lawlessness, but he caught more than a whiff of the mob in the Milford air. His talks with local officials, black leaders and students, and some of the more brutish white element reconfirmed his faith in the conclusions he had reached. . . . Indecisive in the face of heavily marshaled and vocal opposition, the Milford school board had succumbed to the threat of violence. Bloodshed was prevented not so much by the board's backing down in the face of the mob as by a firm law-and-order stand by the Milford mayor and police chief. The black youngsters themselves had been received without friction at the formerly all-white school, but adult pro-segregationists fanned the flames from the sidelines as local and then, more damagingly, state officials wavered. The lessons of Milford, Delaware, were clear to Clark as he reported back to Marshall after his three-day mission to the front lines: only unflinching community leadership, strictly enforcing its will and policy, would assure successful desegregation in areas of entrenched enmity to the changeover.

. . .

Clark's recommendation . . . was both legally and emotionally justifiable, but it struck [Columbia law professor and NAACP legal advisor Jack] Weinstein, for one, as perhaps rather rash and, in the long run, perhaps not the most prudent course. He shared his concerns with his erstwhile Columbia associate Charles Black, Jr., who had moved to Yale:

> . . . Kenneth [Clark], as you know, takes the position that it is unwise to attempt any preparation of the people in a locality for desegregation. He feels that a direct order from above, calling for immediate desegregation, is best. I have a good deal of doubt about his conclusion, not only because its implications with respect to the democratic process against authoritarianism is quite disturbing, but because I think his data is far from conclusive. In this respect, I think we must consider not only recent examples but also what happened after the Civil War.

Marshall himself was admittedly uncertain about whether to take the militant route and demand immediate desegregation across the board . . . or to return to the Court with a more moderate, gradualist position. His own instincts were for the former, but the constitutional lawyer in him argued that the Justices would surely look more kindly on the NAACP's brief if it took a "realistic" view. . . .

NAACP branches throughout the South were due to report to Marshall by the beginning of October on desegregation attitudes and progress, if any, in their areas. He wanted as wide a sampling as possible before settling on a policy that was to be more than mere personal willfulness. His task was made no easier in mid-October by a pair of back-to-back letters he received from William Coleman, who . . . was [one of] the advisor[s] he leaned on most heavily. Coleman sent him a rough draft for a section of the implementation brief and tried to work it around Kenneth Clark's data and conclusions. But his own effort, in Coleman's opinion, was a failure because "I just cannot bring myself to stress that material in the brief since I think it will not persuade the Court and, in fact, will irritate it. . . ." After staying awake half the next night, Coleman dispatched a longer, stronger letter to Marshall. In it, he said he kept coming back to the position that "we would be much better off under a decree which would permit the States to file for Court approval plans which would permit . . . gradual effective transition."

Coleman proceeded to spell out how it might well be to the NAACP's advantage to take the gradualist view, though on the face of it that might seem the timid course. The Court, he noted, had exercised "great statesmanship." . . . Similar statesmanship on the NAACP's part would require the black camp to offer a delay in the swingover to integrated schools instead of demanding it at once. Such a show of sweet reasonableness might very well help lure the Southern states into submitting plans and a timetable of their own for carrying out desegregation instead of truculently resisting NAACP demands for immediate integration and obliging the Court to impose a program of its own upon defiant multitudes. If the South went for the bait, "the Court would feel that the [state] officials would be in the position where they would have to carry out the plans since they could not argue impossibility, the plans being their own."

It was a shrewd and accurate reading of the . . . strategy [eventually adopted by Chief Justice Earl Warren]. And it was clearly advice that Coleman did not relish giving. "God knows that I am not a gradualist," he wrote, but he thought "it would be a pyrrhic victory to get a forthwith decree and yet two or three years will elapse before the first child goes to a school in South Carolina on a non-segregated basis. . . . I realize that as a great constitutional lawyer who has spent the major part of his adult life . . . trying to establish the principles which the Court finally accepted, it is difficult for you to even contemplate taking a position which would be construed as a retreat." But in his own judgment, Coleman concluded, it was not a retreat but calculated wisdom.

The South, digging in for the siege, was beset by no such nuanced skull-wracking. Anger and frustration were apparent in the last-ditch briefs that began moving to the Court in mid-November from the attorneys general of the Southern states which were participating in the final round of argument. Virginia, proud and unapologetic throughout the litigation, perhaps best relayed the region's sentiments.

The Court's May 17 decision had been based not on solid reasoning or legal precedent but on "psychological evidence," Virginia charged. And so long as the Court was so concerned with the psyche, it had best consider also the state of mind of white Virginians who "feel a sense of bewilderment that traditions and systems that have operated with judicial approval since 1870, and, in fact, since 1619, can be so readily swept away." More than time would be needed to bring about integrated education in Virginia: "It will require a complete change in the feelings of the people," the brief declared and invoked the Ashmore book on the importance of favorable community attitudes as a prelude to successful desegregation. As a measure of the depth of hostility to the Court's decision, the brief cited the text of a resolution, passed two months after *Brown* came down, by the Prince Edward Board of Supervisors, the county's governing body, stating that it was "unalterably opposed to the operation of nonsegregated public schools in the Commonwealth of Virginia," that it believed the operation of such schools to be not only impractical but impossible in Virginia, and that it intended to use "its power, authority and efforts to insure a continuation of a segregated school system. . . ." More than half the counties in the state had passed such resolutions by the time the Court heard the final round of arguments.

. . . Virginia . . . urged the Court to consider "the general level of educational capacity and attainment between the two races" as well as "general standards of health and morals." And it trotted out statistics to reinforce the unmistakable innuendo that Negroes were a lower order of humanity. In standard eighth-grade silent-reading tests given to 31,000 Virginia schoolchildren of both races, the lowest quarter of the white test group performed at a higher level than the top quarter of the Negro group. In IQ tests given to Virginia high-school seniors, the bottom quarter of the whites averaged 71.2 while the highest quarter of the Negro group averaged 63.9. Tuberculosis, an infectious disease, was twice as prevalent among Negroes as among whites, and Negroes, composing 22 percent of Virginia's population, contracted about 80 percent of all reported cases of venereal disease in the state. One out of every fifty white children born in Virginia was illegitimate; one out of five black children was.

That the degrading treatment in the form of economic, political, and social exploitation suffered by Virginia's Negroes for nearly three and a half centuries had been the white population's lasting contribution to those statistics was in no way acknowledged, of course. Nor was there any reference to figures just released by the federal government stating that it would cost $2 billion to bring black school buildings up to the level of white ones throughout the segregating South—and that current operating budgets would have to rise by $200 million a year to equalize teaching, transportation, and supplies at the nation's colored schools. What Virginia did say quite eloquently was that the Court must not set a deadline for the desegregation process, but "must permit a now indeterminable period to elapse before requiring integration of the races in Virginia's public schools." The state had "no plan or panacea that will result in complete solution of this problem. We do not foresee a complete solution at any future time."

Of the six segregating states that chose to join the final *Brown* argument— Arkansas, Florida, Maryland, North Carolina, Oklahoma, and Texas— Florida submitted the most extensive and spirited brief and offered some wrinkles that seemed to have been beneath Virginia's dignity.

Like the Old Dominion, Florida pursued the "community attitudes" argument that Ashmore's non-partisan group had espoused. The only hope to end segregated schooling in the Sunshine State without destroying public education itself was for "the Court to restrain the use of coercive measures where necessary until the hard core of public opinion has softened. . . ." After all, the school-segregation law had been "rigidly" enforced for the previous sixty-nine years in Florida, and "an immediate inrush of turbulent ideas" might cause "a tornado which would devastate the entire school system"—easily the best use of regional imagery in any of the Southern briefs. But this entire line of argument that a change in public opinion had to precede desegregation failed to acknowledge that if hostile public opinion might alone justify delaying the integration process, the hostility was likely to prove permanent.

To measure public opinion, Florida spent $10,000 on a poll which showed that three-quarters of "the white leaders" in the state disagreed in principle with the *Brown* decision, that 30 percent disagreed "violently," and—most ominous—only 13 percent of the peace officers polled said they would enforce state attendance laws at racially mixed schools. Only time would change matters, Florida said and cited many instances in which the Court had granted a good deal of time for the implementation of its decrees. These ranged from eight months in the 1911 antitrust case of *United States v. American Tobacco Company* to nine years in the so-called *Gaseous Nuisance Cases* that began in 1907 when Justice Holmes, writing for the Court, granted the Tennessee Copper Company "a reasonable time" to complete plant changes that would reduce the gaseous discharges destroying forest, orchard, and crop lands in five counties of Georgia.

The South's skill at erecting legal barriers to slow the desegregation process was foreshadowed by Florida's suggested "plan" to implement the Court's decision. Under it, even the most ungainly camel in Islam would have had an easier time passing through the eye of a needle than a black child getting into a white school in Florida. First, the petitioner would have had to show that admission to the white school had been sought within a "reasonable" (unde-fined) time before the beginning of the school term and that "all other admin-istrative remedies such as appeal to the State Board of Education" had been exhausted in the event the local school board turned down the petitioning black schoolchild. Then "the court of first instance" (presumably the U.S. Dis-trict Court) would conduct hearings and take testimony to determine, among other things, whether (1) state school authorities and the legislature had had "a reasonable amount of time" (undefined) to reorganize the state school structure; (2) sufficient progress had been made to overcome "practical, ad-ministrative problems" that naturally arose in integrating schools; (3) citizens' educational and interracial committees were improving the climate of racial relations in the communities affected in litigation; (4) "a strong degree of sin-cere opposition and sustained hostility on the part of the public to granting the petitioner's application . . . would [not] cause a disruption of the school system or create emotional responses among the children which would seri-ously interfere with their education"; (5) the black petitioner's application "was made in good faith and not for capricious reasons" and was "not moti-vated . . . solely by a desire for the advancement of a racial group on eco-nomic, social or political grounds, as distinguished from his personal legal right to equality in public school education. . . ." Throughout this obstacle course, the burden of proof would have rested entirely upon the Negro peti-tioner, while local and state officials would have had a vast repertoire of vague and arbitrary standards at their disposal to thrust into the desegregation ma-chinery anywhere along the line and jam it.

Having proposed that horror chamber of legal restraints, Florida then wound up its brief by asserting, "The Court stands not in need of the whip and the scourge of compulsion to drive our people to obedience. . . ."

. . .

Mediating between the positions of the Southern states, which did not want the Court to tell them when or how to desegregate, and the Negro plaintiffs in *Brown,* who insisted that the process begin by the fall term of 1955 and be completed by the fall term of 1956—the compromise position that Marshall reached . . . —was the United States government. The final U.S. brief in *Brown* took essentially the . . . position . . . [that] the Court could be flexible in set-ting down a timetable for desegregation and ought to let the District Courts oversee the process, since they were a lot closer to varying local conditions that might dictate a faster or slower pace. In urging the Court to bear in mind that school segregation was not an isolated phenomenon but "part of a larger social pattern of racial relationships," the . . . government brief in *Brown* stressed that the Justices had best proceed cautiously since the social institu-tion they had just outlawed had "existed for a long time in many areas throughout the country." Precisely at that point in the brief, an insertion was apparently made by the President of the United States, according to Anthony Lewis, who covered the Supreme Court for the *New York Times* and says he saw Mr. [Dwight D.] Eisenhower's handwriting on a draft copy of the Justice Department's brief. Eisenhower, according to Lewis, made this contribution to the brief:

> —an institution, it may be noted, which during its existence not only has had the sanction of decisions of this Court but has been fervently supported by great numbers of people as justifiable on legal and moral grounds. The Court's holding in the present cases that segregation is a denial of constitutional rights involved an express recognition of the importance of psychological and emotional factors; the impact of segregation upon children, the Court found, can so affect their lives as to preclude their full enjoyment of constitutional rights. In similar fashion, psychological and emotional factors are involved—and must be met with understanding and good will—in the alterations that must now take place in order to bring about compliance with the Court's decision.

The wording was almost surely drafted by White House lawyers, or perhaps Attorney General [Herbert] Brownell himself, but the sentiment accurately reflected the hands-off-the-South attitude that President Eisenhower would exhibit throughout his White House tenure.

But the American government's brief was hardly an open invitation to Southern defiance of the Court's decision. "Popular hostility, where found to exist, is a problem that needs to be recognized and faced with understanding," said the brief, . . . "but it can afford no legal justification for a failure to end school segregation. Racial segregation in public schools is unconstitutional and will have to be terminated as quickly as feasible, regardless of how much it may be favored by some people in the community. There can be no 'local option' on that question, which has now been finally settled by the tribunal empowered under the Constitution to decide it." Citizen-education programs, pupil-placement tests, and remedial instruction were among the steps suggested to facilitate the civic and administrative problems the process was likely to bring.

The government's key suggestion to the Court was not to enslave itself to the calendar. Surely the Court ought to make clear to segregating school districts that they could not delay integration indefinitely, but "we do not think it would be feasible" for the Justices to specify outside time limits to the desegregation process. "Apart from the fact that there is no way of judging at this point what integration will involve in the particular area," said the brief, "maximum periods tend to become minimum periods. The Court should not enter any order which might have the practical effect of slowing down desegregation where it could be swiftly accomplished." In other words, setting a deadline had the negative effect of encouraging segregation to continue until the last minute.

What the Court ought to do, said the government, is to insist upon "an immediate and substantial start toward desegregation" everywhere. The lower courts should at once direct the defendant school boards "to submit within 90 days a plan for ending, as soon as feasible, racial segregation of pupils in public schools, subject to their authority or control." The burden should be on the defendants "on the question of whether, and how long, an interval of time in carrying out full desegregation is required." The lower courts should require the defendant school districts to submit detailed periodic reports showing the progress made in ending segregation. Finally:

> The responsibility for achieving compliance with the Court's decision in these cases does not rest on the judiciary alone. Every officer and agency of government, federal, state, and local, is likewise charged with the duty of enforcing the Constitution and the rights guaranteed under it. . . .

The command of this concluding passage, ensuing events would suggest, seemed to have escaped the attention of the President of the United States. The NAACP's hopes that at least some of the Southern states might submit a desegregation plan to the Court were unfulfilled on the eve of the final round of argument in *Brown*. The closest thing to a plan was Florida's blueprint for intransigence, which the NAACP's reply brief called "not a plan for granting rights, but a plan for denying them just as long as can possibly be done without a direct overruling of the May 17th ruling." Indeed, all that the Southern states seemed to care about in their remarks to the Court, the NAACP argued, were reasons for delaying desegregation: ". . . the affirmative problem gets virtually no attention."

But the settlement of Negro rights could not be postponed, the NAACP brief insisted. Nor was there any reason "for supposing that delay can minimize whatever unpleasant consequences might follow from the eradication of this great evil"—a view that clearly reflected Kenneth Clark's thinking. To the contention that community attitudes in the South had to change before integration could be contemplated, the NAACP said that this was no more than arguing that desegregation should be delayed "just as long as the conditions exist which [the South] formerly regarded as sufficient grounds for imposing segregation as a matter of legal right." In short, the whites wanted to keep denying the blacks their rights until the former, of their own volition, decided to stop the bullying. It was not sufficient for the South that the Court had commanded the practice to cease.

That the Court's decision would have wide effects on the public school systems of many states was no reason to delay granting the "personal and present rights" of the black plaintiffs, the NAACP brief insisted. There was obviously nothing in "mere numerousness as such which has any tendency whatever to create or destroy rights to efficacious legal relief. Behind every numeral is a Negro child, suffering the effects spoken of by the Court on May 17. It is a manifest inconsequence to say that the rights or remedial needs of each child are diminished merely because others are in the same position." In response to

Virginia's contention that Negro children on average had far lower academic and moral standards, the NAACP brief lashed back: "That the Negro is so disadvantaged educationally and culturally in the states where segregation is required is the strongest argument against its continuation for any period of time. Yet those who use this argument as a basis for interminable delay in the elimination of segregation in reality are seeking to utilize the product of their own wrongdoing as a justification for continued malfeasance." Besides, average differences in student groups had no relevance to the individual rights of pupils; current academic disabilities could be compensated for through homogeneous grouping of students by academic proficiency and other administrative measures. No excuses could be tolerated for postponing the enjoyment of constitutional rights once declared by the Court, for the Constitution was not a document that applied in some sections of the country more than others. Beyond that, *Brown* was a great beacon in the black man's struggle for equality, the NAACP said in its last written words in the school-segregation cases, because

> ... The fate of other great constitutional freedoms, whether secured by the Fourteenth Amendment or by other provisions, is inevitably bound up in the resolution to be made in these cases. For delay in enforcement of these rights invites the insidious prospect that a moratorium may equally be placed on the enjoyment of other constitutional rights.

Still riding on the momentum of the May 1954 decision, Marshall and his associates performed with marked confidence and vigor in the final round of argument before the Court that began on April 11, 1955, and lasted for thirteen hours and twenty minutes spaced over four days.

. . .

The members of the Court had been contemplating the implementation problem for the better part of two years when they assembled after the . . . argument. . . . They looked naturally now to the Chief Justice as their leader.

. . .

[In the summer of 1954] Warren [had] designated six clerks to prepare an advisory report on desegregation and how it might best be accomplished. The group . . . worked away at the project throughout the 1954 Term, absorbing all available literature and undertaking fresh research, such as mapping out every home in a typical Southern city—Spartanburg, third-largest city in South Carolina, was the guinea pig—to see how readily the existing white and colored school districts could be integrated. They also developed eight other maps of school tax and attendance districts in six other states to demonstrate to the Justices the effects of various desegregation plans. The day before the Court heard the final round of oral arguments, the clerks filed their recommendations with the Court. . . .

On the crucial question of timing . . . the clerks were of four different minds. One clerk opposed all gradualism; he argued that it would be an extreme injustice to condemn half a generation of Negro schoolchildren to a segregated system, would "greatly weaken the Court's moral position," and would not pacify militant segregationists. The other five clerks agreed that a Court order of immediate desegregation was "impractical" and was likely to be ignored by almost all elements in the South as clearly arbitrary and unreasonable. On the other hand, all five clerks felt that "the mere passage of time without any guidance and requirements by the courts produces rather than reduces friction. It smacks of indecisiveness, and gives the extremists more time to operate." One of the five clerks thought it best to leave the matter of timing entirely in the hands of the District Courts "in light of local conditions and sentiment." Another of the five, while encouraging immediate compliance, would have allowed school districts to submit plans contemplating no desegregation at all for several years just so long as the process itself was completed within twelve years (i.e., one full school cycle). The three remaining clerks opposed that drawn-out scheme on the ground that "we see nothing to be gained by sanctioning years of inaction; we fear that this would increase opposition, inhibit communities ready to move more quickly, and insult those officials who have already begun to desegregate." This trio favored, instead, allowing segregated school districts one year of grace, during which they did not have to do any integrating at all but could complete whatever planning and administrative changes were necessary; after the year, though, they would have to take some "immediate" steps toward desegregation that would be sufficient to support a finding by the supervising District Courts of good-faith compliance. Even if the desegregating districts then proceeded at the pace of only one class per year, consuming twelve years to integrate their entire systems, that would be permissible, though the Court should not advertise so conciliatory an attitude in its decree.

Among those most interested in the clerks' efforts was Felix Frankfurter, who had been pondering the mechanics of desegregation and passing around memos on the subject to his brethren for a year and a half. An early advocate of the idea that the Court might appoint "masters" to oversee the desegregation process, Frankfurter had apparently backed off from that notion by November of 1954, when he drafted a proposed decree that favored returning the cases to the District Courts, which would work out detailed decrees that "should take into account prevailing local attitudes and customs, but in no event may the desegregation process take longer than one school cycle of twelve years." He had not made up his mind to the wisdom of having the lower courts establish a terminal date in their decrees, but he called for periodic progress reports to be made to the courts by desegregating school boards, which were to establish "compact, nongerrymandered districts" and not to refuse Negro students admission "to any school where they are situated similarly to white students in respect to distance from school, natural or manmade barriers or hazards, and other relevant educational criteria."

By April 14, 1955, at the close of the Court's marathon final oral arguments in *Brown*, Frankfurter had composed a final memo to his fellow Justices that included some of the language from his memo of the previous November, including his conviction that the Court must not function as a "super-school board" in monitoring the desegregation process. . . .

The Justices convened in conference on April 16, 1955, to try to settle the delicate and highly ramified issue. Earl Warren, presiding, showed in his opening remarks that he had picked and chosen eclectically from the blended caution and resoluteness of the Justice Department brief, from the bifurcated conclusions of the six-clerk research committee the Court had appointed, from the canny ruminations of Felix Frankfurter, from the fervent fears of the Court's Southern contingent . . . and from the most astute outside commentators on the problem, such as Harry Ashmore. [Warren's] suggestions, as recorded in the notes of Burton and Frankfurter, leave little doubt that he was the Court's driving force in resolving the Brown decree.

. . .

What the Chief Justice did favor was a combined opinion and decree citing a number of factors that the courts below should take into consideration. This would be a more useful mechanism than a formal decree, for it would give the lower courts guidance without too narrowly circumscribing them. It would be "rather cruel" to shift the burden of implementation back to the lower courts and let them flounder without any guidelines from above. Among the factors he would suggest that the lower courts take into consideration were financial problems and problems involving the physical plant within any given school district; he would not suggest mentioning "psychological" or "sociological" attitudes. In approving any plan offered by a desegregating district, the lower court had to consider whether a serious effort was being made to get the process started and whether genuine progress was being made. Overall, the Court's main goal should be, according to Burton's notes of the Chief's remarks: "Give District Courts as much latitude as we can but also as much support as we can."

Hugo Black, speaking second, told the conference that he had no fixed ideas, either, but the ones he did have were somewhat different from the Chief Justice's. One thing he was sure of, though: the Court should do "everything possible to achieve a unanimous result" in settling the matter.

In general, according to Burton, Black thought that "the less we say, the better off we are." He was brought up in an atmosphere distinctly hostile to federal officials, he said, and the Deep South was only just beginning to manifest respect for their authority; the caution of the region was rooted in the race question, and what progress there had been would be dissipated if the desegregation process was forced harshly upon the South. One of his law clerks came from Lowndes County, outside of Montgomery, Alabama, said Black, and was convinced that Negro and white children would not go to school together "in this generation." Frankfurter's notes have Black saying: "Nothing more important than that this Court should not issue what it cannot enforce." The Court, he said, should take a lesson from Prohibition, which the government had finally abandoned because of its unenforceability. It was futile, moreover, for the Court to think that in these cases, at a single stroke, "we can settle segregation in the South." . . . He had little confidence in leaving the whole question in the laps of the District Courts, said Black, because he knew all the Southern judges in the federal system and none of them, so far as he could tell, was in favor of the Court's *Brown* decision. The best that the Court could hope for at the moment, he foresaw, was glacial movement in the integration process.

. . .

Sherman Minton, like Hugo Black, said he thought it vital that the Court remain unanimous in this phase of the case. He felt it important that they not talk big in the opinion and small in the decree—that would be weaseling, he said. The Court's main goal should be to get the desegregation process started without, in the process, revealing its own impotence to make it happen.

The newcomer to the Court, John Marshall Harlan, was not reticent. . . . He thought the Justices might be mistaken in underestimating the value of a gracefully written opinion to transmit the Court's basic approach to the whole issue in preference to handing down a decree that might come across as too cold and heavy-handed. Harlan favored combining the opinion and decree in a single statement that placed no time limit on desegregation.

That matter of the time limit remained the most difficult one of all. Any date was necessarily an arbitrary one. Any date, except perhaps one in the twenty-first century, was certain to antagonize the South. And wholesale defiance of whatever date the Justices might settle on would gravely undermine the authority of the Court and the entire judicial system. But what kind of equal justice under law was it that granted some Americans their rights but then told them they would have to wait a while, perhaps a long while, before they might exercise them? Thurgood Marshall's words could not be tuned out. The very numerousness of Negroes should not be used against them to postpone their rights. The objection of whites to having their children mingle with colored children was not a valid reason to hold off the process.

And yet more than reason was involved here, as all the Court grasped. The Justices stood at the very interface of man's susceptibility to destructive private impulse and his longing for reasoned social order. . . . Unless the two forces are resolved, chaos follows. But law, in a democracy, cannot impose that resolution by the force of the state alone. Democracy is too unruly for that. That is its great weapon against the would-be tyrant; that is the agony it imposes on the most enlightened reformer. Law in a democracy must contend with reality. It has to persuade. It has to induce compliance by its appeal to shared human values and social goals. How well law succeeds in winning, however reluctantly, the abandonment of unjust private advantage is perhaps the severest, and best, measure of that society's humanity. Few nations in history have ever aspired to such a massive reconciliation of public needs and private impulses. It is, frankly, a cumbersome process; no ruler would turn to it gladly. Yet America has known no other, and perhaps no other process is possible in so pluralistic a society. But the process breaks down without leaders who understand that it must be primed and lubricated to function well. Earl Warren was such a leader. . . .

In settling down to the punishing task of drafting an opinion of the Court, Earl Warren seized upon a phrase far too subtle to have been his own invention but one that he recognized as useful in solving the dilemma of how to spur the desegregation process without fixing a firm timetable for its completion. In the first argument of the cases in 1952, the U.S. government brief had suggested that the Court might instruct segregating school districts to abolish the practice "with deliberate speed."

. . .

Whatever the precise genesis of the phrase, it appealed to Warren when Frankfurter suggested its appropriateness to *Brown*. The ironic use in combination of contradictory or incongruous words for epigrammatic effect—such as "cruel kindness" or "wise fool"—is a rhetorical device known to linguists as "oxymoron." Though this sort of thing was normally as foreign to Earl Warren's guileless writing as a horde of umlauts, it appealed to him, he later explained, "because we realized that under our federal system there were so many blocks preventing an immediate solution of the thing in reality that the best we could look for would be a progression of action—and to keep it going, in a proper manner, we adopted that phrase." Perhaps, too, the phrase seemed an apt description of the pace set by the tortoise in his fabled race with the hare; and the tortoise, moving with all deliberate speed, of course triumphed.

On May 31, 1955, the last day of the 1954 Term, Chief Justice Earl Warren delivered the unanimous opinion of the Supreme Court implementing its previous decision in *Brown v. Board of Education*. It ran just seven paragraphs. Nowhere in it did the words "segregation" or "desegregation" appear.

Warren began by recalling the Court's opinion of May 17, 1954, "declaring the fundamental principle that racial discrimination in public education is unconstitutional" and added: "All provisions of federal, state, or local law requiring or permitting such discrimination must yield to this principle."

Then he turned to the manner in which relief was to be accorded. He noted that the Court had found it "informative and helpful" to hear from a number of states in its consideration of the complexities involved in the "transition to a system of public education freed of racial discrimination." Substantial steps toward that goal had already been taken by several states, Warren also noted. And then he got to the nuts and bolts of the problem. First, the Chief Justice established firmly that the Court was not about to usurp local prerogatives in commanding the end of segregation:

> Full implementation of these constitutional principles may require solution of varied local school problems. School authorities have the primary responsibility for

elucidating, assessing, and solving these problems; courts will have to consider whether the action of school authorities constitutes good faith implementation of the governing constitutional principles. Because of their proximity to local conditions and the possible need for further hearings, the courts which originally heard these cases can best perform this judicial appraisal. Accordingly, we believe it appropriate to remand the cases to those courts.

The opinion then walked the tightrope between acknowledging the relevance of community attitudes and yielding to them the right to delay the exercise of anybody's constitutional rights. The courts below, in fashioning their decrees, Warren wrote, were to be guided by "equitable principles" that traditionally had been marked by "a practical flexibility" in the shaping of remedies. At stake in the cases before them was "the personal interest of the plaintiffs in admission to public schools as soon as practicable on a nondiscriminatory basis." But "practicable" was a relative term:

> . . . To effectuate this interest may call for elimination of a variety of obstacles. . . . Courts of equity may properly take into account the public interest in the elimination of such obstacles in a systematic and effective manner. But it should go without saying that the vitality of these constitutional principles cannot be allowed to yield simply because of disagreement with them.

The courts below were then ordered to "require that the defendants make a prompt and reasonable start toward full compliance with our May 17, 1954 ruling." Once that start had been made, additional time might be granted for carrying out the desegregation process in an effective manner, but the burden would then rest with the defendants to show that the extension was "in the public interest and is consistent with good faith compliance at the earliest practicable date." Among the "problems related to administration" that the courts were free to consider in determining the timetable were those "arising from the physical condition of the school plant, the school transportation system, personnel, revision of school districts and attendance areas into compact units to achieve a system of determining admission to the public schools on a nonracial basis, and revision of local laws and regulations which may be necessary in solving the foregoing problems." (The opinion said nothing about community attitudes or public opinion.) During the transition period, the courts below were to retain jurisdiction of the cases. Finally, the Court wound up with its ambiguous catch phrase that told the nation to make haste slowly in this momentous business:

> . . . [T]he cases are remanded to the District Courts to take such proceedings and enter such orders and decrees consistent with this opinion as are necessary and proper to admit to public schools on a racially nondiscriminatory basis with all deliberate speed the parties to these cases.

CHAPTER 22

The Warren Court

The Supreme Court's caution in separating the implementation phase of the *Brown* decision and the moderation of its "all deliberate speed" decree paid off in some states—largely in border states—where steps were taken without delay and without turmoil toward the integration of schools. But much of the white South resisted, some to the point of violence, and many political leaders who had the potential to calm the situation—through persuasion or the exercise of legal authority—either did little or actively abetted opposition to the Court's decision. President Eisenhower commented that morality cannot be changed by law, and all but three members of Congress from southern states signed a "manifesto" in opposition to the *Brown* decision. State governments throughout the South took action to thwart desegregation. At the extreme, some localities abolished public education, extending encouragement to segregated private schools.

Those calling for resistance to *Brown* warned that the attack on segregation was not going to stop at schools—and they were right. The year following the *Brown* decision, a black boycott in Montgomery, Alabama, under the leadership the young Reverend Martin Luther King, Jr., desegregated local buses, and federal court opinions from 1955 to 1958 ordered the desegregation of other public facilities such as parks, beaches, and public libraries.

But the focus remained on education, and that issue came to a climax in 1957. When mob violence in Little Rock, Arkansas, prevented the implementation of a federal court order to integrate the local high school, President Eisenhower reluctantly sent federal troops to restore order. Other federal enforcement activity followed the inauguration of John F. Kennedy as president in 1961. State universities in Mississippi and Alabama were ordered by federal courts to admit black applicants in 1962 and 1963, but it took federal troops in both instances to enforce compliance.

The Kennedy administration, however, was slow to take new initiatives as black protests mounted and white reaction became more and more repressive. Following nonviolent tactics espoused by Martin Luther King, Jr., college students organized "sit ins" at segregated lunch counters in North Carolina; "freedom riders" challenged segregated bus terminals throughout the South; and Martin Luther King., Jr., himself led boycotts and marches in Birmingham, Alabama. After a Birmingham march was brutally attacked by police, protest marches spread to other cities.

In this atmosphere of tension, the Kennedy administration called on Congress in 1963 to enact a Civil Rights Act "to move this problem from the streets to the courts." The act did not pass until after the assassination of President Kennedy when, on a wave of sympathy, Congress not only enacted the act but strengthened it as proposed by the new president, Lyndon B. Johnson, formerly a senator from Texas and one of the three southern congressmen who did not sign the 1954 anti-*Brown* manifesto. The sympathy vote carried over to the election of 1964, which Johnson won overwhelmingly.

In the following years, racial tensions erupted into destructive riots in Los Angeles, Newark, and other cities. Impatient with slow progress, some civil-rights leaders called for "black power" and the abandonment of Dr. King's program of nonviolence. After another police attack on a peaceful civil-rights march—in Selma, Alabama—Congress passed the Voting Rights Act of 1965, and voting registration became a focus of the civil-rights movement. Growing black electoral strength led to more moderate voices in politics—and some black elected officials. Throughout the nation, affirmative-action programs were adopted, through litigation or voluntarily, to help overcome the affects of past or continuing racial discrimination in education, employment, and government contracting. In 1968 Congress passed a new Civil Rights Act—the last major legislative achievement of the Johnson presidency in civil rights. But 1969 brought a marked change in the nation with the retirement of Chief Justice Earl Warren and the inauguration of Richard Nixon as president.

The decision in *Brown* v. *Board of Education* was the emblematic achievement of the Warren Court, but the years between 1954 and 1969 saw many other historic decisions. Especially productive was the year 1962: In *Baker* v. *Carr*, the Court required the reapportionment of state legislative districts to give equal weight to urban and rural voters; in *Engel* v. *Vitale*, officially mandated school prayer was declared unconstitutional; and in *Russell* v. *United States*, the Court struck down the contempt convictions of six witnesses who refused to cooperate with the House Un-American Activities Committee. Among other highlights of the era, the Court, in *Roth* v. *United* States (1957) and subsequent cases, abandoned the legal definition of "obscenity" inherited from the Victorian era and, instead, took into account "contemporary community standards," the "dominant theme of the material as a whole," and the material's "redeeming social value." In 1964 the Court overturned an Alabama libel award to a police chief who was criticized in an advertisement for subjecting civil-rights activists to a "wave of terror;" the case, *New York Times* v. *Sullivan* (1964), increased constitutional protection for criticism of public figures. In *Griswold* v. *Connecticut* (1965), the Court struck down a Connecticut statute prohibiting contraception, finding a "right to privacy" in "penumbras" and "emanations" of the Constitution.

The pathbreaking opinions of the Warren Court led to billboards calling for the impeachment of Chief Justice Warren. The decisions also presented a challenge for legal theorists. The Court's grafting of right after right onto the Constitution raised questions about the sources of the rights and about the Court's authority to declare them. The Court's innovations clashed with the positions of those—such as Professor Herbert Wechsler—who urged judges to limit their decisions to "neutral principles" and leave questions involving value choices to legislatures. Other critics of judicial innovation—such as Professors Henry M. Hart, Jr., and Albert Sacks—emphasized institutional divisions of authority and respect for "legal process," but they left some room for judicial decisions to reflect changing social policies if supported by "reasoned elaboration." Yet others—most notably Professors John Rawls and Ronald Dworkin—came to the Court's defense, articulating a theory of "fundamental rights" based on the "shared values" of the community as legitimate sources for innovative decisions by the judiciary.

Criticism of the Court's "activism" increased as the Court sparked another "revolution" described in *Popular Justice: A History of American Criminal Justice* (1980) by Samuel Walker:

> The U.S. Supreme Court, in a series of landmark decisions, reexamined the entire criminal-justice system in the 1960s. Under the leadership of Chief Justice Earl Warren, the Court greatly expanded the rights of individuals and placed limitations on the power of criminal-justice officials. Together these decisions constituted a "due-process revolution," the introduction of a new era of individual rights into the administration of criminal justice. (pp. 229–30)

The "revolution" in criminal law included *Mapp* v. *Ohio* (1961), holding evidence uncovered in the course of an illegal police search inadmissible in a state criminal proceeding; *Gideon* v. *Wainwright* (1963), granting indigent defendants the right to court-appointed counsel in felony cases; *Escobedo* v. *Illinois* (1964), holding a confession obtained before the defendant was allowed to see his attorney inadmissible; and *Miranda* v. *Arizona* (1966), requiring police to inform suspects of their rights. Many criticized these decisions for "coddling criminals" and "tying the hands of the police" and, on a more fundamental level, for overruling precedents and altering the relation-ship between the states and the federal government.

The case of *Gideon* v. *Wainwright* received special attention from *New York Times* columnist Anthony Lewis. In an absorbing account that has become a classic, he set forth the issues at stake in the case. The surface issue was clear enough. The precedent challenged in *Gideon* was the 1942 decision in *Betts* v. *Brady,* in which the Court had held that a state court is required to appoint an attorney for an indigent defendant only when the lack of counsel would deprive the defendant of a fair trial as judged on a case-by-case basis. But much was at stake beneath the surface.

Integration Supreme Court.

Painting by Ben Shahn, 1963. Des Moines Art Center. Copyright © Estate of Ben Shahn/Licensed by VAGA, New York, NY. Reprinted by permission of VAGA (Visual Artists and Galleries Association, Inc.). Edmundson Art Foundation, Inc.

THE RIGHT TO COUNSEL

from Anthony Lewis, *Gideon's Trumpet*
(New York: Random House, 1964), pp. 79–94.
Copyright © 1964 and renewed 1992 by Anthony Lewis.
Reprinted by permission of Random House, Inc., and Anthony Lewis.

"The question is very simple. I requested the court to appoint me attorney and the court refused." So [Clarence Earl] Gideon had written to the Supreme Court in support of his claim that the Constitution entitled the poor man charged with crime to have a lawyer at his side. Most Americans would probably have agreed with him. To even the best-informed person unfamiliar with the law it seemed inconceivable, in the year 1962, that the Constitution would allow a man to be tried without a lawyer because he could not afford one.

But the question was really as far from simple as it could imaginably be. Behind it there was a long history—a history that until recently had seemed resolutely opposed to Gideon's claim but now had started to turn and move in his direction. The question that Gideon presented could not be resolved without reference to issues that had been fought over by judges and statesmen and political philosophers—issues going to the nature of our constitutional system and to the role played in it by the Supreme Court.

We have come to take it for granted in this country that courts, especially the Supreme Court, have the power to review the actions of governors, legislators, even Presidents, and set them aside as unconstitutional. But this power of judicial review, as it is called, has been given to judges in few other countries—and nowhere, at any time, to the extent that our history has confided it in the Supreme Court. In the guise of legal questions there come to the Supreme Court many of the most fundamental and divisive issues of every era, issues which judges in other lands would never dream of having to decide.

The consequences are great for Court and country. For the justices power means responsibility, a responsibility the more weighty because the Supreme Court so often has the last word. Deciding cases is never easy, but a judge may sleep more soundly after sentencing a man to death—or invalidating a President's seizure of the nation's steel mills—if he knows there is an appeal to a higher court. Justices of the Supreme Court do not have that luxury.

"We are not final because we are infallible," Justice Jackson wrote, "but we are infallible only because we are final." Men who know their own fallibility may find it hard to bear the burden of final decision. A few months before the Supreme Court agreed to hear Gideon's case, Justice Charles Evans Whittaker retired after only five years on the Court, explaining candidly that he found the strain of its work too great. He told friends that when he wrote an opinion, he felt as if he were carving his words into granite.

Other men may not be bothered by judicial power, may indeed revel in it. But the existence of power so great inevitably raises questions. Is it consistent with democracy to let nine men, appointed for life and directly answerable to no constituency, make ultimate decisions about the direction of our society? How free should a judge feel to set above the will of the people's elected representatives the principles that he finds in the Constitution? How does he find them, given the Constitution's vague words and the conflicting interpretations of them by judges of the past?

The very legitimacy of judicial review has been questioned repeatedly from the time the Supreme Court first held a federal statute unconstitutional, in *Marbury v. Madison* in 1803. The Jeffersonians accused John Marshall of usurpation. Liberals said the same of the Court in the 1930s, and revisionist historians of that day tried to prove that it really had not been given the power of judicial review. Today the epithets come from extremists of the right, disaffected by the Court's decisions on individual liberty and racial equality.

Scholarly opinion has long since dismissed the charge that judicial review was illicitly imported into our system by John Marshall or anyone else. The Constitution does not explicitly provide for its enforcement by the federal courts, but the text—including the grant of jurisdiction over cases arising under the Constitution—indicates that expectation. The records of the Philadelphia Convention of 1787 point the same way; at least a substantial number of the delegates assumed that the Supreme Court would pass on the constitutionality of state and federal acts that came before it in law suits. The delegates, in fact, considered a proposal to go further and have the Court share the President's veto power in a Council of Revision, but that suggestion was rejected on the ground that the Court already had a "sufficient check" by its power to declare laws unconstitutional. The very conception of a written constitution binding on governments as well as citizens, the great American contribution to political history, presupposed some institution to enforce the rules. Theoretically that could have been Congress, but the episodic and political nature of the legislative process would have made that choice doubtful. In fact we have lived for one hundred and seventy-five years with the Supreme Court as the final interpreter of our fundamental law, and our whole system of government is now built on that assumption. Justice Jackson, no starry-eyed admirer of judicial review, wrote in 1954: "The real strength of the position of the Court is probably in its indispensability to government under a written Constitution. It is difficult to see how the provisions of a one-hundred-and-fifty-year-old written document can have much vitality if there is not some permanent institution to translate them into current commands. . . ."

But if the issue of legitimacy is foreclosed, there remain very live questions of when and how the Supreme Court should exercise its great power to nullify what other branches of government have done. These questions have been the subject of a fierce and unending debate among commentators and among the justices themselves. The opposing positions can best be summarized in terms of the two uncommonly able and determined justices who led the debate for a generation, Felix Frankfurter and Hugo L. Black.

Justice Frankfurter's motto was "judicial self-restraint." He counseled judges to defer to Congress and the states, even where their actions seemed unwise; to be cautious in reading prohibitions into the Constitution; to respect history; to balance against the interest of the individual the interest of society. Justice Frankfurter warned that relying too much on judges to protect our freedoms sapped the strength of democracy by distracting attention from the political forum where unwise policies should be corrected. He felt the Court was often less equipped to deal with a problem than expert administrators or politicians closer to the public will. He was motivated also by a deep concern for the Supreme Court as an institution, a fear that it might destroy itself if it pressed its power too far. He and others remembered the 1930's, when a self-willed Court tried to stand against history by stopping urgent economic and social measures and thus brought itself to the brink of drastic reform—reform which it avoided only by a political change of course. Not that Justice Frankfurter never found state or federal action unconstitutional. His vote to invalidate school segregation, his concern for the freedom of commerce from state barriers, and his careful scrutiny of police behavior and of state assistance to religion all testify to his acceptance of the Court's role as enforcer of the Constitution. But right up to his retirement in 1962 his opinions preached judicial caution, self-examination and restraint. Since then his restraining role has been carried on by others, especially his friend Justice John Marshall Harlan, who in a notable speech in 1963 criticized what he called the "cosmic" view of the judicial function—the idea "that all deficiencies in our society which have failed of correction by other means should find a cure in the courts."

Justice Black, by contrast, has emphasized the duty of judges to preserve individual liberty, and has argued that excessive deference to other branches of government amounts to abdication of that responsibility. In the Black view, the framers of the Constitution made the decision to protect individuals from governmental repression, so a judge should not feel timid or self-conscious about doing so. Particularly obnoxious to Justice Black is the Frankfurter thesis that the Court must balance individual interests against the needs of government and uphold any reasonable governmental course of action. Justice Black argues that this weighing and balancing of what is reasonable leaves judges too much at large. He looks to history and finds definite rules in the Constitution—"absolutes," as he has called them. His favorite example is the First Amendment: "Congress shall make no law respecting an establishment of religion, or prohibiting the free exercise thereof; or abridging the freedom of speech, or of the press. . . ." To Justice Black, as he has put it, "no law means *no law.*" Thus he has gone much farther in finding violations of the First Amendment than almost any other justice, past or present. He has argued, in dissent, that no government has the power to censor obscenity. And he has repeatedly dissented from decisions upholding federal action against the Communist party and its members, decisions in which the majority found the injury to free speech outbalanced by the need of society to protect itself against an international conspiracy.

Sometimes the debate between Justices Black and Frankfurter, or between the schools of thought they represent, has seemed abstract—more words than real ideas. No one, not even a Supreme Court justice, is always perfectly logical in applying his own theories, so it is dangerous to build too many expectations on stated judicial philosophies. Justice Frankfurter, for example, was willing when Justice Black was not to strike down wiretapping as unconstitutional and to forbid the use of state funds for parochial-school buses. But for purposes of the Gideon case the general difference in the Black and Frankfurter approaches was a relevant, inescapable consideration.

As Abe Fortas* began to think about the case in the summer of 1962, before Justice Frankfurter's retirement, it was clear to him that overruling *Betts v. Brady* would not come easily to Justice Frankfurter or others of his view. This was true not only because of their judicial philosophy in general, but because of the way they had applied it on specific matters. One of these was the question of precedent.

"In most matters it is more important that the applicable rule of law be settled than that it be settled right." Justice Brandeis thus succinctly stated the basic reason for *stare decisis,* the judicial doctrine of following precedents. In literal translation the Latin words mean "to stand by what has been decided." Anglo-American law is built on the expectation that courts generally will follow what they have said in the past; on that assumption contracts are signed, wills made, lives planned. But *stare decisis* is not an iron rule in the courts of this country, as it is in England. Justice Brandeis went on:

> But in cases involving the Federal Constitution, where correction through legislative action is practically impossible, this Court has often overruled its earlier decisions. The Court bows to the lessons of experience and the force of better reasoning.

While constitutional cases do present the special considerations mentioned by Brandeis, the Court has not in fact restricted to that area its willingness to re-examine past decisions. More than almost any court it looks beneath prece-

---

*Gideon filed his petition himself, but after the Supreme Court decided to hear his case, it appointed the Washington attorney—and future Supreme Court justice—Abe Fortas to represent him.

dents for the policy they represent. It might be said to be minding the caustic words of Justice Holmes: "It is revolting to have no better reason for a rule of law than that so it was laid down in the time of Henry IV. It is still more revolting if the grounds upon which it was laid down have vanished long since, and the rule simply persists from blind imitation of the past."

Approximately one hundred times in its history the Supreme Court has overruled a prior decision. That is often enough, but overruling has not by any means become a routine step, to be taken casually. Certainty and repose in the law still have their appeal. Changes of mind on the part of the Court have been met by strong dissent—by, among others, Justice Frankfurter.

Justice Frankfurter joined in the most famous of recent overruling cases, the School Segregation decision of 1954, which abandoned the separate-but-equal doctrine laid down in 1896. He was not, therefore, unyieldingly attached to the doctrine of *stare decisis*. But his instinct was to give great weight to the demands of continuity with the past in the law. A 1958 law-review study showed that Justice Frankfurter had dissented thirteen times from decisions overruling prior cases. Abe Fortas would have to produce compelling reasons to overcome the respect for precedent felt by Justice Frankfurter and others sharing his view. Justice Black, by contrast, felt much freer to turn from past doctrine. In 1958, for example, he unhesitatingly urged the Court—in dissent—to abandon one hundred and fifty years of decisions holding that jury trials were not required in prosecutions for contempt of court. He was unlikely to feel bound by what he considered an erroneous past interpretation of the Constitution.

Another issue between Justices Black and Frankfurter cut even deeper than *stare decisis,* and closer to Gideon's case. This was their attitude toward federalism—the independence of the states in our federal system of government.

The relationship of the Federal Government to the states was a central concern of the men who wrote the Constitution. They created a remarkable political structure which made Americans subject to two sovereignties, state and nation. To the states was reserved power over the ordinary affairs of men as they appeared in the Eighteenth Century—birth, marriage, death, business, crime. To the Federal Government went control over interstate commerce, foreign relations, war and other matters necessarily of national scope. By thus dividing governmental power the framers sought to lessen the dangers of centralized authority, which they had seen become tyranny in the hands of English kings. They also succeeded in giving us what John Quincy Adams called "the most complicated government on the face of the earth."

Sorting out the complications has been the job of the Supreme Court. From the beginning the Court has been faced with lawsuits requiring it to draw the boundaries of power between state and nation. At first the great cases tended to raise questions of the extent of the Federal Government's power. Did the Constitution authorize Congress to charter a bank? That was the question

Marshall decided in 1819, in *McCulloch v. Maryland,* and his answer in favor of the Federal Government permanently enlarged its domain.

In the Twentieth Century events have transformed the federal-state issues that come before the Court. The growth of a national economy and the emergence of the United States as a world power have inevitably made us more a nation, and have necessarily increased federal authority. The Supreme Court tried for a time to stand against that current, holding in New Deal days that Congress had no power under the Constitution to deal with the economic crisis in the country's coal mines or farms, but in 1937 it gave up that attempt.

The main arena of controversy today is not the extent of Congressional power but the limitations placed by the Constitution on state governmental action. State officials use the phrase "states' rights." By that they mean the right to handle such matters as race relations and the criminal law as they wish, without restraint by the Federal Constitution. The imposing of restraints on state action has evoked great resentment on the part of many state officials, judges not least. In 1958 the Conference of (State) Chief Justices approved a committee report excoriating the Supreme Court for what was termed an "overall tendency" to "press the extension of federal power and press it rapidly." The report did not deal with the issue of racial segregation, although many thought that was its real inspiration. It put major critical emphasis on Supreme Court decisions laying down minimal guarantees of fairness in criminal proceedings.

The chief justices' report was no scholarly contribution to the debate about the role of the Supreme Court. It passed over significant areas in which the modern Court has significantly enlarged state power, notably the power to tax and regulate the economy. But it did indicate how much emotion may arise over issues of federalism—and most interestingly, in relation to Gideon's case, over the right of the states to run their criminal law without worrying about uniform national standards. For Gideon was asking the Supreme Court to impose on the fifty states a uniform rule of criminal procedure, the universal requirement that counsel be supplied to poor criminal defendants. And that claim inevitably clashed with the belief that diversity among the states was as important a theme in the Constitution as individual rights—a belief held by, among others, Felix Frankfurter.

"Whatever inconveniences and embarrassments may be involved," Justice Frankfurter wrote in 1958, "they are the price we pay for our federalism, for having our people amenable to—as well as served and protected by—two governments." As a strong believer in the independence of the states, Justice Frankfurter was reluctant to impose new restraints on them even in the name of individual liberty. Justice Black was always much readier to cut through the duality and enlarge protections for the individual against any government.

The contrast in views was graphically illustrated in the case of Alfonse Bartkus, the Illinois prisoner who had been tried by a federal and then an Illinois jury for the same bank robbery. Justice Frankfurter, writing for the Supreme Court majority that upheld the second prosecution, said the result was commanded by our system of dual sovereignties. "The greatest self-restraint is necessary," he said in the opinion, "when that federal system yields results with which a court is in little sympathy." Justice Black viewed the case not as a problem in governmental structure but as one of fairness to Alfonse Bartkus. "The Court apparently takes the position," he said in dissent, "that a second trial for the same act is somehow less offensive if one of the trials is conducted by the Federal Government and the other by a state. Looked at from the standpoint of the individual who is being prosecuted, this notion is too subtle for me to grasp."

Underlying the Bartkus case was one of the great issues of federalism, a subject of conflict in the Supreme Court for nearly a century. This was the question of what provisions of the Constitution's Bill of Rights, if any, applied to the states. The average American would probably have thought that Bartkus's second trial, by the state of Illinois, was barred by the double-jeopardy clause of the Fifth Amendment: "nor shall any person be subject for the same offence to be twice put in jeopardy of life or limb." But that clause had been held to cover only *federal,* not state, criminal proceedings.

The Bill of Rights is the name collectively given to the first ten amendments to the Constitution, all proposed by the First Congress of the United States in 1789 and ratified in 1791. The first eight contain the guarantees of individual liberty with which we are so familiar: freedom of speech, press, religion and assembly; protection for the privacy of the home; assurance against double jeopardy and compulsory self-incrimination; the right to counsel and to trial by jury; freedom from cruel and unusual punishments. At the time of their adoption it was universally agreed that these eight amendments limited only the Federal Government and its processes. Fear of the new central government had been the reason for their adoption, some states even refusing to ratify the Constitution until assured that the Federal Government would be restrained by a Bill of Rights.

James Madison, who as a member of the House was a principal draftsman of the amendments, actually included one to guarantee individual rights against the states. It read: "No State shall infringe the right of trial by Jury in criminal cases, nor the rights of conscience, nor the freedom of speech, or of the press." Madison thought it "the most valuable amendment in the whole list," seeing more danger of abuse "by the State Governments than by the Government of the United States." But the Senate rejected his proposal, and the original Bill of Rights limited only federal action. In 1833, in the case of *Barron v. Baltimore,* Chief Justice Marshall wrote the common understanding into law with a specific decision that the Bill of Rights did not cover the states.

There matters stood until the Fourteenth Amendment became part of the Constitution in 1868. A product of the Civil War, it was specifically designed to prevent abuse of individuals by state governments. Section I provided: "No State shall make or enforce any law which shall abridge the privileges or immunities of citizens of the United States; nor shall any State deprive any person of life, liberty, or property, without due process of law; nor deny to any person within its jurisdiction the equal protection of the laws." Soon the claim was advanced that this section had been designed by its framers to *incorporate,* and apply to the states, all the provisions of the first eight amendments.

This theory of wholesale incorporation of the Bill of Rights has been adopted by one or more Supreme Court justices from time to time, but never a majority. The climactic battle came in 1947, in *Adamson v. California,* when four justices read the Fourteenth Amendment as including the entire Bill of Rights—Justices Black, Douglas, Frank Murphy and Wiley B. Rutledge. That five-to-four defeat was the high-water mark of the contention that the first eight amendments were incorporated in toto in the Fourteenth.

But if wholesale incorporation has been rejected, the Supreme Court has used the Fourteenth Amendment to apply provisions of the Bill of Rights to the states *selectively.* The vehicle has been the clause assuring individuals due process of law. The Court has said that state denial of any right deemed "fundamental" by society amounts to a denial of due process and hence violates the Fourteenth Amendment. . . .

The historical process by which provisions of the original Bill of Rights have thus been applied to state as well as federal action was described by Justice Benjamin N. Cardozo as a "process of absorption" of those rights "implicit in the concept of ordered liberty." It is an ironic note that Justice Black, who had just come on the Court, joined the 1937 Cardozo opinion advancing that formula. As his own philosophy developed, he rejected the "absorption" idea, feeling that it left judges too much at large, and found greater certainty in the thesis of wholesale incorporation. But "absorption" has been and remains the accepted process.

The difficult question has been which provisions of the first eight amendments to absorb. At first the Court was most reluctant to read any into the due-process clause of the Fourteenth. By the year 1900 the justices had refused to apply virtually every guarantee in the Bill of Rights to the states. As late as 1922 the Court said that the protections of the First Amendment—of free speech, press, religion and assembly—did not apply to the states. "But it is one thing to slam the door of the due-process clause and another to keep it shut," Professor Paul A. Freund has written. In 1925 [in *Gitlow v. New York*] the Court changed its mind and said free speech was so fundamental that a state could not deny it without denying due process of law and violating the Fourteenth Amendment. The other freedoms of the First Amendment followed.

The Court has been much more reluctant to apply to the states the guarantees of fair criminal procedure in the first eight amendments. It evidently felt, over many decades, that the one area in which the states were most clearly entitled to independence was in the application of their criminal law. Nothing could seem more obvious to us today than that to convict a man in an unfair criminal trial is to deprive him of life, liberty or property without due process of law. Yet it was not until 1923 that the Court specifically said unfair methods in a criminal trial were forbidden by the Fourteenth Amendment. That was an extreme case—five Arkansas Negroes condemned to death after a mob-dominated trial and on testimony said to have been extorted by brutality. Justice Holmes suggested that the entire proceeding was "a mask," with "counsel, judge and jury . . . swept to the fatal end by an irresistible wave of public passion." The decision was only to let the prisoners come into federal court and try to prove their charges of unconstitutional treatment, not to set aside their convictions. Even at that, Justice James C. McReynolds dissented, saying: "The fact that petitioners are poor and ignorant and black naturally arouses sympathy; but that does not release us from enforcing principles which are essential to the orderly operation of our federal system." (The five prisoners eventually had their sentences commuted by state authorities without final legal action.)

Over the years the Supreme Court steadfastly resisted all efforts to apply to the states the specific criminal-law guarantees of the Bill of Rights, such as the Sixth Amendment's provision for trial by jury and assistance of counsel and the Fifth Amendment's ban on double jeopardy and self-incrimination. In 1949 the Fourth Amendment's prohibition on illegal searches and seizures was dealt with in a notable opinion by Justice Frankfurter. He deeply opposed illegal police intrusion on the home—"the knock at the door," he called it—but he could not put aside his firm belief in state independence. In this dilemma he took a curious compromise position. He held that the "core" of the Fourth Amendment was absorbed into the due-process clause of the Fourteenth. But he refused to apply to the states the essential enforcement device that had bound the federal courts since 1914, the rule that illegally seized material must be excluded from evidence at a man's trial.

History, then, showed a special reluctance on the part of the Supreme Court to impose on the states uniform national standards of fair criminal procedure. But there were signs of change in that history. Beginning in 1936, the Court had struck down state criminal convictions based on confessions coerced from the defendant. At first the third degree—physical brutality—was condemned. Over the years the Court gradually raised its standards of decency, condemning psychological as well as physical coercion of prisoners. By the 1950's it was clear that the due-process clause of the Fourteenth Amendment was a pervasive guarantee against convictions based on extorted confessions, whether or not there was external evidence to support the truthfulness of the confession. The aim was not just to rule out suspect confessions but to discourage illegal police practices. That attitude on the part of the Court signaled more vigilance toward state criminal procedure in general.

Another long step was taken in 1956, in the case of *Griffin v. Illinois*. Under the law of Illinois a person desiring to appeal his criminal conviction had to supply to the appellate court a transcript of his trial. A man too poor to buy one could not appeal. The Supreme Court held, five to four, that such a distinction between rich and poor denied the equal protection of the laws guaranteed by the Fourteenth Amendment; a state must provide a free transcript to poor prisoners, or some less elaborate trial record that would furnish a basis for appeal.

The Griffin case marked a significant increase in the Court's willingness to impose minimum standards of fairness on state criminal process. It was met by bitter criticism, from the Conference of Chief Justices among other state sources, but the trend continued.

In 1961, just a year before it granted Clarence Earl Gideon's petition for review, the Court took the step that Justice Frankfurter and a majority had been unwilling to take on illegal searches in 1949. In the case of *Mapp v. Ohio* it overruled the earlier decision and held that the Fourth Amendment was now fully applicable to the states: No illegally seized evidence could be admitted at state criminal trials. Justice Frankfurter, joined by Justices Harlan and Whittaker, dissented.

Mapp v. Ohio certainly had import for the Gideon case. A majority had been willing to overrule a recent decision, and to do so in the face of strongly pressed claims of federalism. The Court had been warned that imposing a uniform national prohibition on illegal evidence would cripple state law enforcement and empty the jails, just as it could expect to be told in the Gideon case about the baleful effects of a uniform counsel requirement.

The ruling in *Mapp*, together with the long series of coerced confession cases and the protection given the poor prisoner in *Griffin v. Illinois,* suggested a broad movement of the Supreme Court away from regard for state independence as a primary value in the constitutional law of criminal procedure. Younger justices, brought up in a United States that had become a nation, were concerned less about federalism and more about national ideals of fairness. Justice Brennan indicated the difference in attitude in a speech a few months before *Mapp v. Ohio* was decided. "Federalism should not be raised to the plane of an absolute," he said, "nor the Bill of Rights be reduced to a precatory trust. . . . Far too many cases come from the states to the Supreme Court presenting dismal pictures of official lawlessness, of illegal searches and seizures, illegal detentions attended by prolonged interrogation and coerced admissions of guilt, of the denial of counsel."

CHAPTER 23

The Vietnam War

As the decade of the 1960s wore on, contentions over civil rights, criminal justice, free speech, church and state, privacy, and other issues tackled by the Warren Court were increasingly overshadowed by the U.S. involvement in Vietnam. Military intervention started during the Kennedy presidency, but it escalated greatly under President Lyndon B. Johnson.

Johnson took over as president with a strong program of domestic reforms. His "Great Society" program included the initiation of Medicare, the creation of the Department of Housing and Urban Development, greatly increased federal aid to education, a "war on poverty," and other attempts to use the federal government for social betterment. Formerly a skillful legislator, he managed to have most of his programs enacted by Congress, but he was defeated by foreign affairs. Despite his domestic successes, in 1968 he announced he would not run for a second full term, largely because of the unpopularity of his policy in Vietnam.

The escalation of the war in Vietnam started before the 1964 election. In August of that year, a North Vietnamese ship allegedly fired on a U.S. ship in international waters in the Gulf of Tonkin. Later investigations have raised doubts that the attack actually occurred, but the Congress believed it did and, in response, authorized President Johnson to "take all necessary measures to repel any armed attack against the forces of the United States and to prevent further aggression." Under authority of that resolution, hundreds of thousands of troops eventually were dispatched to Vietnam, North Vietnamese harbors were mined, and North Vietnam—and neighboring Cambodia as well—were subject to waves of bombings. But, contrary to President Johnson's expectations, the commitment of massive strength did not bring quick victory and, as the war dragged on—and U.S. casualties

mounted into the tens of thousands—dissent at home reached unprecedented proportions.

Dissenters sought the aid of the law to stop the war. In most cases, the
courts were willing to support the right to dissent: in *Bond* v. *Floyd* (1966)
the Georgia legislature was ordered not to exclude a legislator who opposed
the war; in *Tinker* v. *Des Moines School District* (1969) the right of students to
wear armbands to school to protest the war was upheld; in *New York Times*
v. *United States* (1971) the Supreme Court refused to enjoin the publication
of a "leaked" classified government study, known as the "Pentagon Papers,"
critical of the war. But the courts avoided ruling on the legality of the war itself. When draft resisters challenged the use of conscription without a formal
declaration of war by Congress, only Justice Douglas on the Supreme Court
was in favor of hearing the issue. Thus, protestors turned to the political
arena. As one of the prosecutors at the Nuremberg trials, Telford Taylor,
wrote in *Nuremberg and Vietnam: An American Tragedy* (1970):

> [T]he predicament itself is not, I believe, susceptible to solution by judicial de-
> cree. There is no such simple way to end the Vietnam tragedy, for the Supreme
> Court is not a *deus ex machina*. This war, and the agony and rancor that are its
> product, have been the work of the President and the Congress—the people's
> elected agents—and the war can be ended only by action of the national will,
> exerted through political, not judicial, channels. (pp. 120–21)

In the political arena, dissenters found a champion in Senator Eugene Mc-
Carthy of Wisconsin. He entered early Democratic party presidential pri-
maries in 1968 as a "peace candidate" and did well enough to make him a
serious contender, but he did not manage to get enough delegates to secure the party's nomination. The nomination went, instead, to Vice President Hubert Humphrey.

As delegates to the 1968 Democratic Party Convention gathered in
Chicago, so did thousands of antiwar protestors. The unsympathetic local
government of Chicago, headed by longtime Mayor Richard J. Daley, denied
protestors assembly and parade permits. Repeated encounters with Chicago
police boiled over on the evening of August 28, as the police trapped and
clubbed protestors in front of television cameras. A government commission
later referred to the events of that evening as a "police riot." Eight policemen were indicted by a federal grand jury. Symmetrically, eight protestors
were also indicted as "leaders" and charged with conspiracy to cross state
lines with the intent to cause a riot and with having crossed state lines with
the intent to cause a riot. Seven of the policemen were acquitted and one
had his case dropped. The eight protestors were also reduced to seven when
the case of Bobby Seale, national chair of the Black Panther Party, was sev-
ered. (Seale demanded to act as his own lawyer after the judge—Judge

Julius Hoffman—refused to postpone the case to give time for Seale's chosen attorney to recover from a surgery. In response to repeated protests from Seale, Judge Hoffman had Seale bound and gagged before declaring a mistrial, sentencing Seale to four years for contempt of court, and severing his case.) The remaining seven were Rennard Davis, David Dellinger, John Froines, Thomas Hayden, Abbott (Abbie) Hoffman, Jerry Rubin, and Lee Weiner. They were represented by attorneys William Kunstler and Leonard Weinglass. U.S. Attorney Thomas Foran and Assistant U.S. Attorney John Schultz served as prosecutors. The trial of the "Chicago Eight" became a national *cause célèbre*.

Bobby Seale bound and gagged.

Drawing by Jules Feiffer. Copyright © 1969 by Jules Feiffer. Reprinted by permission of United Press Syndicate.

THE TRIAL OF
THE "CHICAGO EIGHT"

from Jason Epstein, *The Great Conspiracy Trial:*
An Essay on Law, Liberty and the Constitution
(New York: Random House, 1970), pp. 397–431.
Copyright © 1970 by Jason Epstein.
Reprinted by permission of Jason Epstein.

The Trial Ends

. . .

[T]he defendants were frightened, angry, and exhausted as the ordeal of the trial approached its end and the terror and mystery of their inevitable imprisonment rose up before them. Though Abbie Hoffman had said that the bright ceiling lights made the courtroom a "neon oven," the atmosphere in these final days was gloomy. The courtroom had come to seem no more than an entrance chamber to the federal prison system.

On February 4, James Riordan, a deputy chief of the Chicago police, took the stand. He testified that on Wednesday, August 28, he saw Dellinger leave the band shell in Grant Park and walk "with the head of the group that were carrying the flags."

"Oh, bullshit," Dellinger said, in a flat, somewhat reflective voice, as if the idea of the witness' duplicity had taken him by surprise. The word seemed to tumble from his lips of its own volition.

"Did you get that, Miss Reporter?" the judge asked.

"That is an absolute lie," Dellinger added, with somewhat more vigor, the quavering impediment catching at his words.

"Did you get that, Miss Reporter?" the judge asked again.

"Let's argue about what I stand for and you stand for, but let's not make up things like that," Dellinger said to the witness.

"All of these remarks were made in the presence of the Court and the jury by Mr. Dellinger," Judge Hoffman said to the reporter.

"Sometimes the human spirit can stand so much," Kunstler pleaded from the lectern, "and I think Mr. Dellinger reached the end of his."

379

The judge replied, "I have never, in more than a half century at the bar, heard a man using profanity in this court or in a courtroom. I never did."

That afternoon, after the judge had dismissed the jury for the day, he asked the defendants and the lawyers to stay. The spectators also remained. "I have some observations to make here, gentlemen," he said. "I have demonstrated great patience during this trial in trying to insure a fair trial for both the government and for the defendants. . . . Time and again, as the record reveals, the defendant Dellinger has disrupted sessions of this court with the use of vile and insulting language. Today again he used vile and obscene language. I propose to try to end the use of such language if possible and such conduct by terminating the bail of this defendant."

The judge then admitted that ". . . it has been said by some that the purpose of bail is to insure the attendance of a defendant at the trial. That is one of the purposes." But he added that a judge may also revoke bail if a defendant's behavior, in or out of the courtroom, jeopardizes the fair administration of justice. The case he cited was that of *Carbo v. United States,* in which the defendant was suspected of having threatened the lives of government witnesses.

Kunstler rose to reply, but the judge cut him short and remanded Dellinger to the custody of the United States marshal.

"Your Honor," Kunstler pleaded, "is there not to be any argument on this?"

"No argument," the judge replied.

But Kunstler persisted. "Your Honor's act is completely and utterly vindictive. . . . There is no authority that says because a defendant blurts out a word in court—"

"I won't argue this," the judge repeated.

"This court is bullshit!" Davis called out from the defense table.

"Everything in this court is bullshit!" Rubin shouted.

"I associate myself with Dave Dellinger," Davis said, "completely 100 percent. This is the most obscene court I have ever seen."

"Take us all!" Rubin shouted. "Show us what a big man you are."

"Your Honor," Schultz interrupted, "I ask that you do not do them the favor that they ask." What Schultz presumably feared was that the jurors who sympathized with the defense would be all the more sympathetic if all seven of the defendants were to be put in jail. "Don't do them that favor," Schultz insisted.

"You don't think that I would," the judge replied.

By now, several spectators had stood up. Some stood on the benches to get a better view. Some began to shout indignantly. Six marshals rushed into the courtroom from the corridor outside to augment the twenty or so who were already there. A reporter whispered, "My God! Someone's going to get killed in here!"

"You can jail a revolutionary," Davis shouted over the turmoil, "but you can't jail the revolution!"

"You are a disgrace to the Jews," Abbie Hoffman yelled at the judge. "You would have served Hitler better," but his words were hardly audible over the din in the spectators' section, where the marshals were struggling with the friends and relatives of the defendants. "You little prick!" a woman cried out, shaking her fist at the judge, as a marshal dragged her through the swinging doors at the rear of the courtroom.

"Clear the court," the judge shouted, banging his palm on the bench. The marshals then ejected the last of the unruly spectators and led Dellinger through the door to the lockup.

That evening, Hoffman and Rubin argued with the four other defendants that they should all do whatever they could on the following day to disrupt the trial. They felt, Hayden later explained, "that if all the defendants were jailed together, it would help Dellinger get out. It would also create the right image to mobilize people for action at the trial's end." As for himself, however, Hayden said that "of all the defendants I probably advocated the most careful behavior in the courtroom." His reason was that he wanted to "cultivate support within the jury of middle class Americans." He had a further reason as well. The principle of "moral witness" and guerrilla "theater, at the root of the pacifist and Yippie politics . . . can expose institutions, but they can never prevent repression and punishment. . . . We would strip away the court's authority but not its power. So it seemed," Hayden concluded, "a senseless sacrifice to accumulate prison time for spontaneous outbursts."

At three-thirty that morning, Dellinger, like the other prisoners who were to be taken that day to federal court, was awakened in Cook County Jail. Then, as he later described the routine, he was "led through a series of way stations. Everywhere you go, you stand and wait. . . . And then you wait another twenty minutes or a half hour. At last you're taken to the pump room, which is so jammed with humanity that after I'd been there ten minutes I looked around to see if anybody was suffocating. And then you move from there to the next station. Everytime you leave, you're stripped. Your anus is examined. 'Lift your right foot. Lift your left foot. Spread your cheeks. Turn around. Jump up and down. Stick your tongue out.'"

Finally he was put in a van with the other federal prisoners, driven some five miles across the city, and deposited in the lockup on the twenty-fourth floor of the Federal Building. . . .

Soon after Court convened that morning, Weinglass petitioned the judge to hear arguments on the question of Dellinger's bail. "You are keeping a man in custody," he said, "and you are not permitting a lawyer to make arguments for his freedom. This is unheard of. That is unprecedented in law."

"I have considered the matter carefully," the judge replied.

"You have not considered it," Weinglass said, "because you have not heard the argument."

"Mr. Marshal," the judge ordered, "will you ask that man to sit down?"

"You put him in jail because you lost faith in the jury system," Hoffman shouted at the judge. "That's why you're throwing us in jail this way. Contempt is the tyranny of the court and you're a tyrant. *Schtunk!*" he screamed.

"Black robes of death!" Rubin added.

"We should have done this long ago when you chained and gagged Bobby Seale. Mafia-controlled pigs," Hoffman said.

"Mr. Marshal," the judge asked, "will you have Mr. Hoffman remain quiet, please. Order him to remain quiet."

"Order us?" Hoffman replied. "You got to cut our tongues out to quiet us, Julie."

Later that day the judge decided that he would, after all, hear a motion by the defense to restore Dellinger's bail. Weinglass argued that the Carbo Case concerned a defendant with a long criminal record. In an earlier trial of the same defendant, the chief government witness was murdered before he could testify. In the trial in question, the chief government witness had received more than a hundred threatening phone calls. It was for these reasons, Weinglass argued, that Carbo had been denied bail. Moreover, the judge in the case had said that he had no faith Carbo would appear in Court unless his bail were revoked. Even so, Weinglass added, the Appeals Court reversed the trial judge.

Judge Hoffman, however, did not respond to the legal argument that Weinglass made. Instead, he said he had ". . . beseeched you and Mr. Kunstler throughout this trial, beginning with the Seale episode, to please try and get your clients to behave in this courtroom. At no time did you lift a finger or speak a word to any of them."

Weinglass, returning to his legal argument, replied that the Court could use its contempt power to punish Dellinger for what he had said, but that it had no power to revoke bail.

"I have more power than that," the judge interrupted. He added, "I don't like the word 'power.' I never use the word 'power' if I can avoid it." Then he explained that bail is "a privilege," not an "absolute right."

"That is called justice?" Rubin asked.

"Your Honor is not going to hear my argument?" Weinglass asked over the uproar that had once again broken out in the courtroom.

"I deny the motion—" the judge said.

"My argument—" Weinglass tried to say.

"That will be all, sir," the judge ordered.

"This is disgraceful!" Kunstler shouted. The judge asked the reporter to be sure to make a record of Kunstler's remark.

"Of course I said it," Kunstler said angrily. "How can I say anything but that?"

"My argument—" Weinglass persisted.

"Mr. Marshal," the judge ordered, "please have that lawyer sit down." Then he turned to Weinglass and Kunstler and said, "I ask you to sit down and there will be no further argument."

"Your idea of justice is the only obscenity in this room!" Hoffman shouted at the judge. "You *schtunck!*" Then he accused him in Yiddish of behaving disgracefully in the presence of gentiles.

"Julius Hoffman equals Adolph Hitler," Rubin added.

Above the shouting, Kunstler asked the judge to instruct the jury that Mr. Dellinger was now in custody. "We would like an opportunity," he added, "to tell the jury exactly why the defense considers him held in contempt."

"You will not have that opportunity," the judge replied.

"And will the defendants and the defendants' attorneys be instructed," Schultz asked the judge, "to make no reference to this in the presence of the jury? That's right!"

"You know you can't win this fucking case!" Hoffman shouted at Schultz. "The only way you can win is to put us away for contempt. We have contempt for this court and for you, Schultz, and for this whole rotten system."

"I order the defendants and their counsel to make no reference to this motion made," the judge shouted over the din.

"And the reason," Rubin said, "is because it is a hung jury and you know it. You know you are losing the jury trial, but you've got to get us in jail, because the people will decide that we're not guilty, so you are going to railroad us into jail."

Soon thereafter, when it appeared that the other defendants would not continue to join in their attacks, Hoffman and Rubin subsided. The jury was then admitted.

"Ladies and gentlemen of the jury, good morning," the judge said pleasantly.

"Good morning, Your Honor," the jurors replied.

"Good morning," Dellinger added.

On the following day, the Seventh Circuit Court of Appeals denied a motion by the defense to reinstate Dellinger's bail. In a conversation with a reporter, Weinglass said that the appellate judges were wrong to have upheld Judge Hoffman. "Bail," he said, "cannot be revoked for punitive reasons. But the appellate judges probably felt that they had to protect the dignity of Judge Hoffman, their man in the field, against the insults of Abbie and Jerry." They could not, Weinglass explained, add their rebuke to the tirades of the defendants.

On February 9, the testimony of the government's rebuttal witnesses came to an end, and on the following day Schultz presented his closing argument to the jury. . . . He [told] the jury that the real aim of the defendants had been to establish an arm of the Viet Cong in America.

That afternoon, Weinglass replied for the defense that the trial was staged in order to shift the blame from the police to the demonstrators for the riots during the convention. Chicago, he said, "had to find a scapegoat." As for the intentions of the defendants, the government, he argued, had proven nothing. The question of their intentions, he told the jurors, was implicit in the negotiations for permits. If the jurors believed that the defendants had negotiated in good faith, while the city had been obstructive and dilatory, then the defendants must be found innocent. He then attacked the government witnesses. Undercover agents and police spies, he said, are deceitful by profession. Furthermore, they don't speak the same language as the defendants. Thus they had been unable to understand what the defendants' speeches had actually meant. . . .

Weinglass then quoted from Lincoln's speech opposing the Mexican War and advocating rebellion. "Lincoln was so vilified for this speech," he explained, "that he had to resign temporarily from politics. But history vindicated him, and it will vindicate these defendants," he said. He added that he hoped the jury would spare history the trouble.

. . .

Foran's summation was the most aggressive of the four.

"There are millions of kids," he told the jurors, "who resent authority, who are impatient for change. And there is another thing about the kid," he added, "his attraction to evil. Evil is exciting." He paused for a moment. . . . "It is knowledge of kids like that," he resumed, "that these sophisticated, educated psychology majors know about. They know how to draw kids together and maneuver them, and use them to accomplish their purposes.

"Kids in the system are disillusioned. They feel that John Kennedy went; Bobby Kennedy went; and Martin Luther King went and the kids feel that the lights have gone out in Camelot, the banners are furled and the parade is over." He paused again. . . .

"These guys," he continued, "take advantage of them—personally, intentionally and evilly—to corrupt those kids. They use them for their purposes and their interests.

"What has happened to us?" Foran asked the courtroom at large. "The bad people are the policemen, the FBI agents. The bad people are the ones who give their lives to government. You are only a good guy if you like the homosexual poetry of Allen Ginsberg. We can't let people use our kids like that. What they want is to stand on the rubble of a destroyed system of government. . . . And these men would have you believe that the issue in this case is whether or not they really wanted permits—so that they could fuck in the grass and smoke dope. I don't like to use language like that," he apologized to the jurors, "but that's what Hoffman said." Then his voice grew sharp. "Public authority couldn't give them permits to use that park; and these men," he said, pointing now toward the defense table, "are sophisticated. And they are smart and they are educated. And they are as evil as they can be."

Again Foran paused. Then he said, "We have got a crazy age on us now. We have got a time when a man can achieve the most he has ever been able to in all the world; and at the same time he is creating instruments of destruction that could destroy the world in a moment. We will have a guy actually walking on the moon and instead," he paused again, turned and faced the defendants, "they burrow downward toward the primitive, in obscenity, vulgarity and hate.

"They would have us believe that their revolution is in a lofty cause, and so they can break the laws to achieve it. The consequences of that thinking is the legitimation of violence and it would destroy this country.

"The First Amendment is not now and never was intended to protect those who violate the law. When a protest becomes a violent, deliberate and forcible assault on public order, it never can be excused or tolerated. . . . To permit factions to resort to force when they feel a particular law or policy is wrong would be to renounce our own experience and the experience of our forefathers. True freedom and substantial justice don't come from violent altercation and incendiary dissent.

"The First Amendment," Foran continued, "permits advocacy, not incitement. You can't," he explained, "[say] fight the police. To incite is not protected by the law."

"These men have named St. Matthew and Jesus and they have named Lincoln and Martin Luther King. Can you imagine these men supporting these men? . . . "

"Yes, I can!" a young woman shouted from the front row of the spectators' benches. "I can imagine it because it is true."

"Remove those people, Mr. Marshal," the judge ordered.

"That's my daughter!" Dellinger cried as the marshals pounced on the young woman. She hooked her arms over the back of the bench and vigorously kicked at the marshals who were trying to pry her loose.

"I don't have to listen to any more of these disgusting lies," another young woman shouted.

"That's my other daughter!" Dellinger cried out again. "Thank you. Right on! Right on!" Meanwhile the marshals continued to struggle with the first daughter, who persisted in kicking at them defiantly.

"Don't hit my daughter that way," Dellinger shouted. "That man hit her on the head for speaking the truth in here."

"The marshal will maintain order," the judge reassured Dellinger.

"Yes, but they don't have to hit a thirteen-year-old girl who knows I was close to Martin Luther King," he replied.

"Isn't it interesting?" Foran cried out over the turmoil that had engulfed the courtroom once more, "that these believers in free speech do not believe that the United States Attorney has the same right?"

Soon the marshal succeeded in removing the young Dellingers, along with several other spectators who had joined the shouting, and Foran concluded his remarks. "If this country should ever reach the stage where any man or group of men by force or violence, or with the threat of force, can long defy the commands of our law, then no citizen will be safe or his neighbors.

"The lights that Camelot kids believe in need not go out," he said. "The banners can snap in the breeze again. The parade will never be over if people will remember what Jefferson said: 'Obedience to the law is the major part of patriotism.'

"These seven men," he concluded, "have been proven guilty beyond any doubt. Do your duty."

. . .

On the following day, Saturday, February 14, the judge read his instructions to the jurors, who then left to commence their deliberations. As soon as the jurors were gone, the judge proceeded to sentence the defendants for contempt. He began with Dellinger, whom he found guilty of thirty-two separate contemptuous acts.

Before the judge passed sentence, however, Kunstler rose and attempted to argue the law of contempt. The judge said he would not hear such arguments, but Kunstler persisted, and finally the judge permitted him to make his case. "The Bloom decision," Kunstler argued, "held that the power of summary contempt should not be exercised after a trial; summary contempt is only a method of preventing disturbances during a trial; after the trial a man is entitled to a jury."

Then Kunstler quoted the decision of the Supreme Court in Bloom. "We are not persuaded," the Court ruled, "that the additional time and expense possibly involved in submitting serious contempts to juries will seriously handicap the effective functioning of the courts. We do not deny that serious punishment might sometimes be imposed for contempt, but we reject the contention that such punishment must be imposed without a right to jury trial."

"I do not share your view," the judge told Kunstler simply. He then asked Dellinger if he had anything to say before sentencing. Dellinger rose and said that . . . war and racism were once more the issues. The judge refused to hear Dellinger further on this subject. "I hope you will excuse me, sir," he requested politely. "You are not speaking strictly to what I gave you the privilege of speaking to. I ask you to say what you want to say with respect to punishment."

Dellinger insisted that his remarks were relevant to his punishment, whereupon the judge ordered him to be seated. Nevertheless, Dellinger continued to speak.

"You want us to be like good Germans, supporting the evils of our decade," he told the judge, "and now you want us to be good Jews and go quietly and politely to the gas chamber while you and this court suppress freedom and truth. The fact is, I am not prepared to do that. You want us to stay in our place like black people—"

"Mr. Marshal," the judge commanded, "I will ask you to have Mr. Dellinger sit down."

"This is a travesty on justice," Dellinger continued, "and if you had any sense at all you would know that the record that you just read condemns you and not us. I am an old man and I am just speaking feebly and not too well, but I reflect the spirit that will echo—"

"Take him out," the judge ordered, and the Court once more erupted in turmoil and shouting.

"Tyrants! Tyrants!" spectators cried as the marshals began to drag people from the courtroom.

"That's what you have done, Judge Hoffman. That's what you have done," a woman cried as the marshals tugged at Dellinger's daughters.

Rubin meanwhile had jumped up from his chair at the defense table and marched rigidly toward the judge's bench, his right arm held stiffly out. "Heil Hitler! Heil Hitler! Heil Hitler!" he screamed. "I hope you're satisfied."

Hayden slouched deep in his chair and glanced balefully at Schultz, who was smiling broadly.

Kunstler rushed to the lectern and fell upon it, his forehead, for a moment, touching its surface. "My life has come to nothing," he wept. "I am not anything any more. You have destroyed me and everybody else. Put me in jail now, for God's sake, and get me out of this place. Come to mine now, judge, please. I beg you. Come to mine. Do me, too. I don't want to be out."

The judge sat impassively throughout this outburst. When Kunstler had returned to his chair and the marshals had restored order, he began to read the sentences for each of Dellinger's contempts. . . . Altogether he sentenced Dellinger to twenty-nine months and thirteen days.

He then proceeded to deal with Davis, whom he sentenced to twenty-five months and fourteen days on twenty-three counts of contempt. For calling Schultz a disgrace, Davis was sentenced to three months. For failing to restrict his replies on cross-examination to the scope of the government's questions, Davis was sentenced to six months. Before he passed sentence, the judge asked Davis to speak on the question of his punishment. Davis began by saying that he and the other defendants had come to Court hoping to win their case, even though they knew the law was unconstitutional. But the judge would not hear him on this point and ordered him to address himself only to the question of punishment. "Judge," Davis said, "you represent all that is old, ugly, bigoted and repressive in this country, and I will tell you that the spirit at this defense table is going to devour your sickness in the next generation." Davis was then taken by the marshals though the door to the lockup, where he was placed in a cell with Dellinger.

The judge next sentenced Hayden to fourteen months and fourteen days for eleven separate contempts. For rising to object that Bobby Seale "should not be put in a position of slavery" he was sentenced to three months. He was sentenced to four months for saying in the presence of the jury that the marshals were beating Seale. He was sentenced to six months for saying loudly enough for the jury to hear him that Ramsey Clark [U.S. Attorney General in the Kennedy administration] had not been allowed to testify. When Hayden rose to speak he told the judge that American youth had turned its back on the system represented by the Court. "Before your eyes," he said, "you see the most vital element of your system collapsing."

"Oh, don't be so pessimistic," the judge replied in a good humored voice. "Our system isn't collapsing. Fellows as smart as you could do awfully well under the system." Hayden seemed to pay no attention. He was staring down at the defense table.

"We don't want a place in the regiment, Julie!" Hoffman called out.

"What did you say?" the judge asked. "Your turn's coming up."

"I'm being patient, Julie," Hoffman answered.

"He thinks that annoys me," the judge said, turning to the spectators and smiling, "addressing me by a name . . . he doesn't know that years ago when I was his age or younger that's what my friends called me."

. . .

Abbie Hoffman was then found guilty of twenty-four counts of contempt, but he was sentenced to only eight months and six days. For saying that he could not respect the law when "it's a tyranny," and for adding that he no longer used his last name, he was sentenced to four months. But for speaking up in defense of Seale he was sentenced to only two months, whereas Hayden, for his part in the same episode, received four months. The judge offered no explanation of this apparent discrepancy, and a few reporters assumed that perhaps the lengthy recitation of the preceding contempt citation had exhausted him, so that he misread the sentences in Hoffman's case. Others, including some of the defendants themselves, thought that the judge had a special affection for Hoffman.

Hoffman's statement on the question of his punishment was restrained. "The only dignity that free men have," he said, "is the right to speak out . . . when the law is tyranny, the only order is insurrection." Then he too was led away. Once he was gone, the judge recessed the Court, leaving Rubin, Froines, Weiner, and the two lawyers to be charged and sentenced on the following day, Sunday.

Though Rubin was found guilty of only fifteen acts of contempt—nine fewer than Hoffman—he was sentenced to twenty-five months and twenty-three days. He received a sentence of six months for complaining aloud when the marshals took his wife from the courtroom. He received another six months for saying to the judge, "Take us all. Show us what a big man you are." When he was asked to speak, he said, ". . . by punishing us you are going to have ten million more." He too was led away.

Weiner was sentenced to two months and eighteen days for seven counts of contempt. Froines received five months and fifteen days for ten counts. . . .

Finally the judge came to the citations against the two lawyers, who were now sitting alone at the defense table. He began by saying he had never held a lawyer in contempt "and only on one occasion did I hold someone who was not a lawyer in contempt." This was not true. He had held the four pretrial lawyers in the present case in contempt until his warrant had been found defective. There was also the case in 1950 in which he had incorrectly imposed summary punishment for the indirect contempt committed by one of the disputants who fell to quarreling outside his courtroom. Moreover, in 1966, he had sentenced a juror to three years in jail for having read and discussed a magazine article concerning a pending trial. In 1968, Judge Hoffman had sentenced a woman named Shirleen Janata to three months in jail for calling him a "son of a bitch." Finally, there was the case of Bobby Seale.

Judge Hoffman sentenced Kunstler to three months for calling the Court a "medieval torture chamber" when Seale was being beaten by the marshals. For arguing "in an angry tone" . . . that Court should not be recessed early, as Foran had requested, Kunstler was sentenced to three months. For asking Mayor Daley "eighty-three questions that were objectionable" he received six months. In all, Kunstler was sentenced to four years and thirteen days in prison for twenty-four counts of contempt.

Kunstler then walked to the lectern and read from a prepared statement. "I am sorry if I disturbed the decorum of the courtroom, but I am not ashamed of my conduct in this Court, for which I am about to be punished.

"I have tried with all my heart faithfully to represent my clients in the face of what I considered and still consider repressive and unjust conduct toward them. If I have to pay with my liberty for such representation, then that is the price of my beliefs and my sensibilities.

"I can only hope that my fate does not deter other lawyers throughout the country who, in the difficult days that lie ahead, will be asked to defend clients against a steadily increasing government encroachment upon their most fundamental liberties. If they are so deterred, then my punishment will have the effect of such terrifying consequences that I dread to contemplate the future domestic and foreign course of this country. However, I have the utmost faith that my beloved brethren at the bar, young and old alike, will not allow themselves to be frightened out of defending the poor, the persecuted, the radicals and militant, the black people, the pacifists, and the political pariahs of this, our common land.

"To those lawyers who may, in learning of what may happen to me, waver, I can only say this: stand firm, remain true to those ideals of the law which, even if openly violated here and in other places, are true and glorious goals, and above all, never desert those principles of equality, justice and freedom, without which life has little, if any, meaning.

"I may not be the greatest lawyer in the world, Your Honor, but I think that I am this moment, along with my colleague, Leonard Weinglass, the most privileged. We are being punished for what we believe in.

"Your Honor, I am ready, sir, to be sentenced, and I would appreciate it if I could be permitted to remain standing at this lectern, where I have spent the greater part of the past five months, while you do so. Thank you."

The spectators began to applaud and cheer. The judge ordered the marshals to remove them, and then said, "I approach my responsibility here just as unhappily as you indicated you are," though Kunstler did not seem unhappy as he spoke. Then the judge said that he was going to make "a rather unorthodox statement. First of all," he began, "there is a lot of crime. I know because I have a lot of criminal cases to try. I am one of those who believes that crime, if it is on the increase . . . is due in large part to the fact that waiting in the wings are lawyers who are willing to go beyond professional responsibility . . . in their defense of a defendant, and the fact that a defendant or some defendants know that such a lawyer is waiting in the wings, I think, has a rather stimulating effect on the increase in crime.

"I have literally thousands of editorials," the judge continued, "back there in my chambers—I know you won't believe this—that are complimentary about decisions I have made over the years. But as for you, to have sat through that Bobby Seale incident and not lifted your arm or a chair, not spoken a word, and he could have been spoken to, and your appearance was on file as his lawyer, you spoke for him as a defendant, even if I were wrong, if I were wrong, even if the many times he called me the vile names that he called me . . . I don't know how it could be proven that a man of my faith was a pig," he said plaintively, ". . . but for you . . . never to have made an attempt to say something like this to him, 'Bobby, hush. Cool it. Sit down now.' But you let him go on. . . . He was your client. Even in the way you describe it, he was your client at one time, and you made no effort to have him keep from calling a judge of the United States District Court a pig, a fascist pig, a racist pig. . . . The only reason I mention the Seale episode is that I didn't want anyone here to get the impression that I was obtuse and didn't know what was going on. I didn't want the ladies and gentlemen of the press to get the impression that I didn't know what was really the time of day."

"Your Honor," Kunstler said, when the judge had finished, "I am glad Your Honor spoke, because I suddenly feel nothing but compassion for you. Everything else has dropped away."

The judge then turned to Weinglass, whom he sentenced to twenty months and nine days for fourteen counts of contempt. Weinglass received four months for repeatedly asking questions . . . after the judge had ruled that such questions were beyond the scope of the direct examination. He was sentenced to five months for continuing to argue after the judge had ruled that he could not. . . .

When the judge had completed his charges, Weinglass rose to say that this was his first trial in a federal court. Yet he felt that he had done his best. As for the contempts with which he had been charged, "each and every one," he said, "had occurred in the course of a legal argument. I have been called in the course of these legal arguments—and Your Honor will recall those words— phony and two-faced." But he said that he did not hold these insults against Mr. Foran or Mr. Schultz. "This has been a long, difficult, highly contested proceeding in which all of us, at one time or another, have lost their sense of professional control and judgment.

"What the court has chosen to label as direct contempt, I cite as nothing more than argument of counsel in the heat of battle. . . . I confess that at times I should have stopped. [But] if Your Honor looks through this record with a balanced eye . . . you will see that on a number of occasions our adversary counsel argued after rulings in several instances. They were even asked to cease their arguments by the court for the very same reason and if counsel are not permitted that small leeway in the conduct of a defense, then I think you do a disservice to the profession and you unbalance the balance in the adversary proceedings—"

The judge interrupted to say that he disagreed that he had been unfair, and told Weinglass that he deserved more respect than the defendants and their lawyers had shown him.

Weinglass replied, "With respect to our different understandings of respect, I was hopeful when I came here that after twenty weeks the court would know my name and I didn't receive that which I thought was the minimum—"

"Well, I am going to tell you about that," the judge interrupted. "I have got a very good friend named Weinruss and I know nobody by the name of Weinrob, and somehow the name Weinruss stuck in my mind. . . ."

Weinglass said nothing about the fact that his name was not Weinrob, any more than it was Weinruss. Instead, he told the judge, "My natural instincts are and have always been to avoid a protracted fight. I am not as strong a man as Bill Kunstler and I think I am more vulnerable to what I perceive as intimidation . . . and I have had to fight that instinct here in court, not only because I thought that the rights of other men were involved but because the inspiration I drew from Bill Kunstler—"

"Did you ever feel like tapping one of those defendants," the judge interrupted, "when they were assailing me with vile epithets to say, 'Hey, hey, be quiet'?"

"Does Your Honor really believe," Weinglass replied, "that what was in conflict here in this courtroom could have been dissipated by an admonishment from Bill Kunstler or myself?"

"I judge your whole attitude toward the Court by your omission to do that," the judge replied.

Weinglass concluded his remarks by saying that he had "come to this city as a stranger. But I say to this court that [the people from Chicago who have worked with the defense] have been sleeping on the floor of my apartment . . . have been receiving a sum of $20.00 a week for their maintenance and no more; have worked until three and four o'clock in the morning, and have given up all the opportunities that are available to them, and, like the defendants, America's best was before them. They only had to seize it."

"I think I would have paid out of my own pocket," the judge interrupted, "for a good bed in a respectable place if you had set them a good example by at least trying to get these men to refrain from the personal epithets hurled at the court."

The judge then passed sentence and Weinglass returned to his place at the defense table.... The two lawyers were granted bail until April. This would give them time, the judge told them, to file appeals for their clients. As for the defendants, the judge, as was his custom, denied them bail.

In the courtroom, no one spoke. A few reporters stood silently beside the defense table as Kunstler and Weinglass gathered up their papers. The spectators drifted out into the corridor. The judge returned to his chambers. It was a frozen Sunday afternoon. The streets outside the Federal Building were deserted except for a line of young pickets who moved slowly past the Federal Building with caricatures of the judge on their signs. They chanted, "Two-four-six-eight. Jail Hoffman. Smash the state." Across the street, a police car waited, its blue beacon slowly turning. In a room on the twenty-third floor, the jury was deliberating for the second day, unaware that the seven defendants and their lawyers had already been sentenced to a total of fifteen years and five days for contempt.

Judge Hoffman had prepared his charge to the jury carefully. On Saturday morning he had spent two hours reading it to the jurors before he sent them out to deliberate. He explained that a defendant charged with conspiracy need not have known every detail of the alleged plot in order to be found guilty. It is enough that the government prove that each defendant was "aware of the common purpose," and that he joined the plot willingly and knowingly. Moreover, the government need not prove that the purpose of the plot had been achieved.

The judge then attempted to explain to the jurors the extent to which the First Amendment protects a defendant's speech. "The law," he said, "distinguishes between mere advocacy of lawlessness ... and advocacy of the use of force or illegality where such advocacy is directed to inciting, promoting, or encouraging lawless actions. The essential distinction," he explained, is between advocacy that urges people "to do something now or in the immediate future, rather than merely to believe in something." ...

Then, to the surprise of the defendants, he instructed the jurors ... "It is a constitutional exercise of the rights of free speech and assembly," he told them, "to march or hold a rally without a permit where applications for permits were made in good faith ... and the permits were denied arbitrarily or discriminatorily."

The defendants were also pleased that the judge told the jurors not to be "influenced by any possible antagonism you may have toward the defendants or any of them because of their dress, hair styles, speech, reputation, court-room demeanor, personal philosophy or life style."

Thus instructed, the jurors began their deliberations at twelve-thirty in the afternoon on St. Valentine's Day. From the beginning, they were divided. Eight wanted to convict the defendants on all counts, and four wanted to acquit them on all counts. One of the jurors felt that the police should have shot the demonstrators in Lincoln Park at the time of the convention and thus spared the government the cost of the trial. Mrs. Peterson, ignoring the judge's in-structions, complained that the defendants had put their feet on the govern-ment's furniture and that they needed a bath. Mrs. Fritz also ignored what the judge had said. She argued that the law was unconstitutional. But Kay Richards, who was in favor of conviction, reminded her that the jurors were not supposed to consider the law; they must confine themselves to questions of fact.

Mrs. Fritz, however, was adamant. Not only were the defendants innocent in her opinion, but she agreed with them that the government had placed itself above the law. "I came to fear our government for the first time," she later ad-mitted, a view that she shared with Shirley Seaholm, another juror who stood for acquittal. Mrs. Seaholm had been bothered by the heavy police guard that accompanied Mayor Daley to Court on the day he testified. "It frightened me," she said after the trial, "that the mayor of my city felt that he needed such security." Mrs. Robbins, another juror who believed that the defendants were innocent, had also been troubled by the mayor's day in Court. She no-ticed that the marshals brought him his drinking water in a glass rather than in the paper cups that the other witnesses used. Mrs. Robbins was reminded by the trial of the persecution of innocent people by the Nazis and she was an-gry that such injustices were now committed in American Courts. Mrs. Butler, the fourth juror in favor of acquittal, felt that the defendants were probably guilty of something, but not what they had been indicted for.

Like Mrs. Robbins, Mrs. Fritz was alarmed by the undercover activities of the police. "What was frightening to me," she later said, "was that there are young people who will go to college and let their hair grow long and then report back. What is happening in our country when your roommate in col-lege may be reporting back to the government?" she asked John Schultz, a Chicago author who interviewed her several months after the trial. What does it mean, she asked, "when the government can tap anybody's phone? Or do anything it wants to do?" Mrs. Seaholm told John Schultz that she had never understood why Seale had not been permitted to defend himself. Often throughout the trial she had wanted to ask the judge, "Why can't Bobby Seale defend himself?"

By Sunday, February 15, the deadlock seemed to be immovable. Thus Mr. Kratzke, who had been elected foreman—because, as Mrs. Robbins later ex-plained, he was a man—sent a notice to the judge that the jury was hung. The judge, however, ignored this information, as he did a similar message that was sent to him by the jurors on the following day. Mrs. Fritz recalled, in her interview with John Schultz, that after this second message had been submitted but had elicited no response, a marshal explained that "the judge can keep you here as long as he wants." Thereafter, the jurors did not deliberate but sat together in bitter silence. By Monday evening, the two factions adjourned to separate rooms at the Palmer House, and Kay Richards began to consider the possibility of a compromise verdict on which both factions might agree.

Meanwhile Mrs. Fritz was convinced that if there were a hung jury, the defendants would inevitably be retried. She feared that the jury in the second trial might not include members who favored acquittal. Mrs. Fritz had served as an alternate juror in a trial that had concluded in a hung jury a few days before the Conspiracy Trial had begun, and she recalled having seen in a newspaper that this trial had been rescheduled for October 8, 1969. Presumably she concluded from this that any trial that ends in a hung jury is retried automatically. In fact, such decisions are at the discretion of the government. And while it was likely that the case would be retried, it was by no means certain. "If we had known that the government would not try this case again, or if we'd known about the contempt proceedings, we would still be in that deliberating room to this day if that was the way Judge Hoffman had wanted it," she explained to Schultz.

Kay Richards was also apprehensive of a hung jury. "I felt as a responsible juror," she later explained, "that I had to come up with a solution. So I became the negotiator. At first I had been a hard liner," she said. But to avoid a hung jury, she "went soft." Of all the jurors, Mrs. Peterson was the most reluctant to compromise. The defendants, she said, "needed a good bath and a hairwash. They should have respected their elders. They should have respected the judge who is so much older and wiser than them or us." Nevertheless, she agreed at last to compromise, "because we hated to see all that money gone and time wasted. Most of us," she later admitted, "would have found all of the defendants guilty on both counts, but we didn't want a hung jury." So finally she too agreed that "half a chicken is better than none." Then she added that if it had not been for Kay Richards, "we'd still be there deliberating."

But Mrs. Fritz later admitted that the four jurors who favored acquittal "felt funny about Kay from the beginning. We didn't trust her and we didn't know why." Mrs. Robbins, however, felt Miss Richards' fiance, who worked for City Hall, may have influenced her against the defendants.

The compromise that Kay Richards proposed became the verdict that the jury submitted on Wednesday morning, February 18. All the defendants were acquitted of conspiracy. Froines and Weiner were found innocent of teaching and demonstrating the use of incendiary devices. The other five defendants were found guilty of the substantive charges that they had crossed state lines with the intention to incite a riot. Except for Miss Richards, none of the jurors was content with the compromise. According to Mrs. Fritz, the jurors who favored conviction believed that the defendants were "evil," as Foran had argued, and that they had no right to come into Chicago's "living room." Mrs. Fritz later admitted, "What we did—and this I'll never get over—we gave in to ourselves. We compromised with ourselves. Kay didn't have anything to do with our decision. You might say that we used her as much as she used us. We didn't know if it was a hung jury that they wouldn't be tried again."

By Tuesday night, the compromise had been agreed upon. On Wednesday morning, Kunstler stood before the judge to argue for a mistrial on the ground that the jury was deadlocked. . . . Thus the defendants, who had been brought to Court from Cook County Jail to be present at the motion for a mistrial, were in a confident mood when Kunstler approached the lectern. But before Kunstler could begin his argument, a marshal entered the courtroom to announce that the jury had reached its verdict. The defendants were taken by surprise. So were the government lawyers. But Schultz had prepared himself for such an event. He proposed to the judge that the defendants' relatives be excluded from the courtroom when the jury gave its verdict. They could not be depended upon, Schultz argued, to behave properly in Court. The judge agreed and the spectators, including the defendants' relatives, were removed.

As she was taken from the courtroom, Abbie Hoffman's wife shouted, "The ten of you will be avenged. They will dance on your grave, Julie, and on the grave of the pig empire."

As soon as the verdicts were rendered and the jurors had returned to the jury room, Mrs. Fritz and the three other women who had favored acquittal broke down and wept. "I went to pieces," Mrs. Fritz recalled. "I started to cry, and I couldn't stop. I kept saying over and over again, 'I just voted five men guilty on speeches I don't even remember.'" Kay Richards and a federal marshal attempted to comfort the four sobbing women. "I don't see how you could have done anything else," the marshal told them.

As soon as the jury had left, the judge announced that he would deny the defendants bail. "I have heard the evidence here. I have watched all of the defendants. . . . From the evidence and from their conduct in this trial, I find they are dangerous men to be at large."

Kunstler then moved to poll the jurors to determine whether they had reached their verdict by compromise and not by a finding of guilt beyond a reasonable doubt.

"I deny that," the judge ruled.

"There may be a question of compromise here," Kunstler insisted.

"I order the defendants and their counsel not to talk to them," the judge replied.

"But, Your Honor, one of the appellate points may be that the jury reached a compromise, that some members wanted to hang the jury. . . ."

"I order you not to do it and that's that," the judge answered.

The judge then adjourned Court until Friday, February 20. On that day he delivered his ruling on the wiretap motion that the defendants had filed the summer before and that the judge said he would not hear until the trial was over. This was the motion in which the defendants had asked to examine the illegal wiretaps withheld by the government for reasons of national security. In the same motion they had also asked the Court to determine whether the illegal wiretaps that had been revealed by the government had "tainted" any of the evidence submitted against them.

On the twentieth, the judge denied the motion of the defense to examine the withheld taps. Attorney General [John] Mitchell had argued that these taps should not be revealed because they had been "employed to gather foreign intelligence information or to gather intelligence information concerning domestic organizations which seek to use force and other unlawful means to attack and subvert the existing structure of the government." The judge admitted that the Alderman decision obliged the government to turn over to the defense all wiretaps for which valid warrants had not been issued. But he also observed that the Supreme Court had not gone so far as to say that its ruling applied to taps that had been made in the interest of national security. To the defendants, the Court's silence on this point suggested that the Alderman ruling was meant to apply to all illegal surveillance, but Judge Hoffman read the intentions of the Court differently. He ruled that ". . . the matter of when electronic surveillance is reasonably necessary . . . to protect the national security is a matter not suitable to judicial determination, but is rather best left to the . . . President or to the Attorney General. I conclude that the electronic surveillance in national security cases is not subject to the warrant requirements of the Fourth Amendment."

The judge then denied the further defense motion that a hearing be held at some future time to determine whether the government's evidence had been tainted by the taps that had not involved national security. With respect to these taps, the judge ruled that the burden was on the defense to demonstrate "taint," and that it was up to the appellate Court to make the final determination based on the defense showing.

Once he had disposed of this matter, the judge announced his intention to pass sentence on the five defendants whom the jury had found guilty. The defendants were once more taken by surprise. Kunstler objected that the judge had allowed himself no time to consider reports from the probation service that might help him determine appropriate terms for the guilty defendants. "The whole purpose of presentence reports [by the probation service] is to indicate what the sentence shall be," Kunstler argued. "You are not even using the facilities of the court to determine that."

"I shall have to do without the services of our wonderful probation department in this case," the judge replied.

Kunstler then pleaded that "the defendants had no way of knowing they are going to be sentenced today. Their families are not even present, which would seem to me in common decency would be permitted."

"The reason they were kept out," the judge replied, "is that my life was threatened by one of the members of the family. I was told they would dance on my grave last week."

"Your Honor," Kunstler asked, "are you serious?"

"Yes I am, sir," the judge replied. He then sentenced each of the five defendants to the maximum term of five years in jail and a fine of $5,000. Furthermore, the defendants were to pay the costs of the prosecution and "to stand committed until the fine and the costs have been paid." Though the sentences were the maximum permitted under the law, and the imposition of the applicable costs of the prosecution—a sum estimated to be about $40,000—was a burden the defense had not expected, the judge was merciful to the extent that the sentences he imposed under the anti-riot statute were to run concurrently with the sentences for contempt.

In their speeches before sentencing, the defendants repeated substantially what they had said when they were sentenced for contempt. Dellinger compared the present proceedings to the Moscow purge trials, but he admitted that he found the judge "spunky," if misguided. "I only wish," he concluded, "that we were all not just more eloquent. I wish we were smarter, more dedicated, more united. I wish we could reach out to the Forans and the Schultzs and the Hoffmans and convince them of the necessity of revolution." Foran and Schultz were sitting with their backs to the defendants. The judge, his eyes shut, was slouched in his chair. A reporter whispered to a colleague, "What revolution?"

Davis said that he looked "to the jury that is in the streets. My jury will be in the streets tomorrow all across this country and the verdict from my jury will keep coming in over the next five years that you are about to give me in prison." Davis then added that in 1977, when he gets out of jail, he is going to move next door to Foran. "I am going to be the boy next door and we are going to turn the sons and daughters of the ruling class into Viet Cong."

Though Hayden promised to make a short statement, he spoke for more than half an hour. It was the police and the FBI, he said, who had made heroes and martyrs of the defendants. "We were invented. We were chosen by the government to serve as scapegoats for all that they wanted to prevent happening in the 1970's." He then said that for four of the jurors to have believed in the innocence of the defendants, despite the efforts of the government lawyers and their police witnesses, "is the testimony of the ability of people to wake up from the nightmare of American life." But it was a "tragedy," he added, that the four jurors "do not yet know how to hold out, and probably never will—do not know how to fight to the end." He then asked why, if the government had not wanted to make martyrs of the defendants, it had indicted them. "If you wanted to keep it cool, why didn't you give us a permit? If you had given us a permit, very little would have happened in Chicago. . . . And you know that if this prosecution had never been undertaken, it would have been better for those in power. It would have left them in power a little longer. You know by doing this to us, it speeds up the end for those people who do it to us."

When Hoffman spoke he addressed himself to the pictures on the wall behind the judge. "I know those guys on the wall," he said. "They grew up twenty miles from my home in Massachusetts. I played with Sam Adams on the Concord Bridge. I was there when Paul Revere rode right up on his motorcycle and said, 'The pigs are coming. The pigs are coming.' I know Sam Adams. Sam Adams was an evil man. So was Thomas Jefferson. He called for revolution every ten years. He had an agrarian reform program that made Mao Tse-tung look like a liberal.

"Hamilton?" he continued. "Well, I don't dig the Federalists. Maybe he deserved to have his brains blown out. . . . As for Lincoln, if he had given his first inaugural speech in Lincoln Park, he would be on trial right here in this courtroom, because that is an inciteful speech."

He then described conditions in Cook County Jail. The food, he said, was inedible. "There's no light. It's not a nice place for a Jewish boy to be, with a college education." The judge smiled. Hoffman continued, "So they shave your heads and tomorrow morning they take our hair. They can have it. It's just hair. And they will go outside the prison walls and they will sell it. Sell our hair."

Rubin offered the judge an inscribed copy of his new book, which had been published that day. On the flyleaf he had written, "Dear Julius, the demonstrations in Chicago in 1968 were the first steps in the revolution. What happened in the courtroom is the second step. Julius, you radicalized more young people than we ever could. You're the country's top Yippie."

When Rubin returned to his chair, the judge imposed sentence. When he told Hoffman that his fine would be $5,000, Hoffman said, "Five thousand dollars, Judge? Could you make that three-fifty?"

"Five thousand," the judge repeated.

"How about three and a half?" Hoffman asked again, but the moment was solemn, and the judge continued without further interruption until the last defendant had been sentenced.

On the following day, as Hoffman had predicted, the defendants' hair was cut. A day later Sheriff [Joseph I.] Woods of Cook County displayed a photograph of the shorn defendants before a rally of the Elk Grove Republican Organization. "This is just to show you that we Republicans get things done," Sheriff Woods told his cheering audience.

In Washington on the same day some two thousand demonstrators descended upon the apartment house where Attorney General Mitchell lived, and six hundred police were required to disperse them. Five thousand marched in Boston. In Chicago three thousand demonstrators assembled in front of Cook County Jail. Through their lawyers, the defendants urged these demonstrators to avoid violence. They feared that a riot at the jail would jeopardize their appeal for bail.

On February 23, the American Civil Liberties Union had filed a brief with the Seventh Circuit Court of Appeals, arguing that Judge Hoffman's denial of bail violated the First, Fifth, Sixth, and Eighth Amendments to the Constitution. Among the lawyers who signed their names to the ACLU brief were Ramsey Clark and Burke Marshall, a former head of the Civil Rights Division of the Justice Department under President Kennedy.

By Friday, February 27, the appeals court had overruled Judge Hoffman and denied the argument of the government that the defendants and their lawyers are "a danger and a threat to the community." The appellate decision was withheld, however, until Saturday the twenty-eighth. The appellate judges did not want to interfere with a celebration attended by Judge Hoffman and Mayor Daley, among others, on Friday in the Federal Building to honor Judge [William J.] Campbell on his retirement.

Thus the defendants were released on the following day. At first their plan was to perpetrate themselves as The Conspiracy and become a permanent revolutionary party. Though, by the spring, their divergent interests had forced them to abandon this scheme, they nevertheless agreed to come together in New Haven on May 1 to protest the forthcoming trial of Bobby Seale, who had been taken to Connecticut. . . . On May 1 the defendants, along with some five thousand other demonstrators, gathered in New Haven with the implied approval of Yale's president, Kingman Brewster, who had said that he was no longer sure that a black radical could be fairly tried in the United States. With the cooperation of the police and the city officials, together with the Panthers, who helped to maintain order among the demonstrators, the rally passed peacefully.

Judge Hoffman, once the trial was over, went to Palm Beach, where his sojourn was interrupted by an invitation to visit the White House. There he attended a breakfast prayer meeting led by the evangelist Billy Graham. On the previous evening he had been an honored guest at the Gridiron Club banquet, an illustrious event sponsored by the Washington press corps. On this occasion, the judge was cheered by the correspondents and the politicians, who regard it an honor to be invited to the annual Gridiron celebration. Among the entertainments that evening was a sketch that included the observation that it hardly mattered if the country ignores the First Amendment; there are still twenty-three left. For the final entertainment of the evening President Nixon and Vice President [Spiro] Agnew put on a sort of minstrel show in which the Vice President assumed the accent of a Southern politician as he played Dixie on the piano. The two men concluded their performance by singing "God Bless America."

CHAPTER 24

From Protests to Scandals

In appeals of the Chicago Eight convictions, the constitutionality of the Anti-Riot statute was upheld, but the convictions of the defendants were overturned and a new separate trial was ordered for each defendant due to errors by Judge Hoffman and the "demeanors of the judge and the prosecutor." The government chose not to hold new trials and dropped the charges.

Trials by a judge other than Judge Hoffman were also ordered for the contempt citations of Bobby Seale, the other seven defendants, and the two defense attorneys. The government dropped the case against Bobby Seale, but the others were tried in 1973. Contempt citations against four of the defendants and against Attorney Weinglass were dismissed; the remaining three defendants were held guilty of eleven contempts and Attorney Kunstler of two—but the convictions were simply allowed to stand without sentences.

During and after the Chicago Eight trials, protests against the war continued. At Kent State University in Ohio, National Guard troops fired on protesting students, killing four. Two other students were shot to death by troops at Jackson State University in Mississippi. In the election campaign of 1968, Richard Nixon claimed to have a "secret plan" to end the war, but after his narrow victory, the war continued. In January 1971 Congress revoked the Gulf of Tonkin resolution, but President Nixon continued the war—and even extended it in Cambodia and, secretly, in Laos—on what he asserted to be his inherent presidential authority. Nevertheless, President Nixon easily defeated the Democratic party's candidate, George McGovern, in the election of 1972.

But President Nixon was not to serve out his second term. During the 1972 election campaign, five persons were caught planting wiretaps in the

Democratic party headquarters in the Watergate apartment complex in Washington. The five were arrested, tried, and sentenced to prison for the break-in. But one of the five implicated higher-ups—all the way to the White House. The resulting scandal caused the resignations of top White House aides. Several aides and former Attorney General John Mitchell were indicted on criminal charges and a special prosecutor—Harvard Law professor Archibald Cox—was appointed to investigate both the incident and allegations of an attempted "cover-up." At the same time, hearings by the Senate and House Judiciary Committees led them to consider impeaching the president.

During one of the congressional hearings, a former White House aide revealed that President Nixon had the White House equipped with recording devices to preserve conversations for history. The Senate Judiciary Committee promptly subpoenaed the tapes, as did the special prosecutor. President Nixon refused the subpoenas on the ground of "executive privilege," and both the Senate Committee and the special prosecutor turned to the judiciary. The federal district court refused to get between two co-equal branches of government but upheld the subpoena of the special prosecutor. President Nixon responded by having the special prosecutor fired (after first forcing out the attorney general and the assistant attorney general—both of whom refused to carry out his orders to fire the special prosecutor—in what came to be known as the "Saturday night massacre"). In the following uproar, the president was forced to have a new special prosecutor appointed. The new special prosecutor—Texas attorney Leon Jaworski—promptly took the president to court again to get the tapes. On July 8, 1974, the case reached the Supreme Court.

The Supreme Court by then had four justices who had been appointed by President Nixon, including the chief justice, Warren Burger. Although Chief Justice Earl Warren had submitted his resignation in the last year of the Johnson presidency, nominating his successor had fallen to President Nixon after President Johnson's nominee, Justice Abe Fortas, ran into charges that he had maintained an improper advisory relationship with the White House. When charges of financial improprieties were added, Justice Fortas not only abandoned the quest for the chief justiceship, but resigned from the Court.

Abe Fortas had been appointed to the Court by President Johnson in 1965. His fall has been analyzed by Bruce Allen Murphy in *Fortas: The Rise and Ruin of a Supreme Court Justice* (1988):

> Greed, ambition, normative insensitivity, occasional dishonesty, and overconfidence are not normally fatal diseases in Washington. If they were, the city would now be empty. These qualities were just contributing causes to [Fortas's] demise. In actuality, there were much larger forces at work that were well beyond his, or anyone else's, control.

. . .

There was chaos in 1968 and 1969. Institutionally, Congress was signaling that it was beginning to take power back from the "imperial presidency," which had kept the nation in a nearly constant state of undeclared executive war in Korea and Vietnam. . . .

From the political standpoint, . . . Senate conservatives from the South and the Republican party would have held up almost any Supreme Court nomination by Lyndon Johnson in the hope that they could control the seat in the fall.

. . .

In the end, . . . Fortas became inextricably linked with the Texan's dying presidency. So closely were they linked that LBJ's vulnerabilities became Fortas's, and the president's political death was matched by the justice's. (pp. 592–96)

President Nixon, thus, had two seats to fill on taking office. Later in his first term, retirements gave him two more seats. The "Burger Court," however, became a disappointment to President Nixon. The Court failed to turn away from the activist legacy of the Warren era and even seemed to extend it—most notably in the case of *Roe* v. *Wade* (1973), recognizing the "privacy" rights of women to abortions, written by Nixon-appointee Justice Harry Blackmun. In the case of *United States* v. *Nixon* the president was to be disappointed again.

Protestors outside the White House, 1973.
Photo from United Press International.

U.S. v. NIXON

from Stanley I. Kutler, *The Wars of Watergate: The Last Crisis of Richard Nixon* (New York: Alfred A. Knopf, 1990), pp. 506–17. Copyright © 1990 by Stanley Kutler. Reprinted by permission of Alfred A. Knopf, Inc.

"Scarcely any question arises in the United States that is not resolved, sooner or later, into a judicial question," noted Alexis de Tocqueville in 1837. By 1974 Tocqueville's brilliant insight had metamorphosed into an unwritten constitutional corollary. Americans preferred legions of lawyers to battalions of soldiers, and they looked to the Supreme Court as the ultimate locale for the peaceful resolution of political and policy disputes. However contradictory the Court and its power were to democratic theory and impulses, its role had served the nation well for nearly two hundred years. From the time of John Marshall, the Court frequently has fallen afoul of particular interests, yet it has displayed resilience, and its authority has steadily grown. Except in periods of emotional assault upon the institution from those momentarily aggrieved by a decision, the Court's prestige consistently has remained high among the American people.

In 1857, the Supreme Court, dominated by a majority of slaveholders, attempted to impress pro-slavery doctrines on constitutional law in the Dred Scott Case. Chief Justice Roger B. Taney's decision upholding Scott's master provoked protests throughout the North and the West. The vituperative denunciations of the Court at the time have attracted a great deal of historical attention—at the cost of ignoring a powerful current of opinion that deplored the Dred Scott decision yet recognized the need for maintaining the authority of the Court. "We are a lost people when the supreme tribunal of the law has lost our respect," ran a typical comment that urged Americans to maintain faith in the efficacy of the Court, despite its momentary lapse. Following the Supreme Court's desegregation decision in 1954, segregation advocates regularly denounced the Court, yet they persisted in pursuing judicial solutions. So, too, antiabortion activists, infuriated by *Roe v. Wade* (1973), nevertheless have pressed for a new judicial determination of the question.

Political battle cries for judicial restraint generally amount to little more than convenient appeals to rally the faithful. "What would we do without the Supreme Court?" asked those who stood between the defenders and root-and-branch critics of the Supreme Court following the Dred Scott decision. The Court had long before firmly established itself as an indispensable component of the American governmental apparatus. "Without some arbiter whose decision should be final the whole system would have collapsed," Judge Learned Hand once observed.

Despite the Supreme Court's popular image as the ultimate constitutional arbiter, only rarely has it been called upon to consider the limitations of presidential power. The modern benchmark for such judicial determination was made in 1952 when the Justices rejected President Harry Truman's claim of "inherent powers" to justify his seizure of steel mills to prevent a strike that he believed would impair the Korean War effort. When the steel companies sued to regain control of their property, six of the nine Justices ruled that in the absence of congressional authorization, the President had no such power. In a concurring opinion, Justice Robert H. Jackson eloquently underlined the rule of law: "With all its defects, delays and inconveniences, men have discovered no technique for long preserving free government except that the Executive be under the law, and the law be made by parliamentary deliberations."

William Rehnquist, a Jackson clerk at the time of the Steel Seizure Case, later recalled it as "one of those celebrated constitutional cases where what might be called the tide of public opinion suddenly began to run against the government, for a number of reasons, and . . . this tide of public opinion had a considerable influence on the Court." In 1974 Rehnquist implicitly applied that observation to his eight sitting colleagues who considered President Nixon's appeals that they legitimate his efforts to retain control of the remaining White House tapes. Rehnquist recused himself in the case, citing his past association with the Nixon Administration. Ironically, as Jackson's clerk he had listened to the arguments in the steel case; as an Associate Justice, he never heard those in *U.S. v. Nixon* lest he give the appearance of secret participation. . . .

While the Judiciary Committee weighed the President's political future, the Supreme Court dealt only with his claims of executive privilege to keep his tapes from the Special Prosecutor. The issue was not literally framed as deciding Nixon's ultimate fate, but the reality was plain. The constitutional process concurrently playing in the House inevitably had the burden of "politics" or "partisanship." On the other hand, despite the political bearing of the Court's role, the public to a large extent perceived the Justices as being above politics and parties—serving as disinterested constitutional arbiters. As the Court listened to arguments in *U.S. v. Nixon,* the editorial writers of the *Wall Street Journal* asserted that the President's fate should not be resolved "by a unilateral assertion" of the impeachment power; "only the courts can draw an ongoing body of standards, that is, a body of law, to balance executive privilege against other necessary principles." Richard Nixon himself had said in 1969 that "Respect for law in a nation is the most priceless asset a free people can have, and the Chief Justice and his associates are the ultimate custodians and guardians of that priceless asset."

The Justices acknowledged the need to give the President his day in court by allowing three hours of argument instead of the normal one hour. As [James D.] St. Clair [counsel to the president] began his presentation on July 8, he recognized the Court's potential for damaging the President's credibility. He told Chief Justice Warren Burger that "no one could stand here and argue with any candor that a decision of this Court would have no impact whatsoever on the pending inquiry before the House of Representatives concerning the impeachment of the President." St. Clair sought to persuade the Court to deny the justiciability of the case and so to leave Nixon's fate to the House alone. The White House much preferred Congress as an adversary. For his part, [Special Prosecutor Leon] Jaworski appealed to the Justices to invoke the most sacred phrases in the Court's constitutional liturgy. John Marshall had written in *Marbury v. Madison* (1803) that "[i]t is emphatically the province and duty of the judicial department to say what the law is." Protecting and interpreting the Constitution, said Marshall, was "of the very essence of judicial duty." St. Clair to the contrary, that is also what the nation looked for in July 1974.

. . . St. Clair now . . . asked the Justices to dismiss the suit because of "the co-pendency of impeachment proceedings." One Justice interrupted St. Clair, suggesting that this was not the Court's problem. St. Clair thought otherwise. The Court, he insisted, had a long tradition of not deciding "political questions," a doctrine that generally provided an escape route from deciding questions best determined by the political branches of government. St. Clair acknowledged that when it had decided "political" matters, as, for example, the legislative reapportionment cases of the 1960s, the Court had acted to strengthen individual rights and the democratic process. But no such consideration was involved in this case, he argued; instead, a decision would affect the proper duties of Congress. Furthermore, St. Clair went on, a decision against Nixon would "diminish" the democratic process, for it would limit the ability of the President to hold confidential discussions with his aides and thus deprive him of the power, duties, and responsibilities given to other presidents.

St. Clair came perilously close to suggesting that his client stood above the law—a claim that a zealous government lawyer had advanced on behalf of President Truman in the steel controversy in 1952 much to Truman's embarrassment and the annoyance of the Justices. St. Clair conceded that the President was not above the law, yet argued that he had a constitutional standing within the law different from anyone else's. He might be impeached while in office, but not indicted—and by implication, he might not be forced to diminish his authority. Meanwhile, St. Clair squared the circle: the President alone might decide what material would go to the House; if a court examined any of that material, it would infringe on the separation of powers, for only the

House might impeach. Justice William Brennan was mystified. How did judicial consideration of taped conversations held for purposes of criminal actions interfere with impeachment? St. Clair replied only that an unfavorable verdict in the criminal proceedings would unduly influence the House. Justice William O. Douglas neatly turned the tables, countering that the material might well help the defendants in various Watergate-related trials now pending. The President's counsel found himself arguing for naked official power as opposed to the rights of individuals.

Defending Nixon's control of the tapes also left St. Clair in the uncomfortable position of protecting matters which the President preferred to hide. Another Justice pressed the counsel to the point that St. Clair admitted that Nixon might claim privilege over any Watergate conversation. What, demanded Justice Thurgood Marshall, was the constitutional authorization for that position? "Well," St. Clair responded, "I would suggest you should find it in the Constitution. And it need not be explicit. It can well be implied." Throughout, St. Clair sought to persuade the Court that the Constitution granted a body of privileges to the executive, just as it did to Congress. The difference, of course, was that the privileges of Congress were enumerated, while those of the President were implicit.

The constitutional privileges and rights of "the presidency" were central to St. Clair's argument—and they proved his Achilles' heel. He contended that the preservation of candor in presidential conversations represented an overriding public interest; such materials could be released only at the President's discretion. But what public interest was there in preserving secrecy regarding a criminal conspiracy, Justice Lewis Powell asked? St. Clair could only beg the question: "The answer, sir, is that a criminal conspiracy is criminal only after it's proven to be criminal." Another questioner posed the hypothetical situation of a soon-to-be-appointed judge who negotiated a deal in which he would give the President money. No, St. Clair said, the conversation remained privileged; the only clear remedy would be to impeach the President. Almost in exasperation, Marshall homed in: "How are you going to impeach him if you don't know about it?" Then there would be no case, St. Clair responded. "So there you are," Marshall said. "You're on the prongs of a dilemma, huh? . . . You lose me some place along there."

Jaworski's deputy, Philip A. Lacovara, followed St. Clair to close the Special Prosecutor's arguments. His task was simpler and less abstract. Lacovara dismissed St. Clair's "co-pendency" argument, requiring the Court to subordinate the criminal case to the impeachment process, as unsupported by "sound constitutional law" or by history. He appealed to the Court's independence and courage, and to its history. The Court had only rarely taken refuge in the doctrine barring decisions of "political questions." Instead, it had regularly decided "political" matters, as in cases concerning reapportionment, civil rights, and the procedural rights of the criminally accused. The Court had understood "its duty to interpret the Constitution"; "that's all we ask for today," Lacovara concluded.

...

St. Clair "lost" the Justices while Jaworski and Lacovara successfully persuaded them of the "very essence of judicial duty." As Rehnquist had noted, the Justices did not live in a vacuum. Watergate had captured their attention, as it had that of the nation. The Justices and their clerks avidly followed the Senate hearings, and the daily revelations of Administration wrongdoing had been a frequent topic of conversation. As they absorbed the Jaworski and St. Clair briefs, a consensus emerged: the President might not enjoy an absolute privilege over the tapes. The Special Prosecutor's arguments had provided the Court with compelling reasons to order Nixon to release the tapes in question. Since the Justices differed as to the scope of their ruling, St. Clair might perhaps have been able to exploit those differences and produce a divided opinion, rather than the "definitive" pronouncement that Nixon said he would obey. But St. Clair did not.

William Brennan, a Democrat appointed by Eisenhower, had operated as a major force within the Warren Court, infusing liberal values into jerry-built coalitions. Some of that influence had declined under Chief Justice Burger, but Brennan now sensed an opportunity to revitalize his old role. When he learned that Potter Stewart, Lewis Powell, and Harry Blackmun had decided to vote against the President, Brennan realized the importance of uniting the Court behind one opinion. . . .

Burger, however, assigned the opinion to himself. He was in a bind as he confronted a case affecting the future political well-being of the man who appointed him. White House gossip in 1973 and 1974 reported that he "had assured the President that the tapes would not be taken away." Burger's closeness to Nixon and the Administration was well known—a situation riddled with irony since the Senate had rejected Lyndon Johnson's nomination of Abe Fortas to be Chief Justice, in part because of charges of cronyism. "The C.J. needs to talk with you *urgently*," the President's Appointments Secretary told Nixon in May 1968. John Ehrlichman recorded in 1971 that Burger had "met periodically" with the President, Mitchell, and himself "to discuss issues of the day and to join a general discussion of current events." Just after the Court took the tapes case in 1974, the *Washington Post* disclosed correspondence between Burger and John Mitchell, indicating a close, "confidential" relationship between the Chief Justice and the Administration.

Burger's decision to write the opinion raised numerous questions. Would he soften the decision? Did he not face a conflict, given his constitutional responsibility as Chief Justice to preside in an impeachment trial? Indeed, for some time Burger had had clerks secretly researching impeachment trials, so that he would be prepared for that contingency. Perhaps he saw the opportunity to establish his independence from the Administration. Whatever his motives, a great deal of ego was involved—as it undoubtedly was for those colleagues who wanted the opinion for themselves. After the Justices assembled in conference the morning after the oral arguments, they quickly revealed their unanimity of judgment; deciding the scope of the opinion proved far more difficult.

Later that day Brennan visited Earl Warren, hospitalized after a series of heart attacks, and told him about the developments. Warren had long disliked and distrusted Nixon, and had been dismayed as the President sniped at Warren Court decisions. Several hours after Brennan's visit, Warren suffered a fatal heart attack. Brennan nonetheless was certain that his news had comforted his old comrade.

The Court's opinion emerged after several weeks of editorial emendation and intensive lobbying among the Justices. Douglas . . . pressed Burger whenever it appeared that he might be willing to assert a too-permissive view of presidential powers. The Chief Justice at one point had suggested that the federal rule allowing courts to subpoena evidence considered potentially relevant and admissible, must be applied more strictly for issuing a subpoena against the President. Douglas would have none of it: "My difficulty is that when the President is discussing crimes to be committed and/or crimes already committed with and/or by him or by his orders, he stands no higher than the Mafia with respect to those confidences." Justice Stewart eventually provided a draft of the key section that satisfactorily maneuvered between the constitutional rights of the various Watergate defendants and the President's demands for privileged communications.

In the end, Brennan and the others certainly had the input they had wanted all along; meanwhile, Burger alone had his name on an opinion that united the Court: the President must surrender the tapes. The Court met for its final conference on July 23, and the Chief Justice issued a press release noting that it would convene the next morning. Leon Jaworski had some trepidations; he knew the decision was about to come down. He also knew that if the Court ruled in the President's favor, he would have "to close shop." St. Clair was in San Clemente with his client.

The next morning Alexander Haig [White House chief of staff] called the President to report that he had the complete text of the Supreme Court's decision. "Unanimous?" the President asked. "Unanimous. There's no air in it at all." "None at all?" the President persisted. "It's as tight as a drum," said Haig.

Richard Nixon . . . knew he could not defy the Court; perhaps he could still devise a plan for deleting some material. . . . While St. Clair made the President's case to the Judiciary Committee on July 18, Nixon admitted that his greatest concern was "the Supreme Court thing." On July 23 he talked to Haig and Ziegler about resigning. . . .

The immediate reaction to the Court's ruling in *U.S. v. Nixon* focused on the Court's order that the President surrender the tapes. Although Nixon had lost the battle, . . . the misty concepts of executive privilege Nixon and St. Clair had battled to protect finally received the Supreme Court's imprimatur. The Justices did not concede privilege enough to protect President Nixon in this case, but they did provide some precedent and underpinning for future claims. The Court's opinion . . . clearly revealed that the criminal implications in the case, and the pressing political confrontation it had produced, forced the outcome. The Court recognized presidential rights to some confidentiality, but it found in the present case "a sufficient preliminary showing that each of the subpoenaed tapes contains evidence admissible with respect to the offenses charged in the indictment."

U.S. v. Nixon is another milestone marking the unique power of the Supreme Court. The heart of the opinion confronted St. Clair's contention that separation-of-powers doctrine precluded judicial review of presidential claims of privilege—that the case, in short, was nonjusticiable. Politely but firmly, the Court invoked John Marshall's 170-year-old dictum that the judiciary's duty was "to say what the law is."

In its partial vindication of the President, the Court agreed that confidentiality had validity—it could be "constitutionally based"; indeed, the opinion noted, the framers of the Constitution had met in secret. But the Justices refused to concede that the President's claims completely insulated him from the judicial process. They would grant him great deference in the exercise of executive privilege, but when his claim depended "solely on the broad, undifferentiated claim of public interest in the confidentiality of such conversations, a confrontation with other values arises." The case did not present a military or national-security matter; hence the Justices contended that confidentiality would not be "significantly diminished" if the President produced the tapes for an *in camera* scrutiny by the judiciary.

In practice, separation of powers, the Court noted, depended greatly on "interdependence," on what Justice Jackson had called in the Steel Seizure Case the need to ensure a "workable government." Nixon's "undifferentiated" claims for confidentiality would "upset the constitutional balance" needed for a "workable government" and, not incidentally, "gravely impair" the judiciary's role under Article III of the Constitution.

The Court conceded a "presumptive privilege" of confidentiality to the President, but the Justices insisted on a balance with the commitment to the rule of law. Here the Court followed the path suggested by Justice Douglas and turned the case against the President into one on behalf of the claims of those criminally indicted . . . : "The generalized assertion for privilege must yield to the demonstrated, specific need for evidence in a pending criminal trial."

. . .

Typically, Nixon interpreted the decision as a setback for the "presidency," something the Supreme Court had carefully attempted to ensure it was not.

After he learned of the Court's action, Nixon closeted himself with Haig and St. Clair. For how long and just how far the President considered resistance to the Court's decision, remains somewhat cloudy.

. . .

Nixon discussed the option of "abiding" by the decision while continuing to withhold materials, thinking that there was some Jeffersonian precedent for doing so. He dropped the idea after some supporters warned that "full compliance was the only option." St. Clair always thought that even now the President "didn't have to turn over the tapes, maybe. I don't know." That "maybe" was predicated on St. Clair's belief that the presidency and the judiciary were two equal and separate branches, a belief traceable to Jefferson and to Andrew Jackson's notion of concurrent powers, under which some actions of the judiciary were not necessarily binding on the executive. During oral arguments before the Supreme Court, when one of the Justices had approached the question of compliance, St. Clair had carefully avoided committing the President. Nixon "was good at dissembling," St. Clair remembered.

The White House's public-relations men had tried to anticipate strategy for reaction to the Supreme Court. . . . But late in the day of the decision, the President had touch with the reality that prevailed in Washington. Eight Republican congressmen dispatched a telegram urging him to comply. "We have confidence that your affirmative response to this order will be consistent with the unparalleled significance of this development." That afternoon, Nixon put on a brave front, trying to salvage some victory from the ashes. "I am gratified," he said, "to note that the Court reaffirmed both the validity and the importance of the principle of executive privilege, the principle I had sought to maintain."

The nation barely had time to absorb the impact of the Supreme Court's decision, for that same evening, July 24, the House Judiciary Committee reassembled to continue its impeachment inquiry. Now its debates would be aired on prime-time television. . . .

As the debate opened, Chairman Peter Rodino waited, gavel poised in midair, for the television prompter to signal the start of the proceedings, just as if he were officiating at an athletic event. The air was thick with real drama. For so long, impeachment had been unimaginable; now, the nation was to be a witness to proceedings that might lead to that very end. The Supreme Court news did not overshadow the evening's events in the Judiciary Committee, yet it was pervasive. Moreover, the Court's opinion neutralized contentions that partisan Democrats alone opposed the President, as Nixon's own Chief Justice had rendered the opinion. . . .

The Chairman's speech had been carefully crafted by his aides. It spoke for fairness and education, with a sense of the occasion. "Make no mistake about it," Rodino said. "This is a turning point, whatever we decide." He at once broadened and narrowed the problem before the committee. The House inquiry was not that of a court of law, he told the audience. Quoting Edmund Burke's 1788 definition of impeachment, Rodino said that the inquiry involved accusation and judgment by statesmen of other statesmen who had abused power, and it was not dependent "upon the niceties of a narrow jurisprudence, but upon the enlarged and solid principles of state morality." The narrow question centered on whether the President had told the truth when he said he had been deceived by subordinates, and whether or not he himself had participated in a design systematically to cover up the role of his agents and associates in an illegal political-intelligence operation, together with related activities—whether he, in short, had engaged in a course of conduct that had impeded his faithful execution of the laws and had done this for his own political interest and protection. Finally, Rodino pointedly underlined the constitutional nature of the proceeding. No one welcomed such a test of constitutional practices, he said; still, "our own public trust, our own commitment to the Constitution," were at stake.

Edward Hutchinson [the ranking Republican member of the Committee] briefly responded. His educational homily for the audience focused on the "political" nature of impeachment. He revealed that the committee had not even agreed on the nature and scope of an impeachable crime, as if to discredit impeachment itself as well as the process at hand. Taking his assignment one step further, Hutchinson reflected on the awesome burden of impeachment; conviction allowed for no discretion to fit the punishment to the crime: removal was the only course. Evidence of a serious offense might exist, yet such an offense, he suggested, might not warrant so extreme a measure. He warned his colleagues—and the public—that the offense should be of "sufficient gravity" to justify removal. Finally, Hutchinson took note of the day's events in the Supreme Court and suggested that the Chairman consider postponement until the President yielded additional evidence. Rodino ignored him and instead turned to the committee's senior Democrat, Harold D. Donohue, who introduced a resolution and two articles of charges against Nixon. For the first time in more than a century, Congress confronted the President of the United States with the very real possibility of impeachment.

CHAPTER 25

The Expansion of Civil Rights

Exactly one month after the Supreme Court arguments on the White House tapes, on August 8, 1974, President Nixon resigned rather than face an impeachment trial in the U.S. Senate. By then, his vice president, Spiro Agnew, had also resigned under tax and corruption charges unrelated to the Watergate break-in, and House Speaker Gerald Ford had become the vice president to succeed to the presidency. In addition to the threat of impeachment, ex-president Nixon could have been charged in criminal proceedings, but that possibility was headed off by a pardon from President Ford.

The Watergate scandal reflected especially poorly on the legal profession. Richard L. Abel, in *American Lawyers* (1989), has noted:

> [In] response to the Watergate scandal, which involved an embarrassing number of lawyers from the President on down, . . . the ABA compelled approved law schools to require instruction in professional responsibility and many states also made it a separate subject on the bar examination. (p. 142)

The scandal also reflected poorly on the Republican party, and voters exacted punishment in the election of 1976, electing Democrat Jimmy Carter over President Ford.

The Vietnam War ended during the Ford administration, and the tensions of the 1960s subsided. But some trends of the 1960s continued. In particular, widespread respect for the achievements of the black civil-rights movement strengthened movements for the legal rights of other disadvantaged groups. Among the most active, Mexican-American civil-rights issues were joined with concerns for the rights of migratory workers under union leader César Chávez; Native Americans pressed for redress of land claims and other grievances—most dramatically in the occupations of the Bureau of Indian

Affairs offices in Washington, Alcatraz Island off San Francisco, and the hamlet of Wounded Knee in South Dakota; and several groups organized to campaign for the elimination of discrimination on the basis of gender or sexual preference.

The campaign for women's rights had as one of its major goals the enactment of an Equal Rights Amendment to the Constitution. The amendment was introduced in Congress after the victory of the suffrage movement in 1920 and was renewed annually. But it languished.

Achieving the right to vote had not substantially reduced discrimination against women in education, in employment, nor even before the law, but women's organizations disagreed on how to address these issues. Some opposed the drive for equal rights, since inequality was not entirely one-sided. While laws disadvantaged women in many ways, some also conferred special benefits such as exemption from military conscription, entitlement to alimony and child-custody preferences in divorce, and protective labor conditions.

Some legal advances were made by women in addition to the right to vote. The ancient common law doctrine of "coverture," under which married women were not allowed to contract, to sue, to own separate property, or even to control their own wages, had been eliminated by "Married Women's Acts" enacted in the nineteenth century. During the Second World War, many women temporarily entered the workforce, including traditionally male-dominated occupations. A substantial number gave up their jobs as peace returned, but the percentage of women in the workforce rose steadily after 1945. In 1961 President Kennedy appointed a National Commission on Women, which reported on the extent of discrimination against women. Although the commission did not endorse an Equal Rights Amendment, its work resulted in a federal Equal Pay Act in 1963 and the establishment of a commission to deal with women's issues in each state.

Women also won some significant victories in courts, such as the elimination of gender-specific job ads in newspapers, the recognition of equal rights as estate administrators, and equal pension benefits. Gender relationships were also altered by the success of reformers seeking changes in divorce laws. Nearly all states adopted statutes granting divorces without either party having to prove the "fault" of the other for the breakdown of the marriage.

In 1966 the National Organization for Women was formed under the lead of Betty Friedan, author of *The Feminine Mystique* (1963), a work that broke new ground for the women's movement. But the goal of an Equal Rights Amendment remained elusive.

Illinois delegation to the first National Women's Conference, Houston, 1977.

Photo from National Commission on the Observance of International Women's Year, *The Spirit of Houston*, (1977).

from Deborah L. Rhode, *Justice and Gender: Sex Discrimination and the Law* (Cambridge, Mass.: Harvard University Press, 1989), pp. 63–78. Copyright © 1989 by the President and Fellows of Harvard College. Reprinted by permission of Harvard University Press.

The Equal Rights Campaign

An objective common to much legal and historical research is . . . "to achieve an intuitive sense of how things do not happen." From this perspective, the campaign for an Equal Rights Amendment to the United States Constitution is a particularly illuminating case study. . . . [T]he difficulties surrounding the campaign are not entirely of recent vintage. For a half-century supporters introduced some variant of a constitutional prohibition against sex discrimination in every congressional term. When, in 1972, the House and Senate finally passed an amendment, the struggle for state ratification foundered on much the same conflicts that have plagued American feminism throughout its history. In part, the dispute involved concerns about preferential treatment that had crystallized during the protective-labor debates of the 1920s. Underlying those controversies were more fundamental questions about the importance of formal rights and sexual differences—questions on which the women's movement has always been divided. . . .

After its initial introduction in the early twenties, the Equal Rights Amendment provoked sporadic legislative disputes and opposition from such unlikely bedfellows as the John Birch Society, the Communist Party, the AFL-CIO, Calvin Coolidge, and Eleanor Roosevelt. An equally eclectic coalition of supporters gradually increased; by the early 1970s it included the ACLU, the Teamsters Union, the Women's Christian Temperance Union, George Wallace, and George McGovern. According to public-opinion polls, a solid majority of Americans supported the amendment, although many appeared uninformed or unenthusiastic about some of its likely consequences.

. . . Against this . . . backdrop, the 1972 Congress overwhelmingly endorsed an amendment providing that "[e]quality of rights under the law shall not be denied or abridged by the United States or any state on account of sex." At that point, the prospect for early and uneventful state ratification appeared promising. Within months after congressional approval, some twenty state legislatures had ratified the provision, often with only minutes of perfunctory debate.

In Illinois, the momentum suddenly ceased. Phyllis Schlafly, a conservative resident with no national prominence, launched a "Stop ERA" campaign that succeeded, first in Illinois, and then in enough other states to block ratification. Despite a three-year extension, the ratification deadline expired without the necessary endorsements from three-quarters of the states. Fifteen states never endorsed the amendment and five attempted to rescind their ratification.

That reversal is instructive both about the status of American women and the dynamics of constitutional change. At issue in the ERA campaign were fundamental questions about the meaning of sexual equality and the means of attaining it. Those questions had both an instrumental and symbolic dimension. On an instrumental level, the issue was whether the amendment's ban on gender classifications would in fact improve women's legal status. On a symbolic level, the campaign became a referendum on a host of other issues concerning sexual differences, social roles, and feminist politics.

That is not to imply a sharp disjuncture between these levels. Many of those who stressed the ERA's symbolic significance did so because they believed that it would have tangible, if indirect, effects on legal institutions and cultural patterns. It was also commonly assumed that the amendment's practical consequences would carry a broader symbolic message and ultimately affect actions beyond the reach of constitutional scrutiny. However, to understand the evolution of the ERA campaign, it is useful to separate these claims and to focus on the way opponents reframed debate on both instrumental and symbolic levels.

. . .

Instrumental Claims

Proponents' primary argument in support of a constitutional amendment was that it would provide the most effective means of combating sex-based classifications in areas such as employment, education, welfare, credit, pensions, domestic relations, and military service. To seek piecemeal legislative or judicial remedies against each discriminatory action could result in interminable delay and inordinate expense, while offering no protection against future abuses. It would, as one supporter put it, be like "enforcing the Emancipation Proclamation plantation by plantation."

Moreover, court decisions under existing statutory and constitutional provisions had produced "uneven developments marked by sharply divided opinions." According to many proponents, that result stemmed from the Supreme Court's unwillingness to view sex, like race, as a "suspect classification" triggering "strict scrutiny." Such scrutiny requires that the challenged classification serve a "compelling" state interest that cannot be achieved by less burdensome means. Few discriminatory practices have survived this test. Accordingly, proponents hoped that an equal-rights amendment would mandate a comparable level of scrutiny for sex-based classifications and thus promote a more egalitarian social order.

. . .

. . . While supporters appealed to women's aspirations, opponents appealed to women's fears. According to Schlafly, a constitutional mandate of equal treatment would jeopardize a host of "precious rights," particularly those related to family and military service obligations.

Opponents claimed, for example, that wives would lose entitlement to support during or after marriage and would have a *"legal obligation* to go out to work to provide half the family income." Such predictions evoked broad concerns. Wives with unstable marriages or few marketable skills complained that the amendment might be "all right for a younger woman," but that they were unsure how to support themselves and their children under an equal-rights amendment. To traditional homemakers, a constitutional mandate seemed to offer an unnecessary and unwelcome exchange: they would pay the price of expanding some abstract set of opportunities that they had never experienced and would never enjoy.

Opposition arguments concerning family law were among those most irritating to ERA proponents. Given Schlafly's training as a lawyer, her claims appeared somewhat disingenuous. As supporters pointed out, the amendment would cover only state action; it would not dictate families' private financial arrangements or require wives to work. Nor would it materially alter husbands' support obligations. Under current laws, courts virtually never enforced such obligations in ongoing marriages; and once a marriage terminated, judges would still be free under sex-blind provisions to require support for dependent homemakers. Even without the ERA, most state legislatures were already enacting gender-neutral family laws, and judicial decisions barring sex-based alimony statutes were accelerating that trend. As proponents noted, such statutory modifications had not produced the "radical" upheavals in family life that Schlafly predicted.

These rejoinders were not entirely effective in allaying public concerns. . . . [T]raditional homemakers have not always fared well under gender-neutral family law reforms. Although such provisions have avoided sex-based stereotyping, they have also failed to address sex-based disadvantages. The real weakness in Schlafly's claim was that most wives already were, and always had been, less secure than she implied, and gender-neutral mandates were not the cause. The difficulty was not with reforms such as those replacing "wife" with "spouse" in alimony statutes that authorized "equitable" awards. Rather the difficulty lay in decisionmakers' interpretations of what "equity" meant, interpretations that undervalued domestic work and its effect on an individual's earning potential. Such judicial biases were as apparent under sex-specific statutes as under their gender-neutral replacements. But that message was unwelcome in many quarters. Many homemakers were more inclined to reject the messenger than to acknowledge their own vulnerability.

Opponents' other most effective argument involved military service. Equality in the workplace was one thing; equality in the trenches was quite another. Throughout state capitols, legislators visualized their daughters sharing barracks, bunkers, or latrines with hardened combat troops, and having their "fair forms blasted into fragments" by "bayonets, bombs, [and] bullets." The issue was not only the future of womanhood but the security of the nation. According to politicians such as Illinois Representative Webber Borchers, women's "inadequate hip structure . . . tender [feet]," and inability "to press the attack" would "hamstring" the infantry.

On this issue, proponents never developed a consistent response. The most common rejoinder—that Congress already had power to draft women—was hardly adequate to the occasion. According to Schlafly, the ERA would require women to assume the same military obligations as men, including combat service. The legal basis for that assertion was, however, open to dispute, as a subsequent Supreme Court decision permitting sex-based draft registration suggested. Thus, some proponents took the position that the ERA would not mandate women in combat; under the Constitution's War Powers clause, judges could properly defer to military leaders' resolution of the issue.

Other ERA supporters, including the authors of a highly influential *Yale Law Journal* article, maintained that the amendment would mandate sex-neutral treatment in the armed forces. This position was consistent with Congress' refusal on several occasions to endorse an equal rights amendment with exemptions for military service. Proponents also cited evidence indicating that women were capable of performing many combat jobs and that their exclusion from such positions had adverse effects on military and civilian opportunities. From this perspective, until women were prepared to accept the full responsibilities of citizenship, including the draft, they would have difficulty claiming its full entitlements. Most Americans, however, took a different view. According to public-opinion polls, a majority of respondents opposed equal treatment for men and women in the military, and state legislators did not appear to be an exception.

A final cluster of arguments that proved effective with some groups involved sexuality, reproduction, and privacy. Catholic and fundamentalist leaders often linked the ERA with legalized abortion, homosexual marriage, and the related evils of a "singles society." Although proponents generally denied those connections, their position was not unproblematic. Supporters were, of course, correct in noting that the Supreme Court had based abortion rights on considerations of privacy rather than equality. However, as opponents also pointed out, feminists had invoked state equal-rights amendments and federal equal-protection guarantees as a justification for governmental funding of abortion. On issues of sexual preference, proponents often noted that courts generally had not interpreted legal mandates against gender discrimination to bar discrimination against gays or lesbians as long as males and females were treated similarly. But some feminists opposed those rulings and were reluctant to relinquish the ERA as a potential ground for challenging them.

Opponents' privacy arguments had less legal substance, though many members of their audience may not have recognized as much. The most notorious example involved Schlafly's account of the ERA's effects on public bathrooms. In her view, "the only reason that this nation has separate restrooms for men and women and boys and girls is sex. Consequently, being a distinction based on sex, the ERA would abolish the power of the Federal Government and the power of the 50 states to require separate facilities of this nature for persons of different sexes." With comparable logic, other opponents projected the demise of sex-segregated locker rooms, saunas, hospital facilities, and homes for wayward girls.

Such arguments ignored the legislative history of the amendment, which clearly preserved an exception for privacy-related regulation. Moreover, the triviality of the argument invited ridicule. Within some constituencies, opponents' resort to "potty politics" was counterproductive. ERA supporters capitalized on the fact that Schlafly herself had apparently managed to survive the ordeal of undifferentiated restrooms during her frequent airline excursions to testify against the amendment. Other proponents claimed that women's greatest risk concerning single-sex bathrooms was that women would be cleaning them. Yet the persistence of some privacy-related claims suggests that they may have touched deeper nerves than proponents generally acknowledged. Although the particular examples opponents cited may not have had great independent significance, when taken together, they evoked a vision of androgyny that threatened core American values.

Symbolic Underpinnings

For both sides in the ratification campaign, the ERA became a stand-in for more fundamental concerns and a battleground for symbolic politics. To proponents, the amendment represented a significant affirmation of equality as well as a means for attaining it. To opponents, the ERA appeared as a "unisex" mandate, a tool to "nullify . . . distinction[s] between the sexes," and to transform the United States into a "gender-free society." . . .

. . . In the world as ERA opponents conceived it, men and women assumed unique roles, dictated by nature and sanctified by scripture. Or, as Schlafly succinctly put it, "Women have babies so men should support them." Despite the fact that over half of all women were in the workforce, "marriage and the home [remained] the greatest liberation for women."

The claim was not without irony, particularly given the source. The Supreme Court had, a century earlier, invoked precisely the same argument about women's maternal mission when it denied female applicants entry to Schlafly's chosen profession. . . .

. . . Public-opinion polls throughout the 1970s indicated that most Americans did not view the organized feminist movement in a favorable light, even though many supported certain central feminist objectives. Opposition to that movement galvanized opposition to constitutional change. To members of groups such as the Feminine Anti-Feminists, Gigi Gals Galore Against the ERA, Winsome Wives and Homemakers, and Women Who Want to Be Women, Schlafly's message appeared flattering and reassuring. It exalted their values and ennobled their station. By contrast, much feminist rhetoric implied that these women had made the wrong choices and demanded reappraisal of their self-image, priorities, and daily lives.

. . .

For other women whose lives were less traditional, but whose opportunities appeared limited, the assumptions of the women's movement appeared to be out of touch with daily realities. Among those who lacked adequate skills, mobility, or employment opportunities, the feminist agenda seemed elitist and irrelevant. Particularly among minority women, many of whom confronted constant problems of racism, poverty, and violence, a campaign for constitutional symbols seemed largely beside the point.

. . .

Other grounds for opposition included resistance to change in general and to women's advancement in particular. Within some conservative constituencies, the amendment became an all-purpose symbolic scapegoat. According to many opponents, the ERA, by weakening women's traditional role, would also weaken traditional values. In tones reminiscent of antisuffragist rhetoric, opponents predicted that the ultimate result of equal rights would be an array of social problems including increased "divorce . . . desertion . . . alcoholism, suicide, and possible deviation." The principal beneficiaries of constitutional change would be "offbeats and deadbeats": the "homosexual who wants the same rights as husbands, the husband who wants to escape supporting his wife and children, the coward who wants to get out of military service by giving his place to a woman."

Extremist right-wing organizations imbued the amendment with even more subversive overtones. Despite the Communist Party's long-standing opposition to the ERA, the John Birch Society perceived the amendment as an integral part of "Communist plans . . . at work in a now vast effort to reduce human beings to living at the same level as animals." Other opponents, less certain about the ERA's conspiratorial origins, nonetheless perceived it as promoting a "communistic way of life." In Southern states, conservative leaders also identified the amendment as yet another assault on states' rights and recalled the federal government's enforcement of comparably open-textured mandates in civil rights cases.

. . .

Among conservative constituencies the ERA fell victim to a general backlash against the radicalism of the 1960s. Calls for emancipation rekindled fears, if not of revolution, of severe dislocations in a congenial way of life. . . .

. . .

Political Strategies

. . . For personal lobbying, Schlafly and her colleagues devised a uniquely domesticated approach that captured both public and legislative attention. ERA opponents arrived in state capitols bearing gifts of identifiably femine manufacture, most often home-baked bread and similar culinary offerings. These strategies were effective in several respects. Not only were they a relatively inexpensive means of arousing media attention, they also appealed to women who lacked experience and interest in more conventional forms of political persuasion. Such approaches helped offset proponents' financial resources and organizational support from well established women's associations.

. . .

[T]he more moderate pro-ERA leaders mounted their own culinary campaign, matching their foes muffin for muffin. . . . [S]eventy-five mature housewives assembled to serve Eggs Benedict to Illinois Representatives and Senators. Neither the opposition nor the press let the event pass unnoticed. The day before the brunch, Schlafly and her followers distributed to all legislators small loaves of home-baked bread labeled "Let us stay in the kitchen." Not surprisingly, this juxtaposition proved irresistible to reporters. In their accounts the affair became a playful contest among rival hausfraus. . . .

Undaunted by such jocular press reviews, proponents continued to offer variations on the same theme. Legislators across the nation received a barrage of breads, pastries, valentines, tea roses, forget-me-nots, and the like. Many recipients appeared more bemused than moved. The gestures seemed "unprofessional" and, as caricatured by the press, made the amendment appear unworthy of serious substantive debate. An inevitable, if unintended, consequence of these quiche and cookie crusades was to trivialize the issue and deflect attention from serious questions of gender inequality.

Moreover, supporters taking this feminine approach were repeatedly upstaged by their more radical colleagues. Some feminists remained unconvinced that the most direct route to a legislator's vote was through his stomach. They pursued a different path, with public denunciations in animal blood or spray paint and gifts such as chicken manure and a child's potty. Such gestures, however cathartic for the converted, did little to persuade those most in need of persuasion.

Although more moderate ERA proponents attempted to dismiss these tactics as the harmless antics of a few extremists, that effort received a significant setback in 1977. Live on national television, delegates to the International Women's Year Conference in Houston endorsed the ERA—along with subsidized abortion, gay rights, and a host of other controversial planks and placards (such as "Mother Nature is a Lesbian"). Just in case any legislators from a nonratifying state had missed the festivities, Schlafly thoughtfully mailed them all a full account. Other anti-ERA leaders brought home conference souvenirs for display in state capitols, to ensure that no one could overlook the connection between equal rights, vibrators, and sex education in the public schools. The point was widely taken. According to one Illinois representative, who switched his vote after the conference, "the resolutions adopted there [show] what these people think the ERA stands for . . . I can't tolerate those things—and neither can my constituents."

. . .

[T]he constitutional campaign remains significant as a cultural text. From a political and jurisprudential standpoint, the debate has offered insights about the dynamics of constitutional change. Most significantly, it has illustrated the difficulty of achieving informed public analysis of legal issues carrying substantial symbolic freight. From a more sociological vantage, the dialogue has illuminated cultural assumptions and aspirations; in particular, it has exposed the lack of consensus regarding social institutions that seek to reinforce or suppress sex-linked differences. And finally, from and instrumental perspective, the results may have exerted some short-term influence over the continuing reformulation of women's legal rights and social status.

CHAPTER 26

Consumerism and Environmentalism

Civil rights, the Vietnam war, and women's rights were the focal points of the social protests of the 1960s and 1970s. But the critical attitude of the time also raised other challenges to the "establishment," including the rights of consumers and protection of the environment.

The movement for consumer rights had its antecedents in the nineteenth and early twentieth centuries, but the revitalization of the consumer movement in the 1960s had a specific starting point. It can be traced to a book: *Unsafe at Any Speed,* published in 1965 by a then-recent graduate of Harvard Law School, Ralph Nader. The book charged General Motors with knowingly marketing an automobile with hazardous design defects. The book became a best-seller, and Nader gained celebrity status—not only from the book, but also from GM's reaction to it. GM hired a detective agency to have Nader investigated and apparently hired women to attempt to entice Nader into compromising sexual liaisons. Kelley Griffin's *Ralph Nader Presents More Action for a Change* (1987) recounts part of the history:

Nader was disturbed that a corporation could wield its power in this manner, so after lengthy consideration, he decided to sue for invasion of privacy. Any award, he announced at the outset, would be used to establish an organization to pursue auto safety issues and other consumer concerns. The legal battle lasted four years. In the end, documents had surfaced proving that GM had hired the detective to find whatever he could to discredit Nader, to "shut him up." As GM officials admit, and the investigation reports show, Nader's profile came out clean, but not GM's. In 1970, GM settled the case for $425,000, an amount thirty times greater than any court had ever awarded in an invasion of privacy case. (p. 4)

The proceeds of the settlement were used to establish a variety of organizations. Nader himself has devoted his time and his funds ever since to consumer-oriented causes. Nader and his "Raiders" went on to document not only the threats to the public's health, safety, and pocketbooks from businesses, but also the failures of regulatory agencies to protect the public. Studies by Nader's groups led to shake-ups in the Federal Trade Commission, the Interstate Commerce Commission, the Food and Drug Administration, the Federal Power Commission, and other agencies.

Success with regulatory agencies was accompanied by success in Congress. Nader's organizations were involved in the enactment of the Truth in Lending Act, the Poison Prevention Packaging Act, the Hazardous Substances Act, and the Occupational Safety and Health Act; the extension of the Flammable Fabrics Act; and the establishment of the Consumer Product Safety Commission. Proposals to establish a more far-reaching Consumer Protection Agency, however, did not succeed, as Nader encountered opposition and charges of overzealousness.

Among the studies published by the organizations founded by Nader, several concerned the deterioration of the environment due to industrial pollution. But other organizations became the central players on this issue as environmentalism also became a "movement." The organizations include the Sierra Club, the National Audubon Society, Friends of the Earth, the Natural Resources Defense Council, the Nature Conservancy, the Environmental Law Institute, and the Environmental Defense Fund. Their major legislative accomplishment came in 1969 with the National Environmental Protection Act, which established the Environmental Protection Agency for enforcement and the Council on Environmental Quality to collect information and recommend legislative or regulatory action. Another major legislative step came in 1980 with the passage of the Comprehensive Environmental Response, Compensation and Liability Act, which established a "Superfund" for the cleanup of hazardous waste sites.

Like consumerism, environmentalism has a history reaching back to the nineteenth century, and it, too, was revitalized in the 1960s by a book: Rachael Carson's *Silent Spring* (1962) aroused the nation with its description of the devastation caused by agricultural insecticides. Other books followed, detailing the pollution caused by industries, automobiles, and other sources, and the depletion of natural resources caused by overuse of water, overlogging, and other excesses.

Among the most shocking cases of environmental pollution uncovered in the 1960s and 1970s were those involving toxic chemicals—some lethal—as exemplified in the industrial city of Woburn, on the Aberjona River, in Massachusetts. In the 1960s, Woburn experienced water shortages, and the city government had two new wells—Wells G and H—added to the six wells then serving the city. In the 1970s, several children living in the sections of the city served by Wells G and H came down with fatal cases of leukemia, a form of cancer.

Some parents suspected a connection between the illness of their children and Wells G and H. Most active among them were Anne Anderson, whose son Jimmy was one of the first fatalities, and her neighbor, Donna Robbins, whose baby was born with physical defects and also died of leukemia. With the aid of the local Episcopal minister, the Reverend Mr. Bruce Young, the parents organized and succeeded in getting the attention not only of the city government, but also of the Massachusetts Department of Public Health, the Centers for Disease Control, and the Environmental Protection Agency.

All three agencies verified the existence of what health experts consider a "leukemia cluster." They undertook studies of Wells G and H and found that the wells contained a chemical popularly known as TCE, which was suspected of being a carcinogen. The TCE was traced to industries near the wells belonging to the W. R. Grace Company and the Beatrice Food Company. But proving the link between the activities of these companies and the leukemia of the Woburn children in a way sufficient to establish legal liability remained difficult.

The Woburn parents turned to a Boston attorney, Joseph Mulligan, of the firm of Reed & Mulligan, who assigned the case to a young attorney in the firm, Jan Schlichtmann. The case aroused the interest of a writer, Jonathan Harr, who joined Schlichtmann as "an observer from within" and produced an engrossing account of the case.

John Travolta as Jan Schlichtmann in Touchstone Pictures' film, *A Civil Action*.
Reprinted by permission of John Travolta.

from Jonathan Harr, *A Civil Action*
(New York: Random House, 1996), pp. 62–82.
Copyright © 1995 by Jonathan Harr.
Reprinted by permission of Random House, Inc.

Four months had passed since Mulligan had signed up the families in the Woburn case, and Anne Anderson [and Donna Robbins] had begun calling the office. . . . Mulligan answered most of the calls at first. "These things take time," he'd explain. . . . After a while Mulligan let his secretary handle most of the calls. She would tell Anne or Donna that Joe was out of the office or in a meeting. The secretary began feeling sorry for the women. After making yet another excuse, she'd walk into the office of one of the firm's associates and say, "What are we going to do with these poor people?" But the associate was a lowly member of the firm. He could only shrug. The case wasn't his.

Reed & Mulligan had many personal injury cases in its files. Mulligan was fond of calling especially promising cases "gold mines." A new case might look promising at first, but further investigation sometimes revealed a fatal flaw, and the case would die quietly in the files. Many cases in many firms across the nation expired in such a fashion.

Mulligan still regarded Woburn as a potential "gold mine," but he had done little work on the case. He had gone once to speak with the state environmental people, hoping they could tell him who had contaminated the wells. But they'd been "tight" (as he later put it) with information. He had also hired at minimum wage two students from Suffolk Law School, where he himself had gotten his degree, night division. He had instructed the students to collect whatever pertinent information they could find in Woburn, and he'd left them to work on their own. One of them quit after a few weeks, and the other one did little more than clip newspaper articles from the *Woburn Daily Times*.

Mulligan . . . was impressed with Schlichtmann's industry, and he decided to recruit the young lawyer for the Woburn case. One evening that winter, before leaving the office, he stopped at the library and invited Schlichtmann out for a drink. "I'll be at the Littlest," said Mulligan. "Meet me there."

The Littlest Bar on Province Street was Mulligan's favorite haunt. It was not only tiny but also subterranean, down six steps from the street. By dusk on a winter evening, the Littlest was crowded with men, most of them Irish, many of them lawyers, a tight nest smelling of whiskey and tobacco. Mulligan cut a huge swath in the Littlest. He towered over the bar and his stentorian voice rose above the babble. Among some patrons at the Littlest, word had it that [the] hero in *The Verdict* [a film starring Paul Newman], the dissolute but principled lawyer, was modeled after Mulligan. Mulligan never denied it.

When Schlichtmann arrived at the Littlest that evening, Mulligan bought him a drink and introduced him around. He put his arm around Schlichtmann's shoulder (he was taller by several inches than Schlichtmann, who himself stood well above an average crowd) and steered him to a stool in the corner of the bar. He began talking about [another] case, telling Schlichtmann that he was impressed by how quickly he'd put it together. "There are other good cases in the office," Mulligan continued. "I've got one in particular I'd like you to look at, a mass-disaster case, best case in the office. This one could be a real gold mine. It'll require some hard work, but you're just the sort of guy to develop it." Mulligan began describing the Woburn case.

Schlichtmann had read in *The Boston Globe* about the leukemia cluster, but he hadn't known that Mulligan was involved, or that there was even a case. He felt flattered that Mulligan would ask him to work on a case of such importance and celebrity. "When can I see the file?" he asked.

Mulligan said he'd have his secretary get it for him tomorrow. "A lot of pieces are still missing from the puzzle," Mulligan confided. They talked about Woburn for an hour over drinks. Mulligan told Schlichtmann several times he was "delighted" to have him working on the case.

On the conference room table the next morning Schlichtmann saw a slender manila file labeled "Woburn Cases." The file, less than an inch thick, looked very thin for a mass-disaster case. . . . Schlichtmann opened the Woburn file and saw newspaper clippings and Mulligan's contingency fee agreements, standard forms in which the lawyer had agreed "to do any and all necessary things in the prosecution of any claims which the client may have against"—here Mulligan had filled in the words—"any and all Defendants identified by the attorneys."

The only other item in the file was the report of the investigation by the Centers for Disease Control and the state department of health. Schlichtmann started reading the report. Some of it seemed promising—the fact, for instance, that it was very unlikely the cluster of childhood leukemias in east Woburn could have occurred merely by chance. But other items in the report gave Schlichtmann pause. "With few exceptions," said the report, "investigations of leukemia clusters have failed to demonstrate significant associations or even promising leads as to environmental causes. . . . None of the chemicals found in Wells G and H are known to be leukemogenic, although trichloroethylene and tetrachloroethylene have been found to cause tumors in laboratory animals. The source of the present contaminants is unknown."

When he finished reading, Schlichtmann felt dismayed. A dozen questions went through his head: Whose chemicals had polluted the wells? Who had dumped these chemicals, and when had they gotten into the water supply? Had they in fact caused leukemia? The file was silent on almost every question. It was apparent that Mulligan had spent little time on the case.

Schlichtmann . . . could not even pronounce the names of the chemicals in the Woburn wells, but he felt instinctively that they probably had caused the cluster of leukemias. He himself had always been vigilant about what he ate and drank. . . . Schlichtmann never took any drug stronger than aspirin, nor had he ever smoked or drunk coffee. He rarely ate red meat and he avoided tap water, preferring instead bottled water, the more expensive the better.

At a glance, the Woburn case did look, as Mulligan had said, quite promising—polluted drinking water had apparently caused an epidemic of leukemia. But Schlichtmann knew that such a claim would be difficult to prove. He'd have to delve into the question of what causes leukemia, a question that medical science itself had not yet resolved. And it would be expensive. . . . At this point in his career, Schlichtmann had been practicing law for only three years. He had taken only one case to trial. Woburn was too big, he told himself, too expensive, too complicated.

Mulligan's secretary began directing the phone calls from Anne and Donna to Schlichtmann. The message slips soon grew into a small pile. One evening that spring, Schlichtmann went out to Woburn to meet the families. It was dusk when he left the office. . . . When he arrived at Anne's house, the families were gathered in the living room, awaiting him. He introduced himself and explained that Mulligan had asked him to work on the case.

He knew that these people wanted to hear what progress he and Mulligan had made. He explained that he had no basis yet for filing a lawsuit. That action would have to wait until the government agencies had identified the source of the contaminants in the wells. "Toxic waste dumps are surfacing all over the country," he told the families. "The EPA [Environmental Protection Agency] doesn't have the capacity or the leadership to investigate each one. You have to organize, you have to force them to do their job. This is a political battle now, not a legal one. We're not ready for the legal battle yet."

He stayed at Anne's house for nearly two hours, answering questions, getting a sense of his new clients. Anne's child had died four months earlier, and she looked pale, her eyes rimmed in red as if she had been crying just moments ago. But Schlichtmann was struck by her forcefulness and the intelligence of her questions. He talked for a while with Richard and Mary Toomey, whose son Patrick had also died earlier that year. Richard, a sheet-metal worker for nearly thirty years, was a reserved man, but he had a blunt, honest face, and Schlichtmann liked him immediately. "We're not in this for money," Toomey told Schlichtmann. "We just want information. No one will tell us anything."

Schlichtmann left the meeting feeling sorry for these people. But he also felt he could do little to help them.

. . .

In the files at Reed & Mulligan, Schlichtmann found dozens of other cases, many of them gathering dust, waiting for someone to take interest. They were, he thought, like unpolished stones, like lumps of coal. Many were of such small value . . . that they would barely justify his labor. A few were completely worthless. But some looked as if they might contain a diamond at the core. He kept searching for the most promising ones. Soon the Woburn file was buried beneath the other cases.

Assisting Schlichtmann was a lawyer who occupied a small cubicle next to Mulligan's office. The lawyer's name was Kevin Conway. He was in his mid-thirties, several years older than Schlichtmann, short and stoutly built, with a belly that was edging toward portliness. He had a manner, unpracticed and unconscious, of conveying warmth and concern. The office workers all seemed to come to Conway with their troubles. When, for instance, Mulligan's secretary became upset by the plight of the Woburn mothers, she went to Conway.

Conway had been at Reed & Mulligan for two years, doing piecework, getting paid by the case. The job was his third since graduating in the top half of his class at Georgetown University Law School. He had started his career working for a big company in New York, where he'd had an office with a view and made a handsome salary. But after six years there, he'd felt as if life were passing him by. He had no sense of accomplishment. He'd looked at the people around him, people who'd spent their lives working for the company, and he'd realized that if he didn't leave soon, he might never get away.

Conway had decided to go into practice for himself. He descended from a position of relative prestige in the legal world—from an office on the fiftieth floor of a fancy building in New York—to the lowly status of a solo practitioner, close to the legal profession's bottommost rung. He moved into the basement of a century-old building in Belmont, a suburb of Boston. From the window of his office in Cushing Square, he had a pavement-level view of a working-class neighborhood of small shops. He knew this world well. He'd grown up near Belmont, not far from his new office, the second of nine children, the son of a schoolteacher. There had never been much money in the Conway family, but there had always been plenty of warmth and conviviality. Every Sunday afternoon the entire Conway clan would assemble in the living room with their musical instruments for a concert. The house was always a thick tangle of kids, crowded with Conways, but so inviting that many neighborhood kids gathered there, too.

For his new office in Belmont, Conway hired a secretary, a pretty woman in her early thirties named Peggy Vecchione who had once dated Conway's younger brother. By her own admission, Peggy could barely type and she knew nothing about legal work. But she needed a job badly. She had recently gotten divorced and had two children to support. Conway didn't think twice about hiring her.

Together they handled the legal problems of anyone who walked in Conway's door. Most of these problems were simple matters—wills, minor criminal infractions, house closings. Also some divorces, though Conway did not like divorces because they saddened him and he invariably spent too much time trying to reconcile the unhappy spouses. Peggy watched one couple walk out the door, irritated by Conway's counseling. "Don't you understand?" the man said, his voice raised. "We want a divorce!" Peggy told Conway he must have done a good job. "At least they're angry at you instead of each other," she said.

Conway came dutifully to work every day, even though there wasn't always much to do. He'd consult with Peggy about how much to charge a client. For a will of moderate complexity, she would advise one hundred fifty dollars. "They can't afford that," Conway would say of an elderly couple. He would charge fifty dollars. He'd ask Peggy how long it would take her to type the will, and she'd say, anticipating many errors and retyping, "Oh, about a week?" Conway would respond, "Hmm, that long?" But he wouldn't complain. When business was slow, he went to the arraignment courts and represented indigent defendants. For each case, he got paid seventy five dollars by the state. He made only as much as he needed, and his needs weren't great.

After a few years in Belmont, Conway married a woman he'd courted since his New York days, and his needs grew slightly greater. He had known Joe Mulligan for several years, and when Mulligan invited him to come work at his firm, Conway accepted. He brought Peggy along with him. He didn't draw a salary. He got paid only from the proceeds of cases he helped to resolve.

He'd been at Reed & Mulligan two years, working out of a small cubicle, when Schlichtmann showed up. Peggy would never forget that day. "Kevin used to tell me, 'There's no passion in my life.' He was bored with what he was doing. Then Jan burst into the office. . . . He was overpowering. Kevin was stunned by him. Kevin said, 'Jan's exactly like what you hope you're going to be when you get out of law school.'"

. . . When Schlichtmann began digging through the files at Reed & Mulligan, Conway was his guide. Conway unearthed a case in which a three-year-old girl, vomiting and with a high fever, was examined by a doctor, treated with aspirin, and sent home. She developed fulminant meningitis and suffered brain damage as a result. Schlichtmann and Conway settled the case for $675,000. They worked together every day. In the evening they'd go downstairs to the Emperor of China restaurant on Tremont Street for dinner and then come back to the office and work some more. They took on a case in which a hospital incubator had overheated, causing brain damage in a newborn infant. They settled that case for $1.15 million. When an insurance company refused to settle a claim in which a surgical clamp had been left for nine years in the abdomen of a elderly man, Conway and Schlichtmann prepared for trial. It was an Essex County case, on the north shore of Massachusetts. . . . They rented a room at a cheap motel near the Essex County courthouse. They lived there for two weeks, amid piles of lawbooks, medical texts, and legal pads. On the bureau was a portable typewriter, on which Schlichtmann typed last-minute motions. They ate their meals at a diner next to the motel, keeping company with long-haul truck drivers. They worked until two or three o'clock in the morning, and then got up to go to court. Conway felt punchy from lack of sleep, but he also felt exhilarated. "Working with Jan," Conway said of that time, "was the difference between being alive and being dead." The jury awarded their client $492,000.

Conway felt as close to Schlichtmann as a brother, although in most respects they appeared to be complete opposites. Schlichtmann was tall and slender, Conway short and stout. Schlichtmann's shoes were always polished to a high gloss, Conway's were always scuffed. Schlichtmann's tailored shirts were perfectly pressed, Conway's were taut over his substantial belly and billowed out of the back of his pants. Schlichtmann's tie, perfectly knotted, was held in place with a gold collarpin. The knot in Conway's tie had usually descended an inch or two by the time he arrived at work. Schlichtmann, fastidious about health and diet, watched Conway eat doughnuts for breakfast and drink "gallons" of coffee. "You treat your digestive tract like a sewer," Schlichtmann once told him. Conway had a kind word for everyone he encountered—the receptionist, the filing clerk, the office boy—while Schlichtmann, impatient and always hurrying, often failed to observe even common civilities. Conway tried never to judge anyone harshly. "You can never know enough about why someone acts the way they do," he would say.

They differed in their approach to money, too. Conway lived frugally, saving to buy a house and start a family. Schlichtmann spent every penny he earned. Conway noticed that Schlichtmann usually seemed depressed when he had money in the bank. He seemed driven by a need to get rid of money as quickly as possible, and when he had spent it all, he would burrow into another case and his spirits would rise.

Conway found the cases in the files of Reed & Mulligan and got Schlichtmann interested in them. But Conway didn't like the Woburn case. Whenever Schlichtmann mentioned it, Conway tried to steer him away. "It's a black hole," he'd warn Schlichtmann. Conway had never met the families, and he could view the case in a cold, unemotional light. He had learned by then that Schlichtmann never did anything in half measures, and the full measure of Woburn—the size, the complexity and the cost—scared Conway. "We don't want that one," he would say when he and Schlichtmann went downstairs after work to the Emperor of China restaurant and discussed new cases.

. . .

For a time after her son's death, Anne Anderson had rarely left the house, fearful she would break down and weep in public. She used to dream that Jimmy was still alive, and then she would awake, stunned by the fresh realization that he was gone. In the grocery store she'd see something he had liked and her tears would start to flow.

She recovered slowly. A few months after Jimmy's death, she began working at her brother's stonecutting business in Somerville, partly to pay the bills, but also to try to get her mind off Jimmy. She worked in the office, answering telephones and keeping accounts. But her thoughts kept returning to the contaminated wells. She wanted answers, and she wanted to bring to account whoever had caused her son's illness and suffering. As far as she could see, neither Mulligan nor Schlichtmann had done anything. Schlichtmann didn't even return her phone calls.

Driving home from work one afternoon in the fall of 1981, Anne turned on the radio and began listening to the Jerry Williams talk show on WRKO. The subject that day was lawyers. Listeners were invited to call in and ask questions of two lawyers who were guests on the show. Anne was listening with half an ear when she realized that one of the voices was familiar. It was Schlichtmann's voice. Here he was, on the radio, pontificating about the law, about serving clients, and she could never even get him on the phone. She drove home as fast as she dared. She ran into the house, picked up the kitchen phone and dialed the station without pausing to take her coat off.

"I've got a question for Mr. Schlichtmann."

"Go ahead, please," said the talk show host.

"What should you do when your lawyer never calls you back?"

"Wait a minute!" said Schlichtmann. "I know this voice. Is this Anne?"

"Jan, I call and call and never get to talk with you."

Over the air, Schlichtmann laughed painfully. "Your messages are right next to my mother's," he said. "I haven't called her back either." Then he added, "You can talk with Kathy, you know."

"Kathy doesn't have the answers," said Anne.

Schlichtmann didn't have any answers either, but he did not say so. He promised to call Anne the next morning.

Anne hung up the phone and then she picked it up again and called Donna Robbins. "Guess what I just did," Anne said.

Despite all its difficulties, the case tantalized Schlichtmann. He believed that it had merit. He kept thinking that if he was destined for something great in life, this case might be his opportunity. If he were to win it, he would set new legal precedents and gain a national reputation among his fellow plaintiffs' lawyers. He would no doubt make a lot of money. And he would have helped the families of east Woburn. Fame, fortune, and doing good—those were, in combination, goals worth striving for, he thought.

But by the winter of 1982 Schlichtmann still had not made a decision on the case. The statute of limitations—three years for a personal injury action in Massachusetts—had begun to run on the day the Woburn wells had closed, on May 22, 1979. If he was going to drop the case, he had to tell the families soon. If not, he had to start working quickly to prepare the complaint. As ambitious as he was, he also liked to think of himself as a businessman, a pragmatist. Conway had called this case a "black hole," and Conway was probably right. Schlichtmann decided there were other worthy cases he could devote himself to, cases he could win.

So in February he called Anne and asked her to arrange a meeting with the families at Trinity Episcopal. On the evening of the meeting, as Schlichtmann prepared to leave for Woburn, Conway came into his office. Conway made him promise that this time he would level with the families. He'd tell them that he didn't have sufficient basis to file a lawsuit. Conway followed Schlichtmann to the door. "When you come back, we won't have the Woburn case anymore. Right, Jan?"

"Right," said Schlichtmann.

At Trinity Episcopal, the small gathering of men and women sat in metal folding chairs around a long wooden banquet table that was usually used for church suppers. Reverend Young sat among them. The church hall was dimly lit and cold. Some of the women kept their coats on. Everyone but Anne thought that Schlichtmann had come to inform them of new developments in the case. She alone suspected that he had come to wash his hands of it, but she had not voiced her suspicion to the others, not even to Donna or Reverend Young.

Schlichtmann sat across from the families and recited the now familiar litany of difficulties—the absence of a defendant, the problem of proving that the chemicals had caused the leukemias, and the cost, especially the cost. "There are a lot of questions," said Schlichtmann, "and we don't have any of the answers yet. I'm afraid the resources to pursue this simply aren't there."

A sense of bleakness came over the group. Anne thought to herself, He's done everything but say good-bye.

For a moment, no one spoke. Schlichtmann, it seemed, couldn't bring himself to say good-bye, to get up and leave. Then Reverend Young cleared his throat and said, "What if I told you I know where we can get some money?"

Schlichtmann looked doubtfully at the minister. This was not a case that could be financed by church bake sales.

Reverend Young explained that he had spoken that very afternoon with a lawyer in Washington, D.C., the executive director of a new public-interest law firm called Trial Lawyers for Public Justice.

Schlichtmann grew suddenly alert. He knew about the firm! he exclaimed to Reverend Young. He was, in fact, one of its founding members! Six months ago, at a convention of trial lawyers in San Francisco, he had contributed a thousand dollars to help get the organization started. He had, of course, liked the name, and he was sympathetic to the goal of using the legal system to bring about social change.

The conversation with the Washington lawyer, continued Young, had come about by coincidence, the result of a call from a staff member in Senator Edward Kennedy's office. The staffer had read that Trial Lawyers for Public Justice was looking for a good environmental case. Woburn had come to her mind. She'd called Reverend Young, and then, at four o'clock that afternoon, she'd set up a conference call between him and the executive director, whose name was Anthony Roisman. Over the phone, Young had described the situation in Woburn, and Roisman had said the case sounded interesting. Moreover, Trial Lawyers for Public Justice had some funds already earmarked for an environmental case. But, Roisman had also said, he could not just step in and take the case away from another lawyer.

And that, Reverend Young told the gathering at Trinity Episcopal, was why he had not mentioned the conversation until this moment.

Schlichtmann, greatly animated now, questioned the minister closely about every detail of his conversation with Roisman. He remarked several times on the "amazing" coincidence of events. He told the families he would call Roisman the first thing tomorrow morning. He hoped that he and Roisman could work together on the case. When he left Trinity Episcopal that evening, the mood among the families was no longer somber.

The next morning Conway appeared at the door of Schlichtmann's office. "Well?" Conway said.

"We've still got the case," said Schlichtmann. "I couldn't say no."

. . .

Roisman flew up to Boston the following week. He and Schlichtmann spent two days together. Roisman was in his early forties, a Harvard Law School graduate who had been head of the U.S. Justice Department's Hazardous Waste Enforcement Section during the Carter administration. He knew how to assemble a complicated environmental case, and he thought that based on everything he had heard so far Woburn appeared most promising.

Schlichtmann invited Roisman to take over as lead counsel in the case. Roisman accepted, and asked Schlichtmann to remain on as local counsel. This arrangement suited Schlichtmann perfectly. He'd still be involved in an important case, and there was much he could learn working alongside a man of Roisman's experience. They agreed to split equally the costs of preparing the case. Roisman's organization would receive two thirds of any fee that might result from a settlement or a verdict, and Schlichtmann and Mulligan would split the other third.

After almost two years of little more than talk, events suddenly began to move swiftly. One of Roisman's assistants collected medical and scientific studies on TCE and the other chemicals in the city wells. Using the Freedom of Information Act, Roisman obtained from the Environmental Protection Agency a preliminary report of its east Woburn investigation. The agency had narrowed its focus to a single square mile of the Aberjona River valley, some 450 acres surrounding Wells G and H. Contractors for the EPA had drilled test wells along the periphery of that square mile. On the northeast side, chemical analysis of the groundwater revealed high concentrations of TCE migrating through the soil in a featherlike plume toward Wells G and H. Even higher concentrations of TCE were found in groundwater to the west of the two wells, under fifteen acres of wooded, undeveloped land alongside the Aberjona River. The EPA listed the names of several industries situated around the perimeter of the square mile, but it did not identify which of those were responsible for the contamination. "Further study is required," stated the report.

The EPA did, however, put the east Woburn aquifer on its National Priorities List, more commonly known as the Superfund. The agency ranked each site by a formula that involved the proximity of the polluted area to residential areas, the nature of the chemicals involved, and whether or not drinking water had been contaminated. By 1982 there were 418 sites on the EPA list. The east Woburn well field, the newest addition, was ranked thirty-ninth.

The EPA report was highly technical, filled with maps of bedrock and groundwater contours, well logs, and scientific jargon. To decipher it, Roisman hired a Princeton University professor, an expert in groundwater contamination and hazardous wastes. The professor told Roisman and Schlichtmann that the underground plume of TCE coming from the northeast appeared to originate at a manufacturing plant owned by W. R. Grace, the multinational chemical company. The other source of contamination, to the west of Wells G and H, came from the fifteen acres of wooded land that was owned by the John J. Riley Tannery. And the tannery, it turned out, was itself owned by the giant Chicago conglomerate Beatrice Foods, producer of dozens of consumer goods, from Samsonite luggage to Playtex bras, Peter Pan peanut butter and Tropicana orange juice.

Both companies ranked high in the Fortune 500. In the lexicon of personal injury lawyers, they had "deep pockets," and this fact had weight for Schlichtmann and Roisman. Personal injury law is not a charitable enterprise. To a lawyer working on a contingency fee and paying the expenses of a case himself, it is crucial that the defendant either have assets, preferably a lot of them, or a big insurance policy. To Schlichtmann, having Grace and Beatrice as defendants in the case was like learning that a woman his mother kept trying to set him up with had a huge trust fund.

. . .

Roisman had started composing the lengthy complaint that would form the basis of a lawsuit against W. R. Grace and Beatrice Foods. Schlichtmann, who knew more than Roisman about Massachusetts personal injury and wrongful death law, assisted him. The complaint asserted that subsidiaries owned by Grace and Beatrice had poisoned the plaintiffs' drinking water with toxic chemicals. These chemicals included TCE, which the complaint described as "a potent central nervous system depressant that can cause severe neurological symptoms such as dizziness, loss of appetite, and loss of motor coordination. It can produce liver damage and cause cell mutations and cancer." The poisoned water, stated the complaint, had resulted in a cluster of leukemia, the deaths of five children, and injuries to all of the family members who were party to the lawsuit, including "an increased risk of leukemia and other cancers, liver disease, central nervous system disorders, and other unknown illnesses and disease." The plaintiffs sought compensation for these injuries, and punitive damages for the willful and grossly negligent acts of the two companies.

Roisman and Schlichtmann finished the complaint on May 14, 1982, eight days before the statute of limitations expired. Schlichtmann took the complaint by hand to Superior Court in Boston and filed it.

One week later a story about the lawsuit appeared in *The Boston Globe*. Alerted by that story, crews from two local television stations arrived at Reed & Mulligan to interview Schlichtmann. The camera crews set up their equipment in the firm's library. Conway watched from the door as first one television reporter and then another talked to Schlichtmann. Conway felt glad that he wasn't the one being interviewed. The cameras and lights would have made him nervous, but he could see that Schlichtmann basked in them.

That evening they went downstairs to the Emperor of China restaurant and ordered drinks at the bar. Schlichtmann asked the bartender to turn on the news so he could watch himself. He made the bartender flip the channel back and forth between the two stations so that he'd miss none of his performance.

While Schlichtmann watched himself on the news, Conway watched Schlichtmann. He knew that Schlichtmann would spend a good deal of time on this case, but he reminded himself that Roisman would be in charge. Roisman would do most of the work. They were just the local contact. Conway told himself he wasn't worried.

CHAPTER 27

The Late Twentieth Century

The Woburn case consumed a decade of Jan Schlichtmann's professional life—and even more of Jonathan Harr's. During that time, the nation became increasingly aware of hazardous pollutants through such events as the discovery of contaminated soil under the western New York community of Love Canal, the tragic release of poisoned fumes in Bhopal, India, and a giant oil spill by the tanker Valdez off the coast of Alaska. In 1986 Congress strengthened the Superfund law to clean up hazardous wastes—but the law has not been without its critics.

The Republican party campaign of 1980 promised to "get government off the backs of business." The victory of the party's presidential candidate, Ronald Reagan, brought a turn toward deregulation. Some environmental regulations were among the Republican targets, but deregulation in the environmental area was overshadowed by the loosening of controls over corporate business activities. Scandals ensued when the easing of regulation led to an era of "leveraged buy-outs," "junk bonds," and savings-and-loan failures. But President Reagan's personal popularity remained high.

The Republican party campaign also called for the reduction of social programs. One of President Reagan's special targets was the Legal Services Corporation, started in the 1960s to provide legal representation to people who could not afford private attorneys. In *The Law Firm and the Public Good* (1995), edited by Robert A. Katzmann, author Esther F. Lardent recounts:

The Reagan administration's attempt to eliminate all federal funding for legal services to the poor, at a time when the number of Americans living in poverty was at an all-time high, generated strong opposition from the organized bar. Under the leadership of the American Bar Association, state and local bars became key players in the effort to save the Legal Services Corporation. When the corporation was saved but stripped of 25 percent of its funding, the organized bar, once again at the urging of the ABA, became actively involved in the expansion of pro bono resources to supplement the federal funds available for legal services. (p. 75)

The era was also characterized by tensions between the executive branch and Congress as Congress became increasingly assertive. For example, the "Bolland amendments" of 1982 to 1985 prohibited aid to the rightist Contra rebels in Nicaragua; and in the "Gramm-Rudman resolution" of 1985 Congress insisted on progress toward a balanced budget.

Some felt strongly enough about a balanced budget to call for a convention to draft a Balanced Budget Amendment to the Constitution. Some favored a constitutional convention for other purposes—including the prohibition of abortion and the permission of prayer in public schools. President Reagan favored both amendments. But they did not get far.

President Reagan, during his first term, was also unsuccessful in altering the Supreme Court. In four years, only one vacancy appeared on the Court, to which President Reagan appointed the first female justice, Sandra Day O'Connor.

Even before that point, seven of the nine justices were Republican appointees. But they took such varied positions that they merely created a split court, not a controlling majority. Many decisions were made five-to-four, and a tendency in one direction was sometimes offset by a subsequent narrowing or seemingly contrary decision.

In perhaps the most publicized decision of the late 1970s, *Regents of the University of California* v. *Bakke* (1978), four justices voted to uphold a school admission program that set aside a number of seats for minority applicants; four other justices considered the program racially discriminatory and prohibited by the language of the 1964 Civil Rights Act; and the decisive vote was cast by Justice Lewis F. Powell, who voted to strike down numeric set-asides, but maintained that racial minorities may be given preferences to achieve diversity in student enrollments.

In subsequent years, some have seen a retreat in civil rights. A leading civil-rights scholar, Derrick Bell, has charged that by the late 1980s achievements in civil rights had been "eroded." In his book, *And We Are Not Saved: The Elusive Quest for Racial Justice* (1987), he wrote:

Today, while all manner of civil rights laws and precedents are in place, the protection they provide is diluted by lax enforcement, by the establishment of difficult-to-meet standards of proof, and, worst of all, by the increasing irrelevance of antidiscrimination laws to race-related disadvantage, now likely to be a result as much of social class as of color. (p. 5)

In the 1990s the State of California eliminated race-based affirmative action programs, and the Regents of the University of California mandated, in their place, special consideration for socioeconomically disadvantaged university applicants. In *Hopwood* v. *Texas* (1996), a challenge to the admissions policies of the Law School of the University of Texas, the Federal Court of Appeals ruled against race-based affirmative action by state schools in the states of the Fifth Circuit.

In other newsworthy areas, the Supreme Court prohibited the imposition of the death penalty in the 1972 case of *Furman* v. *Georgia* when it found that the states were sentencing defendants to death in an "arbitrary and capricious" manner; in *Gregg* v. *Georgia* (1976) the death penalty was reinstated as states passed statutes seemingly requiring greater consistency. In 1980, in *Stone* v. *Graham*, the Court prohibited the display of the Ten Commandments in a public school classroom; four years later, in *Lynch* v. *Donnelly*, the display of a nativity scene in a public park was approved.

Narrow majorities and seeming flip-flops led a number of commentators to note that even one more appointment to the Court could change it fundamentally. Then, in the middle of his second term, President Reagan had his second, and last, opportunity for a Supreme Court appointment—an opportunity to appoint a chief justice.

Chief Justice William H. Rehnquist, Chief Justice Warren E. Berger, and Justice Antonin Scalia, September 26, 1986.

Photo by Dane A. Penland from Smithsonian Institution Photographic Services. Reprinted by permission of the United States Supreme Court Curator's Office.

THE REHNQUIST COURT

from David G. Savage, *Turning Right: The Making of the Rehnquist Supreme Court*
(New York: John Wiley & Sons, 1992), pp. 3–25.
Copyright © 1992 by David G. Savage.
Reprinted by permission of John Wiley & Sons.

It was just past noon when the new chief justice of the United States stepped from behind the marble columns of the Supreme Court and out into the bright September sun. A week earlier, on September 17, 1986, Associate Justice William H. Rehnquist had been confirmed by the Senate to become the nation's sixteenth chief justice, after a long, rancorous debate and a divided vote. The senators, exhausted, then quickly approved without opposition the bright and bold Antonin Scalia to fill Rehnquist's seat as the ninth justice.

September 26 was a day for taking oaths and posing for pictures. In the morning, Rehnquist and Scalia went to the White House to stand next to the president as they pledged their allegiance to the U.S. Constitution. Ronald Reagan predicted that Rehnquist "will be a chief justice of historic stature." The justices then traveled back to Capitol Hill and stood at the front of the ornate courtroom, where they swore to "do equal right to the poor and to the rich."

Shortly afterward, like a wedding party, Rehnquist and Scalia moved out into the sunlight and down the long steps toward the waiting photographers. A "photo opportunity" is a rarity at the Supreme Court. Cameras and microphones are barred from the building, and the justices generally refuse to appear on television. Once a year, photographers are allowed inside to snap the formal photo of the Court. There, the justices appear as "nine black-robed figures who look as if their heads are interchangeable," Rehnquist once joked.

The restriction on cameras suited Rehnquist perfectly well. Before crowds or photographers, he looked stiff and uncomfortable. His hands fidgeted awkwardly. As he paused for a moment on the steps during the photo session, the new chief justice hooked his thumbs in his pockets, with his fingers pointed outward. Scalia, on the other hand, delighted in being the focus of attention. Short and stocky, with jet black hair, he had a confident, steady gaze and a jutting lower lip.

Between them stood the retiring chief justice, Warren E. Burger. Though 79 years old and slightly stooped, Burger still looked as though he had been cast by Hollywood for the part of chief justice. His snow-white hair, well-chiseled chin, and deep voice spoke of gravity and somber judgment.

Inside the dark chambers of the Court, however, where law and the Constitution were debated, Burger had not fared as well. He had been long-winded and ponderous, to the irritation of his colleagues. His pompous manner offended them; he could be spiteful and petty to those who disagreed with him.

His 17-year tenure had been considered a failure, especially by conservatives. In 1969, President Richard Nixon had chosen him to lead a conservative counterrevolution at the Court. Three other Nixon appointees soon followed, but the counterrevolution did not. Indeed, the 1970s saw landmark victories for the liberals. The supposedly conservative Court gave a green light to city-wide busing for school desegregation, struck down the death penalty, legalized abortion, and upheld "affirmative" preferences for racial minorities. Unable to secure the votes—or even the decent regard—of the majority of his colleagues, Burger presided over a fractured, uncertain Court.

Four months before, in late May of 1986, he had paid a quiet visit to the White House to talk with President Reagan about the upcoming 200th anniversary of the Constitution. It was Burger's favorite topic of conversation. . . . Burger had high hopes for the bicentennial. He wanted the schoolchildren of the nation to appreciate the significance of the "separation of powers" concept.

As their conversation drew to a close, Reagan suddenly became alert. The bicentennial celebration was behind schedule and in deep trouble, Burger said. . . . He had decided to retire from the Supreme Court to devote all his efforts to the bicentennial. The President had had no previous warning of Burger's intentions, but he did not try to change his mind. Reagan praised his service on the Court and his devotion to the constitutional celebration and accepted the resignation. As the outgoing chief was ushered from the Oval Office, an aide was dispatched to call Attorney General Edwin Meese III with the news.

At last, the moment had come, a chance finally to change the complexion of the Supreme Court. After two landslide victories and nearly six years in the White House, the "Reagan revolution" had swept across most of Washington but had stopped at the steps of the Court. As a result, the Reagan social agenda on abortion, school prayer, civil rights, and crime had remained dormant. So far, Reagan had replaced only one of the nine justices. In the first six months of his first term, Reagan picked Sandra Day O'Connor, the first woman to sit on the high court. The nomination had won praise from all quarters except from the core of Reagan's conservative constituency. At the Justice Department, she was known derisively as an "80 percenter." Though generally conservative, she deserted the Administration at crucial moments. She had cast a vote or two to permit affirmative action for blacks and women, she had joined a ruling striking down a voluntary prayer law for the schools, and even on the abortion issue, her support was in doubt.

The conservatives had grown frustrated. Year after year, the Supreme Court had rebuffed Reagan's advances. His Justice Department attorneys had gone to the Court seeking new restrictions on abortion and affirmative action but came back empty handed. Now, time was running out. The old liberals, with fortitude and good health, were determined to hang on. For a time, it looked as though 1960s-style legal liberalism might well outlast the Reagan era of the 1980s. Burger's surprise resignation suddenly changed that picture. At the Justice Department, however, Reagan's appointees had long been ready for this.

"When Brad and I went out jogging, we often talked about 'What if?'" said Charles Cooper, a young Alabaman who had risen to the top of the Justice Department. Cooper referred to William Bradford Reynolds, chief of the Civil Rights Division, Meese's closest adviser and the enforcer of the Reagan-Meese legal ideology. At first glance, Cooper and Reynolds made for an odd couple. Athletically built, Cooper sported a broad smile and a hearty handshake. Reynolds was tall, gaunt, and balding, with a stiff, humorless demeanor.

Nonetheless, the two friends shared a common view of the law. An extraordinary cadre of young, bright, and committed conservatives had been drawn to the Reagan Justice Department. Unlike in earlier administrations, where lawyers took positions in the Justice Department to fight crime, defend civil rights, or pad a resume for a later career in private practice, the Reagan administration attracted attorneys who cared deeply about legal ideology. Simply put, they believed that for a generation, the Supreme Court had abandoned its role as an arbiter of narrow legal issues and had instead become the engine of a liberal social revolution. In their view, the left-leaning Court cared more about protecting pornography in the streets than about prayer in the schools. It enforced busing orders for schoolchildren but refused to enforce the death penalty for murderers. The Court's priorities were those of the liberal left in America, as they saw it, and they meant to change that.

Reagan himself had never understood how the Supreme Court could decide it was unconstitutional to provide a daily moment of prayer for schoolchildren. Meese, a former Oakland prosecutor, never understood why it was unconstitutional to make use of a suspect's voluntary confession, whether or not he had been warned to remain silent. For a later generation of conservatives, the *Roe* v. *Wade* ruling symbolized a Court run amok. They felt that the liberals, rather than abide by the Constitution as written, had created a right to abortion that had not previously existed.

For Cooper, the "crystallizing moment" had come in 1979. As a top graduate of the University of Alabama law school, he had won a Supreme Court clerkship with the most conservative justice, William H. Rehnquist. That term, the Court was called upon to decide whether federal law permitted employers to give preferences to blacks or women—at the expense of white males. The Civil Rights Act of 1964 said that employers may not "discriminate against any individual . . . because of such individual's race, color, religion, sex or national origin." Brian Weber, a white steelworker from Louisiana, brought his case to the Supreme Court, contending that he had lost a promotion because of his race. Fewer than 2 percent of the skilled workers at his Kaiser Steel plant were black, even though 39 percent of the local work force were black. To remedy that imbalance, the company and the steelworkers union negotiated a plan to offer blacks 50 percent of the new apprenticeships for skilled jobs. When Weber lost out to a somewhat less experienced black employee, he filed a reverse discrimination suit against the union.

Rehnquist and his clerk Cooper pored over the congressional debates on the 1964 law and were convinced it meant just what it said: no discrimination against anyone, black or white. Senator Hubert Humphrey, the primary sponsor, had said on the Senate floor, "The truth is that this title forbids discriminating against anyone on account of race." Humphrey sought to put to rest what he called "the bugaboo" that the new law would force employers "to meet a racial quota or to achieve a certain balance."

When the votes were counted in the Supreme Court, though, Justice William J. Brennan, Jr., the leading liberal, had a five-vote majority to uphold "voluntary affirmative action" by employers. He, too, quoted Senator Humphrey as saying that the law was spurred by "the plight of the Negro in our economy." For a century after slavery was abolished, blacks had been denied an equal chance to enter white workplaces. It would be a tragic irony, Brennan wrote, if the landmark law intended to finally give them that chance were interpreted to bar a voluntary effort by an employer or a union to "break down old patterns of racial segregation and hierarchy."

Rehnquist wrote a biting dissent. He called the Brennan opinion "a tour de force reminiscent not of jurists such as Hale, Holmes, or Hughes, but of escape artists such as Houdini." Both the language and the intent of the law could not have been more clear, he said. "Congress outlawed ALL racial discrimination, recognizing that no discrimination based on race is benign, that no action disadvantaging a person because of his color is affirmative," he wrote.

"I had my eyes opened," Cooper said. "Bill Rehnquist had gone over every scrap of evidence. He demonstrated that no one could reasonably believe the law meant what Brennan said it meant. The law was about equal opportunity for all, not about creating a racial spoils system." Cooper also drew a lesson from the experience: The only way to change the law in the Supreme Court was to change the people who served there.

The corollary to Cooper's rule was just as important: Promote judges to the Supreme Court who were reliable—not "80 percenters" or good Republicans whose sole virtue was that they had friends in high places—certainly not those lawyers who were described as "open minded."

After all, the Reagan revolution had been thwarted largely because Richard Nixon and Gerald Ford failed to pick true conservatives. Of Nixon's four appointments, two were outright mistakes in the view of hard-core conservatives: First, Lewis F. Powell, a courtly Virginian, had been picked by Nixon for his law-and-order beliefs. As expected, Powell proved to be generally conservative on crime and the death penalty, but he often sided with the liberals on matters of civil rights, religion, and abortion. The second "mistake," Harry A. Blackmun, a Minnesota Republican, turned out to be even worse, from the conservative's point of view. After barely two years on the Court, he wrote the *Roe* v. *Wade* opinion giving pregnant women a constitutional right to abortion. Burger, Nixon's chief justice, had been conservative but ineffectual.

Only Rehnquist, among the Nixon appointees, fully lived up to the conservatives' hopes. From his first day, he took up the position on the ideological far right. . . . He never wavered or played to the liberal press, nor did he seem fazed by criticism from lawyers or legal academics. On a Court dominated by liberals and moderates, he stood alone on the right. His clerks dubbed him "The Lone Ranger."

As Cooper saw it, no one could be better at leading a Reagan Court than William H. Rehnquist. He had a powerful legal mind, reliably conservative views, the respect of his colleagues, and 14 years of Court experience. Reynolds, Cooper's jogging partner, agreed entirely. In the Nixon Justice Department, Reynolds had an office just down the hall from then-Assistant Attorney General Rehnquist. He was now a neighbor of Rehnquist's in north Arlington, across the river from Washington.

"But Bill didn't need friendship to get the appointment. He was quite clearly the justice who most represented the judicial views of the Reagan administration," Reynolds said.

Even during its most embarrassing moments, the Administration had had a loyal ally in Rehnquist. In their first year in office, Reynolds and Meese, then the White House counselor, stumbled into a hornet's nest. Since the early 1970s, the Internal Revenue Service (IRS) had denied charitable tax exemptions to private schools and colleges that were racially segregated. Bob Jones University in South Carolina, along with several private academies that practiced segregation, challenged this policy in court, and Reynolds and Meese brought the Reagan Administration into the case on the schools' side. As the new civil rights chief, Reynolds was promoting a new "color-blind" policy—in contrast, he said, to recent favoritism for selected minorities. However, the fight against the IRS policy looked like the old-style conservative blindness to racism of the worst sort. When the Bob Jones University case came before the Supreme Court, Reynolds, Meese, and the segregated academies picked up only one vote: Justice Rehnquist.

Armed with the still-secret news of Burger's retirement, Meese and Reynolds got together to talk over lunch. They quickly settled on a form of the double steal in baseball: Promote Rehnquist to chief justice, and replace him with a younger conservative. Previously, presidents had usually looked outside the Court to find a new chief justice, in part because promoting one of the brethren could sow dissent and jealousy. . . .

Reagan had his own views on who he wanted to send to the Supreme Court. As governor of California, he had come to distrust politicians as judges. They were unpredictable and unreliable. He made it clear he wanted to promote experienced judges whose views were known. Rehnquist easily passed that test. Like Reagan, Rehnquist had enunciated the same beliefs throughout his career. Indeed, his college friends were convinced that his views were already fully formed when he was an undergraduate at Stanford University and had not shifted since then. Through 14 years as an associate justice, he never seemed to agonize over decisions and never deviated from the conservative side. Regardless of the case that came before the Court, it would be hard to imagine Rehnquist voting to oppose the death penalty or to expand civil rights.

If Rehnquist were the chief justice, could he lead the other justices? Reagan's advisers certainly thought he could. Unlike Burger, Rehnquist had a notably quick, incisive legal mind. No matter how complicated or muddy the legal dispute, he could penetrate to the heart of the matter and distill the key issue at stake. What amazed his colleagues, too, was that Rehnquist did not require the hours of study that they—also experienced and learned in the law—needed to get ready to hear a case.

"Bill Rehnquist is the quickest lawyer I ever met," said Lewis Powell, who joined him on the high court in 1972, after four decades of private practice. In conference, Rehnquist also had a unique ability to recite phrases from past cases or from literature. "I've probably known people who knew more literature than him, but I don't think I know anyone who recalled more of it," Powell added.

One concern was whether Rehnquist could match wits and charm, as well as brains, with William J. Brennan, the unquestioned leader of the liberal faction of the Court. Brennan, a tiny Irishman with twinkling eyes and a warm handshake, had become a legendary figure among law clerks, civil libertarians, and constitutional scholars. Somehow, year after year, despite a parade of new Republican appointees, Brennan managed to put together liberal majorities to win the big cases. Unknown to the general public, during the 1960s he had been the behind-the-scenes architect for many of the landmark rulings of the Court's liberal era—in desegregation, school prayer, the rights of crime suspects, the freedom of the press, women's rights, and the right to abortion. Since then, the nation had moved to the right, but the Supreme Court had not—in large measure because of William Brennan.

Like Rehnquist, Brennan knew exactly what he believed and never wavered. He was a champion of the underdog, the defender of the minority. Where Rehnquist thought the Court should uphold the will of the majority, Brennan took a nearly opposite approach. He revered the Bill of Rights and held it up as a secular Ten Commandments. He was determined to make these ideals a reality. It was the Court's duty, he preached, to enforce the rights of the lowliest of Americans, regardless of the wishes of the majority. Whether the case involved an inmate on Death Row seeking the right to appeal a conviction, a black child seeking the right to attend an integrated school, a political dissident seeking the right to protest freely, or a woman seeking the right to end her pregnancy, Brennan had taken up their causes. . . .

He had also exasperated conservatives. In their view, Brennan was less a defender of the Constitution than a liberal activist in black robes. Brennan's style of judging made the Supreme Court all-powerful, they complained. Two Reagan administration attorneys wrote of Brennan in 1984, "There is no individual in this country, on or off the Court, who has had a more profound and sustained impact on public policy in the United States over the past 27 years." Their tone was one of despair. How could a mere judge exercise so much power? they asked.

. . .

Both Rehnquist and Brennan had a practical view of how the Court worked. Neither sought to portray it as a genuinely deliberative body, which, after deep thought and intense debate, arrived at the true meaning of the Constitution. They were both too realistic to hold that view. Each year, Brennan would ask his new batch of law clerks whether they knew the most important rule of the Supreme Court. Usually, they were stumped. After a moment, he would hold up his hand, palm open and fingers spread wide. "It takes five votes to do anything in the Supreme Court," he told them.

. . .

During Burger's years, Brennan continued to surprise Court experts. Though he and the liberals had their heyday during the Warren Court of the 1960s, he still won the major battles of the 1970s. Though the Equal Rights Amendment for women died before ratification by three-fourths of the states, Brennan found a five-vote majority to rule that the Constitution's guarantee of the "equal protection of the laws" prohibited nearly all discrimination against women. In 1972, he wrote an opinion in a Massachusetts case involving the sale of contraceptives to unmarried persons, in which he said that the right to privacy in the Constitution means that "the individual, married or single, [is] free from unwarranted governmental intrusion into matters so fundamentally affecting a person as the decision whether to bear or beget a child." Those words served as a springboard the next year for the *Roe* v. *Wade* ruling. In the late 1970s, he found a slim majority to agree that the Constitution and federal civil rights law permit universities and employers to give an edge to minority applicants. Through the first half of the 1980s, he blocked the Reagan administration's moves to roll back abortion rights and affirmative action and, to permit a return of school prayer.

"[Brennan] fought one of the greatest rear-guard actions in history," University of Michigan law professor Yale Kamisar said. However, the aging liberal disliked being called a "play-maker" at the Court. "The implication is that . . . you go running about the building talking, shaking hands, putting your arm around everyone," he said in an interview. "Only once did I go around and talk to everybody, and that was on the Nixon tapes case" in 1974. He sought a single, unanimous opinion, such as the Court had given in 1954, in the landmark *Brown* v. *Board of Education* case that outlawed official segregation. . . .

In Brennan's view, he owed his success more to intellectual persuasion than to arm twisting. "It really isn't very mysterious or complex. You try to get a sense of what will sell, what the others will accept. Will this be rejected by Lewis Powell or Harry Blackmun? Will Thurgood [Marshall] agree with this? Has John Stevens written any cases which may suggest how he is thinking? What does Sandra [O'Connor] think? And you write it that way," he said. . . .

In conversation, the Reagan administration attorneys groused about the little Irishman. How much longer could he survive? Brad Reynolds even took to denouncing him by name in speeches, accusing the aging justice of espousing what he called "radical egalitarianism."

Nonetheless, speeches and denunciations had no impact on Brennan or the Court. Reynolds and the other Reagan attorneys knew they needed a chief justice who could counter Brennan. They felt that Rehnquist was ideal. He not only had the firm views and the quick legal mind of his liberal adversary but also displayed a down-to-earth charm that had endeared him to his colleagues. Even the liberal tandem of Brennan and Marshall spoke well of Rehnquist. "I don't agree with him on much, but he's a great guy," Marshall told a friend.

Many who met Rehnquist for the first time came away surprised. In his writing for the Court, he could be cold and cutting. Certainly no one accused him of being sensitive or unduly compassionate. Yet in person, he was invariably genial and displayed an old-fashioned courtesy. He bowed slightly at the waist to greet new-comers. Unlike Brennan, Rehnquist did not wrap his arm around the shoulder of acquaintances or pump their hands; he was more reserved. Rehnquist, after having met Reagan at a White House reception, observed that the president was a man with "no edges"; he was straightforward and good-spirited, with no air of superiority; he had no quirks or pomposity. Much the same could be said about Rehnquist.

On May 29, just two days after Burger announced his intention to retire, Meese went by the White House to meet with the President, Chief of Staff Donald Regan, and White House counsel Peter Wallison. They went over a few of Reagan's ground rules. The president wanted to appoint a judge, not a politician, to the Supreme Court vacancy. He also wanted someone who believed in "judicial restraint," a judge who would leave the lawmaking to the elected officials. There was little talk of specific names and no talk of issues, including abortion, nor was there any need for such talk. The views of the leading candidates were already well known. In addition, Chief of Staff Regan stressed the importance of keeping the discussion confined to only a few top advisers. So far, the news of Burger's resignation had not leaked out.

Meese, like the president, barely knew Rehnquist, but Reynolds and Cooper had convinced him that Rehnquist would make the best chief for a Reagan Court. "That turned out to be the easy decision," Reynolds said later. "We thought Rehnquist was a pretty safe bet" for confirmation in the Senate, he added. "He was already on the Court. He was well liked by his colleagues. The only thing they could raise was that old memo he wrote as a clerk in 1952" in which a young Bill Rehnquist questioned the wisdom of overturning the "separate but equal" doctrine, the pillar of Southern segregation.

A few days later, when the White House group met next, Meese strongly recommended that Rehnquist be elevated to chief justice. He was smart, experienced, reliably conservative, and well liked by his colleagues. Meese had only one cautionary warning: He may not want the job. "That was my only real fear—that he would say 'No,'" Cooper said.

At age 61 and with more than 14 years on the Court, Rehnquist was nearing the time when he could retire with a full pension. For years, he had talked openly of doing just that. Often, he was bored and frustrated with the Court. "I've heard, all this before," he exclaimed in disgust at the end of one long conference session. Year after year, it seemed to him, the justices squabbled over the same issues and finally compromised with utterly confusing rulings that failed to decide the issues.

One example of these conflicting rulings related to the death penalty. A decade earlier, the Court had ruled that capital punishment was constitutional. Nonetheless, the liberals never gave up trying to ban capital punishment, and each year the Court would "tinker" some more, as Rehnquist put it. New, intricate procedural rules would be announced, which in turn would prompt more litigation in the Supreme Court to define the limits of those new rules. "The ball game never ends in our Court," Rehnquist once observed ruefully.

In addition, his intention to quit went beyond the politics of the Court. He wanted to leave before he was too old. He enjoyed reading and writing history and was interested in teaching. "Do not let the law be too jealous a mistress," he told one law school graduating class. "You must give yourself time not only to do a variety of things, but [also] to allow yourself time to appreciate and enjoy what you are doing."

Rehnquist followed his own advice. He usually left the Court by 3 P.M. In the afternoons, he swam or played tennis. He took up painting, too. Once, as Ronald Reagan delivered his State of the Union address, the cameras panned the assembled dignitaries and showed that only eight members of the Supreme Court were in attendance. Apparently, the White House had scheduled Reagan's speech on the same night as Rehnquist's painting class at the Arlington County adult education center, and Rehnquist had gone to class.

. . .

Though Rehnquist took his legal work seriously, he did not want to die a bitter old man on the Supreme Court. His wife, Nan, had been battling cancer, and Rehnquist wanted to be with her when she needed him. For years, he had been the lone conservative on a Court that congealed in the middle. If nothing changed, he had no desire to stay much longer. Still, Meese and Reynolds figured that the chance to be chief justice might change Rehnquist's mind. Without question, Rehnquist deserved the first offer.

The harder decision for the Administration was, Who should be nominated to fill the vacant ninth seat?

A team of young Justice Department attorneys had spent years preparing for this decision. They had systematically scrutinized the decisions and the records of hundreds of judges and lawyers. Some were recommended as federal trial judges, others to sit on the regional U.S. appellate courts. At least a dozen names were also on the list of potential candidates for the Supreme Court. At the top stood two names: Robert H. Bork and Antonin Scalia.

In legal circles, the two were usually mentioned in the same sentence, as if they were a tag team. Bork and Scalia were Reagan-appointed judges on the U.S. appeals court in Washington, D.C., often considered the nation's second most important court. Public interest lawyers who challenged federal regulations usually filed suit in Washington, and their cases eventually landed in the 12-member U.S. Court of Appeals for the District of Columbia.

Neither Bork nor Scalia aspired to a career of deciding regulatory cases. For both, the appellate court was seen as a stepping stone to the Supreme Court. Both had academic backgrounds, as well as government experience in the Nixon and Ford administrations. They were conservative, intellectually oriented, and committed to reshaping the role of the federal courts. Bork was 59, and Scalia was 50.

Both were ideal candidates. They were good writers and thought in broad ideological terms. They would not just decide narrow cases; their opinions would change the law. Bork had more experience in government, but Scalia was younger. It was noted, too, that Bork was overweight and a heavy smoker. How many years could he serve? the Administration's lawyers wondered.

Reynolds leaned toward Scalia because he worried that a Rehnquist-Bork combination could provoke a huge confirmation fight in the Senate. Bork had made a cameo appearance during the Watergate scandal as the Justice Department official who carried out Richard Nixon's order to fire Special Prosecutor Archibald Cox. That incident would provide ammunition for his critics. Moreover, he had spent years on the lecture circuit delivering provocatively conservative speeches.

"If we put the two of them [Rehnquist and Bork] up there together, they would have made a big target," Reynolds said. If Scalia were picked now, Bork could be nominated for the next seat, he argued. White House counsel

Peter Wallison argued the opposite view. Rehnquist would draw most of the fire and shield Bork, he contended, while the younger Scalia could be selected for the next seat. However, if Bork were picked next, the civil rights groups would gang up on him, he contended.

As Reagan listened to the back-and-forth discussion, he heard something that caught his attention: Scalia would be the first Italian-American to sit on the Supreme Court. He had been assured that Scalia was just as conservative as Bork. Everyone remembered an appointment that was a "first." Lyndon Johnson got credit for naming the first black to the Court in Thurgood Marshall. Reagan had been lauded across the political spectrum for naming the first woman, Sandra Day O'Connor. Why not take advantage of the opportunity to put the first Italian-American on the Court? While his advisers talked on about the confirmation prospects, Reagan seemed to have made up his mind.

Let's get Rehnquist in here to see whether he'll take the job; then, we'll talk to Scalia, Reagan concluded.

Don Regan put in a call to Rehnquist to tell him of the offer. The justice asked for a chance to think it over. The job would entail lots of administrative and ceremonial duties, which Rehnquist tended to view as a waste of time. The Court itself operated as a self-contained institution, with 300 employees. It had a library, a cafeteria, a gym, and a print shop. The curator's office handled exhibits throughout the building, while the police force patrolled the halls and the grounds. The chief justice not only presided over this small bureaucracy but also headed the entire federal judicial system. Burger had relished this aspect of the job, and even his critics conceded that he had been a fine administrator. He had helped move the judiciary from the era of the quill pen to that of the computer.

Rehnquist was bored by administrative chores, but most of those tasks could be delegated to others. He kept his eye on the law. The chief justice could put his stamp on an entire legal era. . . . For someone who had stubbornly pressed his view of the Constitution when he stood nearly alone, the opportunity to be chief justice could not be passed up. . . . He called the White House to make an appointment to see the President.

Reagan tried his usual assortment of jokes and one-liners, but the reticent Rehnquist sat stiffly through most of their meeting. He . . . told Reagan he would be honored to accept the president's nomination. A few days later, the irrepressible Scalia drove himself to the White House in his own car and exchanged jokes with Reagan.

No one had leaked the story to the press. Chief of Staff Don Regan delighted in the fact that Burger, Rehnquist, and Scalia had all visited the Oval Office without being spotted by the reporters waiting nearby. No one knew of the impending change on the nation's highest court, other than a handful of Reagan's top aides. At midday on June 17, White House reporters were told to gather in the cramped press room for an important announcement. At the Court, the justices were called to gather in the conference room. There, on a television set, they, along with the rest of the nation, learned of Burger's retirement and Reagan's nominations.

The President, with Burger, Rehnquist, and Scalia standing behind him, delivered a rather bare-bones statement, describing Rehnquist as a justice "noted for his intellectual power and the lucidity of his opinions." Of Scalia, he said, "His great personal energy, the force of his intellect, and the depth of his understanding of our constitutional jurisprudence uniquely qualify him for elevation to our highest court." There was no mention that both men had quite conservative views. After Reagan refused to answer questions, the reporters turned to Rehnquist and Scalia. Both said they would not comment further until the Senate hearings. Only Burger would talk, and what he wanted to talk about was the bicentennial of the Constitution. After a few moments, the press conference was adjourned.

. . .

At the White House and the Justice Department, Reagan's advisers were confident Rehnquist would win a comfortable confirmation in the Senate, although not without a struggle. In 1971, 26 Senators, mostly liberal Democrats, had voted against his appointment as an associate justice. His performance on the Court since then certainly had not won over the Democratic left. Nonetheless, the times had changed, too. Rehnquist now went before the Senate with the backing of a hugely popular president. He had also been on the Court for 14 years. No one could quibble over his qualifications. In addition, the Republicans now controlled the Senate majority. The Senate Judiciary Committee was in especially friendly hands. Its chair was the old South Carolinian Strom Thurmond, the long-time segregationist and fervent foe of civil rights laws of the 1960s. By the 1980s, Thurmond had reconstructed himself as a politician of the new South, seeking out black votes as well as white ones, but he never abandoned his conservative heritage. Through the first six years of the Reagan Administration, hundreds of Republican court appointees came before Thurmond's panel for confirmation. Old Strom took them under his wing as if they were sweet, young debutantes who could be flustered by tough-talking Democrats, and he guided them through the sometimes treacherous confirmation process.

Rehnquist and Scalia had a simple strategy: to say as little as possible. . . . During his years in the Nixon administration, Rehnquist had seen plenty of Senate confirmation hearings, several of them disastrous for the nominee. He had become convinced that nominees could lose votes at a Senate hearing, but none could win votes there. It would be better to sit like a mute defendant on trial rather than to pontificate freely from the witness stand.

Their strategy made for a one-sided battle through the summer of 1986. For weeks prior to the Senate hearing, Rehnquist was pummeled in the press for his record of opposing civil rights and civil liberties. The NAACP Legal Defense Fund tallied 83 cases in which a divided Supreme Court, including Rehnquist, was called upon to vote on a civil rights matter affecting racial minorities, women, or the elderly. It found Rehnquist had voted against these plaintiffs 82 times. After the hearing began, it only got worse. Senator Edward Kennedy denounced Rehnquist as "an extremist" who was "out of the mainstream." Other Democrats followed his lead. Republicans Strom Thurmond and Orrin Hatch (of Utah) rose to his defense, but only to argue that the charges were unfair or exaggerated. Curiously missing was any forceful advocate arguing that Rehnquist's conservative views were correct.

Two episodes proved embarrassing: First, the Democrats revealed that the deed to Rehnquist's summer home in Vermont, which he purchased in 1974, included a prohibition on its sale or rental "to any member of the Hebrew race." In addition, the FBI learned that his Phoenix home in the 1960s had a deed restriction barring its sale or rental to "any person not of the white or Caucasian race." Though one of the nation's most prominent lawyers, Rehnquist told the committee he had not examined his deeds and knew nothing of these restrictive covenants.

Meanwhile, a former U.S. attorney joined several Phoenix Democrats to testify that he had seen Rehnquist at polling places in 1962 or 1964 challenging the credentials of black voters. Such challenges were not outlawed until later, but Rehnquist in 1971 had denied that he personally challenged or "harassed" any voter. He repeated that denial during the 1986 hearing. Certainly he had been active in Republican campaigns and had served as a legal adviser to their so-called ballot security teams. Several Republican activists testifying in Rehnquiet's defense said he may have visited polling places on election day, but only to advise poll watchers, not to question or harass likely Democratic voters.

The hearings created an unease among many senators, but not enough to peel away many votes from the president's nominee. In early August, the Judiciary Committee approved the nomination on a 13–5 vote. Rehnquist heard the news via a note handed him during a law class in the hills of Malibu, near Los Angeles. Rather than sweat out the confirmation battle in Washington, he had chosen to go ahead with a previous commitment to teach a summer class at the Pepperdine University Law School.

Back in Washington, though, the fight was not over. Usually, a nominee approved by the Judiciary Committee wins routine approval by the full Senate. However, liberal activists were convinced that more damaging information—perhaps suggesting that Rehnquist had not told the full truth to the committee—could still block his confirmation. The Leadership Conference on Civil Rights thought it already had ample evidence to justify rejecting his confirmation. Rehnquist had compiled "a 35-year history of hostility to victims of discrimination," the group said.

When the nomination went to the Senate floor in mid-September, Democrats renewed their attack. Even some Republicans were having second thoughts. Senator Charles Mathias, the second-ranking Republican on the Judiciary Committee, changed his mind and decided to vote against confirmation. Leading the defense, Hatch lambasted the Democrats. "They have left no stone unthrown," he said. Debates on the Senate floor are often deceptive, though. Those who dominate the discussion usually do so because they have not lined up the votes needed to win. When it was time to count the votes on the evening of September 17, the Republicans poured onto the floor and ensured Rehnquist's victory. The final tally was 65 in favor and 33 against, the most votes ever cast against a chief justice.

While Rehnquist had taken a thrashing, Scalia had been mostly ignored. He came to the Senate hearings with an air of confidence that implied, "I'm the smartest fellow in this room." As the Judiciary Committee members questioned him, he lit up a pipe and puffed serenely. . . .

No one was going to lay a glove on "Nino" Scalia. After several rounds of questioning, Scalia emerged unscathed and won the committee's approval with ease.

. . .

. . . He would be the first true academic to sit on the Court since Felix Frankfurter. On the night of September 17, when the Senate finally gave its approval to Rehnquist's nomination, Scalia's name was brought up quickly and approved unanimously.

After the last votes were cast, Senate Majority Leader Bob Dole left the floor to put in a late-evening call to Reagan to tell him the result. The president had watched some of the debate in his bedroom and said he was grateful his nominees survived. "It looked like they were forming a lynch mob," he told Dole.

Rehnquist indeed had escaped just in time. Two months later, the Republicans were battered at the polls, and the Democrats retook control of the Senate. Later in November, it was revealed that Ronald Reagan had secretly sold arms to the terrorist state of Iran, while his aides funneled the profits to the Contras in Nicaragua in defiance of a congressional ban on such aid. Reagan's endorsement would never again carry the same weight on Capitol Hill.

None of that would matter to Rehnquist and Scalia, though. As they stood on the Court steps on September 26, they had good reason to smile. They possessed a power that was unique to the American system of government. With their colleagues, they would determine the meaning of the Constitution as well as of the laws passed by Congress. It was certainly a power any politician would envy. They need not pay any attention to the public, and this power was theirs for as long as they chose to exercise it.

When they reached the bottom of the steps, Burger quietly stepped aside and walked away. For an uncertain moment, Rehnquist and Scalia stood apart, staring at the assembled photographers. Then, they turned to each other and clasped hands with a broad smile. The Burger Court was now history. The era of the Rehnquist Court had begun.

PART III

American Law in the Twenty-First Century

CHAPTER 28

The Legal Profession

The approach of a new millennium has given rise to a spate of "futurist" writings. In law, perhaps the most prevalent are writings deploring the state of the legal profession and calling for renewal or reform.

According to one commentator, Professor Russell G. Pearce, lawyers earned their status as a "profession" by tacitly accepting an altruistic role, placing the interests of their clients above their own interests and the interests of society above both their own interests and the interests of their clients. In return, the government has prohibited nonlawyers from practicing law while leaving the legal profession largely unregulated. The bar, therefore, has had the autonomy to regulate itself through licensing, ethics codes, disciplinary committees, and limits on competitive practices—most notably, minimum fee schedules and prohibitions on advertising.

According to Professor Pearce and other commentators, all this began to unravel in the 1970s. Courts struck down bar-sponsored fee schedules and advertising bans; the population of lawyers took a sharp turn upward; and law firms began to adopt "business" practices, endangering both the quality of service to clients and the commitment of lawyers to the common good. As Professor Pearce expressed it (quoting a number of commentators):

> By the 1990s, . . . the "common perception among legal commentators . . . [became] that lawyers [were] primarily motivated by self-interest and the desire to make money." In large law firms, the profits a lawyer generated by procuring business or producing billable hours, and not professional excellence, determined that lawyer's rewards. Fewer lawyers appeared to engage in public service, and those who did found that it brought them little favor at their firms. Some lawyers took advantage of this atmosphere to "generat[e] the highest possible fee," rather than provide the best possible service. This pursuit of fees became "a major cause of procedural incivilities." It also became the catalyst for

law firms to take on the forms of business. They added managers, business plans, marketing directors, and financially driven strategies to maximize efficiency in making profits. The press eulogized the death of law firms that were not able to adjust from a "professional" to a "business" approach. ("The Professional Paradigm Shift," 70 *New York University Law Review,* pp. 1229, 1251–52 [1995].)

In the same era, the pay of partners at many leading law firms dramatically increased; some firms started providing "ancillary" services such as lobbying and financial advising; and, as revealed in the savings-and-loans scandals of the 1980s and 1990s, some firms went "beyond maximizing the goals within the bounds of the law."

At the same time, the demographic makeup of the legal profession was also changing. Beginning in the late 1960s, the increasing numbers of graduates from law schools included significant numbers of women and members of minority groups. The newcomers—more than those already in the system—questioned the growing business orientation of law practice not only because of its possible effects on the profession's monopoly, its autonomy, and its public image, but also because of its effect on the quality of their lives.

from Carrie Menkel-Meadow, "Culture Clash in the Quality of Life in the Law: Changes in the Economics, Diversification and Organization of Lawyering," 44 *Case Western Reserve Law Review*, pp. 621–55 (1994).
Copyright © 1994 by Case Western Law Review.
Reprinted by permission of Case Western Law Review.

I. Introduction:
The Cultures of Change in the Legal Profession

There is no question that law practice has changed in recent decades. More lawyers work in larger units or newer forms of practice. Increasing numbers of lawyers come from previously excluded groups, including both women and minority demographic groups. . . . [T]he forms of law practice organization and billing for legal work are being renegotiated, and rates of dissatisfaction with the practice of law [are increasing], especially among younger and newer lawyers. These are just some of the changes, broadly labeled, by this writer and others, as "transformations" in the legal profession, that have undoubtedly inspired the current effort to understand what the legal profession of the 21st Century will look like. These changes in the structure and organization of lawyering will have a profound effect on the way in which people labor as lawyers.

As one who is generally skeptical about the predictions of "futurists," because I do not think we can accurately predict how various "trends" will interact with each other, I find my task . . . particularly difficult. Change in the legal profession is clearly afoot—but how the various changes outlined above will interact with each other is difficult to assess.

. . .

. . . In my view, the quality of life in the legal profession needs improvement, if lawyers are to lead socially useful and productive lives, for their clients, for their colleagues, for their families, and for themselves, as well as for the future of our legal system. There is room for hope in achieving positive changes for the profession with the entrance and contribution of more diverse members of the profession. However, it is also clear that a variety of other factors, such as the economics of law practice, resistant occupational structures, and persis-

tent, but outmoded, ideologies may have countervailing influences on the innovations most likely to improve the quality of life and work environments of
lawyers. . . .

II. A Brief History of Organizational, Economic and Demographic Changes in the Legal Profession

A. Demographic Trends in the Growth of the Legal Profession

. . . The early years of American legal history set the tone for the ongoing cultural ambivalence about lawyers we feel today. Lawyers in the colonial era
were needed, feared, despised, and banned in some colonies, for many reasons, such as their attachment to the State of the mother country. Following
the Revolution, many states prohibited "attornies" from their courts and dispute resolution tribunals, for reasons having to do with hatred of the adversary system, class hatred, or a desire to conduct legal business without agents.
But attorneys were necessary to conduct and rationalize the interstate commerce of the new nation and to create the documents and institutions of the
new governments, processes which lawyers, as well as landowners, dominated. A second wave of strong anti-lawyer sentiment accompanied the Jacksonian Populist era which some say lasted until after the Civil War. Early
American lawyers were almost all educated by apprenticeship. . . . Apprenticeship did much more than train lawyers (if it did that effectively at all); it
served as an efficient instrument of social control, as a device to limit the number of lawyers and assure enough work and a decent to comfortable living for
those who made it through. . . . The legal profession, though subject to the
ebbs and flows of the national economy, remained relatively homogeneous in
terms of race and class. However, there was some movement over time from a
totally upper class-derived profession to a greater representation of middle-
class sons of shopkeepers, teachers, small businessmen and some farmers. As
de Tocqueville noted, American lawyers sought to fill the vacuum created by
having no aristocracy of birth by creating an aristocracy of profession—that
of the middleman—the connecting link between the two great classes of society. Yet, as the nineteenth century unfolded, this "aristocratic" class grew
from a legal profession of about 20,000 in 1850, to 60,000 by 1880 and increased again to about 115,000 in 1900.

The story of the development of the legal profession in the United States in
the nineteenth century is the oft told tale of limited competition and increased
barriers to entrance to the profession, characterized by the movement from
apprenticeships to proprietary schools and increasingly to formal requirements for university and law school formal education, state examinations, and
licensing and certifications. Whether seen as an economic project to limit competition or a social project to keep out immigrant and non-"nativist" men, the

tale of the nineteenth century is an exclusionary one. . . . [T]he lawyer to population ratio was about the same . . . in 1960 as in 1885. Between 1960 and 1980, the legal profession experienced growth; law school enrollment increased three times, bar admissions four times, and the lawyer to population ratio halved. The last ten years have seen some leveling off of this expansive growth period. . . .

Entry barriers to immigrants, blacks and women were both "official" and more subtle. Blacks and women were formally excluded from legal education and from licensure, while some immigrant groups persevered through night schools and the development of their own law firms to service their own constituencies. Particularly successful were Catholics and Jews, who began with separatism in their own law firms, but eventually gave way to an assimilationist strategy.

By the late 1960s, women began entering the profession in greater numbers. They currently represent about 40% of the student body and just under 20% of the profession. On the other hand, entrance into the profession has been less successful for minorities—putting Blacks, Hispanic-Americans, Asian-Pacific Islanders and American Indians together, all minorities constitute just about 10% of the total enrollment in law schools and much less than 10% of total bar membership. . . . [O]nly 3% of all partners in our largest firms are minorities (compared to about 8–9% for women).

More important than the total numbers are the indications of an occupationally segregated profession. As the practice of law has changed in structure and organization, women and minorities find themselves disproportionately located in particular segments of the profession. . . . [W]hen one aggregates all of the tasks that women lawyers do, one finds that women can do it all. However, when one asks what a particular legal culture values, women will be seen to be doing that which is not valued—the same can be said of many minority lawyers. As the percentage of lawyers working in large private firms has increased over time, women and minorities are still more likely to be working in the public sector, in small firms and in solo practice, and if in large firms, they are disproportionately associates. . . .

B. Trends in the Economics and Organization of Law Practice

Of the almost 800,000 lawyers in the United States in 1990, most still work in small units of solo practice or small law firms. However, the percentage of lawyers working in large units has increased steadily since the founding of the first big law firms to handle the business of industrialization and railroad building in the nineteenth century. The number of law firms of more than 100 lawyers has almost tripled since 1980. . . . In addition to the proportional increase of lawyers in big firms, more lawyers today work in large units of law practice, in governmental settings, and in-house for corporations. . . .

... Several important and influential studies in recent years have attempted to understand the phenomenon of the growth, "transformation," and economic structure of the big firm. It is equally important, however, to recognize that some of the important economic and other innovations (such as the use of technology to deliver large volumes of service) ... have also been developed in the sites of small or solo practice. Finally, some non-economic transformations of the profession, particularly relevant to a consideration of the quality of work life, may occur when critical masses of innovative or "different" lawyers work together (such as in certain segments of governmental or public interest work) or where certain "trend-setters" push the envelope of what is acceptable in legal practice (advertising) or possible (technological innovation).

. . .

With an increased emphasis on "billable hours" as the measure of success within a [large] law firm, there have been several important developments for lawyers on both economic and quality of life grounds. To the extent that the bottom line or billable hours control evaluation (in more polite law firm lingo this is called "productivity"), more quantitative than qualitative decisions are made about partnerships. This increases predictability for associates but often creates some instability for the law firm, by reducing "bonding" by senior partners with particular associates and creates what some critics have labeled a "time famine." Billable hours continue to rise to such levels that at least one study documents that over 50% of associates bill more than 2400 hours a year and take less than two weeks of vacation a year. Associates claim that law firms require total commitment such that their family and other aspects of their outside lives are almost non-existent, as their every minute is clocked and monitored in the law firm. The emphasis on individual billable hours has also had the effect of decreasing some forms of collective action in the law firm, including both sociability and collegiality, as well as more altruistic, pro bono and public interest activities.

. . .

While most of the attention on the economics of law practice has focused on the large law firm, a few scholars have focused their attention on what may be the source of real innovation in the profession—the new forms of entrepreneurial lawyers consisting of solos, small firm practices, or pre-paid legal plans or clinics that attempt to deliver volume legal services. Following the decision of *Bates v. State Bar* [a 1977 case holding that advertising by attorneys may not be subjected to blanket suppression], lawyers began advertising to attract directly volumes of middle and lower income clients who had previously been thought to have inadequate access to the expensive, bar-fixed rates of private lawyers. This "revolution" in client-getting techniques, accompanied by the Supreme Court's approval of a variety of group and pre-paid legal plans has resulted in a number of economic and technological innovations in how law is practiced, that affects other dimensions of the quality of life choices for lawyers.

Early pioneers in this movement (the "legal clinic" movement) undertook considerable economic and personal risk to capitalize their practices, engage in advertising and marketing strategies, and purchase the first generations of computers for volume legal work. . . . As the legal clinics (such as Hyatt Legal Services, Jacoby & Meyers, etc.), pre-paid plans, and other forms of group legal services have developed, however, they have created two classes of lawyers—a managerial class, which attempts to monitor the productivity of work, and a laboring (dare I say a proletarian?) class of lawyers who "perform" the daily tasks of interviewing, form preparation and court hearings for large volumes of clients. . . . Laboring lawyers work on salary, usually for a relatively "normal" and predictable work week, reporting to a clear line of supervisory command, thus distinguishing the "work style" . . . from the greedy institution of the large law firm. Some lawyers report that working in legal clinics or pre-paid plans is, in effect, an extension of work in a legal aid or other direct service government office. Yet these lawyers, like a new group of entrepreneurial solo practitioners, report that they work mostly alone on large numbers of direct service cases. They report somewhat greater feelings of control over their caseload and personal lives, even as they know they are being monitored. In some instances, they can become "partners" through profit sharing plans or even formal partnership.

These new forms of practice are also distinguished by their demographic profile—a larger proportion of these lawyers are women and in urban areas greater numbers of minority lawyers will be found in this form of practice. For many women and minorities disenchanted with the ways of the large firm, these new forms of practice provide an alternative that allows them to use their "personal qualities" to deal directly with clients, master a new form of professional knowledge (the technology of computer delivery of services), and maintain a less totalized personal existence. . . .

Every once in a while a creative lawyer or group of lawyers may experiment with law practice organization and these innovations should be of particular interest to those of us who look for change in the legal profession. In one sense, Cravath, Swain & Moore's management of the IBM anti-trust litigation was one of these moments of law practice innovation. Separating a group of lawyers and paralegals and other professional and staff personnel to handle one large and complex case served to reorganize the practice in a number of ways. First, some lawyers were hired specifically to work on one case. This led to the employment of less-elite trained law students, more paralegals, differentiated (and in some cases higher) compensation packages, and an explicit no-partnership track, leading some to pursue permanent associate jobs and others to develop the "contract lawyer" track. Second, for at least some time, these personnel worked directly on site, much as accountants travel to the "field" and in essence, "bonded" more closely with clients than with other members of the firm. With the increase in large scale litigation, particularly mass torts, other innovations, such forms of specialized and routinized law practice, may have pre-figured the era of specialized or client-based break-away and boutique law firms.

The 1970s saw the development of "alternative law collectives" of political and ideological commitments in which work was shared, salaries divided evenly among professional and non-professional staff, and cases were taken purely for their law reform potential, rather than for their economic value. While few of these offices survived the era of greed in the 1980s, they continue to provide evocative visions of how law practice could be alternatively arranged.

. . .

III. Innovation in Law Practice from Diversity

A. Sources of Innovation . . .

. . . [S]ome have argued that the legal profession needs to adapt to the particular needs of its new entrants and that greater diversification of the profession will be beneficial not just to the new entrants but to the clients served, as well as the profession at large. It is less clear that the profession has been hospitable to these proposed changes.

. . .

Perhaps the place to begin is with the most controversial claim . . . —will women or other previously excluded groups (as "outsiders") contribute particular perspectives or practices to the legal profession (or the substance of law and doctrine) that can be attributed to their status or qualities as women or minorities? . . .

Most simply stated, those who have made claims that women will make changes in the legal profession because of their gender argue: (1) that women may be more likely to adopt less confrontational, more mediational approaches to dispute resolution, as well as transaction planning; (2) that women will be more sensitive to client's needs and interests, as well as to the needs and interests of those who are in relation to each other (client's families, employees, etc.); (3) that women employ different moral and ethical sensibilities in the practice of law; (4) that women will employ less hierarchial managerial styles; (5) that women are more likely to have social justice or altruistic motives in practicing law than total devotion to monetary gain; and (6) that women will be more likely to develop greater integration between their work and family lives. . . .

[B]eyond some of the process claims about practice . . . women or other excluded groups in the profession have had or will have an impact on the substantive law. . . . [F]eminists argue that their position as outsiders and as the "acted upon" in law allows them to see other possibilities of legal regulation and definition.

. . .

B. Benefits to the Legal Profession in Diversification

. . .

The inclusion of women and others in the profession has also the obvious benefit of providing lawyers who can serve the previously under or unrepresented. . . . I do not mean to suggest that women lawyers should serve only women clients or native group lawyers should serve only natives, but that in some cases, comfort with a same-group representative may facilitate the expression of legal needs and desires that might be repressed with more conventional, dominant group representation.

. . . [When] disparate treatment of some groups is perceived by the general public . . . the legitimacy of the entire system is compromised. . . . When the public observes court proceedings, such as through jury service, and through being a witness or observer (and these days through non-fictional television programming of actual trials . . . as well as the fictional accounts . . .) adverse treatment of particular individuals because of their social characteristics becomes evident. . . . Thus, public attention to issues of gender and racial differential treatment . . . serves to illuminate in a public way what is going on in private and in turn may result in pressures to the profession to "clean up its act" if the profession wishes to improve its already tarnished reputation.

Finally, attention to gender issues and the issues that women are more likely to raise with respect to quality of life issues may cause the profession as a whole to reevaluate the demand of its "greedy institutions" that seem to require so much devotion to work. In some instances, the development of parental or healthcare leaves has occurred because of the activism of some male attorneys who also seek to spend more time with their families and to humanize their commitments to work. . . . [T]he demands for an improved quality of life, coupled with the now charged political agenda of "family values" has produced strange sources of innovation and change. In my own research into law firm policies I have uncovered instances of middle-aged men who have become innovators on issues of leave, either because their daughters have become lawyers and they now understand more fully the impediments of the "glass ceiling" as it affects mothers or because of their own needs to spend time with families, often second families they have begun in their more mellow middle years. For some, the aggravating wear and tear of adversarial legal practice leads to mid-life evaluation and changes in what is desirable in legal practice. . . .

IV. Economic and Social Barriers to Innovation

A. *Economic Realities*

Barriers to the recognition, never mind achievement, of some of these innovations come from a variety of sources. . . . [S]ome would argue that law firm resistance to part-time or flexible work is, in effect, intentional discrimination to avoid certain kinds of workers. . . . Indeed, rather than reducing expenses by hiring more part-time lawyers (with fewer fringe benefits), law firms seem to be requiring more hours of fewer and fewer associates. . . . In addition to the economic and quality of life issues addressed here, there is the question of the quality of the work produced under these economic conditions.

Thus, economic pressures to use fewer lawyers to bill for greater numbers of hours prevents the growth and development of workplace innovations addressing the issues presented by work and family responsibilities. . . . [T]he work cycle of the typical lawyer, particularly the big firm lawyer, is incompatible with the birth-fertility-child-rearing cycles of most women's lives. This recognition . . . led to the cultural debate, some would say "explosion," about the "mommy track." . . . The debate which followed the naming of the "mommy track" demonstrates the deep ambivalence that feminists, policy makers, and all employers and employees feel about the inevitable tensions and conflicts between the allegiances owed to work and family. . . . Several commentators have suggested that the profession officially acknowledge that all careers are "phased" with layers and variations of productivity throughout the life cycle. The economics of law practice are in fact far more complex and the demand for total commitment to work needs to be understood as a complex of economic and non-economic demands and needs, including client preferences for "on-call" professionals, the economics of providing fringe and other benefits to workers, and an underlying culture of work that some might label "masculinist."

    . . .

B. *Social and Cultural Barriers: Continuing Discrimination*

In the United States, over thirty states and now two federal jurisdictions have commissioned Gender Bias Task Forces to study the possible sources of bias and discrimination in the practice of law. Several states, affected by the leadership of the ABA in developing a Commission on Minorities in the Profession, have established similar task forces designed to uncover problems encountered by minority lawyers. Initially conceived as a more limited look at how women lawyers, witnesses, jurors, judges and employees were treated in the court system, most Gender Bias Task Force studies have been expanded to consider the gender biases that exist in the relevant substantive law as well. Thus, for example, the California Gender Bias Task Force issued a report which called for substantive changes in the law of divorce and spousal and child support, certain crimes and torts related to violence against women, as well as procedural changes in court rules and practices.

One of the most significant findings of the Task Force Reports is the existence of two (almost separate perceptual or cultural) worlds. Women actors in the legal system continue to report discrimination and the perception of being treated differently from men ... in the legal system, while men report either lack of consciousness or awareness of discriminatory practices or a belief that the system does operate fairly and neutrally.

...

V. What Has Been and Can Be Done to Change the Legal Profession: Change Agents

...

... Gender Bias Task Force studies have fully documented the widespread discrimination experienced by women in the legal system in arenas ranging from professional courtesy and niceties to substantive doctrinal treatment in the law. ...

Some states ... have begun a second round of work in establishing committees of judges, lawyers and other legal administrators to implement the proposals suggested in those reports. In California, for example, specific committees have been delegated with the function of reforming particular areas of the law or drafting new court rules that will explicitly deal with some of the objectionable conduct.

One of the major efforts in the United States to track the progress of women's participation in the legal profession has been the American Bar Association's Commission on Women in the Profession. ... [T]he ABA Commission on the Status of Women has developed a policy guide for implementing parental leave, alternative work schedules and sexual harassment policies for lawyers designed to improve the quality of life for all lawyers. The ABA Commission has also been effective in monitoring the position of women in leadership positions in both the ABA itself and in local and state bar associations. Bar association activity is important for monitoring such issues as judicial selection as well. ... Similar efforts are now underway for minority lawyers, including mandating diversity workshops, training programs and official mentoring programs in law firms.

In addition to these institutional efforts, other developments have increased the visibility of women's participation in the legal profession and other professions, such as the growing number of very visible lawsuits against law firms for partnership denials, which challenge the sex stereotypic ways in which decisions are made. In addition, growing numbers of women and minorities are being appointed to the bench. Minnesota, for example, is the first state with a majority of women on the Supreme Court. Thus, the good news is that there is a great deal of attention being paid to the issues of women's participation in the legal profession and slowly the number of women is growing and accreting.

Yet the bad news is that partnership rates for women and minorities are still lower than their participation and length of time in the profession would predict and women and minorities remain highly segregated in different parts of the profession. And, the new threat of the formally recognized "Mommy Track" might serve to encrust this dangerous division of women permanently.
. . .

Perhaps what is needed for the legal profession as a whole is . . . an explication of feminist theory and jurisprudence accessible to non-specialists in feminist issues. Efforts at judicial education have attempted to explain to judges what women's and racial and ethnic minorities' experiences are and how they should come to understand them before they judge them. Similar efforts at educating lawyers and the public will be essential before gender, racial and ethnic bias can be eliminated. The difficult part of effecting social change in the legal profession is the interlocking webs of client expectations and law firm and judicial system structures, in which the status quo is sadly and constantly reinforced.

CHAPTER 29

Access to Law

In 1975 a conference was held at Stanford University to predict changes in the law. The proceedings of the conference were published as *Law and the American Future* (1976). In the introduction, the editor, Murray L. Schwartz, referred to "Newton's Third Law of Motion":

> To every action there is always opposed and equal reaction. If we have solved our health problems, we are faced with overpopulation; if our cities seem more attractive than life on the farm, they become uninhabitable; if industrialization and production have produced a higher standard of living for more human beings than ever before, they may also have made that living progressively hard to endure. But whatever we may think of the Laws of Motion, we must ask whether a system of law conceived in its fundamentals in the . . . environment of 1790 can be appropriate, let alone optimal, for the . . . environment of 1975 or of 2000. (p. 3)

The conference identified "representation of the unrepresented" as the most challenging issue for the future, a challenge exacerbated by the growing complexity of law.

Complaints about needless legal complexities have been heard throughout history. In the late twentieth century such complaints have emphasized the burdens created by regulatory agencies. Presidents Jimmy Carter and Ronald Reagan made much of their policies of consolidating and simplifying federal administrative agencies and their regulations. During the presidency of George Bush, "moratorium" periods were declared, during which federal agencies were prohibited from issuing nonemergency regulations. In some fields, such as public utilities, air transportation, and estate administration, legislatures passed measures to reduce regulation. Deregulation has been accompanied by privatization, turning some government functions—including prisons and schools in some communities—into private, for-profit enterprises.

In face of the trend toward reduced legal regulation, President Bill Clinton, elected in 1992, proposed a complicated legislative overhaul of the nation's health care system to extend insurance coverage to those not covered by health insurance through their jobs. The proposal lost in Congress as much for its complexity and bureaucratic nature as for its substance. The major legislative enactment of the first Clinton term—the reform of the federal welfare law—went in the opposite direction, drastically reducing and simplifying federal welfare benefits and regulations. The enactment of welfare reform prompted President Clinton to declare "The era of big government is over." Taking his message to heart, some have called for further reductions, including abolition of the Internal Revenue Service and enactment of a "flat tax."

Accompanying the trend toward less law and simplified law, the call of the 1975 conference for greater access to legal representation has been addressed in a variety of ways. The Legal Services Corporation survived the attacks of the 1980s, albeit with reduced funding; some with low and mid-level incomes gained access to lawyers through prepaid legal service plans and group legal services; and a portion of the need was met by pro-bono programs of law firms. Growing specialization and the use of paraprofessionals also increased the efficiency of law practice.

The movement for "representation of the unrepresented" has also had an impact on legal education. In the 1960s and 1970s the Ford Foundation launched a program to provide "seed money" to law schools throughout the country to develop law clinics, state legislatures enacted measures to permit law students to represent clients under the supervision of attorneys, and clinical legal education became a standard feature of most U.S. law schools. Clinical legal education, however, requires low student/faculty ratios—much lower than the twenty-to-one ratios at the average law school—and clinical legal education is costly to the law schools in other respects. Clinical education, therefore, has become merely an elective—not a required—part of most law school curriculums. A 1992 report of a Task Force of the American Bar Association, known as the "MacCrate Report" (after the chair of the Task Force, Robert MacCrate), called for increased commitment by law schools to "instruction in skills and values."

But all the efforts of the bar and legal educators—combined with significant increases in the number of lawyers—have not kept pace with the need for legal services. Some, therefore, have looked for other measures.

from Linda R. Singer, *Settling Disputes: Conflict Resolution in Business, Families, and the Legal System*, 2d ed. (Boulder, Colo.: Westview Press, 1994), pp. 1–14. Copyright © 1994 by Linda Singer. Reprinted by permission of Westview Press, a member of Perseus Books, L.L.C.

Origin and Growth of the Dispute Settlement Movement

A quiet revolution is taking place in the methods Americans have available to them for dealing with conflict. Innovations, almost all of them fewer than fifteen years old, are being developed not only to settle disputes out of court, but to supplement or replace the processes used by legislatures to budget funds, by businesses to manage employees, by therapists to treat families, and by diplomats to respond to global crises. There also are new institutions and new methods for resolving conflicts, such as those between neighboring families or countries, that once could be dealt with only by fighting it out with lawyers, with fists, or with armies.

From the beginning, America has been a nation of fighters, with a tradition of every man—and sometimes woman—for himself. Our culture is permeated with the language of sports—and of war. Perhaps it is our history of bountiful land and ever-expanding frontiers. Perhaps it is the perceived opportunity to get rich within a single generation, unaided by family or community. Whatever the explanation, our tradition of individualism also has spawned a history of confrontation. Except for countries actively undergoing revolution, the United States has the highest incidence of violent crime in the world.

The way we deal with lawbreakers also reflects our frontier and individualistic heritage. Except for the former Soviet Union and South Africa, we lock up more people, for longer periods of time, than any other country in the world.

Our civil as well as our criminal courts have been heavily used throughout our history. The public perception of a litigation explosion is not new. De Tocqueville wrote 150 years ago, "Scarcely any political question arises in the United States that is not resolved, sooner or later, into a judicial question."

Early Americans distrusted lawyers. The Fundamental Constitutions of Carolina termed pleading a case for a fee "a base and vile thing." Yet there are many more lawyers in the United States today than in any other country, both in absolute numbers and relative to the size of our total population. While the United States accounts for about 5 percent of the world's population, we have at least 35 percent of the world's lawyers. According to a speech by Harvard Law School Dean Robert Clark, the percentage of the U.S. gross national product devoted to legal services more than doubled between 1988 and 1993. Historian Jerold Auerbach has written, "Five hundred years from now, when historians sift through twentieth-century artifacts, they doubtless will have as little comprehension of American legal piety as most Americans now display toward medieval religious zeal. The analogy is illuminating: the courtroom is our cathedral, where contemporary passion plays are enacted."

Several developments have contributed to the public perception of a litigation explosion. Although the actual number of cases filed in state courts has grown only in proportion to population, . . . [f]ederal legislation designed to regulate business, to ensure civil rights, and, more recently, to protect the public from hazardous products and polluted air and water all have contributed to a significant increase in the business of our federal courts. Whatever the reason, the number of civil suits filed in federal courts alone has nearly tripled since 1970. This trend has been exacerbated by the sharp upturn in the criminal matters brought to federal courts, which in many parts of the country makes it difficult to have civil claims heard at all.

The nature of the disputes litigated also has changed, from a predominance of private business and property cases to personal injury accident claims and cases involving products liability, domestic relations, criminal law, and government regulatory actions. With the creation of products such as asbestos insulation, Bendectin, and Agent Orange, which have the potential of injuring huge numbers of people, and the invention of legal techniques (especially class actions) for bringing large numbers of cases involving accident victims or injured workers or consumers to court at a time, court battles affect the lives of many more people than they once did. They also require greater technical expertise. Demand for expert witnesses has increased markedly; witness brokers and clearinghouses can locate experts willing to testify on almost any subject. Despite the proliferation of new types of lawsuits, some of them with far-reaching implications, preliminary data from an ongoing study of federal litigation between 1971 and 1991 indicate that contract disputes among Fortune 1000 companies constituted the largest category of lawsuits filed in federal court.

When Americans must use the system—for example, to handle corporate conflicts over substantial sums or personal problems such as accidents, discrimination, or divorce—court or administrative action displaces our power over our own disputes. The legal process distorts reality; not only speed and economy but the real issues in dispute and the treatment of disputants by the professional dispute resolvers escape our control. Even top corporate managers feel as if their business problems take on a legal life of their own once they turn them over to lawyers and courts.

Despite the well-documented flaws in the system, which have attracted increased attention in recent years, it would be shortsighted to overlook the system's enormous benefits in establishing critical principles—principles many of us consider vital to our individual freedoms. Over the past forty years, for example, the courts have served as the last resort for racial and other minorities whose interests do not command a majority vote. Schools and workplaces have been desegregated; blacks and women have made political, economic, and social gains; public institutions, such as prisons and mental hospitals, have received far greater scrutiny. Courts also have improved the environment, increased safety in the workplace, and deterred manufacturers from injuring consumers through negligence or fraud. For example, the flood of litigation to compensate workers exposed to asbestos undoubtedly brought about safer handling—and eventual banning—of the insulation material sooner than would otherwise have been the case.

But all lawsuits do not involve important legal principles. In a large urban court, it can take years for even the simplest case to come to trial. Lengthy, complex procedures, both costly and time-consuming, make the courts appear to be exclusively the province of the rich, the patient, and the hearty. As early as 1926, Judge Learned Hand confessed, "I must say that, as a litigant, I should dread a lawsuit beyond anything else short of sickness and death."

Costs and delays, coupled with occasional multimillion-dollar verdicts (and, some charge, trial lawyers' and insurance companies' greed), have caused the rates of liability coverage for doctors, lawyers, car owners, and even architects to skyrocket. Yet awards made to the injured who use the courts to obtain compensation also are consumed by these same costs and delays. According to a study of the costs of compensating accident victims through litigation, victims receive only 45 cents in net compensation for every dollar spent on a lawsuit by the parties, their insurance companies, and the public.

Even administrative agencies, established to cope with such widespread, immediate problems as employment discrimination or consumer fraud in a faster, more accessible way than courts, have become courtlike, with long waits, complex procedures, and trial-like proceedings. Our large and complex society no longer can be run like a New England town meeting. The enactment of legislation and regulations, even at the local level, is so remote that it is completely removed from the lives of most Americans.

Even if our legal system of justice were more efficient, it would not satisfy some participants' most critical interests. The emphasis of courts and other traditional forums on pronouncing right and wrong and naming winners and losers necessarily destroys almost any preexisting relationship between the people involved. Whether the parties are a divorcing husband and wife who must continue to share the parenting of their children, businesses that want to retain their customers and suppliers, or employers and employees who want to keep their jobs, it is virtually impossible to maintain a civil relationship once people have confronted one another across a courtroom.

At the same time that use of the official system for resolving disputes is so forbidding, other traditional methods of settling conflict have lost much of their effectiveness. In a nation where moving from neighborhood to neighborhood, city to city, and job to job has become the norm, the mediating roles once played by the extended family, by churches, and by respected citizens in small towns persist only in a few homogeneous, cohesive communities. For Orthodox Jews in New York and residents in Chinatown in San Francisco, dispute resolution by rabbis or by community elders still remains a possibility. For the rest of us, such traditions, if they ever existed at all, belong to the distant past.

Then what do we do when we have a complaint of nonpayment on a bill or a contract, mistreatment on our jobs, or pollution of our air? Most of us recoil from fighting. Except for large corporations, hiring a lawyer seems far beyond our means: According to a survey by the American Bar Association, approximately 1 percent of the U.S. population receives 95 percent of the country's legal services.

So, in the words of legal anthropologist William Felstiner, most of us "lump it." We take out our frustrations on family and friends. We may even write occasional letters to our representatives in Congress. But generally we do nothing at all. The less money we have, the less likely we are to complain—whether directly to sellers or to third parties such as newspapers or television, consumer complaint centers, or civil courts. The costs, the stresses, and the inaccessibility of ways to resolve conflict other than through the polar alternatives of fight or flight cause some of us to drop out or to seek extreme techniques to make our points.

No less a member of the legal establishment than Derek Bok, former president of Harvard University and former dean of the Harvard Law School, described our system for resolving disputes as "strewn with the disappointed hopes of those who find [it] too complicated to understand, too quixotic to command respect, and too expensive to be of much practical use." Harvard law professor Laurence Tribe adds that the results do not justify the costs: "Too much law, too little justice; too many rules, too few results. . . ."

The Move Toward Alternatives

Against this backdrop, new methods of settling disputes are emerging both in and out of courts, in businesses, in diplomacy, and in communities. Diverse though they are, the innovations have a number of characteristics in common:

- They all exist somewhere between the polar alternatives of doing nothing or of escalating conflict.
- They are less formal and generally more private than ritualized court battles.
- They permit people with disputes to have more active participation in and more control over the processes for solving their own problems than do traditional methods of dealing with conflict.
- Most of the new methods have been developed in the private sector, although courts and administrative agencies now are borrowing and adapting some of the more successful techniques.

The movement by now has earned its own awkward acronym: "ADR," for "alternative dispute resolution." It draws on the history of tightly knit religious and immigrant ethnic groups, beginning with the Puritans in the 1600s and including the Dutch in New Amsterdam, the Jews on Manhattan's East Side, the Scandinavians in Minnesota, and the Chinese on the West Coast. All of these groups resolved differences within the community through mediation by ministers or elders.

The movement also draws on our commercial history. In settings such as the maritime, securities, fur, and silk industries, where firms dealt regularly with one another on an ongoing basis, businesses and trade associations early established private channels for resolving their differences. Commercial arbitration was born in 1768, when the New York Chamber of Commerce set up its own way of settling business disputes according to trade practice rather than legal principles.

This trend reached the personal level as well. George Washington put an arbitration clause in his will to resolve disputes among his heirs. Abraham Lincoln, while practicing law, arbitrated a boundary dispute between two farmers.

More recently, labor unions and employers developed an entire system of resolving work-related disputes as an alternative to violence or costly strikes. Although Congress authorized the secretary of labor to appoint "commissioners of conciliation" as early as 1913 when it created the United States Department of Labor, authority in U.S. industrial society before World War II, to quote labor arbitrator George Nicolau, was "unilateral and unreviewable." Workers resorted to direct action to challenge management's authority, which was "personal, arbitrary, and virtually unrestrained." Violent seizures of property, sit-downs, and bloody strikes were common. Characterized as unlawful, these actions more often than not were met with force by private security guards, state police, or the National Guard.

In the 1930s and early 1940s, several states and a few cities initiated publicly sponsored mediation services to settle labor-management disputes. During World War II, when Congress determined that industrial strife was too costly to the war effort to be tolerated, the War Labor Board was born. Griev-ance procedures, binding arbitration, and other innovations for solving indus-trial disputes became the norm throughout most of the United States. In 1947 Congress created an independent agency to settle labor disputes: the Federal Mediation and Conciliation Service.

The still-evolving history of resolving conflict in nonunionized corporations and in urban communities, prisons, schools, and universities reflects many of the same events. Yet only in dealing with conflicts between unionized labor and management have we actually developed well-defined institutions for re-solving disputes, a set of laws that help to achieve settlement, a cadre of pro-fessional dispute settlers (negotiators, mediators, and arbitrators), and the re-sulting expectation that disputes will be settled peacefully and fairly.

. . . Some of the same methods are being used today in corporations, in uni-versities, and in public schools and are being discussed as essential compo-nents of a revamped health-care system. A few years later, those . . . who were involved in creating the first "neighborhood justice centers," where commu-nity volunteers help people to settle their own disputes, looked both to . . . ex-perience with various types of organizations and to the traditional roles of clergy and village elders in tightly knit communities. The pioneers in settling environmental and government-related disputes built on these experiences and took additional inspiration from New England town meetings.

Some of these disparate efforts to develop new methods of dealing with conflict began to coalesce in April 1976, when Warren E. Burger, then chief justice of the Supreme Court, convened the Roscoe E. Pound Conference on the Causes of Popular Dissatisfaction with the Administration of Justice in Saint Paul. (In 1906, speaking in Saint Paul . . . , Pound already had voiced concern about the irrelevance of the legal system to the problems of most Americans.) Expressing the fear that "we may well be on our way to a society overrun by hordes of lawyers, hungry as locusts, and brigades of judges in numbers never before contemplated," and that "we have reached the point where our systems of justice—both state and federal—may literally break down before the end of this century," Burger invited an unusual mixture of people to reconsider Pound's wisdom.

The meeting attracted members of the judicial establishment who were con-cerned about the volume of litigation in general and the presence of cases with which courts were growing increasingly uncomfortable: environmental litiga-tion, class actions, cases brought to reform public institutions, and so-called minor disputes involving small amounts of money. Also present at the meeting were a few veterans of the civil rights movement, together with public interest lawyers concerned about increasing people's access to the legal system and the fairness of procedures. These strange bedfellows were joined by academics in-tent on developing better solutions to increasingly complex scientific or social problems. Absent from the conference, but active throughout the early devel-opment of the field, were the peace groups and grassroots community organizers, intent on empowering communities and enabling people to resolve their own conflicts.

The Pound Conference served to spark the interest of the legal establishment in alternative ways of settling disputes. But the different, and sometimes conflicting, values and goals of its participants have remained alive as the movement has gathered force. Not surprisingly, these differences have resulted in a diversity of settlement philosophies and techniques. For example, corporate minitrials coexist, sometimes uncomfortably, with community dispute centers as part of the same overall movement. The unusual alliance that makes up the ADR movement also has produced tensions among those who advocate the use of the same processes: There is no consensus on whether the primary benefits of settlement devices are the savings of time and money, the increase in the parties' participation, or the achievement of better results.

Since the Pound Conference, the proliferation of techniques for settling disputes and the emergence of new institutions and professionals to use them have constituted a major phenomenon of social change. In a varied and often unorganized way, discrete efforts are evolving into a new system for handling conflict.

1. Corporate executives are signing up for training courses in negotiation to learn to deal directly with their employees, customers, and competition. They also are attending seminars in mediation. Business school offerings are changing to reflect executives' different orientation. More than half of all business schools now offer courses in ADR. Although managers may have the power to order subordinates to take certain courses of action, they often find it more effective to reach consensus, whether by negotiating or mediating among employees who disagree with their bosses or with one another. High success rates and participant satisfaction have made these skills essential for managers and a permanent part of their job descriptions.

When faced with disputes with consumers or other corporations, business executives increasingly insist that their lawyers reduce cost, delay, and bruised feelings by settling cases through negotiation, mediation, or minitrials. Businesses can bind themselves and those who deal with them to specific methods of resolving future disputes by including agreements to mediate and/or arbitrate in their contracts; some will not sign a contract unless it contains such a provision. As a result of such devices, the number of federal lawsuits over alleged breaches of contract, which peaked at over 10,000 in 1987, dropped 30 percent to just over 7,000 in 1991.

Businesses also have begun to use corporate ombudspeople, mediators, or peer review panels to attempt resolution of complaints by employees or customers. Even the U.S. Senate has implemented a multistep dispute resolution program to resolve complaints of employment discrimination.

Insurance companies used ADR to handle claims arising from Hurricane Andrew [in 1992] and the devastating fire that destroyed much of Oakland, California [in 1991]. As a result, an estimated $20 million will be saved in transaction costs related to Hurricane Andrew victims alone, not to mention the months or years that otherwise would have separated them from much-needed compensation.

In response to their clients' demands, a growing number of law firms are appointing ADR coordinators; a few have separate departments of settlement or negotiation that operate independently of the firm's litigators. Led by Colorado, several states have adopted new ethics rules for lawyers, which strongly encourage or require them to advise their clients of alternatives to litigation. Profit-making dispute settlement firms, such as Judicial Arbitration and Mediation Service, Endispute, and ADR Associates, have sprung up to take advantage of the business market.

2. Troubled families used to go to court or to therapists. Now they can go to mediation—with the same therapists, with lawyers, or with community volunteers. The idea is to use the third party, who has no power to make decisions, to help settle disputes between husbands and wives, between parents and children, and, increasingly, between divorcing spouses. Some psychiatrists report that the emphasis of their entire practice has shifted from therapy to dispute settlement.

Following this trend, a number of jurisdictions require divorcing couples to try mediation before the courts will resolve their disputes for them. The proponents of mandatory mediation believe that the open communication and resolve-it-yourself nature of mediation make the process ideal for handling divorce settlements, especially where couples have children. Opponents caution that mediation probably works best when the parties engage in it voluntarily.

3. Approximately 350 neighborhood justice centers have been created throughout the United States in the past fifteen years, in sites ranging from storefronts to public schools and courthouses. These centers, sometimes called mediation services or "community boards," use community volunteers to settle landlord-tenant conflicts, neighborhood disputes, family rifts, and disputes involving the education of handicapped children. Some of them mediate between criminal defendants and their victims, either as an alternative to trial or as part of the sentence. In New York City alone, over 14,000 such disputes are handled through mediation each year.

4. Growing numbers of enforcement agencies, such as the Equal Employment Opportunity Commission and local consumer protection departments, require complaining employees and consumers to participate with businesses in settlement attempts presided over by the agency, before claims are investigated. The EEOC contracted with the Center for Dispute Settlement in Washington, D.C., to conduct a successful experiment with offering outside mediators to complainants and employers in an attempt at early settlements of selected charges filed in Washington, D.C., Philadelphia, Houston, and New Orleans. Some businesses have gone a step further and hired private mediators to help them settle disputes with dissatisfied current or former employees ei-

ther before or after they are brought to enforcement agencies or courts. In Maryland, the state attorney general's office recruits citizen volunteers to arbitrate complaints against businesses instead of prosecuting them.

5. In the United States, 95 percent of the law schools, as well as rapidly increasing numbers of schools of business, planning, and public policy, offer some alternative dispute resolution courses as part of their curricula. Publishers of law school textbooks now include ADR in publications on civil procedure, contracts, torts, and family law. Of the practicing lawyers, judges, and law teachers who sign up for Harvard Law School's Program of Instruction for Lawyers each June, more than half choose the oversubscribed offerings in mediation or negotiation. ADR has become a permanent part of the curriculum at the National Judicial College. Corporate lawyers recently were invited to learn about new ways of resolving cases on board a ship cruising around the Hawaiian islands. Most of them settle for the increasing numbers of ADR offerings in seminars offered by local bar associations or professional dispute resolvers.

6. Growing numbers of high schools and junior high schools across the country are developing courses in conflict resolution. Students are applying their new knowledge to resolving other students' disputes, including the fistfights that once would have guaranteed suspension. Working in teams with newly trained teachers, they also settle differences between students and teachers. Some have mediated conflicts between teenagers and their parents.

7. Congress in late 1990 passed the Administrative Dispute Resolution Act, which requires all federal agencies to develop policies on the use of ADR, appoint an ADR specialist, and provide appropriate employees with training in ADR. Spurred by the legislation, and by a 1991 executive order requiring federal agencies that litigate to use negotiation or third-party settlement techniques in appropriate cases when the federal government is involved in litigation, several federal agencies have developed programs that use a variety of ADR methods to handle disagreements with employees, contractors, taxpayers, or regulated businesses.

8. Increasingly, federal agencies, state public utility commissions, and even local sanitation departments are issuing new regulations through what they call "negotiated rulemaking." In this new process, representatives of opposing special interest groups from industry, consumer, and environmental organizations sit down with one another and with the agencies involved and negotiate government regulations. The negotiating committee that devised the penalties prescribed for violation of the Clean Air Act by the manufacturers of diesel engines, for example, included representatives of competing manufacturers, operators and importers of diesel engines, environmentalists, state agencies, the Environmental Protection Agency, and the Office of Management and Budget. A statute, enacted in 1990, specifically authorized federal agencies to employ this process.

9. In a related process, called "negotiated investment strategies," local, state, and federal officials negotiate with private interests over the allocation of government money for social services and public works projects. Resulting agreements have distributed the state budget for providing social services in Connecticut, established priorities for funding public works in Saint Paul, and provided government aid for industrial growth in Gary, Indiana.

10. The Civil Justice Reform Act, also passed in 1990, requires all federal district courts to create advisory committees to consider ways of reducing the cost and delay of civil litigation. The legislation specifically directs each committee to consider the use of ADR to reduce cost and delay. As a result of the committees' work, many (if not most) federal courts are instituting some sort of mediation, arbitration, or early neutral evaluation programs (many of them mandatory) to assist litigants in what is hoped will be earlier, less costly resolution of their cases.

11. Lawyers, therapists, retired judges, and entrepreneurs with no particular professional identity are hanging out shingles as mediators or judges for hire. Large numbers of students, together with professionals tired of other careers, are trying to build new careers in dispute resolution. They are helped by the public attention being generated by such events as court-sponsored "Settlement Weeks," when all judicial business stops to allow judges and volunteer mediators to help parties to settle cases, and statewide "Dispute Resolution Weeks," the first of which was proclaimed by the governor of Texas in 1985.

12. In 1978 President Jimmy Carter spent thirteen days at Camp David as a mediator between Menachem Begin and Anwar el-Sadat. (For the last ten days, Begin and Sadat never spoke to each other, although their cottages were only about one hundred yards apart.) Carter's unusual efforts produced the first comprehensive agreement between Egypt and a Jewish nation for more than two thousand years. . . .

Fifteen years after the historic Camp David agreement, perhaps an even greater breakthrough in the Middle East was achieved with an agreement between Israel and the Palestine Liberation Organization (PLO) [facilitated by the foreign minister of Norway]. The negotiations, held in secret, were particularly tricky because neither group recognized the other's right to exist and it was a longstanding policy on both sides not to negotiate with the other.
. . .

13. ADR has spread from North America, England, and Australia to Vietnam, South Africa, Russia, several Central European countries, Sri Lanka, and the Philippines. These countries are developing innovative conflict management programs, specific to their own cultures, in areas ranging from civil dispute mediation to environmental protection. Countries also are using ADR to resolve disputes in their ongoing relations with one another. The U.S.-Canada Free Trade Agreement and the North American Free Trade Agreement contain explicit dispute resolution procedures.

The Growth of Settlement Options

What do all these developments have in common? What unites the disparate cadre of volunteers and professionals, ranging from former housewives to retired judges, who crowd into meetings of the burgeoning International Society of Professionals in Dispute Resolution, which only a few years ago limited its membership to professional labor mediators and arbitrators? And what of the even more motley crowd of law and sociology professors, psychologists, and community organizers (complete with their sleeping bags) who gathered periodically at the National Conferences on Peacemaking and Conflict Resolution?

Settlements reached through negotiation, mediation, or arbitration promise faster results than do traditional legal, managerial, or bureaucratic processes—and at a fraction of the cost. There is some hard evidence to support these claims. Yet savings in cost and time are not the sole reason for much of the rapidly increasing enthusiasm for settling disputes. The core of the excitement lies in the reactions of disputants and dispute resolvers alike: People—from squabbling neighbors to corporate managers to Begin and Sadat—gain satisfaction from taking an active role in settling both their own and other people's conflicts. A national survey conducted by the Wirthlin Group, in which 80 percent of the respondents said they would choose mediation or arbitration over litigation, found that active participation in solving problems and the opportunity to reach a fair conclusion were even more important to disputants than savings in time and cost.

Many disputants care about preserving relationships even where they differ. All of us care about controlling the outcome of our own disputes. Even corporate executives with high-priced lawyers are more satisfied with both the process and the results when they are actively involved in shaping outcomes than when their affairs are placed in the hands of outsiders.

Decisions produced by collaboration among those who must live with the results can be tailored to the parties' needs. A schedule for caring for their children that is devised by divorcing parents themselves, for example, is more likely to take account of their preferences and other commitments than is a schedule imposed by a judge or even negotiated by their own lawyers. The resolution of a dispute between two corporations over late delivery of equipment or failure to pay for parts or labor can include agreements about long-term supply or service arrangements; a court could award only money. . . .

Negotiated or mediated settlements also are far more likely to preserve any continuing relationship between the parties than is a court battle. For some disputants, their ongoing relationship provides the most persuasive reason to attempt various settlement efforts. This is so not only in disputes among family members or neighbors; a continuing relationship may be the critical consideration between an employee and employer or between a business and a customer or critical supplier. Concern for preserving their long-term relationship with customers, for example, has been one of the primary incentives motivating automobile manufacturers to develop accessible mediation and arbitration procedures for the buyers of new cars claimed to be defective.

Finally, there is growing evidence that people who reach agreements themselves are more likely to abide by them than are people who are told what to do, whether by a judge, a supervisor, or a therapist. They also may be more willing to renegotiate their agreement as circumstances change. This observation has implications for a broad range of people and problems, from fathers who refuse to pay child support to companies whose products poison the environment.

Of course, together with the many advantages, informal dispute settlement can have significant disadvantages. Negotiated settlements do not develop standards to govern the behavior of others involved in similar disputes in the future. They do not punish lawbreakers or cheaters (although negotiated agreements can provide penalties for a later breach). They often do not obviate the need for lawyers, whether to give advice or to participate in negotiations. Nor do they serve to equalize the bargaining power between participants, such as husbands and wives or corporations and their employees, who may have markedly different resources or sophistication. Indeed, serious controversy exists over whether informal settlement is appropriate for parties of significantly unequal power or whether it reinforces their differences and thereby produces unfair results.

CHAPTER 30

Science and Technology

Perhaps the most productive period in the application of science and technology was the half-century from the 1850s to the 1900s. The innovations of those five decades included the light bulb, the phonograph, the telephone, the typewriter, the radio, the refrigerator, the diesel engine, and the Bessemer steelmaking process. In 1869 the continental railroad was completed; in the 1880s the automobile appeared; in the same period cities installed subways and elevated trains; in 1903 the Wright brothers flew their airplane at Kitty Hawk.

In 1937 a group of leading American scientists was called together by the federal government to identify the trends in science most likely to affect the future. Their report did not foresee the splitting of the atom, computers, radar, or the jet engine. Thirty-five years later, two legal scholars, David Loth and Morris L. Ernst, published *The Taming of Technology* (1972), in which they discussed the legal implications of a variety of other scientific developments, many of which would have surprised the authors of the 1937 report, including space exploration, weather modification, ocean-floor mining, nuclear energy, birth control, artificial insemination, organ transplants, genetic engineering, wiretapping, and truth drugs.

When Loth and Ernst wrote of computers, they had in mind large mainframes. Two years after the publication of their book, such mainframes were used to develop the first massive, full-text legal information storage system, LEXIS, followed in a few years by a rival system, Westlaw. But Loth and Ernst did not foresee the personalization of the computer, nor the worldwide linkage of computers through the Internet. In the subsequent quarter century, perhaps no technological development has had a greater impact on law, on society, and on individuals. As M. Ethan Katsh has written in his *Law in a Digital World* (1995):

Technology is changing rapidly, and it increasingly will be asked whether our legal doctrines and our ways of using or applying law can be extended to activities in this new place. . . . For example, can employers and online service providers look at e-mail messages received by an employee or a subscriber? Or, what kind of responsibility is assumed by someone who runs an electronic bulletin board on which copyrighted information is uploaded and downloaded without the owner's knowledge? Or, since a finding of obscenity must take into account local community standards, which community's standards apply when someone in Tennessee downloads questionable material from an electronic bulletin board in California?

Such questions will inevitably dominate public discussion about law in the new environment. There will be important and difficult questions of this type since tranquility and harmony do not appear to be natural conditions of cyberspace. Yet, . . . there is a second category [of questions]—one concerning new values and expectations, new ways of speaking and thinking, new relationships being formed, new concerns of style and culture. (p. 240)

Advances of science and technology have affected not only the substantive rules of law, but also the institutions of the legal system. As complexity has increased, legislatures have become less and less able to formulate needed legal controls with specificity, leaving more and more to be filled in by regulatory agencies and by judges. Ideally, regulatory agencies are staffed by technocrats with expertise in the area being regulated. But judges must interpret and apply the often vague provisions of legislation and must review challenged regulations and actions of administrative agencies without the help of expert staffs.

Proposals have been made for specialized "science courts," and some have speculated that computer-applied artificial intelligence systems may ease the tasks of judging complex cases (although such systems are more likely, at least initially, to be applied to the simplest cases). But if the court system continues to be staffed and run as at the end of the twentieth century, judges and juries must continue to grapple with cases involving scientific issues, however complex, aided only by the information in the case records provided by the opposing lawyers and by commonly known facts subject to "judicial notice" outside the records.

GRINDING GEARS

from Sheila Jasanoff, *Science at the Bar*
(Cambridge, Mass.: Harvard University Press, 1995), pp. 204–23.
Copyright © 1995 by The Twentieth Century Foundation.
Reprinted by permission of The Twentieth Century Foundation, New York.

Is the relationship between science, technology, and the law an essential alliance or a reluctant embrace, a collaboration or an unhappy marriage? Is it a "culture clash" that can be bridged only by individuals or institutions with multicultural expertise? Are scientists who participate in the legal process tolerated meddlers or essential contributors? The neat epithets of scholars and journalists scarcely do justice to the complex archaeology of modern courtroom conflicts over science and technology and the social yearnings and unrest that underlie them. Ranging from the narrowly technical to the morally divisive, from the structural and persistent to the contingent and evanescent, these controversies defy simple categorization because they embrace the totality of contemporary society's attempts to understand and control perceived threats to its stability and identity. Science and scientists are drawn into the courtroom not merely as adjuncts to legal fact finding, but because human technological ingenuity continually gives birth to new and unruly forms of life, outstripping the equally human craving for predictability and repose.

. . . How does litigation advance and how does it hinder policymaking for science and technology in a democratic society? What are the most problematic consequences of using adjudication to resolve disputes among technical experts? What institutional features in law, science, technology, or the political process account for these problems, and how can or should they be remedied? Only by systematically working through these questions can we hope to assess whether fundamental changes are needed in the legal system's methods of dealing with science, technology, and social change.

. . . Courts often . . . appear uncertain about or resistant to quantitative methods and principles that scientists take for granted, such as concepts of causation, probability, and statistical significance. They seem even less systematically aware of modern science as a social institution, whose claims and credibility are produced through complicated negotiations within the community and with external institutions. Case-by-case adjudication leads to incoherent results in the evaluation of technical evidence, producing uncertainty

487

for businesses and professional communities as well as for innocent victims. . . .

In spite of these deficits, . . . courts . . . remain an indispensable and often appealing forum for resolving technical controversies. . . . [There have been] many instances in which courts almost by default were required to take the lead in constructing new social and political orderings around science and technology. Thus, Congress' deliberate unwillingness to act left the courts in charge of devising complex litigation procedures and rules of liability to meet the needs of victims of toxic exposure. Changes in biomedical technology and practice likewise elicited only slow and faltering responses from state and national legislatures. From surrogate motherhood to the right to die, the task of articulating policy fell in the first instance to the judiciary. Legislatures frequently held back from acting until landmark cases . . . spotlighted problems whose urgency could no longer be denied. A court decision . . . played a seminal role in the commercialization of biotechnology. The most powerful new forensic technique of recent decades—DNA fingerprinting—began to be debated in national scientific and law-enforcement circles only after state court proceedings exposed its eminently contestable claims to reliability.

Lawsuits, we must conclude, are an essential part of the process by which American society comes to grips with the moral, material, and institutional dimensions of technological change. . . . The pressing question for policy, then, is how litigation can be made to work better when confronted by problems with significant scientific or technical dimensions. . . .

The Myths of "Mainstream Science"

[T]he unexamined though widely held conviction that "mainstream science" could dispel most of the legal system's problems in handing sociotechnical conflicts . . . rests upon fundamental misconceptions about the links between scientific and legal decisionmaking. Contrary to the professed beliefs of many in science and industry, good science is not a commodity that courts can conveniently shop for in some extrasocietal marketplace of pure knowledge. There is no way for the law to access a domain of facts untouched by values or social interests. Scientific claims that are imported into the legal process are colored not only by the interests of the offering parties but also by the social, cultural, and political commitments of other actors in society: for example, the reluctance of experts to breach disciplinary solidarity, the law's desire to cloak morally difficult judgments with the "objective" authority of experts and instruments, and the public's demand for decisions that seem both open and rational. Historically, sociologically, and politically, the proposal that courts should increase their reliance on a value-neutral mainstream science is therefore extremely problematic.

Scientific closure and legal controversy do not, to begin with, stand in a predictably linear chronological relationship. Disagreement is endemic in science, and knowledge claims as often as not remain open-ended within the scientific community at times when they must be subjected to further testing in court. Scientific research is undertaken in many cases only after litigation pinpoints a possible causal connection. Where research exists, data still need to be aggregated and reanalyzed, sometimes through controversial scientific methods . . . in order to address the issues relevant to litigation. Context-specific information must be compiled to fill evidentiary gaps in cases ranging from employment discrimination to industrial and environmental disasters to patent infringement. Given its often limited relevance to scientific discovery, such information may never be independently reviewed or published, and publication if it occurs at all may postdate the needs of the legal process. Accordingly, the rule that courts should simply adopt the prevailing scientific opinion is often unworkable in practice. Consensus positions may develop around recurrent or widely distributed problems, but only after years of litigation and many interim efforts to produce definitive knowledge. . . .

At any given moment, moreover, the law's view of what constitutes the "mainstream" position in science may be an artifact of the legal system's limited and highly contingent ability to interrogate the scientific community. The fallibility of DNA typing, for example, was publicly demonstrated only after the technique had been deferred to in nearly two hundred trials. . . .

The production of scientific testimony for the courtroom is bound up with cross-cutting institutional and political imperatives that complicate the notion of science as a free-standing culture, independent of the law. The adversary process, the pressure to reach definite conclusions, and the selective use of knowledge by interested parties are only the most obvious social influences on the conversion of claims and observations into scientific evidence suitable for use in court. Less well attested but no less significant is the reorientation of scientific practices to suit the real or imagined needs of the legal system, from the initiation of strategic research to the adoption of unconventional modes of peer review and publication. Examples . . . testify to the scientific community's deep interest in constructing "mainstream" positions with an eye to their eventual adoption by the legal system. Science done (or interpreted) under these circumstances can scarcely be counted upon to maintain a persuasive impartiality when openly tested in court.

Further, textbook science—the body of knowledge that is already in the public domain, having passed through science's critical filters—is rarely enough to satisfy the law's need for contextualized knowledge. In toxic tort cases, for example, even a large (though often undigested) body of literature on general causation typically will not answer the question of specific or individual causation upon which plaintiffs rest their claims for damages. Mass torts, such as environmental disasters, require the production of site-specific knowledge, creating potential conflicts between knowledge considered valid by professional scientists and the knowledge compiled by local victims' groups. Different types of evidence routinely elicit different credibility judgments from fact-finders: thus, epidemiological data may be favored over animal studies, a treating physician's testimony over a toxicologist's, a doctor's assessment of reasonableness over a patient's perceptions, and an instrumental reading over a police officer's or a coworker's reporting of individual experience. . . . [S]uch credibility judgments incorporate the fact-finder's own tacit understandings of science and expertise, although these private judgments may be hidden from critical review. . . .

If legally relevant knowledge is always interest-laden, then the choice between alternative scientific accounts necessarily involves normative, even political, judgments. Willingness to accept a particular knowledge claim amounts to an expression of confidence in the institutions and practices that produced it. The researcher from the elite university, the representative of the powerful professional society, or the expert from the state agency may be judged as more authoritative than the "mere technician," who possesses neither Ph.D. nor publication record. In other contexts, the consultant employed by a corporate defendant or the university scientist whose work was supported by grants from industry may be dismissed as less credible than a disinterested-seeming witness with lesser professional credentials. . . .

In sum, courts, like regulatory agencies, conduct the bulk of their scientific inquiries "at the frontiers of scientific knowledge," where claims are uncertain, contested, and fluid, rather than against a backdrop of largely settled "mainstream" knowledge. . . . Other forms of guidance are needed, more realistically attuned to the indeterminacy of scientific knowledge in the actual contexts of litigation, and mindful of the institutional strengths and weaknesses of judicial dispute resolution.

The Record of Judicial Accomplishment

How have legal institutions performed in facilitating the wide-ranging social readjustments that accompany, and indeed help define, scientific and technological change? Our responses . . . can usefully be grouped under the headings of *deconstruction, civic education,* and *effectiveness.*
. . .

Deconstructing Expert Authority

The phrase "science at the bar" conjures up the image of a blustering, overconfident, perhaps inebriated science that has been called to account at the bar of justice. Indeed, the deconstruction of expert testimony by cross-examining attorneys is perhaps the most widely discussed aspect of science's relations with the law. But what does cross-examination really achieve? The credibility of science could in principle be assailed at many levels: specific scientific claims, their individual proponents, the methods and assumptions underlying the claims, and the institutions that certified those methods and assumptions. In reality, however, courtroom challenges to expertise are rather more selectively targeted, with the personal credibility of witnesses bearing the brunt of attack. Cross-examination . . . assumes that there is a substrate of "truth" to be precipitated out from "covert, extraneous bias (including values or opinions) or incompetence" in the presentation of testimony. The law's institutional commitment to preserving the fact/value distinction (even if its artificiality is recognized by sophisticated practitioners) drives cross-examination toward an almost obsessive concern with inconsistencies in the witness's testimony and with biases, such as ties to economic interests, that are considered important in commonsense tests of credibility. The technical practices of lawyering thus shore up a deeper commitment to the notion of science as a reservoir of determinable facts. Science as a whole does not lie; it is only the occasional dishonest scientist on the witness stand who is culpable.

Not surprisingly, then, we find that the legal process exposes the cognitive and social commitments of individual expert witnesses more predictably than it identifies structurally or institutionally conditioned contingencies in scientific knowledge. . . .

[However,] the deconstructive force of the law operates not only at the micro level of individual claims and controversies, but also at the macro level, where the law, as an institutionalized embodiment of distrust, challenges science's equally institutionalized claims to superior authority. Scientists, we know, are vigorous critics of each other's work, but this criticism is effective only within a basic envelope of trust that cannot be challenged without threatening the integrity of the entire scientific pursuit. . . . With different institutional commitments, and with an equally powerful skeptical rhetoric at its command, the law can render transparent domains of contingency and constructedness in science that science's culturally bounded querying procedures could not have brought to light. Through repeated and incremental, if conflictual, interactions with science and technology, the legal system plays a vital part in exposing the presumptions of experts and holding them accountable to changing public values and expectations.

But what of the law's reflexive ability to deconstruct its own conceptions of science and expertise, especially when these conceptions are encoded within legal categories such as property, gender, causation, rationality, and, indeed, facts? Just as scientific peer review is constrained by the norms of science, so legal self-criticism, which proceeds through techniques of reasoning from and distinguishing among precedents, is constrained by the institutional commitments of the law. There are tantalizing hints from a wide range of cases that legal criticism only inconsistently opens up judicial understandings of science and technology. . . . Most of all, the legal system jealously guards its power to declare what counts as science for purposes of the law. The extraordinarily undifferentiated and uncritical accounts of scientific methods and cultures found in much of the legal academic literature provide important intellectual support for this strategy.

Civic Education

At their most effective, legal proceedings have the capacity not only to bring to light the divergent technical understandings of experts but also to disclose their underlying normative and social commitments in ways that permit intelligent evaluation by lay persons. Adversary procedures, however, can be indiscriminately deconstructive in their impact and can obfuscate as well as advance critical inquiry. To what extent has litigation served to improve the quality of public debate on scientific and technological issues, whether by increasing participation, providing appropriate discursive and conceptual resources, or otherwise fostering deliberation?

. . . Review by generalist judges symbolizes this nation's continued adherence to the principle that all governmental actions, however arcane or esoteric, must be explained in terms that are comprehensible to nonexpert audiences. By insisting on their prerogatives in this regard, courts have repeatedly affirmed that the ultimate power to guide technology policy is vested not in experts but in the citizenry. . . . [T]he overall effect of maintaining a dialogue between experts and the people, mediated by the legal process, appears to have been salutary. American attitudes toward science and technology remain generally optimistic, and the pervasive alienation from and mistrust of technology discernible in some segments of Western European polities to date have found no strong echoes in the United States.

Although courts have succeeded, sometimes brilliantly, in bringing to the surface public fears, concerns, and demands relating to technology, their record in transmitting these messages to other deliberative arenas remains equivocal. Right-to-die cases . . . engaged the capacity of courts to provide "detached but passionate investigation and decision" on a matter of individual liberty. Courts were relatively successful over time both at conceptual clarification and at transferring policy responsibility to less adversarial institutions, such as ethics committees, professional societies, and legislatures. Other democratizing trends in judicial decisionmaking, however, . . . arguably reached a point of diminishing returns.

. . .

Effectiveness

Apart from deconstructing expert authority and providing another language and forum for political discourse, how effectively have courts answered to public demands for equity, efficiency, and responsiveness in decisions involving science and technology? . . .

The much-maligned inefficiency of the adjudicatory system, and the frequent second-fiddling by legislatures, assume a relatively benign cast when looked at through the lenses of federalism and pluralism. Modern technology raises wrenching questions about life and death, human nature and social relationships, to which twentieth-century America seems singularly reluctant to provide collective answers until multiple possible responses have been articulated in many discrete controversies. Given the religious, cultural, and ethical diversity of U.S. society, addressing claims at smaller units of discourse—the individual, the family, or the state—holds undeniable advantages. There is much to be gained in a pluralistic society by addressing value-laden technological disputes away from the glare and publicity of national legislation. Courts, for all their weaknesses as policymakers, possess certain offsetting virtues as mediators of conflicting values. The relatively decentralized, small-scale, and ad hoc character of judicial decisionmaking permits a more leisurely consideration of moral and ethical questions than is generally possible in the legislative arena.

Responsiveness is another of the legal system's great virtues, even though an overall assessment of judicial performance with regard to science and technology might fault the courts for participating too uncritically in the public steering of science and technology. Judicial fears about toxic chemicals and increased risk, coupled with judicial optimism about nuclear power and biotechnology, display much the same unreflective ambivalence that is revealed in public opinion surveys. Nonetheless, a fair evaluation of the judicial record counters the charge that courts by and large have dampened the development of science and technology. In cases ranging from patenting new life forms to regulating surrogacy, courts demonstrated their institutional capacity for breaking up policy stalemates and forcing legislatures to confront problems of growing public anxiety. Even where legislation came first, as in areas of environmental law, it fell to courts to supply the detailed and nuanced interpretive principles that the relatively blunt instrument of legislation could not provide. . . .

Policy Reform: Criticism with Credibility

However positively one views the democratizing influence of courts, one cannot ignore the widespread perception at this century's end that something in the American legal system's handling of science and technology is broken badly enough to need fixing. Proliferating proposals for improving judicial decisionmaking reveal at least three strands of thought about the nature of the problem and its possible solutions: (1) that courts should defer more to external sources of scientific authority ("mainstream science"); (2) that the legal system's established mechanisms for dealing with technical questions should be strengthened; and (3) that more alternatives to litigation should be sought, including litigation over scientific and technological issues. Each proposition calls for evaluation. . . .

Separatist Schemes

Although many observers of the legal process see the worlds—or cultures—of law and science as separate, at least at the "core," the notion of a "science court" or specialized branch of the judiciary with expertise in science and technology commands little political appeal. The historical commitment to generalist courts authorized by Article III of the Constitution and the legal system's hostility to the idea of "scientific separatism" create formidable barriers against institutional bifurcation. Even the Court of Appeals for the Federal Circuit, whose jurisdiction over patent appeals makes it the most technical and specialized of the federal appellate courts, remains firmly tied to a holistic conception of the law.

Separatism, however, finds other expressions as well. One form is the injunction that judges should learn to "think like scientists" and should use specified, uniformly applicable criteria to determine whether the evidence before them is truly scientific. . . .

A less intrusive form of separatism is the preparation of handbooks, manuals, or panel reports that seek to systematize bodies of knowledge for use in resolving common types of scientific disputes. Such works are able to elucidate, without significant mythmaking, both substantive problems (such as toxic torts and DNA fingerprinting) and the processes by which science produces facts (such as replication and peer review). Thus, a reference manual on scientific evidence published in 1994 . . . provides reference guides on seven areas of expert testimony: epidemiology, toxicology, survey research, forensic analysis of DNA, statistical inference, multiple regression analysis, and estimation of economic loss.

Apart from obsolescence, the main risk of this approach is that judges will fail to question the origins and foundations of the consensus that a manual or report purports to represent. What work was done to create the document? Does it make sense to accept its findings without further challenge . . . ? The history of the first National Research Council study of DNA typing illustrates the reasons for concern. A panelist who participated in the study later reported that "the committee members had agreed to *let the report speak for itself* to avoid the emergence of conflicting gospels according to different members" (emphasis added). A court that failed to look behind such possibly self-serving vows of silence could hardly meet its normative obligations, especially where, as in the case of DNA typing, guilt, innocence, and human lives might hang in the balance.

Finally, some scholars would like to connect the allegedly separate domains of law and science through new institutions rather than keep them distinct on the model of the science court. Bridging institutions or individuals such as "science counselors" would be entrusted to carry information and critical perceptions back and forth across the perceived cultural divide. . . . [S]uch proposals would simply substitute one process of social construction for another. Courts . . . are themselves a quintessential form of "bridging institution": they are places where scientists, lawyers, and lay persons participate in the production of legally relevant knowledge under particular, ritualized conventions for establishing credibility and authority. Why should one substitute for these tried-and-true "multicultural" institutions other, possibly less tested models of constructing knowledge and legal order?

A partial answer is that under certain circumstances nonadversarial institutions may serve both science and democratic values better than courts do. The objectives of criticism and civic education, for instance, are not always best entrusted to litigation. Scientific advisory bodies, in particular, have demonstrated their capacity to synthesize a common knowledge that satisfies norms of scientific, legal, and political accountability. At their best, such bodies can provide a "hard look" at the available evidence without falling prey to endless technical deconstruction. . . .

Training Judges and Informing Juries

Many methods have been proposed to strengthen the capacity of courts to evaluate scientific and technological controversies. The focus usually is on judges, because they are best positioned to help juries to weigh and contextualize scientific evidence, although the idea of blue-ribbon juries also deserves attention. Generally, these approaches hold promise because they combine flexibility with the potential for enhancing the fact-finder's awareness of the intertwined normative and technical issues in litigation.

The most radical scheme would require expert witnesses to be appointed by the court and answerable to the judge alone, as in European civil law jurisdictions. This prospect, however, holds little more than theoretical interest in a common law culture wedded to the virtues of party autonomy. Cross-cultural borrowings that seek to graft isolated procedural devices from one legal system onto another offer in any case only the slimmest hope of success; law, like language, is a system in which the elements are mutually interdependent in ways that only a "native speaker" can fully appreciate. . . . Pretrial hearings offer another popular procedural device for increasing the give-and-take among scientific experts and broadening the range of expertise beyond the polarized extremes usually sought by the parties. As in the context of administrative rulemaking, hearings may create a more informative record than the more formal rituals of trial-type examination and cross-examination.

Although solutions such as these offer only incremental relief for what some see as a massive structural problem, there are strong reasons to favor incrementalism in the interactions between law, science, and technology. First, one of the greatest strengths of legal proceedings is precisely the ability to produce localized, context-specific epistemological and normative understandings that are not subordinated to inappropriately universal claims and standards. Second, . . . the deconstruction of expertise often happens most effectively through repeated encounters between scientists and lawyers, with the facts, the participating experts, and the legal rules of the game all changing from one disputing context to another. Both considerations would favor reforms that respect the diversity of problem-solving approaches currently represented in the American legal system.

Alternatives to Litigation

Trajectories of conflict such as those over abortion, fetal research, or the right to die point to the need for policymaking bodies that are less unwieldy than legislatures, as sensitive to values as courts, and yet better able to forge political compromises than a nonelected judiciary. In the United States, as in Britain, the blue-ribbon commission has been a favorite device for filling the institutional gap between courts and legislatures, but the effectiveness of such panels depends critically on the nature of their linkage to the larger political process. For example, Congress in 1988 created a bioethics committee to study the legal and ethical implications of the human genome project and to offer guidance on sensitive policy issues arising at the frontiers of the biomedical sciences. But the committee's operations were stalled when Congress proved unable to fill a vacancy. . . . By contrast, a less political bioethics task force appointed in 1985 by Governor Mario Cuomo of New York successfully mediated among religious and ethnic groups and played a constructive role in political consensus-building. Hospital ethics committees and the ethics advisory panels of scientific and technical societies can also serve as valuable adjuncts to the legal system. Free from the immediate pressures of litigation, such bodies are well positioned to carry out the dispassionate inquiry into professional standards and practices that so often eludes the reach of chronically overburdened courts.

More generally, currents in the law that have little to do with science or technology may lead to reforms. . . . Concerns about the complexity, cost, and inefficiency of litigation have been growing steadily for more than two decades, bringing far-reaching changes in the way law is practiced in America. The increasing acceptance of no-fault insurance schemes, negotiated rulemaking, complex litigation, pretrial disclosure, and methods of alternative dispute resolution testifies to a gradual movement away from the strictly adversarial approach to dealing with society's formal grievances. At the same time, increased monitoring of judicial performance and an emphasis on out-of-court settlements are beginning to expedite cases that do make their way into the legal arena. In the end, these macropolitical trends may do more to alleviate some of the grinding of gears between law, science, and technology than utopian schemes for marrying perfect rationality with perfect justice.

CHAPTER 31

The World Community

Fundamental changes in the international environment in the last decade of the twentieth century illustrate the difficulty of making predictions: Even expert kremlinologists failed to predict the collapse of the Soviet Union.

Among those who attempt to predict how the world community will evolve in the twenty-first century, the favorite buzz-word is "globalization." "Globalization" is distinguished from "internationalization." Internationalization is traceable back to antiquity in the interaction of nations in trade, diplomacy, war, and other contacts. Laws regulating such interactions emerged from customary practices and from treaties, although obedience to such laws could depend on little more than fear and mutual self-interest. Scholars contributed to the development of internationalization to such an extent that the commentaries of some are considered to be sources of international law alongside customs and treaties.

Treaties have not only created rules for dealings between states, they have also created international organizations with lives of their own as international actors. Multilateral cooperation in Europe dates from the Peace of Westphalia, which ended the Thirty Years War in 1648. Two of the major powers of the time, France and Sweden, were designated as guarantors of the peace. Similarly, in 1815, after the defeat of Napoleon, the Congress of Vienna established a "Concert" of great powers to guarantee the terms of the peace. The Congress also established the first permanent international organization—the Commission for the Navigation of the Rhine. Throughout the nineteenth century other conferences and other international organizations dealt with specific issues such as telegraph transmission, mail, rail passage, and safety at sea.

Conferences at The Hague in 1899 and 1907 sought to institutionalize a system of arbitration to avoid future wars. After the First World War, the

League of Nations became the first standing representative assembly of nations. After the Second World War, the same model was followed in the establishment of the United Nations.

International courts were appended to both the League and the UN, but the jurisdiction of each was limited to the voluntary submissions of nations. The UN also helped to bring about the General Agreement on Tariffs and Trade to reduce trade barriers around the world through a series of negotiating "rounds."

Attempts to reduce trade barriers met with greatest success on the regional level. The prime example is the European Community. Regional organizations exist for other purposes as well: the North Atlantic Treaty Organization, a military defense alliance, not only survived the end of the Cold War but expanded its membership to some formerly Communist states and took collective action in Bosnia and Yugoslavia; the Organization of American States coordinates policies on such issues as refugees, drug trafficking, and terrorism; similarly, the Organization of African Unity and the Arab League meet to discuss and coordinate policies of mutual interest.

International law has also made room for nongovernmental organizations (NGOs). A number of NGOs have received limited representation at the UN and some, such as Amnesty International and Greenpeace, have achieved considerable international influence. Individuals, too, have achieved legal standing in international law in limited instances, as in the European Court of Human Rights. The development of internationalization, however, remains for the most part dependent upon the relations of sovereign states.

Globalization goes beyond traditional concepts of international law and international organizations. A German scholar, Jost Delbruck, has described the distinction:

> [T]he term *globalization* has entered into the vocabulary of scholars as well as political practitioners. Although it seems, at times, as if the new term is rather carelessly used as a trendy synonym for the word "internationalization," such interpretation of the term "globalization" would fall short of its distinct meaning. For instance, certain serious threats to the environment such as ozone layer depletion or climate change caused by the so-called "greenhouse effect" are of *global* rather than *international* concern since they affect humankind everywhere, regardless of national boundaries. Similarly, today's financial markets are globalizing rather than internationalizing (which they did in earlier decades) since, for instance, the movement of capital has largely become independent of the sovereign control of state agencies. Thus, it seems that globalization . . . denotes a process of *denationalization* of clusters of political, economic and social activities. Internationalization, on the other hand, refers to cooperative activities of *national* actors, public or private, on a level beyond the nation-state but in the last resort under its control. Another difference between the two notions is that internationalization serves as a supplement to the nation-state's efforts to

satisfy the needs of its people, i.e., the *national interest*. On the other hand, at least ideally, globalization is to serve the *common good of mankind*, e.g., the preservation of a viable environment or the provision of general economic and social welfare. ("Globalization of Law, Politics, and Markets—Implications for Domestic Law—A European Perspective," 1 *Indiana Journal of Global Legal Studies*, pp. 9, 10–11 [1993].)

GLOBALIZATION

from Martin Shapiro, "The Globalization of Law,"
1 *Indiana Journal of Global Legal Studies*, pp. 37–64 (1993).
Copyright © 1993 by Indiana Journal of Global Legal Studies.
Reprinted by permission of the Indiana Journal of Global Legal Studies.

I. Globalization of Commercial and Contract Law and the Proliferation of Lawyers

We speak of globalization of law in reference to a number of interrelated phenomena. As a concomitant of the globalization of markets and the organization and business practices of the multi-national corporations that operate in those markets, there has been some movement toward a relatively uniform global contract and commercial law. It is commonplace that, by their very nature, contracts are a kind of private lawmaking system. The two or more contracting parties create a set of rules to govern their future relationships. These are the various substantive provisions of the contract. Such a system of private lawmaking can exist transnationally even when there is no transnational court or transnational sovereign to resolve disputes between the contracting parties and to enforce those resolutions. The contracting parties may have specified in the contract itself some nongovernmental arbitration mechanism or the courts of some particular nation state, or both, to resolve contract disputes. Typically they also specify the contract and commercial law of some particular country as the law under which any contract dispute between them shall be resolved. So long as the courts and law of individual nation states are available, and the courts and law of each or most are prepared to recognize and enforce the judgments of the others, a global commercial law can come into being by private lawmaking. This event occurs when the standard incentives for uniformity, predictability, and transparency of law that are at play in all capitalist contract regimes move the substantial, but not enormous, number of significant multi-national, corporate, private lawmakers to generate a relative uniform set of contract provisions. Thus, there emerges a global commercial law independent of any global law giver or enforcer, although dependent on national legal and judicial institutions already long in place.

Given the place of the United States in the world economy, this globalization of law through private corporate lawmaking rather naturally takes the form of the global Americanization of commercial law. Often when we speak of globalization we mean that certain American legal practices are being diffused throughout the world (for instance, the legal device of franchising). It may be not only American economic power, but some particular receptivity of common law to contract, and other commercial law innovation that is the engine of globalization in this sense. . . . For whatever reasons, it is now possible to argue that American business law has become a kind of global *jus commune* incorporated explicitly or implicitly into transnational contracts and, beginning to be incorporated into the case law and even the statutes of many other nations.

After World War II, a long run of relatively steady economic growth, the expansion of world trade, the communications and data processing revolutions, and the mergers and acquisition movement of the 1980s contributed to an enormous acceleration in business activity. More transactions conducted more quickly necessarily leads to more lawyers and more litigation if we choose law and lawyers as one of the means of perfecting such transactions and resolving conflicts about them when we do not achieve perfection.

One reason that choice was made has to do with enterprise organization. In the period before and just after World War II, vertical integration was the model of business organization. . . . [B]usiness theory changed some time after World War II. The vision of the corporation as a rationalized, vertically integrated producer and marketer of a single or complementary line of products was replaced by the vision of the corporation as a bundle of capital and executive intelligence seeking profit wherever and however it was to be found. . . . Whatever arrangement promised to maximize profit (acquisition, joint venture, license, franchise, job shop, independent contractor, subsidiary, spin-off, long-term supply contract, patent pool, or bank coordinated interlocking financing) was the appropriate strategy. Nothing was forever, or indeed, for very long. Not building the boundaries, but pushing the envelope, became the corporate creed.

In the world of the vertically integrated firm as in the world of socialism, economic relationships are determined by internal command. The inter-office memo, rather than the contract, is the mode of communication. Internal negotiation is among principals and is set in a hierarchical command structure. . . . In such a firm there may be many rules, but there is little room for lawyers and none for judges. At most there is a kind of inspectorate that sees that rules are obeyed and forwards observed uncertainties and disputes about rules to higher executive authority for resolution.

The new, open corporation is essentially a deal maker. Instead of taking the form of internal directives, decisions are much more in the nature of negotiated agreements with outsiders or quasi-outsiders. . . . Common corporate culture, common expertise, shared hierarchy, and even a common expectation of future long-term relationships are often absent. In the absence of such commonalities, principals are less likely to negotiate with one another and more likely to seek go-betweens who specialize in bridging gaps between differing perspectives.

. . .

It often has been claimed that from colonial times Americans have been particularly litigious. Certainly lawyers have played a particularly large role in American public life. It is also claimed that American business style is particularly adversarial. The absence in America of an aristocracy, and the absence of a small elite based on education in a handful of prestigious institutions such as in England and France, the predominance of fee simple ownership of small agricultural holdings over much of American history, the multiplicity of governments, the relatively low level of cartelization of industry and banking compared to Europe, the geographic dispersal of corporate headquarters, and the fact that the American political capital and its business and culture capital are not in the same place, all may be factors in the American propensity to deal through lawyer go-betweens.

When a handful of powerful men of common class background, who were all literally at school together, who all live in the same neighborhood of the same city and whose families intermarry, run the dozen or so major industrial concentrations and the handful of financial giants that dominate the national economy, and also control the nation's highly centralized government, then there is little room for lawyer go-betweens, because there is little desire for arms-length transactions. Business and government are intimate affairs to be conducted by a small circle of intimates in a style of muted, mutual accommodation that fits such a circle. This has traditionally been the situation in most of the industrialized states other than the United States. America may use so many lawyers in business and governmental dealings less because we have a special affection for lawyers, than because economic and political power has been widely dispersed among scattered, disparate elites who cannot get together at their club or countryhouse, because they do not have one, and who would find that they had little in common upon which to build mutual trust even if they did have a meeting place. Where there are no gentlemen, there have to be contracts, rather than gentlemen's agreements.

Of course, the argument is one of degree. America has had the trusts, and the Ivy League and Wall Street and the money aristocracy of Vanderbilts, Carnegies, and Rockefellers, but it has had neither the degree of concentration nor the degree of intimacy among the concentrators that has existed in Europe.

Perhaps another rather mysterious chicken and egg dimension ought to be added. . . . European lawyers have had certain singular difficulties in serving business, particularly big business, which American lawyers have not experienced. From the revival of the civil law in Italy, continental legal education and those who received it were particularly tied to government service. Law as a body of learning flowered quickly and massively because the possessors of that learning proved to be ideal recruits for the bureaucracies that princes and emperors were building as key instruments in the recentralization of political power after the dispersions of feudalism. The bulk and the best of the law graduates entered government civil or judicial services. The remainder who exercised their learning at all went to private practice; private practice itself, however, particularly in the Latin countries, was viewed as a public office. Lawyers were a kind of nobility of the robe holding independent positions of honor from which legal advice was bestowed as a kind of public benefaction from the learned to the unlearned. Until very recently in most European countries, being an employee was incompatible with membership in the bar. . . . People with law degrees were not lawyers, but jurists. Most did not practice law. Most who did not enter government service entered the general world of affairs, not the special practice of law.

The result was first that the European lawyer could not display quite the enthusiasm for the getting and spending of trade that his plebeian American counterpart was never embarrassed about. Business advising and contract writing tended to be left to separate and lesser branches of the profession, the advocate reserving himself for litigation. More importantly, European lawyers have experienced great difficulty in adjusting to corporate business.

. . .

Thus, viewed either as the result of peculiar American traits or peculiar European ones, the intrusiveness of law, particularly in business dealings, is often seen as particularly American and the globalization of this intrusiveness as Americanization. European lawyers are now profoundly interested in the growth of the large law firm, both the movement of American firms into Europe and the increasing size of European firms. The difficulties of continental lawyers in providing legal services to corporate business are now being consciously addressed. Multi-national corporations are moving toward demanding the incredibly detailed, completely researched, contracts in Europe that they are accustomed to in the United States. The growth of multi-nationals, the growth of European-wide business, the movement of regulatory authority from national capitals to Brussels [the headquarters of the European Community], the incursion of foreign competition on former national quasi-cartels, the existence of flagship firms, etc., all reduce the intimacy of business and business government dealings. The American style of more arms-length, more legalized, business dealings is growing apace in Europe.

II. Globalization of Public Law

Certain global commonalities in law develop from a universal, and apparently growing, popular distrust of government, or more precisely, of bureaucratic discretion based on claimed expertise. The century from 1850 to 1950 is roughly the period of technocratic government. Bureaucracies grew enormously in size and policy-making authority and were legitimated on the basis of their technical expertise at accounting, war, engineering, and the like. . . . Although clearly ultimate policy discretion in all states has to be wielded by some political authority—the people, the party, the leader—most of the day-to-day activity of government has become essentially a technical enterprise to be conducted by experts in the various sciences and technologies, including the social sciences and the science of public administration. In the United States, the Progressive movement and the New Deal were central vehicles for the acclaim of bureaucratic expertise. . . . The most dramatic recent assertion of the superiority of technocratic government is to be seen in the European Community, where the Commission claims the central role in Community policy making as a kind of technocratic juggernaut.

For a number of reasons, faith in technocracy waned after World War II. In the West, experts began to be seen less as neutral truth seekers above the fray of interest group politics and more as themselves, interest bearers who sought their own advantages from government. The military-industrial complex was the first technocracy denounced. The green movement then discovered that the government agronomists, chemists, and foresters were more like allies rather than restrainers of the evil, corporate, nature destroyers. . . .

No one, however, proposes doing away with bureaucratic government or even proposes that the defining characteristic of bureaucracies should cease to be technical expertise. Instead, what is sought globally is increased transparency of, and increased public participation in, bureaucratic decision-making. . . .

Globalization and Americanization go together here precisely because the almost frantic pace of American innovation put the United States well "ahead" of the rest of the world. In the 1960s, 1970s, and 1980s, American federal courts, seconded by Congress, created an enormous new apparatus of administrative law designed to maximize both the participation of interest groups in the bureaucratic policy-making process and the obligation of bureaucracies to make public every bit of their fact gathering, analysis, and policy choice processes and to prove publicly their every claim of expertise. . . . American judges of the 1940s and 1950s deferred to bureaucratic expertise because the experts knew everything and the judge nothing. By the 1980s, those same judges were demanding that the bureaucrats fully, completely, and publicly explain what they were doing and do so in such a way that the judge, a person totally devoid of technological training and knowledge, could understand. It is clear that the American felt need for transparency and [public participation] is now felt across the industrialized world. It is also clear that across that world attention is being paid to the use of law to achieve those goals. . . .

The promotion of the judge into the position of a kind of anti-bureaucratic hero may have been seen as part of what comparative politics scholars speak of as a "legitimacy crisis." In democratic states, where polling data can be somewhat trusted, there do appear to be rather long-term and steep declines in public approval of government institutions. . . . From another perspective, we are looking at the same phenomenon when we observe the recent worldwide preoccupation with new written constitutions dividing government powers and guaranteeing individual rights, the spread of constitutional courts and constitutional judicial review, and the fervor and effectiveness of the human rights movement. Here again, Americanization and globalization partially overlap. The American constitutional experience, including the Bill of Rights and judicial review, has appeared to be singularly innovative and successful and thus serves as a world model. For a time after World War II, as new constitutions with bills of rights and judicial review appeared, it could be argued whether they were emulations of the American model or simply the imposed products of American conquest. But that particular hallmark of American constitutionalism, constitutional judicial review, has certainly now come to flourish endogenously in Germany and Italy. Even more notably, France, whose legal and political culture has been most resistant to constitutional judicial review and who was a World War II ally of the United States, not a conquered enemy, now finds itself with an active constitutional court and a constitutional bill of rights. The Court of Justice of the European Community has turned itself into a constitutional court with human rights jurisdiction, and that magic could hardly have been accomplished unless constitutions and rights had become a European habit. . . . The transmuted Eastern European states have adopted constitutional judicial review almost automatically, as have Asian post-Leninist states like Mongolia.

. . .

. . . Post–World War II constitutions tend to be replete not only with negative rights, but also with positive ones such as the right to education, housing, health care, and employment. Here the demand is not that the government stay out of things, but rather that it act positively to assure the well-being of the citizens. Such constitutional provisions really exhibit the same distrust of government. Nearly all of the nations in which pressure has been experienced to put welfare rights in the constitution already have, or clearly anticipate having, systems of economic and social rights secured by statute. The push toward constitutionalizing these rights is far less a movement to endow government with new tasks than an expression of lack of trust in legislatures to adequately fund and bureaucracies to adequately implement mere statutory rights programs.

III. Globalization of Protective Law

The constitutional rights movement is one aspect of a global movement that goes beyond distrust of government to distrust of all hierarchical authority and concentrations of power. The individual is seen as needing protection from all the larger forces that threaten to crush him, not simply from the governmental ones. Law is seen as one instrument for such protection. Thus, in speaking of globalization, we move from the realm of constitutional law to the more mundane realm of torts, product standards, consumer protection, and occupational health and safety. Of course, most legal systems around the world have always dealt with personal injury, fraud, and shoddy goods. The industrial revolution brought together men and man-maiming machines; Twentieth-Century technology generated the most maiming of all, the automobile, plus a host of consumer goods so complex that the rule of caveat emptor [buyer beware] was no longer fair. The same may be said for business organization and finance, areas where securities and corporate governance law expanded to protect the investor. Globalization here refers to a worldwide increase of legal protection against the ill effects of technical, economic, and social devices too complex, distant, or powerful to make individual self-protection possible. The most recent manifestation of this movement is the great outburst of environmental protection law that is partially fueled by a concern with nature itself but tends to achieve its greatest impetus when that concern is coupled with putative injury to individuals from pollutants.

Global patterns are, however, far from uniform here. The United States has experienced a tort explosion. Many other nations have not. American experience has not become global in this area, except as a cautionary tale, in part because most other industrialized nations have more developed systems of tax-supported health care and income maintenance that reduce the impact on individuals of personal injuries. The American securities market has also become a global cautionary tale, but one that is generating a worldwide move to certain American securities law innovations, such as the ban on insider trading. There has been an enormous, global flood of product standards and other consumer protection law, but not only are developments much faster in some nations than in others, but the substantive standards and rules adopted also vary widely.

Perhaps globalization is clearest and most dramatic in environmental law. As it became increasingly clear that the externalities of environmental degradation crossed national boundaries and that some of them, like ozone depletion, were truly global, parallel developments in national environmental law accelerated as did efforts at multi-national and/or international environmental protection law. Given the global uniformity of the industrial technologies threatening the environment, a considerable substantive uniformity emerges even in national environmental rules.

When we consider the collective impact of consumer protection and environmental law, a major potential conflict is identifiable between the globalization of markets and the globalization of law. As various movements toward free trade (such as the General Agreement on Tariffs and Trade and the initial European Community treaties) break down tariff barriers to global markets, the large numbers of differing national product standards and rules on advertising and marketing intentionally or unintentionally become final and often very effective barriers to global trade. National economic sectors disadvantaged by global competition, which once experienced all this consumer protection law as meddlesome government regulation, now foster it as the last dike against the invasion of cheap and shoddy foreign goods and services.

. . .

Developments in the European Community provide a microcosm of these potential global dynamics. The initial Community treaties attacked tariffs in order to create, or at least aim at, a European quasi-customs union. Disadvantaged national economic sectors then retreated to vigorous enforcement of national product standards, actively aided and abetted by national customs bureaucracies who were about to lose their missions and their jobs. Popular national support could be generated in the name of the traditional national quality of beer or carving knives that could not have been engendered in the name of tariff-protected higher prices. For many years the principal political institution of European Community building was the Court of Justice. In one of its most famous cases, it struck at this new protectionism by announcing the Community law doctrine of mutual recognition. Each member of the Community must recognize the product standards of every other so that products lawfully manufactured in any member state must be admitted for sale in all of the others.

Later, when national political and economic elites within the Community concluded that they wanted to go forward in Community-wide market building, this principle of mutual recognition became the cornerstone of the Single Act, or "1992," agreement. Under the Single Act, by 1992 an attempt would be made to harmonize, that is, enact Community-wide product standards. All standards not harmonized were to be subject to the rule of mutual recognition.

. . .

Yet, at the same time the Single Act moves toward debilitating consumer protection law as a trade barrier, it sets up a potential move to environmental law as a trade barrier. . . . [S]pecific provisions of the Act allow member states to enact more rigorous environmental regulations than those of the Community as a whole, even if such deviations from uniformity incidentally hamper free trade. These provisions are, of course, worded in such a way that the Court of Justice may strike down sham national environmental laws that are nothing more than new trade barriers in disguise. But it is not always easy to unmask such shams. . . .

IV. Global Acceleration of Law and Lawyers

Yet one more phenomenon that leads to talk of globalization is a step-level increase in the sheer volume and penetration of law. The bureaucratic state generates legal rules at a rate quite beyond the capacity of legislatures or courts. The regulatory state keeps expanding its reach through law in spite of talk of deregulation. . . . The citizens of modern democratic states expect their governments to cope with whatever becomes defined as a social problem, from child abuse to the aging of symphony audiences. When the government can cope, and even more when it cannot, it passes a law as one step toward satisfying those demands. . . .

If the bureaucratic and regulatory welfare state manufactures legal rules at an astounding rate and pushes them into more and more human relationships, it may be argued that the private sector does not lag far behind. There are more lawyers, more lawsuits, and more law talk all the time. Newspapers and magazines now carry regular law sections next to their music sections. Everybody knows about the litigation explosion. The crowd of lawyers becomes so prominent that it can serve as a target in presidential campaigns. The number of lawyers and the size of law firms expands exponentially.

It is notoriously difficult to achieve reliable data on litigation rates either over time in one country, or comparatively between countries. It may well be that there is no litigation explosion in relative terms, but it is only that modern industrial states multiply so greatly the number of human interactions that provide the potential for litigation, that the absolute amount of litigation grows. With or without the litigation explosion, however, there does seem to be an increased worldwide prominence of law, lawyers, and judges in both private and public affairs.

This prominence may be the result of a host of developments that have little direct relation to one another. . . . As we multiply litigation opportunities in order to achieve greater transparency, participation, and protection, those who lose economic, social, or political struggles go to court to attempt to recoup their losses.

There are other causes of lawyer, judge, and court prominence. . . . For instance, the rapid expansion of European university education after World War II and the sudden opening of law as a plausible education and career for women led to a sudden surge in the total number of persons trained in the law in the industrialized world during the 1970s and 1980s.
. . .

Some nations, like Japan, may successfully pursue a policy of limiting legalism by using draconian measures to shut their citizens off from lawyers and courts. The globalization of markets, however, means that even in these nations the many companies linked to international transactions will need and acquire legal services, if necessary. Under such circumstances, it seems unlikely that regimes that profess some level of democracy can keep lawyers away from their domestic affairs indefinitely. The one exception, and of course a very important one, is China. . . . [Chinese] legal tradition, combined with the country's incredible size, population, and authoritarian regime, will almost certainly allow China to enter global markets while shielding most of its population from the globalization of law, unless it eventually experiences the collapse of the regime that has overtaken other Leninist states.

The post-Leninist states will almost certainly experience major increases in lawyers and litigation. . . . One of the central tasks of post-Leninist reconstruction is to introduce the fundamental practice, which is almost taken for granted in the West, that requires public officials to obey laws and their own rules and calls them to account when they do not. Western consultants on law and constitutional organization must remind themselves that Western institutions designed to achieve the rule of law, such as judicial review, presuppose the existence of a prosperous, active, private bar.

. . .

V. Globalization of Law and the Growth of U.S. Law

We have been looking at the globalization of law along a number of vectors. The global distrust of hierarchical authority and concentrated public and private power generates growth in administrative law, constitutional, and other rights law, and in legal regulation of economic enterprise. The global desire to protect the individual generates growth in personal injury, consumer protection, environmental law, and even family law. The globalization of markets and business enterprise generates the growth of a worldwide law of business transactions. The global multiplication of exterior business relationships and the growth of arms-length regulatory styles fuel a growing demand for lawyers and their involvement in more and more social, economic, and political relationships. Frequently, we have encountered a certain overlap between globalization and Americanization.

While in some instances U.S. responses to various global needs may have served as models to be diffused, in others our experience may well be a cautionary tale involving the traditional U.S. vice of excess. We may have too much distrust of governmental and corporate power, too much rights talk, too much adversarial, confrontational regulation, too much administrative and constitutional law, and indeed too much law, lawyers, and litigation in general. U.S. legal experts are rushing into the post-Leninist states to help them establish the rule of law. The European Community inquires about American regulatory style. Business firms everywhere look to the legal services provided by the big American-style law firm. All this occurs at the very time that U.S. citizens are increasingly uneasy about "too many lawyers" and "too much litigation."

. . . Should we be particularly anxious to export our free-wheeling, open, lawyer-lubricated style of corporate development . . . ? Ought we warn outside emulators that the large U.S. law firms may be about to implode as a result of having committed themselves to practices that generate geometric growth rates that cannot be sustained indefinitely? Should not our corporations warn their transnational brethren to control their legal costs, as U.S. corporations are beginning to do?

. . . [T]he worldwide adoption of certain aspects of U.S. style law as applied to business transactions, certainly provides opportunities for U.S. lawyers, particularly those in the large law firms. The globalization of environmental law may pose large threats to the United States economy because, as the largest and most profligate national industrial entity, the United States must be the principal regulatory target. Certain moves toward internationally uniform and enforceable bodies of law, such as the law of intellectual property, entail potentially great costs and benefits for U.S. interests. . . .

On the whole, however, . . . [f]or all the internationalist talk, it remains true now, as it long has, that law and the political structures that produce and sustain it are far more national and far less international than are trade and politics as such. There are more nations now than there have ever been and more are emerging daily. The tendency toward finer and finer ethnic political subdivision is one of the most striking features of the new global politics and is probably being accelerated by the expansion of global markets. . . . In short, . . . our domestic legal regime may have to respond to global changes in markets and in politics far more often than to global changes in law.

For the most part, national regimes of law and lawyering will remain self-generating. They will be self-generating, however, in response to certain aforementioned globally perceived needs, such as the need to limit technocratic-bureaucratic discretion. Thus, U.S. lawyers and lawmakers may find comparative legal studies more fruitful than they have in the past. There may be somewhat more rapid legal borrowing and diffusion among national legal systems than there has been in the past. But, except in certain special areas, which no doubt will be the duty of globalization of law specialists to identify, the American agenda of legal change will continue to be built largely out of domestic legal materials. It may be true that a certain degree of U.S. style law is a real feature of the globalization of law. It is highly unlikely, however, that the traffic will flow equally in both directions, that there will be much Europeanization, let alone Asianization or Africanization of U.S. law. For the United States, globalization of law will be much more a matter of parallel development than of direct borrowing or response. . . . [T]he globalization of markets and of the politics of the environment may indeed drive much legal change in the United States, but most of the change is likely to come from domestic, rather than global, legal materials.

The enormous costs and failures of the U.S. style of adversary legalism are coupled with the continued American enthusiasm for rights and our continued derogation of political authority, most recently evidenced by the popularity of legislative term limitations. This dynamic sets the agenda for legal change in the United States. It is highly unlikely that we will respond to the pathologies of legalism by moving toward less law, although just possibly we may move toward fewer courts or less active court intervention in policy making. Alternative dispute resolution and judicially facilitated settlement are much bruited. We may have passed the peak of judicial policymaking in both constitutional and administrative judicial review. Yet, most reforms are likely to move toward different, rather than less, law. In shaping legal reform, it may be of some help to appreciate that certain phenomena are now globally common and generate globally parallel legal responses. We may have increasing confidence that the successes and failures of legal innovations in country A will be predictive for country B. In certain special areas of law, globally common and globally enforceable rules are beginning to emerge. For the most part, however, U.S. law will indubitably continue to resemble traditional U.S. law, generated by domestic responses to perceived domestic problems, although many of those domestic problems are generated by our global interrelationships. The whole world marches into the international future with its feet firmly planted in the ever more fertile soil of nationalism, as a glance at any day's newspaper will make clear. Studies of globalization of law will depend as much on a subtle appreciation of differences among peoples of the globe as on similarities.

CHAPTER 32

The Last Frontier

Watching the evening news on October 10, 1957, Americans were shocked to learn that the Soviet Union had launched a space satellite named *Sputnik* ("fellow traveler" in Russian). The resulting political pressure led to the acceleration in the American space program and the first American satellite, *Explorer I*, less than four months later. But the Soviets maintained their lead and, on April 12, 1961, launched the first astronaut, Yuri A. Gagarin, into orbit. Less than one month later, the United States followed with the flight of Alan Shepard, Jr., but with merely a lob into space, not a full orbit.

The new American president, John F. Kennedy, was determined to overtake the Soviets in space, but he did not live to see the result of his determination. It took nearly a decade, but the United States took a decisive lead on July 20, 1969, when two Americans—Neil A. Armstrong and Edwin Aldrin— walked on the moon.

Armstrong and Aldrin planted the American flag on the moon, much as Columbus planted the Spanish flag when he reached land in the Western Hemisphere. But, unlike Columbus, the American astronauts did not utter words claiming the territory for their nation.

Between 1957 and the moon landing, the international community had been at work formulating a body of law to answer a variety of questions which arose following the launching of *Sputnik:*

- Given the Cold War, the Soviet-American space race was unavoidably thought of in military terms. Could outer space be used for military purposes?
- The two Cold War rivals were contaminating their own national territories with nuclear tests. Could tests be conducted in outer space?

- Nuclear programs were creating nuclear wastes, some of which were being buried, some dumped into the oceans. Could outer space become a nuclear-waste dump site?
- Could satellites be used for spying?
- If an astronaut or a satellite launched by one nation returns to earth and lands on the territory of another nation, could the latter nation refuse to return either to the launching nation?
- Could space nations use satellites for telecommunication without coordination with each other and with earth-bound telecommunications?
- Could they claim sovereignty over space resources?

The answer to all above questions was "yes." With the exception of some limited analogies from the law of the sea, space was essentially lawless territory. Only the development of an explicit body of legal rules could prevent the undesirable uses of space.

The United Nations played a major role in the development of space law. In 1958, the United Nations General Assembly established the Ad Hoc Committee on Peaceful Uses of Outer Space (COPUOS), which prepared an extensive report and became a standing body to monitor space activities. Under the committee's sponsorship, five space treaties were concluded between 1967 and 1979. The most extensive of these was the treaty of 1967.

But questions remained regarding spy satellites, the demarcation between national air space and international outer space, rights to mining celestial bodies, and other issues. Since 1979 space initiatives have included communications satellites in stationary orbits, shuttle flights, a space station, unmanned landings on Mars, and deep-space probes of Venus and Jupiter. And nations other than the United States and Russia have become involved in space research. Each new development has brought its own set of legal concerns. Nonetheless, in 1991 an American legal scholar, Carl Q. Christol, in his book *Space Law: Past, Present, and Future,* could write:

> [I]t is possible to be optimistic about the success of future space activities if one takes law seriously. Among law's many qualities is its capacity to provide a service function. It can offer an identifiable process contributing to the achievement of mutually acceptable goals. It is useful in the clarification of values. It can facilitate the identification of acceptable norms. It can provide stability and certainty of expectations. All of these factors are particularly important in the area of international relations. (p. 482)

THE LAW OF OUTER SPACE

from Siegfried Wiessner, "Human Activities in Outer Space: A Framework
for Decision-Making," in Tanja L. Zwaan, ed., *Space Law: Views of the Future*
(Deventer, Neth.: Kluwer Law and Tax Publishers, 1988), pp. 8–20.
Copyright © 1988 Kluwer Law and Tax Publishers.
Reprinted by permission of Kluwer Law and Tax Publishers.

. . . As flowers eventually break through concrete, even the most hardened legal prescriptions, "written in stone," have to give way to new configurations of social behaviour if new facts and new opinions so demand. These changes are sometimes delayed, branding the lawyer, and, especially, the judge, conservative elements in society. Ever so often, the adjustments do not come about without a fight.

The need for this systemic ability to change is most critical in arenas where today's feat in technology is only a stepping-stone for tomorrow's breakthrough. This is true for the awesome number of ethical and legal problems created by, say, genetic engineering and the broader field of biotechnology. Problems of that kind are faced, and solved, by and within the authoritative and effective decision-making processes of given territorial communities. We tread into more uncertain, but equally critical fields when we talk about the conquest of outer space as the last frontier the human race is overcoming.

For, then, we enter the realm of international law. First, activities of humans relating to outer space take place, or have effects, in an arena that is perceived to be beyond the reach of appropriation by any nation-state. Outer space is—still—regarded as "international," although that consensus may be shattered over time. Secondly, the uses made of and the activities performed in this common area may conflict and may lead to harmful consequences if not channelled into some form of coordinated behaviour.

Without a structure of vertical decision-making in the relations between nation-states, that channelling may either be done by treaty, bilateral or multilateral. Or it may arise out of a dialectic process of claim by one state, counterclaim by another, and judgment by the rest of the world as to which claim should prevail. That judgment, continually reconsidered in the world's constitutive process of decision-making, enunciates what we traditionally call the customary international law of any given time.

. . .

The dawn of the Space Age has produced quite an assortment of multilateral treaties dealing with human activities in this newly-conquered arena. The most inclusive such document is the Treaty on Principles Governing the Activities of States in the Exploration and Use of Outer Space, Including the Moon and Other Celestial Bodies of 27 January 1967. Its broad and general nature and content made that agreement, for a long time, the "constitution" of outer space, boasting membership of 93 states including all the spacefaring nations. . . .

This consensus about the Outer Space Treaty may be waning. It was the product of high-flying dreams of its time, but it was also limited to the then-present technology and the then-held expectations about future technology and human aspirations. Among other issues, the Treaty failed to foresee, and thus take into account, the scramble for scarce resources in the geostationary orbit, the problems of privacy and national security to be created by rampant remote sensing, and the filling of the near-Earth environment with "exotic" battle stations.

. . .

I. Problems with the 1967 Treaty

1. The first, unresolved problem revolves around the scope of application of this agreement: What do we mean when we refer to *outer space?* Wisely, the international community did not delve into the various demarcation lines suggested by the so-called "spatialist" school for the clearcut separation of airspace and outer space, the realm of state sovereignty, and the domain of international law, respectively. With the impending development of the aerospace plane, the "functionalists" advocating a flexible approach depending on the type of activity conducted seem to have gained a decisive upper hand.

2. At the beginning of the Space Age, expectations flew high that outer space was *to be used exclusively for peaceful purposes.* In the late fifties, the General Assembly of the United Nations, as well as the top leaders of the spacefaring nations, expressed this as a common aspiration that would have outlawed any kind of military activities in outer space. The United States and the Soviet Union, however, soon toned down the rhetoric. In the early sixties, they pressed for U.N. General Assembly resolutions adopting a more limited view of "peaceful purposes" and split up the legal regime of outer space into differently treated arenas.

The 1967 Treaty follows this line. . . . The only teeth that were put into this Treaty with respect to military uses of outer space were mild and enumerated in Article IV:

(1) States Parties to the Treaty undertake not to place in orbit around the Earth any objects carrying nuclear weapons or any other kinds of weapons of mass

destruction, install such weapons on celestial bodies, or station such weapons in outer space in any other manner.

(2) The moon and other celestial bodies shall be used by all States Parties to the Treaty exclusively for peaceful purposes. The establishment of military bases, installations and fortifications, the testing of any type of weapons and the conduct of military manoeuvres on celestial bodies shall be forbidden.

Thus, the only parts of outer space which were to be "demilitarized" were the moon and other celestial bodies. Nuclear weapons and other weapons of mass destruction were banned from being *stationed* in outer space. Thus, [the Treaty] did not prevent the buildup of . . . nuclear missiles that employ the medium of outer space merely to reach their targets.

Beyond that, the U.S. and the USSR have put into Earth orbit a barrage of "national technical means of verification" which are crucial for gathering intelligence about the military strengths and movements of the other side, for verification of arms control agreements, and for early warning of nuclear attacks. In fact, such missiles and reconnaissance satellites have been considered essential for the maintaining of international peace and security, under the superpowers' "open skies" policy.

The next step, beyond the passive reconnaissance function, was the stationing of antisatellite systems (ASATs) in outer space. Their presence was justified as defensive, perfectly legitimate "non-aggressive military use" of outer space. Scientists soon pointed out that such devices could easily be used for offensive purposes. Ultimately, however, any weapon may be perceived as contributing to the overall balance of deterrence designed to uphold the peace.

New military strategies go far beyond mere ASAT capability. The U.S. Strategic Defense Initiative [SDT—also known as "Star Wars"] . . . would employ weapons systems in outer space that can be used offensively as well as defensively. They include nuclear-driven devices such as particle beams, microwaves, hypervelocity pellets, X-ray lasers, and optical lasers. In particular, the proposed X-ray laser would not only be powered by nuclear energy, but would set free a nuclear explosion if operated. It has thus been called a "third generation nuclear weapon." As such, the X-ray laser would seem to violate the proscription against nuclear weapons in Earth orbit, laid down in Article IV (1) of the 1967 Treaty.

. . .

3. The universalistic spirit of the 1967 Treaty also found its expression in Article I (1):

The exploration and use of outer space . . . shall be carried out for the benefit and in the interests of all countries, irrespective of their degree of economic or scientific development, and shall be the *province of all mankind.*

What does this clause mean? In the U.S. Senate hearings on advice and consent to the Treaty, it was made clear that this prescription would not translate into obligations by the haves of space technology to the have-nots. At best, the term "province of all mankind" was "embryonic." It did not carry with it the distinctive connotations of equitable sharing and common inclusive management which are packed in the standard of a "common heritage of mankind." The latter term, used in the 1979 Moon Agreement, was decisively rejected by the space superpowers, together with the Moon Agreement itself. Outer space thus remains a free-for-all; the benefits clause of Article I (1) vanishes into legal nirvana before the freedoms of use, exploration and exploitation of outer space as enumerated in Article I (2) and (3). This is another example of the inadequacies of the 1967 text.

4. A fundamental presumption of the 1967 Treaty is that outer space and the celestial bodies *cannot be appropriated*. In the context of SDI, it has been contended that the array of objects to be placed in Earth orbit and the necessity to create "keep-out" zones around them would constitute an appropriation of outer space.... If so, what about the semi-permanent satellite positions on the geostationary orbit and their assigned latitudes? Is that not also an appropriation of outer space? If not, how large must the zones be to be considered "appropriations"? Should the difference between these security zones be one of quality rather than quantity, depending on the intent of the parties?

Another issue concerning appropriation arises in the context of possible future space mining. It may lead not only to the exploitation of valuable parts of the moon, but to the virtual consumption of entire asteroids. By what twist of the language can this still be called mere "use," and not "appropriation," of the celestial body?

5. The 1967 Treaty fails to take into account, to the extent needed, the numerous activities of *private enterprise* which enter into the use of outer space.... The 1967 Treaty is largely State-oriented: Article VI provides that a State has to "authorise and supervise" the activities of its non-governmental entities in outer space. Article VII establishes liability by the launching state, and Article VIII requires retention of jurisdiction and control over space objects by the States "on whose registry" such objects are launched.

One does notice private parties operating in the first commercial arena: communications satellites. Important business needs are satisfied by these space stations. They provide for telephone, telex, and record traffic, but also tv, radio, data transmissions, videoconferencing, weather forecasting, and navigation. Remote sensing is being privatised. ... The media are considering operating their own satellite, raising grave concerns of national security and foreign policy ... and individual privacy. The future aerospace plane will be a most appreciated means of intercontinental transportation.... Even launching may be taken over by private parties. Materials processing will take place on the space station envisaged by President Reagan.

All these activities presuppose some kind of supervision and control of the participant private parties' activities by nation-states.... [T]he issue of the minimum degree of control of a nation-state over its private "national" space object remains as it was—barely touched on by the 1967 Treaty.

6. The problem of *liability* is addressed only most generally in the 1967 Treaty. Article VII provides that the launching State is internationally liable for the damage caused by its space object. The 1971 Liability Convention provides more detail. New issues, however, will arise with the advent of the aerospace plane. Should liability for its operation and its registration be determined by the established rules of air law or space law, or should we strive to tailor a special regime for that particular object?

7. *Space debris* has become a major threat to human activities in outer space. Current regimes of liability, based as they are on negligence theories of negative obligations, duties *not* to commit certain acts, even the 1967 Treaty's strict liability for the harmful effects emanating from one's own space object, might no longer be enough—in view of both the increasing "contamination" of the area, and the increasing difficulties in identifying whose country's space object has caused the damage. It seems to be advisable to contemplate *positive* duties to remove dangerous debris, similar to the duty to perform necessary repairs in domestic property law. This duty might be incumbent upon a country that is predominantly active in one particular area of outer space, or on the international community as a whole who might commission such mine-sweeping missions from the leading space powers.

8. This, by necessity, incomplete list of problems may be concluded for now by reference to the novel legal issues created by the establishment of an international space station. Looming large are the *jurisdictional and substantive law conflicts* on such a complex, "international" space structure. Who owns the station? Who decides which disputes where? On board the station? According to which law?

9. One may conclude that the 1967 Treaty fails to address major novel issues of space law, and that some of its fundamental policies are honoured today only in their breach. This state of things will worsen in the future. . . . Thus, beyond the 1967 Treaty, it is up to scholars to ascertain what are the expectations about lawfulness or unlawfulness of specific human activities in outer space. Where evidence on the outcome of the world's constitutive process of decision-making in relation to a particular problem is lacking or inconclusive, it is the critical task of scholars to advance solutions in the global common interest. Such recommendations should ideally promote the abundant and economic use of great sharable resources for the benefit of the whole of humankind. To complete this task successfully, scholars must employ an adequate methodological framework.

II. Towards an Adequate Framework for Decision-Making

To determine what the present expectations of the world community are on which human activities in outer space are "right" or "wrong" and what the law is or should be, one has to be clear about one's conception of "the law."

... [L]aw is essentially designed to govern the activities of and the interaction between human beings. ... This characterization encompasses not only direct human actions beyond the Earth's atmosphere, but covers any chain of events set in motion by human beings and having effects on the medium, such as the journey of *Voyager* through the Solar System. The characterization would have to be revised once the human race enters into some kind of interaction with extraterrestrial intelligence.

Starting from this premise, we have to realise that law relating to outer space is, at present, *created on Earth*. This might change with the establishment of permanent space habitats for humans. But now, and for the foreseeable future, space law is created in the same processes and within the same structures of decision-making as other compounds of legal prescription. What, then, is the "law" created on this planet?

...

Law arises from [the] process of claim and counterclaim, from von Jhering's "battle for law," in which we all have a moral duty, a vocation to fight for the interests and values we want to see preserved. This dynamic nature of the law is most pronounced in the area of international law where little or no vertical structure of decision-making is in place. Instead, we face a highly imbalanced array of actors, with greatly varying bases of power, perspectives and strategies, in often complex situations. They interact to create the fragmented set of rules that we term "international law."

... To investigate this process of decision-making with the utmost degree of professional veracity, one ... has to delve into the real world and analyse how the international community's decision-making processes resolve the issues confronting them.

Methodologically, one has to complete five intellectual tasks:

...

(1) Lawyers, as experts in decision-making, have to demarcate the particular *problem* society is facing and investigate the factual parameters, using the methods favoured by the sciences most apt to deal with the issue. To understand a particular problem, for example the scarcity of the twin resource of the geostationary satellite orbit (orbital locations and frequencies), one has to grasp the *facts* by employing the assistance of the universe of knowledge with its own competent methodologies (in this instance of scientists and engineers) to determine the activities involved, the nature and type of the resource concerned, *etc.* In this example, facts calling for analysis would include the present and future use of the geostationary orbit, the physical constraints on its utilization, and the degree of regulation necessitated by these conditions.

(2) A necessary second step is the identification of claimants and their *claims* in the struggle for law in any given set of problems. In the case of the geostationary orbit, one would have to state the demands to the unrestricted use of this resource, on a first-come-first-served basis, by the major spacefaring nations; the claims of most equatorial countries to exclusive control over

that valuable band in outer space; and the rising demands of the Third World to equitable sharing via planning the use of the orbit.

(3) The outcomes of the continuing battles have to be addressed in the display and analysis of *past trends in decision.* How did the world community as a whole react to the competing claims? . . .

This part of the inquiry comes closest to the traditional analysis of international law, in any given set of problems. It is, however, more comprehensive than the exclusive, normativist focus on the behaviour of nation-states. To obtain a full picture of the decision-making process, one has to understand its dynamics, its *conditioning factors.* The analysis of these factors makes one better equipped to not only understand, but also predict the outcomes of particular conflicts of interest in particular historical situations.

Factors to be analysed are both environmental and predispositional:

- the situation of decision (geographical, historical, cultural and technological ramifications);
- the participants in the decision-making process (international officials, governments, private groups and individuals);
- their perspectives (value demands, identifications, expectations);
- their bases of power (armies, wealth, resources, technology, loyalties, etc.);
- their range of available strategies; and
- the short-range outcomes of options in decision and longer-term effects of each decision.

(4) To *predict future decisions,* their constraints and consequences, one does not only have to look to decisions of the past and their conditioning factors, but also to the changes within these parameters of decision, including new conditioning factors, that may have occurred. . . . In the context of the geostationary orbit, for example, it would behoove us to take into account alternatives of conflict resolution based on technological innovation, the relative bases of power of states and private citizens/corporations involved, as well as their interest or need to reach an agreement.

(5) The preceding intellectual tasks have been largely descriptive, scientific, analytical. The fifth step in the framework of decision-making is *prescriptive.* It culminates in the choice among options in decision. Through it one endeavours to work out, on the basis of the information accumulated, a solution to the problem that is in the global common interest. In order to gain the most widespread acceptance of the prescriptive proposal, the policies on which it is based have to be clarified and related to the particular instance. To be aware of the often underlying value judgments, the author, in particular one writing in scholarly function, should use a process of introspection to identify his or her preconceptions, predilections, and particular views engrained by upbringing and environment, which might influence his or her judgment.

Ideally, the proposals advanced reflect both the aspirations of the individual who advances them, and the aspirations of humankind as a whole. This outcome is most probable when the aspirations of humankind are formulated in a broad and general fashion. As an example, again we might turn to the policies of equitable sharing, flexibility, efficient and economic use on which the world community agrees concerning the use of the geostationary satellite orbit.

III. Conclusion

This inclusive analysis of facts, claims, and trends in decision enables one to reach a comprehensive picture from which to draw conclusions and to make recommendations suited to gain community consensus. This framework helps to complete the most critical task of a scholar in the field of law: to contribute to the minimisation of the use of force and the preservation of human dignity by advancing practical solutions to pressing social problems in the global common interest—to be a warrior in the strife, sometimes quixotic, for legal order in a violent world.

CHAPTER 33

Legal Philosophy

Friedrich Nietzsche identified philosophers as both historians and futurists. He wrote that philosophers "reach for the future with a creative hand, and everything that is or has been becomes for them a means, an instrument, a hammer." In American legal philosophy—whether the formalist, "scientific" approach of Christopher Columbus Langdell or the instrumental, "experi-ence"-based outlook of Oliver Wendell Holmes, Jr., or the skepticism of the Legal Realists or the "judicial self-restraint" counseled by those looking to "neutral principles" and "legal process" or the "fundamental rights" es-poused by those seeking more normative values in the law—no school of legal philosophy can be considered dead. All continue to influence legal thought.

From Langdell and Holmes to Rawls and Dworkin, American legal philoso-phers shared a belief in the existence of universal, "foundational" rules of law that are neutral and objective and can lead to principled, consistent de-cisionmaking. Some on the radical fringe of the Legal Realist movement questioned this belief, but the rise of Legal Realism in the 1920s and 1930s coincided with the rise of the social sciences, and the mainstream of the Re-alists turned to these new disciplines to provide the objectivity they found missing in the law as then proclaimed by the *Lochner*-era courts. Optimistic belief in the social sciences was more than theoretical: legal scholars of the New Deal era wrote of the uses of law for "social engineering" and provided many of the ideas for the New Deal's "brain trust"; in law schools, interdisci-plinary "Law and . . ." courses came into vogue.

Among the social sciences, one caught on as a source for legal analysis more than any other—but decades after the New Deal. In 1960 economist Ronald Coase published the article "The Problem of Social Cost" in the *Jour-nal of Law and Economics* (which was then only three years old). The following year, law professor Guido Calabresi published an economic analysis of tort law in the *Yale Law Journal*. The two articles attracted a generation of "Law and Economics" scholars who analyzed legal rules for their "efficiency" and "profit maximization" and thereby provided an empirical standard for evaluation. Predictably, the Law and Economics movement attracted both adherents and critics.

Many of the critics of Law and Economics came from a loosely organized movement labeled "Critical Legal Studies" (CLS), which began to meet at annual conferences in 1977. CLS scholars (or "Crits") debunked (or "trashed") not only Law and Economics but other legal theories as well. With many variations in detail, Crits declared law to be inherently political, an indeterminate tool for self-legitimization of the hierarchy with the power to manipulate it. Crits had little difficulty demonstrating "contradictions" in legal rules or finding legal rules to "deconstruct," revealing the biases at the cores of most rules; they have had a more difficult time formulating alternative concepts for decisionmaking. This has led some to accuse Crits of nihilism. But Crits have also been identified with the ideological values of the left (while Law and Economics has been identified with the right). In *A Guide to Critical Legal Studies* (1987), Mark Kelman has written:

> Critical Legal Studies is not infrequently paired in observers' minds with Law and Economics, in part because both became prominent as academic movements at the elite law schools in the middle and late 1970s, in part because each represented an attack on the dominant law school stance. . . . Moreover, Law and Economics was frequently thought to represent not just a new *method* of thinking about legal issues but a *substantive* attack from the right on the consensus views of the propriety of mildly liberal political policy, while CLS was often seen as the attack from the left on these same policies. (p. 114)

Also linked to Critical Legal Studies are scholars who criticize dominant legal theories (and other critical scholarship as well) from the perspective of those who have been excluded from power. Writings by scholars of "Feminist Legal Theory," "Critical Race Theory," and "Queer Theory" attribute the inequities underlying legal rules not only to class interests, but to gender, race, and sexual-orientation biases as well. Their writings have used not only the traditional materials of legal analysis but also autobiographical details and "stories" as expressive of experiences not sufficiently represented in the traditional published sources.

Another group exploring sources of legal analysis beyond statutes, cases, regulations, and traditional legal scholarship has been labeled the "Law and Literature" movement. Drawing on imaginative literature, and applying techniques of literary interpretation to the interpretation of laws, Law and Literature scholars have appealed to values and emotions missing from the "hard" empiricism of Law and Economics and the negativism of Critical Legal Studies. But some have seen enough similarities between Law and Economics, Critical Legal Studies, Law and Literature, and the group-based theories developed since the 1970s to link them under the umbrella of "Postmodernism."

POSTMODERNISM

from Gary Minda, *Postmodern Legal Movements: Law and Jurisprudence at Century's End* (New York: New York University Press, 1995), pp. 224–57.
Copyright © 1995 by New York University.
Reprinted by permission of New York University Press and the author.

Postmodernism is an elusive idea that is not easily defined. Postmodernism is neither a theory nor a concept; it is rather a skeptical attitude or aesthetic that "distrusts all attempts to create large-scale, totalizing theories in order to explain social phenomena." Postmodernists resist the idea that "there is a 'real' world or legal system 'out there,' perfected, formed, complete and coherent, waiting to be discovered by theory." As developed in linguistics, literary theory, art, and architecture, post-modernism is also a style that signals the end of an era, the passing of the modern age. . . .

Modernity . . . relies upon a foundational concept of reason identified with the spirit of the Enlightenment. At one time, this spirit was expressed in the romantic confidence of philosophers like Kant and Hegel who thought that human emancipation could be achieved through reason. Today, modernity . . . clings to the belief in the ability of "man" to emancipate humanity through empirical knowledge, scientific innovation, and rational thought. Modernists attempted to bring order and stability to the world through the rational construction of meta-theories. A central characteristic of modernity is the belief . . . that knowledge can be justified only if it rests on indubitable foundations.

In law, modernity characterizes the view of traditional jurisprudential scholars who shared a common belief in the possibility of systematizing legal knowledge using coherent and verifiable propositions about the nature of law and adjudication. . . . Legal moderns thought about law . . . as an autonomous, self-generating activity. . . . They believed that a distinct legal method is discoverable and that such a method could unlock the door to the ultimate truths of the law. The legal scholar's responsibility was to discover, develop, and refine that method. . . .

While the distinctive discourse of modernity is aimed at prediction and control, postmodernism brings out the diversity of multiple discourses and is skeptical of all universal knowledge claims. . . . Postmoderns claim that there is no logical correspondence between language and the "objective" world because "language is socially and culturally constructed, it is [thus] inherently incapable of representing or corresponding to reality; hence all propositions and all interpretations, even texts, are themselves social constructions." Postmodernists do not deny that there can be knowledge of reality; what they deny is that we can rely on theory and language to objectively fix the meaning of reality.

. . .

The Postmodern Condition

Postmoderns say that we are now living in . . . a time that entails new conditions and requires new critical techniques of investigation. One way to understand this claim is to consider how individual identities of subjects are constructed in the dominant electronic media of our culture, television. A shift in cultural images can be seen by considering how the cultural images of the fifties generation compare to those of the contemporary generation. . . .

The popular mid-fifties sitcom, *The Adventures of Ozzie and Harriet*, depicted the average American family (the Nelsons) as having "no economic crises, no class divisions or resentments, no ethnic tensions, few if any hyphenated Americans, few, if any, minority characters." The Cleaver family portrayed similar images in the popular 1950s TV comedy *Leave It to Beaver*. The Cleavers, like the Nelsons, also lived in television suburbia. No one knew in which state or suburb they lived, or what Ward Cleaver and Ozzie Nelson did for a living, except that they were respectable, and they dressed in a white shirt, tie, and suits. The cultural images of the families in these TV sitcoms suggested that America was a well-ordered and good society. . . .

By the late 1970s, television imitated the diverse, fragmented, and confusing cultural images of social life. The 1979 *Saturday Night Live* late-night television comedy made fun of the fifties sitcoms in a show featuring a special guest appearance by Ricky Nelson, who played the wholesome all-American teenager in the Ozzie and Harriet show. The *Saturday Night Live* skit turned the suburban world of Ozzie and Harriet into the Twilight Zone.

. . .

Postmoderns attempt to . . . expose how the postindustrial process of commodification and consumerization has disintegrated the cultural symbols of the fifties generation and recombined those values in ironic new combinations to produce a postmodern system of bureaucratic thought. Diversity and fragmentation of jurisprudential theories signal the postmodern condition.

The Two Sides of Postmodernism

In law, postmodern criticism has come to represent two dominant perspectives. One group of postmodern social critics adopted a neopragmatic stance framed by the antifoundational philosophy of Richard Rorty.

. . .

When applied to legal studies, neopragmatism forms the academic perspective of scholars who reject all foundational claims of legal theory but remain committed to the view that legal theory can be useful for resolving legal problems. . . .

Another group of postmodern critics, the *ironists*, attempt to facilitate the crisis and fragmentation of modern theory by employing postmodern criticism to "displace, decenter, and weaken" central concepts of modern legal Western thought. They are ironists because they claim that the discourse of modern Western thought has been effective—very effective—but not for the reason modernists imagine. Ironists assert that the significance of modernism lies not in specific prescriptions or social tasks, but rather that it lies in the intellectual pursuit of theory as an end to itself. . . .

Ironists attempt to "intensify the irony" of modern discourse by exposing how the descriptions and prescriptions of the discourse fail to support the objective truth claims that the theorists make for advancing social progress. . . . Postmoderns such as Jacques Derrida, Michel Foucault, and Edward Said thus employ deconstructive practices and other critical techniques for displacing and decentering the modes, categories, and normative concepts of Western thought.

Derrida's deconstruction of Western philosophy and literature attempts to . . . reveal how Western reason excludes different self-identities and life-styles. Foucault and Said attempt to show how Western concepts of humanism and reason have functioned to define social identities in ways that exclude the social conventions and identities of other groups. *Postmodern ironists* attempt to expose exclusionary effects of rational thought by bringing attention to the relationship between knowledge and power.

. . .

Postmodern Jurisprudence

. . .

As an intellectual and political practice, postmodernism views knowledge as mediated by the current social, cultural, linguistic, and historical condition of our time. Postmoderns understand truth and knowledge as contingent social constructions, incapable of being grasped by a fixed, determinate theory or conceptional construct. . . . Thus, postmodern jurisprudence is not a theory of law, but a kind of *antitheory*—an antitheory that strives, however problematically, to resist the adjudicatory impulse, the regulatory obsession of modern legal thought.

Postmodern jurisprudence can be found within the legal scholarship of postmoderns who have adopted either the neopragmatist or ironist stance in their legal criticism. Richard Posner is the best-known neopragmatic postmodern legal scholar in the academy today. Pierre Schlag is the leading champion of ironist legal criticism. To understand how these postmodern scholars practice their postmodern criticism, it is helpful to examine how they position themselves in relation to ideas about the nature of theory, language, knowledge, and the identity of the subject.

The Nature of Theory

. . . Posner believes the pragmatic approach is a "middle way." . . . Instead of relying on abstract propositions of "theory," Posner argues that judges should rely on instrumental logic; he uses theory and legal reasoning as tools to get a job done. His true test of every legal analytic is whether it "works" instrumentally in maximizing human goals and aspirations. Posner justifies the application of economics to law on a practical level; economics wins because it "gets the job done" better than any other method.

Richard Posner's pragmatism exhibits what Thomas Grey calls "freedom from theory guilt," a scholarly temperament liberated from the necessity of devising a theory of law rooted in some total perspective. . . . Postmodern pragmatists argue that their "real interest is not in truth at all but in belief justified by social need."

. . .

. . . Neopragmatists have accepted two paradoxical ideas about law: first, that it is possible to know the truth without accepting the idea of universal essences; and second, that it is possible to reach principled decisions even though there are *no* right answers. These ideas are not really paradoxes for legal pragmatists since they reject the philosophy of foundationalism upon which universal truth and right answers rest.

Ironists . . . believe that there is no way to avoid the predicaments of modern theory because no "middle ground" exists. These nonpragmatic postmoderns have given up on the Enlightenment idea of normative or regulative theory altogether, and attempt to look beyond theory to recognize and redescribe the normative narratives and discourses of law.

. . .

Neopragmatism's foundation is the intuition and common sense of the situated pragmatist. Ironists attempt to decenter the foundation of neopragmatism by revealing how pragmatic judgment reflects the view of a situated subject who tries to be very pragmatic in reacting to the postmodern condition. As Schlag has amusingly put it: "The pragmatist subject, understood in pragmatic terms, is the shopper at the universal mall making meaning with the commodified signs of our traditions and culture while the social aesthetics of techno-bureaucratic strategies are making him think he means something. Everything else is just nostalgia."

. . .

The Nature of Language

Modern legal scholars uncritically assume that language is like a mirror capable of accurately reflecting the meaning of objects in reality. The metaphor that captures the modernists' view of language is *conduit*—language is viewed as a *conduit* used by lawyers and judges to "get their message across." In this schema, words are (re)presented as *containers* of meaning. Postmoderns reject this objectivist view of language. They argue that language must be understood in relation to the cognitive processes of the people who speak it. Postmodern neopragmatists argue that language must be understood as a "language game" based on socially contingent rules for determining the truth or falsity of judgments. Ironists adopt a similar stance in arguing that language in the law is a "normative language game."

. . .

The Nature of Knowledge

While postmoderns agree that "truth" is a relative concept, they disagree on the possibility of progress through "knowledge." Neopragmatist believe that practical reason is a form of knowledge that exists and can be relied on in reaching judgment. Legal neopragmatists believe that knowledge of the world can be obtained through the trial and error process of experiences. As Richard Posner states: "There is knowledge if not ultimate truth, and a fallibilist theory of knowledge emphasizes, as preconditions to the growth of scientific and other forms of knowledge, the continual testing and retesting of accepted 'truths,' the constant kicking over of sacred cows—in short, a commitment to robust and free-wheeling inquiry with no intellectual quarter asked or given." Postmodern neopragmatists believe that "[t]he soundness of legal interpretations and other legal propositions is best gauged . . . therefore, by an examination of their consequences in the world of fact."

Ironists have a different orientation toward knowledge. Taking Foucault's mandate that "power comes from everywhere" seriously, ironists argue that law is a form of knowledge that creates and constitutes power. . . .

Ironists thus try to decenter, displace, and weaken the knowledge claims of conceptual and normative jurisprudence. Their goal is to uncover how bias, prejudices, and normative perspectives affect theories of evaluation and types of knowledge. The point is not merely criticism. It is to show how limits are set, how possibilities are established—in short, to show how law works. . . .

Identity of the Self

Of the four key ideas relevant for understanding postmodern legal criticism, the concept of self is critical. . . . The concept of self in modern theory defines

the legal subject or person "back there" in control of the analysis and reason of the law. In modern legal theory, the subject is the judge who engages in "reasoned elaboration" and applies "neutral principles." . . . As Schlag puts it, he "*is* the idealized self-image of the legal academic who by virtue of his intellectual prowess and his commitment to the rule of law applies his overarching legal knowledge to rewrite the case law in a way that is morally appealing."
. . .

While modern legal theory adopted a "centered sense of the self," postmodern critics adopted either a *situated* or *decentered* concept of self. The idea of the *situated self* is based on an understanding of subjectivity that "emphasizes that self is formed only through a relationship with others." The implications of situated subjectivity can be found in Posner's postmodern legal pragmatism. . . . The individual is seen as an economic rational actor in the context of transactions with other individuals. The economic concept of self is thus defined by a theory of behaviorism of situated individuals. As Posner explained: "The law is not interested in the soul or even the mind. It has adopted a severely behaviorist concept of human activity as sufficient to its ends and traceable to its means." . . .

Ironists are committed to a decentered form of subjectivity. They believe there is no core component of the self, only a shifting set of unstable references of multiple identities, and attempt to bring out the multiple identities of human subjects that contemporary legal scholars have uncritically ignored. As Schlag stated: "Postmodernism questions the integrity, the coherence, and the actual identity of the humanist individual self—the knowing sort of self produced by Enlightenment epistemology and featured so often as the dominant self-image of the professional academic."

Ironists' legal criticism is thus based on the idea that the "subject is a problem." "The problem arises as each school (of jurisprudence) recognizes that its own intellectual architecture, its own normative ambitions rest upon the presupposition of a subject—a subject whose epistemic, ontological, and normative status is now very much in question." The goal of postmodern criticism is to decenter the subject so that the human agents of law can appreciate their responsibility for the normativity of law.
. . .

Rejecting the possibility of finding "correct" solutions to legal problems based on conceptual formulations of some ideal Rule of Law, postmodernists argue for new understandings derived from an awareness of the reciprocal nature of law, culture, and individual subjectivity. Ironist criticism has inspired legal scholars to contemplate the possibility of a new framework of analysis . . . , one that offers a transformed concept of what it means to solve legal and theoretical issues generally. What is different about postmodernists is their unabashed acceptance of the impossibility of solving legal problems under an ideal set of conceptual solutions.

. . .

Postmodern Politics

It would be misleading to say that everyone finds the postmodern developments in jurisprudence attractive. To the contrary, judging from the academic
hype in the general university, postmodernism is held responsible for a multitude of ills in the modern university—multicultural curricula, political correct-
ness, affirmative action, restrictions on hate speech, and the general disinterest
in the great classics of Western culture. In the legal academy, the most frequently voiced objection to postmodernism is that it is a nihilistic scholarly
movement that is a recipe for inaction. Modern legal scholars tend to see postmodernism as threatening the progress of modern jurisprudence by destabiliz-
ing and rendering uncertain the process of interpretation. Progressives worry
that postmodernism may undermine the collective optimism necessary for
progressive resistance and renewal.

. . .

Postmodernism thus challenges legal thinkers to reconsider their most basic
understanding of the nature of law and politics—their belief in an objective
and autonomous law. Postmoderns argue that decision making according to
rule is not possible, because rules are dependent upon language, and language
is socially and culturally constructed and hence incapable of directing decision
makers to make consistent and objective choices. Objectivity is possible only if
agreement or consensus about different interpretive practices can be reached.
Consensus about acceptable meanings of words is possible, but only if legal
interpreters can agree about the "correct" method for legal interpretation.
The proliferation of different interpretive methods in law means that consensus is no longer possible.

. . .

Conclusion: Jurisprudence at Century's End

. . .

. . . Contemporary legal academics are becoming more cynical and skeptical
as they realize that legal theorists have been participating in a "recycling
process" in which "[e]ach [new] generation . . . offers a different metatheory
to explain or understand legal phenomena, rejecting the perspectives of the
previous generation in the hope of more successfully solving [law's] paradox."
Cynicism comes with the realization that each succeeding generation of modern legal scholars has merely recycled the work of the previous generation,
moving from new and improved conceptual theories to increasingly more
complex normative theories, without ever achieving a successful conceptual or
normative theory that can withstand the criticism of the next generation. In

the face of this, mainstream legal scholars proclaim that chaos is "good," that the future will be secured by the development of a new "chaos theory" for law.

Postmoderns assert that the current mood of the cynic is quite normal and to be expected. They assert that this cynicism is what the current postmodern condition in legal studies signifies. To better appreciate the significance of this condition, postmodern legal critics persuade students of the law (professors and law students) to adopt a new metaphor for legal studies. They favor metaphors like "law as a theater," because they believe that modern legal thought is "a kind of theater." Postmodern legal critics argue that the problem with normative legal thought is that "[t]he rhetorical script . . . is already written, the social scene is already set and play after play, article after article, year after year, normative legal thought [repetitively] requires [us] to choose: 'what should we do? Where should we go?'" Postmoderns argue that these are the wrong questions. What is needed is a drama and a new kind of "scene, *agon*, and actors." The theater of modern jurisprudence has not permitted other stories to be told, until now.

There are now many different stories being told in the law, different theaters and rich new plots and scenes depicting new vantage points for understanding previously ignored characteristics and subjects of the law. While at one time the study of jurisprudence reflected the 1950s pluralist consensus of the legal process school, the idea of social consensus has long been discarded as legal scholars turn to new, diverse, and eclectic approaches in theory and practice. The "theater" of the 1950s generation of legal scholars reflected the values and consensus of television sitcoms such as *The Adventures of Ozzie and Harriet*. Like the Nelsons, the 1950s generation was optimistic about the future and believed that progress was possible through the legal system. . . .

Like Ricky Nelson on *Saturday Night Live*, the student of jurisprudence today . . . is confronted with fragmented and somewhat confusing images and stories about law. These diverse images and stories require the current generation of law students to think more explicitly about the difficulties and opportunities of reaching agreement and consensus in a multicultural world. The experience of this may be unsettling and may even be described as being schizophrenic. The "schizophrenia" of modern jurisprudence, however, may be another *signification* of the breakdown in the recycling chain of modern discourse.

. . .

[P]ostmodern trends in legal scholarship have generated considerable anxiety and discomfort. In challenging traditional notions of jurisprudence, postmodern criticism seems to challenge the very idea of law itself. If decision makers cannot render decisions according to law, then how can we expect "law" to protect us against the many injustices and invasions of the day? If the Rule of Law depends on different normative and theoretical perspectives, how will "law" protect itself against the subjective desires of legal subjects? As we approach the next millennium, it seems certain that anxiety about these questions will heighten.

. . .

It may be that the temperament of contemporary jurisprudence evidences a general cultural anxiety that occurs whenever a century ends. In moving from one century to the next, it is hard not to believe that an era is ending and that the old ways are exhausted. Perhaps the current postmodern condition is part of a historically anxious, contingent moment. In the next millennium, new frontiers and new energy may reinvigorate the quest for answers to the dilemmas of modernism.

What may seem to be "impending annihilation" may in fact be the basis for satisfaction, hope, and new intellectual inquiry in the next millennium. Constructive engagement between the different jurisprudential movements may lead to new jurisprudential insights about law. . . .

. . . However, postmoderns would be quick to remind us that we can never go back to the good old days of political and intellectual consensus. They would warn us that all canons of law are man-made and thus always subject to reinterpretation. They would resist the idea of a postmodern theory of jurisprudence; they would instead emphasize diversity, contradiction, and paradox. Postmoderns would say that the future of jurisprudence remains in our hands, that it is up to us to build the legal world we wish to inhabit.

It is a critical time for jurisprudential studies in America. It is a time for self-reflection and reevaluation of methodological and theoretical legacies in the law. At stake is not only the status of modern jurisprudence, but also the validity of the Rule of Law itself. In the current era of academic diversity and disagreement, the time has come to seriously consider the transformative changes now unfolding in American legal thought. The challenge for the next century will certainly involve new ways of understanding how the legal system can preserve the authority of the Rule of Law while responding to the different perspectives and interests of multicultural communities. It is without a doubt an anxious and exciting time for jurisprudence.

BIBLIOGRAPHY

Abel, Richard L. *American Lawyers*. New York: Oxford University Press, 1989.

Allport, Gordon. *The Nature of Prejudice*. Cambridge, Mass.: Addison-Wesley, 1954.

Ashmore, Harry. *The Negro and the Schools*. Chapel Hill: University of North Carolina Press, 1954.

Auerbach, Jerold S. *Unequal Justice: Lawyers and Social Change in America*. New York: Oxford University Press, 1976, pp. 231–261.

Baker, J. H. *An Introduction to English Legal History*, 3d ed. London: Butterworths, 1990.

Baker, Leonard. *Brandeis and Frankfurter: A Dual Biography*. New York: Harper & Row, 1984.

Bell, Derrick A. *And We Are Not Saved: The Elusive Quest for Racial Justice*. New York: Basic Books, 1987.

Bernstein, Richard B. *Are We to Be a Nation?* Cambridge, Mass.: Harvard University Press, 1987, pp. 149–181.

Bickel, Alexander. *The Least Dangerous Branch*, 2d ed. New Haven, Conn.: Yale University Press, 1986.

Bloomfield, Maxwell. *American Lawyers in a Changing Society*. Cambridge, Mass.: Harvard University Press, 1976.

Boorstin, Daniel J. *The Mysterious Science of the Law*. Boston: Beacon Press, 1941.

Bowen, Catherine Drinker. *The Lion and the Throne: The Life and Times of Sir Edward Coke*. New York: Little Brown, 1956, pp. 478–507.

Burkhart, Ann M. and Robert A. Stein. *How to Study Law and Take Law Exams in a Nutshell*. St. Paul, Minn.: West, 1996.

Calabresi, Guido. "Some Thoughts on Risk Distribution and the Law of Torts," 70 *Yale Law Journal* (1961), p. 499.

Carson, Rachael. *Silent Spring*. Boston: Houghton Mifflin, 1962.

Chafee, Zechariah, Jr. *Free Speech in the United States*. Cambridge, Mass.: Harvard University Press, 1941.

Christol, Carl Q. *Space Law: Past, Present, and Future*. Boston: Kluwer Law and Tax Publishers, 1991.

Coase, Ronald. "The Problem of Social Cost," 3 *Journal of Law and Economics* (1960), p. 1.

Cray, Ed. *Chief Justice: A Biography of Earl Warren*. New York: Simon & Schuster, 1997.

Delbruck, Jost. "Globalization of Law, Politics and Markets—Implications for Domestic Law—A European Perspective," 1 *Indiana Journal of Global Legal Studies* (1993), p. 9.

Ehrlich, Thomas and Geoffrey C. Hazard, Jr. *Going to Law School? Readings on a Legal Career.* Boston: Little Brown, 1975.

Epstein, Jason. *The Great Conspiracy Trial: An Essay on Law, Liberty and the Constitution.* New York: Random House, 1970, pp. 397–431.

Fehrenbacher, Don E. *Slavery, Law, and Politics: The Dred Scott Case in Historical Perspective.* New York: Oxford University Press, 1981.

Ferguson, Robert A. *Law and Letters in American Culture.* Cambridge, Mass.: Harvard University Press, 1984, pp. 11–285.

Fetner, Gerald L. *Ordered Liberty: Legal Reform in the Twentieth Century.* New York: Alfred A. Knopf, 1983.

Fraenkel, Osmond K. *The Sacco-Vanzetti Case.* New York: Alfred A. Knopf, 1931, pp. 3–25.

Frank, Steven J. *Learning the Law: Success in Law School and Beyond,* rev. ed. Secaucus, N.J.: Carol Publishing Group, 1997.

Friedan, Betty. *The Feminine Mystique.* New York: Norton, 1963.

Friedman, Lawrence M. *A History of American Law,* 2d ed. New York: Simon & Schuster, 1985.

Gillers, Stephen, ed. *Looking at Law School: A Student Guide from the Society of American Law Teachers,* 4th ed. New York: Meridian, 1997.

Gilmore, Grant. *The Ages of American Law.* New Haven, Conn.: Yale University Press, 1977.

Griffin, Kelley. *Ralph Nader Presents More Action for a Change.* New York: Dembner Books, 1987.

Gunther, Gerald. *Learned Hand: The Man and the Judge.* New York: Alfred A. Knopf, 1994, pp. 118–221.

Hall, Kermit L. *The Magic Mirror: Law in American History.* New York: Oxford University Press, 1989.

Harr, Jonathan. *A Civil Action.* New York: Random House, 1996, pp. 62–82.

Higginbotham, A. Leon, Jr. *In the Matter of Color: The Colonial Period.* New York: Oxford University Press, 1978.

Honnold, John. *The Life of the Law.* Glencoe, Ill.: The Free Press, 1964.

Horwitz, Morton J. *The Transformation of American Law, 1780–1860.* Cambridge, Mass.: Harvard University Press, 1977.

Hurst, James Willard. *Law and the Conditions of Freedom in Nineteenth Century United States.* Madison: University of Wisconsin Press, 1956.

Irons, Peter. *Justice at War.* New York: Oxford University Press, 1983, pp. 227–252.

Jasanoff, Sheila. *Science at the Bar.* Cambridge, Mass.: Harvard University Press, 1995, pp. 204–223.

Jones, Gareth. *The Sovereignty of the Law: Selections from Blackstone's Commentaries on the Laws of England.* Toronto: University of Toronto Press, 1973, pp. ix–xiii.

Kalman, Laura. *Legal Realism at Yale, 1927–1960.* Chapel Hill: University of North Carolina Press, 1986.

Katsh, M. Ethan. *Law in a Digital World.* New York: Oxford University Press, 1995.

Katzmann, Robert A. *The Law Firm and the Public Good.* Washington, D.C.: Brookings Institution, 1995.

Kelly, J. M. *A Short History of Western Legal Theory.* Oxford, Eng.: Clarendon Press, 1992, pp. 1–82.

Kelman, Mark. *A Guide to Critical Legal Studies.* Cambridge, Mass.: Harvard University Press, 1987.

Kluger, Richard. *Simple Justice: The History of* Brown *v.* Board of Education *and Black America's Struggle of Equality.* New York: Alfred A. Knopf, 1976, pp. 714–745.

Kronman, Anthony T. *The Lost Lawyer: Failing Ideals of the Legal Profession.* Cambridge, Mass.: Harvard University Press, 1993.

Kutler, Stanley I. *The Wars of Watergate: The Last Crisis of Richard Nixon.* New York: Alfred A. Knopf, 1990, pp. 506–517.

Leuchtenburg, William E. "The Case of the Wanatchee Chambermaid," *in* Garraty, John A., ed. *Quarrels That Have Shaped the Constitution,* rev. ed. New York: Harper & Row, 1987, pp. 266–283.

Levi, Edward H. *An Introduction to Legal Reasoning.* Chicago: University of Chicago Press, 1948.

Levy, Leonard W. *The Law of the Commonwealth and Chief Justice Shaw.* Cambridge, Mass.: Harvard University Press, 1957, pp. 72–108.

Lewis, Anthony. *Gideon's Trumpet.* New York: Random House, 1964, pp. 79–94.

Llewellyn, Karl N. *The Bramble Bush.* New York: Oceana, 1930.

Llewellyn, Karl N. and E. Adamson Hoebel. *The Cheyenne Way.* Norman: University of Oklahoma Press, 1941.

Loth, David and Morris L. Ernst. *The Taming of Technology.* New York: Simon & Schuster, 1972.

Maine, Henry Sumner. *Ancient Law.* London: J. Murray, 1861.

Margulies, Sheldon. *Learning Law: The Mastery of Legal Logic.* Durham, N.C.: Carolina Academic Press, 1993.

Marke, Julius J. and Edward J. Bander. *Dean's List of Recommended Reading for Prelaw and Law Students Selected by the Deans and Faculties of American Law Schools,* 2d ed. New York: Oceana, 1984.

McCraw, Thomas K. *Prophets of Regulation.* Cambridge, Mass.: Harvard University Press, 1984, pp. 80–142.

McKnight, Jean Sinclair. *Law for the Layperson: An Annotated Bibliography of Self-Help Law Books,* 2d ed. Littleton, Colo.: F. B. Rothman, 1997.

Menkel-Meadow, Carrie. "Culture Clash in the Quality of Life in the Law: Changes in the Economics, Diversification and Organization of Lawyering," 44 *Case Western Law Review* (1994), pp. 621–655.

Minda, Gary. *Postmodern Legal Movements: Law and Jurisprudence at the Century's End.* New York: New York University Press, 1995, pp. 224–257.

Murphy, Bruce Allen. *Fortas: The Rise and Ruin of a Supreme Court Justice.* New York: W. Morrow, 1988.

Murphy, Paul L. *The Constitution in Crisis Times: 1918–1969.* New York: Harper & Row, 1972.

Nader, Ralph. *Unsafe at Any Speed.* New York: Grossman, 1965.

Navasky, Victor S. *Naming Names.* New York: Viking Press, 1982.

Neely, Mark E., Jr. *The Fate of Liberty: Abraham Lincoln and Civil Liberties.* New York: Oxford University Press, 1991, pp. 210–222.

Nelson, William E. *Americanization of the Common Law: The Impact of Legal Change on Massachusetts Society, 1760–1830,* 2d ed. Athens: University of Georgia Press, 1994, pp. 117–144.

Newmyer, Kent R. *The Supreme Court Under Marshall and Taney.* New York: Thomas Y. Crowell, 1968, pp. 18–38.

Nygren, Carol J. *Starting Off Right in Law School.* Durham, N.C.: Carolina Academic Press, 1997.

Osborn, John, Jr. *The Paper Chase.* Boston: Houghton Mifflin, 1971.

Oxford Companion to Law, The. Oxford, Eng.: Clarendon Press, 1980.

Oxford Dictionary of American Legal Quotations, The. New York: Oxford University Press, 1993.

Pearce, Russell G. "The Professional Paradigm Shift," 70 *New York University Law Review* (1995), p. 1229.

Pollock, Frederick and Frederic William Maitland. *The History of English Law Before the Time of Edward I,* 2d ed. Cambridge, Eng.: Cambridge University Press, 1911.

Reid, John Phillip. *A Better Kind of Hatchet: Law, Trade and Diplomacy in the Cherokee Nation During the Early Years of European Contact.* University Park: The Pennsylvania State University Press, 1976, pp. 1–12.

Rhode, Deborah L. *Justice and Gender: Sex Discrimination and the Law.* Cambridge, Mass.: Harvard University Press, 1989, pp. 63–78.

Savage, David G. *Turning Right: The Making of the Rehnquist Supreme Court.* New York: John Wiley & Sons, 1992, pp. 3–25.

Schwartz, Bernard. *The American Heritage History of the Law in America.* New York: American Heritage, 1974.

———. *Main Currents in American Legal Thought.* Durham, N.C.: Carolina Academic Press, 1993, pp. 376–392.

Schwartz, Murray L. *Law and the American Future.* Englewood Cliffs, N.J.: Prentice-Hall, 1976.

Shapiro, Martin. "The Globalization of Law," 1 *Indiana Journal of Global Legal Studies* (1993), pp. 37–64.

Shapo, Helene S. and Marshall Shapo. *Law School Without Fear: Strategies of Success.* Westbury, N.Y.: Foundation Press, 1996.

Singer, Linda R. *Settling Disputes: Conflict Resolution in Business, Families, and the Legal System.* Boulder, Colo.: Westview Press, 1994, pp. 1–14.

Stampp, Kenneth M. *The Peculiar Institution: Slavery in the Ante-Bellum South.* New York: Alfred A. Knopf, 1956.

Stevens, Robert. *Law School: Legal Education in America from the 1850s to the 1980s.* Chapel Hill: University of North Carolina Press, 1983.

Strickland, Rennard. *Fire and the Spirits: Cherokee Law from Clan to Court.* Norman: University of Oklahoma Press, 1975.

Taylor, Telford. *Nuremberg and Vietnam: An American Tragedy.* Chicago: Quadrangle Books, 1970.

Turow, Scott. *One L.* New York: Putnam, 1977.

Tusa, Ann and John Tusa. *The Nuremberg Trial.* London: Macmillan, 1983, pp. 20–60.

Urofsky, Melvyn I. *A March of Liberty: A Constitutional History of the United States.* New York: Alfred A. Knopf, 1988.

U.S. President's Committee on Civil Rights. *To Secure These Rights.* Washington, D.C.: U.S. Government Printing Office, 1947.

Van Caenegem, R. C. *The Birth of the English Common Law,* 2d ed. Cambridge, Eng.: Cambridge University Press, 1988, pp. 85–110.

Walker, Samuel. *Popular Justice: A History of American Criminal Justice.* New York: Oxford University Press, 1980.

West's Encyclopedia of American Law. St. Paul, Minn.: West, 1997–1998.

White, G. Edward. *The American Judicial Tradition,* exp. ed. New York: Oxford University Press, 1988, pp. 92–108.

Wiessner, Siegfried. "Human Activities in Outer Space: A Framework for Decision-Making," *in* Zwaan, Tanja L., ed. *Space Law: Views of the Future.* Deventer, The Netherlands: Kluwer Law & Tax Publishers, 1988, pp. 8–20.

Wright, Quincy. *International Law and the United Nations.* New York: Asia Publishing House, 1960; reprinted Westport, Conn.: Greenwood Press, 1976.

INDEX OF CASES

INDEX

Italic numerals refer to illustrations.